# Interactive Multimedia Music Technologies

Kia Ng
*University of Leeds, UK*

Paolo Nesi
*University of Florence, Italy*

**INFORMATION SCIENCE REFERENCE**

Hershey · New York

| Acquisitions Editor: | Kristin Klinger |
| Development Editor: | Kristin M. Roth |
| Editorial Assistant: | Jessica Thompson |
| Senior Managing Editor: | Jennifer Neidig |
| Managing Editor: | Sara Reed |
| Copy Editor: | Angela Thor |
| Typesetter: | Lindsay Bergman |
| Cover Design: | Lisa Tosheff |
| Printed at: | Yurchak Printing Inc. |

Published in the United States of America by
    Information Science Reference (an imprint of IGI Global)
    701 E. Chocolate Avenue, Suite 200
    Hershey PA 17033
    Tel: 717-533-8845
    Fax: 717-533-8661
    E-mail: cust@igi-global.com
    Web site: http://www.igi-global.com/reference

and in the United Kingdom by
    Information Science Reference (an imprint of IGI Global)
    3 Henrietta Street
    Covent Garden
    London WC2E 8LU
    Tel: 44 20 7240 0856
    Fax: 44 20 7379 0609
    Web site: http://www.eurospanonline.com

Library of Congress Cataloging-in-Publication Data

Interactive multimedia music technologies / Kia Ng & Paolo Nesi, editors.
    p. cm.
  Summary: "This book illustrates how interactive music can be used for valorizing cultural heritage, content and archives not currently distributed due to lack of safety, suitable coding, or conversion technologies. It explains new methods of promoting music for entertainment, teaching, commercial and non-commercial purposes, and provides new services for those connected via PCs, mobile devices, whether sighted or print-impaired"--Provided by publisher.
  Includes bibliographical references and index.
  ISBN 978-1-59904-150-6 (hardcover) -- ISBN 978-1-59904-152-0 (ebook)
  1. Music--Data processing. 2. Interactive multimedia. I. Ng, Kia. II. Nesi, Paolo.
  ML74.I57 2008
  780.285--dc22
                    2007023452

British Cataloguing in Publication Data
A Cataloguing in Publication record for this book is available from the British Library.

All work contributed to this book set is new, previously-unpublished material. The views expressed in this book are those of the authors, but not necessarily of the publisher.

# Table of Contents

# Detailed Table of Contents

**Chapter I**

The MUSICNETWORK project was cosupported by the European Commission to bring music industry and related research areas into the interactive multimedia era. It represented a virtual Centre of Excellence during the period of the project, and today an international association where music content providers, cultural institutions, industry, and research institutions work together, drawing on their collective assets and mutual interests, to exploit the potential of multimedia music contents with new technologies, tools, products, formats, and models. Due to large gaps between needs and real products and solutions, many products in the market fail to exploit the potential of new multimedia technologies effectively. MU-SICNETWORK helps research solutions to reach the market by seeking agreements between different actors and formats, by bringing together research institutions, industries, small and medium enterprises (SMEs), and experts to build the required momentum to study and define multimedia music modelling and coding for the new age. MUSICNETWORK activities, actions and services are provided through the project Web site, which can be found online at http://www.interactivemusicnetwork.org.

**Chapter II**

The evolution of digital communication devices and formats has recently produced fundamental changes in the practical approach to music representation and notation, transforming them from a simple visual coding model for sheet music into a composite tool for modelling music in computer and multimedia applications in general. As a consequence, a multilayer model of music representation is needed for several purposes in addition to sheet music production or visual display, such as audio rendering, entertainment, music analysis, database query, music performance coding, music distance learning, and so forth.

The symbolic music representation is a standard for modelling music notations, proposed inside the MPEG multimedia framework. Symbolic music representation generalizes the main music notation concepts to model the visual aspects of a music score, and audio information or annotations related to the music piece, allowing integration with other audiovisual elements by multimedia references. The Symbolic Music Representation standard overcomes the limitations of a widely accepted format like MIDI, which is in line with its main purpose to model music events, whereas it reveals important limitations in producing audio and visual representations with satisfactory results.

The evolution of information technology has changed the use of music representation and notation in software applications, transforming and extending them from a simple visual coding model for music scores into a tool for modelling music for computer programs and electronic devices in general (e.g., keyboards), to support the exploitation of the multimedia characteristics lying behind music notation and representation. The MPEG symbolic music representation (MPEG-SMR) is a new emerging standard for modelling music notation within the MPEG multimedia framework. MPEG-SMR provides an XML-based language to model most of the music notation in terms of the visual and audio aspects, as well as music score annotations. MPEG-SMR also provides a language to define the music score formatting rules, supporting personalisation for the score visual presentation, custom symbols, and control visual rendering of the common notation symbols.

This chapter presents the applications and practices in the domain of music imaging for musical scores (music sheets and music manuscripts), which include music sheet digitisation, optical music recognition (OMR), and optical music restoration.

With a general background of optical music recognition (OMR), the chapter discusses typical obstacles in this domain, and reports currently available commercial OMR software. It reports hardware and software related to music imaging, discusses the SharpEye optical music recognition system, and provides an evaluation of a number of OMR systems.

Besides the main focus on the transformation from images of music scores to symbolic format, this chapter also discusses optical music image restoration and the application of music imaging techniques for graphical preservation and potential applications for cross-media integration.

Optical music recognition is a key problem for coding western music sheets in the digital world. This problem has been addressed in several manners, obtaining suitable results only when simple music constructs are processed. To this end, several different strategies have been followed to pass from the simple music sheet image to a complete and consistent representation of music notation symbols (symbolic music notation or representation). Typically, image processing, pattern recognition and symbolic reconstruction are the technologies that have to be considered and applied in several manners the architecture of the so-called OMR (optical music recognition) systems. In this chapter, the O³MR (object oriented optical music recognition) system is presented. It allows producing, from the image of a music sheet, the symbolic representation and save it in XML format (WEDELMUSIC XML and MUSICXML). The algorithms used in this process are those of the image processing, image segmentation, neural network pattern recognition, and symbolic reconstruction and reasoning. Most of the solutions can be applied in other fields of image understanding. The development of the O³MR solution with all its algorithms has been partially supported by the European Commission, in the IMUTUS Research and Development project, while the related music notation editor has been partially funded by the research and development WEDELMUSIC project of the European Commission. The chapter also includes a methodology for the assessment of other OMR systems. The set of metrics proposed has been used to assess the quality of results produce by the O³MR with respect to the best OMR on market.

## Chapter VI

XML-based languages for music have constraints not applicable to typical XML applications, such as for standard text documents or data sets. Music contains numerous simultaneous events across several dimensions, including time. The document model for a piece of music would thus look very different from serialised text documents. Most existing XML-based music markup languages mark music typography, following the print traditions of music scores. A general music markup language should include much more than mere print. Some of the challenges designing an XML-based markup language for music are considered. An SVG-based music symbol design grid is proposed to meet the challenge of music typology. An XML-based Music Symbol Language is used to design symbols on this grid. Resulting symbols are positioned in 3-D music space, which is introduced to address the challenge of topography.

## Chapter VII

Design goals determine the particular structure of a markup language, while the philosophy of what markup languages are about determine the framework within which its structure is developed. Most existing markup languages for music reflect low-level design strategies, compared to design that adheres to the high-level philosophy of markup languages. An approach to an XML-based music markup language from the perspective of SGML would differ from an approach from a markup language such as HTML. An ideal structure for a general markup language for music is proposed that follows a purist approach and that results in a different kind of XML-based music markup language than most present music markup languages offer.

This chapter considers the development of systems to deliver multimedia content for new opera. After a short overview of the history of multimedia in opera, the specific requirements of opera are analysed, with emphasis on the fundamental musicality of operatic performance. Having considered the place of multimedia elements in the narrative and acting space, the relevance of previous practice in electroacoustic music and VJing is considered as a model for a working approach. Several software and hardware configurations explored, including the use of gestural control by the actors themselves. The creation of a keyboard based "video instrument" with a dedicated performer, capable of integration into the pre-existing musical ensemble, is recommended as the most effective and practical solution.

An overview on problems and methods to map performers' actions to a synthesized sound is presented. Approaches incorporating the audio signal are described, and a synthesis method called "audio signal driven sound synthesis" is introduced. It uses the raw audio signal of a traditional instrument to drive a synthesis algorithm. The system tries to support musicians with satisfying instrument-specific playability. In contrast to common methods that try to increase openness for the player's input, openness of the system is achieved here by leaving essential playing parameters nonformalized as far as possible. Three implementations of the method and one application are described. An empirical study and experiences with users testing the system implemented for a bowed string instrument are presented. This implementation represents a specific case of a broader range of approaches to the treatment of user input, which has applications in a wide variety of contexts involving human-computer interaction.

From the authors' perspective, technology is both a tool and a developing factor that can foster culture and learning development. This chapter focuses on the interrelations that interleave education, technology, content accessibility, and intercultural issues. With an introduction and related background, language learning is used as an example further to explain these issues. This chapter then discusses authoring and content development for e-learning applications (including authoring tools, virtual communities, and forums), and examines technology and accessibility issues in this context. The current state of e-learning is introduced along with a description of different tools and approaches. The chapter concludes with an overview of e-learning and the marketplace.

Our work bridges two interesting topics: the research in the area of Web-based applications and the area of learning technologies. We give an overall picture of the current development in Web-based music intelligent tutoring system (WMITS). The term WMITS is coined by us to describe the two main areas in our focus. In this chapter, we address the following issues: (i) the pedagogical aspect of teaching and learning music, (ii) the background of music intelligent tutoring system, and (iii) our WMITS system for teaching music theories. A Web-based environment offers strengths in terms of accessibility and self-paced learning. However, the environment has a great drawback in terms of interactivities between the users and the system. Our design addresses this issue by developing a specialised client tool. The client tool provides an interactive environment for score editing, which is crucial for learning music theories. The system incorporates three major inference techniques (i.e., deductive, inductive, and Bayesian inference) in dealing with music theories and uncertain knowledge such as students' understanding.

This chapter discusses technologies and standards related to digital rights management (DRM). Firstly, it presents DRM systems that are multimedia information management systems that take into account digital rights and protection. These systems enable the controlled distribution and use of multimedia content through the digital value chain. Then, this chapter presents current initiatives, standard and proprietary, that specify a DRM system. It focuses in the MPEG-21 standard initiative, mainly in the parts of this standard that normatively specify the different pieces and formats needed by a complete DRM system. Finally, this chapter presents one of the key components of DRM systems, rights expression languages (RELs), that have been defined to express content usage rules.

This chapter explains the fundamental principles of audiovisual content protection. It explains the basic knowledge that is needed to understand the fundamentals of digital rights management (DRM) systems and their problems. Starting with a general introduction about copyright and content protection, available protection technologies are described and analyzed. The basic concepts of DRM solutions are explained and problems discussed. Potentials and practical limitations are analysed based on the digital music industry value chain. An outlook is given on solutions that are under development and that stronger consider the needs of the customers. In the conclusion, future solutions are discussed.

This chapter analyses multiple aspects of online music distribution, investigating the major problems, the different approaches and business models, considering the different points of view and perspectives, presenting the emerging technologies and digital rights management standards, analysing issues for rights clearing, intellectual property protection, content retrieval, and metadata management.

The chapter presents the structure of the developing market of digital music and multimedia content distribution, considering all the stakeholders and their mutual relationships, as well as the legal framework. It highlights the importance of the needs of end-users and consumers of music when considering the major problems, as well as the new behaviours and possibilities originated by the availability of music in digital form

This chapter is aimed at many different audiences, from policy makers to music end-users and consumers, to content creators, publishers, and distributors, as well as technology providers, and in general, to all the players in the digital music content value chain.

# Preface

Currently, there is a wide range of interactive multimedia technologies that can help evolve the music market to the next level; to enhance and to provide musical content in a more effective, more readily accessible, faster, and more easy-to-use manner.

Content owners, producers, and distributors such as publishers, archives, libraries, conservatories, music shops, music information-technology industries, and educators recognise the usefulness and potential of these developments. There are many opportunities to exploit these novel technologies and a great deal of interest from the relevant parties. However, there are concerns about losing the rights and ownership of content. This obstacle is further increased by the widening gap and the lack of effective knowledge transfer between the industrial and research communities.

Many multimedia music content owners and distributors are converting their archives of music scores from paper into digital formats, such as images and machine-readable symbolic notation, in order to excel in the market. Typically problems arise due to the requirements of archives that have been organised differently, where several other related digital objects are collected (e.g., images, documents, lyrics, videos, etc.). Issues such as standards and formats (machine representations), integrated cross-media datasets, digital rights management, and tools are important considerations and invaluable knowledge. The new functionalities of multimedia interactive music can be used for:

- Valorising cultural heritage, content, and archives that are not currently distributed due to digital rights issues, suitable coding models, and conversion technologies.
- Promoting music and products for entertainment, for distance teaching, for archives, for commercial and noncommercial purposes.
- Providing new services for consumers connected via personal computers, mobiles, and other devices, and widening accessibility for impaired users.

This book aims to provide the latest insights and future directions integrating relevant experiences, information, and knowledge in these domains to help bring the music content industries, information technology companies, and research communities closer, and to bring music into the interactive multimedia era. With a primary focus on the activities and findings of the MUSICNETWORK (see http://www.interactivemusicnetwork.org), cosupported by the European Commission, this book consists of analyses, knowledge, and application scenarios, as surveyed, analysed, and tested. These include music representations and the developments in the standardization of machine-readable symbolic music notation representations of MPEG ISO; music imaging (e.g., optical music recognition); with informative discussions on efficient mechanisms for distributing and sharing multimedia music content (such as e-commerce, mobile applications, etc.); rights control and management, towards more secure and new formats to exploit new functionalities with interactive multimedia technologies. These subject areas are useful to professionals and researchers working in the field of interactive multimedia-related technologies, computer music, music technology, publishers, librarians, e-business, digital media, digital rights, music representations, cultural, learning and teaching, and many other interdisciplinary domains, including students, researchers, businesses, and SMEs (small and medium enterprises).

To provide the background context and motivations, this book starts with an introductory chapter, "Interactive Multimedia MUSICNETWORK: An Introduction," to present the MUSICNETWORK that was cosupported by the European Community under the fifth framework programme. The aim of the MUSICNETWORK is to help bring the music content providers, cultural institutions, industry, and research institutions to work together, to reduce the barriers between the technology and content providers, and to improve the exploitation of new interactive multimedia technologies. It brings together research institutions, industries, SMEs, and experts to build the required momentum in order to study and define multimedia music modelling and coding for the digital era, and finally to open new markets and possibilities with new technologies and solutions.

With a large number of participants, the MUSICNETWORK addressed several aspects of music within a set of working groups including:

- **Music notation:** Examines all aspect of coding music notation, such as modern music notation, format conversion, fonts, and defining standards for music symbols, and started the work on MPEG Symbolic Music Representation (MPEG SMR).
- **Music libraries:** This group has a cross-domain perspective including museums, archives, industry catalogues, and other collections.
- **Music multimedia standards:** Studies and analyses of multimedia standards for music coding, including audio and video coding (e.g., MPEG7, MPEG21, etc.), portable Internet formats, media integration, and other standardization aspects, with MPEG and others.
- **Music distribution:** Examines the distribution of coded music including streaming, Internet, distribution models (B2B, B2C, P2P, etc.), mobile systems, WEB-TV, and transaction models (online, off-line, kiosks, etc.).
- **Music protection:** Focuses on issues related to the protection of coded music, such as encryption, fingerprint, watermark, digital rights management, profiling functionalities, active and passive protection, and other security issues.
- **Music accessibility:** Examines music coding for print-impaired people (visually impaired, dyslexic, etc.), and studies accessibility issues, user interfaces, computer-assisted software and devices, and the provision of music in alternative formats.
- **Music imaging:** Concentrates on issues relating to imaging and processing of sheet music, printed music scores, and handwritten manuscripts, including music image acquisition, acquisition of music with different types of page support, digitising ancient music, coding for images, optical restoration and preservation, and optical music recognition (OMR, also known as optical character recognition for music) and evaluation of OMR systems.
- **Music audio:** This working group is focused on audio processing aspects such as conversion from audio to music notation, query by content, beat tracking, audio shrinking and stretching, audio recognition, and so forth.
- **Music education:** This group analyses and works on educational aspects of music with the support of the information technology and pedagogical aspects. In particular it deals with the aspects of cooperative work on music notation, performances, playing instruments by using Internet support, e-learning, distance teaching, courseware tools, assessing music performances, self learning, software tools for music education, and so forth.

- **Music culture:** This working group addresses the cultural aspects of music and musicology. It considers historical interpretation, context, and so forth.

The chapters of this book present a selection of the most relevant activities in the previously mentioned sectors, highlight key achievements, and analyze main results. Most of the results produced by the project have a strong international value and involved many participants globally.

As one of the main results of the MUSICNETWORK, Chapter II on "MPEG Symbolic Music Representation: A Solution for Multimedia Music Applications" by Pierfrancesco Bellini, Paolo Nesi, and Giorgio Zoia presents an overview of the development of the MPEG SMR (Symbolic Music Representation) standard that was started by the MUSICNETWORK and has recently been accepted by the MPEG ISO global multimedia standard organization. The chapter discusses the MPEG SMR design and development including its decoder for the MPEG-4 standard, for interactive TV, PC, and mobiles. A large part of the work performed in this area has been coordinated by the MUSICNETWORK. The authors believe that the MPEG SMR development represents a crucial step that will bring the next phase of multimedia music development into all forms of electronic devices that will further support interoperability and widen accessibility to music enjoyment, research, culture, as well as education.

Music notation and representation is one of the fundamental aspects of the new knowledge presented in this book. Chapter III "XML Music Notation Modelling for Multimedia: MPEG-SMR" by Pierfrancesco Bellini outlines the structure of the forthcoming MPEG SMR ISO standard, and proposes the formalization in terms of XML for music representation and provides several examples. This chapter discusses the continuous growth of the MPEG SMR (XML and binary formats), which includes modelling of music representation, multilingual lyrics, integration of music representation and multimedia, formalization of a language for the automatic formatting of music representation, music representation streaming, and so forth.

In order to take advantage of new interactive multimedia capabilities and possibilities such as those discussed in this book, paper-based music scores have to be transformed into machine-readable representations. This book devotes two chapters to music imaging issues and presents two OMR systems.

Chapter IV "Optical Music Imaging: Music Document Digitisation, Recognition, Evaluation, and Restoration" by Graham Jones, Bee Ong, Ivan Bruno, and Kia Ng, introduces the background of music imaging-related issues including digitisation, processing, restoration, and automatic transcription of digitised music score to recognise musical features (from the image of the digitised score), and convert them into machine-readable formats (e.g., MPEG SMR). With a general overview, the chapter discusses challenges in this domain, digitisation issues, and necessary components including hardware and software. It also presents the design and development of SharpEye, which is one of the most popular commercial OMR systems. After that, the chapter presents an approach for the evaluation of OMR systems and evaluates a number of systems (SharpEye, SmartScore, and O³MR) using this approach. This chapter also presents automated recognition and graphical restoration issues that are important for the preservation of a vast amount of invaluable paper-based heritage, including printed music scores and handwritten manuscripts that are deteriorating over time due to natural decaying of paper and chemical reaction (e.g., printing ink and paper).

Following the theme of OMR, Chapter V "Optical Music Recognition: Architecture and Algorithms" by Pierfrancesco Bellini, Ivan Bruno, and Paolo Nesi, presents the design and development of the O³MR system for optical music recognition. The O³MR solution has been realised with a large set of methods and technologies to analyse and process images of music scores. Experimental results reported demonstrate a high efficiency in the correct location of basic symbols. With a neural-network-based classifier, a rule-based music grammar, and iterative aggregation process, the system supports reconstruction of notation of varying complexity, which is represented with the WEDELMUSIC XML model.

In Chapter VI "Challenges of Designing a Markup Language for Music," Jacques Steyn analyses the background development of music representations using markup languages. Steyn makes comparisons with other representations (e.g., text and mathematics markup languages) and discusses considerations such as paged or scrolled rendering, writing systems, and reusability and scalability issues. This chapter highlights the particular challenges of markup languages for music, such as multiple and simultaneous events that need to be synchronised.

This is followed by a chapter on "Alternative Design Goals for a General Music Markup Language" by the same author. In this chapter, Steyn notes that "Design goals determine the particular structure of a markup language, while the philosophy of what markup languages are about determine the framework within which its structure is developed." In this context, this chapter presents brief surveys of related representations including SGML, DSSSL, HyTime, and SMDL, together with HTML and XML. With several XML-based music applications examples, the author proposed an ideal structure of XML for music, and discusses design criteria and application issues.

Chapter VIII "Interactive Systems for Multimedia Opera" by Michael Oliva, presents current trends towards technology-enhanced performing arts, exploring interactive multimedia technologies for stage performance and how they increase artistic possibilities. It describes the background, the design, and the development of several software applications and hardware systems to deliver multimedia content for operas, and discusses gestural control interfaces. It analyses requirements, presents a recent performance, and recommends effective and practical approaches to these issues. The author believes that the requirements and integrations of these new elements should be performed centrally from the beginning and not simply applied "atmospherically or decoratively."

Chapter IX "Driving Sound Synthesis with a Live Audio Signal," Cornelius Poepel discusses issues of musical expression, challenges of real-time computer-based systems. The chapter introduces an audio synthesis method called "audio signal driven sound synthesis" that uses the raw audio signal of a traditional instrument to drive a synthesis algorithm. This method can be used for the augmentation to various existing musical instruments as well as new instruments.

The author discusses an application of the method with a bodiless viola that allows the player to explore new sonic dimensions of electronic sounds with an interface (the playing of the instrument) that is already familiar to the player. Since the synthesis engine is driven by the audio signal of the bodiless instrument, nuances of articulation and playing technique can be represented in the synthesized sound even if not tracked, as it is necessary in common parameter driven approaches. The chapter also reports user tests and comments from expert players who have tested the system and discusses plausible future directions.

Chapter X "How Technology Can Support Culture and Learning" by David Luigi Fuschi, Bee Ong, and David Crombie discusses the interleaving interrelations of education, technology, content accessibility, and intercultural issues. It presents a wide range of related background for contextualisation, and uses language learning as an example for the discussions. The authors suggest that technology is both a tool and a factor that can foster cultural and learning development, and presents the evolution of educational models and developments with respect to technological innovations. The chapter also considers accessibility issues, together with tools and approaches to e-learning, considerations on the market sectors, standards, regulation, and related issues.

Chapter XI "Web-Based Music Intelligent Tutoring Systems" by Somnuk Phon-Amnuaisuk and Chee Keh Siong, presents a Web-based, intelligent music-tutoring system for music theory. It considers the pedagogical aspects of music learning and teaching, and discusses the pros and cons of Web-based systems for learning and teaching. The chapter discusses the key challenges including the lack of domain specific content authoring tools, intelligent feedback, and presents the design and development of an interactive multimedia environment for music score editing. In order to provide further understand of the performance of individual students and to analyse students' behaviours and performances, monitoring functionalities and modelling of learning (using a Bayesian network) are explored. With the framework, technical details, and results analysis, the chapter also discusses several potential future trends, including multimodal interface, standardisation requirements of teaching materials for music, and intelligent systems for music theory tutoring.

DRM systems can be viewed as multimedia information management systems that take into account digital rights and protection functionalities. They enable controlled distribution and usages of the multimedia content through the digital value chain. In Chapter XII "Digital Rights Management Technologies and Standards," Jaime Delgado and Eva Rodríguez discuss the background, state-of-the-art developments, and requirements related to digital rights management (DRM), with particular focus on the technological advancements and standardisation activities.

The chapter discusses a number of selected initiatives (standard and proprietary) that specify a DRM system or the elements that form a DRM system, including MPEG-21, Open Mobile Alliance (OMA) DRM, TV-Anytime DRM, DReamM, and so forth. It also presents current industry solutions, such as Windows Media DRM 10 and Helix DRM, and discusses their components and architecture. It further describes the MPEG-21 standard initiative, with particular focus on the different pieces and formats that normatively specify and are needed by a complete DRM system, such as the digital item declaration, rights expression language, intellectual property management, and protection and event reporting. The chapter presents the Rights Expression Languages (RELs) in detail, as one of the key components of DRM system that define the content usage rules, and addresses interoperability issues between RELs.

Following the theme on DRM, Chapter XIII "Possibilities, Limitations, and the Future of Audiovisual Content Protection," by Martin Schmucker, briefly discusses DRM and presents several key developments of technologies for the protection of digital content including the so-called passive protection technologies, particularly on watermarking and fingerprinting (perceptual hashing). These passive protection technologies are less interfering with content usage and enable new protection applications. For each method, the general principle, characteristics, requirements, and limitations are described.

The chapter further considers different application contexts and discusses issues from related parties, such as the content owner and consumer, and discusses examples of conflicts between security requirements and consumer issues. It analyses current technological possibilities and practical limitations, studies the music industry value chain, and the influences of DRM. The final section discusses potential future trends and solutions.

Chapter XIV "Online Music Distribution," by Francesco Spadoni, presents the development of online music distributions and related issues including its challenges, business models, market structure, new technologies, and distribution media, together with DRM issues including rights clearing, intellectual property protection, content retrieval, and metadata management. It also discusses the legal framework and the developing market of digital music, and the quality and accessibility aspects of online music distribution services. In the final section, this chapter summarizes the findings and projects towards plausible future trends.

This book consists of a collection of selected chapters that encompass information, experiences, and knowledge to bring the music industries and research communities closer, and to bring music into the interactive multimedia era. With a wide range of background research and introductory materials that are supported by relevant references for further reading, this book aims to show the latest possibilities and to ponder potential future directions. Real-life application scenarios are used to explain the concepts and provide further understanding on how to apply the new knowledge provided. This book covers key ele-

# Acknowledgment

We very much appreciate the effort, collaboration, and participation of many people, including colleagues and friends, a long list of partners, institutions, organisations, and over 1,000 registered members without whom MUSICNETWORK and this book would not exist. Thanks to all the authors who submitted chapters and all the reviewers for their invaluable help and insightful contributions. Thanks to the European Commission IST 5th Framework Programme for cosupporting the MUSICNETWORK project, and the EC project officer Ian Pigott.

Thanks to many special people working behind the scenes who have helped and supported us over the course of the project and during postproject activities (such as the establishment of the MUSICNETWORK International Association and the completion of this book), including the DSI team at the University of Florence, the ICSRiM team at the University of Leeds, and many others.

A special thanks to all the staff at the IGI Global, particularly to Kristin Roth, Ross Miller, Jessica Thompson, and Jan Travers, for their assistance and guidance.

Last but not least, we would like to thank our families for their support and understanding throughout this project.

*Kia Ng, PhD*
*ICSRiM, University of Leeds, UK*
*http://www.kcng.org*

*Paolo Nesi, PhD*
*DSI, University of Florence, Italy*
*http://www.dsi.unifi.it/~nesi*

# Chapter I
# Interactive Multimedia
# MUSICNETWORK:
## An Introduction

**Kia Ng**
*University of Leeds, UK*

**Paolo Nesi**
*University of Florence, Italy*

## ABSTRACT

*The MUSICNETWORK project was cosupported by the European Commission to bring music industry and related research areas into the interactive multimedia era. It represented a virtual Centre of Excellence during the period of the project, and today an international association, where music content providers, cultural institutions, industry, and research institutions work together, drawing on their collective assets and mutual interests, to exploit the potential of multimedia music contents with new technologies, tools, products, formats, and models. Due to large gaps between needs and real products and solutions, many products in the market fail to exploit the potential of new multimedia technologies effectively. MUSICNETWORK helps research solutions to reach the market by seeking agreements between different actors and formats by bringing together research institutions, industries, small and medium enterprises (SMEs), and experts to build the required momentum to study and define multimedia music modelling and coding for the new age. MUSICNETWORK activities, actions, and services are provided through the project Web site, which can be found online at http://www.interactivemusicnetwork.org.*

## INTRODUCTION

The main achievement of the MUSICNETWORK has been the creation of an effective community to bring European music industries and content providers into the interactive multimedia era. This is the result of a collaborative effort by many people from different contexts, including content providers, institutions, research centres, industries, and experts in the field of multimedia music. Since the early beginning of its establishment, the MUSICNETWORK community has been pursuing a common goal to study different aspects of music coding, protection, and distribution in order to improve the existing standards and to foster wider exploitation of music related contents, tools, and applications.

What has been clear since the beginning was the need to identify suitable models and solutions to integrate and make available the knowledge coming from music publishers, digital libraries, universities, standardisation bodies, research institutions, music associations, end-users, music schools, information technology companies, commercial content distributors, and other players in music industry. To address this need, the MUSICNETWORK project implemented concrete actions for integrating these types of knowledge and bringing music into the interactive media era (see Figure 1). A set of activities was implemented to provide a better understanding of the real requirements, to better assess to the state-of-the-art research and technology, to integrate currently available technologies, and to strategically steer all these activities toward the project's objectives.

From what has been done over the last few years, we believed that these activities have accelerated the process of development and adoption of

applications in the area of multimedia music, and also in the area of digitisation and conversion of archives and digital collections by both reducing technical problems and creating awareness about the capabilities offered by present technologies and solutions.

## MUSIC IS NOT ONLY AN AUDITORY EXPERIENCE

Music is part of an integrated multimodal communication. It can be integrated with many other related aspects of the music piece to provide necessary contextual information to enrich the experience of the user. For example, a handwritten music score can be shown in synchronisation with actions of a performer, such as a soloist or a conductor, during a live performance. Besides music scores, other related information, such as a composer's biography, can also be associated with the music and/or performance. All these additions can offer the user a wider view and greater knowledge about a musical piece and/or the composer. This approach can introduce different musical genres to a wider audience and enhance cultural understanding and knowledge.

Another important application of interactive multimedia music lies within the context of music

*Figure 1. The MUSICNETWORK activities, © MUSICNETWORK*

education. Interactive multimedia technology can enrich the students' learning activities with improved effectiveness, better experiences, and greater enjoyment. For this purpose, interactive multimedia music should have the following aspects:

- Coding of symbolic music notation, symbolic music representation.
- Coding of music score image sequences.
- music descriptors.
- Multilingual lyrics linked to symbolic notation.
- Music notation symbols or lyric related images.
- Video related/synchronised to music notation symbols, image scores, documents, or lyric text.
- Audio files related and synchronized with music in symbolic format and images of music scores.
- Protection aspects of audio and/or video and/or music scores such as watermarking or fingerprint.
- Verbal description of videos and documents, and scores for visually impaired users.

The MUSICNETWORK identified a lack of coordination and standardization in the area of multimedia music modelling, and most of the available multimedia standards neglect music notation. Therefore, recognising the relevance of the integration of music and multimedia as an enabling technology for developing new applications and markets, the MUSICNETWORK started an activity to integrate a symbolic music representation (SMR) into the MPEG standard. This activity has achieved successful results within the MPEG forum. Currently, a draft of the MPEG SMR standard has been produced. More information can be obtained from the Web site of MPEG *ad hoc* Group (AHG) on SMR hosted by the MUSICNETWORK at http://www.inter-activemusicnetwork.org/mpeg-ahg/

## MUSICNETWORK'S ACTIVITIES AND SERVICES

MUSICNETWORK offers a unique set of services to the community:

- Innovation and stimulation:
  - Stimulating new services and exploitation of new multimedia functionalities
  - Opening new markets for content distribution, for example, e-publishing, advertising, entertainment, edutainment, infotainment, with mobile and pervasive systems
  - Suggesting models and formats for interactive multimedia music coding, distribution, and protection
  - Promoting guidelines for the adoption of standards in connection with standards bodies such as the ISO MPEG
- Knowledge and information:
  - Giving a clear view of the present market and state-of-the-art technologies, best practices and trends
  - Providing access to a large state-of-the-art database, requirements, technologies, and solutions
  - Providing information and support on European Commission initiatives in interactive multimedia music area
  - Offering training on latest technologies, standards, and solutions
- Visibility and accessibility:
  - Offering wider visibility for research and technology innovations
  - Offering free access for everyone to all kinds of information
  - Creating an environment where skills of partners can easily be identified and located
- Consultation and standardization:
  - Collecting and surveying challenges and proposing solutions for obstacles

concerning interactive multimedia music and innovative technologies

- ○ Mediating the work of companies and research centres with the work of standardisation bodies
- ○ Identification of requirements
- ○ Production of call-for-technologies with the standard bodies

These technical objectives have been, and are addressed by, a set of activities in order to create a collaborative environment where content providers and corporate users may access research results and technological solutions to make the technology transfer easier and simpler. These activities include:

- Coordinating a set of expert working groups on the most important topics and producing guidelines, state-of-the-art reports, and so forth, in order to understand the obstacles and challenges in bringing music coding, distribution, and protection into the interactive multimedia era.
- Managing an MPEG *Ad Hoc* Group on Symbolic Music Representation. Further information, events, and documents are available at http://www.interactivemusic-network.org/mpeg-ahg/.
- Organising a set of workshops and conferences and inviting experts and decision makers to highlight and discuss the technical and business challenges.
- Organising a set of open workshops that often colocated with other conferences, including Web Delivering of Music (WE-DELMUSIC) 2003 and 2004, MPEG Meeting (March 2004), International Association of Music Libraries (IAML), International Association of Music Information Centre (IAMIC), Automatic Production of Cross Media Content for Multi-Channel Distribution (AXMEDIS2005, in Florence, Italy, and

AXMEDIS2006 in Leeds, UK), Allegro con Bit 2006 in Rome (Italy), and others

- Maintaining a Web portal for supporting all of the above-mentioned services (see http://www.interactivemusicnetwork.org).

## THE WORKING GROUPS (WG)

The MUSICNETWORK addresses several aspects of music involving a large group of participants, from many different countries, with different cultures and a wide range of technological skills. Participation is always welcome from everyone interested in the subject areas, with no limitation on geographical or cultural issues. Hence, most (if not all) of the results of the project are valuable for European countries and beyond.

The MUSICNETWORK has established several different working groups to focus on issues of particular importance, and to provide opportunities for the experts and practitioners, as well as all interested parties, to get involved in the work. The WGs include:

- **Music notation:** This group examines each and every aspect of coding music notation, including modern music notation, format conversion, lyric modelling (multilingual aspects), fonts, and defining standards for music symbols, standardization into MPEG, and other bodies.
- **Music libraries:** This group has a cross-domain perspective including museums, archives, industry catalogues, and other collections. It deals with metadata; information- and content-based retrieval; digital libraries; technological, legal, and standardization developments; sharing documents and contents.
- **Music in multimedia standards:** This working group examines multimedia standards for music coding, including audio

and video coding (MPEG-7, MPEG-21, etc.), portable formats for the Internet, synchronization, media integration, and other standardization aspects with MPEG and other bodies.

- **Music distribution:** This group examines the distribution of coded music, including streaming, Internet, distribution models (B2B, B2C, P2P, etc.), mobile systems, WEB-TV, mobile, and transaction models (online, off-line, kiosks, virtual shops).
- **Music protection:** This group is devoted to issues related to the protection of coded music, such as encryption, fingerprint, watermark, digital rights management (DRM), profiling functionalities, active and passive protection, and other security issues.
- **Music accessibility:** This working group examines music coding for print-impaired people (visually impaired, dyslexic, etc.), and studies accessibility issues, user interfaces, computer-assisted software and devices, and the provision of music in alternative formats.
- **Music imaging:** This working music imaging group focuses on issues related to imaging and processing of music score (printed music scores and handwritten manuscripts), including music image acquisition, acquisition of music with different types of page support, digitising ancient music, coding for images, optical restoration and preservation, and optical music recognition (OMR).
- **Music audio:** This working group is focused on audio processing aspects such as conversion from audio to music notation, query by content, beat tracking, audio shrinking and stretching, audio recognition and comparison for personalization.
- **Music education:** This group analyses and works on educational aspects of music with the support of the information technology and pedagogical aspects. In particular, it deals with cooperative work on music no-

tation, performances, virtual conducting, virtual orchestra, playing instruments by using Internet support, e-learning, distance teaching, courseware tools, assessing music performances, self learning, software tools for music education, and so forth.

- **Music culture:** This working group addresses the cultural aspects of music and musicology. This helps to consider music in the related historical period, and also the interpretation of the music in its related musical context.

## THE MUSICNETWORK PARTICIPANTS

Analysis on the profiles of MUSICNETWORK participants has been regularly performed, during the development of the project, to:

- Refine the services and the models provided to the participants.
- Understand if other needs could be satisfied or emerge.
- Identify the best model for the business plan.

The latest analysis was carried out on a sample of approximately 940 participants from about 230 qualified institutions. The data used for the analysis were collected from questionnaires filled in by participants when they registered and whenever they modified their profiles. Unfortunately, not all participants filled in the questionnaires and hence, the number of data entries actually used for the analysis was smaller than the sample size.

The first set of questions was used to get a better understanding of the participants' profiles. In this document, only country distribution is reported (as illustrated in Figure 3). In the most recent survey, it was found that 70% of the participants are from Europe (18 states), and 12% of the participants from the US and Canada.

*Figure 3. Distribution of MUSICNETWORK participants by country*

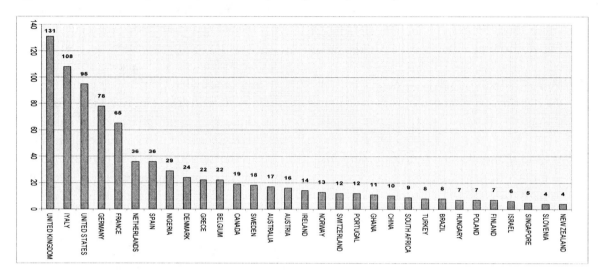

*Figure 4. Distribution of MUSICNETWORK participants by type in percentage*

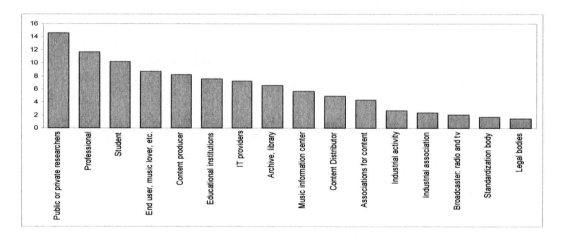

Figure 4 shows the distribution of the participants' different types of affiliations. As can be seen from the distribution chart, the most important groups are researcher, professional, student, and content producer.

We have also studied this set of data by reclassifying them into two groups: (1) participants who registered with the MUSICNETWORK to offer the role of technology provider and (2) participants who are interested as technology consumers. It is interesting to note that MUSICNETWORK has attracted more technology consumers than providers.

This is considered as a success, since the project has mainly been focussed on stimulating the understanding and usage of interactive multimedia music technologies. One of the conclusions could be that the consumers are interested in the technology itself. This is evident from the analysis reported in the next section, which shows what consumers are looking for. This analysis has been performed in two steps: firstly, the general area of interest, and secondly, what kind of services was of greater interest.

This analysis was carried out using the information the users stated during the registration. Fifteen categories on the area of interests that match the subject domains of the WGs have been used to analyse the distributions on the area of interest, so that the technical area of the interest can be identified (see Figure 5).

By "distribution" we mean the technology for distributing content via the Internet, and it is the most requested topic by the analysis. The reason may be found in the distribution of notation (partially), audio files, and other general contents. All these aspects are of great interest to the participants. Hence, protection and copyright should be considered as part of the distribution. From the analysis, it is clear that distribution is

obviously the most dominant aspect for most of the MUSICNETWORK participants. Therefore, some of the WGs may seem to be less relevant than the others. This is natural and expected since their related market is smaller.

The types of services required by the participants have also been analysed. Table 2 lists the type of requirements together with the number of requests.

From the table, it is evident that the most requested services from MUSICNETWORK participants are related to the ease of access to information. Other services, such as discussion forums and contacts, proved to be of less importance.

The number of downloads performed by participants can also be a good measure of their areas of interest. It has been noticed that users

*Table 1. Providers vs. consumers*

|  | Number | % |
| --- | --- | --- |
| Technology Providers | 558 | 41.77 |
| Technology Consumers | 778 | 58.23 |
| **Total** | 1336 | 100 |

*Figure 5. Distribution of MUSICNETWORK participants' interests*

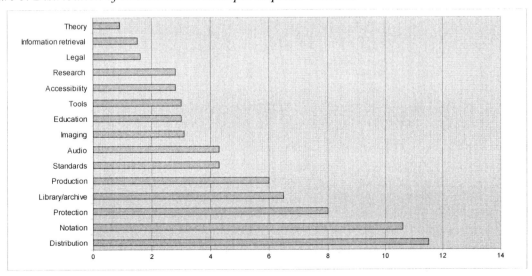

*Table 2. Distribution of MUSICNETWORK participants' needs*

| Description of Services Requested | Number | % |
|---|---|---|
| Information and News on Technology, the future | 111 | 50 |
| Collaboration and Contacts for technical aspects | 78 | 35 |
| Conferences and Workshops | 14 | 6.3 |
| Market and Commercial contacts | 10 | 4.5 |
| Dissemination diffusion of results, and models | 8 | 3.6 |
| **Total** | **221** | |

*Figure 6. Trend of growth of the MUSICNETWORK*

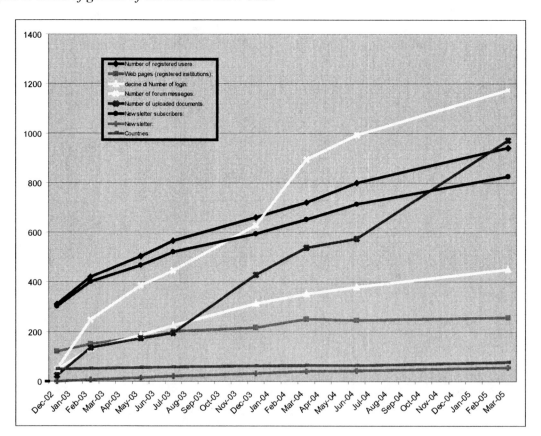

have mainly been focusing on a number of specific areas reported in the next table. The most attractive documents have been those produced in the context of music notation and distribution (around 38,000 downloads in total).

The number of downloads related to the activities and documents produced by each individual working group has also been analysed and presented in Table 4. Notation, Imaging, Protection & Distribution, and Library working groups are

*Table 3. Topics of interest*

| Topics of Interests | Sub Areas | % for Topic |
|---|---|---|
| Music Notation (symbolic and imaging) | Notation | 52.87% |
| | Imaging | |
| | MPEG-AHG | |
| | Glossary | |
| Distribution and protection | Distribution | 11.02% |
| | Protection | |
| Library | Library | 6.54% |
| Standard | Standard | 3.82% |
| Education and Culture | Educational | 4.48% |
| | Culture | |
| Accessibility | Accessibility | 2.45% |
| Audio | Audio | 1.00% |
| Overview | | 1.41% |
| Events | | 16.40% |
| **Total** | | **100%** |

*Table 4. Areas of interest of the MUSICNETWORK participants*

| Area of Interests | Number of Downloads |
|---|---|
| **Imaging** | **16,031** |
| **Notation** | **22,234** |
| AHG | 5,945 |
| WG | 19,688 |
| Glossary | 258 |
| **Protection & Distribution** | **25,633** |
| Distribution | 13,660 |
| Protection | 11,973 |
| Library | **15,298** |
| Education | **5,658** |
| Standards | **6,454** |
| Accessibility | **3,941** |

among the most attractive in terms of participants' interest. Protection & Distribution WGs have been considered jointly since distribution technologies have no sense without protection and DRM.

## THE GROWTH OF THE MUSICNETWORK

Figure 6 illustrates the evolution of a set of very simple metrics over the course of the MUSICNET-WORK project. Together they provide an overview about the evolution of MUSICNETWORK as a whole, since the start of this monitoring process in December 2002, when the first services of the project were activated.

From the graph, it is evident that MUSIC-NETWORK is now still growing, although at a slower speed than it was at the very beginning. Additionally, it seems that, since December 2003, MUSICNETWORK reached the critical mass when the forum activities started.

## CONCLUSION

In this chapter, we have presented, analysed, and discussed the MUSICNETWORK project. From the analysis and evaluation data obtained, we believe that the MUSICNETWORK project has achieved its aim as a Centre/Network of Excellence to bring the music content providers, cultural institutions, industry, and research institutions to work together, to provide a large number of services to SMEs in the area of multimedia music.

Moreover, MUSICNETWORK can help research solutions to reach the potential marketplace and assist in finding the appropriate matches between those who have technical solutions to offer and those who could be benefited from these solutions. This has been achieved, thanks to the support and contribution of many research institutions, industries, SMEs, and experts in the field of multimedia music modelling and coding. The fast and continuous growth of MUSICNET-WORK activities further confirms the success of the project.

The MUSICNETWORK is now an international association with a wide range of partnerships, many members, and many exciting activities that will continue to build on the successful achievements of the project so far. If you are interested in the activities, membership, and services of the association, you are welcome to join the association to participate in the activities and development of the MUSICNETWORK association for the advancement and success of this interdisciplinary domain.

## ACKNOWLEDGMENT

The authors would like to acknowledge all the partners of the MUSICNETWORK project, including over 1,000 participants and more than 260 institutions and companies that are registered with the MUSICNETWORK to collaborate and to contribute to its work and growth.

## REFERENCES

Bellini, P., Crombie, D., & Nesi, P. (2003). MU-SICNETWORK: To bring music industry into the interactive multimedia age. In *Proceedings of the EVA* Florence, Italy.

Bellini, P., & Nesi, P. (2001, November 23-24). WEDELMUSIC FORMAT: An XML music notation format for emerging applications. In *Proceedings of the 1st International Conference of Web Delivering of Music*, Florence, Italy (pp. 79-86). IEEE Press.

CANTATE project. (1994). *Deliverable 3.3: Report on SMDL evaluation, WP3*. CANTATE. Retrieved from http://projects.fnb.nl

CUIDADO. *Processing of music and Mpeg7.* Retrieved from http://www.ircam.fr/cuidad/

Delgado, J., Nesi, P., & Ng, K. C. (Eds.). (2004). In *Proceedings of the Fourth International Conference on WEB Delivering of Music (WEDEL-MUSIC-2004).* Barcelona, Spain: IEEE Computer Society Press, .

Good, M. (2001). MusicXML for notation and Analysis. In W. B. Hewlett & E. Selfridge-Field (Eds.), *The virtual score representation, retrieval, restoration* (pp. 113-124). Cambridge, MA: The MIT Press.

HARMONICA. Retrieved from http://projects.fnb.nl/harmonica

I-MAESTRO project. Retrieved from http://www.i-maestro.org

MOODS project. Retrieved from http://www.dsi.unifi.it/~moods

Mitolo, N., Nesi, P., & Ng, K. C. (Eds.). (2005, July 2-4). In *Proceedings of the 5th MUSICNET-WORK Open Workshop,* Universität für Musik und darstellende Kunst Wien, Vienna, Austria.

Nesi, P., Ng, K., & Delgado, J. (Eds). (2005, Nov 30 - Dec 2). In *Proceedings of the 1st International Conference on Automating Production of Cross Media Content for Multi-channel Distribution Conference* (AXMEDIS 2005): Workshops and Industrial, Convitto della Calza, Florence, Italy. Firenze University Press.

Ng, K. C., Busch, C., & Nesi, P. (Eds.). (2003). In *Proceedings of the third International Conference on WEB Delivering of Music (WEDELMUSIC-2003),* Leeds, UK.

Ng, K. C. (Ed.). (2005). *Journal of New Music Research (JNMR), 34*(2).

Ng, K.C. (Ed.). (2006, May 9-10). In *Proceedings of the COST287-ConGAS 2nd International Symposium on Gesture Interface for Multimedia Systems (GIMS2006),* Leeds, UK.

Ng, K. C., Badii, A., & Bellini, P. (Eds). (2006, December 13-15. In *Proceedings of the 2nd International Conference on Automated Production of Cross Media Content for Multi-channel Distribution.* University of Leeds, UK: Firenze University Press.

Ng, K. C., Crombie, D., Bellini, P., & Nesi, P. (2003). Musicnetwork: Music industry with interactive multimedia technology. In *Proceedings of Electronic Imaging and the Visual Arts (EVA London 2003),* UCL, London.

NIFF. (1995). *NIFF 6a: Notation Interchange File Format.*

Selfridge-Field, E. (Ed.). (1997). *Beyond MIDI—The handbook of musical codes.* London: The MIT Press.

SMDL ISO/IEC. (1995). *Standard Music Description Language.* ISO/IEC DIS 10743.

Smith, L. (1997). SCORE. In E. Selfridge-Field, Ed. *Beyond MIDI - The handbook of musical codes,* London: The MIT Press.

WEDELMUSIC. Retrieved from http://www.wedelmusic.org

# Chapter II
# MPEG Symbolic Music Representation:
## A Solution for Multimedia Music Applications

**Pierfrancesco Bellini**
*University of Florence, Italy*

**Paolo Nesi**
*University of Florence, Italy*

**Giorgio Zoia**
*EPFL, Switzerland*

## ABSTRACT

*The evolution of digital communication devices and formats has recently produced fundamental changes in the practical approach to music representation and notation, transforming them from a simple visual coding model for sheet music into a composite tool for modelling music in computer and multimedia applications in general. As a consequence, a multilayer model of music representation is needed for several purposes in addition to sheet music production or visual display, such as audio rendering, entertainment, music analysis, database query, music performance coding, music distance learning, and so forth. Symbolic music representation is a standard for modelling music notations, proposed inside the MPEG multimedia framework. Symbolic music representation generalizes the main music notation concepts to model the visual aspects of a music score, along with audio information or annotations related to the music piece, allowing integration with other audiovisual elements by multimedia references. The symbolic music representation standard overcomes the limitations of a widely accepted format like MIDI, which is in line with its main purpose to model music events whereas it reveals important limitations in producing audio and visual representations with satisfactory results.*

## INTRODUCTION

Music is mainly accessed through its audible representation, while music notations have been developed to visually represent the information needed by performers to play, through specific instruments, the musical work and reproduce music as intended by the author. The visual representation of music has reached the present format by means of many years of evolution. Thus, the edition of music scores for professional publishing and visualization is one of the earliest applications of music notation on computers, and it is mainly focussed on visual arrangement and rendering of music symbols (Blostein & Haken, 1991; CANTATE, 1994; Selfridge-Field, 1997), (many commercial applications exist: Sibelius (http://www.sibelius.com), Finale of Coda (http://www.finalemusic.com/), Capella (Capella, 2005)). Sheet music publishing requires the production of high-quality music scores, in terms of visual rendering.

The evolution of information technology has recently produced changes in the usage of music representation in practice, transforming music notation from a simple visual coding model for music score to a tool for modelling music in computer programs and electronic tools in general. In the last few years, several XML-compliant mark-up languages for music modelling have been presented (and a review is also reported in this book), among them: MNML (musical notation markup language), MusicML, MML (music markup language), MusicXML (Good, 2001), WEDELMUSIC (http://www.wedelmusic.org) (Bellini, Della Santa, & Nesi, 2001; Bellini & Nesi, 2001), CAPXML (Capella, 2005), and so forth. Most of them are mainly focused on modelling the music elements to preserve and interchange them among other applications. Past efforts for standardizing music notation were attempted in the past with SMDL (SMDL, 1995) and NIFF (NIFF Consortium, 2005). Only a few of the mentioned formats can cope with part of the needs of the innovative and emerging applications in interactive multimedia music, as highlighted in the MPEG requirements on symbolic music representation (ISO document ISO/IEC SC29WG11, W6689). The most relevant among these requirements are briefly reported and commented on in this chapter. Some of the innovative applications integrate 3-D virtual reality, complex animations, and synchronizations, and they are already spreading in everyday life, together with many emerging prototypes and tools from research and development projects that explore new areas and possibilities. These new applications can be categorised briefly as:

- Multimedia music systems for music tuition, for example: VOYETRA, SMARTSCORE, PLAYPRO, PIANOTUTOR, IMUTUS (self-tuition system for recorder in which the pupil has the possibility of receiving suggestions and observing the correct posture of the hands provided by a 3-D scene reconstruction) (http://www.exodus.gr/imutus/), MUSICALIS (self-tuition system for several instruments in which the user may receive suggestions and other information) (http://www.musicalis.fr/), Freehands (allowing the visualization and the annotation of music scores, http://www.freehandsystems.com/), Yamaha tools for music education (http://www.digitalmusicnotebook.com/home/), and so forth.
- Multimedia music tools for edutainment and infotainment in archives such as WEDELMUSIC (integrating music notation and multimedia for building and distributing multimedia music cultural content with digital rights management) (http://www.wedelmusic.org) (Bellini, Barthelemy, Bruno, Nesi, & Spinu, 2003), or for producing multimedia content to document and assist the user in theatres such as in OPENDRAMA (http://www.iua.upf.es/mtg/opendrama/).

- Cooperative music editing: tools to support rehearsals and musical practice in orchestras and music schools, such as MOODS solution and tools (http://www.dsi.unifi.it/~moods ), (Bellini Fioravanti, F., & Nesi, 1999), (Bellini, Nesi, & Spinu, 2002), and now with the I-MAESTRO solution for cooperative support for music education and performance control integrated into the Max/MSP environment (http://www.i-maestro.org) (Ong, Ng, Mitolo, & Nesi, 2006).

Many users have discovered and are attracted to the multimedia experience. The traditional music notation model has been, in many cases, replaced with more suitable multimedia representations of music. Many new applications are getting the market attention. Unfortunately, these innovative experiences are mainly based on incompatible technologies in which the music content is recreated for each product, and for which the information exchange between products is difficult and strongly limited to subsets of the notational part. The lack of a standardized symbolic music representation format, integrated with multimedia, results in each developer implementing their own solution that varies in efficiency, scope, features, quality, and complexity. Thus, a new concept of multimedia interactive music is growing also thanks to the MUSICNETWORK (http://www.interactivemusicnetwork.org) and to the several innovative R&D projects of the European Commission: CANTATE, MOODS, IMUTUS, WEDELMUSIC, PLAY, PLAY2, CUIDADO, I-MAESTRO, OPENDRAMA, and so forth.

In addition to the simple representation format, the need for a unique and comprehensive representation of music information that can be integrated with other media has arisen. This is particularly needed to support and enable the realization of a wide range of diverse applications. To this end,

several problems, ranging from information modelling to integration of the music representation, have to be taken into account. The main problems are related to the organization of music elements and symbols in a suitable and acceptable form to cope with the more general concepts of music elements and relationships with the several aspects of audiovisual content.

Finally, there is also a need of representing nonwestern music notation, such as music from the Far East countries (including China, Korea, Japan), Middle East (Arabia, Northern Africa), Northern Africa, and so forth. In order to support these music representations, the music model has to be kept sufficiently flexible and general.

## GOALS OF SYMBOLIC MUSIC REPRESENTATION

MPEG symbolic music representation (SMR) aims at generalizing music notation to model not only the visual aspects of a music score, but also audio information or annotations related with a music piece. SMR is a multilayer logical structure based on symbolic elements that represent audiovisual events: the relationship between those events, and aspects of rendering those events. There are many symbolic representations of music, including different styles of Chant, Renaissance, Classic, Romantic, Jazz, Rock, and Pop styles, percussion notation, as well as simplified notations for children, Braille, and so forth.

The integration of SMR into the MPEG multimedia framework with technologies that range from video, audio, interactivity, and digital rights management enables the development of a large number of new applications, like those mentioned earlier in this document and in Bellini et al. (Bellini, Nesi, & Zoia, 2005). MPEG SMR (officially MPEG-4 Part 23) enables the synchronization of symbolic music elements with audiovisual events that are represented and rendered using existing

MPEG technology. The MPEG standards for multimedia representation, coding, and playback with SMR provide content interoperability.

With the insertion of SMR, MPEG is opening the way for realising new applications for music notation, mainly in the areas of entertainment, edutainment, infotainment, that may be also exploited on set-top boxes (STB) for interactive TV, personal computers, and mobiles systems. All of these applications of interactive multimedia music representation may take advantage of MPEG SMR technology for the standard multimedia integration, presenting the possibility of distributing content in a variety of forms in a completely integrated manner (see, for example, OPENDRAMA). The insertion of symbolic music representation in MPEG-4 is going to open the usage of music representation on a large set of devices based on MPEG such as DVD players, decoders, and so forth. They have a large penetration, and this may lead to have music scores appearing on many applications on our TV sets for interactive TV.

## SMR FOR EDUCATIONAL AND EDUTAINMENT

One of the most interesting applications of MPEG SMR is in the area of educational applications. In these cases, we have the integration of SMR with audio, lyrics, annotations, different semantics for visual and audible renderings (different notations, parts and main scores, ancient and common western notation), synchronization with audiovisual such as video, audio, images, and also the 3-D virtual rendering of the position of the hands and body (posture and/or gesture), or of the scene with the actors, and so forth (see Figure 1).

Music education and edutainment are currently the largest markets for music representation. In the same way that a text can be synchronized to images and sounds in commercial DVDs; audio, video, and music representation can be synchronized as well, for various (or separate) instruments and voices, and with various models or rendering aspects (common western music notation, tablature, Braille, etc.).

*Figure 1. A tool mock-up for exploiting MPEG SMR for education, edutainment, suitable for assisted learning, self-learning, on i-TV, tablet PC, and so forth coded in MPEG-4 with SMR support*

Music courseware needs to have music representation integrated with video, images, documents, animation, audio, and so forth. In addition, a music course may present some exercises that require special music notation symbols (e.g., given by the teacher for annotating the student work) and/or audio processing (e.g., play training assessment, theory training assessment, etc.). For these reasons, for music education and courseware production, the users on the client (music content usage) and server (content generation) sides may have different visual representations of the same musical model (with full access to the same logical aspects and additional personalized or customized semantics information for visual and audio rendering), with full capabilities of music manipulation, and a support for establishing relationships and synchronizations with other media.. Therefore, the system and model have to provide the possibility of:

- Navigation among music representation features and multimedia elements.
- Music editing, transposing, playing, formatting, piano reduction, and so forth.
- Selection of one lyric from the collection of multilingual lyrics for the same music representation.
- Synchronization of audiovisual events with the play/execution of music representation elements.
- Display of the video of the teachers or of the 3-D rendering of the correct gesture of the hands while playing the instrument synchronously with the music notation.
- Playing along: automatic accompaniment of the user by having the computer play selected voices/parts.
- Specific formatting of music with different quality and resolution, or for rendering on different platforms, possibly characterized by different formats or by different capture and actuation devices: Braille, spoken or talked music, tablature, guitar tablatures, Korean music, and so forth.

## MPEG SMR ASPECTS

In MPEG-4, some technologies are already available to code and render audio and graphics. SMR addresses logical and visual aspects of music, taking into account what is already present in MPEG. These aspects (audio, graphics, logical, and visual) are applied to symbolic elements in different ways, according to the specific implementation or distribution model. Each aspect must be addressed by separate chunks of information so that the SMR can be rendered in different ways:

- The logical aspect of SMR contains symbolic elements and their relationships and dependencies, without including exact spatial or temporal information. The Logical aspect contains no precise, absolute values such as centimetres, inches, seconds, milliseconds, and so forth. The Logical aspect of music is a concept that was missing so far in current MPEG technology.
- The Audio aspect of SMR is the temporal information that allows the logical aspects of a symbolic element to be rendered as audio. Audio rendering can be performed by using MPEG capabilities associated to scene description and media "nodes," similar to what is done in MPEG-4 structured audio (SA) (Lazzaro & Wawrzynek, 2000), another subpart of the standard that allows specifying sound as a combination of a sound generation algorithm and associated events to be "executed." MPEG4-SA is based on a language for describing audio algorithms (SAOL, structured audio orchestra language) and can be driven by a musical score language (SASL, structured audio score language), as well as by simpler standard MIDI events.

SMR adds to the MPEG SA solution the capability of representing complex symbolic music content by using a logic model and a concise visual representation such as those used by musicians; at the same time, it provides, through the scene description layer (see remarks on Scene Description later on), a straightforward interoperability with MIDI files embedded in SA streams (possibly with real SA in future) in terms of audio rendering or representation capabilities.

- The Visual aspect of SMR is abstract visual information providing hints to decoders about how to render the symbolic elements. The visual aspects do not care about the client's rendering screen or support. In common western SMR, visual aspects include the direction of a stem, the direction of the beams, the position up or down with respect to the note of qualifiers, the cue note, the visualisation and representation of complex music structures with simple symbols, and so forth, all aspects that are missing in MIDI and also in the MPEG SA.

- The Graphical aspect of SMR is the precise spatial information that allows the logical aspect of a symbolic element to be rendered graphically. Graphical information consists of precise coordinates, line thicknesses, type and sizes, and so forth, described in some absolute unit of measurement (e.g., centimetres, inches, points, etc.). In common, western music notation, graphical information permits the detailed rendering of staff lines, clefs, sharps, and so forth, and all symbols in general.

For example:

- An SMR Audio renderer takes both the Logical and Audio aspects of SMR elements and it interfaces to audio devices in synergy with other structured forms of coding (MIDI, MPEG SA, MPEG Text To Speech). If the audio aspects are missing, the SMR Audio renderer may infer them in some way from the logic aspects and some default values.

- An SMR graphics renderer takes the Logical and Visual aspects, or Logical and Graphical aspects, or Logical and Visual and Graphical aspects of SMR elements, and produces graphic information (through MPEG-4 scene description to a graphics application program interface). If the decoder receives insufficient visual or graphical information, it may infer this information in some way from default values. Examples of SMR graphics renderers are those which can produce a print out of the full score, a voice-part or set of voice-parts, Braille music scores, special tablatures, and so forth.

## FORMALIZATION OF MAJOR REQUIREMENTS

The requirements have been divided into the following groups:

- General requirements
- Decoding and rendering (including interactivity) requirements
- MPEG integration requirements

The requirements are also organized in two main categories. Those that are mandatory (major needs), and those that are conditional (minor needs).

The major general requirements are reported in the following, stating that the SMR model and tools have to:

- Support common western symbolic music representations (CWSMR), including Classical, Romantic, Jazz, and Pop/Rock forms.
- Allow coding of different representations of music, such as accessible music (spoken music, Braille [Krolick, 2000], etc.), early

European neumes, Renaissance, Baroque, tablatures, 20th century experimental notations, Schenkerian analysis, Orthodox Chant, Arabic, Indian, East Asian, and so forth.

- Be extensible. It must allow new symbolic elements to be defined. Note that this requirement also allows one to define new symbolic elements outside the pure music concepts, for example, for the multimedia annotation or other means.
- Allow SMRs to be rendered both audibly and visually. An SMR player may include only audio rendering (such as spoken music, which is a verbal description of the music info, and can be also played as MIDI generation), or present both visual and audio aspects; the model can cope with both of them.
- Allow symbolic elements to be linked to audio and/or visual information.
- Allow interoperability in the sense that SMR has to be suitable to be rendered on different devices with different capabilities.
- Support both measured (barred) and unmeasured (unbarred) SMRs.
- Allow each symbolic element to be accessed uniquely. This capability is essential for navigating, establishing relationships among different symbolic elements, establishing relationships between symbolic elements and their audio and visual counterparts.
- Support symbolic events such as SMR context and change of SMR context, whose values may provide the necessary information for deducing the meaning of other symbols. According to the general requirement of scalability, SMRs may define default values, so that SMR context information can be omitted in streams and when rendering.
- Be able to cope with multiple representations of pitch while preserving the original logical information. Note, this could be useful for modelling, transposing, and scordatura,

while maintaining separate audio and logical information.

Regarding the major SMR decoding and rendering (including interactivity) requirements, the SMR model and tools have to:

- Allow rendering of SMRs visually on the basis of the logical information.
- Allow linear browsing of SMR (for example, next/previous paging).
- Allow rendering of SMRs as audio, on the basis of the logical information.
- Support SMR qualifiers and their definition to provide the necessary information for deducing the meaning of associated symbolic events. According to the general requirement of scalability, SMRs may define default meanings, so that these can be omitted in streams and when rendering.
- Allow full scores and sets of voice parts and/or SMR symbolic selections to be transposed.
- Allow the user to add annotations to symbolic elements, such as simple text, audiovisual objects, other symbolic elements, or simple URL links. Note that the annotation format for SMR has to be normative, as well as the way annotations are issued by the end user; on the other hand, the ability to save/load annotations will not be normative and thus, player dependent.
- Support multilingual lyrics so that content can be localized. Any language should be modelled as a sequence of syllables (textual or graphical) associated with symbolic events.
- Enable full scores (also called main score, partitura) and their component voices and/or parts to be easily related in terms of symbolic elements.
- Be able to include and describe several symbolic selections.

The major requirements for the integration of SMR model and tools into MPEG have to:

- Allow SMR to be integrated into the MPEG-4 systems architecture with no modifications and minimum additions to the other parts of MPEG-4.
- Allow SMR streaming using the tools provided by MPEG-4 Systems.
- Allow synchronizing SMR with any MPEG-4 audiovisual object type by using the tools provided by MPEG-4 systems such as access units (AU), decoding time stamps (DTS), composition time stamps (CTS), and so forth.
- Support random access to symbolic elements without requiring complete decoding of the SMR stream or file.
- Allow MPEG-4 audio information to be generated from the SMR. The solution will allow both SASL and MIDI generation and subsequent decoding and presentation via MPEG-4 audio decoder.

- Allow decoding SMR even if the decoder is not aware of the other MPEG-4 audiovisual object types.
- Support both an XML-based and a binary format. For example, as in the BIFS (MPEG-4 binary format for scene description) (Kim, Lee, & Ki, 2002) and/or XMT-A (equivalent extensible text format) (Joung & Kim, 2002; Kim & Wood, N.D; Kim, Wood, & Cheok, 2000).

## THE SMR DECODER AND ITS INTEGRATION IN MPEG-4

Moving from the requirements identified previously, integration of SMR into MPEG-4 allows creation of a large range of very rich content. At the same time, the nature of the SMR itself, a music (then related and "synchronized" with audio) format rendered by visual and graphic symbols and possibly, at the same time, by structured audio events, implies several relationships with

*Figure 2. MPEG-4 Player Architecture containing SMR*

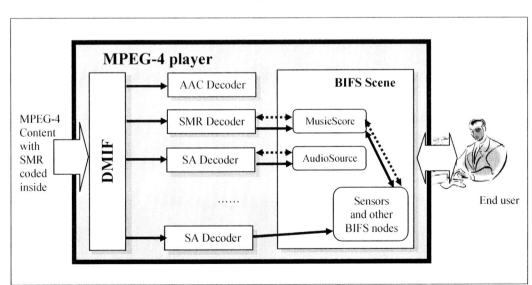

*Figure 3. MPEG SMR decoder*

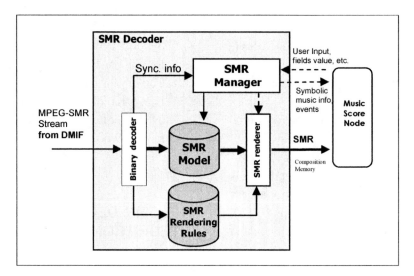

other existing tools in order to fully exploit its potential richness.

Fundamental among these relationships, allowing composition and synchronization with all other media types, is, of course, the one with MPEG-4 systems and the tightly related scene description parts. Systems carries all the necessary configuration and synchronisation information, the media streaming-data structures, and the possibility to encapsulate all this information in an adequate file format; the Scene Description allows, instead, an audiovisual layout design in space and time through a mark-up language.

As mentioned earlier, it is straightforward to enhance the richness and flexibility of the SMR toolset by direct usage of MIDI, this being a protocol based on symbolic information (even if not notation information, as noted previously); a native support inside MPEG-4 SA (through which MIDI information can be carried over MPEG-4) allows this synergy; the SMR decoder provides a direct support of SA streams containing MIDI object (see Figure 2).

Figure 2 shows a simple example of an MPEG-4 player supporting MPEG-4 SMR.

The player uses the *MusicScore* SMR node (a node is the basic element of MPEG-4 scene description hierarchical trees) to attach the symbolic music information to the scene (or even by exploiting functionality of other MPEG-4 BIFS nodes) as decoded by the SMR decoder. The user can also interact with the SMR content (to change a page, view, transpose, and so on) using sensors in association with other nodes defining the audiovisual interactive content, and routing them to MusicScore. The user sends commands from the SMR node fields to the SMR decoder (dashed lines in the figure), which generates a new view to be displayed in the scene. In addition, the user client tool automatically converts MIDI files (through a specific algorithm) into SMR on the client side and renders them. Similarly, the server might only deliver the SMR. In these cases, the client can generate the MIDI information from SMR for use with MIDI-compliant devices. This is particularly important to guarantee straightforward adaptation of current devices.

The general architecture of an SMR decoder is presented in Figure 3.

An SMR decoder is instantiated as a consequence of the opening of an SMR elementary stream or file, which also contains the configuration in its header. Then the decoder is capable of parsing the decoder configuration information into its chunk components, decoding and using them. The decoder is capable of coping with several chunks: main score, single parts, formatting rules, synchronisation information, lyrics, and fonts (or even MIDI files).

## SCORE RENDERING

The rendering engine can process the SMR information, represented through SM-XF (for SMR extensible format) chunks, on the basis of the formatting rules to produce the resulting output of the SMR in the visual and audible domains. For the visual rendering, the model and algorithms described in Bellini et al. (Bellini, Bruno, & Nesi, 2005) is used.

The formatting engine for SMR rendering and sheet music production is divided into two main systems: the insertion and positioning engine, and the justification and line-breaking module (see Figure 4). In Figure 4, the general architecture of formatting and justification engines is shown. The rendered music score is both the source and the result of the formatting and justification engines. In an SMR tool, the music score is modelled by using an object-oriented model, including main score and part within the same model. The parts are used to build the main score. The additional information for the main score organization is contained in a separate file. Music notation symbols retain all the relationships among the notation symbols and music structure in general, disregarding the values of graphic details concerning the music formatting on the rendering device (e.g., absolute or relative coordinates).

The MPEG symbolic music formatting language (SM-FL) is defined to allow describing the insertion point and positioning of music symbols.

It specifies a rule-based formatting language and engine that is used to describe sets of rules and conditions interpreted in real time by an inferential engine at the moment that the position of symbols have to be estimated. The SM-FL rules define formatting actions: they assign specific values to specific parameters related to the visual rendering of the music symbols. For example, a rule states that the stem is characterized by a given length, or by a model to estimate its length on the basis of the position. The actions to be performed are activated by the conditions based on the music context of the symbol that is under evaluation. These conditions are expressed in terms of conditional sentences, and allow identifying a music scenario (configuration/arrangement of music elements). For example, a conditional sentence recognising a certain music scenario could consist in the conjunction of conditions for detecting if a note does not belong to a chord, that is, nonpolyphonic, and present a height within a certain range. The verification of a music scenario described by a conditional sentence leads to the application of a certain formatting rule to the symbol under evaluation.

When the SM-FL engine for the automatic formatting is activated, the process of placing a symbol in the score involves some computation of conditions, and activates the corresponding rules. The conditions depend on the music context. For example, the stem direction of notes may depend on the note height in the staff. In the object-oriented model, there are permanent parameters; therefore, the value is computed only once at the very insertion of the symbol in the score or on demand. Furthermore, dynamic parameters are computed every time the rendered image of the score is produced. This is very important when the score is visualized in a computer window (or in any resizable window of a device); whereas it is less important when the goal of the algorithm is to arrange the score for producing a music sheet or an image.

*Figure 4. General architecture of an SMR decoder formatting engine*

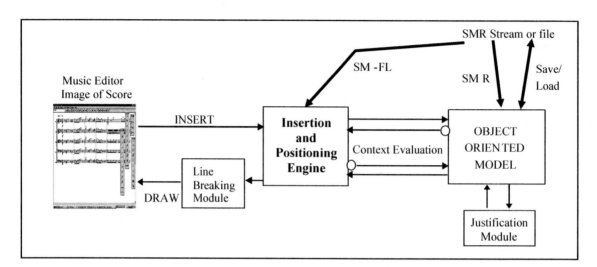

In order to make the process of music score visualization shorter, the SM-FL formatting engine has been conceived as being made up of two parts:

- The Insertion Engine evaluates permanent parameters and it is invoked every time a new music element is added to the model, mainly in the authoring phase.
- The Positioning Engine is invoked every time the rendering of the music score has to be redrawn (for example, on image resizing or on score scrolling). This allows estimation of the dynamic parameters related to symbols positioning.

The formatting engine estimates the context needed in order to assess the conditions, according to the music notation symbol involved. To perform the context evaluation, the SM-FL engine makes queries to the object-oriented model of music. The context evaluation permits the identification of rules to be applied for setting the parameters of the symbol being inserted or positioned with the appropriate values. Each activated rule points at the value to be set for the parameter under evalu-

ation. For example, the stem height, the starting position of the slur, and so forth.

Conditions and rules are written in SM-FL language and are included within a unique file loaded when the decoder is invoked. The entire set of SM-FL rules and conditions can be re-loaded/resent so as to permit the possibility of changing rules and reapplying them to the same music score.

Parameters related to the visualization of SM-XF information are computed by the decoder in real time on the basis of the SM-FL Positioning conditions. Some formatting parameters of the music notation symbols (for example, direction of the note stems) may be stored in the SM-FL and expressed in terms of simple symbolic relationships (for example, flipping up/down the stem, above and below for expressions concerning the note they are referred to). This is useful in order to cope with exceptions instead of computing them on the basis of SM-FL rules at run time. The context evaluation and the estimation of positioning parameters are based on the analysis of other music symbols in the score. Therefore, the rendering is strictly dependent on the positioning engine of the formatting engine.

The parameters set by the justification engine are the spaces between the score symbols. They are not related to the formatting parameters set with SM-FL rules since the SM-FL estimates only relative displacements with respect to the other symbols. When music symbols are horizontally spaced by the justification module and formatted by SM-FL positioning engine, the line-breaking module is capable of arranging music score in order to fill the page/view margins. The three modules set different parameters, thus contributing to the resulting visualization of the music score on the computer screen as well as on the print page.

## CONCLUSION

Integration of symbolic music representation (SMR) in multimedia frameworks, and particularly in MPEG, is opening a way to realize a large set of new music-based applications in the areas of education, entertainment, and cultural development. Most of these applications are not available yet on many devices accessible to the mass population, such as I-TV, mobiles, and so forth, while those available on PC are not based on standard content formats. This constrains content producers to reshape any functionality from scratch by creating specific solutions adapted to each tool. This represents a strong limitation for the diffusion of music culture and knowledge and for the market of music education. Moreover, the integration of SMR in MPEG permits creative developers to implement and distribute new, extended functionality that can be made accessible to a larger number of citizens, enabling the development of a huge number of completely new applications in several domains, from education through distance learning, to rehearsal and musical practice at home, and any imaginable form of music enjoyment.

Some of these new applications have been presented, and issues related to integration in MPEG have been discussed. We have shown that a seamless integration is possible, and that music, and more precisely any music notation, could greatly benefit from this integration. On the other hand, MPEG SMR may become a way for multimedia frameworks, and particularly MPEG, to express a great potential in the domain of music enjoyment and fruition, and particularly in widespread market areas like music education and practice.

Further information on MPEG SMR can be found on the Web pages of the MPEG interest group on SMR: http://www.interactivemusicne twork.org/mpeg-ahg. From this URL, you have access to a large collection of documents on requirements, scenarios, examples, and links.

## ACKNOWLEDGMENT

We would like to acknowledge everybody who has participated in the discussions on the reflector of the MPEG ad-hoc group on SMR, and members of the MUSICNETWORK WG on music notation and everyone who have attended joined meetings of MPEG and MUSICNETWORK. Special thanks to (in no particular order): Jerome Barthelemy, Kia Ng, Tom White, James Ingram, Martin Ross, Eleanor Selfridge Filed, Neil McKenzie, David Crombie, Hartmut Ring, Tillmann Weyde, Jacques Steyn, Steve Newcomb, Perry Roland, Matthew Dovey, and many, many others. Apologies to many more who have not been mentioned. Part of the development on SMR has been performed under the i-Maestro EC IST project co-supported by the European Commission under the 6th Framework Programme.

## REFERENCES

Bellini, P., Barthelemy, J., Bruno, I., Nesi, P., & Spinu, M. B., (2003). Multimedia music sharing among mediateques: Archives and distribution to their attendees. *Journal on Applied Artificial Intelligence*. Retrieved from http://www.wedel-music.org

Bellini, P., Bruno, I., & Nesi, P., (2005). Automatic formatting of music sheets through MILLA rule-based language and engine. *Journal of New Music Research*.

Bellini, P., Della Santa, R., & Nesi, P. (2001, November 23-24). Automatic formatting of music sheet. In *Proceedings of the First International Conference on WEB Delivering of Music, WEDELMUSIC-2001* Florence, Italy (pp. 170-177) .

Bellini, P., Fioravanti, F., & Nesi, P. (1999). Managing music in orchestras. *IEEE Computer, September*, 26-34. Retrieved from http://www.dsi.unifi.it/~moods/

Bellini, P., Nesi, P., & Spinu, M. B. (2002). Cooperative visual manipulation of music notation. *ACM Transactions on Computer-Human Interaction, 9*(3), 194-237.

Bellini, P., & Nesi, P., (2001, November 23-24). WEDELMUSIC FORMAT: An XML music notation format for emerging applications. In *Proceedings of the 1st International Conference of Web Delivering of Music* Florence, Italy (pp. 79-86) .

Bellini, P., Nesi, P., & Zoia, G. (2005). Symbolic music representation in MPEG for new multimedia applications. *IEEE Multimedia*.

Blostein, D., & Haken, L. (1991). Justification of printed music. *Communications of the ACM, 34*(3), 88-99.

CANTATE project. (1994). Deliverable 3.3: Report on SMDL evaluation, WP3. Retrieved from http://projects.fnb.nl

Capella. (2005). CAPXML. Retrieved from http://www.whc.de/capella.cfm

CUIDADO project. *Processing of music and Mpeg7*. Retrieved from http://www.ircam.fr/cuidad/

Finale of Coda. Retrieved from http://www.finalemusic.com/

Freehand. Retrieved from http://www.freehand-systems.com/

Good, M. (2001). MusicXML for notation and analysis. In W. B. Hewlett & E. Selfridge-Field (Eds.), *The virtual score representation, retrieval, restoration* (pp. 113-124). Cambridge, MA: The MIT Press. Retrieved from http://www.recordare.com

I-MAETRO project. *EC IST FP6*. Retrieved from http://www.i-maestro.org

IMUTUS project. Retrieved from http://www.exodus.gr/imutus/

*ISO/IEC JTC1/SC29/WG11 W6689*. Call for proposals on symbolic music representation, Audio Subgroup, July 2004, Redmond, USA.

Joung, Y., & Kim, K. (2002, December). An XMT API for generation of the MPEG-4 scene description. In *Proceedings of the Tenth ACM International Conference on Multimedia*.

Kim, K., Lee, I., & Ki, M. (2002, December). Interactive contents authoring system based on XMT and BIFS. In *Proceedings of the Tenth ACM International Conference on Multimedia*.

Kim, M., & Wood, S. *XMT: MPEG-4 textual format for cross-standard interoperability*. Retrieved from http://www.research.ibm.com/mpeg4/Projects/XMTInterop.htm

Kim, M., Wood, S., & Cheok, L. T.. (2000, November). Extensible MPEG-4 textual format (XMT). International Multimedia Conference. In *Proceedings of the 2000 ACM workshops on Multimedia*.

Krolick B. (2000). *New international manual of braille music notation, braille music.* Subcommittee of the World Blind Union. Retrieved from http://www.opustec.com/products/newintl/newprint.html

Lazzaro, J., & Wawrzynek, K. (2000). *MPEG-4 structured audio.* Retrieved from http://www.cs.berkeley.edu/~lazzaro/sa/book/index.html=

MOODS project. Retrieved from http://www.dsi.unifi.it/~moods

MPEG ISO SMR group web page. Retrieved from http://www.interactivemusicnetwork.org/mpeg-ahg

MUSICALIS project. Retrieved from http://www.musicalis.fr/

NIFF Consortium. (1995). *NIFF 6a: Notation interchange file format.*

Ong, B., Ng, K., Mitolo, N., & Nesi, P. (2006). i-Maestro: Interactive multimedia environments for music education. In Kia Ng, Atta Badii, & Pierfrancesco Bellini (Eds.), In *Proceedings of the AXMEDIS2006 International Conference on Automated Production of Cross Media Content for Multi-channel Distribution, 2nd i-Maestro Workshop* (pp. 87-91). Firenze, Italy: Firenze University Press.

OPENDRAMA project. Retrieved from http://www.iua.upf.es/mtg/opendrama/

Pereira, F., & Ebrahimi, T. (Eds.). (2002). *The MEPG-4 Book.* IMSC Press.

Selfridge-Field E. (Ed.). (1997). *Beyond MIDI— The handbook of musical codes.* London: The MIT Press.

SIBELIUS. Retrieved from http://www.sibelius.com

SMDL. (1995). *ISO/IEC, standard music description language.* ISO/IEC DIS 10743.

WEDELMUSIC project and tools. Retrieved from http://www.wedelmusic.org

# Chapter III
# XML Music Notation Modelling for Multimedia:
## MPEG–SMR

**Pierfrancesco Bellini**
*University of Florence, Italy*

## ABSTRACT

*The evolution of information technology has changed the use of music representation and notation in software applications, transforming and extending them from a simple visual coding model for music scores into a tool for modelling music for computer programs and electronic devices in general (e.g., keyboards), to support the exploitation of the multimedia characteristics lying behind music notation and representation. The MPEG symbolic music representation (MPEG-SMR) is a new emerging standard for modelling music notation within the MPEG multimedia framework. MPEG-SMR provides an XML-based language to model most of the music notation in terms of the visual and audio aspects, as well as music score annotations. MPEG-SMR also provides a language to define the music score formatting rules, supporting personalisation for the score visual presentation, custom symbols, and control visual rendering of the common notation symbols.*

## INTRODUCTION

Music in multimedia applications and frameworks is often considered only for its audible dimensions, while neglecting the important issues on the representation of the symbolic aspects. This could be due to historical cultural effects, since many popular and earlier multimedia tools are built for entertainment applications, and not focused on education, preservation, or research purposes.

Music notation is an abstraction of the music. Not all performers use notations, and music notations have many different styles and forms. Currently, multimedia tools frequently use simple symbolic representations of music to represent the production of sound/music – for example, notes produced by an instrument.

Notations for the representation of music symbols have been developed over the years and ages to visually represent the pieces of information needed by a performer to play the music piece and reproduce the music as the author/composer intended. The production of music notation scores for professional publishing on paper is one of the most traditional applications of music notation on computers (Blostein & Haken, 1991; Rader, 1996; Selfridge-Field, 1997).

The evolution of multimedia applications is accelerating relevant changes in the usages of music representation and notation in computer-based applications. Nowadays, it is no longer unusual to see music notation and modelling integrated into professional and educational music/audio applications (Bellini & Nesi, 2004; Byrd, 1984). In the past, several XML-based languages for music modelling have been proposed, including MNML (Musical Notation Markup Language), MusicML, MML (Music Markup Language), MusicXML (Good, 2001), WEDELMUSIC (http://www.wedelmusic.org) (Bellini & Nesi, 2001; Bellini, Della Santa, & Nesi, 2001), CAPXML (Capella, 2005), and so forth. Past efforts for music notation standardization were SMDL (SMDL, 1995) and NIFF (NIFF, 2005). Most of them are mainly focused on modelling the music elements to preserve and interchange the notation format and information among different applications (for editing and rendering of music scores), rather than to provide features that could support the integration of music notation with multimedia, for example, synchronisation with audiovisual and 3-D rendering, references and hyperlinks, multilingual lyrics, automatic formatting and rendering, and so forth. These features are clearly required and can be seen in tools from industrial projects, and R&D areas:

- Multimedia music for music tuition, such as VOYETRA, SMARTSCORE, PLAYPRO, MUSICALIS.
- Multimedia music for edutainment and infotainment, such as WEDELMUSIC

(integrating music notation and multimedia to build and distribute multimedia-music cultural content with digital rights management), or to produce multimedia content for theatres: OPENDRAMA (http://www.iua.upf.es/mtg/opendrama/);

- Cooperative music editing, such as in MOODS (http://www.dsi.unifi.it/~moods), (Bellini, Fioravanti, & Nesi, 1999; Bellini, Nesi, & Spinu, 2002), and more recently using MAX/MSP with I-MAESTRO project (http://www.i-maestro.org).

Most of the applications mentioned are based on a multimedia music content format that is specific for each product. This is why any information exchange among the products can be so difficult, and it is strongly restricted to subsets of the notational part, for example, in MIDI. The lack of standardized symbolic music representation integrated with multimedia content results in each developer/company implementing their own solution, which may vary in efficiency, scope, features, quality, and complexity.

In this context, the MUSICNETWORK (http://www.interactivemusicnetwork.org) project began in 2002 to support a group of experts to identify a standard format for music representation for multimedia applications. The MUSICNETWORK started to work with ISO MPEG on the SMR (symbolic music representation), as described in another chapter of this book. The integration of SMR in MPEG multimedia framework, with technologies ranging from video, audio, interactivity, and digital rights management, has enabled the development of many new applications like those mentioned earlier and in Bellini, Nesi and Zoia (2005).

An overview of the MPEG-SMR standard is presented in this chapter.

## MPEG SYMBOLIC MUSIC REPRESENTATION

The MPEG symbolic music representation (SMR), as specified in ISO/IEC 14496-23, is composed of three different languages:

- The Symbolic Music Extensible Format (SM-XF) to encode main score, single parts, and lyrics.
- The Symbolic Music Formatting Language (SM-FL) to customize music formatting style.
- The Symbolic Music Synchronization Information (SM-SI) that is used to provide synchronization information with the multimedia scene.

Figure 1 shows the relationships among the SMR data in the event of a music score with three parts, and how the SMR data is used by an MPEG-4 player to produce a synchronized multimedia presentation. Both SM-XF and SM-FL are XML languages defined using XML schemas, while SM-SI is binary encoded.

Interactivity features that may be implemented by an SMR-enabled MPEG-4 player are specified in an amendment to the BIFS (BInary Format for Scene representation) specification (ISO/IEC 14496-11:2005 AMD5), which is used to describe the multimedia scene.

## SM-XF: SYMBOLIC MUSIC EXTENSIBLE FORMAT

Symbolic music extensible format is an XML application for encoding main scores, single parts, as well as multilingual lyrics. In Figure 2, a simplified UML diagram of the SMR model is presented. At an abstract level, the main score consists of single parts, each single part consists of a sequence of measures, and each measure consists of parallel layers containing sequences of notes, rests, and other timed and untimed symbols that are organized horizontally on a staff. Each symbol (e.g., notes, rests, chords, etc.) can be associated with some qualifier symbols to

*Figure 1. Example of structure and relationship among MPEG-SMR data and how a SMR enabled MPEG-4 player should use it*

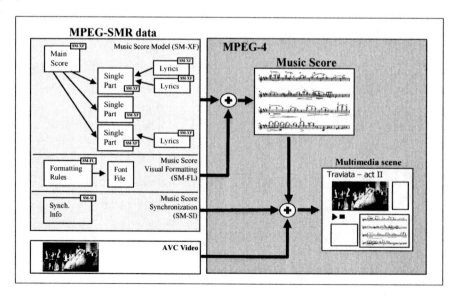

*Figure 2. SMR abstract UML model*

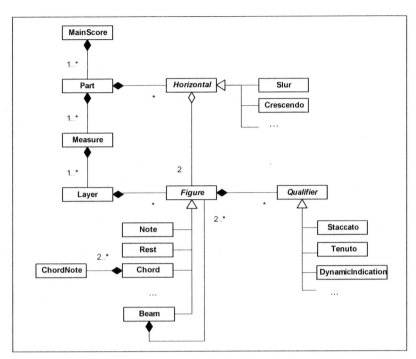

represent some additional pieces of information on the symbol itself, such as expression symbols. A chord is modelled as a sequence of chord notes (one for each note head), and beamed notes are modelled as containers of musical figures. Additionally, there are other symbols, called horizontal symbols, spanning over multiple timed symbols (e.g., slurs, crescendo, diminuendo), that start at a specific musical figure and end at another musical figure. The horizontal symbols are contained inside the single part and referred to the start/end figures/locations.

The MainScore representation is built from the Parts representation. Other formats use different representations for MainScore and Parts; thus, having a strong duplication (each part is provided twice, in the main score and in the single instrumental part). If the main score is built from parts, it reduces the size of the data (to be sent to the client) and supports a synchronized visualization of parts and main score (a modification made on a part in a main score view is reproduced mirror-like in the part shown in the single part view). In some cases, the main score and the parts are encoded differently, and some musical elements are present, specifically for the view (e.g., small guideline indications are used in the single parts) or different instruments are merged on a single staff in the main score representation. In such cases, the representation can be duplicated, and the main score and parts can be represented separately.

In SMR, a measure is represented as a container of musical figures. This is different from other formats such as CapXML (Capella, 2005), which does not group musical figures in measures and have the barline as another symbol among musical figures. However, the structural subdivision in measures enables subdivision of the content in chunks to be delivered to clients. In MPEG-4, all the media content (and subsequently also SMR) is delivered to clients in subdivided Access Units. The Decoder receives the Access Units one after another and it has to decode them, passing the decoded data to the renderer. In SMR, each Access Unit delivered to the terminals can contain one or more measures for the different parts. The whole score can be provided in one Access Unit or subdivided in many Access Units, thus enabling the device to start rendering the score without being restricted to wait for the whole score (consider the case of an opera containing hundreds or thousands of measures).

One of the main requirements in the language design consisted in each element (Part, Measure, Layer, Note, Rest, Chord, ChordNote, ...) being identified in a unique way to allow musical elements to be referred directly in the score.

This feature is used in:

- Horizontal symbols (e.g., slurs, dynamics) to indicate the start/end element of the symbol.
- Lyrics to indicate the note a syllable is connected to.
- Annotations to indicate to which musical symbols the annotation is related/associated to.

In all these occurrences, the information is stored outside the score itself. This feature allows a primary musical structure to associate additional information, such as annotations. Moreover, the musical element identification has to work, even if it does not have in memory the whole score (this is particularly useful for low-memory footprint devices), and the identifier has to be valid even after score manipulation (therefore, element position cannot be used as identifier). For these reasons, each element has been identified with a numeric ID that is unique in the parent element (Part in Main Score, Measure in Part, Layer in Measure, Figure in Layer, ChordNote in Chord). Hence, an element can be identified by using a sequence of IDs that specify the path to be followed in order to locate the element. The path is valid even if new measures/figures are added before the identified element. If each element is easily identified, this

allows for things such as separate files for Lyrics or Annotations that can be applied without any modifications to the score.

Beams are modelled as containers of Figures inside Layers, thus not allowing beaming across measures. Hence, a kind of horizontal symbol used to beam notes from a start note to an end note has been introduced. In this case, the end note can be in another measure, to support beams across measures. This feature has been added only recently and both approaches can be used.

For instruments using more than one staff (like piano and organ), the staves are considered as belonging to the same score (other XML formats, like CapXML, encode each staff separately). The score has an attribute stating how many staves are used by the instrument, and each figure in a layer has an attribute indicating which staff the note/rest belongs to. Therefore, layers can go from one staff to another and can easily represent beaming across staff.

What follows is a set of selected examples on how the basic musical symbols are represented in SMR, starting from the bottom level (a note) and going up to a single part and a main score. The complete description of the XML language can be found in the ISO/IEC MPEG Specification (ISO/IEC 14496-23 FDIS).

In Figure 3, a brief explanation of the notation used to represent XML elements is reported.

## Note

The musical note is modelled in XML with the note element, as described in Figure 4 (attributes documentation is missing). A note element may contain:

- An optional pitch element with the note pitch indication.
- Accidental symbols (like sharp, flat, etc.).
- Augmentation information that modifies the note duration.
- A sequence of qualifier symbols like fermata, dynamic text, markers, and so forth.

*Figure 3. Notation used to represent XML element structure*

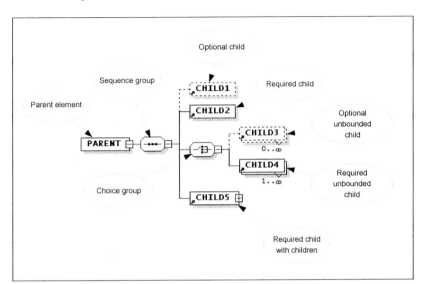

• An optional user spacing with the distance with respect to the next figure.

If the pitch is missing, it can be deduced from the HEIGHT attribute containing the position of the note on the staff, from the accidental symbols, if any, and from the clef and key signature currently active. If both the height attribute and the pitch element exist, the height is used for visual rendering and the pitch information is used for audio rendering. In the event that the height attribute is not specified, the latter is deduced from the pitch and from the clef and key signature.

Some of the attributes of the note element are:

• The HEIGHT containing the position of the note on the staff ( 0 for the lowest staff line, 1 for the first space, 2 for the second staff line, etc.).
• The DURATION with the note duration (e.g., D1_8 for an eighth note).
• The ID, which identifies the note within the layer.
• The STEM to indicate the direction of the stem (up or down).

• The STAFF to indicate the staff where the note has to be positioned.

Figure 4 (on the right side) reports an example on how a note is represented in XML.

## Rest

A rest symbol is represented in XML with the rest element, which may contain the augmentation information so as to change the rest duration. It may contain zero or more qualifier symbols, such as fermata, dynamic text, textual indication, annotation, pay attention symbol (glasses), piano symbol, and fretboard symbol. Moreover, it may contain the userspacing element expressing the distance from the next figure.

The rest element contains attributes such as the rest DURATION, the HEIGHT with the position of the rest on the staff, and the rest ID to identify the rest in the layer.

## Chord

A chord is represented in XML with the chord element containing a sequence of chordnote ele-

*Figure 4. XML model of a note (on the left) and an example (on the right)*

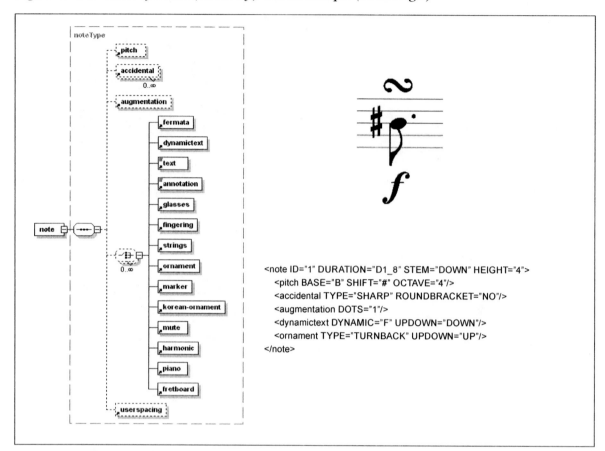

*Figure 5. XML model of a rest (on the left) and an example (on the right)*

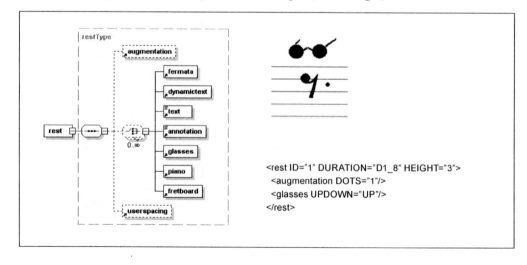

ments, with the information related to each note head of the chord (accidentals, fingering, pitch, position on the staff, staff, …). The chord element contains the same elements of the note (fermata, dynamics, text, etc.), since they refer to the chord as a whole. The arpeggio element is specific for chords to indicate how to play the chord. Figure 6 depicts the XML element structure with an example of a chord.

## Beam

The beam is modelled as a container of notes, chords, rests, anchorages, and change clefs elements. The anchorage element represents a point in the score where other symbols (mainly horizontal symbols) can be logically attached. With this kind of model, a beam crossing the bar line cannot be represented; for this reason a specific horizontal symbol can be used (see later on). Therefore, a beam can be represented both as container and horizontal.

## Measure

The measure represents the classical subdivision of a score; it is modelled with the measure element, which contains a sequence of layers containing the notes, rests, chords, beams, and so forth.

With some further details, the measure may contain:

- Justification information on how to position the notes/rests on the available space (e.g., linear or logarithmic with a tuning parameter).
- An optional label for the measure (e.g., rehearsal marks or "segno/coda" signs).
- An optional jump indication to indicate the successive measure to be executed (e.g., da capo al fine).
- A header with the clef and key signature for each staff.
- The time signature of the measure (e.g., 3/4).

*Figure 6. XML model of a chord (on the left) and an example (on the right)*

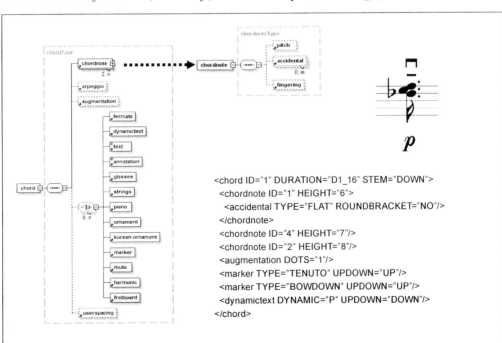

*Figure 7. XML model of a beam with an example*

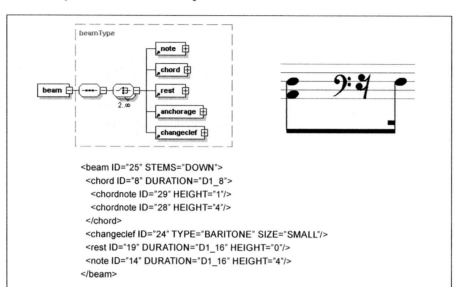

```
<beam ID="25" STEMS="DOWN">
  <chord ID="8" DURATION="D1_8">
    <chordnote ID="29" HEIGHT="1"/>
    <chordnote ID="28" HEIGHT="4"/>
  </chord>
  <changeclef ID="24" TYPE="BARITONE" SIZE="SMALL"/>
  <rest ID="19" DURATION="D1_16" HEIGHT="0"/>
  <note ID="14" DURATION="D1_16" HEIGHT="4"/>
</beam>
```

- A beat scan indication.
- An optional metronome indication that applies starting from the measure until another metronome change.
- The different layers with the musical figures.
- The bar line to be used (e.g., single, double, refrain start/end, invisible).

Some of the attributes of the measure element are:

- An ID to identify the measure in the score.
- A progressive number;
- The number of staves to be used (1, 2 for piano, or 3 for organ).

Figure 9 provides an example of a measure spanning on two staves. Please note that two layers are used, one for the notes on the upper staff and one for the notes on the lower staff, and in the second layer there are two beams with notes belonging to different staves.

## Score and Horizontal Symbols

The score is modelled as a container of both a sequence of measures and horizontal symbols. Horizontal symbols are the ones spanning over the score from a start event/position up to an end event/position (e.g., slurs, crescendo/diminuendo). The start/end event/position may correspond to a musical figure, such as a note, rest, or chord, or to an anchorage point that represents an event between two musical figures. Since horizontal symbols are not stored within the measures but outside, what is needed is a way to logically identify the start/end element of the symbol. In order to refer to the start/end figure of the score, a set of identifiers is used in the address element:

- The ID of the measure where the start/end figure is.
- The number of the layer where the figure is.
- The ID of the beam/chord/note/rest within the layer containing the addressed figure.

*Figure 8. XML model of the measure*

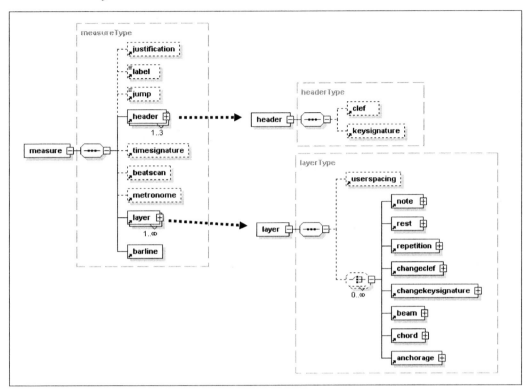

*Figure 9. An example of measure*

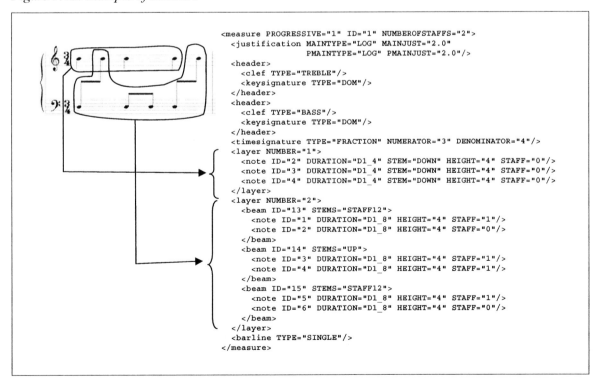

*Figure 10. The XML model of the score element*

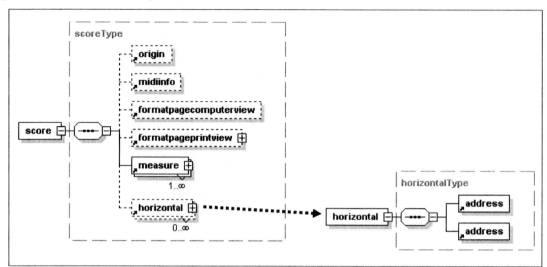

- The optional ID of the note within the chord or the ID of the note/rest/chord within the beam.
- The optional ID of the note within the chord in a beam.

Horizontal symbols are used for:

- Slurs
- Ties
- Tuplets (e.g., terzine)
- Octave change (8va, 8ba, 15ma, 15ba)
- Beaming across measures
- Crescendo/diminuendo
- Trill with a wavy line
- Bend
- A wavy line
- An arrow
- Refrain change
- Piano pedal indication

The score is represented in XML as illustrated in Figure 10. The score element can contain:

- Some optional origin information (e.g., the software tool used to produce the score).

- Some optional MIDI information on the instrument, volume, and channel to be used for MIDI execution.
- Some optional information on how to format the page for computer view and for print view (e.g., margins, distance between staves, number of systems per page).
- The sequence of measures building the score.
- The sequence of horizontal symbols, each one with two addresses identifying the start/end figure/event.

Attributes of the score element include:

- The score ID identifying the score
- The score type (e.g., normal, percussion, tablature)
- The instrument name
- The number of staves to be used (e.g., 1, 2 or 3)
- …

Figure 11 presents an example of a score with a slur connecting two notes.

*Figure 11. An example of an MPEG-SMR score*

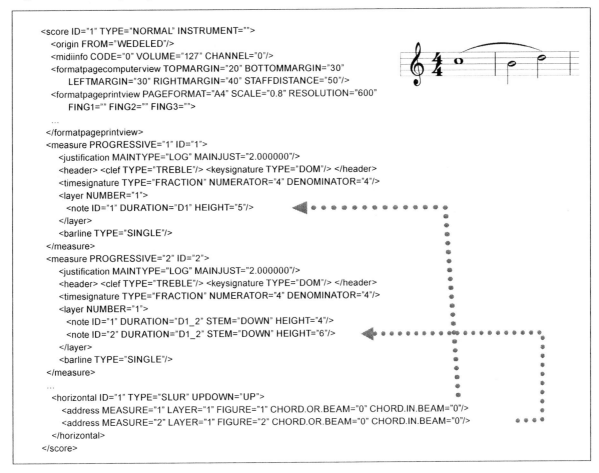

## Single-Part Score

The single part contains the musical information for one executor, and it is modelled with the SMXF_Part element. It contains the score element with the musical information and some general identification and classification information (as XML elements), some preferences for some specific decoder, and additional pieces of information for printing the score as a single part. The printpages element has textbox and imagebox elements, to be used when printing each page.

## Main Score

The main score contains the musical information of the whole score and subsequently, it contains the information about all the single parts of the instruments playing the music piece.

Like the single part, the main score may contain identification and classification information and custom preferences for specific decoders. Moreover, the main score contains:

- References to the single parts making the main score (using the score IDs).
- Some general MIDI information (e.g., how to map to MIDI dynamic symbols).
- Some formatting information for the computer view and for print view (e.g., margins, distance between staves, number of systems per page).
- A sequence of brackets used to group visually different parts (e.g., string instruments).

- Additional "graphical" elements (image and text boxes) for print view.
- An optional sequence of selections used to associate annotations (as text, URL, or any XML elements), with a subset of musical symbols of the different parts.

Selections are used to group together a subset of musical figures being included in the score, and to annotate them with textual descriptions (in different languages) or reference to a digital resource via URLs (e.g., an image contained in the MPEG-4 file), or with any customized XML content. A selection may be defined with extad-

*Figure 12. XML model for the single part*

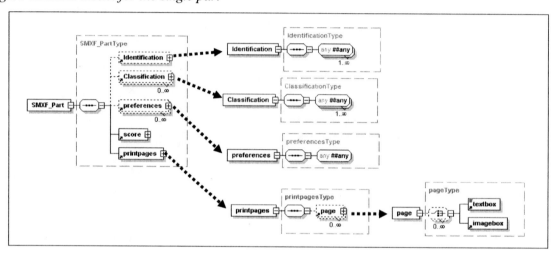

*Figure 13. XML model of the main score*

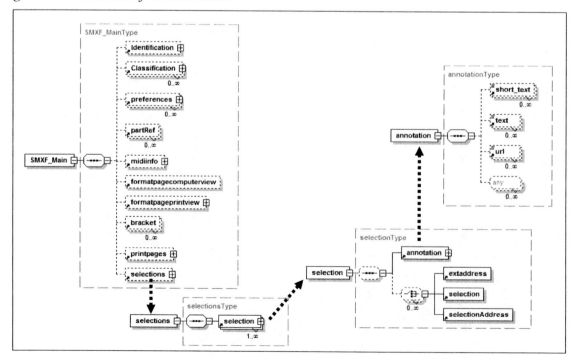

dress elements that refer to the musical figures in the score (the extaddress contains the score ID that is not included in the address element of the horizontal symbols). Moreover, the selection can be built also by embedding other selections so as to form a hierarchical structure, or by referring to other selections using an ID (using the selectionAddress element).

Selections are useful in music education in order to mark specific passages or to give audio/visual performance indications.

## Lyrics

The lyrics are modelled in a way similar to the horizontal symbols; the syllables of the lyrics are not spread over the notes in the score (like many other music notation formats) but are kept separate, and they refer to the notes they are associated with (using the same mechanisms of addresses, as it happens with the horizontal symbols). In this way, different lyrics (e.g., in different languages) can be plugged on a score without changing the score. Moreover, the original lyrics can be reconstructed as plain text, out of the lyrics model. This method to model lyrics is explained with further details in Bellini et al. (Bellini, Bruno, & Nesi, 2004).

The SMXF_Lyric element contains:

- An ID to identify the lyrics.
- The language used for the lyrics.

- A sequence of mixed text and syllable elements, where the text elements contain some accompanying text that should not appear in the score (e.g., some formatting text), and syllable elements containing information on the syllable.

The syllable element contains:

- The syllable text.
- A reference to the note the syllable is associated with (the start element).
- An optional end position in case of syllable prolongation like in melisma, where the same syllable is sung over more notes.
- An attribute with the row where the syllable has to be positioned, to be used in case of refrains.

In Figure 15, an example of lyrics is reported.

## SM-FL: SMR FORMATTING LANGUAGE

The symbolic music formatting language (SM-FL) is defined to allow the description of the insertion point and the positioning of common music symbols (stem, ornaments, expression, etc.), as well as the definition of new symbols. It specifies

*Figure 14. XML model for the lyrics*

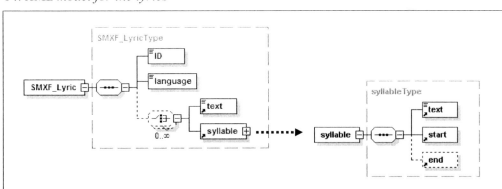

*Figure 15. An example of MPEG-SMR SM-XF lyrics*

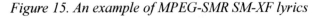
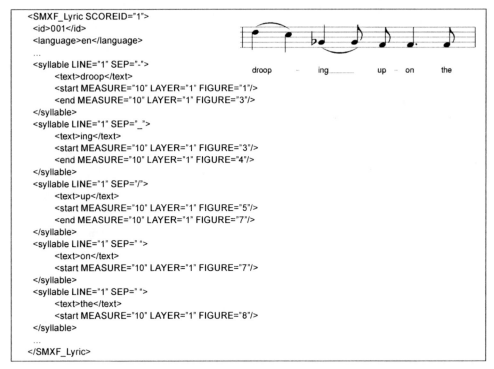

a rule-based formatting language and engine that is used to describe sets of rules and conditions to be applied and interpreted whenever the position of symbols has to be estimated. The SM-FL rules define formatting actions; they assign specific values to specific parameters related to the visual rendering of the music symbols. For example, a rule is used to define the stem length of a note. The rule to be applied is identified on the basis of the conditions met in the music context of the symbol under evaluation. These conditions describe a music scenario. For example, a music scenario could consist of a note not belonging to a chord, that is, nonpolyphonic, and with a height set within a certain range. The verification of a music scenario defined by a conditional sentence leads to the application of a certain formatting rule to the symbol under evaluation.

SM-FL can be used to define rules to customize:

- Stem length and direction
- Beam slope and direction
- Automatic beaming rules
- Note head shape
- Stem start position
- Symbols' position and direction
- Symbols' positioning order (w.r.t. the note)
- Shape of any symbol

SM-FL can be used to define new symbols associated with a note and rules to cope with their position in the score. The SM-FL is an XML language derived from the MILLA language used in WEDELMUSIC editor (Bellini et al., 2005). In Figure 16, the structure of an SMFL rule file is reported, it contains:

- A sequence of font-mapping definition elements where the shape of some classical symbols (clefs, alterations, etc.) can be redefined (those represented using fonts).

- A sequence of group definitions allowing to define new groups containing custom symbols.
- In any order: rule definition elements to set a particular aspect of the score (note head shape, stem direction, stem length, beam direction and slope, etc.) and rule application elements defining the condition for a specific rule's application.

The only rule that is not conditional is the SymbolOrderRule, which is used to state the position of symbols with respect to the note head. In order to be applied, all the other rules need a condition to be satisfied.

For example, an insertion rule "StemUp," which sets the stem upward with respect to the note head, can be stated as:

```
<stemDirectionRule ruleId="StemUp">
    <stemUp/>
</stemDirectionRule>
```

A condition to activate this rule can be very simple. The condition could state that the rule "StemUp" is applied whenever the note is found below the middle line of the staff:

```
<applyRule rule="StemUp">
    <condition>
        <note>
                <heightLT>0</heightLT>
        </note>
    <condition>
</stemDirectionRule>
```

A different condition may state that the rule "StemUp" is invoked if the note belongs to the upper voice for a measure having polyphony (In-

*Figure 16. XML model for SM-FL*

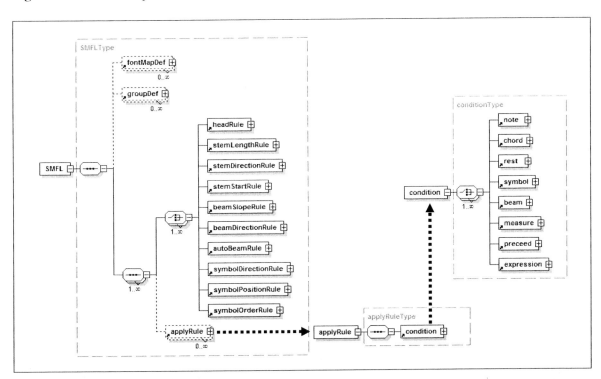

*Figure 17. The stem of notes and chords in single layer and in polyphony*

MultivoiceUpper) as a feature. The upper voice is the one presenting the note with the highest pitch among those to be played at the same time:

```
<applyRule rule="StemUp">
  <condition>
    <note>
      <inMultivoiceUpper/>
    </note>
  <condition>
</applyRule>
```

Another case is when the note is in a single layer and is included in a chord:

```
<applyRule rule="StemUp">
  <condition>
    <note>
     <inSinglevoice/>
     <inChord/>
    </note>
    <expression>
     <lt>
       <minus><chord.upperd/><chord.lowerd/></minus>
       <value>0</value>
     </lt>
    </expression>
  <condition>
</applyRule>
```

Such conditions are met in the second measure of Figure 17. The notes belong to a chord (inChord), only one voice is present (inSinglevoice), and the difference between the highest and the lowest

notes of the chord defines the "centre of gravity" of the chord, either above or below the middle line, that is (upperd-lowerd>0), where: upperd is the absolute value based on the distance between the highest note of the chord and the middle line of the staff, and lowerd is the absolute value based on the distance between the lowest note of the chord and the middle line of the staff.

Specific rules can be provided to set the stem length. The basic unit for stem length is the space defined as the distance between two staff lines. In this way, the standard length of the stem is 3.5 spaces, while it has to assume different values, depending on the note height. In Figure 18, the following rules and conditions have been used for some notes:

```
<stemLengthRule ruleId="Stem3_5">
    <length>3.5</length>
</stemLengthRule>
<stemLengthRule ruleId="StemHeight">
    <noteHeight/>
</stemLengthRule>

<applyRule rule="Stem3_5">
    <condition>
       <note>
          <heightGE>0</heightGE>
          <heightLE>7</heightLE>
          <stemDown/>
       </note>
    <condition>
</applyRule>
<applyRule rule="StemHeight">
```

*Figure 18. Example for stem length*

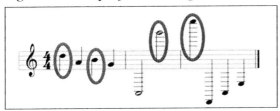

*Figure 19. An example of order rule application*

```
<condition>
  <note>
    <heightGE>8</heightGE>
    <stemDown/>
  </note>
<condition>
</applyRule>
```

The first condition is verified for the first note of the first measure of Figure 18, while the second condition is true for the second note of the second measure and for the first of the third measure, which sets the use of a stem with a length equal to the note height divided by two.

Markers and other symbols may accompany the same note. In this case, the SymbolOrderRule defines the order of symbols' positioning.

To change the order rule is a procedure that can be used to change the order of symbols without modifying the symbolic description of music score. The order rule appears as a list of symbol identifiers shown in decreasing order of priority. For example:

```
<symbolOrderRule>
    <symbol>STAC</symbol>
    <symbol>TEN</symbol>
    <symbol>SLUR</symbol>
    <symbol>MARTF</symbol>
    <symbol>ACCE</symbol>
    <symbol>SFOR</symbol>
    <symbol>MART</symbol>
    <symbol>ARCO</symbol>
    <symbol>PUNTA</symbol>
    <symbol>TALLONE</symbol>
```

```
    <symbol>PONTICELLO</symbol>
    <symbol>TASTIERA</symbol>
    <symbol>ARCATASU</symbol>
    <symbol>ARCATAGIU</symbol>
    <symbol>CORDA</symbol>
    <symbol>PIZZICATO</symbol>
    ...
</symbolOrderRule>
```

Therefore, the staccato symbol (STAC, if any) is the symbol closest to the note head, the tenuto symbol (TEN) the second closest one, and so forth.

The SM-FL allows the definition of new symbols, which are considered as generic expression symbols related to a note. For these new symbols, rules can be defined. Since symbol rules are usually very similar, symbols are grouped and rules are defined for groups of symbols. However, specific rules can be defined as well.

A new symbol can be defined using the symbolDef element inside a groupDef element:

```
<groupDef name="faces" font="mysym.ttf">
    <symbolDef name="smile">
        <code>33</code>
        <dimension>
            <toTop>20</toTop>
            <toBottom>20</toBottom>
            <toLeft>20</toLeft>
            <toRight>20</toRight>
            <dx>-20</dx>
            <dy>-20</dy>
        </dimension>
    </symbolDef>
```

```
<symbolDef name="sad">
    <code>34</code>
    <dimension> ... </dimension>
</symbolDef>
<symbolDef name="star5">
    <code>35</code>
    <dimension> ... </dimension>
</symbolDef>
</groupDef>
```

specifying:

- The name of the symbol (e.g., "smile").
- The group it belongs to (e.g., "faces").
- The name of the font where the symbol can be found (e.g., "mysym.ttf").
- The code of the character representing symbol in the font file (e.g., code 36).
- The bounding box of the symbol in the dimension element (see Figure 20 for the meaning of the elements).

The rules for a group of symbols or for a specific symbol can be defined in the same way as for other symbols related to a note; for example, considering that the symbols in the group have to be positioned opposite to the stem in single voice and on the stem when in multivoice:

```
<symbolDirectionRule ruleId="facesOppStem">
    <group>faces</group>
    <oppositeToStem/>
</symbolDirectionRule>
```

*Figure 20. meaning of dimension elements*

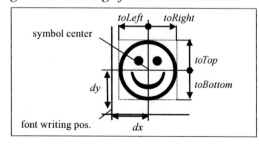

```
<symbolDirectionRule ruleId="facesOnStem">
    <group>faces</group>
    <onStem/>
</symbolDirectionRule>

<applyRule rule="facesOppStem">
    <condition>
        <note>
            <inSingleVoice/>
        </note>
    </condition>
</applyRule>
<applyRule rule="facesOnStem">
    <condition>
        <note>
            <inMultivoice/>
        </note>
    </condition>
</applyRule>
```

As to the symbol position, other constraints can be specified: it has to be positioned on a space (not on a staff line) and outside the staff. This in both cases that the symbol is on the stem or opposite to stem:

```
<symbolPositionRule ruleId="facesPos">
    <group>faces</group>
    <onSpace/>
    <outsideStaff/>
    <dx>0</dx>
    <dy>0</dy>
</symbolPositionRule>

<applyRule rule="facesPos">
    <condition>
        <symbol>
            <oppositeToStem/>
        </symbol>
    </condition>
</applyRule>
<applyRule rule="facesPos">
    <condition>
        <symbol>
```

```
            <onStem/>
         </symbol>
      </condition>
   </applyRule>
...
```

The symbol name (and not the group name) has to be used in the order rule to state the vertical relation of the symbol with other symbols, when it is placed on a note/chord:

```
<symbolOrderRule>
      <symbol>STAC</symbol>
      <symbol>TEN</symbol>
      <symbol>LEG</symbol>
      <symbol>MARTF</symbol>
...
      <symbol>PIZZICATO</symbol>
      <symbol>smile</symbol>
      <symbol>star5</symbol>
      <symbol>sad</symbol>
      <symbol>STRING</symbol>
...
</symbolOrderRule>
```

hence, the "smile" symbol has to be over the pizzicato and below the "star5" symbol.

## SM-SI: SMR SYNCHRONIZATION INFORMATION

The SM-SI format contains information about the synchronization of the music score display with the whole multimedia scene where the music score is shown. For example, a multimedia scene may contain a video of an opera to be displayed synchronously with the music score of the same opera. Another possible case could be that the opera is a live event streamed over the network or through satellite and the music score has to be shown in synchronization with the live event.

The SM-SI is a binary format used inside MPEG-4 access units to provide to the SMR

*Figure 21. Notes with user defined symbols*

decoder the information needed to manage the synchronization. It has a different representation when it comes to synchronization with an off-line scene and with an online scene. In case of an off-line scene, the SM-SI data contain the sequence of measure numbers to be shown, with their corresponding duration expressed in milliseconds. Please note that the same measure can be repeated (with different durations) as it occurs with refrains. In the case of an online scene, the access unit coming from the transport layer (e.g., the network) with the SM-SI content contains the measure number to be displayed.

## AUDIO GENERATION AND USER INTERACTION

It is possible to generate a MIDI representation of the music score by using the information contained in the score, namely, the metronome indication, the clef, and key signature currently active, while considering the dynamic indications included in the score. For transposed instruments, it is possible to indicate the transposition that should be used when generating the audio description. Moreover, each note can have both a visual indication of the note position on the staff and the note pitch. Whenever one of the two is missing, the other is calculated using the contextual information (clef and key signature). If the two elements are in contrast, the pitch is used for audio generation and the note position is used for rendering. Some parameters control the volume of dynamic

*Figure 22. Off-line and online synchronisation using MPEG-SMR SM-SI*

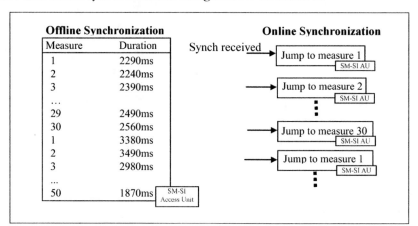

indications (e.g., "f," "p," "mp," etc.), the MIDI instrument to be used for the score, the volume to be used for the instrument, and so forth.

The MIDI generated may be used as a score language by the structured audio engine, and together with the orchestra language (defining how to produce the audio), it can produce the synthetic audio.

The SMR format encoded as MPEG-4 files can be used by any application and not necessarily restricted to MPEG-4 conformant players only. For these applications, no specific requirements for user interaction are present. However, an MPEG-4 conformant player that supports BIFS scene representation (a binarization of a VRML extension) can use the MusicScore node (defined in ISO/IEC 14496-11 AMD 5) to display the music score, coming from an SMR stream, into the multimedia scene. The player can display the score synchronously with other media (natural audio, natural video, or 3-D models), and allows some interaction with the SMR content.

The MusicScore node manages the rendering and display of the score, and supports the following functionalities:

- Browse the score (jump to a label, jump to a measure, jump to a given time).
- Choose which parts/views to see (single parts, main score, main score with only some parts).
- Choose the lyrics to be displayed (in case of lyrics in different languages).
- Generate an event when a music element with an associated link is selected.
- Start/stop play the score in synch with the multimedia scene, highlighting the current playing position in the score.
- Transpose the score.
- Perform some editing of the score (e.g., add textual annotation, add/remove notes, add/remove symbols, ...).

Using the MusicScore node with the other nodes managing user interaction, like the Touch-Sensor node, the MPEG-4 Player can realize an interactive scene where the user can use and manipulate the SMR content. Figure 23 presents a snapshot of the IM1 MPEG-4 player (part of the MPEG-4 reference software) showing the MusicScore node.

*Figure 23. IM1 MPEG-4 Player showing a music score*

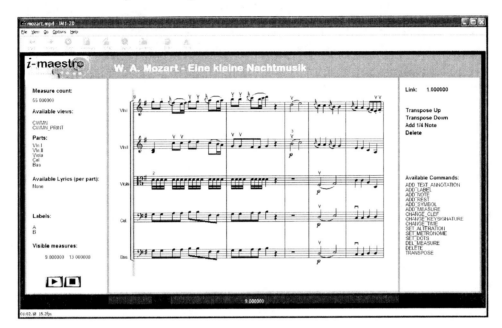

## CONCLUSION

This chapter presented the MPEG-SMR music representation formats that are under standardization in the ISO/IEC MPEG group. The SM-XF, SM-FL, and the SM-SI languages have been discussed in some details with a number of examples. SM-XF XML language is used to model the music notation as main score, single parts, and lyrics, while SM-FL is used to represent the formatting rules of SMR, and SM-SI binary format is used to transport synchronisation information with the multimedia scene. Other aspects of the integration with the other MPEG tools, like BIFS, are treated in another chapter of this book.

The presence of MPEG-SMR will enable and support the realisation of many new applications in the areas of education, entertainment, and cultural valorisation. Currently, most of these applications are not available on devices such as I-TV, mobiles, and so forth, and applications available on PC are not based on standard content formats. The absence of such a standard is constraining producers

to create their own formats. This is one of the key challenges for the diffusion of music knowledge and for the market of music education.

It is hoped that SMR will become a way for multimedia frameworks, and particularly for MPEG to express a great potential in the domain of music enjoyment and fruition, and also in all its related usages and practices, including music education and musical performance.

Further information on MPEG SMR can be found via the MPEG ad-hoc group on SMR Web page, http://www.interactivemusicnetwork.org/mpeg-ahg, where a large collection of documents reporting requirements, scenarios, examples, and links are available.

## ACKNOWLEDGMENT

Thanks to Paolo Nesi and Giorgio Zoia for the help provided, and thanks to everybody who has participated in the discussions on the reflector of the MPEG ad-hoc group on SMR, all members of the

MUSICNETWORK WG on Music Notation, and everyone who attended joined meetings of MPEG and MUSICNETWORK. Special thanks (in no particular order) to Jerome Barthelemy, Kia Ng, Tom White, James Ingram, Martin Ross, Eleanor Selfridge Field, Neil McKenzie, David Crombie, Hartmut Ring, Tillmann Weyde, Jacques Steyn, Steve Newcomb, Perry Roland, Matthew Dovey, and many, many others (apologies for not being able to mention everyone involved here).

Part of the development on SMR has been performed under the i-Maestro EC IST project cosupported by the European Commission under the 6th Framework Programme.

## REFERENCES

Bellini, P., Barthelemy, J., Bruno, I., Nesi, P., & Spinu, M. B. (2003). Multimedia music sharing among mediateques: Archives and distribution to their attendees. *Journal on Applied Artificial Intelligence, 17*(8-9), 773-795.

Bellini, P., Bruno, I., & Nesi, P. (2004). Multilingual lyric modeling and management. In S. E. George (Ed.), *Visual perception of music notation: On-line and off-line recognition.* Hershey, PA: IRM Press.

Bellini, P., Bruno, I., & Nesi, P. (2005). Automatic formatting of music sheets through MILLA rule-based language and engine. *Journal of New Music Research, 34*(3), 237-257.

Bellini, P., Della Santa, R., & Nesi, P. (2001, November 23-24). Automatic formatting of music sheet. In *Proceedings of the 1st International Conference on WEB Delivering of Music* (pp. 170-177). Florence, Italy: IEEE Press.

Bellini, P., Fioravanti, F., & Nesi, P. (1999). Managing music in orchestras. *IEEE Computer*, September, 26-34. Retrieved from http://www.dsi.unifi.it/~moods/

Bellini, P., & Nesi, P. (2001). WEDELMUSIC FORMAT: An XML music notation format for emerging applications. In *Proceedings of the 1st International Conference of Web Delivering of Music* (pp. 79-86). Florence, Italy: IEEE press.

Bellini, P., & Nesi, P. (2004). Modeling music notation in the Internet multimedia age. In S. E. George (Ed.), *Visual perception of music notation: On-line and off-line recognition.* Hershey, PA: IRM Press.

Bellini, P., Nesi, P., & Spinu, M. B. (2002). Co-operative visual manipulation of music notation. *ACM Transactions on Computer-Human Interaction, 9*(3), 194-237.

Bellini, P., Nesi, P., & Zoia, G. (2005). Symbolic music representation in MPEG for new multimedia applications. *IEEE Multimedia, 12*(4), 42-49.

Blostein, D. & Haken, L. (1991). Justification of printed music. *Communications of the ACM, 34*(3), 88-99.

Byrd, D. A. (1984). Music notation by computer. (Doctoral Dissertation, Indiana University). *UMI, Dissertation Service.* Retrieved from http://umi.com

CANTATE project. (1994). Deliverable 3.3: Report on SMDL evaluation, *WP3*. Retrieved from http://projects.fnb.nl

Capella. (2005). *CAPXML.* Retrieved from http://www.whc.de/capella.cfm

CUIDADO: *Processing of music and Mpeg7.* Retrieved from http://www.ircam.fr/cuidad/

Good, M. (2001). MusicXML for notation and analysis. In W. B. Hewlett & E. Selfridge-Field (Eds.), *The virtual score representation, retrieval, restoration* (pp. 113-124). Cambridge, MA: The MIT Press.

IMUTUS project. Retrieved from http://www.exodus.gr/imutus/

*MOODS project.* Retrieved from http://www.dsi. unifi.it/~moods

*MPEG SMR AHG Web page.* Retrieved from http:// www.interactivemusicnetwork.org/mpeg-ahg

NIFF Consortium. (1995). *NIFF 6a: Notation interchange file format.*

Pereira, F., & Ebrahimi, T. (Eds.) (2002). *The MPEG-4 book.* Los Angeles, CA: IMSC Press.

Rader, G. M. (1996). Creating printed music automatically. *IEEE Computer,* June, 61-68.

Selfridge-Field, E. (Ed.) (1997). *Beyond MIDI— The handbook of musical codes.* London: The MIT Press.

SMDL ISO/IEC. (1995). *Standard music description language.* ISO/IEC DIS 10743.

# Chapter IV
# Optical Music Imaging:
## Music Document Digitisation, Recognition, Evaluation, and Restoration

**Graham Jones**
*Sight Synthesis, UK*

**Bee Ong**
*University of Leeds, UK*

**Ivan Bruno**
*University of Florence, Italy*

**Kia Ng**
*University of Leeds, UK*

## ABSTRACT

*This chapter presents the applications and practices in the domain of music imaging for musical scores (music sheets and music manuscripts), which include music sheet digitisation, optical music recognition (OMR), and optical music restoration. With a general background of optical music recognition (OMR), the chapter discusses typical obstacles in this domain, and reports currently available commercial OMR software. It reports hardware and software related to music imaging, discusses the SharpEye optical music recognition system, and provides an evaluation of a number of OMR systems. Besides the main focus on the transformation from images of music scores to symbolic format, this chapter also discusses optical music image restoration, and the application of music imaging techniques for graphical preservation and potential applications for cross-media integration.*

## INTRODUCTION

The chapter addresses some issues on the digitisation, restoration, and automatic transcription of music documents, converting paper-based music documents into machine-readable formats in order to make full use of the latest interactive and multimedia technologies for many different applications including reprinting, restoration, and preservation of musical documents (such as sheet music, handwritten manuscripts, and ancient music scores).

With the rapid advancement of digitisation and information technologies, document analysis and optical character recognition (OCR) technologies are now popularly used from automated form processing to handwritten postal-address recognitions. Automatic document imaging, analysis, and understanding is complex. There have been large developments and progress for optical character recognition systems for printed text, with many currently commercially available printed text recognition systems. However, these systems are still under active development since the processes are fragile and sensitive to noise and inconsistencies on printed materials, which are almost unnoticeable to human eyes. Typical problems between automated character recognition for text also apply to automated music recognition, with additional challenges due to the additional complexities inherent to the graphical, symbolic, music notation structure and layout.

There are a vast amount of invaluable paper-based heritage, including printed music scores and handwritten manuscripts, that are deteriorating over time due to natural decaying of paper and chemical reaction (e.g., printing ink and paper), similar to many other paper-based items in library and museum archives. In order to introduce interactive multimedia music capabilities and functionalities, machine-readable representation is required. Hence, one of the main steps is to create a digital version of these paper-based heritage materials for further processing (restoration, encoding, recognition etc.) in order to allow long-term preservation, and to enable wider and more effective distribution methods, such as the Internet. Various efforts have been focused on this issue in order to preserve the record of the invaluable heritage; for example, manual and high-skilled *paper-splitting* technique used to

conserve Bach's manuscripts (Porck & Teygeler, 2000; Wächter, Liers, & Becker, 1996).

## BACKGROUND

Digitisation has been commonly used as a tool for preservation. Although the digital copy may not conserve the original document, it can preserve the data in the document, with the benefits of easy replications, distribution, and digital processing.

Optical music recognition (OMR), also commonly known as OCR for music (optical character recognition for music) was first attempted in the 1960s, and since then, there have been a wide range of research and development in this interdisciplinary domain. Currently, there are various commercially available products as well as research systems for OMR. OMR system transforms paper-based, printed, music scores and handwritten music manuscripts into a machine-readable symbolic format. An ideal system that could reliably "read" and "understand" music notations could provide a wide range of applications for interactive multimedia music, bringing paper-based music to the new multimedia era.

As mentioned earlier, OMR was first attempted over 30 years ago (Pruslin, 1966). It has received much attention over the last 15 years (Bainbridge & Wijaya, 1999; Bellini, Bruno, & Nesi, 2001; Bruno & Nesi 2002; Ng, 1995; Ng, 2002; Ng & Boyle, 1992; Ng, Cooper, Stefani, Boyle, & Bailey, 1999; etc. See Section "OMR Bibliography"), and the list of commercially available packages includes capella-scan (capella-scan), Optical Music easy Reader (OMeR), PhotoScore (PhotoScore), SharpEye (SharpEye), SmartScore (SmartScore), and Vivaldi Scan (Vivaldi Scan). However, there is still much room for improvement in many aspects. Reviews and background on the development of various OMR systems can be found in Bainbridge and Carter (1997), Blostein and Baird (1992), and Selfridge-Field (1994). An online bibliography on OMR can be found at the Interactive MUSICNETWORK project Web site (http://www.interactiveMUSICNETWORK. org) and http://www.kcng.org/omrbib/ (Crombie, Fuschi, Mitolo, Nesi, Ng, & Ong, 2005; Mitolo, Nesi, & Ng, 2005; Ng, Ong, Nesi, Mitolo, Fuschi, & Crombie, 2005).

## OBSTACLES WITH MUSIC NOTATION

Optical character recognition (OCR) is perhaps the best-known, related, document image-processing problem, but OMR can be critically different. The visual problem might seem simple since writing is normally black on white paper. However, OMR introduces an additional layer of complexity due to the diversity of possible shape variation resulted from interconnections and groupings of symbols. Furthermore, there may be other symbols (e.g., expressive signs, fingerings, bowing, texts, etc.) that are positioned around, and sometimes overlaid part of other music symbols, for example, a tie crossing a stem or touching a note-head.

Music notation is inherently opened ended. Even if generally considered as stable for the period of the eighteenth and nineteenth centuries in the Western world, there are several exceptions, such as "unmeasured notation" (for cadenzas and so on), approximate rhythmic notation (several examples can be found in works of authors like Chopin, Schumann, or Mendelssohn), or slight enhancements to traditional notation (slurs without ending note, noncanonical time signatures, etc.). In the earlier centuries, with neumatic or Gregorian notation, music notation was very far from a standardised system, and in the twentieth century, music notation has exploded, and deviated noticeably from that model commonly known as common western music notation.

Direct recognition of musical symbols is difficult due to the design of the notation. In general, OMR system uses divide-and-conquer approaches to separate musical features before recognition. For example, stave lines are detected and marked before/after note head in order to separate one feature from the other.

Basic musical syntax (e.g., time signature) and domain-knowledge enhancement, such as rhythmical analysis, have been explored to improve recognition performance. Fahmy and Blostein (1994, 1998) propose a graph-rewriting approach for OMR enhancement. Stückelberg et al. (Stückelberg, Pellegrini, & Hilario, 1997) propose an architecture for OMR with high-level domain knowledge, and Stückelberg and Doermann (1999) explore probabilistic reasoning for musical score recognition. Coüasnon (2002) comments that existing OMR software is not suitable for industrial context due to time-consuming and tedious manual proofreading, and proposes a system that is capable of self-diagnostic to detect error (Coüasnon & Rétif, 1995). The chapter discusses the application of musical knowledge of music writing to enhance OMR processing and recognition using description of modification of segmentation (DMOS), a generic recognition approach for structured document analysis with grammatical formalism enhanced position formalism (EPF).

## MUSIC DIGITALISATION

### Hardware

Document digitisation systems, such as optical flatbed scanners, are nowadays available at a constantly decreasing cost, as manufacturers face fierce competition. There are a wide range of commercial products from manufacturers such as Fujitsu, Agfa, HP, Cannon, Epson, UMAX,

Microtek, Visioneer, and many more. Currently available commercial products are equipped with USB, FireWire (IEEE1394), parallel, or SCSI interfaces. Some of these products support dual interfaces.

Many of these products are capable of more than 600 d.p.i. (dot per inch) optical scan resolution with grey, or up to 48-bit colour depth with surplus general requirement for OMR processing. Increasingly, digital photocopiers are also equipped with optical scanner, which provides high-speed digitisation. Examples include products from Ricoh and Canon.

Drum scanners are less commonly being used in this domain. Besides professional flatbed scanners (such as Creo Scitex, Heidelberg, and others), industrial music imaging applications for archiving (bitmap images) also use a digital-camera-back or digital camera with a copy-stand setup that ranges from simply a board for document placement to include a fully pneumatically controlled book cradle system as well as a complex robotic control automatic page-turning system. Examples of overhead scanning products are illustrated in Table 1.

With increasing pixel count and decreasing cost, one-shot digital camera systems are increasingly used in this domain, for example:

- PhaseOne, http://www.phaseone.com
- BetterLight, http://www.betterlight.com
- Imacon, http://www.imacon.dk
- Fujitsu, http://www.fujitsu.com and
- others

*Table 1. Examples of overhead scanning products*

| Company | Product | Notes |
| --- | --- | --- |
| Kirtas Technologies, Inc. (USA) | APT BookScan 1200 | World's first automatic book scanner |
| 4DigitalBooks | "DIGITIZING LINE" | Automatic digitizing system |
| Zeutschel GmbH | various MONISCAN models | Large format colour scanner OMNISCAN9000 |
| Solar Imaging Systems, UK | M3 & M5 digital camera systems | Maximum optical resolution 8192x12000 pixels |
| Icam Archive Systems, UK | GUARDIAN | Various models, including Guardian, that use Phase One camera backs |
| Konica Minolta | Minolta PS7000 book scanner | up to A2, 256 greyscales |
| InfoSys GmbH | Alpha librae | up to 900 pp/hour, greyscale & colour model |
| ImageWare Components GmbH | Bookeye products | Oversize formats up to 350 x 720 x 470 mm |
| Imaging Business Solutions | SMA ScanFox | A1 and A2 |
| Lumiere Technology | Jumbo Scan | 30,000x12,000 pixels |
| Cruse Digital Equipment | Various models including Synchron Table Scanners | CS 175P, which accepts originals as large as 40"x60" |
| Zeutschel GmbH | Zeutschel Omniscan 10000 | Books, newspapers, and large-format documents (maps, drawings, posters) 10,424x 7,300 pixels and 24 bit/pixel |

## Digitisation Guidelines

There are a vast amount of settings and options for the digitisation technologies, and many issues to consider in order to carry out a digitisation operation effectively, for example, image representations (formats), compression, choice of resolutions, colour depth, colour management, storage requirement, long-term preservation, and other issues. These issues are addressed in various digitisation-related projects and institutions. Proposed guidelines for digitisation can be found from the outcomes of these projects and institutions, such as:

- **MINERVA:** http://www.minervaeurope.org
- **PULMAN:** http://www.pulmanweb.org
- **AHDS:** (Arts and Humanities Data Service), UK at http://www.ahds.ac.uk
- **British Library:** http://www.bl.uk/services/preservation/freeandpaid.html
- **CLIR (Council on Libraries and Information Resources):** *Building and sustaining digital collections: Models for libraries and archives* at http://www.clir.org
- **DLF (Digital Library Federation):** *Digital library standards and practices* at http://www.diglib.org/standards.htm
- **Library of Congress:** A framework of guidance for building good digital collections at http://www.nap.edu/catalog/9940.html
- **UNESCO/ICA/IFLA:** Guidelines for digitization projects for collection and holdings in the public domain, particularly those held by libraries and archives at http://www.ifla.org/VII/s19/pubs/digit-guide.pdf
- **DI.MU.SE project:** (Ministero per i Beni e le Attività Culturali and Palatina Library of Parma) provided guidelines for the digitalisation of 150,000 music manuscript pages, at http://www.bibpal.unipr.it

As with other document-imaging processes such as OCR, OMR is not particularly demanding on currently available optical document scanners. Typically, for sheet music, 300 d.p.i. optical resolution and 8-bit grey is sufficient for the purpose of OMR (Selfridge-Field, 1994). Fujinaga and Riley (2002) reported that 600 dpi is a sufficient resolution for all significant details, and suggested that further increase in resolution is not necessary for OMR.

Generally, the first process in a document analysis system is to threshold a given grey input image into a binary image. Some systems used binary input images produced by the scanner. For the DI.MU.SE project, the digitalisation parameters for the music manuscript is fixed at 300-d.p.i. optical resolution, with colour depth at 24-bit RGB, and the TIFF format is used to store the digitised image.

## OPTICAL MUSIC RECOGNITION (OMR)

### Commercial OMR Systems

Currently, there are a number of commercially available OMR software, including:

- Capella-scan
- Optical Music easy Reader (OMeR)
- SharpEye Music Reader
- SmartScore
- Neuratron, PhotoScore
- BraeburnSoftware, Music Publisher system
- Vivaldi Scan (derived from SharpEye)
- Musitek, SmartScore
- Scorscan of NPC Imaging http://www.npci-imaging.com/scscinfo/scscinfo.html
- MIDI-Connections Scan, http://www.midi-connections.com/Product_Scan.htm

The accuracy specified by each distributor is generally over 90%. However, due to the complexities of music notation, simple recognition rate (as in OCR) does not offer good nor meaningful measure for OMR system. In a later section, this chapter discusses current obstacles on evaluating these systems, proposes an evaluation method to provide a meaningful assessment for OMR system, and presents results obtained from the proposed evaluation.

For a more technically detailed discussion on optical music recognition, the next section presents one of the most well known optical music recognition systems—SharpEye by Graham Jones.

## OVERVIEW OF THE SharpEye MUSIC OCR SYSTEM

### Introduction

This section of the chapter presents the experience of developing a commercial music OCR program, called SharpEye (SharpEye), by Graham Jones over many years. The description has a top-down structure, starting with a brief summary of the complete recognition engine. Section "Finding Staves and Ledge Lines" to Section "Final Interpretations and Output" fill in details of the most important stages. Section "Low Level Module" covers some lower level modules that are used throughout.

The input to the recognition engine is a black and white bitmap. The output can be one of several formats, as described in Section "Finding Interpretations and Output."

### Top Level Description

#### Main Parts of Algorithm

1.  Locate staves and systems. ***
2.  Calculate the overall scale and skew of the image from the locations of the staves. *
3.  Find ledger lines. **
4.  Find bar lines. **
5.  Find note heads (except breves). ***
6.  Find text (lyrics, musical directions, textual guitar chords). ****
7.  Add text objects to the MOCG. *
8.  Find hairpins (wedges). *
9.  Find beams. **
10.  Find stems. **
11.  Find slurs. **
12.  Add LNH objects to the MOCG. *
13.  Erase staves from bitmap. **
14.  Erase LNH objects from bitmap, keeping copies of some. ***
15.  Find FSS objects. ****
16.  Add FSS objects to MOCG. *
17.  Identify key signatures in MOCG and remove them. *
18.  Resolve conflicting interpretations in MOCG. ***
19.  Remove poorly recognised objects from MOCG. *
20.  Deal with "two voice clumps." *
21.  Locate and interpret measures, forming beamed groups, etc. ***
22.  Interpret slurs and ties, lyrics, and dynamics. *
23.  Assign times and voices to notes. **
24.  Produce output. *

Here "MOCG" is an abbreviation for "musical-object-candidate graph." It is a graph in which vertices represent possible interpretations of regions in the image, and edges represent geometrical relationships between nearby regions. Thus, one vertex might represent the interpretation of a black blob as a solid note head, and an edge from this vertex to another could represent the fact that this blob touches a vertical line interpreted as a stem. Musical objects are divided into two main types: "LNH" and "FSS." "LNH" means "linear and note head" and these objects are open and solid note heads, including grace notes and whole notes, as well as beams, stems, slurs, ties, barlines, and hairpins. LNH objects are found before the stave lines are erased. "FSS" means "fixed shape symbols," and these objects include rests, clefs, key and time signatures, accidentals, augmentation dots, articulations, and dynamics such as "mp." FSS objects are found after staves and LNH objects are erased.

The word "find" in this list should be understood as meaning "locate a region in the bitmap and assign a possible interpretation to it." The stars are meant to give a rough indication of the complexity of each stage.

*Figure 1. A "two-voice clump"*

## General Comments

Every interpretation of a region in the bitmap as being a particular symbol is given a cost. These are of the form $-\log(P(x \in C \mid x \in C \cup X))$, where $x$ is a region, $C$ is the class of the symbol, and $X$ is the outlier class consisting of noise, unknown symbols, and mis-segmentations (referred to later as "nonsymbols"). For symbols classified using the shape classifier (note heads, FSS objects, text), the probability estimates $P(x \in C \mid x \in C \cup X)$ are calibrated posterior probabilities derived from the classifier. (Details are in "Using a Shape Classifier as Part of a Larger System" (Jones, 2007)). As an example, a dot in the image could have an associated probability $P(dot\ is\ a\ staccato\ sign\mid dot\ is\ a\ staccato\ sign\ or\ a\ nonsymbol)$. The same dot might have similar associated probabilities for being a dot in a repeat sign; an augmentation dot; or a full stop in text. Other symbols, such as beams and slurs, are also given a cost, but the method of deriving them is more ad hoc, and varies from symbol to symbol.

It would be nice to be able to say that all region interpretations are placed in the MOCG, and a single algorithm then finds the best self-consistent interpretation among all the possibilities. In practice this would take too long, even if it worked well. Quite a lot of weeding out is, therefore, done before objects are put into the MOCG, and

there are some "wrinkles" that require separate treatment. The worst of these is that FSS objects cannot be reliably segmented until the LNH objects have been erased; LNH objects cannot be usefully erased until they have been reliably identified; and before the FSS objects are found, there is not as much information as one would like to resolve ambiguities among the LNH objects. Music OCR presents many such circular problems! (See section "Erasure" for how this is tackled.) Two minor issues are that key signatures and "two voice clumps" (see Figure 1) are dealt with separately. The "two voice clumps" are often found by earlier stages as a single stem with two note heads attached, and so do not obey the normal rules (see section "Resolving ambiguities in the MOCG") for stems and heads.

The bitmap is never "deskewed." Instead, the skew is estimated and any calculations requiring knowing what "horizontal" or "vertical" means use this estimate. This avoids damaging symbols by rotating them. The recognition engine can cope with about two degrees of skew. Stave lines are often not exactly straight or parallel, so they do not follow the skew angle exactly. After staves have been found, more accurate stave-relative positions can be used.

## Finding Staves and Ledger Lines

### Finding Staves

Considerable care is used when finding the staves, since all later stages depend on how well this is done, and there is no provision for recovering from errors in this stage. Here is the algorithm:

1.  Vertical black runs are merged (when fairly short and horizontally adjacent) to form "stave-line-parts." A stave-line-part is, roughly speaking, a contiguous bare portion of a stave line. Of course, there will be some nonstave objects included, but staves are almost always the dominant contributors. From these, a global estimate of stave line thickness is found, and an initial estimate of the skew of the image is found. Stave-line-parts that are inconsistent with the global thickness or skew are removed, and new estimates of thickness and skew are found. The stave-line-parts are then discarded; only the estimates of thickness and skew are used later.

2.  Now "stave-vertical-elements" are found. These are sets of five approximately equi-distant short black runs, so match a verti-cal slice through a stave. Since stave lines can be obscured (especially by beams) for considerable distances, it is permissable for one of the five lines to be missing, as long as it is black at the appropriate point.

3.  Stave-vertical-elements are merged in two stages. In the first stage, only horizontally adjacent stave-vertical-elements are allowed to merge. In the second stage, horizontal jumps are allowed. The merges in both stages are done on a "best merge first," A cost is calculated between every pair of elements, the pair with the least cost is merged, and new costs calculated from the newly merged object to all others. (This is potentially slow, but there are ways of doing it quickly—see

section "Merging Algorithm.") The costs in the second stage are based on the degree of geometrical misalignment between the two stave-vertical-elements and the number of white pixels encountered when joining up the five lines.

4.  Models for each stave are created. The model contains the left and right end positions, and for each pixel between, an estimate (to subpixel accuracy) of the vertical position of each of the five lines. It also has an esti-mate of the stave line thickness and of the noisiness of the stave line edges.

5.  An iterative method is used to improve the fit of the model to each stave. The basic iterative step is smooth the vertical posi-tions, then assign vertical black runs to the stave lines. The smoothing is done with a large-scale Gaussian, so that the vertical position estimates are replaced by a weighted average of nearby estimates. The assign-ment of vertical black runs checks whether a black run has top and bottom sufficiently close to the vertical position estimates for a stave line, taking into account the stave line thickness and the noisiness of the stave line edges. During this process, the staves can also grow or shrink horizontally.

6.  It is possible for two or more stave models to be found for a single true stave. This can happen when a stave has a large number of ledger lines; so, the next step is to weed out stave models that overlap one another by removing the worst of any stave models that overlap.

7.  In the final stage of finding staves, the domi-nant spacing of stave lines is found. This is used in many later calculations where a size or distance is required. A final estimate of global skew is also derived from the stave positions. The left and right ends are located using an algorithm that starts at a "good" place in the stave and searches left and right. Systems are then found, looking for a

systemic bar line, or other bar lines joining the staves.

## Finding Ledger Lines

Horizontal black runs near stave lines (approximately one stave-line-spacing away) are found. The black runs do not have to be exactly horizontal, but are one pixel in height. These are then merged when they are vertically adjacent and horizontally overlap. The merged objects are then tested for looking like a ledger line (particularly by looking at top and bottom edges of the shape). Those that pass the test are stored as candidate ledger lines. Ledger lines further away from the staves are found recursively by looking near ones already found.

## Finding LNH Objects

## Finding Bar Lines

Each stave is examined for bar lines. A horizontal projection of black pixels is made, looking only in the four gaps between stave lines at each horizontal position. The positions of (local) maxima in the projection are identified. The positions of the left and right edges of the candidates bar lines are refined by looking at the maxima and minima of the "first derivative" of the projection. Then the bar line is evaluated by looking at the left and right edges and at any white gaps in the line to provide a "cost."

If the cost is small enough, the bar line is stored. These bar-line candidates are then joined to others, in nearby staves, where they line up, and the line between is mainly black. Then bar lines that appear to continue above or below the stave, but are not joined to others, are deleted (assume they must be stems). Surviving bar lines are stored; ones that successfully join ones in other staves have their cost reduced.

## Finding Note Heads

Note heads are found before stave lines are erased. They are found in two stages. Firstly, possible positions are located; then subimages are extracted and sent to a shape classifier.

The possible positions are located using models for the left and right edges of a note head. The models are constructed for each stave (since they are scale dependent) and for each note type (solid, open, whole note, and grace). Since these models must cope with stems and neighbouring note heads in chords, they are quite complex. These models are then tried at each horizontal position along each stave line and each ledger line, and likely positions for left and right edges of heads identified. These are then paired (one left edge with one right edge).

For each pair of head edges, a rectangular area (somewhat larger than the note head appears to be) is extracted from the image and classified, using the shape classifier. The classifier is trained on a large number of artificially generated images that cover all the possibilities for the region near the note head, that is, the stave or ledger lines, the stem, and other nearby note heads in a chord. These training images also include variations due to different fonts and distortions that mimic variations in printing and scanning. The shape classifier provides a cost for each classification. Extra costs are then added on the basis of width, by finding the width of the best-recognized solid heads, and if this width is sufficiently well defined, adding costs to solid heads with very different widths from this "good width," to grace notes that are too wide, and to open heads that are too narrow.

Note that it is possible to have overlapping regions that are interpreted as being the same type of note head, as well as overlapping or identical regions that are interpreted as being different types of note head. Since ledger lines are already "attached" to staves, and note heads are found only along staves and ledger lines, heads can be attached to staves. This forms the starting point for assigning other objects, such as stems and beams to the appropriate stave.

## Finding Beams

Beams are found by merging vertical black runs. Black runs that belong to a stave line are ignored, as are ones that are too short or long. This is a two-stage merge. In the first stage, a cautious merge of shapes (initially the black runs) that are horizontally adjacent and vertically near-matches is carried out. The second merging, which allows shapes to join across gaps, is done. The gaps may be due to stems that produce very long vertical black runs, or due to the beam passing through a stave line, which produces an apparent sudden change in thickness. The merging is done on a "best merge first" basis, as with stave lines. This allows the reliable parts of the beam to join together, despite interruptions from stems, stave lines, or anything else.

The candidate beams are evaluated by looking at the straightness of the beam (as measured by the mean square error of a straight-line fit); by counting white pixels just beyond the edges of a parallelogram that is fitted to the shape; and by looking at the image for whiteness in the supposed beam area.

## Finding Stems

Horizontal black runs are merged in two stages, in a similar manner to beams. They are evaluated by looking at the image row by row, and matching against models for bare stem, bare on right, bare on left, obscured both sides, and so getting a weighted sum of "good length"; also a measure of average quality, which are combined to make cost.

## Finding Slurs and Ties

Vertical black runs not belonging to staves are cautiously merged (if they are vertically near-matches and horizontally adjacent); then these shapes, if big enough, are "grown" to left and right using a fairly local model of slur as a parabola.

Ones that are too straight are weeded out, and costs are assigned for being short; being too thick in comparison with length; and for wandering both sides of the straight line joining endpoints. (The recognition engine does not deal with "S" shaped slurs.)

The clump-growing method can produce a lot of overlapping candidates (near duplicates), so these are weeded out.

## Finding Text

Text, in this context, means lyrics, musical directions such as "Andante," and textual guitar chords such as "Bm" or "D♯7." It does not include dynamics such as "mp" and "ff." Text is assumed not to collide with other symbols. Lyrics are found as complete lines rather than individual syllables.

Lyrics are searched for first. Connected components from the bitmap are first merged into "short text lines" using the same general method as for beams and stems. These are then read using text OCR, but the results are only used to locate the baseline of the text (if any) in each short text line. These baselines are projected (taking into account skew) to form a vertical histogram. The histogram is smoothed, maxima near a bigger one are suppressed, then for each maximum remaining, and positioned beneath a stave, connected components near the maximum are collected and formed into a de-skewed image of the complete line and sent to the text OCR routine. The result is analyzed to decide whether it is a line of lyrics or other text, or not text at all. If it is determined to be lyrics, the result is stored, and the corresponding connected components are removed from further consideration.

The remaining connected components are merged into short text lines and sent to the text OCR routine. These short text lines are then classified as musical directions or chords.

Note that while there is no overlap between different kinds of text, there may be overlaps between text and other objects. For example, articulations may be interpreted as text and (later) interpreted as articulations.

## Storing the Results

All LNH objects are placed in the MOCG. Each interpretation of each region becomes a vertex, and edges are added to represent overlapping (and therefore conflicting) interpretations. Edges are also added to represent geometric relations between nearby LNH objects. (See section "Resolving Ambiguities in the MOCG" for more details.)

## Erasure

### Erasing Staves

Every black pixel near a stave line is examined by looking upwards and downwards from it in a "fan" of angles between North-West and North-East, and between South-West and South-East, until white is found or a limit reached in each direction. The distances traveled are combined to make a score for each pixel. These scores are painted into a grey-level image, with higher

*Figure 2. Ambiguous note head and stem (before and after stave erasure)*

scores being darker. Black pixels not near a stave line and all white pixels are copied into the grey-level version and "masked." Then the unmasked region of the grey-level image is smoothed and thresholded.

### Erasing LNH Objects

Each type of LNH object has its own special erasure routine. In general, these erase an area somewhat larger than the object appears to be, since it is preferable to remove small parts of other objects than to leave little bits unerased. Two issues make this erasure complicated. The first is that overlapping objects are usually found, such as note heads, in similar positions. It is not good to erase every possible object, given that many may be clearly false. The second issue is that some LNH objects can be confused with some FSS objects, for example, a curve found as a slur might really be part of a fermata sign; a supposed bar line might be part of a C clef; and a note head (usually poorly recognized) may be found in several FSS objects.

To deal with the first issue the strategy is to (temporarily) resolve ambiguities in the LNH objects found so far, using rules such as "a stem must have a head touching it." The ambiguity resolution algorithm is the same as used later (see section "Resolving Ambiguities in the MOCG").

Then a decision is made about whether to store copies of the shapes erased. If they are "safe," that is, very unlikely to be an FSS object, or part thereof, they are simply erased. Otherwise, copies are made of them and the list of these is merged later with the list of connected components that will be found in the erased bitmap. The objects regarded as "unsafe" include short slurs; poorly recognized note heads; poorly recognized stems with only one head; and one-stave bar lines. Figure 2 shows an example of a poorly recognised head and stem that occurs in a sharp sign. A music recognition must consider such shapes if it is to recognise notes in complex crowded music in scores of moderate quality.

Note that this erasure helps segment FSS objects, for example, where accidentals touch heads or slurs touch flags. All text is left in the image so that it can also be recognized as FSS objects, since there are ambiguities here (some supposed text might be an articulation). However, it is not useful to erase and make copies of text objects, since it is unlikely to help with segmentation.

Once the erasure decision has been made, the ambiguity resolution is "undone" so that when it is redone later, it can benefit from more information available from FSS objects.

## Finding FSS Objects

The input to this stage is a list of shapes, mostly connected components in the erased image, plus some ambiguous LNH objects that were found earlier when erasing them. Some connected components are split; this is necessary, for example, with key signatures and nearby accidentals that can remain "stuck" to one another, even after stave line erasure (see Figure 2 for an example). After this splitting, the resulting shapes are called "FSS atoms," since they are never further subdivided. The main problem dealt with by this stage is deciding how groups of FSS atoms should be combined. Naturally, this is guided by trying to recognize various combinations of atoms as music symbols using a shape classifier. Note, however, that this stage does not make final interpretations, only final segmentations.

### Clustering Connected Components

The FSS atoms are clustered using a distance measure that looks in eight directions for short lines that connect two atoms. The clusters are restricted to, at most, 10 FSS atoms, and are restricted in their geometrical size. Each cluster is then dealt with separately. The restriction to 10 FSS atoms

per cluster is to avoid a combinatorial explosion. Even with 10 FSS atoms, there are 1,023 ways of choosing atoms to form a single shape.

### Finding Decompositions of Clusters

The potential number of ways that the atoms in a cluster can be decomposed into shapes is huge, over 100,000 for 10 atoms. Note that text OCR often uses a similar over-segmentation strategy; the difference there is that there is a left-to-right ordering that drastically reduces the number of plausible combinations. Here, the number is brought under control by an algorithm that uses a graph in which vertices are atoms, and an edge is present between a pair of atoms if the distance (as used in making the clusters) is small enough. A connected subgraph now represents a plausible combination of atoms; shapes containing large white gaps are not connected as subgraphs. Now, every connected subgraph is found, and every possible decomposition (disjoint union) of the graph into connected subgraphs is found (to a maximum of 1,000 decompositions).

### Choosing a Decomposition

Each shape corresponding to a connected subgraph is then classified as an FSS object using the shape classifier. If it also has an LNH interpretation, this is added to the shortlist of candidates. The shape classifier supplies a cost for each recognizable shape; some shapes will be classified as rejects.

Then the best decomposition is found, using the classifier costs as a guide. To evaluate the decomposition, an edit cost is calculated, which is an estimate of the expected amount of editing required to correct the output. More details are in the paper by Jones (2007). The decision about the best decomposition is final, and all other decompositions are ignored from this point.

## Storing the Results

For each cluster, all FSS candidates on the short list for each shape are added to the MOCG. Edges representing overlaps between FSS candidates for the same shapes are added, as well as overlaps between FSS candidates and LNH objects; so, if a shape has three possible interpretations as an FSS object, and one as an LNH object, there will be 4 vertices and 10 edges. Edges are also added to represent geometric relations between nearby LNH and FSS objects.

Finally, LNH objects that were possibly FSS objects, but that have been rejected by this process (do not appear in best decomposition) are then deleted.

## Resolving Ambiguities in the MOCG

### Edges in the MOCG

At this stage in the recognition process, a large amount of information has been collected, and most of it is stored in the MOCG. Vertices represent possible interpretations of regions in the image as LNH or FSS objects, or as text, and edges represent geometrical relationships between nearby regions. There are two types of edges. There are negative ones that join vertices that cannot both be true interpretations, and there are positive ones where an interpretation at one vertex supports the interpretation at a neighbouring vertex. The negative edges are Boolean: they either exist or do not. The positive edges are weighted and may have a type as well. For example, an edge joining a note head to a stem will have a weight depending on how well the objects match geometrically. It will also have a type that indicates whether the head meets the stem on its left or right, and whether the stem meets the head at the top, bottom, or middle.

Every vertex has a value, associated with it, that represents an estimate of the probability that the interpretation is correct. As mentioned in section "General comments," they are estimates of $P(x \in C \mid x \in C \cup X)$ where $x$ is a region, $C$ is the class of the symbol, and $X$ is the outlier class consisting of noise, unknown symbols, and mis-segmentations. Objects enter the MOCG when these probabilities are greater than 0.1. Using the positive edges, a contextual probability can be calculated so that, for example, a poorly recognized note head may gain support from a neighbouring stem (if the stem is well recognized and the join between them is good). The contextual probability may therefore be bigger than 0.5 even if the context-free estimate is near 0.1.

The negative edges implement the following rules:

1. Two objects must not overlap. (This is the most important one.)
2. Heads cannot be too close to a flag or beam on same stem.
3. A head of one type cannot be on same stem as another (except cue/solid).
4. A head must not have two stems in same direction (both up or both down).
5. Long rests cannot be too close to a stem or bar line.
6. A key signature should have no intervening notes between itself and the bar line or left-of-stave to its left.
7. A time signature should have no intervening notes between itself and the bar line or left-of-stave to its left.
8. Whole notes cannot be close to a stem or bar line.
9. A stem cannot have heads at both ends.
10. No head can be very close to a bar line.

There are also rules expressed by the *lack* of a positive edge between vertices:

1. A note head (other than a whole or double-whole note) needs a stem.
2. Stems need a note head at one end.
3. Flags need stems.

62

4. A full beam needs a stem at both ends.
5. A half beam needs stem at one end.
6. A half beam needs another half beam, or a full beam on a stem nearby.
7. A ledger line needs another ledger line beyond it, or a note head on or just beyond it (moving away from the stave).
8. A note head on the "wrong side" of a stem needs a note head on the normal side of the same stem one staff step away.
9. A slur or tie needs a note head or a stave-end at left and right ends.
10. An augmentation dot needs a note head.
11. An accidental needs a note head.
12. Articulations need note heads.
13. A repeat dot needs another repeat dot.
14. A repeat dot needs a bar line.
15. A time signature top number needs a bottom number, and vice-versa.
16. Sharp and flat signs in key signatures have quite a complex relationship with one another, stave, and clefs.

The positive edges implement the following kinds of support:

1. Stems support, and are supported by, solid, open, and grace heads.
2. Stems support, and are supported by, beams.
3. Stems support, and are supported by, flags.
4. Sharp signs and flat signs in key signatures support one another.
5. Repeat dots support one another.
6. Stave-position supports repeat dots, long rests.
7. Time signature top numbers and bottom numbers support one another.

## Finding Contextual Probabilities

Consider a candidate stem $s$, and a candidate head $h$. Let $S$ be the class of stems, $H$ the class of heads, and $X$ the class of nonsymbols. Suppose $g$ is the event that a particular geometric relationship holds between $s$ and $h$. Let $k$ be $(g \wedge h \in H)$, the event that there is a true head nearby. Then:

$$P(s \in S \mid s \in S \cup X \wedge k)$$

$$= P(s \in S \cup X \wedge k \wedge s \in S) \, / \, P(s \in S \cup X \wedge k)$$

$$= P(s \in S \wedge k) \, / \, (P(s \in S \wedge k) + P(s \in X \wedge k))$$

$$= P(k \mid s \in S) P(s \in S) \, / \, (P(k \mid s \in S) P(s \in S) + P(k \mid s \in X) P(s \in X))$$

$$= \omega P(s \in S) \, / \, (\omega P(s \in S) + P(s \in X))$$

where $\omega = P(k \mid s \cup S) \, / \, P(k \mid s \in X)$. This $\omega$ can be estimated (in principle via some training method, but currently ad hoc formulas for different objects types are used) for any $g$, that is, for any geometric relationship. It will be at least one (it is assumed that the presence of a nearby head cannot decrease the likelihood of $s$ being a stem), and will be larger for a better join.

If $h \notin H$, it is assumed this has no effect on the likelihood of $s$ being a stem so the estimate of $P(s \in S \mid s \in S \cup X)$ should not change. Putting this together:

$$P(s \in S \mid s \in S \cup X \wedge g)$$

$$= P(h \in H) \omega P(s \in S) \, / \, (\omega P(s \in S) + P(s \in X)) + (1 - P(h \in H)) P(s \in S \mid s \in S \cup X)$$

This is a typical formula used to calculate a contextual probability estimate in the MOCG. If there was also candidate flag near $s$, a more complicated, but similar, formula is used. The contextual probabilities are not applied recursively.

## The Ambiguity Resolution Algorithm

The main algorithm for resolving ambiguity is a discrete relaxation algorithm. Vertices are progressively deleted until there are no more conflicts between interpretations. Vertices can be deleted for two reasons, corresponding to the two types of rule described in section "Edges in the MOCG." The rules expressed by the lack of an edge are easy to deal with. Since the ambiguity resolution starts with "too many" vertices and only deletes them, it is always "safe" to apply these rules, in the sense that it will not make a mistake that could be recovered from. These rules are, therefore, applied frequently during the discrete relaxation.

The other type of rule, expressed as a negative edge, is harder to deal with, and an optimal choice of deletions would be extremely time-consuming to find. Instead, the algorithm iteratively finds "good" vertices to remove. In principle, one can imagine that the least ambiguous conflict between pairs of conflicting vertices is found and one of the pair is removed. (In practice, some short cuts are taken.) The least ambiguous conflict is found using the contextual probability values for two conflicting objects: loosely, it is the pair with the biggest difference between contextual probabilities. When a deletion has been done, new contextual probabilities may need to be calculated, and there may be vertices that can be removed due to lack of an edge.

Once no further conflicts remain, objects having a contextual probability of less than 0.5 are removed.

## Final Interpretations and Output

## Measures and Notes

The main work is putting together the interpretations of individual shapes into musical objects (joining stems to heads, stems to beams, etc.). Bar lines are found and grouped to identify double bar lines, and repeat signs are formed. Objects are assigned to staves, starting with heads (which are already done) from which stems, beams, and flags can be assigned. Beamed groups are found, and the number of beams meeting stems are found. The search for things attached to heads looks for stems and beamed groups that may extend into lower staves, and these groups are split up into one-stave objects. Articulations, accidentals, and augmentation dots are converted into properties of note heads. Within each stave, objects are assigned to measures.

Note that information about the timing of notes, or the voice they belong to, is not calculated at this stage.

## Other Objects

Slurs and ties, text, and dynamics do not belong to a single measure. Slurs and ties are only assigned to a system, text, and dynamics are assigned to a stave.

## Producing Output

The recognition engine can produce output in four formats: its own format, MIDI, NIFF, and MusicXML. Its own format is graphical in nature, with no start times or voices for notes, and the minimum of interpretation. For example, slurs and ties are not attached to notes. It essentially contains the information found so far.

The other three formats require more interpretation. The main work is assigning times and voices for notes; the assignment of times and voices is highly intertwined. This task is more difficult than it might seem at first sight. The rules of music notation "should" make the task a mere matter of calculation, but in practice, unmarked triplets, partial measures (pickup measures and ones with double bar lines or repeat signs), incomplete voices, and some "bending" of the correct rules cause problems. There is also the issue of trying to do the best in the presence of recognition errors.

Other interpretation issues include attaching slurs, ties, and lyric syllables to notes; joining slurs and ties across systems; and converting textual chords like "Am7" into a logical format.

## Low-Level Modules

Two important low-level modules are the merging algorithm, which does the bottom-up merging of shapes to form staves, beams, and so forth, and the shape classifier, which is used to categorize and give a cost to note heads, FSS symbols, and characters in text. (The segmentation of text into characters is another significant problem, not discussed here.)

### Merging Algorithm

In principle, the algorithm is easy:

1. Find distances between all pairs of shapes.
2. Choose the nearest pair and merge them.
3. Find new distances from the newly merged shape to the remaining shapes.
4. Repeat 2 and 3 until the nearest pair is too distant.

The difficulty is doing this in a reasonable amount of time. For example, when finding stave lines, there may be $n=100,000$ elementary shapes to merge, and the algorithm, which is $O(n^3)$, is impractical. The calculation of distances can be speeded up by taking advantage of the geometrical nature of the problem. Most pairs of shapes are too far apart to ever merge, and by using a grid-based search algorithm, most of these distances need never be calculated. The other slow part is finding the nearest pair to merge. A priority queue of potential merges is used to speed this up. A potential merge is essentially a triplet (shape, nearest neighbour, distance). However, there is considerable complexity involved in maintaining the priority queue structure as merges take place.

Two further aspects should be mentioned. The shapes to be merged are kept sorted (for example, from left to right for stave lines), and many of the merging operations are done in two stages in which only merges between adjacent shapes are allowed in the first stage. Together this means that in the first stage, closest neighbours can readily be updated, and in the second stage, merging of noncontiguous objects is facilitated.

### Shape Classifier

Images that are sent to the shape classifier are converted into feature vectors. The image is scaled to a standard size and slightly smoothed. The main feature vectors are gradient-based. At each pixel, the angle and magnitude of the edge is found and converted to eight nonnegative values, giving edge-strength in eight directions. These are summed over various subimages to give a total of about 100 features. Classes are modeled as normal mixtures, and the classifications and costs are derived from density estimates in feature space. Jones (2007) has more detail about how the classifier is used. It is worth making the comment that although a discriminative classifier (such as a support vector machine) might have a better error rate, a generative classifier is arguably preferable when accurate posterior probability estimates are required, and where it is important to be able to reject noise and mis-segmentations.

## OMR EVALUATION

### Obstacles

The optical music recognition process is more complex than OCR. Despite the availability of several commercially available OMR systems such as SharpEye, SmartScore, Photoscore, Capella-scan, and so forth, the precision and reliability of these systems is still in need of further improvements and enhancements in order to provide a real time-saving automated process without too much manual correction and intervention. It is arguable that corrections require more time than direct data entry and hence, the accuracy of such systems must be near perfect before they are really applicable in large operations.

The accuracy of the commercially available OMR systems, as declared by the distributor, is generally around 90%, but this value is usually obtained by using a limited number of typical music sheets. This estimation is not objective. In other image recognition fields, such as the optical character recognition or the face recognition domain, there are many large ground-truth datasets that enable recognition results to be evaluated automatically and objectively. At the time of writing, there is neither a standard dataset for OMR nor a set of standard terminology for comparative study. If a new recognition algorithm or system were proposed, it could not be compared with the other algorithms or systems since the results would have to be traditionally evaluated with different scores and different methods. Taking these facts into consideration, it is indispensable to make a master music score dataset that can be used to objectively and automatically evaluate the music score recognition system. At the same time, a set of rules and metrics are required in order to define the aspects that have to be considered in the evaluation process.

In general, the currently available commercial OMR systems are linked to specific proprietary music notational software. For example, PhotoScore (OMR system) outputs directly into Sibelius (music notation software). It is not easy to assess the performance of the OMR system alone without interaction with the interface provided by the notational software. It is not always possible to access to the output from the OMR system itself directly. This problem is further complicated by the lack of a commonly accepted standard for music notation.

Existing OMR systems offer capture facilities to communicate directly with the scanner. This adds another complication, since it is not easy to make sure that the input images for all OMR systems are exactly the same (pixel perfect). For the OMR assessment, file input is clearly preferred, however, the complications here include:

- Different input format support.
- Different optimum resolution required.
- Different image-depth requirement (e.g., 2-bit, 8-bit, etc.) and different preprocessing approaches.

Besides differences of input and format representation, differences in output formats, due to the lack of a commonly accepted standard for musical notation, present another layer of complication. Generally, output can only be obtained in a proprietary format of the music notation software. For example, ".mus" or the Enigma format for the Finale software, the Sibelius format for the Sibelius software, and so on. Some of these formats are proprietary with no publicly available documentation.

The NIFF format, which was designed for the purpose of exchanging music notation between different music notation software, noticeably OMR and music notation software, is starting to be used by a few notation software. However, this is still very much underexploited, particularly in OMR systems.

In general, all music notation software can export in the MIDI format. However, MIDI does not represent all features of music notation as they appear (visually) on the music score. For example, the MIDI format does not capture the rhythmic features. MIDI files output from different music notation software can be slightly different, depending on the music software.

It is not easy to compare results output in different formats due to their individual designs and capabilities. Due to these complications, "scan once, use many" methodology may not be easily applied.

Furthermore, the fundamental unit of music notation (the note) is itself a complex object. A note may consist of a note head, a stem, a flag and/or a beam, and associated to possibly one or more accidental signs, dynamic markings, and expressive marking such as staccato dot.

Additionally there are global and environmental factors that can further modify the fundamental semantic of this object (a note), for example, the clef, key and time signature, and so forth. The results of the comparison can be distorted by contexture errors that cannot be taken in account by direct comparisons. A better methodology for comparing results must involve definition of different ratios for each kind of error. An error recognition of a clef sign, for example, would result in an error for each note in the output, but this error can easily be corrected by just one correction in the notation format.

The measurement and correction should be done in order, with a priority list with global features before more local features. For example, the clef sign error must be corrected at the beginning of the process, since the error induces many more corrections and artefacts introduced by software at a later step (for example, error in time signature could introduce completion of measures in notation software, by introduction of incorrect rests for completion of measures). In the same manner, a normalisation must be done at an earlier stage to correct possible errors of global features, such as time signature, that could introduce many differences in the final output.

Although MIDI does not represent the layout and format of a music score, it is still useful to setup a methodology based on the MIDI format since most of the software support this format. Ideally, a full featured interchange format, such as NIFF, is required, but MIDI is currently the most common denominator. In order to make full use of the methodology with the MIDI, it is necessary to normalise the data before exporting to MIDI, followed by an import in a reference software.

The proposed methodology for comparing OMR software consists of the following steps:

1. Input of a scanned image with different resolutions, different format support, different image depth
2. First step of correction for contexture errors, for example, clef, time signature, key signature.
3. Normalisation of context for nontested (and nonsignificant) features, for example, tempo marking
4. Output in music notation software
5. Second step of correction for contexture errors (if this is not possible in the earlier stage)
6. Normalization of context for nontested features (if not possible at an earlier stage)
7. MIDI export
8. MIDI import in a reference software— Normalisation of context (tempo markings—dynamics—MIDI instruments and parts)—first evaluation of the accuracy rates
9. Correction of errors on the first-rated result, and generation (MIDI export) of a reference file
10. MIDI export

The comparison tests can be made:

• Manually, to detect errors at step 8 (MIDI import) as described previously.
• Automatically, software-based comparison of the results obtained at step 10, with the reference file obtained in 9.

This methodology can only be applied to those basic features that are part of the MIDI standard, and cannot be applied to features that are not part of the standard, such as dynamic markings (hairpins, staccato, tenuto…).

## Evaluation of Performance Based on Complete Music Symbols and Relationships Reconstruction

This section discussed a performance evaluation approach for the assessment of OMR system that takes into account the "important-ness" of each musical feature to offer a representative measure for benchmarking.

### Definition of the Test Set

Due to the lack of a standard ground-truth dataset, as discussed earlier, to condition the choice of tests, seven images have been selected from the archive of DSI at the University of Florence with the following features:

- Monophonic music
- Font variability
- Music symbols frequently used in the classic music repertory
- Variable density of music symbols
- Irregular groups (e.g., triplets, etc.)
- Small note with or without accidentals (e.g., grace notes)
- Different types of barlines (e.g., single barline, double barline, etc.)
- Clef and time signature change
- Ornaments (mordent, turn, and trill)
- Slurs (single and nested).

The set of complete symbols and relationships are listed and described in Figure 3. This evaluation set is by no mean complete for all genres of music score. It can be extended in order to include many other aspects (structural, symbolic, etc...). The proposed list is adequate to describe the monophonic music score and relationships, and the most important and frequently occurred symbols.

The test cases can be found online at http://www.interactivemusicnetwork.org/documenti/view_document.php?file_id=475

## Criteria for Evaluation

This section discusses evaluation criteria to address the correctness and effectiveness aspects of an OMR system. Assessment of effectiveness and correctness involve the following considerations:

1. The ability in recognizing music symbols.
2. The accuracy in reconstructing music symbols and relationship (from their components/primitives).

A complete music symbol is the final result of recognition and reconstruction from its basic components (or graphical primitives) and its association/relationships from the basic components. Some basic components/symbols are also complete music symbols (e.g., rests, clef, etc.), whereas others are lower-level components (e.g., a beam, an augmentation dot, etc...) of a complete music symbol. Correct recognition of lower-level components does not imply correct recognition of the complete music symbols, since from the point of view of final result, the music symbol has to be identified and characterized by its music features and relationships with other symbols. For example, the identification of an isolated note head does not imply the complete recognition of the note that is characterized by its pitch, duration, and if an accidental (if found) is correctly assigned, if it is in a group of note, and so forth. The realization of a group of beamed notes is an indication of the capability to determine the semantic relationships amongst a group of notes. To this end, an evaluation set of complete music symbols and relationships among symbols have been identified. For each category $i$, the following metrics are defined:

1. *expected* $N^{(i)}$ is the occurrence number of complete symbols or relationships counted in the original score.

*Figure 3. List of complete symbols and relationship for the OMR performance evaluation*

| Categories | Weight | Aim |
|---|---|---|
| Note with pitch and duration | 10 | Evaluate the note reconstruction correctness in terms of pitch and duration. |
| Rests | 10 | Evaluate the recognition of rests. |
| Note with accidentals | 7 | Evaluate the association of accidentals (sharp, flat, double sharp, natural, double flat) with a note. |
| Groups of beamed notes | 10 | Evaluate the capability in reconstructing beamed notes |
| Time signature and time change | 10 | Evaluate the capability in identifying and reconstructing the time indication by recognised numbers involved in the fraction. |
| Key signature and key signature change | 10 | Evaluate the capability in identifying and reconstructing the key signature (tonality). The tonality is linked to the number of accidentals used in representing the key signature. |
| Symbols below or above notes | 5 | Evaluate the capability in identifying and linking ornaments symbols and accents (staccato, accent, turn, mordent, trill, tenuto, etc...). |
| Grace notes | 5 | Evaluate the capability in recognising grace notes: acciaccatura and appoggiatura are related to a single symbol while multiple grace notes define a group of notes. The multiple notes are considered a unique symbol. |
| Slurs and bends | 7 | Evaluate the reconstruction of horizontal symbols: slurs (and ties) and bends. |
| Augmentation dots | 10 | Evaluate the augmentation dots linking to notes. |
| Clefs | 10 | Evaluate the recognition of clefs and clef changes. |
| Irregular notes groups | 10 | Evaluate the capability in recognising tuplets. |
| Number of measures | 10 | Evaluate the capability in recognising the bar line and the number of measures. |
| Number of staves | 10 | Evaluate the capability in recognising staves. |

2. *correct* $n_t^{(i)}$ is the occurrence number of complete symbols or relationships observed in the reconstructed score considering the original score.
3. *added* $n_a^{(i)}$ is the occurrence number of complete symbols or relationships introduced into the reconstructed score considering the original score.
4. *fault* $n_f^{(i)}$ is the occurrence number of complete symbols or relationships that are recognized incorrectly but are counted in the reconstructed score considering the original score.
5. *missed* $n_m^{(i)}$ is the occurrence number of complete symbols or relationships that are being overlooked but are present in the original score. They are counted in the reconstructed score considering the original score.

For category $i$, the following equation is valid:

$$N^{(i)} = n_t^{(i)} + n_f^{(i)} + n_m^{(i)}$$

This evaluation method is characterized by an accurate analysis. A music symbol or a relationship is considered correct only if the basic components/symbols and music symbols that are involved in the relationship are correct.

Considering:

- $M$, the total number of categories.
- $E_{tot} = \sum_{i=1}^{M} N_i$, the total number of expected symbols and relationships.

the following cumulative evaluation indices have been defined:

1.  Percentage reconstruction rate

$$T_{Rec} = \frac{\sum_{i=1}^{M} n_t^{(i)}}{E_{tot}} 100$$

2.  Weighted percentage reconstruction rate

$$TP_{Rec} = \frac{1}{E_{tot}} \frac{\sum_{i=1}^{M} p_i n_t^{(i)}}{\sum_{i=1}^{M} p_i} 100$$

where:

- $p_i$ stands for the relevance (weight) given to each basic symbol or relationship. The range for weights is [1,10], where 10 means high relevance.

3.  Percentage reconstruction error

$$E_{Rec} = \frac{\sum_{i=1}^{M} n_f^{(i)} + n_a^{(i)} + n_m^{(i)}}{E_{tot}}$$

The indices in Table 2 have been used to evaluate the performance over the whole set of test images by considering the percentage rate for correct, incorrect, missed, and added symbols and relationships.

The relevance of each category is represented by a weight. The weights (important-ness) have been collected from questionnaire feedback of an expert group at the second MUSICNETWORK workshop. These weights have been estimated as the median values of relevance values collected. The set of complete symbols and relationships and values of weights are reported in Figure 3.

*Table 2. Indices used to evaluate the performance over the whole set of test images*

| Percentage rate for correct (True) symbols | Percentage rate for incorrect (Fault) symbols |
|---|---|
| $$TT_{Rec} = \frac{\sum_{i=1}^{L} n_t^{(i)}}{\sum_{i=1}^{L} N_i} 100$$ | $$TF_{Rec} = \frac{\sum_{i=1}^{L} n_f^{(i)}}{\sum_{i=1}^{L} N_i} 100$$ |
| Percentage rate for missed (Miss) symbols | Percentage rate for added (Add) symbols |
| $$TM_{Rec} = \frac{\sum_{i=1}^{L} n_m^{(i)}}{\sum_{i=1}^{L} N_i} 100$$ | $$TA_{Rec} = \frac{\sum_{i=1}^{L} n_a^{(i)}}{\sum_{i=1}^{L} N_i} 100$$ |

where:
- $N_i$ stands for the total number of expected symbols for the example $i$;
- $L$ stands for the number of examples of test set used in the evaluation.

## Result Analysis

Three applications have been selected in order to compare the performance in the score recognition: SharpEye2 (Visiv), SmartScore (MusiTek), and O³MR (developed at the DSI—University of Florence).

The results of each of the OMR systems are reported in Figure 4, with global evaluation of the test set, where:

- The **Total** column reports the number of collected occurrences for each category.
- The **True** column reports the percentage rate for correct symbols recognised.
- The **Add** column reports the percentage rate for added symbols.
- The **Fault** column reports the percentage rate for incorrect symbols.

- The **Miss** column reports the percentage rate for missing symbols.

The results show that:

- SmartScore introduces errors in notes reconstruction and adds notes. It detects *tuplets*, but the tendency is to make mistakes. It has difficulty with *slurs, time signature* change, and *key signatures.*
- SharpEye2 does not introduce additional notes. However, it has some problems with *tuplets*. It does not discriminate *appoggiatura* from *acciaccatura*. It considers *grace notes* as *appoggiatura.*
- The main limits for O³MR lies within the recognition of *slurs, tuplets, grace notes,* and *ornaments* symbols. It introduces *slurs* wrongly due to its incorrect decomposition

*Figure 4. Evaluation tables: SmartScore, SharpEye2 and O³MR*

| Complete Music symbols & Relationships | Total | SmartScore | | | | SharpEye2 | | | | O³MR | | | |
|---|---|---|---|---|---|---|---|---|---|---|---|---|---|
| | | % True | % Add | % Fault | % Miss | % True | % Add | % Fault | % Miss | % True | % Add | % Fault | % Miss |
| Notes' shape with right pitch & duration | 1923 | 95.68 | 2.44 | 2.29 | 2.03 | 96.67 | 0.26 | 1.20 | 2.13 | 97.97 | 0.68 | 1.46 | 0.57 |
| Note with right associated accidental | 171 | 88.89 | 5.26 | 2.34 | 8.77 | 95.32 | 0.00 | 0.58 | 4.09 | 80.12 | 2.34 | 2.92 | 16.96 |
| Groups of Notes (Number) | 446 | 98.65 | 0.22 | 0.22 | 1.12 | 96.64 | 0.00 | 0.22 | 3.14 | 98.21 | 0.00 | 0.90 | 0.90 |
| Rests | 192 | 38.54 | 8.85 | 0.00 | 61.46 | 81.77 | 0.00 | 2.60 | 15.63 | 95.31 | 5.73 | 0.00 | 4.69 |
| Time Signature and Time Change | 41 | 31.71 | 2.44 | 14.63 | 53.66 | 63.41 | 4.88 | 4.88 | 31.71 | 68.29 | 0.00 | 2.44 | 29.27 |
| Key Signature | 74 | 32.43 | 0.00 | 35.14 | 32.43 | 90.54 | 10.81 | 9.46 | 0.00 | 93.24 | 0.00 | 6.76 | 0.00 |
| Markers | 117 | 33.33 | 13.68 | 0.00 | 66.67 | 70.09 | 0.85 | 0.00 | 29.91 | 37.61 | 1.71 | 0.00 | 62.39 |
| Grace note | 31 | 0.00 | 0.00 | 0.00 | 100.00 | 12.90 | 0.00 | 67.74 | 19.35 | 0.00 | 0.00 | 0.00 | 100.00 |
| Slur, Tie and Bend | 440 | 61.82 | 9.32 | 9.77 | 28.41 | 82.05 | 0.00 | 8.18 | 9.77 | 60.23 | 3.86 | 19.77 | 20.00 |
| Augmentation Dots | 123 | 89.43 | 66.67 | 0.00 | 10.57 | 91.06 | 11.38 | 0.00 | 8.94 | 80.49 | 2.44 | 0.00 | 19.51 |
| Clefs and Clef change | 145 | 75.17 | 5.52 | 0.00 | 24.83 | 66.21 | 3.45 | 18.62 | 15.17 | 96.55 | 1.38 | 0.69 | 2.76 |
| Tuplets | 87 | 34.48 | 26.44 | 0.00 | 65.52 | 33.33 | 1.15 | 9.20 | 57.47 | 0.00 | 0.00 | 0.00 | 100.00 |
| Number of measures | 275 | 100.00 | 2.18 | 0.00 | 0.00 | 99.27 | 1.45 | 0.00 | 0.73 | 99.64 | 1.45 | 0.00 | 0.36 |
| Number of Staves | 74 | 100.00 | 0.00 | 0.00 | 0.00 | 100.00 | 0.00 | 0.00 | 0.00 | 100.00 | 0.00 | 0.00 | 0.00 |

of symbols. Comparatively, it adds lesser symbols than SmartScore. It obtained the best score in *time signature, key signature,* and *clef* recognitions.

Generally, the recognition of notes and *rests* is the fundamental requirement of an OMR system. They are considered as the most important music symbols, and their recognition has to be robust and reliable.

The bar charts in Figure 5 (a, b, c) illustrate the global evaluation associated with each example:

1. The Weighted Percentage of Reconstruction Rate: it takes into account weights associated with each music symbol and relationship.
2. The Percentage of Reconstruction Rate: in this case music symbols and relationships have the same relevance.

3. The Percentage of Reconstruction Error: it considers missed, added and fault symbols. For this reason it represents a measure of the work has to be done to correct the reconstructed score.

This evaluation shows that SharpEye provides the best performance overall, and the O³MR is comparable to the Smartscore, and the O³MR obtained the best score with the example 5 (93.35%) as shown in Figure 5.

## MUSIC IMAGE RESTORATION

Besides recognition and translation, paper-based music score into machine-readable symbolic representation, as discussed in the earlier sections, graphical representation of music scores and manuscripts can also be useful for various

*Figure 5(a). Evaluation of complete music symbols and relationships reconstruction: The weighted percentage of reconstruction rate*

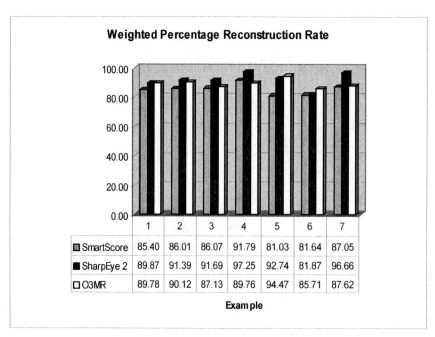

| | 1 | 2 | 3 | 4 | 5 | 6 | 7 |
|---|---|---|---|---|---|---|---|
| ▨ SmartScore | 85.40 | 86.01 | 86.07 | 91.79 | 81.03 | 81.64 | 87.05 |
| ■ SharpEye 2 | 89.87 | 91.39 | 91.69 | 97.25 | 92.74 | 81.87 | 96.66 |
| ☐ O3MR | 89.78 | 90.12 | 87.13 | 89.76 | 94.47 | 85.71 | 87.62 |

*Figure 5(b). Evaluation of complete music symbols and relationships reconstruction: The percentage of reconstruction rate*

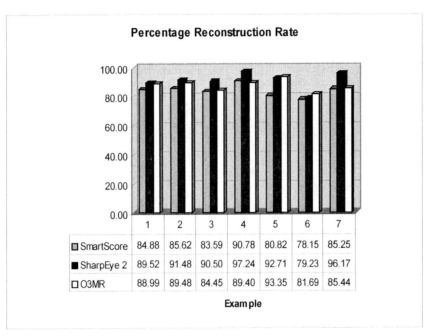

*Figure 5(c). Evaluation of complete music symbols and relationships reconstruction: The percentage of reconstruction error*

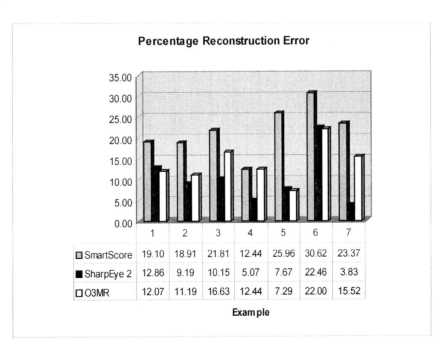

applications, including digital preservation and cross-media integration. The idea is to digitise, extract, and encode the music graphically to preserve the look and feel of the original image from the paper-based input.

This is particularly important for handwritten music manuscripts, since this approach preserves the writing style, and enables scalable reconstruction and visualisation. Suitable vector graphics formats include:

• SVG (Scalable Vector Graphics); which is an XML-based 2D vector graphics file format
• MPEG 4 BIFS
• Postscript
• Adobe PDF
• Flash
• and others

SVG (for scalable vector graphics) is a standard (a recommendation) of the World Wide Web Consortium. SVG is a language for describing two-dimensional graphics and graphical applications in XML. Postscript is a language for description of a printed page. Developed by Adobe in 1985, it has become an industry standard for printing and imaging. The PDF (portable document format) is based on Postscript, and on the ability of almost all software on major operating systems, such as Windows or MacOS, to generate postscript using their widely available Postscript printing device driver. The Flash format, developed by Macromedia, is mainly based on a vector graphics format, similar in functionalities to the Freehand format of the same vendor. It is a proprietary format, even if the specifications are available. MPEG BIFS (binary format for scenes description) makes possible to define so-called "scenes" consisting of several audiovisual objects that can be part of complex interactive multimedia scenarios. The individual objects are encoded and transmitted separately in a scene that is then composed after decoding of individual objects. Objects can be simple shapes such as circles, rectangles, text, or media such as AudioClip or MovieTexture, or even scripts.

Typical enhancements and restorations process include reconstructing broken stave lines and stems, and removing ink spillage and noise (see Figure 6). Working at this level allows minor alteration such as this. However, this is not an

*Figure 6. Typical enhancements and restorations process (before and after processing)*

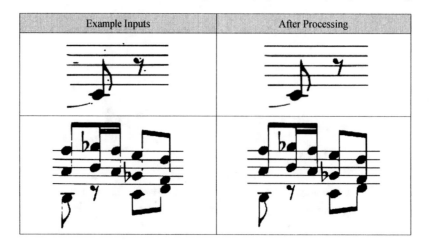

effective approach for modifications involving larger interconnected features or alteration affecting multiple staffs.

The advantage of optical music restoration is that the processes do not jeopardise the original layout of the scores, which have been optimised by the engravers, and normally represents the ideal visual configurations. Since the original spacing of the music is untouched, there is no large modification and hence, it does not require extensive proofreading. However, the process is only concerned with small and local modifications. Larger adjustments, for example insertions or deletions of a group of symbols, cannot be fully automated without altering the original layout. No full recognition is necessary for this process and hence, it does not provide multimedia functionalities such as playback or search. This process is robust and it can improve the visual qualities of the scores and manuscript for reprinting and archiving.

## CONCLUSION AND FUTURE DIRECTIONS

This chapter discussed the background of music imaging, including digitisation, recognition, and restoration. It also described a detail comparative study with three OMR systems that bring "importantness" of the features into account, rather than a single global accuracy value to assess and evaluate the performance of the OMR system.

With an effective and robust OMR system, it can provide an automated and time-saving input method to transform paper-based music scores into a machine readable representation, for a wide range of music software, in the same way as OCR is useful for text-processing applications. Besides direct applications, such as playback, musical analysis, reprinting, editing, and digital archiving, OMR would enable efficient translations, for example, to Braille notations (Dancing dots) or other nonwestern musical notations. It could provide

better access and widen participation of music and, at the same time, introduce new functionalities and capabilities with interactive multimedia technologies, and provide digital preservation of this invaluable paper-based cultural heritage.

With graphical reconstruction processes, paper-based music sheets can be digitised with the original visualisation with the capabilities of cross-media integration, extending useful functionalities for usages and applications in edutainment, long-term preservation, and archiving, as well as widening accessibilities and participations.

Typical applications in the field of cross-media (multimedia) integration include:

- Association of scores and audio performance, with automatic synchronization.
- Association of scores and video excerpts (showing details on execution).
- Association of scores and other visualisations, such as musical summaries, sonagrams...
- Hyperlinking (adding links to graphic symbols in scores).
- Convergence with audio technologies (remix, spatialisation...).
- Content-based queries, and Web-based access to music (query by humming, query by example...).
- Use of the score as a reference point for studies on expressive rendering (comparison of renderings from different performers), and use of score for expressive rendering using audio synthesis software.

Association of scores and musical performance can be made manually, but in the case of a vector-graphics based score, an automatic process can be envisaged. There has been significant progress in the symbolic music representation with audio-visual integration and this has introduced a very exciting prospect to music imaging that translates paper-based materials into machine-readable formats that have the capabilities to enhance music notation with latest interactive multimedia technologies such as the applications described, to widen accessibilities and musical expressivities and to allow long-term preservation of the invaluable music heritage.

## ACKNOWLEDGMENT

Part of this work has been performed under the MUSICNETWORK project, cosupported by the European Communities IST (Information Society Technology) 5th Framework Programme. Many thanks to all the partners and participants of the MUSICNETWORK and the Music Imaging Working Group.

## REFERENCES

Bainbridge, D., & Bell, T. (2001). The challenge of optical music recognition. *Computers and the Humanities, 35*, 95-121.

Bainbridge, D., & Carter, N. (1997). Automatic recognition of music notation. In H. Bunke & P. Wang (Eds.), *Handbook of optical character recognition and document image analysis* (pp. 557-603). Hackensack, NJ: World Scientific.

Bainbridge, D., & Wijaya, K. (1999). Bulk processing of optically scanned music. In *Proceedings of the 7th International Conference on Image Processing and Its Applications* (pp. 474-478).

Bellini, P., Bruno, I., & Nesi, P. (2001). Optical music sheet segmentation. In *Proceedings of the First International Conference on WEB Delivering of MUSIC* (pp. 183-190).

Bellini, P., & Nesi, P. (2001). Wedelmusic format: An XML music notation format for emerging applications. In *Proceedings of the First International Conference on WEB Delivering of MUSIC* (pp. 79-86).

Blostein, D., & Baird, H. S. (1992). A critical survey of music image analysis. In H. S. Baird, H. Bunke, & K. Yamamoto (Eds.), *Structured document image analysis* (pp. 405-434). Berlin: Springer-Verlag.

Bruno, I., & Nesi, P. (2002). *Multimedia music imaging: Digitisation, restoration, recognition and preservation of music scores and music manuscripts*. 1st MUSICNETWORK Open Workshop, Darmstadt, Germany.

capella-scan (n.d.). *capella Software*, Retrieved February 9, 2003, from http://www.whc.de/

Carter, N. P. (1992). Segmentation and preliminary recognition of madrigals notated in white mensural notation. *Machine Vision and Applications, 5*(3), 223-30.

Carter, N. P. (1994). Conversion of the Haydn symphonies into electronic form using automatic score recognition: A pilot study. In L. M. Vincent & T. Pavlidis (Eds.), *Proceedings of the SPIE—Document Recognition*, 2181, (pp. 279-290).

Carter, N. P., & Bacon, R. A. (1990). Automatic recognition of music notation. In *Proceedings of the International Association for Pattern Recognition Workshop on Syntactic and Structural Pattern Recognition*, 482.

Choudhury, G. S., DiLauro, T., Droettboom, M., Fujinaga, I., Harrington, B., & MacMillan, K. (2000). *Optical music recognition system within a large-scale digitization project*. International Conference on Music Information Retrieval.

Cooper, D., Ng, K. C., & Boyle, R. D. (1997). An extension of the MIDI file format: expressive MIDI—expMIDI. In E. Selfridge-Field (Ed.), *Beyond MIDI: The handbook of musical codes* (pp. 80-98) Cambridge, MA: MIT Press.

Coüasnon, B. (2002). *Improving optical music recognition*. Position paper, First MUSICNETWORK Open Workshop, Darmstadt, Germany, 2002.

Coüasnon, B., & Rétif, B. (1995). Using a grammar for a reliable full score recognition system. In *Proceedings of the International Computer Music Conference (ICMC)* (pp. 187-194).

Crombie, D., Fuschi, D., Mitolo, N., Nesi, P., Ng, K., & Ong, B. (2005). Bringing music industry into the interactive multimedia age. *AXMEDIS International Conference*, Florence, Italy. IEEE Computer Society Press.

Dancing dots (n.d.). *Goodfeel Braille Music Translator*. Retrieved August 8, 2002, from http://www.dancingdots.com

Fahmy, H., & Blostein, D. (1994). A graph-rewriting approach to discrete relaxation: Application to music recognition. In *Proceedings of the SPIE*, 2181,(pp. 291-302).

Fahmy, H., & Blostein, D. (1998). A graph-rewriting paradigm for discrete relaxation: Application to sheet-music recognition. *International Journal of Pattern Recognition and Artificial Intelligence, 12*(6), 763-99.

Fujinaga, I. (1996). Exemplar-based learning in adaptive optical music recognition system. In *Proceedings of the International Computer Music Conference* (pp. 55-56).

Fujinaga, I. (1988). *Optical music recognition using projections*. Master Thesis, McGill University, Montreal, Canada.

Fujinaga, I. (2001). An adaptive optical music recognition system. In D. Greer (Ed.). Musicology and sister disciplines. In *Past, Present, Future: Proceedings of the 16th International Congress of the International Musicological Society*. Oxford: Oxford University Press.

Fujinaga, I., Alphonce, B., & Pennycook, B. (1992). Interactive optical music recognition. In *Proceedings of the International Computer Music Conference* (pp. 117-120).

Fujinaga, I., & Riley, J. (2002). Digital image capture of musical scores. In *Proceedings of the 3rd International Conference on Music Information Retrieval (ISMIR 2002), IRCAM*—Centre Pompidou, Paris.

Gezerlis, V. G., & Theodoridis, S. (2000). *An optical music recognition system for the notation of the Orthodox Hellenic Byzantine Music*. International Conference of Pattern Recognition (ICPR-2000), Barcelona, Spain.

Good, M. (2001). MusicXML for notation and analysis. In W. B. Hewlett & E. Selfridge-Field, E. (Eds.), The virtual score: Representation, retrieval, restoration. *Computing in Musicology, 12*, 113-124.

Good, M. (2002). MusicXML in practice: Issues in translation and analysis. In *Proceedings of the 1st International Conference MAX 2002: Musical Application Using XML*, Milan (pp. 47-54).

Hoos, H. H., Hamel, K. A., Renz, K., & Kilian, J. (1998). The GUIDO music notation format—A novel approach for adequately representing score-level music. In *Proceedings of the International Computer Music Conference* (pp. 451-454).

Jones, G. (in press). *Using a shape classifier as part of a larger system.*

Matsushima, T., Harada, T., Sonomoto, I., Kanamori, K., Uesugi, A., Nimura, Y., Hashimoto, S., & Ohteru, S. (1985). Automated recognition system for musical score: The vision system of WABOT-2. *Bulletin of Science and Engineering Research Laboratory*, Waseda University.

Mitolo, N., Nesi, P., & Ng, K. C. (Eds.). (2005, July 2-4). In *Proceedings of the 5th MUSICNETWORK Open Workshop*, Universität für Musik und darstellende Kunst Wien, Vienna, Austria.

Miyao, H., & Haralick, R. M. (2000). *Format of ground truth data used in the evaluation of the results of an optical music recognition system*. IAPR Workshop on Document Analysis Systems.

Ng, K. C. (1995). *Automated computer recognition of music scores*. PhD Thesis, School of Computing, University of Leeds, UK.

Ng, K. C. (2001). Music manuscript tracing. *Proceedings of the Fourth IAPR International Workshop on Graphics Recognition (GREC 2001)*, Canada (pp. 470-481).

Ng, K. C. (2002). Document imaging for music manuscript. In *Proceedings of the Sixth World Multiconference on Systemics, Cybernetics and Informatics* (SCI 2002), Orlando, USA, XVIII (pp. 546-549).

Ng, K. C. (guest editor). (2005). *Journal of New Music Research (JNMR) special issue on Multimedia Music and the World Wide Web, 34*(2).

Ng, K. C., & Boyle, R. D. (1992). Segmentation of music primitives. *Proceedings of the British Machine Vision Conference* (pp. 472-480).

Ng, K. C., & Boyle, R. D. (1996). Reconstruction of music scores from primitives subsegmentation. *Image and Vision Computing*.

Ng, K. C., Boyle, R. D., & Cooper, D. (1996). Automatic detection of tonality using note distribution. *Journal of New Music Research, 25*(4), 369-381.

Ng, K. C., & Cooper D. (2000). *Enhancement of optical music recognition using metric analysis*. Proceedings of the XIII CIM 2000—Colloquium on Musical Informatics, Italy.

Ng, K. C., Cooper, D., Stefani, E., Boyle, R. D., & Bailey, N. (1999). Embracing the composer: Optical recognition of hand-written manuscripts. In *Proceedings of the International Computer Music Conference (ICMC'99)—Embracing Mankind*, Tsinghua University, Beijing, China (pp. 500-503).

Ng, K. C., Ong, S. B., Nesi, P., Mitolo, N., Fuschi, D., & Crombie, D. (2005, July 25-29). *Interactive Multimedia Technologies for Music*, EVA 2005 London International Conference, UK.

OMeR (n.d.). *Optical Music easy Reader, Myriad Software*, Retrieved February 8, 2003, from http://www.myriad-online.com/omer.htm

PhotoScore (n.d.). *Neuratron*. Retrieved February 8, 2003, from http://www.neuratron.com/photo-score.htm

Pinto, J., Vieira, P., Ramalho, M., Mengucci, M., Pina, P., & Muge, F. (2000). *Ancient music recovery for digital libraries*. Fourth European Conference on Research and Advanced Technology for Digital Libraries (ECDL 2000), Lisbon.

Porck, H. J., & Teygeler, R. (2000). *Preservation science survey: An overview of recent developments in research on the conservation of selected analogue library and archival materials*. Washington, DC: Council on Library and Information Resources.

Pruslin, D. H. (1966). *Automated recognition of sheet music*. Doctor of Science dissertation, Massachusetts Institute of Technology.

Roads, C. (1986). The Tsukuba musical robot. *Computer Music Journal, 10*(2), 39-43.

Roth, M. (1994). *An approach to recognition of printed music*. Extended Diploma Thesis, Swiss Federal Institute of Technology, ETH Zürich, CH-8092, Switzerland.

Scorscan (n.d.). *npc Imaging*. Retrieved August 8, 2002, from http://www.npcimaging.com

Selfridge-Field, E. (1994). Optical recognition of music notation: A survey of current work. In W. B. Hewlett & E. Selfridge-Field (Eds.), *Computing in Musicology: An International Directory of Applications, 9*, pp. 109-145.

SharpEye (n.d.). *visiv*. Retrieved August 8, 2002, from http://www.visiv.co.uk

SmartScore (n.d.). *Musitek*. Retrieved February 8, 2002, from http://www.musitek.com/

Stückelberg, M. V., & Doermann, D. (1999). On musical score recognition using probabilistic reasoning. In *Proceedings of the Fifth International Conference on Document Analysis and Recognition*. Bangolore, India.

Stückelberg, M. V., Pellegrini, C., & Hilario, M. (1997). An architecture for musical score recognition using high-level domain knowledge. In *Proceedings of the Fourth International Conference on Document Analysis and Recognition, 2*, (pp. 813-818).

Suen, C. Y., & Wang, P. S. P. (1994). Thinning methodologies for pattern recognition. *Series in Machine Perception and Artificial Intelligence, 8*.

Vivaldi Scan (n.d.). *VivaldiStudio*. Retrieved February 8, 2003, from http://www.vivaldistudio.com/Eng/VivaldiScan.asp

Wächter, W., Liers, J., & Becker, E. (1996). Paper splitting at the German Library in Leipzig. *Development from Craftsmanship to Full Mechanisation. Restaurator, 17*, 32-42.

# Chapter V
# Optical Music Recognition:
## Architecture and Algorithms

**Pierfrancesco Bellini**
*University of Florence, Italy*

**Ivan Bruno**
*University of Florence, Italy*

**Paolo Nesi**
*University of Florence, Italy*

## ABSTRACT

*Optical music recognition is a key problem for coding western music sheets in the digital world. This problem has been addressed in several manners, obtaining suitable results only when simple music constructs are processed. To this end, several different strategies have been followed to pass from the simple music sheet image to a complete and consistent representation of music notation symbols (symbolic music notation or representation). Typically, image processing, pattern recognition, and symbolic reconstruction are the technologies that have to be considered and applied in several manners; the architecture of the so called OMR (optical music recognition) systems. In this chapter, the O³MR (object oriented optical music recognition) system is presented. It allows producing from the image of a music sheet the symbolic representation and saving it in XML format (WEDELMUSIC XML and MUSICXML). The algorithms used in this process are those of the image processing, image segmentation, neural network pattern recognition, and symbolic reconstruction and reasoning. Most of the solutions can be applied in other fields of image understanding. The development of the O³MR solution with all its algorithms has been partially supported by the European Commission in the IMUTUS Research and Development project, while the related music notation editor has been partially funded by the research and development WEDELMUSIC project of the European Commission.*

## INTRODUCTION

Systems for music score recognition are traditionally called OMR (optical music recognition) systems. This term is tightly linked to OCR (optical character recognition) systems that are used for reading textual documents. Strictly speaking, OCR refers to systems based on the segmentation and recognition of single characters. OMR systems are used for many applications of education, cultural heritage, and publishing. The typical application of OMR is for accelerating the conversion of image music sheets to a symbolic music representation that can be manipulated to create new and revised music editions. Also, educational applications use the OMR systems for the same purpose (IMUTUS, 2004), generating, in this way, a customized version of music exercises. A different usage is for the extraction of incipit or full description for the image score retrieval (Byrd, 2001).

Typically, OCR techniques cannot be used in music score recognition since music notation presents a bidimensional structure. In a staff, the horizontal position denotes different duration for notes and the vertical position defines the height of the note (Roth, 1994). Several symbols are placed along these two directions. OMR is quite a complex problem, since several composite symbols are typically arranged around the note head. Despite the various research systems for OMR (Baimbridge, 1996, 2003; Byrd, 2001, 2006; Carter, 1989, 1994; Cooper, Ng, & Boyle, 1997; Coüasnon, 1995; Fujinaga, 1988, 1996; Kobayakawa, 1993; McPherson, 2002, Modayur, 1996; Ng, & Boyle, 1994, 1996; Prerau, 1970; Selfridge-Field, 1993; Tojo, 1982) as well as commercially available products (MIDISCAN, PIANOSCAN, NOTESCAN in Nightingale, SightReader in FINALE, PhotoScore in Sibelius, etc.), none of them is fully satisfactory in terms of precision and reliability. They provide a real efficiency, close to 90%, only if quite regular music sheets are processed and the estimation is not always

objective (Bellini, 2007). This datum justifies the current research work focused on building reliable OMR systems and tools. OMR systems can be classified on the basis of the granulation chosen to recognize the music score's symbols. There are two main approaches to define basic symbols. They can be considered as (1) the connected components remaining after staff lines removal (chord, beam with notes, etc.), or (2) the elementary graphic symbols, such as note heads, rests, hooks, dots, that can be composed to build music notation (Bellini, 1999; Blostein, 1992; Heussenstamm, 1987; Ross, 1970). With the first approach, symbols can be easily isolated out of the music sheet (segmented), and yet, the number of different symbols remains very high. The second approach has to cope with a huge number of different symbols obtained from the composition of basic symbols. This leads to an explosion of complexity for the recognition tool. A compromise is necessary between complexity and the system's capabilities.

The architecture of an OMR system, and the definition of basic symbols to be recognized, are related to the methods considered for symbol extraction/segmentation and recognition. Generally, the OMR process can be divided into four main phases: (1) the segmentation, to detect and extract basic symbols from the music sheet image, (2) the recognition of basic symbols from the segmented image of the music sheet, (3) the reconstruction of music information, to build the logic description of music notation, and finally (4) the building of the music notation model for representing music notation as a symbolic description of the initial music sheet. In this chapter, the architecture, algorithms, methods, and results related to the O³MR system (object oriented optical music recognition) developed at the DSI University of Florence are discussed. The development of the O³MR solution with all its algorithms has been partially supported by the European Commission, in the IMUTUS IST FP5 Research and Development project (IMUTUS, 2004), while the related music notation editor and symbolic format of music notation in XML has been partially funded by the research and development WEDELMUSIC IST FP5 project of the European Commission (Bellini & Nesi, 2001a).

## BACKGROUND

Automatic music recognition systems can be classified and studied under many points of view, since different approaches have been used in literature. Thus, defining the general steps for a music recognition process is not easy at all, and yet, it is possible to identify a list of main activities (Bellini, 2004; Bruno, 2003; Selfridge-Field, 1993):

- Digitalization of music score.
- Early graphic elaboration and filtering (Kato & Inokuchi, 1990; Ng & Boyle, 1994, 1996; Roth, 1994; Tojo, 1992).
- Identification and/or removal of staff lines (Bainbridge, 1996; Carter, 1989; Coüasnon & Camillerapp, 1995; Fujinaga, 1988, 1996; Kato & Inokuchi, 1990; Kobayakawa, 1993; Modayur, 1996; Ng & Boyle, 1994, 1996; Roth, 1994; Tojo, 1992).
- Identification and/or segmentation of elementary music symbols (basic symbols) allowing to build music notation (Bainbridge, 1996; Carter, 1989, 1994; Coüasnon & Camillerapp, 1995; Fujinaga, 1988, 1996; Kato & Inokuchi, 1990; Modayur, 1996; Ng & Boyle, 1994, 1996; Prerau, 1970; Roth, 1994; Tojo, 1992).
- Reconstruction and classification of music symbols (Bainbridge, 1996; Carter, 1989, 1994; Coüasnon & Camillerapp, 1995; Fujinaga, 1988, 1996; Kato & Inokuchi, 1990; Modayur, 1996; Ng & Boyle, 1994, 1996; Prerau, 1970; Roth, 1994; Tojo, 1992).
- Post graphic elaboration for classifying music symbols (Bainbridge, 1996; Coüasnon

& Camillerapp, 1995; Fujinaga, 1988, 1996; Modayur, 1996).
- Coding music information into symbolic format (Bainbridge, 1996; Carter, 1989, 1994; Cooper et al., 1997; Fujinaga, 1988, 1996; Kato & Inokuchi, 1990; Modayur, 1996; Roth, 1994).

The early graphic elaboration and filtering of the image is always considered as the image setup operation and the tuning of the system. The identification and/or the possible removal of staff is held as a mandatory step by many authors. The graphic analysis (which is to say, basic symbols' identification, segmentation, composition, and classification) is the core of OMR systems, and it is the most studied topic in literature. Several techniques and solutions have been proposed, and many of them are strictly connected with pattern recognition techniques, image processing, and methods used in the optical character recognition area. Among emerging techniques, procedures based on the syntactic and semantic knowledge play a fundamental role when it comes to postgraphic elaboration to help in classifying music symbols. The representation of the music information into the music notation symbolic format is nowadays an open problem, since there is not a standard language able to describe music notation thoroughly.

Several factors that influence the realization of OMR systems have different levels of difficulties that mainly relate to the graphic quality of the digitized materials, the object recognition, the music representation, and the complexity of the music piece.

Issues concerning the visual aspects are mainly print faults, such as:

- Nonhorizontal staves lines (with respect to the page margin), and also rotation during digitisation.
- Staves bending, with stave lines that are not straight (this problem can also be found

in the original, and it could also be caused by manual scanners or photocopying machines).

- Staff lines thickness variation or interruption.
- Inaccurate position of music symbols (a note covering both a space and a line).
- Shapes that are not completely drawn or filled (a quaver note having white spots in the note head).
- Spots (noise) that could be misunderstood as other music feature (e.g., dot, slur, etc.)

Issues related to object recognition change according to the adopted approach. Most common problems are:

- Dimension variations among same objects represent a problem for those recognition approaches focused on dimensions. For instance, the stem height and the beam width in ancient music score; or the difference between a grace and a common note; or clef changing within the score.
- Connectivity and overlapping of symbols. For instance, slurs could bring about problems that are bearable only when they concern simply a note stem overlapping; whereas if they touch a note or overlap a dynamic indication, slurs generate objects that are not associated with any graphical music shape.

Two aspects concerning the music piece complexity should be focused: one is related to the distinction between a single part and a main score; the other one deals with "music architecture."

On the first aspect, for most instruments, the single part is made of a melodic line written on a single staff, except piano, harpsichord, and harp scores, which use a double staff, and organ score, which uses three staves. The main score is structured so as to offer a simultaneous view of all single instrument parts, and it is characterized by

systems of staves. To manage a single part having a staff (or at least three) is relatively easier than to deal with a system of staves. A system of staves brings forth a problem related to the method to be used in the staff identification process and in the treatment of the topological information (symbol positions, staff numbering, staff domain, etc.).

On the second aspect, the music notation presents a two-dimensional structure: in a staff, the horizontal position denotes different duration for notes and the vertical positions define pitches. Several symbols are placed along these two directions. This last aspect is linked to the distinction that has to be drawn between monophonic and polyphonic music: a monophonic piece has a single voice (layer) and notes are played sequentially, whereas the polyphonic one has more than a layer/voice and more notes are played simultaneously.

This distinction affects the semantic recognition and consequently the reconstruction step of music content. In both cases, another important issue is the density of music symbols. In fact, in the event of high density, it is hard to obtain a quite good segmentation, since the major difficulty is to isolate fragmented symbols that could be unrecognized or misunderstood.

## GENERAL ARCHITECTURE DESCRIPTION

The architecture of an OMR system and the definition of basic symbols to be recognized are tightly related to the methods considered for symbol extraction/segmentation and recognition. Generally, the OMR process can be regarded as divided into four main phases: (1) the segmentation, to detect and extract basic symbols, (2) the recognition of basic symbols, (3) the reconstruction of music information, and (4) the building of the music notation model to represent the information.

The first phase of segmentation is the most critical of the entire process. Music notation may present very complex constructs and several styles. Music notation symbols are various and can be combined in a different manner to realize several complex configurations, sometimes using not very well-defined formatting rules (Heussen-stamm, 1987; Ross, 1970). This aspect impacts on the complexity of the segmentation problem. A method to cope with the complexity is to consider music notation as a set of basic symbols, the combination of which allows producing the entire set of music notation symbols and their combination. The segmentation of basic symbols has to be independent on the music score style, size, and on the music processed, from simple (sequence of single notes) to complex (chords in beams with grace notes and several alterations, markers, slurs, expression, ornaments, etc.).

A problem addressed in music score segmentation is the management of staff lines that touches the elementary symbols. The removal of overlapping lines requires a complex process of reconstruction of involved symbols (e.g., Kato & Inokuchi, 1990), with a corresponding loss of information. On such grounds, some authors preferred to recognize symbols without removing the portion of lines crossing them. For these purposes, the use of projection profiles is very common.

The general architecture of O³MR (Bellini, 1999; Bellini, Bruno, & Nesi, 2001b, 2004) is based on four main processing modules.

- **Segmentation:** The music sheet is processed aiming at extracting the basic symbols and their positions. From our point of view, the basic symbols are the elementary symbols that can be used for building music notation symbols. For example, the filled note head; the deep lines representing beams, rests, sharps, flats; the empty note head; the accidentals; the thin lines used for drawing the staff, stem, slur, tie, wedges, and so forth. This means that each basic symbol

can be used for building several music notation symbols. The exact identification is performed in the third block of O³MR architecture. The definition of the set of basic symbols has been performed by considering the capability of (1) the segmentation algorithm in automatically extracting the symbols and (2) the phase of recognition.

- **Basic symbol recognition:** The module performs the recognition of basic symbols by using a neural network. It takes, as input, the normalized image segments of the basic symbols. On the basis of the set of basic symbols, a feed–forward neural network has been set and trained to perform the recognition. The output of this module is mainly symbolic. For each recognized basic symbol, the image segment coordinates and the confidence value of recognition is produced. Moreover, when bar lines are recognized, the corresponding image segment is further elaborated, in order to estimate the position of staff lines. This information is extracted and communicated to the successive module to be considered as reference lines.

- **Music notation symbol reconstruction:** In this module, the recognized basic symbols are mapped into the elementary components of music notation symbols. For example, a deep line may be a part of a beam as well as of a rest, and so forth. The decision criterion is based on the recognition context: the position of the basic symbols with respect to the position of staff lines, the confidence level of the first phase of recognition, and so forth. In order to make the identification of elementary symbols simpler, on the basis of their possible relationships, the Music Symbols Visual Rules have been formalized and used during the recognition. According to this process, for each basic symbol, a set of probable elementary symbols is assigned. These elementary notation symbols

*Figure 1. (a) Staff detection (Level 0); (b) Decomposition in basic symbols (Levels 1 and 2)*

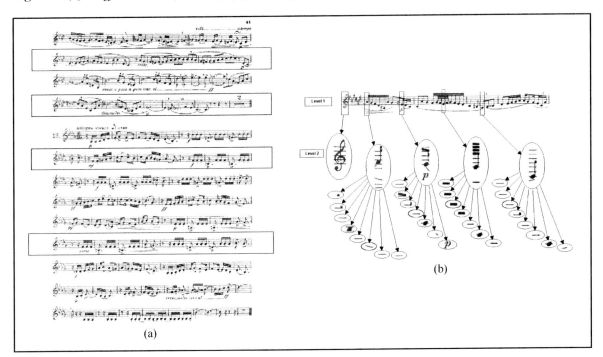

(a)

(b)

estimate the probability to be basic symbols on the basis of the context. This module may request some additional evaluations when the decision cannot be taken with current knowledge, for example, when two music notation symbols are similarly probable. Once the basic notation symbols are identified, their composition is performed using a set of Music Notation Rules.

- **Music notation model:** It is the data model used to represent the reconstructed music symbolic notation. In this context, the $O^3MR$ is totally supported by the WEDELMUSIC editor and object-oriented model (Bellini & Nesi, 2001a) in which the music formatting rules are formalized and the correctness of each measure is easily checked. The symbolic music representation obtained can be saved in XML formats (WEDELMUSIC XML or MUSICXML of Good, 2001) This part will be not discussed in this chapter.

## SEGMENTATION

An image of a music score page grabbed with a scanner is the starting point of the segmentation process. The segmentation method proposed is based on a hierarchical decomposition of the music image. The music sheet image is analyzed and recursively split into smaller blocks by defining a set of horizontal and vertical cut lines that allow isolating/extracting basic symbols (see Figure 1).

In more details, the procedure is based on three elaboration levels depicted in Figure 2 and shortly commented on:

- **Level 0:** The music sheet is segmented to extract subimages, including the single music staff. In addition, a set of image score parameters are estimated for tuning the successive processing phases.

*Figure 2. Elaboration levels*

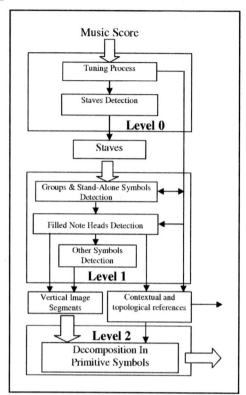

• **Level 1:** The image segment of each staff is processed to extract image segments that include music symbols, and have a width close to that of note heads. This level is performed in three steps: (1) extraction of beams (e.g., group of beamed notes) and stand-alone symbols (e.g., clefs, rest, barline); (2) detection of filled note heads; (3) detection of other music symbols or parts of them.

• **Level 2:** Music symbols, detected at level 1, are decomposed into basic symbols. In this phase, two decomposition methods are used: for image segments containing note heads and for the others where note heads are missing. In this last case, the image segment may contain other symbols.

The segmentation procedure is based on the combined application of the X-Y projection profiles

technique and image processing algorithms. This choice permitted to develop a set of algorithms that recursively operate in small image segments.

## Level 0

It should be noted that the images of the music sheets may have different magnitude. This implies that the dimension of music notation symbols and staves are unknown. This is a problem since the knowledge of the scale allows better identification of the basic symbols. Typically, music adopts well-defined ratio among the features of staff lines and the size of all other music symbols (Blostein & Baird, 1992; Heussenstamm, 1987). Staff lines are graphic symbols that are independent of the music content. They give important information about music sheet features, since thickness of staff lines, n, and the distance between staff lines, d, are useful to tune the segmentation process. In fact, they allow defining thresholds, tolerance values for measurements, and segmentation of basic symbols of the music score. With the thickness of lines and the distance between two lines, it is possible to describe the graphic features of a note head, or to estimate the height of a single staff. For these reasons, differently from others (Bainbridge & Bell, 1996; Bruno, 2003; Carter, 1994; Kato & Inokuchi, 1990; Ross, 1970) in our approach, staff lines are not removed, since they are used in the segmentation process. This avoided the introduction of elaboration phases to fix symbols partially cancelled by the staff lines removal. The knowledge of staff lines' position allows detecting the right pitch of notes in the reconstruction phase. The main goals of Level 0 are the (1) tuning of the segmentation process by the identification of a set of graphic parameters, and (2) detection of image segments in which staffs are included. According to the presented hierarchical structure, the image is decomposed in a set of subimages, each of which includes a staff.

## Tuning Process

The tuning process is performed to estimate the music sheet parameters from the scanned image. These parameters are (1) the thickness, $n$, of staff lines, (2) the distance $d$ between staff lines, and (3) the thickness of a beam, $b$. In order to estimate these values, the score image is processed column by column to generate two histograms in which the size of sequences of black and white pixels are counted as a function of their dimension. In the histograms, the occurrence value and the number of pixels are considered; the number of pixels is positioned on X-axis, while the number of occurrence values is on Y-axis. These histograms represent the profile of vertical contiguous sequences for black and white pixels, respectively. As shown in Figures 3a and 3b, the most frequent values for $d$ and $n$ are the two peak values of those curves, respectively. These features depend on the resolution and on the music formatting style/font. In order to manage variability and noise on the

*Figure 3. (a) Distance between two staff lines, d; (b) Thickness of staff line, n, and beam, b*

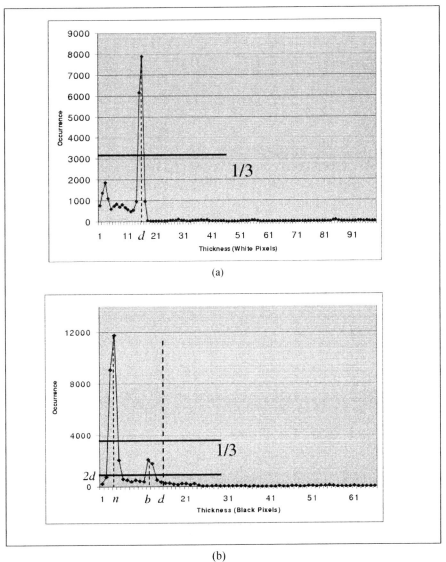

(a)

(b)

values of these parameters, two intervals have been adopted, as follows:

- $n_1$ and $n_2$: The minimum and the maximum values for the staff line thickness, respectively.
- $d_1$ and $d_2$: The minimum and the maximum values for the distance between two staff lines, respectively.

These values are related to the maximum peak of each histogram. The histograms present a peak with a wideness that depends on the image acquisition resolution and on the original staff line thickness. Cutting the peak at 1/3 of its value leads to identify the measure of its wideness. In this view, the thickness of line is assumed to be $[n_1, n_2]$, by taking the approximation for excess of the measure performed. In the same manner, the range of the distance between consecutive lines is obtained $[d_1, d_2]$.

The histogram of Figure 3b shows a second peak located in $n<b<d$. It is due to beams contribution, and represents the thickness, $b$, of a single beam. Since $2d$ is the horizontal minimum length of a single beam connecting two adjacent notes, it is assumed as threshold for cutting the peak and identifying the value of $b$.

These parameters are used in the successive steps of the segmentation process for slicing the image of the music score and extracting basic symbols and defining topological references.

## Staves Detection

The staff detection is the first elaboration phase of the O³MR system. The goal is to identify a rectangular area in which the staff is located in order to process that image segment to extract the contained basic music symbols. The algorithm for detecting the staffs is based on the recognition of the staff line profile. The profile, obtained by applying the Y-projection to a portion of staff lines image, presents a regular pattern in terms of structure, whereas other projections have a variable pattern. In order to distinguish the projection of lines from the other graphic elements, a transformation of profiles has been introduced. In details, the transformation, indicated with $T$, works on the Y-projection of a vertical image segment. The Y-projection is constituted by a set of groups/peaks, each of which is associated with a staff line. For each of them, their width is evaluated. When the width is comparable with values defined by the interval for the thickness of lines, then the position of the mean position for the peak is estimated; otherwise, it is not considered. The position of the mean values defines the position of lines in the T-Profile. They have unitary thickness. In this way, in the presence of staff lines, the projection is transformed into thin lines that allow characterizing the staff during the identification phase. The analysis of the distance between thin lines in T-profile is used to understand if the profile is due to the presence of a staff. The distance between lines of the T-domain is strictly related to the values of the mentioned parameters. In fact, given the $[n_1, n_2]$ range for the thickness of staff lines and the $[d_1, d_2]$ range for the distance between two lines, the distance between mean values expressed in terms of interval $[\alpha, \beta]$ is defined as:

$$\begin{cases} \alpha = d_1 \\ \beta = d_2 + 2(n_2 - (n_2 - n_1)/2) \end{cases}$$

The staff detection algorithm searches for the "five equidistant" lines structure. This is performed by analyzing thin slices of the image sheet. Each slice has a vertical size equal to the whole image score size, and width equal to a few pixels ($dx$); the slices processed performing T-transformation. On each slice, a probe looks for the five lines pattern. The probe is applied on a subsection of the slice and analyzes it from top to bottom. The probe looks for the starting coordinate of the five lines staff. For this reason, its dimension, $I$, has to be comparable with staff height. The $I$ value is defined as a function of the thickness parameters considering the maximum values of $n$ and $d$ ranges:

$$I = 5n_2 + 4d_2$$

In order to cope with possible staff deformations, the value of $I$ has been increased by 20%. The staff detection by means of the probe is performed in two phases: (1) discovering and (2) centering the staff. In the discovering phase, the probe window is used to detect the staff lines and store the starting coordinates of segment in which the staffs are present. In the centering phase, for the staff $i$, a couple of staff coordinates $(y_{sup}, y_{inf})$ are obtained. These are defined in order to fix the cut lines for extracting the staffs contained in the score image. If $n$ is the number of staffs, then each new couple of coordinates $(\hat{y}_{sup}, \hat{y}_{inf})$ has been evaluated as:

$$\begin{cases} \hat{y}_{sup}^{(i)} = \dfrac{y_{sup}^{(i)} + y_{inf}^{(i-1)}}{2} - \varepsilon \\ \hat{y}_{inf}^{(i)} = \dfrac{y_{sup}^{(i+1)} + y_{inf}^{(i)}}{2} + \varepsilon \end{cases}$$

where $i = 2, ..., n-1$, $\varepsilon \geq 0$ (a tolerance value to increase robustness).

The introduction of $\varepsilon$ tolerance allows getting adjacent or partially overlapped image segments containing the staff. In this definition, the coordinates of the first and last staff are excluded. If the top and the bottom margins of the score image are considered and $Y_{max}$ is the height of the image score, the coordinates are:

$$\begin{cases} \hat{y}_{sup}^{(1)} = 0 \\ \hat{y}_{inf}^{(1)} = \dfrac{y_{sup}^{(2)} + y_{inf}^{(1)}}{2} + \varepsilon \end{cases} \qquad \begin{cases} \hat{y}_{inf}^{(1)} = \dfrac{y_{sup}^{(2)} + y_{inf}^{(1)}}{2} + \varepsilon \\ \hat{y}_{inf}^{(n)} = Y_{max} \end{cases}$$

## Level 1

Level 1 works on the image segments produced from Level 0, containing one staff. The aim of this level is to extract the vertical image segments containing music symbols. Level 1 produces the lower level subimage segments in three phases: (1) detection of groups and isolated symbols; (2) detection and labelling of note heads; (3) detection of other music symbols or parts of them. In certain cases, the third phase is not needed.

### Groups and Stand-Alone Symbols Detection

In this phase, groups of figures and single symbols (e.g., clefs, rest, barline) are detected. Image segments, with the staff presenting no symbols, separate groups of figures and single symbols. To this end, the staff detection algorithm is applied to produce the value of the binary function, $F$. The detection process has been realized by considering a running image window. This has the same height of the image segment coming from level 0, given by the difference $(y_{inf} - y_{sup})$, and width, $dx_1$, equal to $\lfloor d/5 \rfloor$. The analysis of the image segment is performed by moving the running window from left to right of one pixel at a time. The presented staff detection algorithm is used on each image segment to verify either the presence or absence of an empty staff. The result of such staff detection sets the values of binary function, $F$. The $F=0$ is associated with the empty staff segment and $F=1$ with image segments contain music symbols. The identification of the empty staff allows processing the corresponding image segment in order to estimate:

- The $x$ refresh horizontal coordinate.
- The $y_i$ vertical coordinates for the staff lines $(y_5 < y_1)$.

*Figure 4. (a) Parameters for the full note head; (b) X-projection for a group*

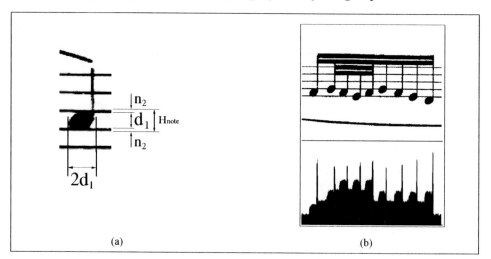

(a)                                                                                     (b)

A *stafflines' position list* permits one to collect the updating of the coordinates along the entire staff length. In this way, the graphic trend of the staff and its end are completely known. They provide also a reference in the pitch detection and a way to cope with the lines skew.

Image segment with $F=1$ is further marked with the Boolean flag *group*. If the segment has a width greater than $5/2d_2$, it could include groups of figures or beamed notes; in this case the label is set to *true*. Otherwise, the image segment includes stand-alone music symbols (clef, barline, time signature, whole notes, accidentals, etc.) and the label is set to *false*. All these vertical image segments have to be processed in the next phase in order to proceed at their decomposition in smaller image segments.

## Filled Note Head Detection

The goal of this phase is to slice the complex image segments produced by the previous phase and marked as $F=1$. The proposed approach is based on searching the presence of single filled note head.

In the western notation, note heads may present at least a diameter equal to the distance between two staff lines. In effect, the note head shape is quite elliptic. Therefore, to consider the note head width equal to $2d_1$ is a reasonable approximation (see Figure 4a). For these reasons, image segments coming from the previous phase are processed on the basis of their width. In this case, only image segments larger than $2d_1$ are considered.

The X-projection of a group of notes presents a typical shape, as shown in Figure 4b. In the projection, it is possible to identify:

- Spikes due to note stems and vertical symbols.
- Offsets due to horizontal symbols like staff lines, beams, slurs, crescendo, and so forth.
- Smoothed dense profile due to note head.

In order to extract the note heads, the dense profile contribution has to be extracted from the X-projection. This means to eliminate the other two contributions. This is possible by using the information provided by the Y-projection. To this end, a thin running window is considered on the image segment containing the staff with symbols (see Figure 5). The running window scans the image with a step equal to 1 pixel. For each step/pixel, the Y-projection (e.g., the distribution reported in the box of Figure 5) is calculated.

In the projection, the presence of a note head is detected on the basis of its width, $H$, which is in the range $[2n_2, 2n_2+d_1]$. Since the aim of the process is to detect the location of note heads, only the maximum value of $H$ along the projection of the running window is considered ($H_{y,6}$ in the example of Figure 5). This value is reported in the final X-projection shown in Figures 5 and 6a.

The filled note heads produce higher peaks since they are deeper than beam lines. On the other hand, when note heads are missing, the maximum value produced from the beam is reported in the X-projection of max Y-projection. The evident difference in the value of such two cases is enhanced by the adoption of a running window that leads to consider several overlapped thin windows of the same note head.

The final step consists in isolating the note heads. This is performed by using a double threshold mechanism to obtain the results shown in Figure 6b. The first threshold (reported as a line in Figure 6a) is defined as the compromise between the dimension of the note head and that of the beams. The second filtering is performed on the width of the remaining peaks. They are considered as due to the presence of notes, only if their width is larger than $d_1/2$.

The result of this double threshold mechanism is shown in Figure 6b. The X-projection has to be processed in order to calculate the points in which the original image segment has to be cut for extracting the segments with single notes. To this end, for each peak the mean position of the peak along the X-projection is estimated. If $C$ is the $x$ coordinate of the mean value, the couple of points is defined as follows:

$$(C-d_1, C+d_1)$$

Each couple of points defines the width of the image segment including the note. In particular,

*Figure 5. X-Projection building*

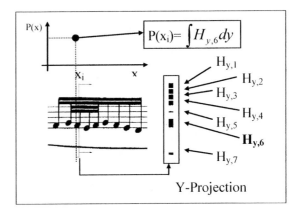

the width is equivalent to that of the note head. In this process, the new image segments inherit the values of flags associated to the initial image segments, and they are further marked by means of the Boolean flag *note*. It is *true* when the new image segment contains a filled note head. Please note that also chords having a note on the same side are managed within this current approach. Chords having note heads on both sides of the stem are managed in the next subsection. Image segments that do not contain note heads are nonsliced by the described process. These are processed with the algorithm described in the next subsection.

## Begin-End Beam Detection

By analyzing values of $F$, *group*, and *note* flags associated with vertical image segments, it is possible to detect image segments including the first note and the last note of a beamed note group. The vertical image segments belonging to a group of beamed notes are characterized by $F=1$ and *group=true*. They are sequentially analyzed to detect the first and the last vertical image segments with *note=true*. All these segments are further marked with the *BeamStatus* status flag. It assumes the following values:

*Figure 6. (a) X-projection before thresholds application; (b) X-projection after thresholds application and ready for extracting image segments with note heads*

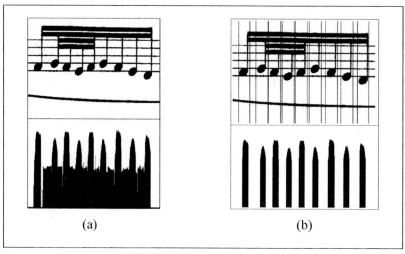

(a)　　　　　　　　(b)

- **Begin:** The vertical image segment contains the start note of the beamed notes group.
- **End:** The vertical image segment contains the final note of the beamed notes group.
- **No:** The vertical image segment does not belong to a beamed notes group.

This information allows defining the spatial extension of beamed notes groups.

## Other Symbols Detection

Image segments that have to be processed typically include groups of symbols very close to each other. In most cases, these symbols are separated by small spaces, generating local minima in the X-projection profile, such as in Figure 7. Thus, detecting these points means to allow slicing the image segment and thus extracting the basic symbols. To this end, an iterative method has been developed. As a first step, a low-pass filter is applied to smooth the profile. The smoothed profile is analyzed in order to find the position of the minima. Its position is used to divide the image segment in two new subimages. The same procedure is applied at the two subimages when

their width is greater than or equal to $d_1/2$. The process stops when the maximum width of the processed image segments is lower than $(5/2)d_1$. The last operation consists of sorting the points for vertical image segment in order to define image segments. In the presence of a "constant" profile (for example, the projection of a large segment with an empty staff), the segmentation process produces image segments with width comparable to that of note heads. Image segments, having a width lower than the staff line thickness, are not passed to the next segmentation level. They are too small images to include relevant information. The new image segments inherit the values of labels associated to the initial image segments. This process can cope with key signatures, and accidentals, since it allows decomposing the image segments nondecomposed in the previous step.

## Level 2

Image segments coming from the Level 1 are decomposed into a set of basic symbols. This phase covers an important role since the recognition and reconstruction are strictly connected to it. Therefore, the produced image segments

*Figure 7. Relation between isolation points and minimums of X-projection*

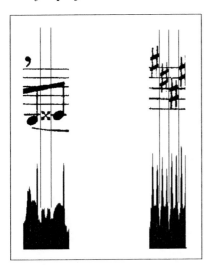

## Images with Black Note Heads

In this phase, notes with filled black head (*note=true*) and basic symbols around them (ornaments and parts of horizontal symbols like slur, crescendo, etc.) are decomposed. The proposed method is focused mainly on the graphical features of notes.

The graphic components of the note are mainly (1) note head, and (2) beams or hooks. Observing the Y-projection of notes, the contribution of the stem adds an offset to the profile of the projection, linking the profile of the note head to beams and hooks. In the case of a quarter note, it is only an offset. The removal of stem contribution allows disconnecting the main components of a note shape. A high-pass filtering is used to separate the note head from beams or hooks since it erases all constant contributes in the Y-projection profile. This filtering does not erase contributions of symbols around note-generated well-defined peaks in the profile of the projection. The cut points for symbols extraction are detected on the filtered projection by means of a threshold mechanism. The procedure of segmentation is made up of the following steps:

must include graphic details: (1) belonging to the set of defined basic symbols, (2) together with additional information needed for their recognition. The first aspect impacts on the reliability of the recognition phase, whereas the second, on the application of the rules of the reconstruction phase. The previous segmentation phase produced different results, depending on the presence or not of the black note head in the image segment. Therefore, in this process, two different segmentation methods are applied to the received image segments: (1) including, and (2) not-including black note heads. This distinction is possible by using the information given by the value of the *note* flag fixed in the filled note head detection phase. Both segmentation methods are based on the Y/X-projection and produce couples of vertical coordinates that allow extracting basic symbols. This level is the last phase of segmentation; the output is a complete graphic decomposition of the initial music score image. The result of the decomposition is described better later on.

1. Y-projection computation.
2. High-pass filtering. This filtering phase by means of an unsharp Gaussian filter with $1.5(4d+5n)$ pixel window allows eliminating the low-frequency components.
3. Extraction points computation. It is based on the computation of extraction points by means of a threshold mechanism applied on the filtered projection. Two different values of threshold are used. They have been defined to cope respectively with beams and hooks. They are expressed in function of the thickness of staff lines and the maximum of the Y-projection as follows:

$$threshold = \begin{cases} \dfrac{3}{4}\dfrac{(n_1+n_2)B}{MaxPy}, & \text{Groups of notes} \\[2ex] \dfrac{n_2 B}{MaxPy}, & \text{Isolated notes} \end{cases}$$

where:

- B is the maximum value for the intensity of black and it is fixed to 255.
- MaxPy is the maximum value of the filtered Y-projection related to the image segment.

4. Extracted areas adjusting. When two successive segments are closer than $n_2$, they are fused in unique segment. After the fusion, the segments are enlarged by adding $n_2$ pixels on the sides in which the image segments present the staff line.

## Other Music Symbols

The image segments to be decomposed contain mainly rests, clefs, accidentals, augmentation dots, pieces of beams, staff lines, pieces of slurs, time indication, barline, whole notes, and half notes. All these symbols, excluding the half note, are extracted directly from the Y-projection by means of a threshold value close to the 1% of the maximum of the projection profile. All image segments with height close to the thickness of staff lines and located in the staff lines vertical coordinates are not considered. In presence of a half note, the threshold value is not valid, since is too low and does not allow disconnecting the note head from the stem. A method to cope with the segment containing the half note is described next.

- **Identification of half notes:** The developed method analyses image segments labeled as isolated and having a width close to $2d$. The stem detection is performed in order to establish the presence of notes. The X-projection is filtered by means of a high pass filter in order to isolate the stem profile. It

could stay on the right if it is upward, or on the left if it is downward, and it is located in correspondence to the maximum of the filtered profile. The magnitude of the pick $A_{max}$ is evaluated and used to define the threshold to be used with the Y-projection. The threshold is defined as follows

$$threshold = \frac{B\max\{n_2, 1.2A_{Max}\}}{MaxPy}$$

where:

- *B* is the maximum value for the intensity of black and it is fixed to 255.
- *MaxPy* is the maximum value of the unfiltered Y-projection related to the image segment.

## The Segmentation Output

The segmentation process provides a graphical decomposition of the music score image, and it associates contextual and topological references with image segments. The topological information is related to the position in the image music score and the dimension of the image segment. In particular, they consist of:

- the absolute coordinates $(x,y)$ related to the left top corner of the image segment.
- width $dx$ and height $dy$ of the image segment.

The contextual information is related to the values of flags provided by the segmentation

*Table 1. Context flags*

| Vertical Image segment |
| --- |
| Context (flags) |
| F= (1 \| 0)<br>group= (true \| false)<br>note= (true \| false)<br>BeamStatus= (Begin \| End \| No) |

94

algorithms, as shown in Table 1. Their meanings are reported as follows:

- *F:* The image segment belongs to a vertical segment including an empty staff ($F=0$) or a group of figures ($F=1$).
- **group:** The image segment belongs to a group of music symbols (*group=true*) or it is a stand-alone symbol (*group=false*).
- **note:** The image segment belongs to a vertical segment including a filled note head (*note=true*).
- **BeamStatus:** It says if the image segment is the beginning (BEGIN) or the end of a beamed group (END).
- **Staff lines position list:** It is the list of staff lines coordinates along the staff length.

## BASIC SYMBOL RECOGNITION

The basic symbol recognition module (see Figure 8) is made up of two components and performs the classification and error recovery phases. The role of this module is to realize the passage from the graphic domain to the music information domain; it performs the transcoding function that converts images to the information they express. This information is extended by associating and combining the topological and contextual information obtained in the segmentation process (staff lines positions, beams, notes, and end of staff). In this way, the output represents a symbolic description of recognized music information. Single components are described hereafter.

## Classification

This module is based on a multilayer perceptons (MLP) back-propagation feed-forward neural network (Rumelhart, Hinton, & McClelland, 1986) that has been set and trained to perform the classification of basic symbols. It takes in input image segments with reduced dimension of 8 x 16 pixels. Images are scaled (zoomed in or out) to match the dimensions of the input, while pixel values are normalized in the [0,1] range with respect to 255. The scaling is an advantage since it allows it to be scale independent in learning the neural network. More than 20,000 basic symbols of different fonts have been collected and distributed into a database constituted of 48 classes of elementary shapes. This set is suitable for classical monophonic music scores. The MLP network structure is fully connected and consists of 128 inputs, a hidden layer of 256 neurons, and 48 output neurons; the neuronal activation function is sigmoidal, with output values in the [0,1]

*Figure 8. Structure of the basic symbols recognition module*

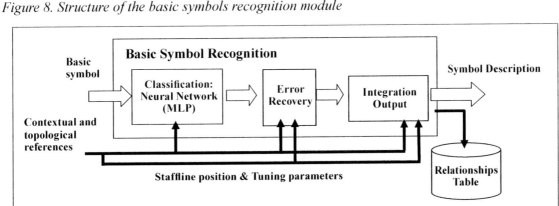

range. The normalized image is vectorized and provided as input. The percentage range of classified symbols oscillates between 80%—90%; this oscillation depends on the different kinds of fonts and on the likeness among different basic symbols (i.e., the augmentation dots and black note heads, beam, and part of slur, etc.). For each input pattern the neural network provides the class and the confidence of classification as output. The classification output is a symbolic description. It is made of a set of descriptors structured as follows:

<Basic symbol name> <X > <Y > <dx > <dy > <conf >

$$(1)$$

where: <Basic symbol name> is the category associated with the neural network, <X> and <Y> are the absolute coordinates related to the left top corner of the image segment, <dx> and <dy> are respectively the width and the height of the image segment, and <conf> is the value of confidence assigned by the neural network.

For example, a treble clef is described as reported in Box 1.

## Error Recovery

The aim of this phase is to increase the classification efficiency. It performs a secondary classification based on the following considerations:

- The neural network provides a class name and a confidence value that represents the recognition likelihood. Images classified with a confidence less than a certain threshold could be considered unreliable and they could represent a classification error.
- The original graphic features of image segments are partially modified during the scaling phase and hence, basic symbols could assume graphic features similar to other symbols (e.g., DOT and FNOTEHEAD).

To avoid reconsidering all basic symbols, the confusion table of the neural network has been analyzed to detect symbols more frequently confused. The analysis produced the subset of basic symbols (class name) shown in table 2.

Observing the table, basic symbols are similar both morphologically and dimensionally and can be confused one to another. Some heuristics rules have been defined to understand which symbol has to be considered. They consider the topological and contextual information associated with the image segment during the segmentation phase; in particular, they take into account:

- If the basic symbol under analysis belongs to an image vertical segment where a black note head has been detected by the segmentation phase.
- If the basic symbol is in a vertical segment belonging to a group of notes.
- The dimension of the bounding box of the image.
- Staff-line parameters: the line's thickness and the distance between two lines.

In the case of symbols, such as a single thin line or a single big line or a single skewed line, the contextual and topological information could

*Box 1. Treble clef*

| Class | X | Y | Width | Height | Confidence |
|---|---|---|---|---|---|
| CLEFTREBLE | 55 | 48 | 57 | 153 | 0.91 |

*Table 2. The sub set of basic symbols involved in the error recovery*

| Basic Symbol | Confused with |
|---|---|
| FNOTEHEAD | DOT, BIGLINE1, THINLINE |
| DOT | FNOTEHEAD |
| THINLINE | BIGLINE1, HOOK1UP |
| BIGLINE1 | THINLINE |
| BIGLINE2 | BIGLINE1 |
| BIGLINE3 | BIGLINE1, FLAT |
| BIGLINE4 | BIGLINE2, FLAT |
| REST4 | SHARP |
| GREATER | THINLINE |
|  | THINLINE, HOOK1UP |

*Table 3. Example of error recovery*

| Error Recovery Output | Neural Classifier output |
|---|---|
| ………<br>FNOTEHEAD 2093 149 30 28 0.99<br>THINLINE 2123 150 10 7 0.98<br>DOT 2133 159 10 10 0.75<br>CLEFALTO 2179 86 30 63 0.95<br>……… | ………<br>FNOTEHEAD 2093 149 30 28 0.99<br>THINLINE 2123 150 10 7 0.98<br>FNOTEHEAD 2133 159 10 10 0.75<br>CLEFALTO 2179 86 30 63 0.95<br>……… |

not be exhaustive for their classification. Their recognition is linked to their thickness. For this reason, the evaluation of the average thickness has been added to define and estimate rules that cope with those symbols. The check in of the line thickness is performed by means of the vertical projection method. The threshold values for thickness of a beam and a thin line are estimated using the tuning process result. In this way, it is possible to distinguish a thin line due to a portion of a slur or staff line from a single or multiple beam, thus, understanding the number of beams. In some cases, the contextual and topological information could be enough to classify the symbol without further graphic elaboration. Generally, this is possible when the information about the context is well defined and not ambiguous. In any case, the verification of a rule is used to confirm the class name associated with the neural network or to replace it with a more appropriate class.

In the example of Table 3, an augmentation dot (DOT) has been confused with a black note head (FNOTEHEAD). Its topology is not characteristic of a black note; in fact, the bounding box is too little to contain a note head. Moreover, the vertical image segment contains only the augmentation dot and, in this case, the black-note head-detection algorithm fails. The following rule replaces the FNOTEHEAD class name with the DOT class.

$$FNOTEHEAD: \neg note \wedge (dy>2n) \wedge (dy<d) \wedge (dx/dy>0.6) \wedge (dy/dx>0.8) \Rightarrow DOT$$

$$(2)$$

where:

- *note* is a Boolean label. It is true when the image segment contains a filled black note head.
- *dx* and *dy* are, respectively, the width and the height of the bounding box.

- $d_2$ is the height of the black note head. It is equal to the maximum distance between two lines.
- $n_2$ is the maximum thickness of a black staff line.
- The constant values 0.6 and 0.8 have been heuristically defined.

## Integration and Basic Symbols Recognition Output

The output of this module is the list of symbolic descriptions. The symbolic descriptions associated with recognized symbols are mixed with the information related to staff lines position; the end of staff, and references concerning groups of beamed notes.

The *staff lines position list* provides the staff lines' coordinates and the staff end. The staff lines are described by the descriptor

$$STAFF5 \ x \ y_1 \ y_2 \ y_3 \ y_4 \ y_5 \qquad (3)$$

where:

- $x$ is the refresh horizontal coordinate where the staff lines have been detected.
- $y_i$ are the vertical coordinates for the staff lines $(y_5 < y_1)$.

The end of staff is marked by the ENDSTAFF descriptor. In case of note groups of beamed notes, the segmentation task provides the start (*Begin*) and the end point (*End*) of notes groups. This information is coded by means of two descriptors: BEGIN and END. These references allow defining the subset of descriptions that are part of a beamed group of notes.

BEGIN
<description 1>
...
<description n>
END

## The Relationships Table

The segmentation process produces graphic primitives that could correspond either to a complete symbol of the music notation or to a peculiar graphic symbol. The classifier could associate the graphic primitives with the corresponding basic symbols or with classes held as the most representative ones. This happens both with the set of symbols used in the neural network training phase and symbols unknown to the network. This behaviour makes the reconstruction process nondeterministic, since each class could represent different symbols: a beam could be mistaken with many other musical symbols, such as a whole-note pause, half-note pause, a piece of slur, and so on; a staff line segment, together with a slur, could be taken as the end tip of a crescendo, a single hook, or an accent. A Relationship Table has been defined in order to cope with these aspects; such a table provides the complete list of symbols associated with classes. The table is built according to the neural network trained on a certain set of basic symbols; whenever a network with a different set of symbols is used, the table defined for that new network has to be adopted. This permits one to enlarge the set of symbols managed for recognition, thus making the system more flexible and pliant. Each line of the table has been defined as follows

<token> <S_confusion_1> | <S_confusion_2> | ... | <S_confusion_n>

where:

- token stands for the name of the output class,
- S_confusion_i stands for the name of an output class or a symbol not among the basic ones, which the token could be mistaken with. "S_" is the prefix used to distinguish the token from the associated symbols.

- "|" stands for a separating element in the list of confusion occurrences. It can be considered as the OR expression.

The whole set of confusion occurrence is called set of associated symbols. The following line:

FNOTEHEAD  S_FNOTEHEAD | S_DOT | S_BEAM1

points out that the graphic primitives associated with FNOTEHEAD (filled black note head) class, in output of the neural network, could correspond to the symbol S_FNOTEHEAD (filled note head symbol), or to an S_DOT (augmentation dot or staccato symbol), or to an S_BEAM1 (single beam symbol).
The classes of basic symbols recognized by the network with high confidence have an associated symbol that stands for the real and direct interpretation of the class itself; this symbol is obtained by adding the "S_" prefix to the class name.

## MUSIC NOTATION SYMBOL RECONSTRUCTION

The aim of the music notation reconstruction module is to rebuild the music score and code the music information in the music notation model. Before starting with the reconstruction, the symbolic description has to be organized in strips according to the image segments produced during the segmentation. Successively, each strip is set up considering the behaviour of previous phases.

The set of mistaken symbols associated with a class by the Relationship Table represents the set of possible interpretations for the basic symbol that the class stands for. They have to be aggregated to rebuild the music notation and the relationship among music symbols. The choice of the right assumption (i.e., bass clef or baritone clef, beam or slur) is made considering basic symbol position in the score and the probability that each mistaken

*Figure 9. Music notation reconstruction module*

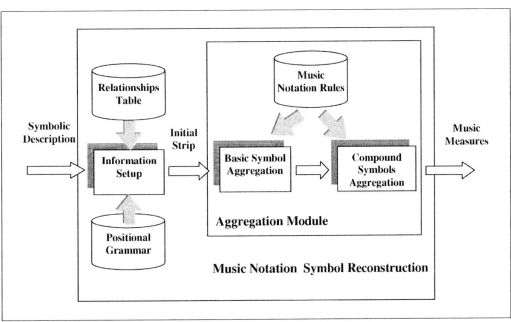

symbol occupys that position. To this end, a rule-based Positional Grammar has been defined.

The architecture of music notation symbol reconstruction module is reported in Figure 9 and consists of two main components:

- **Information set-up:** This phase parses the symbolic description, generating the list of strips. It performs the set-up of strips for the aggregation phase by means of the Relationship Table and the Positional Grammar.
- **Aggregation module:** It performs the symbols aggregation. It is based on vertical and horizontal rules of the Music Notation Rules. The aggregation process is conducted in two steps: (1) *Basic Symbol Aggregation* and (2) *Compound Symbols Aggregation*. During this phase, a single measure is rebuilt considering assembled music symbols and indications of start measure and end measure given by the recognition of bar lines.

## Information Setup

This phase consists of building strips and setting up the aggregation process. The first activity is performed by grouping and parsing the symbolic descriptions of the image segments sharing the $x$ coordinate. In the set-up phase, each element of the strip is associated with a set of basic symbols provided by the Relationship Table. These symbols are the possible interpretations of each element belonging to the strip. The Positional Grammar associates to such symbols the position they are likely to occupy in the score, in relationship with the element they refer to. Each element of the strip may be interpreted in many different ways as the number of associated symbols (according to the Relationship Table); the whole set of possible solutions is a combinatorial set of strips configurations. The structure of a strip is described as follows:

$$E_S = \left\{ \begin{array}{c} X_1(e_1), \\ \dots \\ X_p(e_p) \end{array} \right\}$$

where:

- $E_S$ stands for the strip as a set of elements;
- $e_i$ represents the $i^{th}$ element of $E_S$.
- $X_i(e_i) = \{(x_1, p_1), ..., (x_{m(i)}, p_{m(i)})\}$ is the element defined as a set of symbols/interpretations associated with $e_i$ by the Relationship Table.
- $(x_j, p_j)$ with $j=1,...,m(i)$, stands for the couple made of the associated symbol $x_j$ and the position probability $p_j$ assigned by the Positional Grammar.

## The Positional Grammar

The analysis carried out on the music scores gave evidence that each and every position on the staff lines is not allowed to different music symbols; generally speaking, six positions can be defined:

- $Pos_1$ inside the staff
- $Pos_2$ across the staff
- $Pos_3$ above the staff
- $Pos_4$ below the staff
- $Pos_5$ inside while partially above the staff
- $Pos_6$ inside while partially below the staff

According to the identified positions and the probability for the associated symbol to occupy them, some rules have been defined so as to allow the description of the position properties. The structure of a generic rule is as follows:

<symbol> <P(Pos_1)> ... <P(Pos_6)>

where:

*Box 2. Associated symbol representing a 16ᵗʰ note rest*

| Symbol | $P(Pos_1)$ | $P(Pos_2)$ | $P(Pos_3)$ | $P(Pos_4)$ | $P(Pos_5)$ | $P(Pos_6)$ |
|--------|-----------|-----------|-----------|-----------|-----------|-----------|
| S_REST16 | 0.9 | 0 | 0 | 0 | 0.6 | 0.5 |

- symbol stands for an associated symbol's name
- $P(Pos_i)$ stands for the probability of the symbol to be in $Pos_i$ (position probability).

The whole set of rules represents the Positional Grammar.

In the case of an associated symbol representing a 16ᵗʰ note rest, the definition is as shown in Box 2.

In many cases the pause is positioned inside the staff lines; therefore, the probability value for $Pos_1$ is high. And yet there are cases where the pause is positioned in $Pos_5$ or in $Pos_6$; therefore, the related probability values are lower. The other positions are not allowed and they are marked with a null value.

## Estimation of the Initial Status for Strips

The information set-up phase associates with $X_i(e_i)$ a state $S$ and selects the initial configuration $E_{S,0}$. For each $X_i(e_i)$ element, $E_{S,0}$ considers the most representative associated symbol indicated by $X_{Max}$. The initial configuration is structured as follows:

$$E_{S,0} = \left\{ \begin{array}{c} (X_{Max}^{(1)}, S_0^{(1)}), \\ \ldots \\ (X_{Max}^{(p)}, S_0^{(p)}) \end{array} \right\}$$

The following conditions are used for the construction of $E_{S,0}$.

Certainty condition:

$$\left| X_i(e_i) \right| = 1 \Rightarrow X_{Max}^{(i)} = x_1 \wedge S_0^{(i)} = \text{Certainty}$$

where:

- $|A|$ is the operator returning the number of the included elements belonging to the A set

It means that if $e_i$ has associated only one symbol, the choice of $X_{Max}$ is bound to that symbol and its state is defined as Certainty (C) state.

Probable certainty condition:

$$\left| X_i(e_i) \right| > 1 \wedge (conf(e_i) > th) \wedge (\exists x \in X_i(e_i) \mid x = \hat{e}_i)$$
$$\Rightarrow X_{Max}^{(i)} = \hat{e}_i \wedge S_0^{(i)} = \text{Probable Certainty}$$

where:

- $conf(e_i)$ is the confidence value associated with $e_i$.
- $th$ is a predetermined threshold value.
- $\hat{e}_i$ is the symbol obtained from $e_i$ and adding "S_".

The condition states that if $\hat{e}_i$ could be assigned to $e_i$ and the confidence value provided by the neural network is greater than $th$, $X_{Max}$ is $\hat{e}_i$ and its state is defined as Probable Certainty (P) state.

Uncertainty condition:

$$\left| X_i(e_i) \right| > 1 \wedge (conf(e_i) \leq th) \vee (\forall x \in X_i(e_i)$$
$$\Rightarrow x \neq \hat{e}_i) \Rightarrow X_{Max}^{(i)} = x^* \wedge S_0^{(i)} = \text{Uncertainty}$$

where:

- $x^*$ is the symbol having the highest $p$ position probability (in the event of more symbols, the first one in the list of the symbols' set is considered).

It states that if $e_i$ has more than one associated symbol and one of the following conditions is true:

1. The confidence value is less or equal to *th*.
2. $\hat{e}_i$ does not exist.

$X_{Max}$ is the symbol with highest $p$ position probability ($x^*$) and the state is defined as Uncertainty (U) state.

## Aggregation Module

The aggregation module gathers together the symbols inside the initial strip, so as to rebuild the music symbols. It is based on rules derived from the western music notation grammar. Such rules, which are not only syntactical, focus both on the structure of the symbols belonging to the music notation, like, for instance, the structure of a note, and the way such symbols are associated one to another, for instance, determining where a note alteration must be positioned.

The vertical rules focus on the aggregation of music symbols, both elementary and compound symbols, belonging to the same strip. The horizontal rules address the aggregation of music symbols (both elementary and compound symbols) belonging to different strips. The horizontal rules are used for music symbols involving more than one strip, such as the decrescendo, the accidentals belonging to the key signature, the clef itself, or the accidental associated to a note.

The definition of two disjoint sets of graphic rules depends both on the behavior of the segmentation phase and on the graphic structure of the music language. As to segmentation, the extraction of the graphic primitives is held at level 2 and is obtained according to the strips determined in level 1. This behavior has to refer to reconstruction rules working on the elements belonging to a single strip, so as to allow the rejoining, thus, obtaining

the input music symbol. For music symbols like the slur, the decrescendo, and the crescendo (they are all symbols where the segmentation produces graphic primitives belonging to different strips), any rejoining could happen only according to rules working on different strips.

## Music Notation Rules

In this section, the music notation rule syntax is described. A common rule structure has been defined both for vertical and horizontal rules. A rule header has been defined to distinguish the kind of rule. The term VRULE appears for the set of vertical rules, while the term HRULE is used for the set of horizontal rules. The structure of a generic rule is defined as follows:

Rule header

Required Symbols (conditions)

$\Rightarrow$ Resulting music symbol (assignment);

### Required Symbols

Enclosed between the rule header and the resulting graphic symbol "$\Rightarrow$," there are the symbols necessary to the rule application (see Box 3).

The required symbols stand for the sequence necessary to build the resulting symbol. These symbols can be associated with the data in the brackets. Such data, identified as Conditions and kept separate by a comma, represent those further conditions the symbol has to meet all together (AND), in order to be held as correct.

The graphic markers "[ ]" include symbols that could be present for a minimum number of times equal to 0, and a maximum one that is infinite. Its function provides an option mechanism for the affected symbol and a management mechanism of the music symbols composed of a variable number of elementary symbols of the same type. An example is a note has a stem of variable length, depending on the context, and the number of staff

*Box 3. Required symbols*

| Rule header | VRULE |
|---|---|
| | S_BEAM2 (conf>0.1) |
| Required Symbols (conditions) | [S_STAFFLINESTEM] |
| | ::S_FNOTEHEAD (height>1) |
| ⇒ Resulting music symbol (assignment); | ⇒NOTE(stem:=Up,head:=Fill, Duration:=16,inBeam); |

lines crossing the stem can change. Therefore, the option mechanism allows reducing the number of rules that manage such situations.

Finally, the graphic symbol "::" is used to identify the key symbol of the rule. This symbol is used to find the rule that allows generating a compound symbol by matching the required symbols with the whole or the partial strip. It is used also to index rules inside the archive.

## Resulting Music Symbol or Actions

It is marked by the graphic symbol "⇒" and it is the result of the aggregation, according to which the symbols belonging to a rule can be replaced. The resulting music symbol can have data that are kept in round brackets. Such data, identified as Assignments and separated by a comma, represent the features of the resulting music symbol. As to such features, apart from the assignments of the resultant, they are defined also by the features associated with each single symbol used for the rule application. Therefore, the rule resultant *inherits all the features of the symbols used to apply the rule, together with their related value.*

The following rule allows aggregating two compound symbols:

VRULE
  SYMBOL (isAccent)
  ::NOTE (stem=Up)
  [S_STAFFLINESTEM]
  ⇒ NOTE (withAccent);

The symbol list of the rule consists of:

1.  A compound symbol, indicated by the keyword SYMBOL. The required condition (isAccent) represents an accent symbol.
2.  A generic NOTE having a sole constraint represented by the stem, which must have the Up direction (stem=Up).
3.  Some staff segments, their presence being made optional by the graphic symbol "[ ]."

The resultant of the rule is a NOTE to which a symbol, with accent, is associated; in fact, there is the assignment withAccent.

## Aggregation Process

The aggregation process is divided into two levels:

*   **Basic symbols aggregation:** Aggregations are performed, in an iterative way, by applying vertical rules. Each and every aggregation-producing compound symbols starting from a strip are possible; the remaining nonaggregated symbols are considered in the successive aggregation. The aggregation process is concluded when there are no more symbols to aggregate in the strip, or there are symbols not yet aggregated that can be used as the key symbol of a vertical rule.
*   **Compound symbols aggregation:** Second level applies both vertical and horizontal

rules. The application of vertical rules could happen either between compound symbols and elements of the strip not yet used in previous aggregations, or among compound symbols included in the same strip. Applying horizontal rules allows the aggregation among compound symbols and/or elements not yet aggregated in an adjoining strip. The output is made up of compound symbols or complete music symbols.

The aggregation process allows the generation of more complex symbols. The rule application aggregates compound symbols, obtained in the previous phase, and elementary symbols, producing a great number of combinations among music symbols and determining a lot of alternatives whenever it happens that the reconstructed measure is not correct.

The best aggregation condition is to fuse symbols of configuration all at once. This is not always performed, since it is not certain that the configuration chosen could identify a rule able to aggregate all the elements. More probably, it happens that only a subgroup of strip symbols could match and verify the symbols and conditions required by the rule, and the rule could generate a complete music symbol or a compound one. Therefore, some symbols are involved in an aggregation process, while others are left unaltered. This enables one to carry out an iterative process performing the aggregation by successive levels on the compound symbols and the symbols not yet aggregated, so as to use all the information part of the strip. The vertical and horizontal aggregation processes are based on two joining modes:

1.  **Aggregation without symbols substitution (direct):** Once the key symbol and the rule determined by the strip configuration have been identified, the aggregation is performed involving only the symbols of the strip that match the required symbols and conditions,

leaving unaltered the other symbols. This aggregation is called *Direct Aggregation* (*without symbol substitution*).

2.  **Aggregation with symbols substitution (forced):** If a rule allowing direct aggregation is not determined, it means that the current strip configuration is not valid. Let us suppose that there is a rule where the set of required symbols list differs from the entire configuration, or from a strip subgroup, for one or more symbols. Let us assume that at the level of this invalid symbol, the set of associated symbols, could include the symbol required by the rule. This condition suggests that a replacement of the affected symbol or symbols should be carried out. In this way, a configuration change is performed, allowing the rule application. The aggregation affects only the configuration symbols verifying the list, and leaves unaltered the others. This kind of aggregation is called *Forced Aggregation* (*with symbol substitution*).

Each aggregation is followed by a new strip configuration where all compound symbols and separate symbols are held. This passage is conceived as a change of the *S* state for the affected symbols and for any state definition of the compound symbol. The following states are features of the aggregation evolution:

*   **Forced (F):** It is the state assumed by the symbol when it is submitted to the forced aggregation. The input symbol is replaced with another symbol belonging to the list of associated symbols, as required by the rule. Such a symbol is temporarily considered as if it is used by rule, in order to evaluate conditions for its application, in comparison with other rules that could be potentially used.

*   **Aggregated (A):** It is the state assumed by the symbol when the rule has been applied.

*Box 4. Example of aggregate symbol evolution*

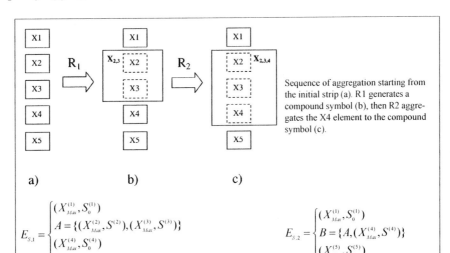

Sequence of aggregation starting from the initial strip (a). R1 generates a compound symbol (b), then R2 aggregates the X4 element to the compound symbol (c).

a)          b)          c)

$$E_{S,1} = \begin{cases} (X_{Max}^{(1)}, S_0^{(1)}) \\ A = \{(X_{Max}^{(2)}, S^{(2)}), (X_{Max}^{(3)}, S^{(3)})\} \\ (X_{Max}^{(4)}, S_0^{(4)}) \\ (X_{Max}^{(5)}, S_0^{(5)}) \end{cases} \qquad E_{S,2} = \begin{cases} (X_{Max}^{(1)}, S_0^{(1)}) \\ B = \{A, (X_{Max}^{(4)}, S^{(4)})\} \\ (X_{Max}^{(5)}, S_0^{(5)}) \end{cases}$$

The symbol obtained by the aggregation takes the name of the symbol associated with the resulting of rule.

Symbols that are not used are left in the initial state, except for those that were temporary, which are moved into the Forced state. Such symbols will be brought back to their initial state $S_0$ in order to evaluate the next rule.

Referring to the example, let us suppose that $R_1$ has $X_2$ as key symbol and it generates the compound symbol $A=X_{2,3}$ (resultant of $R_1$) and the $E_{S,1}$ strip configuration (b). Successively, $R_2$ matches the new key symbol $A$ and aggregates the $X_4$ element to $A$ providing the compound symbol $B=X_{2,3,4}$ (resultant of $R_2$) and the $E_{S,2}$ strip configuration (c). The initial strip configuration changes according to the evolution are reported in Box 4.

The considerations mentioned for the vertical aggregation apply also for the horizontal aggregation defined for two adjacent strips. It is possible to bind the aggregation, defining some conditions concerning the distance among symbols. The affected strips could have a configuration consisting of compound symbols (generated by the vertical rule) and not aggregated symbols. The aggregation is performed by working transversally. In the aggregation order, the reconstruction of horizontal relationships is the last step in the reconstruction process.

## Conditions for Rule Choice

In order to identify the rule to be used, the first step is to determine the symbol matching the rule key. The valuation method has to consider both the aggregation evolution and the state taken by symbols. In the aggregation initial phase, the only indications are those related with the initial state $S_0$. During the aggregation, the evolution towards a compound state means that an aggregation of certain pieces of information is currently taking place, since the process is the result of a rule that uses symbols, starting with the most probable ones; therefore, the generated compound symbol has a higher certainty level. This consideration allows defining selection criteria that relies on the $S$ state and helps in realizing a priority order when choosing. The defined criterion establishes that the selection of the key symbol has to be carried out by choosing, in order, the separate or compound symbol, having the state as follows:

1. Aggregated (used only with compound symbols)
2. Certainty
3. Probable certainty
4. Uncertainty

Once the symbol has been identified, it is used to find rules having it as key symbol. These rules are tested over the strip to find those that match elements belonging to the strip configuration and being, respectively, previous and next to the key element. When the features, which an aggregation rule has to possess, have been clarified, the research of set $R$ containing rules that have the selected symbol as a key can be performed. Among them, only the rules having a close correspondence with the number of symbols above and below the key are considered. The determined set is the set $R_c \subset R$. The rule to be applied is chosen within the set $R_c$, consisting of rules selected with the key. The application conditions of the rule are defined as follows.

Condition 1 $(F_1)$
Rule $r \in R_c$ is applied, if it verifies the formula

$$F_1(R_C) = \arg \min_{r \in R_C} \left[ \frac{N_s(\hat{r})}{N_r(\hat{r})} \right]$$

where:

- $N_s$ is the number of forced associated symbols.
- $N_r$ is the number of symbols required by the rule and thus $N_s(r) \leq N_r(r)$.

Since it is possible to have more rules meeting the $F_1$, the condition generates a set of applicable rules. In this context, the identified rules have to satisfy the following condition.

Condition 2 $(F_2)$
Provided that rules $r_i \in F_1(R_c)$, the applied rule is the one verifying the following relationship:

$$F_2(R_C) = \arg \max_{r_i \in F_1(R_C)} \left[ N_r(r_i) \right]$$

where:

- $N_r$ is the number of symbols required by the rule.

The defined conditions depend on the relationship between the number of forced associated symbols and the number of strip elements that are part of the music symbol. In the event of an unforced aggregation, there are no forced symbols; therefore, the minimum value that could be realized by the $F_1$ is the null value. When there are rules allowing an unforced aggregation, the choice falls on the rule that aggregates more symbols. What is assumed is that the rule is working on aggregating as much information as possible inside the strip. In case of direct aggregation, the choice falls on the rule that can aggregate more symbols, but at the same time, it is very easy to demonstrate that such rules required a fewer number of substitutions. Whenever there are more rules verifying two conditions, the choice falls on the first one being evaluated.

## State Evolution

During the aggregation process, the state of symbols develops into the conditions expressing the kind of aggregation undergone, or it is kept in its own initial state. The state transitions $T$, reported next and depicted in Figure 10, describes and formalizes how the state of a single symbol $e_i$ belonging to the strip $E_{S,0}$ changes when applying or trying to apply a rule $r$.

Let us assume that:

*Figure 10. State diagram and evolution of aggregation for ei*

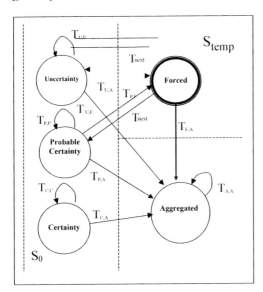

- $r \in R_c$ is the aggregation rule belonging to the $R_c \subset R$ set of rules selected with the key symbol.
- $\gamma(r,i)$ is the symbol required by the rule $r \in R_c$ in correspondence to $e_i$.
- $\rho(r)$ is the result symbol generated by $r$.
- $T_{Si,Sj}$ is the transition from the $S_i$ to the $S_j$ state, whose values could be: $A$ for aggregated, $C$ for certainty, $P$ for probable certainty, and $U$ for uncertainty.
- $p$ and $m$ are the number of symbols respectively previous and next to $e_i$ and so that $N_r = p+m+1$ is equal to the number $N_r$ of symbols required by $r$.
- $\oplus$ stands for the aggregation operator.
- $:=$ stands for the assignment operator after the transition.

The state transitions are defined as follows:

## Transition of Permanence $T_{C,C}$, $T_{P,P}$ and $T_{U,U}$

$$\gamma(r,i) \notin X_i(e_i) \Rightarrow S^{(i)} := S_0^{(i)}$$

The element is left unaltered in its own initial state if it cannot be used by the rule, either in a forced aggregation or in an unforced one. The associated symbol is the one of the initial configuration: $X_{Max}^{(i)}$.

## Forced Transition or Symbol Replacement $T_{U,F}$ and $T_{P,F}$

$$(X^{(i)} = X_{Max} \neq \gamma(r,i)) \wedge (\gamma(r,i) \in X_i(e_i))$$
$$\Rightarrow (S^{(i)} := \text{Forced}) \wedge (X^{(i)} := \gamma(r,i))$$

If the symbol can be replaced with the one required by the rule $r$, then the substitution is temporarily ($S_{temp}$) performed in order to verify whether the rule could be applied or not. The state taken by the symbol is Forced.

## Transition of Rule Application $T_{U,A}$, $T_{P,A}$, $T_{C,A}$, $T_{A,A}$ and $T_{F,A}$

$$(X^{(i)} = \gamma(r,i)) \wedge (r \in F_1(R_c) \wedge r \in F_2(R_c))$$
$$\Rightarrow (S^{(i)} := \text{Aggregated}) \wedge (\bigoplus_{j=i-p}^{i+m} X^{(i)} := \rho(r))$$

If the $X^{(i)}$ associated with $e_i$ matches the symbol required by the rule, and the rule verifies the $F_1$ and $F_2$ conditions, then $X^{(i)}$ is fused together with the $p$ and $m$ symbols required by the rule to realize a new symbol that takes the same name as the rule resultant $\rho(r)$. The state changes to Aggregated.

In event of the $T_{A,A}$ transition, it involves a compound symbol generated by a previous rule. When it occurs, the compound symbol is further aggregated either with other compound symbols or with not yet aggregated symbols.

## Transition of Return Back to Initial State $T_{next}$

$$\neg T_{F,A} \Rightarrow (S^{(i)} := S_0^{(i)}) \wedge (X^{(i)} := X_{Max}^i)$$

If the element has been forced, but the rule cannot be applied, then everything is brought back to the initial state. The associated symbol is the one of initial configuration $X_{Max}^{(i)}$ and a new rule has to be verified.

## CONCLUSION

In this chapter, the complete O³MR system has been described. It is designed to perform the automatic optical recognition of music scores and it consists of four main modules: (1) the segmentation (2) the classification, (3) the reconstruction of music information, and (4) the representation of the logic description of music notation. The described segmentation method has produced interesting results considering both monophonic music score and single voice, and music for piano solo. The tuning phase allows considering images coming from different publishers and acquired by the scanner at different resolutions. According to the parameters fixed by the tuning phase, the staff detection algorithm can cope with problems related to staff inclination, deformation, and indentation. The note head identification and the other symbols' detection algorithms are able to work with image presenting a high density of note per measure. The experimental results have shown a high efficiency in the correct location of basic symbols, and they allowed collecting 48 categories of basic symbols. They are used by a neural-network-based classifier in the recognition phase. A rule-based music grammar and an iterative aggregation process have been defined and are used in the reconstruction phase. They allow the reconstruction of both all music symbols and the spatial and time relationships directly from basic symbols. The music has been represented by using the WEDELMUSIC object-oriented model. Finally, the O³MR performance has been compared with SharpEye2 and SmartScore tools. The assessment has been performed by applying the methodology based on complete music symbols and their relationships described in Bellini et al. (Bellini, Bruno, & Nesi, 2007).

## REFERENCES

Bainbridge, D., & Bell, T.. (1996). An extensible optical music recognition system. *Australian Computer Science Communications, 18*(1), 308-317.

Bainbridge, D., & Bell, T. (2003). A music notation construction engine for optical music recognition. *Software—Practice & Experience, 33*(2), 173-200.

Bellini, P., Bruno, I., & Nesi, P. (2001b). Optical music sheet segmentation. In *Proc. of the 1st International Conference of Web Delivering of Music WEDELMUSIC2001,* (pp.183-190), Florence: IEEE Press.

Bellini, P., Bruno, I., & Nesi, P. (2004). An off-line optical music sheet recognition. In S. E. George (Ed.), *Visual perception of music notation: On-line and off-line recognition.* Hershey, PA: Idea Group Inc.

Bellini, P., Bruno, I., & Nesi, P. Assessing optical music recognition tools. *Computer Music Journal, 31*(1), 68-93.

Bellini, P., & Nesi, P. (2001a). WEDELMUSIC format: An XML music notation format for emerging applications. In *Proc. of the First International Conference on WEB Delivering of Music* (pp. 79-86). Retrieved from http://www.wedelmusic.org

Blostein, D., & Baird, H. S. (1992). A critical survey of music image analysis. In H. S. Baird, H. Bunke, & K. Yamamoto (Eds.), *Structured document image analysis* (pp. 405-434). Berlin: Springer-Verlag.

Bruno, I. (2003). *Music score image analysis: Methods and tools for automatic recognition and indexing.* PhD Thesis, Department of Systems and Informatics, University of Florence, Italy.

Byrd, D. (2001). Music-notation searching and digital libraries. In *Proceedings of 2001 Joint Conference on Digital Libraries (JCDL 2001)* (pp. 239-246).

Byrd, D. (2006). *OMR (Optical Music Recognition) Systems.* School of Informatics and School of Music, Indiana University. Retrieved from http://mypage.iu.edu/~donbyrd/OMRSystemsTable.html

Carter, N. P. (1989). *Automatic recognition of printed music in the context of electronic publishing.* Doctoral dissertation, University of Surrey, UK.

Carter, N. P. (1994). Music score recognition: Problems and prospects. *Computing in Musicology, 9,* 152-158.

Cooper, D., Ng, K. C., & Boyle, R. D. (1997). MIDI extensions for musical notation: Expressive MIDI. In E. Selfridge-Field (Ed.), *Beyond MIDI - The handbook of musical codes* (pp. 402-447). London: The MIT Press.

Coüasnon, B., & Camillerapp, J.. (1995). A way to separate knowledge from program in structured document analysis: Application to optical music recognition. In *International Conference on Document Analysis and Recognition* (pp. 1092-1097).

Fujinaga, I. (1988). *Optical music recognition using projections.* M.A: Thesis.

Fujinaga, I. (1996). *Adaptive optical music recognition.* Ph.D. Dissertation, Music, McGIll University.

Good, M. (2001). MusicXML for notation and analysis. In W. B. Hewlett and E. Selfridge-Field, *The virtual score* (pp. 113-124). Cambridge, MA: MIT Press.

Heussenstamm, G. (1987). *The Norton manual of music notation.* W.W. Norton & Company, Inc.

IMUTUS. (2004). *Interactive Music Tuition System.* Retrieved from http://www.exodus.gr/imutus

Kanai, J., Rice, S. V., Nartker, T. A., & Nagy, G. (1995). Automated evaluation of OCR zoning. *IEEE Transactions on Pattern Analysis and Machine Intelligence, 17*(1), 86-90.

Kato, H., & S. Inokuchi. (1990). The recognition system for printed piano music using musical knowledge and constraints. In *Proceedings of the International Association for Pattern Recognition Workshop on Syntactic and Structural Pattern Recognition* (pp. 231-48).

Kobayakawa, T. (1993). Auto music score recognition system. In *Proceedings SPIE: Character Recognition Technologies 1906* (pp. 112-23).

McPherson, J. R. (2002). *Introducing feedback into an optical music recognition system.* Third International Conference on Music Information Retrieval, Paris.

Miyao, H., & Haralick, R. M. (2000). Format of ground truth data used in the evaluation of the results of an optical music recognition system. In *IAPR Workshop on Document Analysis Systems* (pp. 497-506).

Modayur, B. R. (1996). *Music score recognition - a selective attention approach using mathematical morphology.* Seattle, University of Washington, Electrical Engineering Department.

Musitek (2002). SmartScore. Retrieved from http://www.musitek.com/

Ng, K. C., & Boyle, R. D. (1994). *Reconstruction of music scores from primitive Sub-segmentation.* School of Computer Studies, University of Leeds.

Ng, K. C., & Boyle, R. D. (1996)."Recognition and reconstruction of primitives in music scores. *Image and Vision Computing, 14*(1), 39-46.

Prerau, D. S. (1970). *Computer pattern recognition of standard engraved music notation.* Ph.D. Dissertation, Massachusetts Institute of Technology.

Ross, T. (1970). *The art of music engraving and processing.* Miami: Hansen Books.

Roth, M. (1994). *An approach to recognition of printed music.* Diploma thesis, Department of Computer Science, Swiss Federal Institute of Technology, Zurich, Switzerland.

Rumelhart, D. E., Hinton, G. E., & McClelland, J. L. (1986). A general framework for parallel distributed processing. In D. E. Rumelhart, J. L.

McClelland, and the PDP Research Group (Eds.), *Parallel distributed processing: Explorations in the microstructure of cognition, vol. 1: Foundations.* Cambridge, MA: MIT Press.

Selfridge-Field E., (1997). *Beyond MIDI - The handbook of musical codes.* London: The MIT Press.

Selfridge-Field, E. (1993). Optical recognition of musical notation: A survey of current work. *Computing in Musicology, 9,* 109-145.

Tojo, A., & Aoyama, H. (1982). Automatic recognition of music score. In *Proceedings of 6th International Conference on Pattern Recognition, 1223.*

Visiv. (2005). *Sharpeye.* Retrieved from http://www.visiv.co.uk/

# Chapter VI
# Challenges of Designing a Markup Language for Music

**Jacques Steyn**
*School of Information Technology, Monash University, South Africa*

## ABSTRACT

*XML-based languages for music have constraints not applicable to typical XML applications, such as for standard text documents or data sets. Music contains numerous simultaneous events across several dimensions, including time. The document model for a piece of music would thus look very different from serialised text documents. Most existing XML-based music markup languages mark music typography, following the print traditions of music scores. A general music markup language should include much more than mere print. Some of the challenges designing an XML-based markup language for music are considered. An SVG-based music symbol design grid is proposed to meet the challenge of music typology. An XML-based music symbol language is used to design symbols on this grid. Resulting symbols are positioned in 3-D Music Space, which is introduced to address the challenge of topography.*

## INTRODUCTION

Since the release of the XML specification (Bray, Paoli, Sperberg-McQueen, & Maler, 1998), several applications have been developed focusing on various aspects of music, but mostly on music notation, particularly the typography of common western music notation (CWMN). As XML is a metalanguage that makes it possible to mark any object in the universe that can be expressed with human language, the implication is that every conceivable aspect of music can be marked. The challenge is to develop a marking system that is sensible and economical. The decision as to what should be marked is philosophical. In recent years, the ancient Greek philosophical concept of ontology has been introduced in the markup arena. This was done, as it was realized that the first challenge in developing a markup language is to decide exactly what should be marked: the physics of sound, or a notational system, or a descriptive system, or whatever. And when notational systems are to be marked, which ones? Which of the different cultural systems need to be accounted for?

Music has several unique features that differ from the one-dimensional linear text of ordinary human language, which is not problematic for typical SGML or XML applications. SGML, and thus XML, is a content model, specifically, a text content model, and not an application model. SGML does not specify how nontextual media should be handled. This has implications for a music markup language as music is primarily an audible entity, and its writing systems use many graphic symbols that are nontextual.

The most obvious difference between music and human language textual documents is that several music events can happen simultaneously, while several instruments can each also play several notes simultaneously. Text, on the other hand, operates on one dimension only: it is monoplanar. In addition, in a multimedia context, other types of events need to be mapped and synchronized to music events, and vice versa. This multiple layering on space and time dimensions results in a much more complex phenomenon, which should be marked, than, for example, a markup language focusing on a procurement system. No XML parser can handle this complexity, such as to present multilayered markup in a manner music users have become accustomed to. Such rendering aspects need to be handled programmatically by the application. An easy way out would be to leave it to the application to handle all music aspects, but that would defy the purpose of trying to utilize XML to mark the structured content of music that might then rather not be used at all. One design goal would thus be to make as much as possible explicit through markup that an application can use to render this complexity appropriately.

There is yet a further challenge when it comes to music. Performed music can be measured against absolute time and absolute frequency, but written music (i.e., notation) often lacks explicit reference to time or frequency, except with reference to relative terms that can be interpreted by a performer in many ways. Reference to absolute time is of course very important for synchronization in computing devices, while referencing to frequency is important for computer synthesis playback devices.

## PAGED AND SCROLLED

In the presentation of information on a computer screen, there are two fundamental formats: paged and scrolled. The screen's dimensions serve as a window, or viewport, behind which data of any dimensions can be viewed. Paged representation is not a requirement of the properties of a screen, but rather a relic, transferred from the world of paper publishing. In the early days of human language writing, papyrus surfaces were scrolled. Only when the printing press was introduced was there a technological requirement that printed surfaces do not run continuously, as single sheets were placed on a table to be pressed with characters on their surface. Modern printing presses again operate with long rolls of paper that need to be cut in order to obtain pages. When music was originally written as music notation, the available print surfaces were accepted as norm, and hence, customs developed, such as for staves to be fitted to the width of the printed page. This segmentation of a staff is not an inherent music requirement, but merely a conventional requirement of the printed page, of typography.

Printing of music onto the printed page also gave birth to a complex set of typographical customs. Among attempts to develop an XML-based markup-based language for music, the Holy Grail seems to be to develop a language that could visually render music notation that reflects a manuscript, and its conventions, precisely. Efforts seem to be more concerned with the typography of the visual rendering of music than with the music content itself. Most attempts to mark music try to make explicit the publishing rules of music typography, accepting certain traditions and customs of printing to paper as normative. For an overview of these attempts, see the other contribution in this book, *Alternative design goals for a general music markup language*.

Printing to paged paper operates within the constraint of fixed dimensions. A staff needs to be segmented, and the bars on it need to be either squashed or stretched in order to fit into the predetermined paper size. None of these constraints are applicable to scrolled rendering. A particular part of an entire symphony could be rendered on a single line for screen purposes, while the data can scroll horizontally past the viewport. Different parts can be scrolled vertically. An entire score can thus be presented on a single abstract sheet of data (or "cyber paper") that becomes visible when that "sheet" scrolls past the human viewer's viewport. When the new technology of paper printing became established, many customs developed for representing music notation. Now that a computer screen is socially well established, new customs should be developed for rendering music. From a markup point of view, when the abstract music structure is marked as a core level, that music can be rendered on any type of device with any type of screen of any dimensions. Different style sheets should enable a user to select how the music should be rendered visually.

This approach to marking music implies that something else rather than notation should form the basis of a music markup language. If that "something else" is marked appropriately, it should theoretically be possible to render the markup in any of the many different available cultural music-writing systems. It should also be possible to render it on any screen size, and the appearance of the rendered notation or music symbols would follow the likes and dislikes of the user's applied style sheet.

## MathML

Before discussing the practical challenges for designing a music markup language, it is necessary to consider the value of emphasising an abstract system as opposed to a notation system. To explain this, let us consider MathML. The symbol set used in mathematics differs from symbol sets typically used in human writing systems. There are symbols from several language character sets, such as Greek and Latin, but there are also lines of various dimensions that are used to group symbols together or to separate them, and certain symbols are much larger (spanning several lines) or much smaller (such as super- or subscripts) than the "normal" default symbols. These mathematical symbols cannot be handled by the basic ASCII extended character set or human language Unicode sets (and neither can music symbols—the music symbols of Unicode form a small subset of the possible music symbols). From this perspective, there are commonalities between mathematics and music symbol systems. Both systems are highly graphical and each forms a "character set" different from those used for the many human languages of the world. From a symbol perspective, mathematics and music function like the writing systems of human languages that have their own character sets and syntactic rules.

The developers of MathML distinguished between the presentation level of mathematics and mathematical content. There are about 30 MathML presentation elements, and about 100 content MathML elements (Carlisle, Ion, Miner, & Poppelier, 2003). Mathematics can be expressed with either of these systems or with a hybrid form of both. To cope with the placement of mathematical symbols in relation to one another, the MathML developers chose a box method, where boxes serve as layout containers for symbols. Each symbol, or group of symbols, is placed in a box, and boxes relate to one another in terms of their locations.

Content MathML describes mathematical meaning, while Presentation MathML describes formatting issues. Content MathML is thus what mathematics is really about, while Presentation MathML was developed to address the unique rendering problems of mathematical formulae. If a music markup language could learn from this, it would be to have a core that describes the content of music structures, while presentation aspects are handled separately, even if the system itself is also expressed in XML.

## MARKUP AND MUSIC

Goldfarb defines a markup element as a particular component of the logical structure of a document (Goldfarb & Prescod, 1998). The structure of a document may be represented as a hierarchical nodal structure, a tree diagram with a number of branches and subbranches

A document's marked structure contains a root or document element (the "tree trunk"), while components of the document that are regarded to be on the same logical level of importance follow on the same node level of branches. Elements may contain subbranches.

Additional information about an element is added by using an attribute. Goldfarb acknowledges that it is not always clear when a component should be represented as an element, or as an attribute of another element. But a guideline would be to consider a structural entity as an element if it has a logical structure. Structure is typically marked by an element, while an attribute typically has no structure. Attributes are typically text strings, in terms of the data types of their values. Structure implies order, which means that if the linear order is important, use an element. Where order is not important, an attribute may be used.

These are decisions the DTD designer should make, and the decisions would be made on the basis of how the object that is to be marked is

viewed. In practice, for typical text documents, the guideline is that data that is rendered explicitly should be marked by elements because formatting systems typically print element content by default, and attributes only when specifically and programmatically requested. Note that data refers to semantic content, and not to the formatting of the data. Attributes would represent information of secondary importance. Elements would typically represent parts of a whole document, while attributes would represent the properties of the parts.

What exactly is regarded as an object or its part, on one hand, or its attributes, becomes a philosophical issue involving epistemological and ontological frameworks. In practice anything probably goes—there is no right or wrong, as long as the XML document is well formed and valid—although elegant systems may perform better and have wider application possibilities than their bloated sisters.

## MULTIMEDIA DOCUMENT MODEL

Before a DTD designer decides on which parts of a document should be regarded as elements, the document should be modeled according to document engineering principals. In this process, the document's abstract structure is in focus, and not its presentation. Brueggemann-Klein and Wood (2004) complain that such modeling seems to be quite absent from the XML community. When the modeling process of the document is performed on the semantics of its abstract structure, the resulting DTD is not a thumb suck, but built on the experience of sound, constructed models. The inventor of the Web, Tim Berners-Lee, envisaged the Web to be semantically linked (Berners-Lee, 2000), so it would make sense to take semantics as the point of departure when designing a system. An elegant XML-based language would be one that has followed the principals of document engineering, focusing on an abstract, logical content structure, but also accounting for the requirements of the semantic Web.

The logical structure of a document is typically defined in terms of objects; their hierarchical relationships defined as document models. There are many classes of documents. Their content can be arranged in hierarchical patterns on a highly abstract level. There have been several attempts to develop high-level generic models that could be used to apply to all these classes. For the Web environment the W3C released recommendations for such a generic document object model (DOM 1: Apparao, Byrne, Champion, et al. 1998; DOM 2: Le Hors, Le Hégaret, Wood, Nicol, Robie, Champion, & Byrne, 2000). These models are aimed at serial one-dimensional textual document content, and although they can be applied to XML documents, they lack addressing the requirements of multimedia documents. Boll, Klas and Westerman (1999) provide a summary of some of the requirements of multimedia documents, specifically temporal and spatial models.

There are at least three multimedia temporal models: point-based, interval-based, and event-based models. *Point-based temporal models* map media elements as points on a continuous time scale, which serves as an external clock. *Interval-based models* are typically based on temporal relations between time intervals, of which 13 can be made explicit, but there is still reference to an external clock. None of these two methods can really handle intervals of unknown duration. They would thus not be able to handle music of relative duration, such as music based on notation that does not reference absolute clock time. In an *events-based model,* events are triggered based on certain actions. In their primitive forms, none of these models are suitable for managing micro relationships between events such as consecutive notes. These models focus more on extrinsic multimedia objects, that is, they focus on clips as wholes and relate how clips as wholes should interrelate.

**Extrinsic music control** refers to the properties of the "external" control aspects of music, such as starting and stopping a clip, a CD, or any such device. Extrinsic control means the control operates on the music object or event as a whole. There are already several applications that address this kind of control of music, of which SMIL is an XML-based one.

**Intrinsic music control** refers to the description, management, and manipulation of specific music events and objects *within* a song or music document. This refers to notions such as the instruments in a song, their individual notes, performance guidelines, and a host of other features that are not addressed by applications that focus on extrinsic music events.

Describing "canned" music, or what I call "extrinsic music events" (Steyn, 2002) is not a challenge, as the success of SMIL shows. It is relatively easy to start or stop a clip, or to synchronize a clip as a whole in relation to other multimedia objects. It is much more challenging to describe intrinsic music events within an extrinsic fragment, for example, the relationships between individual notes of an instrument within a song.

Multimedia spatial models focus on the spatial positioning of objects within the viewport. Boll, Klas and Westerman (1999) distinguish between three approaches to spatial modeling: absolute positioning, directional relations, and topographical relations. Perhaps the first model should be called just positioning, as the placement of an object within the viewport could also be relative. For example, if a user resizes the viewport's dimensions, objects adjust their relative position in relation to one another.

In keeping with the philosophy of empowering users, the notion that the user should be in control is supported. From this perspective, the absolute constraints imposed by multimedia and Web authors on their audiences, such as forcing down their own personal choices for the dimensions of viewports, is to be rejected: it shows a total lack of understanding of document object models. Traditional aesthetic design for paper may demand such a fixed-dimensions approach, but the Web is a new medium with new design possibilities and constraints. The Web is neither paper nor broadcasting. Aesthetic designers should develop new design traditions for this new medium and accept the Web as a new mode of communication with its own unique constraints and possibilities: it is not required to duplicate the conventions of other media. Such a new aesthetics would operate on top of a document object model, and not enforce style onto that abstract object. Also, if content rather than appearance is fundamental, the user should be allowed to change dimensions at will, and place and resize multimedia objects within the viewport at will. Absolute positioning fixes objects at specific coordinates within the viewport. Relative positioning would allow a user agent to recalculate relations and adjust the actual distances in the viewport accordingly. This approach would allow multimedia content to adjust itself to the constraints of the specific device that is used to access it.

One consequence of this design approach is that music notation, such as scores, need not necessarily have fixed dimensions, as found in paper printing. If the core of music is marked, the visual rendering of music could take any form, from being represented in paged format to continuous scroll, depending on the choice of the user (not the designer).

This has implications for the rendering of music scores, which then obviously do not need to follow the typographical traditions of paper print. The challenge is to develop an approach that allows for many degrees of freedom when presenting music visually. A user who indeed requires an exact replica of some printed edition should be able to get exactly that while a more casual user should get a much more simplified score containing only the melody line and chords. Both instances are to be rendered form the same data to which different style sheets are applied.

Directional relation spatial models are based on geographical directions that allow up to 169 different directions to be specified in relation to the reference point. Topological spatial models describe positional relations between objects in terms of their placement in three-dimensional space. Some values used in this context are *overlap, cover, contain, inside*, and so forth.

Topological models are important for the visual rendering of the relation of particular music objects to other music objects. If the focus is on the visual representation of music, such as some conventional music notation system, topographical relationships between objects on the presentation area need to be marked explicitly. This could be handled by different methods, as will be explained. Typography, in this context, would refer to the shape of glyphs or symbols (a proposed solution for this is the music symbol design grid to be explained), while topography (for which music space is proposed, as will be explained) would refer to the space within which these symbols are expressed. If audio is in focus, typography is irrelevant, although abstract topology within music space would still be relevant for placement within the audio space. A series of boxes within boxes that have spatial (or topographical) relations with one another is a very effective method to deal with the placement of music objects (both visual and audio). The most elegant design would be one that distinguishes audio from vision, thus implying an abstract intermediate object that can be rendered either way. A domain neutral to typography is thus required, but this domain needs to be topographically sensitive.

Multimedia document models address the macro extrinsic objects of a multimedia document. These multimedia objects are addressed as wholes, while their content is not considered at all. Multimedia document models therefore do not address the internal relationships of internal child objects. If music details, such as a particular note within a particular bar, needs to be marked explicitly, then multimedia document models are not particularly helpful. MathML, particularly its box model, is much more applicable for positioning music objects topographically (Carlisle et al., 2003). For the box model of CSS see Lie and Bos (1996) and Bos, Lie, Lilley, & Jacobs (1998).

## THE NOTION OF ONTOLOGY IN THE CONTEXT OF XML FOR MUSIC

In the context of data management, ontology has quite a different meaning than its use in classical philosophy. To the ancient Greeks, ontology concerned an investigation into the nature of being, while epistemology concerned how we know about things. The basic premise here was that there is a world out there that presents itself as is, and that human investigators merely have to plug into this external objective world with logical tools in order to understand it. Twentieth-century linguistic philosophy showed that the distinction between ontology and epistemology is all a matter of language use, while simultaneously, it was recognized that we impose our mental structures, partly formed by our cultures, onto our interpretation of the world. Some would go as far as to state that we observe the world into being.

The concept of ontology, as used in the context of data management, has absolutely nothing to do with this classical usage of the term. In practical applications, it concerns relationships between special key categories, typically in a hierarchical tree diagram structure, that are, of course, constructed on the whims of developers. Philosophically, such an approach is a captive of early twentieth-century structuralism, originally introduced by Ferdinand de Saussure (Harris, 1987; Saussure, 1916/1986) and which went out of fashion in the latter part of the twentieth century. The linguistic theory on which structuralism is based is suspect, but for practical purposes and Web applications, it is a useful tool that allows

stupid computing devices to relate categories with one another, and consequently, facilitates better information management, such as search results. All literature I found on XML-based ontologies relate to this structural meaning of the word rather than to the Greek philosophical meaning. One example is MIML (Malyankar, 2002).

In this contribution, I would like to use this word in both senses. In scientific investigation, the first step in scientific methodology is to demarcate this huge universe of ours into manageable pieces, and that is a philosophical issue. We decide on which part we wish to focus. These categories are based on our knowledge, and hence, relates to classical epistemology. They also relate to how we observe that demarcated part of the universe we investigate. How we define the object we mark is consequently important, as our markup language will reflect our demarcation. If our object to be marked is music notation, the focus would be very different from a system that marks music from a different perspective. The resulting music markup language thus reflects a particular ontological view of music. It is therefore possible for many different kinds of music markup languages to exist alongside one another. No ontological judgment can be made between these languages, such as that one is better than the other. One language could only be pragmatically better than another, depending on design goals and the resulting coding effort, as well as on usability. Without getting too deeply involved in philosophical issues, for pragmatic purposes, I will assume that it is possible to define music well enough in order to build practical applications, and that it is possible to construct practical, hence meaningful, ontological (in the classical sense) categories.

The first question to be addressed when designing a music markup language is what exactly do we mean when we use the word "music": What is included in this description and what is excluded? Anything expressible in human language can be marked as an XML element. It follows that every possible humanly expressible aspect of music can be marked. This may be an ideal situation, but very impractical, as we might then just as well regard every word in a sentence as a marked word. For computing purposes, and for a streamlined and elegant XML-based application, the set of structural elements also need to be economical, which means that the object needs to be properly demarcated.

The challenge is to describe music in such a manner that is both comprehensive and economical. Instead of focusing on music notation as core, a different object could be chosen, namely, the physics of music, such as explained by Sundberg (1991). There is an interesting dilemma here. XML is text based and consequently, the expression of the physics of music, which is audio, is a visual and textual expression, which implies a translation between modes of communication (from audio to visual, and moreover, symbolic in the terms of ordinary language). Another challenge is thus to translate music as audio into music as text.

So what is music? From a physics point of view, at its core, music is a function of frequency and time, but whether such an expression is regarded as music is culturally and psychologically determined. The average person would not regard John Cage's 4 minutes of "silence" as music, but musicologists and music philosophers would. The social group of listeners preferring top-20 music only would not regard industrial rock as music; based on their value judgments, a strictly eurocentric musical taste would not regard classical Chinese music as proper music. These are, of course, cultural value judgments, but even from a musicological point of view, there is no objective criterion to decide which kind of noise, that is, which frequency, over time, may be regarded as music. Romantic lovers may regard their partner's chuckle as music to their ears, literally and not metaphorically. What is regarded as music is, thus, in the ear of the beholder.

If music has reference to time, it must be acknowledged that philosophically, the notion of time is a problematic one. Newton objecti-

fied time and assumed it is an absolute measure. Einstein, though, showed that time is a construct and depends on the viewpoint of an observer. In fact, time cannot be conceptualized as a separate "entity," but is collapsed into a single concept with space, called *spacetime*. Musical time could, of course, not refer to objective time or spacetime, but to the psychological experience of time by a listener. One could thus distinguish between "sound time" (as philosophical time) and "music time" (as psychologically experienced time). With reference to music time, music events follow on one another experientially, and as we as humans can experience only one moment at a given instance, our experience is that moments follow on one another. This experience of sequential moments we call time.

Despite James Ingram's (1985, 1999) objections to incorporating a notion of time in a music XML, even his "timeless" music is, nevertheless, experienced by listeners as passing through time. Ingram's time thus refers to philosophical time, while time in this contribution refers to psychological time. Perhaps, when measured against a clock, each of the performances of his "timeless" music takes on a different duration because of the mood of the conductor, but for the audience, the music events, nevertheless, unfold through time. Philosophically then, there may be timeless music, but for practical purposes, especially in the realm of computing, time becomes an issue for synchronization in the absence of a human conductor who imposes his interpretation of time onto a composition. The challenge is to map psychological time to the clock time of a computer. In this regard, Honing (2001) provides some useful background information on issues around the representation of time and tempo.

For practical purposes then, when designing a markup language for music, the most comprehensive, as well as the most economical definition of music, is in terms of frequency and time. This should make it possible to describe any event of this type as music, even wind, the clang of a hammer, a bird's whistle (all of these have been used in compositions), and, of course, sound produced by any of the technologically created artifacts we call musical instruments. A further challenge here is to be able to capture the variety of music events through time, a temporal axis, as well as its frequency, simultaneously, without being restricted to absolute time and frequency aspects that are required when using computing devices that are dependent on absolute values. Plus, all this needs to be expressed in linear, monoplanar text-based XML code.

Expressing music sound visually can be done following many different conventions. One typical method is in terms of a Cartesian coordinate grid, where the x-axis represents time, and the y-axis frequency. Music, of course, does not "look" like this, as it is essentially an audible medium, consisting of sound waves. Any visual expression of music is a translation of some of the audio aspects into visual objects. Throughout history, many diverse visual systems have been developed in many different cultures.

## Writing Systems

Writing systems have developed relatively recently (perhaps about 5,000 years ago), compared to the 150,000 years of the history of modern man (*homo sapiens*). The exact origins of writing are lost in the mist of time, but most likely, writing originated in the form of tally keeping, as marks on objects such as sticks (which would quickly decay), bone, and stone (for which there is quite some archaeological evidence—Renfrew & Bahn, 2004). At some stage, the writing marks became conventionalized, and human speech was captured. In this context, writing thus serves to keep record of speech. Writing systems for music are more recent, and more controversial. The foundations of CWMN were developed less than 1,000 years ago.

Music is primarily an audible entity, generated by humans for various reasons. As music consists of sound waves, the physics of sound waves would thus be the most basic scientific approach to music, while its interpretation and analysis would be cultural human endeavours, and on a more hermeneutic plane. Different cultures have developed different music writing styles. The most commonly used music writing system today is probably CWMN, a relatively simple convention that is guided by the Cartesian grid, most likely not consciously so, but nevertheless. Although simple, this is an extremely powerful convention, as variations of it can capture the polyphonic sounds of multiple instruments through a large variation of time. At best, it is an approximation, and suffers

*Figure 1. Sound, or music, expressed in a Cartesian coordinate grid as a function of frequency over time. Common western music notation is used here to express the audio visually.*

the whims of interpretation, while composers who wish to have a much more precise system invent alternative systems. Music conventions in other cultures have been typically monophonic, and the writing systems developed to capture that music are thus also relatively simple, restricted to single instruments or voices, and not as powerful as CWMN. One challenge in this context is to design an XML-based music markup language based on CWMN, yet able to scale up to a more complex notation system, while simultaneously able to scale down to more simplistic conventions. If written music is a visual summary and guideline for interpretation, it should be possible to translate the same piece of music into any of the possible conventions, obviously losing the finer nuances in the process due to the restrictions of a particular convention.

Music notation might have been, historically, an important method for keeping record of music expressions (Rastall, 1983; Williams 1903, 1969), but today, electronic recording techniques provide much better tools for the record keeping of musical compositions. Music notation methods today mostly serve as visual aids for learning music, or as visual cues for performance. The function of music notation has thus, not been made redundant yet.

## Human Language Writing Systems

The human alphabetical writing system is a very successful system. Compared to actual human speech, the alphabetical writing system records it very poorly, as indicated by an analysis of the sound waves of spoken language. Yet this system is used for successful communication, having been used for the creation of many billions of records. One reason for its success is that the same graphic symbol can be used for a very wide range of actual sounds. Consider the character "a." Even in the same language, the actual sound associated with this character varies from context to context. For example, it sounds different in the

words "character" and "same." Different dialects of the same language may also have different pronunciations of the same character, while different languages also assign different sounds to the same character "a."

Linguists have attempted to develop a system of symbols to represent the different sounds of human language more accurately, as provided by the IPA (international phonetic alphabet). This set of symbols is abstract, and although, to a degree, more precise than "ordinary" characters, still a long way from representing actual sound waves. Each of these abstract symbols may have several graphic representations that differ in terms of their designed form. By using different font styles, the same abstract character may be presented by many different looking glyphs.

Taking this as a guideline for music notation, it implies that the same music symbol can be used for many different purposes. This is indeed the case. An abstract note "A" can be played by a saxophone or by a piano, and its exact frequency depends on several factors. There are also many different typographical styles for presenting music writing systems. But there is not a music system like the phonetic system of human language. A notation-like system, such as CWMN, may not reflect sound waves exactly, just as human language characters do not reflect sound waves. But such an approach to representing sound waves, which forms an interpretation layer of abstraction a level above actual sound waves, seems to be a very practical solution to consider what exactly should be marked. Instead of marking actual sound waves, this second layer can be marked successfully, as was done with MML (Steyn, 1999, 2002, 2004). Note that although very similar to notation, this abstract layer is not yet notation. When MML was designed, there was a deliberate decision to use the nomenclature of CWMN, as it is the most widely used and most successful notation system, rather than to introduce novel or complex terms, such as SMDL (Newcomb et al., 1995) had done. The learning curve for users of a music markup system would be less if a system is closer to CWMN, although it must now be admitted that users often misinterpret the abstract MML symbols on the notation level instead of an abstract level.

It is possible to infer structure form typography, as shown by Fuss, Gatzemeier, Kirchhof, and Meyer (2004). But their exercise takes typographical cues, such as font size, to infer structure, which may be absent from a music score. In music typographical notation, there may be many important properties external to the notation system without which it may be impossible to express the score audibly. These external properties, such as frequency, are not referenced explicitly by CWMN. Whether a particular note should express a particular frequency depends on factors external to the notation system. It depends on external customs acquired through extensive training. Some traditions are such as using a particular note as a Reference Note that is then associated with a particular frequency, for example, A=440Hz, or A=442Hz. The frequencies of other notes within a note set are determined by ratios defined by tuning systems, of which there are several. Code (2002) presents an adaptive tuning system for piano, and some of these concepts are relevant in this context as well. These external factors are implied by conventions, and not internal to notation systems such as CWMN. But they are aspects of an ontology of music that need to be addressed and made explicit in music applications as machines, such as computers, are quite dumb and need to be explicitly informed of such matters. A challenge for a markup language is thus to be able to refer an audio rendering system to the frequency of a Reference Note (if applicable), as well as to be able to handle several tuning systems. None of these are expressed in CWMN, which implies that a music markup language should be more comprehensive than CMWN.

Compared to linear text documents, musical expressions have several additional layers of complexity. Human languages express their

data linearly, in sequence, character by character; hence, electronic documents or databases follow the same pattern. Different characters are not displayed simultaneously in the same cognitive space. Different documents are also never rendered simultaneously in the same space to human consumers—this is not referring to having several instances of open documents on a computer workstation. Music events, though, except for monophonic music, is typically expressed by several simultaneous events, expressed by different instruments, which means that a human listener is exposed to several layers of simultaneous music events. This cannot be handled at all by an SGML or XML parser, which means that an additional burden is placed on the renderer to be able to express several linear sequences simultaneously. Such parsers output characters serially. The only human friendly output string would be one that shows data as CDATA element content, but that would be music expressed very simply, and it would have to be according to some convention. It further implies that for proper rendering, due to the linearity of XML, methods need to be built into the parser, as well as rendering engine, to operate ahead in time, to cache markup, to synchronize the various monoplanar linear expressions in order to eventually render multiple simultaneous events. The challenge is thus to translate simple monoplanar linearity into complex, synchronized, simultaneous music events, whether they are audible or visual, or both. Conversely, the challenge is to translate this complexity of music into serialized characters.

## Reusability and Scalability

From an application point of view, a modular approach is the only sensible one to designing a music markup language in order to obtain optimum reusability and scalability. This is not only a present technological device requirement, but a requirement of good information design.

*Figure 2. A modular approach to music with core modules and several optional modules*

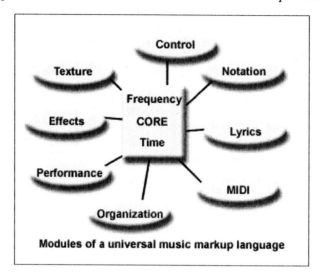

Similarly, the music object should be divided into categories and subcategories of information. The challenge is to develop a music model that could be marked, and which reflects reusability and scalability on all levels. One possible model is the MML model (Steyn, 1999). This model covers all aspects of music, as ontologically defined in this contribution.

The functions of these different modules are briefly:

- **Core:** The core of music consists of references to frequency (or relative pitch) and time (duration or relative tempo)
- **Texture:** For the intensity, envelope, and harmonics of the music core
- **Effects:** A basic sound wave can be altered by changing frequency parameters (such as overtones or undertones) over several time-unit lengths
- **Performance:** To express manipulation by the music core by hand, foot, or breath control. In addition, certain properties of the singing voice need to be described that are not contained in the Lyrics module, which marks basic human text. In the context of

singing speech synthesizers, additional parameters are required for performing lyrics.

- **Organization:** Music can be organized for many different purposes, ranging from describing music albums, play lists, and, of course, a host of metadata. For music synthesis managing, the sounds need to be marked, which is typically done with reference to terms such as timbre, banks of timbre, and combinations of these, as well as preprogrammed sounds. Note that this module does not imply the marking of the actual sound units, but only their organisation. Marking of actual sound units, such as reference to soundwave shapes and so on, should rather be handled by another module, such as the universal synthesizer (Steyn, 1999).
- **Control:** This module describes subtle nuances in the realization of the core through amplification and reproductive methods: accent, volume, and extrinsic characteristics such as starting/stopping the music, volume, channels to be used, and the direction of the sound source (e.g., azimuth, elevation, panning).

- **Notation module:** For music writing systems. It should theoretically be possible to design a music markup language based on a core module that is expressible in any of the possible notation systems.
- **Lyrics module:** Lyrics of a particular song
- **MIDI:** For translating marked music into audio by means of MIDI. Other translation means are possible, but MIDI is so widely used that it would be foolish not to give this special attention.

Using this model, any piece of music will always be described in terms of the Core module of frequency and time, or the lack thereof, as absolute values are not always available. Note that I use the terms *frequency* and *time* as abstract structures, as logical containers that may or may not be referenced to actual frequency or actual time values. The other modules are applied on a needs basis, as defined by a user, implying that not all modules are always explicitly marked. The most comprehensive description of a piece of music would include all of the modules. Yet even when all modules are used, a user may select which ones would be applicable to his needs. This music model should be able to handle the music object, defined in very broad terms, unlike music markup languages that focus only on music notation, which would not be able to address aspects such as sound effects (e.g., room ambiance), which may be important for an electronic playback system, require elaborate translation filters between different notation systems, and cannot handle reference to multimedia objects natively. The challenge is to design a markup language that is capable of handling much more than music notation, where different aspects of music can be handled independently, depending on user needs, and is thus flexible enough to include enough, but not too much music information at its core. Some core module is thus required that could serve as a reference structure for the other modules, of

which notation is not basic, but merely one along several other possibilities.

## Deserializing Simultaneous Events

If music had been as simple as spoken language, taking written language as a model for music writing would have been uncomplicated. In human speech, except perhaps as executed by speech choirs, different speakers do not need to synchronize their expressions precisely. Speech, or Saussure's *parole*, (Saussure, 1916/1986) can be interrupted during turn-taking in conversations. This does not work with music. In speech, the generated content depends on the interests of the producer, while in group music all the music producers need to generate the same content, or variations of the content that are allowed within the specific system. Turn-taking in music is far more regulated than in human speech, literally more orchestrated.

SGML, and consequently XML, were developed to mark the written form of human speech, which has a very long history, and customs and conventions that are very well developed. Human speech is monoplanar, or one-dimensional. SGML, hence XML, is ill-suited for marking music, which is multidimensional, each dimension consisting of its own multiple dimensions. Other shortcomings of SGML are highlighted by Mason (1997). SGML elements mark the written content of human language, but there is no acceptable system for marking the written content of music. This was realized by the father of SGML, Charles Goldfarb, who initiated the development of SMDL (also see SGML SIGhyper, 1994; Sloan, 1993, 2002).

The challenge is to design an elegant system that could deserialize the serial monoplanar markup without placing too much burden on caching, and then to synchronize the deserialized events.

Deserialization involves deciding which of the simultaneous events should be written first, and what the order should be. This applies to coding.

Given a data bank, the first step of information design is to chunk the data into hierarchies and relationships, that is, to impose some order into the data system. Chunking the data of a document can be done in many ways. For example, in music, the group of simultaneous events could be chunked and described by music bar, that is, all bar 1's of all instruments are described first:

```
<bar id="1">
    <instrument id="ins1" />
    <instrument id="ins2" />
...
</bar>
```

Such an approach would enable better cache handling, but when viewed with a standard browser, would be very difficult to read by a human reader, as all the first bars would be rendered, then the second bars. To ensure human readability, it is better to structure the data by instrument:

```
<instrument id="1">
    <bar id="bar1" />
    <bar id="bar2" />
...
</ instrument >
```

All the notes for a particular instrument will, thus, be displayed serially, and could be followed by a human reader.

The converse of deserialization would apply at play back or rendering, when the serial code needs to be reassembled to be presented simultaneously in multiple dimensions, visually as score, or audibly as the simultaneous playing of many different sounds. This involves synchronization.

## Synchronizing Music Events

Perhaps a much more serious challenge than deserialization is synchronizing all these events, either visually or audibly. This challenge regards the marking of overlapping structures, an issue that is addressed in another context, among others, by Sperberg-McQueen and Huitfield (2004). As mentioned previously, SGML represents the logical structure of a document as a tree with child nodes, following the principals of structural linguistics. But even in the text of human language, there are instances where document structure is not linear. Sperberg-McQueen and Huitfield present some methods to handle this overlap, with special emphasis on the GODDAG method, which is an abbreviation for "General Ordered-Descendant Directed Acyclic Graph." But this overlapping is weak compared to the complex overlapping found in music. Although some lessons may be learned from this approach, it is not a final solution for the requirements of music. The challenge for a music XML is that multiple layers of events need to be synchronized as micro-objects, not only the generic high-level multimedia objects, or put in different words, not only the extrinsic music objects and events need to be synchronized, but also the intrinsic music objects and events. We need to consider how multilayered objects should be associated with one another. As proposed next, the best solution for this challenge is a concept, such as the HyTime FCS, or more specifically, the MML Music Space.

During a live performance, the different layers of music parts are synchronized by a human conductor, band leader, drummer, or designated member, who serves as synchronizing "clock." This clock may, of course, not necessarily be synchronized to an absolute clock. During live performances, tempo is often increased, when compared to rehearsals, due to the energy and excitement of the audience, which rubs off on performers.

From a performance perspective, a music markup language should include a descriptive dimension of time. However, if symbolic music representations of music also need to be incorporated in the model, the "time" dimension should be neutral to time, as there is a vast body of visually expressed music with no indication of time at all. In this context, the HyTime Finite-Coordinate-Space (FCS) is a very useful concept to serve as an abstract space that serves to link all the events and objects together. No music markup language would be able to handle the variety of complexities of music time without reference to an abstract reference layer similar to the HyTime FCS.

## Associating Multilayered Events

Visually, music is expressed in some or other notation system, which may vary from CWMN, piano roll type of expression, MIDI information expressed visually in textual format, any of the possible cultural writing systems, 2-D and 3-D representations, and so on. In polyphonic music, music sounds that are executed together are grouped visually in CWMN convention, for example, by bars or binds. This makes sense as our minds can handle only a limited amount of information at a time. It should be possible to express the same music sequence with any of these many different visual systems. The challenge here is to design a system that does not require too much programmatic filtering. Ideally, no filtering should be necessary; the same music core should be expressible in any of these expression systems using style sheets.

For the audio rendering of music XML, the application needs to know how to synchronize all the music events with one another. The HyTime Finite-Coordinate-Space (FCS) seems to be a very good basis for synchronization. The SMI "spine" and MML Music Space are variations of HyTime FCS. Haus and Longari (2002, 2005) introduce the concept of "spine," which is a space-time structure that serves as reference for

their Performance and Notation Layers in their SMI (symbolic music information). Their spine functions as a bidirectional mapping mechanism for synchronization of, for example, notes on a staff and notes in an audio file. In the spine, each event is described with two coordinates relative to the preceding event in its dimension. The first coordinate describes the time passed after the previous event. The second coordinate serves a visual purpose for aligning notes on a staff. They call this coordinate a VLPU (virtual logic position unit). The main focus of SMI's "spine," at present, is to synchronize music notation with recorded soundwaves. It is not clear how other objects will be mapped to the spine. In a sense, the spine acts as an abstract monoplanar timeline, and like SMIL, focuses on extrinsic events, although in this case, mapped to intrinsic events.

Another method, similar in concept, is the MML Music Space (Steyn, 2004), which is a three-dimensional Cartesian coordinate system where the x-axis represents an abstract "time," the y-axis abstract "frequency," and the z-axis layers of simultaneous events. The z-axis allows description not only of music objects and events, but all multimedia objects and events, including entrance cues for actors, positioning of props, and so on. Each z-axis interval serves as a layer, and thus allows expressing a theoretically infinite number of music instruments, each playing various musical themes.

Time and Frequency are regarded as abstract as they are not necessarily absolute. They function as abstract place holders within the coordinate system of Music Space within which any objects may be positioned, including any intrinsic music events or objects. The use of the terms "time" and "frequency" proved to be unfortunate, as MML users interpret the terms literally. Within MML, however, they function much more abstractly. A user specifies whether time is clock-based (thus absolute) or relative (with no reference to a clock), as well as whether frequency is to be mapped to a frequency table (thus absolute) or relative (as pitch

*Figure 3. A 2-D graphical representation of 3-D music space*

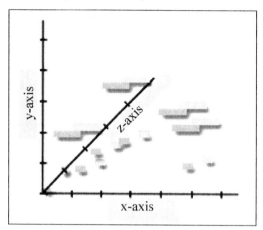

only). Music Space also allows for the simultaneous use of absolute and relative descriptions. As the manipulation of values of these aspects can be handled by the application, a user can easily manipulate them.

The frequency dimension is much more complex than the time dimension, as it contains references to systems such as note sets (e.g., the octave system), and various tuning systems that need to be accounted for.

Music Space is based on the concept of an events-based temporal model, as explained previously. Within this music space, actions and objects are positioned in relation to one another. Only once a user or user agent has made explicit the absolute clock time to follow, are the positions on the x-axis mapped to clock time. It is envisaged that a user agent would calculate a default time, but provide an interface to allow users to change the pace.

If a performed piece of music is described using MML, the user would most likely choose an absolute reference point as frequency, say A=440Hz. If the piece of music is the translation of a score, the reference would most likely be relative, allowing the user to change time (or tempo) or frequency (or pitch, and by implication the Reference Note and Tuning System used) according to his or her preferences, while such changes need to apply on all layers simultaneously.

MML Music Space is one proposed solution to handle the challenge of topography, the relations between events and objects within music space, which is multidimensional, and requires synchronization of all events and objects within all dimensions.

## Handling Diverse Cultural Music Writing Systems

Another challenge for designing a music markup language is to allow for the expression of music in any of the diverse cultural notation conventions. If music indeed consists of soundwaves, these should be universal, while cultural systems, recording such soundwaves in writing, are culturally relative systems of expressions. A music markup language based on soundwaves should thus be expressible with any of the cultural systems that actually operate on top of this base system. This was one of the design goals of MML. It was envisaged that by describing an abstract core of frequency and time, all other aspects of music can be mapped to these two concepts. Different cultural notation systems that are typographically expressible can thus be mapped to the same core description. It should thus be possible to render a simple European folk song, such as *Ring, oh ring of rosies*, visually in any of the notation systems, ranging from piano roll to Korean and Indian music writing systems. This translation from the abstract score of the folksong to a notation system would not be easy if the music markup language is designed around the typographical aspects of a music notation system, as is done by most current XML-based music applications. In other words, music topography should be expressible in any typography, but systems taking a specific typographic convention (such as CWMN) as basis will not provide elegant solutions to this challenge.

By nature, melodies based on more complex tuning systems and notesets are not translatable into simpler systems (e.g., translating and 8-note noteset or "octave" system into a 5-note noteset system). Translation of simpler melodies using a more complex system should, however, be possible. Translating up would be possible, but not translating down. Where polyphonic, multipart music markup needs to be expressed with a monophonic, single-part system, the export filter would handle one theme or instrument at a time. Even if single-part systems cannot express the parts of multipart music simultaneously and synchronized, as can be done with CWMN, parts can, nevertheless, be expressed as different single parts; hence, the entire score can be expressed.

## Music Symbols

Unicode contains a closed set of some CWMN symbols, but the challenge is to develop an open-ended system that allows for the expression of any kind of cultural glyph, including any kind of variations of the CWMN symbols as well as the symbols of more experimental notation systems.

In the latest version of MML, a Music Symbol Design Grid was developed that allows users to

design any music symbol of their liking within the vector environment of SVG (Ferraiolo 2001). In the MML Application, symbols can be designed on a grid similar to that of the MathML box, of which the dimensions can be specified. The grid itself serves as a containing box for the symbol, while the resulting glyph can be inserted into higher-level boxes, such as a position on a staff. An XML-based Music Symbol Language was developed that enables users to design any possible shape symbol. The MML Application is now being extended to use these symbols to render the core structural markup. This symbol layer functions in a similar manner to the font descriptors of CSS (Bos et al., 1998), the difference being that the descriptors themselves are XML compliant. This system is very powerful and allows for the design of any possible shaped music glyphs that can be embedded into one another, or placed in any relationship with one another within Music Space. To address the challenges of typography, Music Symbol Language is used to design symbols on the Music Symbol Design Grid. Resulting symbols are positioned in 3-D Music Space, which is introduced to address the challenge of topography.

The Music Symbol Design Grid is used as follows. A user first specifies the dimensions of a particular symbol on the grid which size is defined in terms in terms of number of columns and rows. A point is selected as the anchor in order to serve as a positioning device for the target parent box. Different SVG properties, such as *line, polyline*, and *circle,* can then be used to draw a symbol on the grid. Child properties, such as *strokewidth, stroke color, angle, length*, and others, can be used to change partial properties of the symbol. In the present MML application, by applying a different style sheet, the properties can then be adapted and rendered according to new style specifications, for example, the color and thickness of different components can be altered; a different color could be used for the stick than for the blob. This method is much more powerful than trying to change attribute values of the XML elements themselves.

Here is the code for a design grid with 7 columns and 8 rows:

```
<grid>
    <height>50</height>
    <width>75</width>
    <cols>7</cols>
    <rows>8</rows>
</grid>
```

An object can be placed on this grid with this markup:

```
<position col="3" row="2"></position>
```

The object can then be angled, filled, offset, and so forth. To change the colour of the strokes of an object, the code is as follows:

```
<stroke color="blue"></stroke>
```

Objects can be shaped by using any of the standard SVG properties.

*Figure 4. A quarter note*

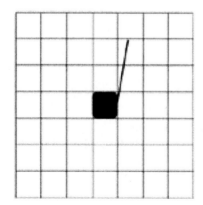

Here is example code of a quarter note with green strokes, orange fill, and a tilted line.

```
<symbol>
    <rectangle>
        <position col="5" row="3" />
        <size cols="1" rows="1" />
        <angle>20</angle>
        <stroke color="green" />
        <fill color="orange" />
        <rounded x="20" y="20" />
    </rectangle>
    <line>
        <stroke color="green" />
        <angle>20</angle>
        <length>2</length>
        <updown>up</updown>
        <strokewidth>3</strokewidth>
    <line>
</symbol>
```

By changing just single descriptors, the visual result can be quite dramatic. Figure 5 is a collage of screenshots of some sample designs of possible variations of CWMN symbols where minor changes in attribute values of the individual symbols have interesting results. This collage of screenshots shows several different notes on different grids. Grid lines are not visible in this reproduction, but the individual note glyph offsets from the horizontal plane should give an indication of how space could be used within grids. Not shown here is the mapping or association of different grids to one another. These examples show the design of individual music symbols. When used within a composition, they are aligned with reference to a larger score grid, according to the axes of 3-D Music Space.

The Design Grid, as well as the symbols designed on it, is vector based, and can be imported as objects into the already existing MML code for the rendering of music by SVG. Although no symbols from other cultural music writing systems are included in the examples above, any possible shape that can be described with the SVG shapes can be expressed on the Music Symbol Design Grid, and then used by an application with an SVG plug-in to express the marked data. These visually expressive symbols function as a layer on top of the basic core frequency and time-based markup, which can also be expressed audibly.

This approach ensures that with a relatively limited functioning MML Application, using standard XML-parsing and SVG engine, most cultural expressions of music, including highly experimental ones, can be handled economically without having to construct elaborative filters or interpretation engines to convert music markup to some or other visual representation. Music objects and events described in music space should be so "neutral" that they can be expressed in any of the many possible modes of expression.

*Figure 5. A collage of different CWMN symbols on their design grids, resulting in different styles when single property values are changed*

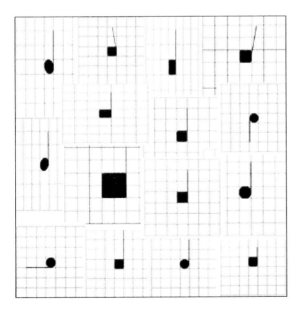

## CONCLUSION

Unlike monoplanar human language documents, music documents are much more complex. SGML/XML were designed for serial, monoplanar human language documents, so from that point of view, such markup languages are not very useful for music. Music documents that are marked on the SGML/XML model cannot be properly represented by typical parsers, so this places tremendous burdens on the application programs of XML-based music languages, and particular challenges to use this serial, monoplanar language.

In the design of a music markup language, the ontology of music determines exactly which aspects of this complex object would be regarded as logical structures to be marked. Although music is, basically, a function of frequency and time, if the approach of human writing systems is followed, it is not necessary to mark visual representations of actual sound waves. A slightly more abstract level of representation, such as provided by abstract notions of "notes," can be marked. This level of representation should, however, not be on the level of traditional notation (which is a typographical system), but more on abstract notions of notes. The reason for this is that the resulting markup can be much more economical, and can be used for a diversity of applications. Following SGML's strict distinction between an abstract logical document object model on one hand, and formatting instructions for rendering, such as visual representation, on the other hand, the result is a more economical markup, as well as the facilitation of translations of the abstract layer into any of the available cultural music notation systems. This design philosophy should result in a more economical design cycle of application systems.

The abstract level of music ontology permits dissecting music into different categories that map easily into practical modules that could be called upon, when required. The abstract core, described in terms of "frequency" (which could either be "real" frequency or relative pitches) and "time" (which could either be absolute time or relative duration), would serve as base generic and universal module that can be expressed in terms of any of the additional modules.

Markup is typically serialized on a monoplanar level, while music consists of many simultaneous layers of events. The most elegant solution is to map these layers by introducing an abstract coordinate system, such as Music Space, which is conceptually similar to the HyTime Finite-Coordinate-Space (FCS) system. In Music Space, the x-axis represents "time," the y-axis "frequency," and the z-axis simultaneous events and objects as layers.

These many layers need to be synchronized with one another. Again, this cannot be handled by a serial monoplanar parser, and an application program needs to synchronize events, but the markup should include the relevant clues and cues that the application program can use for synchronization. Again, the most elegant solution is the HyTime Finite-Coordinate-Space system, as expressed by the SMI Spine (Haus & Longari, 2002), and by the MML Music Space.

Music writing has its own unique set of symbols, and in this context, is similar to MathML. Apart from unique "character sets," the typographical layout of visual music is also much more demanding than the visual representation of human language text. For human language, there are many established character sets such as ASCII and Unicode. The demands of music are not only for existing representation systems, but also for more experimental systems. It would thus be much more practical to design a system that could incorporate any symbols, even privately designed ones. The Music Symbol Design Grid of MML, using the Music Symbol Language for designing the shape and other properties of symbols, is an attempt to address this challenge. Such an approach not only allows symbols to be designed by users, but also to change their style

relatively easily on the user side. This, again, indicates that abstract music structure should be distinguished from stylistic issues.

There are many challenges imposed by the requirements of music on an XML-based markup system. The major ones were addressed here, but there remain several more. The focus here was on challenges of marking general music characteristics that could apply to all the variations and conventions of expressing music visually, yet simultaneously account for music as audio.

## ACKNOLWEDGMENT

Thanks to Damon O'Neill, my research assistant, who developed several components of MML into a workable application, using SVG and Java. Thanks to James Ingram for many interesting conversations about the philosophy of music, particularly around issues of time. Thanks to Paolo Nesi for inviting me to participate in the ISO/MPEG workshops.

## REFERENCES

Apparao, V., Byrne, S., Champion, M., Isaacs, S., Le Hors, A., Nicol, G. et al. (1998). *DOM1: Document object model level 1*. Retrieved March 16, 2006, from http://www.w3.org/TR/REC-DOM-Level-1

Berners-Lee, T. (2000). *Weaving the Web: The past present and future of the World Wide Web by its inventor*. London: Texere.

Boll, S., Klas, U., & Westermann, W. (1999). *A comparison of multimedia document models concerning advanced requirements*. Technical Report—Ulmer Informatik-Berichte No 99-01. Department of Computer Science, University of Ulm, Germany.

Bos, B., Lie, H. W., Lilley, C., & Jacobs, I. (Eds). (1998). *Cascading style sheets, level 2*. Retrieved March 16, 2006, from http://www.w3.org/TR/REC-CSS2

Bray, T., Paoli, J., Sperberg-McQueen, C. M., & Maler, E. (1998). *Extensible markup language (XML) 1.0 (2nd ed.)*. Retrieved March 16, 2006, from http://www.w3.org/TR/REC-xml

Brueggemann-Klein, A., & Wood, D. (2004). A conceptual model for XML. In P. King & E. V. Munson (Eds.). *Digital documents: Systems and principles* (pp. 176-189). Berlin: Springer.

Carlisle, D., Ion, P., Miner, R., & Poppelier, N. (Eds.). (2003). *Mathematical markup language (MathML) version 2.0* (2nd ed.). Retrieved March 16, 2006, from http://www.w3.org/TR/2003/REC-MathML2-20031021/

Code, D. L. (2002). Grove.Max: An adaptive tuning system for MIDI Pianos. *Computer Music Journal, 26*(2), 50-61.

Ferraiolo, J. (2001). *Scalable vector graphics specification*. Retrieved March 16, 2006, from http://www.w3.org/TR/SVG

Fuss, C., Gatzemeier, F., Kirchhof, M., & Meyer, O. (2004). Inferring structure information form typography. In P. King & E. V. Munson (Eds.), *Digital documents: Systems and Principles* (pp. 44-55). Berlin: Springer.

Goldfarb C. F., & Prescod, P. (1998). *The XML handbook*. NJ: Prentice Hall.

Harris, R. (1987). *Reading Saussure*. London: Duckworth.

Haus, G., & Longari, M. (Eds.). (2002). *MAX 2002: Musical applications using XML*. In Proceedings First International Conference. Laboratoria di Informatica Musicale, Computer Science Dept, State University of Milan.

Haus, G., & Longari. M. (2002a). Towards a symbolic/time-based music language based on XML.

In G. Haus & M. Longari (Eds.). *MAX 2002: Musical applications using XML*. In *Proceedings First International Conference* (pp. 38-46). Laboratoria di Informatica Musicale, Computer Science Dept, State University of Milan.

Haus, G., & Longari. M. (2002b). Music information description by mark-up languages within DB-Web applications. In G. Haus & M. Longari (Eds.), *MAX 2002: Musical Applications using XML*. In *Proceedings First International Conference* (pp. 83-90). Laboratoria di Informatica Musicale, Computer Science Dept, State University of Milan.

Haus, G., & Longari. M. (2005). A multi-layered, time-based music description approach based on XML. *Computer Music Journal, 29*(1), 70-85.

Honing, H. (2001). From time to time: The representation of timing and tempo. *Computer Music Journal, 25*(3), 50-61.

Ingram, J. (1985, 1999). *The notation of time*. Personal copy.

Ingram, J. (2002a). *Developing traditions of music notation and performance on the Web*. Personal copy.

Ingram, J. (2002b). *Music notation*. Personal copy.

Ion, P., & Miner, R. (Eds.). (1999). *Mathematical markup language (MathML) 1.01 specification*. Retrieved March 16, 2006, from http://www.w3.org/1999/07/REC-MathML-19990707

IPA International Phonetic Association. Retrieved March 16, 2006, from http://www2.arts.gla.ac.uk/IPA/ipa.html

Le Hors, A., Le Hégaret, P., Wood, L., Nicol, G., Robie, J., Champion, M., & Byrne, S. (2000). *Document object model (DOM) level 2 core specification*. Retrieved March 16, 2006, from http://www.w3.org/TR/DOM-Level-2-Core/

Lie, H. W., & Bos, B. (1996). *Cascading style sheets, level 1*. Retrieved March 16, 2006, from http://www.w3.org/TR/REC-CSS1

Malyankar, R. (2002). *Vocabulary development for markup languages—a case study with maritime information. ACM* 1-58113-449-5/02/0005 674-685.

Mason (1997). SGML and related standards: New directions as the second decade begins. *Journal of American Society of Information Science, 48*(7) 593-596.

Newcomb, S., et al. (1995). *Standard music description language.* ISO/IEC DIS 10743. ftp://ftp.techno.com

Rastall, R. (1983). *The notation of western music.* London: J. M.Dent & Sons Ltd.

Renfrew, C., & Bahn, P. (2004). *Archaeology: Theories, methods and practice.* London: Thames & Hudson.

Saussure, F. de. (1916, 1986). *Course in general linguistics.* Translated by R. Harris. London: Duckworth.

SGML SIGhyper. (1994). A brief history of the development of SMDL and HyTime. Retrieved March, 2006, from http://www.sgmlsource.com/history/hthist.htm

Sloan, D. (1993). Aspects of music representation in HyTime/SMDL. *Computer Music Journal, 17*(4).

Sloan, D. (2002). Learning our lessons from SMDL. In G. Haus & M. Longari (Eds.). *MAX 2002: Musical applications using XML. Proceedings First International Conference* (pp. 69-73). Laboratoria di Informatica Musicale, Computer Science Dept, State University of Milan.

Sperberg-McQueen, C. M., & Huitfield, C. (2004). GODDAG: A data structure for overlapping hierarchies. In P. King & E. V. Munson (Eds.), *Digital documents: Systems and principles* (pp. 139-160). Berlin: Springer.

Steyn, J. (1999). *Music markup language.* Retrieved March 16, 2006, from http://www.musicmarkup.info/

Steyn, J. (2002). Framework for a music markup language. In G. Haus & M. Longari (Eds.), *MAX 2002: Musical applications using XML.* In *Proceedings First International Conference* (pp. 22-29). Laboratoria di Informatica Musicale, Computer Science Dept, State University of Milan

Steyn, J. (2004). *Introducing Music Space.* Retrieved March 16, 2006, from http://www.musicmarkup.info/papers/musicspace/musicspace.html

Sundberg, J. (1991) *The science of musical sounds.* New York: Academic Press, INC.

Williams, C. F. (1903, 1969). *The story of notation.* New York: Haskell House

# Chapter VII
# Alternative Design Goals for a General Music Markup Language

**Jacques Steyn**
*School of Information Technology, Monash University, South Africa*

## ABSTRACT

*Design goals determine the particular structure of a markup language, while the philosophy of what markup languages are about determine the framework within which its structure is developed. Most existing markup languages for music reflect low-level design strategies compared to design that adheres to the high level philosophy of markup languages. An approach to an XML-based music markup language, from the perspective of SGML, would differ from an approach from a markup language such as HTML. An ideal structure for a general markup language for music is proposed that follows a purist approach, and which results in a different kind of XML-based music markup language than most present music markup languages offer.*

## INTRODUCTION

Markup languages have been around for almost half a century, but have experienced an exceptional explosion in the 1990s. Prior to the World Wide Web, of which the content is primarily based on the HTML markup language, markup languages were used in isolated cases. The Web changed all that. By the turn of the century, another language from the markup family, XML, resulted in a further explosion. In the early 2000s, more than a thousand XML applications, as listed by Robin Cover (2006), had already been developed for applications ranging from chemistry, geography, numerous business related systems, to multimedia and music. Important concepts in the development of markup languages provide a framework that should be considered when designing a markup language for music. The architecture of present markup languages for music seems to suggest a lack of consideration of the foundation of markup language philosophy. This is partly to be blamed on the explosion of the World Wide Web, which is extremely forgiving to poor markup techniques. Most present XML developers have learnt the tricks of markup not from an SGML perspective, but from an HTML point of view. Important milestones in the development of markup languages are presented and then brief guidelines for an ideal structure of an XML-based language for music are presented from that perspective.

## BRIEF HISTORY OF SGML

In the late 1960s, Charles Goldfarb was commissioned by IBM to build a central system for data management, particularly for legal documents. These documents had to be stored, found, and published. Even within IBM, there were many systems that could not communicate with one another. Goldfarb, together with Ed Mosher and Ray (Raymond) Lorie, concluded that a common document representation model was needed, while the mechanism would rely on the concept of a markup language, which means that abstract logical aspects of document content would be marked with special characters that a computer could interpret to have special functions. Goldfarb remarks that the initial letters of their surnames and the name of the resulting language, GML, is not coincidental (Goldfarb, 1998).

GML documents are textual documents, and not binary documents, which makes them relatively easy to read by humans. The purpose of GML itself was to handle large and complex documents, and to manage large information repositories, while the purpose of the marking process is:

- To separate the logical elements of the document.
- To specify the processing functions to be performed on those elements.

The elements of GML were marked by embracing text with special terms, called tags, embraced by Backus-Naur Form symbols, developed in the 1960s to specify the syntax of Algol, that are distinguished from content. The validating parser was not developed until 1974, which Goldfarb regards as the proper birth of GML. In 1985, documentation was prepared to turn GML into an ISO standard. The language was eventually accepted in 1986 as Standard Generalized Markup Language (SGML, ISO 8879:1986). For more details about the history of SGML, see the SGML User's Group (1990). For some practical guidelines for SGML, see Herwijnen (1994).

SGML basically distinguishes between three aspects of a document: content, structure, and format. Content is the information used by human readers, who may not be particularly interested in the logical structure of a document, but who may be attracted to a document because of its format. The structure of a document refers to its abstract logical structure, and is particularly relevant for managing documents electronically. There are many different types of documents, and they may have different structures. The structure of a novel differs from that of a postcard or from an office memo. These structures have developed during the course of history of human writing, and have certain widely accepted traditions and conventions. SGML is particularly interested in marking this logical structure. The format of a document refers to its appearance, which is only of interest to human readers. In terms of appearance, there may be many different kinds of postcards, but they would share the same structure, such as a *To Address*, typically a picture on the front side, and an area to write on the back side, that is, for modern postcard formats. An office memo would contain *To* and *From* structural elements, but their positioning on paper (left, center, right, vertical, horizontal) and textual appearance (font character size, color, font family) may follow different formats.

## BRIEF HISTORY OF DSSSL

SGML marks the logical elements of a document (its structure), and is not particularly concerned with the appearance of a document (its format or style). To address the visual appearance of SGML documents, a *Document Style and Semantics Specification Language* (DSSSL, 1996: ISO 10179) was developed and is used for publishing intricate designs. Its syntax is based on the Scheme programming language. DSSSL style sheets are written in a schema-like language. In such a style sheet, an element is declared, and its formatting instructions listed as keywords that could take various predefined values. A keyword could be used, for example, for the distance of the element's top margin, and in this case would be "top-margin" followed by the value of the distance, say 2cm. The anchor location, which is used as reference point from which the distance should be measured, would depend on a higher level style, which is often defined not in the style sheet, but by conventional rules built into processors.

A DSSSL processor builds a tree from the source document, very much along the lines of a document object model (DOM). The processor starts with the document root, then processes down the nodes.

DocBook is an SGML document type definition and has an XML version available (Walsh & Muellner, 1999). It is used for "books," that typically follow the similar logical structures. Some of the DocBook elements of books are *Author, AuthorBlurb, Abstract, BiblioEntry, Bibliography, BeginPage, Blockquote,* and many more. By far the majority of books contain these components. DocBook's major concern is the structure of the content of a document, and relies on style sheet languages, such as DSSSL, for the rendering of the document. For example, it relies on a tool called Jade to apply DSSSL to a DocBook marked document.

## SGML AND DSSSL: STRUCTURE AND FORMAT

Consider the notion of a paragraph to understand the difference between structure and format. The paragraph is a printing convention of relatively recent origin. Ancient written texts have few structural distinguishers and most texts were written as long unbroken sequences. Today the most basic property of a paragraph is white space before and after it. This white space is called "leading" after an extra strip of lead that was inserted into lead printing trays to force the text of different paragraphs apart. The notion of white space is structural in terms of its mere presence in a document, while the actual distance (measured in inches, metric measures, points, or picas) of a particular paragraph instance could be any value within an acceptable range as defined by a user, in this case the layout designer. The fact that certain content should be contained in a paragraph is thus indicated by structural markup, while its specific instance properties are indicated by a style sheet. If the markup philosophy is followed by restricting content structure to be handled by SGML and formatting by DSSSL, then in XML design the XML markup should handle document structure, leaving formatting and typographical issues to a style-sheet language.

One reason for the introduction of a strict distinction between structure and format is to facilitate data display on the many different types of computing devices on the market that handle information differently. Also, if content and appearance are separated, it is very easy to render the same content with different appearance by merely changing the style sheet without having to edit the entire document for each new style. If a document's structure is marked quite apart from its formatting, its content could theoretically be shared by any and by many devices. It would be possible to attach any style sheet of a user's liking to that document and the document would not become inaccessible because of mixing structure and format.

This philosophy worked well until one of the children of SGML, namely HTML, particularly Version 3.2, became a *de facto* standard in 1996. This version confused structure and format. Although there was an attempt to rectify this with HTML 4 (Raggett, Le Hors, & Jacobs, 1999), unfortunately, most Web authors are self-taught, and do not obtain HTML authoring skills via the SGML route. HTML is a very low-level application of SGML, while CSS (Cascading Style Sheets—Bos, Lie, Lilley, &Jacobs, 1998; Lie & Bos, 1996), introduced by the W3C as companion to HTML and XML, particularly XSL, is a simplified child of DSSSL. Given the billions of Web pages out there, most based on no proper distinction between structure and format, this mess will remain with us; a mess in the sense that the content of these documents cannot be reused, both with regards to their structure and their appearance. As most XML authors get into the markup world through HTML, this mess will probably continue in the area of designing XML applications.

## BRIEF HISTORY OF HyTime AND SMDL

In 1984, Charles Goldfarb proposed an extension to the concept of GML to include multimedia documents. In 1985, IBM and Stanford University's Center for Computer Research in Music and Acoustics (CCRMA) held a workshop with 32 participants from the music industry, and produced a document (ANSI X3 SD3-542D, 1985/06/21) that describes several music and hypermedia applications that cannot be handled by SGML:

- Music publishing using modern text processing technology, including the integration of music with text and graphics.

- Business presentations involving customized text, graphics, and music.
- Computer-assisted instruction with music and sound effects employed to enhance communication and to sustain the student's interest.
- Music education systems that sense the student's playing, provide feedback, and adapting the course materials to the student's rate of progress.
- Inclusion of musical performances and soft-copy "sheet music" as part of the product mix for electronic information distribution via teletext and videotext, as well as enhancement of nonmusical product (and advertisements) by musical accompaniment (SGML SIGhyper, 1994).

Development of SDML started after this meeting, but the time synchronization aspect was eventually separated as a more generic aspect of multimedia documents; hence, *HyTime* was developed, which focuses on linking mechanisms within the complex dimensions of multimedia events (DeRose & Durand, 1994; Ferris, 1995; Newcomb et al., 1995). HyTime distinguishes between the objects that need to be linked, and the linking mechanism itself. SDML, on the other hand, focuses more on music-specific aspects. It distinguishes between a logical domain (for structural content), gestural domain (for performance-related aspects), visual domain (for the visual rendering of the logical domain, such as for notation symbols), and an analytical domain (for scholarly and theoretical analyses of music compositions). In the logical domain, the "cantus" represents one axis of the HyTime Finite-Coordinate-Space (FCS) concept, and serves to link modes such as simultaneous and overlapping events (the *thread* child element), lyrics, other FCSs, and sound modification techniques (such as modulation and filters).

In order to deal with multiple multimedia events that occur on different planes within the same timeframe and that simultaneously need to be synchronized with one another, HyTime introduces a finite-coordinate-space (FCS) module onto which multimedia events are mapped. Any number of dimensions can be mapped on the FCS, including time dimensions. Events are placed at points within the FCS; HyTime is thus a point-based timing system. HyTime distinguishes between *musical time* and *real time*. Real time is concrete time and typically clock based. Musical time is an abstract time system where units are relative to one another. Musical time can thus apply to fragments of CWN notation with relative note values, and for which absolute time values are unknown. Both these systems can be applied and synchronized with one another.

Perhaps due to its complicated approach, neither SDML nor HyTime are widely used. Sloan (2002) points out that SDML is essentially a DTD for HyTime, which made it a bit complicated for nontechnical users. While those involved in the initial project changed focus to make HyTime commercially available, nothing much happened on the debugging of the standard. Meanwhile software companies, such as SCORE and ENIGMA, had their own information format and commercial goals, with the result that the technical deficiencies of SDML were never fixed. Since then the World Wide Web exploded, XML entered the arena with new demands, and SDML faded away. Unfortunately, most current XML music applications focus on music typography and ignore the tremendously powerful insights provided by SDML and HyTime. Apart from the SMI (Symbolic Music Information, Haus & Longari, 2002a, 2002b) and MML (Steyn, 1999) applications, none of the present generation of XML-based music applications with public descriptions make use of a coordinate system similar to FCS.

## BRIEF HISTORY OF HTML

To put XML in perspective, it is necessary to very briefly consider the contribution of HTML as it was specifically developed to make the World Wide Web possible, as historically XML followed on the success of HTML.

The concept of HTML was developed by Tim Berners-Lee in 1989 at CERN (European Nuclear Research Facility). HTML 0.0 was made available in 1990 as a much-simplified SGML application, but without validating rules. HTML element types are generalized and descriptive like SGML, and unlike formatting constructs typically found in word processors. HTML 4.x cannot be extended by users beyond the approximately predefined 80 elements, and its marking requirements were not very strict either. Nevertheless, its ease of implementation is one of the major factors resulting in the explosion of the World Wide Web. The first "extension" to HTML was introduced by Netscape in the early 1990s as formatting instructions, such as "center" for centering the layout of a text fragment. This confusion of logical structure and format for appearance was of course a huge mistake.

Following on Netscape's success of introducing new elements, different browser developers began to add their own formatting HTML elements, as the popular audience was used to colour TV and "demanded" Web documents that looked better than 80 character long text lines on the then standard grey background. An intolerable situation developed where elements of one browser could not be understood by another. In order to prevent this situation from developing into total chaos, the W3C decided in 1996 to accept the then *status quo* as the *de facto* "standard" and named it HTML 3.2. Unfortunately, this version of HTML did not follow the SGML philosophy of distinguishing the logical structure of a document from its visual rendering and formatted appearance. Later there was an attempt to rectify this, but the damage had been done. The HTML 4.0 Recommendation was released on 17 Dec 1998 (Raggett et al., 1999), and specifically stated that the "wrong" elements and attributes are deprecated and that style sheets, particularly CSS, should be used for formatting purposes. CSS 1.0 was released on 17 Dec 1996 and CSS 2.0 on 12 May 1998 (Bos et al., 1998; Lie & Bos, 1996). In practice, today, almost a decade later, very few Web documents have implemented this philosophy. What makes matters worse is that many involved in XML development seem to be unaware of this development in HTML 4.x of distinguishing between content and format. There is a consistent confusion between what the logical structure of a document should be and how it should be rendered. In order to introduce HTML to the much stricter world of XML, XHTML was developed (Altheim & McCarron, 2001; Pemberton & Austin et al., 2000 ). XHTML is basically HTML made stricter to comply with XML requirements.

An HTML 4.x (and XHTML 1.x) document is parsed as follows. The text string is passed through the HTML parser, which processes its logical structure, and then renders it by consulting a style engine. This rendering is typically done visually in a Web browser, but could also be done audibly with a text-to-speech synthesizer. CSS 2 in fact contains several properties to describe aural media (Bos et al., 1998).

*Figure 1. The basic parsing and rendering process within an HTML 4 plus CSS environment*

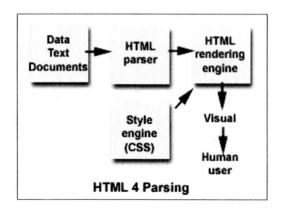

## BRIEF HISTORY OF XML

HTML 4.x consists of 80 predefined elements that are used for the logical representation of the structure of documents. This limited set of elements places severe restrictions on the semantic management of Web content. XML was developed to address some shortcomings of HTML. Jon Bosak summarises the reason why XML was developed as follows:

- **Extensibility:** HTML does not allow users to specify their own tags or attributes in order to parameterize or otherwise semantically qualify their data.
- **Structure:** HTML does not support the specification of deep structures needed to represent database schemas or object-oriented hierarchies.
- **Validation:** HTML is very forgiving and, in practice, basically anything goes, as such documents are not validated (Bosak, 1997).

A W3C SGML workgroup, headed by Jon Bosak, was formed in 1996 to sort out the messy situation HTML found itself in. The goal of the group was to maintain the simplicity of HTML, but to follow the design philosophy of SGML. As this new language would be neither HTML, nor SGML, a new name was needed. Tim Bray (1998) lists the following as some of the names that had been considered: MGML (minimal generalized markup language), SLIM (structured language for internet markup), MAGMA (minimal architecture for generalized markup language), and of course the eventual winner, XML (extensible markup language). XML was, basically, HTML made more SGML-compliant, with extended functionality. XML is HTML on steroids.

In 1997, Bert Bos also wrote the following guidelines for XML, which are basically a rewording of what became the "official" specifications for XML:

- It must be a language that can encode any hierarchical structure in a straightforward way.
- It must be human readable itself, at least to the point that a file in this format can be "debugged" with a text editor.
- It must be particularly suited to marking up documents that are, for the most part, human-readable text (and the marked-up document must still be human readable) .
- When it is used for other documents (databases, knitting patterns, vector graphics) it should not have too much overhead, compared to formats based on predicate logic, S-expressions, or similar.
- It must have a simple grammar and lexical structure, so a parser for it can be written in one day. (This will allow people to write ad-hoc tools and throwaway applications with very little cost.)

These design goals make the design of XML applications quite simple, but its simplicity is also its downfall, as designers now turn everything and anything into XML without understanding the notion of the abstract document structure that should actually be marked.

Tim Bray and CM Sperberg-McQueen wrote most of the original XML specification document, assisted by Paoli and Maler. (Bray, Paoli, Sperberg-McQueen, & Maler, 1998). Prior to this project, Bray worked on the New Oxford English Dictionary Project, and based on the weaknesses of systems then available, he wished to address better solutions in XML.

Although XML is an abbreviated form of SGML, the latter, on one hand, provided many features that were unnecessary for Web purposes, but on the other hand, lacked some network-specific requirements that would be necessary for the Web environment. XML was designed as a metalanguage to make SGML easy and straightforward to use on the Web. The design goal was to make it easy to define documents, to author them, to manage them, to transmit them, and to share them on the Web. It was designed to be interoperable with both SGML and HTML. Given this context, XML is based on the design goals of SGML, but added some functionality.

It was envisaged that XML would:

- Provide database interchange.
- Assist with distributed programming.
- Make it possible for users to decide on how they want to view the data.
- Enable Web agents to pinpoint relevant information.

This vision was based on the notion of the "Semantic Web," driven by the founder of the Web, Tim Berners-Lee (2000).

According to Goldfarb and Prescod (1998), XML is used for the digital representation of documents, implying some kind of computer-readable code to facilitate their storage, processing, searching, transmitting, displaying, and printing. In multimedia XML documents, the XML would not represent the multimedia components. These components will be references and their processing will be done by "native" applications that are specially built to render the data of the specific format. This is because XML merely marks a document's content structure and is not concerned with delivery. This also implies that there are many aspects of a multimedia document that XML cannot render. In order to render audio or typographical aspects of a multimedia document, special applications need to be built that can handle those functions. XML thus focuses on data structures, not on delivery.

XML for visual use is parsed in much the same way as HTML, while its style engine is based on XSL (Adler, Berglund et al., 2001), which includes visual formatting instructions based on CSS 2.0. XSL itself is an XML application and consists of three components: XSLT (Clark, 1999), XPath (Clark & DeRose, 1999) and XSL-FO. For some comments on the early developments of XML,

*Figure 2. The basic parsing and rendering process within an XML plus XSL environment*

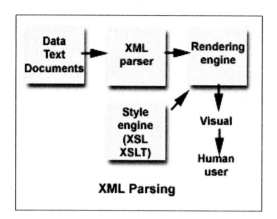

see Bos (1997). For important background information on why certain decisions were made in the XML specification document, see Bray et al. (1998). Also, see an interpretation of XML by the original author of SGML, Goldfarb (Goldfarb & Prescod, 1998). The XML FAQ maintained by Flynn (1999) also gives a good indication of some of the early issues of XML.

The XML standard recommendation focuses on the sequential visual expression of data in text format. Any compliant XML parser will be able to express XML data visually when used in a browser environment. That is the standard approach to XML data for client-side rendering. As music involves other dimensions, a standard XML parser may be able to parse the data, but the result would be useless to a human user. No matter whether the data is to be rendered visually or audibly, an additional application will nevertheless be required to handle this. Such an application program will need to interpret the XML data and render it according to predefined rules built into the application. Ideally the rules should be included in the data, while the application does as little as possible work, otherwise the value of data exchange between different applications is minimal. Unfortunately, most of the present XML applications depend more on the filters

and interpretative engine of the application that the data is mostly useless to other applications without elaborate filtering. I suspect that this is due to the fact that the ontological object chosen by most XML applications for music focuses on the typography of Common Western Music Notation, and not on a more universal or abstract notion of the object of music.

It is possible to visually display XML data with a standard browser along similar lines as HTML is displayed. That was one of the design goals of XML. The XML language is of course much more powerful and is today used on all levels of data management on networks, such as data filtering, instructions to networked computers, data exchange, communications, and more. Today there is hardly a domain of computing that has not been adapted to XML. For any XML document that requires more functionality than a mere extension of HTML-like functionality, some programming is required. A programming module can be inserted in any of the nodes, visualised as boxes in Figure 2. On the client side, much of the programming functionality will be operating on the rendering engine as a browser plug-in.

The XML recommendation had hardly been published when numerous XML-based languages were announced. The first XML languages were chemical markup language or CML (by Peter Murray-Rust) and MathML, developed by several companies and which became a W3C Recommendation much later. Today there are many thousands of XML applications, including several for music.

## SMIL, VERY BRIEFLY

The *synchronized multimedia integration language* (SMIL) is an XML application for interactive multimedia documents released by the W3C (Bulterman, Grassel, Jansen, Koivisto, Layaïda, Michel, et al., 2005; Hoschka, 1998). SMIL allows the control of multimedia objects as wholes. For example, clips can be started, paused, stopped, and synchronized. SMIL was thus designed to control whole objects, and not their internal properties. A general music markup language also needs to address the internal properties of music objects. I therefore distinguish between the extrinsic music properties for control issues, such as start and stop, and intrinsic music properties that describe the micro properties of objects, such as the individual notes within a song, or the instruments associated with MIDI. Such intrinsic details cannot be described by SMIL, and there was thus a gap in XML applications for music that could handle such detail.

## BRIEF OVERVIEW OF XML MUSIC APPLICATIONS

Some early discussions about markup, music, and the Web, can be found in Pennycook (1995a, 1995b). Robin Cover's Cover Pages: XML and Music (2006) lists a number of XML applications for music. I have been following this list since 1999, and several of the Web sites of the entries no longer exist, but are cached on Cover's site. This site is unfortunately not a good source for the history of music markup languages, as in many cases only the latest posting is published on the main page, and not all archived files are linked. For example, postings to the site about MML prior to 2002 are not linked. The brief history presented here is based on my own notes that I have kept over the past few years and there may be gaps, and perhaps even wrong dates, and some may no longer be accessible with their original content.

To my knowledge, the first XML applications for music were Jeroen van Rotterdam's MusicML and R.J Grigaitis' XScore, or eXtensible Score language (Grigaitis,1998; Van Rotterdam, 1998). MusicML's DTD was published in October of 1998, while XScore's draft was published in December 1998, within a couple of months after the publication of the XML 1.0 Recommendation in February of 1998 (Bray et al., 1998). MusicML was an attempt to develop an XML application for sheet music, XScore, as it name indicates, focused on music score. Both these thus focus on the notation system of Common Western Music Notation (CWMN). MusicML requires a Java-enabled browser, and displays only relatively simple notation on a single staff.

In January 1999, Gustavo Frederico released ChordML (also based on CWMN), which as its name indicates, focuses on music chords. It serves as an abbreviated music notation, and includes reference to lyrics and metadata. Frederico later also developed ChordQL for finding chords (Frederico, 1999).

In February 1999, MML was developed by Jacques Steyn (Steyn, 1999; also see 2002, 2004). MML is the most ambitious of all the XML-based music markup languages as it attempts to describe and incorporate all aspects of music in a comprehensive, yet economical manner. It includes a notation module for symbolic representation of music that is regarded as merely one of the possible renderable layers of music. Its approach to music is also different from other XML music applications as the notation layer is handled separately from what is called the core of music events and objects, described in terms of a function of frequency and time. The ontology chosen by MML differs thus quite extensively from the other XML applications that have been developed.

In 2000, the MusicXML definition was released by Michael Good and MusiXML by Gerd Castan (Castan, 2000; Good 2000, 2002). Both MusicXML and MusiXML focus on music notation. FlowML, released by Bert Schiettecatte, also in 2000, is a format for storing synthesis diagrams and their supporting mechanisms to exchange virtual musical instruments between several (non) realtime software synthesizers (Schiettecatte, 2000).

In 2001, 4ML (music and lyrics markup language) was released by Leo Montgomery, and EMNML (enhanced musical notation markup language) by Eric Mosterd, which focuses on sheet music to be transferred via the internet (Montgomery, 2001; Mosterd, 2001).

WEDELMUSIC (undated) is another ambitious development and although its core is based on CWMN, its aim is to address aspects of music such as its management (e.g., distribution) and as a tool for music analysis. It incorporates several multimedia concepts.

Other related applications based on XML are the MEI (music encoding initiative) DTD of Perry Roland, which was developed in 2001 along the lines of the TEI (Text Encoding Initiative) and focusing on music archiving (Roland, 2001, 2002). MuTaTeD (Music Tagging Type Definition), by Carola Boehm (undated), focuses on music metadata.

Today a host of other XML applications for music exist, ranging from mLAN (see undated reference) to adaptations of other commonly used formats (such as MIDI and NIFF) to XML. JScoreML (David Weinkauf - undated) is a Java application, focuses on the music score with MIDI capabilities. MusiqueXML (François Chastanet - undated) uses SVG for displaying CWMN. VMML (virtual musician markup language) of Damien Tardieu (undated), focuses on gestures for virtual musicians.

Another somewhat different approach is that of SMI (symbolic music information) of Goffredo Haus and Maurizio Longari with which they attempt to link audio files with notation (Haus & Longari 2002a, 2002b). SMI adapts the HyTime finite-coordinate-space (FCS) module by introducing a Spine, which acts as the synchronization method between virtual time units and virtual logic position units. The Spine is used to uniquely identify events on a temporal node. This serves to synchronize music notation and audio, such as soundwave files. SMI is thus a very powerful XML application, and its interest is not so much in a music notation system as in its relation to sound waves.

Most XML applications for music focus on the visual representation of music, and more specifically the typographical representation of common western music notation (CWMN) and variations thereof, such as chords. The exceptions are SMI, MML, FlowML (which focuses on synthesis diagrams) and some aspects (such as lyrics, video, distribution, and classification) of WEDELMUSIC, as well as music-related applications such as mLAN and MIDI XML. Marked music that needs to be rendered as a score or as a filter for some audio generator is much more complex than any of the XML applications built for linear, monodimensional data strings. Single music events and objects that can only be described serially with XML need to be rendered simultaneously on several layers in a synchronized fashion. This means that a standard XML parser cannot handle an XML-marked music document. This functionality thus has to be built into the program application.

Most XML applications for music have elaborate application engines, while their XML music cannot be handled by standard XML-enabled

*Figure 3. The basic parsing and rendering process within an XML plus XSL environment, with a music application*

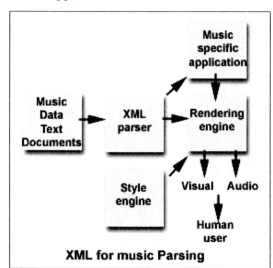

browsers; no content is displayed. The XML of MML as text is still usable even if no application software is available. It renders music events similarly to a simplified jazz score (see Figure 4).

## IDEAL STRUCTURE OF XML FOR MUSIC

XML is a metalanguage based on strict SGML requirements and design philosophy, and may be used to express *any* string of text. There could be as many approaches to a particular object to be described as there are XML application developers. There is no right or wrong serving as guideline to decide between different designs of markup languages. An XML element could be literally anything in the universe that is expressible in human language, including nonconventional "words" such as "*zbrnk*," "*pflik*," or whatever, which could be used as element names. The details of a specific design of an XML language depend on its design goals. The following criteria apply to the design of an XML-based music markup language:

1.  The object of description should be universal and not culture specific; thus not be biased toward CWMN.
2.  Popular use of music should be in focus and not be foreign or difficult to nonmusicologist users.
3.  A standard Web browser with an XML parser should be able to render the core sufficiently enough to be intelligible if no application is available.
4.  Structural content of music should form the core of a music markup language, while rendering, visual or audio, should be handled separately, perhaps as additional modules.
5.  It must be possible to render the markup in any of the available cultural music writing systems, not only CWMN.

6.  Use technologies within the XML-family as far as possible, without too much dependence on add-ons.
7.  Economy of markup should be a goal.

## 1. Universal Music

The design of any XML application depends on which dataset among many possibilities in the universe is described and marked. Exactly what constitutes a good and universal object for music is discussed in another contribution to this book, *Challenges of designing a markup language for music*. It is my contention that an XML-based music markup language should be able to handle all aspects of music in a culturally neutral way. In order to achieve this, I propose that the physics of music, such as presented by Sundberg (1991), should form the basis of a universal music markup language. But just as human language writing characters do not represent sound acoustics faithfully, yet are very efficient to communicate, I maintain that the same level of abstraction would be sufficient for a music markup language. In other words, it is not necessary to mark the exact shape of a sinusoidal complex wave. A symbolic summarised representation, as is done in CWMN (using symbols such as *A...G*) is sufficient. It is of course possible to develop an XML-based language to describe sinusoidal complex waves. That would only interest a small section of a population of users.

## 2. Popular Interest

The Web made information sharing and access democratic, and one of its driving forces was an extremely simplified child of SGML, namely HTML. The parent SGML is most suitable for highly complex document environments, and due to this complexity, mainly used by professionals. HTML is so simple and easy that anyone with a little computer knowledge and a text editor could create a Web page, which is even easier to do with basic application authoring programs.

The same should happen to music. An XML application of music should enable nonprofessionals to distribute, create, play, and organize music. Such applications should not only enable users to manage extrinsic music, as provided by an SMIL-enabled player, but also the intrinsic music events of a piece of music. Extrinsic music management is done by selecting prerecorded songs, playing them and performing other controls such as rewinding, forwarding, adding effects, and so on. Intrinsic music management would apply to manipulating music events within a song by either viewing it in a written format (such as in CWMN), or by associating it with another music sound (such as can be done with a software MIDI sequencer, for example, by changing a piano sound to a saxophone sound). This cannot be done presently with XML applications based on CMWN. It can be done with the prototype developed for MML.

Western European musicologists are very biased to common western music notation, yet music is practiced in all cultures, while many have their own music writing systems. Even in the West, knowledge of music notation is limited among nonspecialist citizens. There are excellent virtuoso musicians that cannot even read CWMN, such as in the jazz environment where jazz scores are used, or in the pop music environment where simplified notation is used for vocals along with chords that instrumentalists must interpret along the lines of a jazz score. In terms of quantity of usage, there are probably more musicians of this type in the world than classically trained musicians who have good knowledge of CWMN. Just as HTML democratized the use of text documents, an XML-based language for music should democratize the use of music on the Web.

One practical implication of this is that a strict distinction should be made between the core of music and its visual rendering. Complex scores need to be interpreted by the musician and/or

conductor. This interpretation is guided by years of training in music notation conventions. A score is thus never a precise rendering of the audio music composition, or what a composer had in mind. A markup language should allow for this. A user should be allowed to select the level of complexity she wants to view. This implies a relatively simple core of music events, with layer on layer of complexity added at each iteration. Such an approach further implies that a modular approach should be followed in the design of a music markup language.

## 3. Standard Web Browser

Another implication of catering for the general Web population is that the core of music should be renderable with a standard XML-enabled Web browser without the requirement of an additional program or plug-in. Users who demand much more sophistication can apply specialized applications, but still use the same basic marked document. In this regard, MML is the only known XML for music application that can render core music in simple text format in a standard XML-compliant browser without the need of any additional software. Music events are expressed in a simplified character symbol system, following CWMN's *A...G* convention. This is done by expressing the core of music as CDATA content of base elements rather than attribute values, which is what all the other XML music applications do. Here is a screenshot of the rendering of Chopin's *Trois Nocturne* when no plug-in is available; obviously it follows the MML convention of presenting pitch and duration.

Due to the different cultural systems of visual symbols of music (i.e., notation systems), and other peculiarities of music as opposed to text, such as simultaneous events, synchronized events, the dual-mode delivery of music as visuals as well as audio, and audio aspects such as tuning systems and note sets (such as octaves and other combinations), a music-specific XML application needs to

*Figure 4. How MML renders CDATA when no plug-in is available. A snippet from Chopin's Trois Nocturne.*

```
5(B C D An B) G
   [F:4]4 G F E C F
     Larghetto
   D:2 B:4 5(B C D An B A Gs A C B Gb) C
   F G En F 5(B An Ab) Gn Gb F Eb Dn Db C D C Bn C F En Eb C F
```

interpret the XML document content by applying filters and translation tables on many different layers. The full complement of music can thus never be achieved through a simple XML parser and browser alone, as additional applications will need to drive all these other complications. Of course it makes no difference to such an application whether such data is CDATA as content of an element, or whether it is the value of an attribute, but it does make a difference to the nonsophisticated end-user. For usability purposes, it makes more sense to make the core music information available to standard browsers than to capture these features as attribute values.

## 4. Structural Content

An XML-based music language should focus on the structural content of music and leave its visual expression to either a subdomain of XML, or to a style-sheet language, or to a combination of both. If this approach is followed, it would be relatively easy to change the core logical music to any possible design requirements facilitate its translation into any of the many possible symbolic music systems available.

Of course typographical music symbols also have structure, and it is possible to develop XML-based languages to express these music symbols, as most of the XML applications thus far developed, show. But this would be similar

to developing a font descriptor language (such as found in CSS2), while marking the logical structure of the music document on a much higher level is not addressed. Such approaches do not result in economical markup code, and neither do they address music ontology on a high enough level of abstraction.

## 5. Cultural Music Writing Systems

If the XML application marks neutral abstract music events, it should be relatively easy to associate any existing cultural symbols, or any symbols yet to be created, with that abstract structure. The reasoning for this is as follows. Music is primarily an auditory music enterprise. The same soundwave melody can be written down in many different notation systems, ranging from CWMN (Rastall, 1983; Williams, 1903/1969) to piano roll representations and the *sol fa* system, or any of the other culturally available systems, as illustrated in Fig. 5. With the exception of CWMN and a few other systems, most music writing systems cannot handle polyphonic music, which would obviously make it impossible to represent a complex symphony score in such systems, but the basic melody line should be expressible in such systems. It should thus be possible to render the same markup fragment in any of the many possible visual representation systems, based on a common abstract core of music.

*Figure 5. Expressing the same marked abstract logical structure of music with a variety of music writing systems*

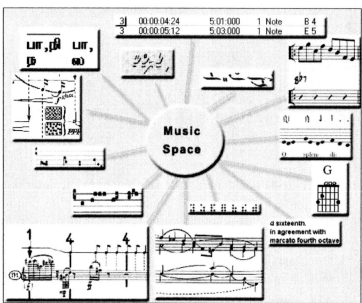

## 6. XML-Family

The "XML-family" refers not to applications built with XML, but to a core set of related basic applications (which are actually themselves XML applications) to make possible quite sophisticated products, except of course music. The mother of all is of course XML, the metalanguage itself, while other members of the family are strictly speaking XML-based applications and include XSL, consisting of XSLT (Clark, 1999), Xlink (DeRose, Maler, Orchard, & Trafford, 2001), Xpath (Clark & DeRose, 1999), Schema (Biron, Permanente, & Malhotra 2004; Thompson, Beech, Maloney, & Mendelsohn, 2004) and their related core, such as the DOM (Apparao, Byrne, Champion et al., 1998; Le Hors, Le Hégaret, Wood, Nicol, Robie, Champion, Byrne, 2000). In addition to this family, there is a basic group of cousins that should be considered: SMIL (Bulterman et al., 2005; Hoschka, 1998;), and SVG (Ferraiolo, 2001).

Presently not a single available browser supports the entire XML-family, with the Mozilla project the closest to supporting all the features. This of course means that a music markup language that wishes to implement features not yet implemented in browsers will not work in its intended way.

## 7. Economy of Markup

There is much less markup code when XML tags handle only logical structure, and a style sheet the appearance of a document. There is a simple reason for this. In a style sheet, the appearance properties are listed once, and can be applied infinite times to an infinite number of documents. If the style sheet language is also of the cascading type, only exceptions to the default need to be specified. On the other hand, if appearance features are attributes of elements, they need to be made explicit at each instance of the element, which results in tons of unnecessary code, and which results in an editing nightmare when values need to be changed. An informal comparison between these approaches shows a manifold saving on code if a style-sheet approach is followed as opposed to an approach marking attribute values in each instance. The reader can test this very simply by saving a document created with a word processor as an HTML file (most word processors will do this following the deprecated HTML 3.2 method), and then clean the code with any of the many available tools that implement CSS, such as Dave Ragget's HTML Tidy tool, available at the W3C's Web site. Now compare the original file size with the new file size. Results will vary according to the number of styles applied within the document, but I have personally reduced a 200Kb file to less than 60Kb by just implementing a style sheet properly. By using an external style sheet, the file size can be further reduced and then reused by an infinite number of files; the same applies to XML. By using an external style sheet, all music scores of the same type could be printed easily following the same style sheet. This method also facilitates the management of styles, as a change in style needs only be applied to the single instance in the style sheet, and the result immediately applies to an infinite number of documents linked to that style sheet file.

in an efficient and economical manner; complex and elaborate filtering and translation applications are required to do this.

MML is the exception among XML applications for music as it approaches the object of music from quite a different angle. Its core can be rendered with standard XML-compliant browsers in a manner similarly to a jazz score, while its additional modules and layers are powerful enough to allow for idiosyncratically designed music symbols in vector format, and which can be used to express the core of markup, all by using established standards such as SVG and CSS. The application engine for MML is thus lightweight and renders aspects handled by standard technologies.

If structure and formatting are separated strictly, as is done in the world of SGML and DSSSL, an XML application for music can handle much more than only the typographical notation of CWMN. Such an approach would result in an economic core set of elements that could be rendered for many different purposes and in many different formats, including the many possible different cultural music writing systems.

## CONCLUSION

The design goals of SGML were briefly considered. XML is a subset of SGML and therefore, the design goals of SGML should, in principal, also apply to XML, while accepting that the specific design goals of XML are more restricted on one hand, and on another extended. The general design philosophy of separating content and format should nevertheless apply to both.

Most XML applications for music focus on CWMN, more specifically, the typography of CWMN. There is, of course, nothing wrong with such an approach. The problem is merely that an approach biased toward CWMN typography cannot handle the varieties of music writing systems, nor can they be easily adapted for other purposes

## REFERENCES

Adler, S., Berglund, A., *et al.* (2001). *Extensible stylesheet language (XSL) Version 1.0.* Retrieved March 16, 2006, from http://www.w3.org/TR/xsl/

Apparao, V., Byrne, S., Champion, M., Isaacs, S., Le Hors, A., Nicol, G. et al. (1998). *DOM1: Document object model level 1.* Retrieved March 16, 2006, from http://www.w3.org/TR/REC-DOM-Level-1

Altheim, M., & McCarron, S. (2001). *XHTML 1.1—Module-based XHTML.* Retrieved March 16, 2006, from http://www.w3.org/TR/xhtml111

Berners-Lee, T. (2000). *Weaving the Web: The past, presend and future of the World Wide Web by its inventor*. London: Texere.

Biron, P. V., Permanente, K., & Malhotra, A. (Eds.). (2004). *XML schema part 2: Datatypes* (2nd ed.). Retrieved March 16, 2006, from http://www.w3.org/TR/xmlschema-2/

Boehm, C. (undated) *MuTaTeD (Music Tagging Type definition)*. Retrieved March 16, 2006, from http://www.music.gla.ac.uk/CMT/projects/MuTaTeD1/mutated.html

Bos, B. (1997). *Some thoughts and software on XML*. Retrieved March 16, 2006, from http://www.w3.org/XML/notes.html

Bos, B., Lie, H. W., Lilley, C., & Jacobs, I. (Eds). (1998). *Cascading style sheets, level 2*. Retrieved from http://www.w3.org/TR/REC-CSS2

Bosak, J. (1997). *XML, Java, and the future of the Web*. Retrieved from http://www.ibiblio.org/pub/sun-info/standards/xml/why/xmlapps.htm

Bosak, J. (1998). Media-independent publishing: Four myths about XML. *IEEE Computer, 31*(10), 120-122.

Bray, T. (1998). *Annotated XML specification*. Retrieved March 16, 2006, from http://www.xml.com/axml/testaxml.htm

Bray, T., Paoli, J., Sperberg-McQueen, C. M., & Maler, E. (1998). *Extensible markup language (XML) 1.0* (2nd ed.). Retrieved from http://www.w3.org/TR/REC-xml

Bulterman, D., Grassel, G., Jansen, J., Koivisto, A., Layaïda, N., Michel, T., Mullender, S., & Zucker, D. (Eds.). (2005). *Synchronized multimedia integration language (SMIL 2.1)*. Retrieved from http://www.w3.org/TR/2005/CR-SMIL2-20050513/

Castan, G. (2000). *MusiXML*. Retrieved March 16, 2006, from http://www.music-notation.info/en/musixml/MusiXML.html

Chastanet, F. (undated) *MusiqueXML* Retrieved March 16, 2006, from http://francois.chastanet.free.fr/musiquexml/MusiqueXML.htm

Clark, J. (1999). *XSL transformations (XSLT) Version 1.0*. Retrieved from http://www.w3.org/TR/1999/REC-xslt-19991116

Clark, J., & DeRose, S. (1999). *XML path language (Xpath) version 1.0*. Retrieved from http://www.w3.org/TR/1999/REC-xpath-19991116

Code, D. L. (2002). Grove.Max: An adaptive tuning system for MIDI pianos. *Computer Music Journal, 26*(2), 50-61.

Cover, R. (2006). *Cover pages: XML and music*. Retrieved March 16, 2006, from http://xml.coverpages.org/xmlMusic.html

DeRose, S. J., & Durand, D. G. (1994). *Making hypermedia work: A user's guide to HyTime*. Boston: Kluwer Academic.

DeRose, S. J., Maler, E., Orchard, D., & Trafford, B. (2001). *XML linking language (Xlink)*. Retrieved from http://www.w3.org/TR/xlink/

DSSSL 1996 (ISO/IEC 10179). Retrieved March, 2006, from http://www.ibiblio.org/pub/sun-info/standards/dsssl/draft/

Ferraiolo, J. (2001). *Scalable vector graphics specification*. Retrieved from http://www.w3.org/TR/SVG

Ferris, R. (1995). *A HyTime application development guide*. Retrieved from ftp://ftp.techno.com/HyTime/Application_Development_Guide

Flynn, P. (Ed.). (1999). *Frequently asked questions about the extensible markup language*. XML Special Interest Group FAQ.

Frederico, G. (1999). ChordML. Retrieved March 16, 2006, from http://www.cifranet.org/xml/ChordML.html

Goldfarb, C., Newcomb, P. J., & Kimberm, W. E. (1997). A reader's guide to the HyTime standard. Retrieved March 16, 2006, from http://www. hytime.org/papers/htguide.html

Goldfarb, C. F., & Prescod, P. (1998). *The XML handbook*. NJ: Prentice Hall.

Good, M. (2000). *MusicXML*. Retrieved March 16, 2006, from http://www.recordare.com

Good, M. (2002). MusicXML in practice: Issues in translation and analysis. In G. Haus & M. Longari (Eds.), *MAX 2002: Musical applications using XML. Proceedings First International Conference* (pp. 47-54). Laboratoria di Informatica Musicale, Computer Science Dept, State University of Milan.

Grigaitis, R. J. (1998). *XScore (eXtensible Score language)*. Retrieved March 16, 2006, from http:// grigaitis.net/xscore/

Haus, G., & Longari, M. (Eds.). (2002). *MAX 2002: Musical applications using XML*. Proceedings First International Conference. Laboratoria di Informatica Musicale, Computer Science Dept, State University of Milan.

Haus, G., & Longari. M. (2002a). *Towards a symbolic/time-based music language based on XML*. In G. Haus & M. Longari (Eds.), *MAX 2002: Musical applications using XML. Proceedings First International Conference* (pp. 38-46). Laboratoria di Informatica Musicale, Computer Science Dept, State University of Milan.

Haus, G., & Longari. M. (2002b). Music information description by mark-up languages within DB-Web applications. In G. Haus & M. Longari (Eds.), *MAX 2002: Musical applications using XML. Proceedings First International Conference* (pp. 83-90). Laboratoria di Informatica Musicale, Computer Science Dept, State University of Milan.

Haus, G., & Longari. M. (2005). A multi-layered, time-based music description approach based on XML. *Computer Music Journal, 29*(1), 70-85.

Herwijnen, E., van (1994). *Practical SGML* (2nd ed.). Boston: Kluwer Academic.

Hoschka, P. (1998). *Synchronized multimedia integration language (SMIL) 1.0 specification*. Retrieved from http://www.w3.org/TR/REC-smil

Le Hors, A., Le Hégaret, P., Wood, L., Nicol, G., Robie, J., Champion, M., & Byrne, S. (2000). *Document object model (DOM) level 2 core specification*. Retrieved from http://www.w3.org/ TR/DOM-Level-2-Core/

Lie, H. W., & Bos, B. (1996). *Cascading style sheets, level 1*. Retrieved from http://www.w3.org/ TR/REC-CSS1

Mason, J. D. (1997). SGML and related standards: New directions as the second decade begins. *Journal of American Society of Information Science, I*(7), 593-596.

mLAN (undated). Retrieved March 16, 2006, from http://www.mlancentral.com/mlan_info/ mlan_ppf.php

Montgomery, L. (2001). *4ML (Music and lyrics markup language)*. Retrieved March 16, 2006, from http://xml.coverpages.org/ni2001-03-03-b.html

Mosterd, E. (2001). *EMNML (Enhanced musical notation markup language)*. Retrieved March 16, 2006, from http://www.usd.edu/csci/research/theses/graduate/sp2001/emosterd.pdf

Newcomb, S., et al. (1995). *Standard music description language*. ISO/IEC DIS 10743. Retrieved from ftp://ftp.techno.com

Pemberton, S, Austin, D. *et al.* (2000). *XHTML™ 1.0 The extensible hypertext markup language* (2nd ed.). Retrieved from http://www.w3.org/ TR/xhtml1

Pennycook, B., *et al.* (1995a). The music library of the future: A pilot project. In *Proceedings of the 1995 International Computer Music Conference*. San Fransisco: ICMA.

Pennycook, B., *et al.* (1995b). Music and audio markup tools for the World Wide Web. In *Proceedings of the 99th Audio Engineering Society*. New York.

Raggett, D., Le Hors, A., & Jacobs, I. (1999). *HTML 4.01 specification*. Retrieved from http://www.w3.org/TR/html401/

Rastall, R. (1983). *The notation of western music*. London: J.M.Dent & Sons Ltd.

Roland, P. (2001). *MEI (Music encoding initiative)*. Retrieved March 16, 2006, from http://www.lib.virginia.edu/digital/resndev/mei/

Roland, P. (2002). The music encoding initiative (MEI). In G. Haus & M. Longari (Eds.), *MAX 2002: Musical applications using XML. Proceedings First International Conference* (pp. 55-59). Laboratoria di Informatica Musicale, Computer Science Dept, State University of Milan.

Schiettecatte, B. (2000). *FlowML*. Retrieved March 16, 2006, from http://xml.coverpages.org/FlowML.html

SGML Users' Group (1990). *A brief history of the development of SGML*. Retrieved from http://www.sgmlsource.com/history/sgmlhist.htm

SGML SIGhyper. (1994). *A brief history of the development of SMDL and HyTime*. Retrieved from http://www.sgmlsorce.com/history/hthist.htm

Sloan, D., (1993). Aspects of music representation in HyTime/SMDL. *Computer Music Journal, 17*(4). MA: MIT.

Sloan, D. (2002). Learning our lessons from SMDL. In G. Haus & M. Longari (Eds.), *MAX 2002: Musical applications using XML. Proceedings First International Conference* (pp. 69-73).

Laboratoria di Informatica Musicale, Computer Science Dept, State University of Milan.

Steyn, J. (1999). *Music markup language*. Retrieved March 16, 2006, from http://www.musicmarkup.info/

Steyn, J. (2002). Framework for a music markup language. In G. Haus & M. Longari (Eds.). *MAX 2002: Musical applications using XML. Proceedings First International Conference* (pp. 22-29). Laboratoria di Informatica Musicale, Computer Science Dept, State University of Milan.

Steyn, J. (2004). *Introducing music space*. Retrieved March 16, 2006, from http://www.musicmarkup.info/papers/musicspace/musicspace.html

Sundberg, J. (1991). *The science of musical sounds*. New York: Academic Press, INC.

Tardieu, D. (undated). *VMML (Virtual musician markup language)*. Retrieved March 16, 2006, from http://vrlab.epfl.ch/research/S_VMML.pdf

Thompson, H. S., Beech, D., Maloney, M., & Mendelsohn, N. (Eds). (2004). *XML schema part 1: Structures* (2nd ed.). Retrieved from http://www.w3.org/TR/xmlschema-1/

Van Rotterdam, J. (1998). *MusicML*. Retrieved March 16, 2006, from http://lists.xml.org/archives/xml-dev/199803/msg00091.html

Walsh, N., & Muellner, L. (1999). *DocBook: The definitive guide*. Cambridge: O'Reilly.

WEDELMUSIC (undated). Retrieved March 16, 2006, from www.wedelmusic.org/

Weinkauf, D. (undated). *JscoreML*. Retrieved March 16, 2006, from http://nide.snow.utoronto.ca/music/

Williams, C. F. (1903, 1969). *The story of notation*. New York: Haskell House.

Chapter VIII
# Interactive Systems for Multimedia Opera

**Michael Oliva**
*Royal College of Music, UK*

## ABSTRACT

*This chapter considers the development of systems to deliver multimedia content for new opera. After a short overview of the history of multimedia in opera, the specific requirements of opera are analysed, with emphasis of the fundamental musicality of operatic performance. Having considered the place of multimedia elements in the narrative and acting space, the relevance of previous practice in electroacoustic music and Vjing is considered as a model for a working approach. Several software and hardware configurations explored, including the use of gestural control by the actors themselves. The creation of a keyboard based "video instrument" with a dedicated performer, capable of integration into the pre-existing musical ensemble, is recommended as the most effective and practical solution.*

## INTRODUCTION

By definition, opera and musical theatre should be the ultimate multimedia experience, and new technologies are bound to become an ever increasingly important part of this art form. Indeed, I would go further and suggest that the inclusion of computer sound and video is essential to the development of the form in our new century, expanding its range hugely and bringing much needed new audiences. In particular, we need to recognize the highly visually sophisticated nature of modern audiences, who have learnt the languages of cinema and television from birth, using these techniques to enhance our storytelling in opera and creating works of contemporary relevance. It is "an honest expression of the life we're living now" as Steve Reich, an important pioneer in this field, says (Reich & Korot, 2001).

Developing suitable interactive systems will be a part of bringing new media into the fold, so that they work successfully with what is there already. At its best, the experience of live opera, both large- and small-scale work, can be overwhelmingly powerful. I am convinced that much of this power derives from the fact that it is live, and that we are aware of the fragility and variability of what we are seeing. Also, the original conception of opera as "drama through music" still applies, not that music is the most important element, all should carry equal weighting, but it is the music that is at the helm, so to speak, and musicality has to be a key principle. It is vitally important not to lose this in the push to include computer sound and video, and this is all too easily done. In particular, the marriage of prerecorded material with live elements needs to be very carefully handled so that the performers do not feel straight jacketed, as this is immediately deadening. As far as possible, the performers and conductor must have the freedom to drive the work along and interpret it as they wish, and any system we use for delivery of the media should enable this, responding to the energy of a particular performance, and functioning in an essentially musical way.

In order to achieve a successful integration, it is just as important that the use of computer sound and video is written into the work from the outset, as an integral part of the story to be told. To use these elements purely atmospherically or decoratively is to miss the point. These additions are capable of so much more than this, creating entire layers of narrative and character, defining worlds for these characters to inhabit, and alternative timelines for them to move in. In parallel with recent instrumental electroacoustic music, the design and implementation of the system itself is a significant part of the score, with the nature of the interface between person and machine informing what is possible. Clearly, what is said will adapt itself to the nature of the medium, and this will have an effect on the content of such works and the way that they are staged.

It also has to be recognised that even small-scale opera involves the collaboration of a rather large number of people, all of them trained specialists, from conductor to stage manager, working together in, hopefully, a highly organised way. Over the centuries, chains of command have developed that are logical and effective. Therefore, careful thought must go into developing systems that are appropriate to this type of collaborative ensemble. What may work for one form of multimedia production may not work here.

Thanks to advances in computer technology, the creation of such works has become a real possibility and, drawing from my own experience of composing and producing multimedia opera and electroacoustic music, I will set out and evaluate the types of interactive systems that might be best suited to the task, exploring in detail the requirements for what is to be achieved and the software and hardware possibilities. I shall investigate the nature of a practical interface with singers, ensemble, and conductor (as well as other elements of stagecraft such as lighting and set design) and how this is to be achieved.

## BACKGROUND

The use of the moving image has a venerable history in opera. During the second phase of composition of *Lulu* (1929-1934), Alban Berg included a "film music interlude" between Act II i and II ii, and inserted a "film music scenario" in the short score of the opera. The film music interlude was to accompany a silent film that continued the action, showing events that could not be shown onstage, with annotations in the score indicating how images and actions would correspond to the music, and this was realised after Bergs death at the 1937 premiere (Weiss, 1966). More recently, Tod Machover' *Valis* (1987) (Richmond, 1989), Steve Reich's *The Cave* (1993) and *Three Tales* (2002)—described by Reich as "music theatre video" works (Reich & Korot, 2001)—and Barry Truax's *Powers of Two* (1995) (Truax, 1996) represent much more complete and successful integrations of video and computer sound into operatic storytelling allowed by considerably more advanced technology.

But in all these cases, video is not generated live, so the incorporation of these elements into theatrical work presents performers with a significant problem: Who owns time? Prerecorded computer sound and video naturally have a tendency to "own time," running, as they are wont to do, at fixed rates. If there is to be close synchronisation, once a sequence has been triggered everyone has to play along. Moment to moment flexibility in tempo and interpretation are largely ruled out, and although there is the possibility of rubato at extremely small scales, depending on the rhythmic quality of the passage in question, there is no interactivity between events onstage and this sort of video or computer generated material.

In my own *Black and Blue* (2004) (Oliva, 2004), this problem was not resolved. The piece uses many long cued video and audio sequences and requires highly accurate synchronisation between image, action, and sound. Initially, the video represents the central character's real-time experiences viewing Web cams and in online video chatrooms, although as the drama unfolds, the narratives of the online, imagined, and real worlds become increasingly confused. The action is fairly evenly spread between these worlds, and integration was achieved by projecting the video onto a gauze screen that filled the front of the stage so that by carefully controlling lighting levels, the singers could be made to appear and disappear within the images. A second gauze at the back of the stage allowed for more complex layering. Video remained entirely in the digital domain, taking the form of a series of Quicktime .mov files on a laptop, organised into a playlist. The laptop was connected directly to a data projector, much as one would for a Powerpoint presentation. In contrast with previous tape-based systems, this allows for frame-accurate synchronisation between the image and music.

*Figure 1. A character watches an online murder in Black and Blue. The video is projected onto a gauze in front of the acting space*

Although sequences were cued in the score to ensure sync with the live performers, the conductor worked to a click track generated by the computer, much as they might in the recording of music for film or TV. This system was simple, using commercial sequencing software that provided instantaneous response for accurate cueing. This worked, was reliable, and given the very driven nature of the story (a sort of high speed Faustian descent into hell) and score, it could be said that the overall effect was successful. However, it also proved incredibly burdensome on the performers, particularly over the large timescales involved (90 minutes).

It could be argued that this was simply a skill for them to learn, one increasingly demanded in modern music making, and this view has some validity, but it is also the case that this method robbed talented performers of some of their most highly developed and cherished skills. To give of their best, singer/actors need to feel ownership of the music and dramatic pacing. This ownership allows them to project personality, which in turn greatly assists in the development of character. Another part of this ownership is that they need to feel safe. Mistakes can and do happen, so there should be the flexibility to allow for recovery in these situations, as is the case in more traditional acoustic performance. This safety relieves stress and lets the singer focus on the fine detail of their acting, leading to much more successful results.

I believe that a truly satisfying operatic or theatrical experience depends fundamentally on the ability of the singer/actors to shape the flow of time, using fluctuation in tempo as an expressive tool both at the level of a single phrase or gesture or over the course of an entire scene or act. My own experience in less technological theatre and music making shows that a work may show large variations in timing from night to night without it being noticeable that one performance was particularly slower or faster than another. An audience's sense of pace is a relative thing, and

context is everything, so the variable, in-the-moment responses of a good performer are a key part of what we seek as members of that audience. This, above all, will draw us into the work and make us care about the characters.

## THE RELEVANCE OF ELECTROACOUSTIC PRACTICE

The development of electroacoustic music incorporating live instruments, over the last 15 years or so, provides an enlightening backdrop to the problem since this field presents us with a microcosm of our problem. It is also an area where a range of effective *musical* practices is beginning to be established and so offers glimpses into our future. Here only electronic or computer sound has to be delivered into a live setting. At a very basic level, adding video will simply be a matter of greater computing power, more disk space, and increased bandwidth, the principles remaining the same.

Without a doubt, the most significant development here has been the creation of flexible computer programming software environments such as MAX/MSP (Tools for New Media, n.d.), Pd (About Pure Data, n.d) and Supercollider (McCartney, n.d.). These provide the ability to process and/or create sound in almost any way imaginable. For example, live sound input from microphones can be processed in an incredibly wide variety of ways, an unlimited number of soundfiles/samples of practically any size can be played on cue, one can build synthesisers or samplers and incoming audio can be analysed and new musical material generated in response to it. The software can be controlled over MIDI (MIDI Manufacturers Association, n.d.) or Open Sound Control (Wright, 1997), high speed digital communications protocols, allowing use of a broad range of hardware controllers. Importantly, one can create a highly customised software configuration (known in MAX/MSP as a patch) for a particular

*Figure 2. Computer (MAX/MSP) interface for Kaija Saariaho's Noa Noa. (1999, Chester Music Ltd. Used with permission.)*

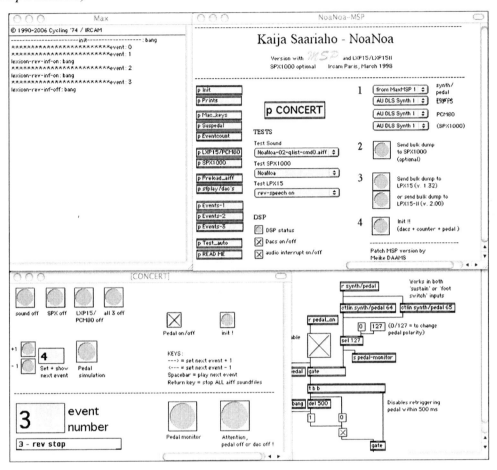

piece, designed to work with a suitable hardware combination. One of the charms of these software packages is that they are absolutely open-ended, since you program from a very low level up. Although this can mean some hard work at the beginning, it has the considerable advantage that, unlike many music applications, no assumptions are made about what you want to achieve or how you might go about it, leaving you at the mercy of your imagination.

Kaija Saariaho's *Noa Noa* (1992) (Noa Noa, n.d.) for solo flute and "electronics" provides a very early but highly successful model of the sorts of interactive system one can build using this sort of software. The original form of the piece requires a single computer running MAX/MSP for sample playback and two Lexicon PCM81 effects units controlled via MIDI, but in subsequent forms, the effects processing has been incorporated into the MAX/MSP patch to minimise the use of hardware. A microphone picks up the flute and passes the sound into the computer to be processed (via a multichannel audio interface); this is mixed with soundfile playback, and distributed over an eight-channel speaker system.

Control of the entire system is effectively in the hands of the flautist by means of a simple MIDI sustain pedal that needs to be depressed at cue points marked in the score. In the course of the roughly 10-minute piece, there are 64 cue points, and what happens at any particular depression of the pedal is entirely dependent on which cue number one is at. One of the 33 soundfiles might be played, the sound may move to a particular position in the eight-speaker array, some form of reverberation or harmonisation (pitch shifting) of the live flute sound may be applied, or perhaps a combination of these elements. To rehearse from anywhere in the score, one simply specifies the next cue point to be hit. This is all written into the patch in what amounts to an extra layer of the score.

The result is an incredibly beautiful, free and moving piece of music that always feels as if the flautist is in control of his or her expression. The way that the prerecorded soundfiles are used is very interesting here. They are all short (ranging in length from 33 to less than 1 second), and in the parts where they are closely spaced, can overlap quite successfully (in the case of a fast performance). As a result, the flautist is always absolutely in control of the rhythm of any section. Many of the sounds are also derived from flute recordings, which creates a very close blend and dialogue with the playing. Combining this with the real-time treatments, it often becomes unclear whether the source is electronic or live. As a result, Saariaho's very careful conception and preparation of materials lets her create an integrated, expressive piece, and the listener hears something complex and vital that definitely belies the use of what might seem like a simple "on" button.

To some, the nature of the interaction between the flautist and computer (the pedal) may seem incredibly simplistic, given that it is now entirely possible to devise systems, such as gestural control, in which extra sensors applied to the instrument could be used to generate data that will control the computer (Diana Young's Hyperbow project for string instruments (Young, 2002) being a very interesting example of this). But it must also be remembered that purely in terms of flute technique, this is already a demanding piece, pushing the limits of what the instrument is capable of. So as far as the flautist is concerned, this simplicity is, in fact, a great strength. It lets them concentrate on their greatest skill, playing the flute beautifully. Many musicians actively dislike being "wired up to complicated systems" (to quote one I have worked with), despite having a real enthusiasm for working with new media. This is not being a Luddite, but rather a concern that their virtuosity and sound will suffer as a result of being distracted. If we want our work to be performed often by more than a just few specialists, we need to accommodate these concerns. Musicians need to enjoy their work to give of their best.

Saariaho's liking for simple interfaces can also be seen in her opera *L'Amour de Loin* (2000) (L'Amour de Loin, n.d.), where she uses a standard full-size MIDI keyboard to cue 88 eight-channel soundfiles. In the course of the entire opera, the pianist in the orchestra (in addition to their other duties playing a normal piano) simply plays a rising chromatic scale from the bottom to the top of the keyboard as indicated in the score- incredibly simple in performance and rehearsal, and incredibly effective.

More recently we have begun to see the development in electroacoustic music of a dedicated performer at the computer (or whichever interface is used), as an equal partner in the ensemble. This approach has much to recommend it. In my own *Xas-Orion* (2001) (New Ground, 2003) for oboe, cor-anglais, and computer, which again uses a MAX/MSP patch, the computer is performed directly from its alphanumeric keyboard using a "next cue" system, similar to that used in *Noa Noa*, combined with direct control of sound processing. So, for example, holding the letter D down will increase input of the oboe into the pitch shifting system, and holding F down will reduce it. This system works well with minimal hardware (just the laptop and PA), but for more intuitive and flexible control, these functions are also mapped to a hardware MIDI fader bank, in my case a Behringer B-Control BCF2000 (B-Control

Fader BCF2000, n.d.), that connects directly to the laptop over USB.

In recent years, there has been an explosion in the use of systems like this, based as they are on relatively cheap, commercially available technology, and they represent a new type of musical instrument in their own right, which needs to be learnt just as one might learn to play the clarinet. This has developed naturally from recording studio technology, where, after all, most electroacoustic composers learn their craft; so these instruments usually combine familiar features from mixing desk and computer operation with the occasional use of MIDI keyboard and foot pedal controls. Subject to evolution over the years, these types of hardware control are not as arbitrary as they may seem. They have proved themselves to be effective, providing (when well engineered) the sensitivity and good tactile feedback we find in other musical instruments. A less common, but highly effective device that can be added to this type of set up is Yamaha's excellent BC3A (Wind Guitar and Foot Controllers, n.d.), which generates MIDI from a small breath-sensitive mouthpiece. With a combination of these tools, we can easily provide enough simultaneous dimensions for control of the software, if this is intelligently laid out, always bearing in mind as we create the work how practically it is to be performed.

As works like *Noa Noa* show, the success or failure of these systems lies much more in how the software has been configured to work for, and as a part of, the piece in question than in the details of the hardware. Quality of content and flexibility of delivery can more than adequately compensate for simplicity of execution.

This instrumental approach also fits naturally into the world of music-making. Whether working from a score or improvising, traditional skills of ensemble playing, listening and response are still used in a way that other musicians can relate to easily and quickly.

## INCORPORATING VIDEO: REQUIREMENTS

Before we can design a system to deliver video elements for opera, we need to have a clear idea of what our ideal requirements are. I believe we should aim to produce works that are highly integrated and utilise the full range of possibilities offered by the moving image. As the most recent addition to an established art form, it is important that video never seems like a tacked-on afterthought, so we have to integrate on three levels: space (in terms of how video works on stage), narrative (content), and time (synchronisation).

The placing of video into the acting space needs careful consideration, and is a significant part of the initial design process. The mismatch between its essentially two-dimensional nature and the three dimensions of the theatre can be problematic, especially if there are significant interactions between what is live and onscreen. Multiple layers, involving several video projectors and the use of gauze screens, can provide a very good solution to this. Flat screens are, of course, not the only surfaces one can project on to, but the use of more interesting shapes may require some form of geometry correction so that the image does not become distorted undesirably (this is often required for situations where the projector is off axis to the screen anyway). Video projectors can do very simple geometry correction to remove keystoning, but anything more complex will have to be handled by computer software. It is also worth remembering that front projection directly onto the actors will throw shadows and can be rather blinding for them, possibly interfering with their ability to see the conductor. This can have disastrous consequences, so if space allows, rear projection is preferable. In my own experience, a combination of rear and front projection can be made to work very well. An additional consideration is whether the actors can

*Figure 3. A simple, but highly flexible, stage layout allowing layering of imagery*

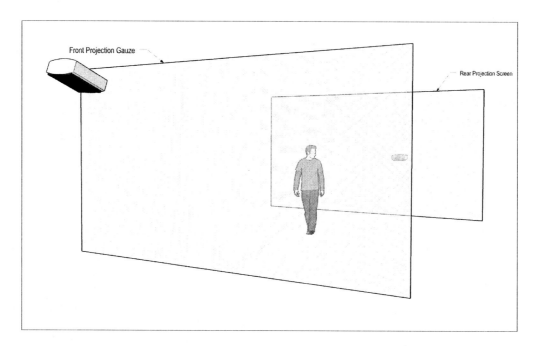

actually see the video they are to interact with, and hidden monitors may have to be provided to assist with this.

Modern audiences are very fluent when it comes to receiving information through imagery, so we do not need to shy away from using video that contains important narrative strands, providing information that is essential to the dramatic development. For an effective blend, information content should be distributed evenly between all the elements of the opera-words, action, images, and sound-and this has to be written into the work, from the outset, with a clear understanding of why any particular piece of information is using a particular medium. Video allows us to incorporate text or graphics (moving or static), be used as an extension of lighting or set design, show our characters participating in events that do not take place on stage, or present them in other places or times. It enables presentation of multiple simultaneous viewpoints. An important part of this is that at different times in the work, we see the actors both live and on screen, and this could be achieved both by filming them beforehand or using live video from cameras that could be on or offstage. Using both, with the ability to composite these video streams live, can produce some startlingly effective results.

Video can be transformed in real time through the use of a very wide range of effects: adjusting colour, position, granulation, and so forth. This is not always as exciting as it may at first appear, and has to be used with caution, but is capable of adding meaning and expression in some very interesting ways.

Tight synchronisation between music, action, and video is essential for opera. Obviously, words and music are completely locked together in that they are sung, and this naturally leads on to synchronisation of action and music. This is a basic condition for this art form, and video must participate on equal terms. As we have already discussed, there is also a need for flexibility in tempo, leading to variability in the flow of time. So we need let the video follow the music (conductor or singer), standing the relationship we are familiar with, from film or TV, on its head. This requires a flexible and accurate cueing system; flexible enough to follow the score in real time and fast enough to respond instantaneously. Drawing again from the example of *Noa Noa*, the best approach would seem to be to use many short cues to piece the video together, but somehow achieve this without producing something choppy and fragmented. The rate at which we cut or dissolve from one image to another has great expressive effect, and is part of the language of film that we all understand, so this has to match the tone of the scene in question. Layers of video that can coexist would seem to be a solution to this problem. The overall effect required is deconstructed into smaller units that are then reassembled in real time. These can be divided over multiple screens or within one projection. If we are using prerecorded clips, it is clear that they need to be of sufficient length to get from onset cue to offset cue at the slowest imaginable tempo (in other words, they should all be longer than is absolutely necessary). In terms of significant information content, these clips need to be "front weighted so that in a particularly fast performance, we do not cut away before the important event or image is shown. Another means of providing variable length for cues is being able to vary the frame rate in real time. This can be very effective, but is not appropriate for all types of material. For example, we are very sensitive to speed when viewing scenes of people in action, so a sense of slow-motion in this kind image may not be appropriate to the nature of the drama at that time. For film of clouds passing overhead, speed variation can be much less noticeable. Live video streams are, of course, inherently flexible, making them ideal in this situation, but there has to be a justification for using them rather than watching it happen on stage, and there are limitations on

what you can set up. Again, a system that allows compositing in real time with other material would have great advantages. As we can see, the nature of the video material, and how it can be de- and reconstructed, is of great importance to the success of building a system that allows temporal flexibility, with content and form working together to achieve this.

Clearly, the use of all these different layers will produce work of considerable complexity that will require careful preparation and planning. For *Black and Blue* (2004), we produced a cinema-style storyboarded script at a very early stage of the creative process, which proved immensely useful. This script was then regularly "cross-checked" with regards to practicality of means of production and design, and updated as our conception of the piece developed during writing and composition, with the rule that whenever we decided to include something, we had to be able to answer the question of how it was going to be done. Later, it became very easy to extract lists of sequences that needed to be filmed; images, graphics, and sounds to be collected; props required; and so forth, from this master script, as we progressed towards production.

Although based in the world of theatre rather than opera, *Super Vision* (2005) provides an inspiring example of what we can hope to achieve. Produced by the New York based Builders Association (The Builders Association, n.d.) and dbox (dbox dialog, strategy and design, 2005), the piece explores how we now live in a "post-private society, where personal electronic information is constantly collected and distributed. The data files collected on us circulate like extra bodies, and these 'data bodies' carry stains that are harder to clean than mud or sin" (Super Vision, n.d.). The piece effectively fulfils the requirements, outlined previously, on all three levels. The design of the stage space and use of multiple layers of projection is beautifully conceived, and the themes of surveillance, digital communication, and identity theft naturally lend themselves to, and provide opportunities for, the chosen media in compelling ways. Synchronisation is seamless and precise, responding organically to the pacing of the scenes. It is a short step from this kind of work to a form of opera that is equally satisfying.

## INCORPORATING VIDEO: PRACTICE

Developments in computer software and hardware have begun to allow live and prerecorded video to be used with the same freedom that has been possible in the audio field. In fact, some of the same software that we have discussed earlier now comes with extensions for video processing and delivery. So, for example, MAX/MSP is now MAX/MSP/Jitter, with Jitter providing this extra functionality (Tools for New Media, n.d.). The fact that these extensions are part of an already well-proven programming environment, with the possibility of using the same control systems and tight integration with sound, makes it immediately attractive for musical multimedia work. Other software more specifically specialised for video work, such as ArKaosVJ MIDI (Arkaos VJ 3.6 MIDI, 2006), Modul8 (Modul8, 2006), and Watchout (Dataton Watchout, n.d.), also offer similar abilities, each with its own particular emphasis.

Using the instrumental approach described earlier, we can perform video just as we can perform electronic music and, of course, VJs have been doing precisely this sort of thing for some years now, so we should expect to be able to derive systems from this field. VJing has its roots in clubbing, a world that is just as driven by the musical experience as opera, so many of the concerns outlined apply here too. What is significantly different to our concerns is a general lack of interest in narrative, which would have little place in a club anyway, so the tendency here is towards an improvisational graphic/abstract quality that suits the club experience. Much use is made of short looping sequences (in harmony

with forms of dance music), with an emphasis on layering, compositing, and video effects. Larger scale media, which might carry dramatic content, are avoided. Given that VJing has always been at the forefront of technology, and has developed an aesthetic incredibly quickly, may also have a lot to do with technical limitations of systems in the past in terms of being able to deal with the very large file sizes.

The tools of the trade are usually a MIDI keyboard-triggering software on a laptop, some additional sources of video, and a vision mixer, using analog signal cabling to connect everything together. Substitute a sound mixer for the vision one and we can see the close connection to the standard electroacoustic set up. A fundamental principle of VJing is building up rich visual textures by layering smaller units. Software like Modul8 has this layering concept at the heart of its design. Here, up to five layers of video or still images are mixed and affected in real time. MIDI control allows accurate synchronised cueing of the entry and departure of these layers into the overall mix, and can control effects settings, playback speed, and layer transparency, among other things. Unfortunately, live video input from a camera does not appear to be possible. ArKaosVJ extends this by offering up to 50 layers and live input streams, and has a more intuitive MIDI interface.

A system like Watchout, which has its roots in corporate presentation rather than VJing, is interesting because of its high-quality support for multiple video projectors. This is achieved by using several computers networked over Ethernet. Each projector is driven by a dedicated computer, and these are all controlled from a separate production machine. The system is scaleable, can use multiple live input streams, and has some attractive features, including the ability to project over large areas using several aligned projectors that are "edge blended" to create a seamless single image, and support for advanced geometry correction to allow the use of curved screens. These make it

*Figure 4. A typical analog VJ system*

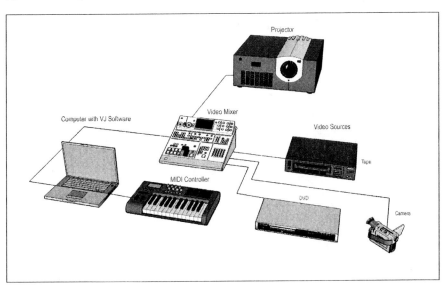

very suitable for theatrical work, but, as yet, there is no support for MIDI or OSC control, which is a serious disadvantage, and the cueing system is not as intuitive as it could be. If we could combine Watchout's attractive features with the ease of use of something like ArKaosVJ and a custom cueing and control system, we would have something truly desirable for our purposes.

Of course, this is possible through the use of a programming environment rather than dedicated software, and MAX/MSP/Jitter provides us with precisely this. The Jitter extensions are highly optimised for video, enable any of the processes outlined, and because the audio and video system for a particular work can coexist in the same patch or in several patches running simultaneously on multiple computers linked via Ethernet and OSC, we can achieve the very high level of integration necessary for opera. Since MAX/MSP/Jitter can generate data as well as receive it, there is also the considerable advantage of being able to merge control of video and stage lighting. These obviously need to work together, and it is relatively straightforward to produce industry standard

DMX protocol commands, to which any decent lighting board will respond.

It is clear to me that along the model of a VJ, we will need some form of dedicated performer to operate the "video instrument" under the direction (and so within sight) of the conductor. Adding this workload to a pre-existing member of the production team or band is not a particularly desirable option, as they all have plenty to do already. A MIDI keyboard, combined with faders, foot pedals, and access to the computer is more than adequate as an interface if, as discussed before, the software is suitably designed, and we make sure that the computer is powerful enough to be instantaneously responsive. There ar,e of course, other possible interfaces. For example, one could be based on a percussion rather than keyboard model, but this one has precedence, and I like to think of it as a distant, highly developed offspring of the "Clavier à Lumière" Alexander Scriabin called for in his orchestral *Prometheus (The Poem of Fire)* as far back as 1911. Playing this "instrument" should feel familiar and easy to someone with experience as a VJ or electroacoustic

*Figure 5. A proposed MAX/MSP/Jitter based system—more computer/projector pairs can be added as necessary*

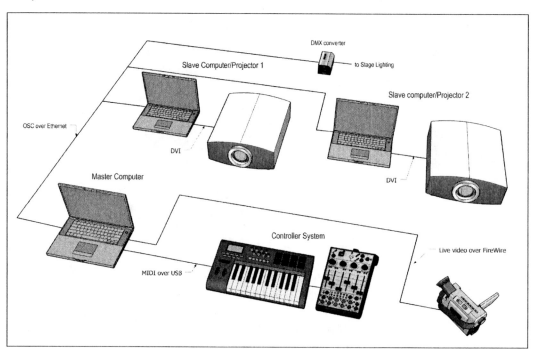

musician, allowing a full range of performance styles from tightly specified writing through to free improvisation. It will be interesting to see how a new practice develops for this "instrument," just as MIDI keyboard technique has grown from previous forms of keyboard skills (piano and organ).

I am developing this approach for my current work, *The Girl Who Liked to be Thrown Around* (2006), my third collaboration with the writer Deepak Kalha. The piece is small in scale, takes the form of a psychological striptease, and is scored for a single woman, alto and bass flutes, and computers with two performers for sound and video, respectively. In contrast to our earlier work on *Black and Blue*, using a video performer in this has led us to think of many of the video elements in expressly musical terms-as notes to be composed and orchestrated–creating, if you will, visual melody, harmony, and counterpoint to

match their counterparts in the story and music. This is not to say that the video is essentially abstract, as music is; far from it, in fact, with video having both diegetic and nondiegetic roles in the narrative. However, it does seem to promote a very nonlinear style of storytelling. This is also having interesting effects on other aspects, such as the dramaturgy and even how the words are put together, encouraging the use of multiple simultaneous layers of deconstructed material that conceal or reveal each other, depending on context.

Given this system of control for video, the directions for the performer might as well also take musical form, with events notated in a score. In the performance of opera, everyone is reading a score, from conductor to stage manager, and those who are not (the singer/actors) have memorised it. It would be simple and natural for the video performer to have a score too. It is worth remembering that the 20th century has seen considerable developments in the forms scores can take: completely standard notation, use of Lutoslawskian "mobiles," proportional notation, or the use of pure graphics provide a range of solutions to any imaginable performance situation that musicians are now quite familiar with, so this is not as limiting as it may seem.

Although it is technically possible to use computer-score-following technology to let us dispense with a performer (Philippe Manoury's *En Echo* (1993) (Manoury, 1993) for soprano and computer is an early and rather beautiful example from electroacoustic music), I completely fail to see what benefit this brings. The computer has to be operated by someone anyway, and in the context of opera, it seems reasonable to expect that person to have well-developed musical skills. More fundamentally, no matter how good the technology gets, the most interactive, intuitive

thing I can think of is a person. Nothing is better at judging the energy of a scene in the moment. Human responses will make for humanity in performance, and when telling stories about people, this is vitally important.

Having said that a dedicated performer is required, putting some of the control into the hands of the singer/actors could have some very interesting results. One of the most appropriate ways of doing this would be through the use of motion tracking and gestural control. The EyesWeb software from InfoMus Lab, University of Genova (Camurri, Hashimoto, Richetti, Trocca, Suzuki, & Volpe, 2000) or Cyclops extensions to Jitter (Tools for New Media, n.d.) offer the ability to analyse incoming video in order to create control data that could be used in any number of ways, allowing the singers on stage to directly control events in the video or audio domain. The system has the advantage that it leaves the performer

*Figure 6. A scene from* The Girl Who Liked To Be Thrown Around, *using rear projection and a plasma screen on stage*

entirely free, there is no need to be wired up with special sensors, and we may well have live video feeds already in place.

A particularly elegant implementation of this is to bathe the stage in infrared light and then use a video camera, fitted with an infrared filter, as the input to the tracking system. This has the great advantage of working independently of any stage lighting, and the infrared light is, of course, invisible. Several actors can be tracked at once, and their interactions can be analysed to a remarkable degree, whether they are touching, moving towards or away from each other, behind or in front, and so forth. It is even possible to individually track different parts of the actor, the head, arms, and legs, and assign different triggering mechanisms to each part. As to the question of what these triggers might do, the possibilities are almost endless. We can control audio and video equally well, setting off sequences, letting imagery follow the actor around the space, defining points to cut from one scene to another, or altering the quality of the image or sound in a myriad of ways.

This can create some fascinating interactions between the live and video worlds, as has already been demonstrated in dance works by companies like Troika Ranch (Farley, 2002), but I do want to emphasise the use of the phrase *some of the control* here. Given the probably very large number of cue events an opera may contain, it would be unreasonable to expect to use this as the only means of control, and there are technical restraints on the amount of useful data that can be generated, since singers are rarely as mobile as dancers. Again, we need to be careful of overburdening our singers, and if we are striving for any form of naturalism in the acting, we will need to be subtle. But with careful planning, this could be used as an effective addition to what is already there. The great immediacy of response can create very striking effects that can be achieved in no other way, and this undoubtedly provides a very attractive way of enhancing the integration between action and video.

## FUTURE TRENDS AND CONCLUSION

It is always surprising to me that opera, the form that always tried to claim the title of "total art work," has been so slow on the uptake when it comes to digital media. Undoubtedly this has much to do with the way culture of opera developed over the course of the 20th century, slowly turning it's gaze backward to the point where many contemporary composers refuse to use the term, preferring a range of inelegant alternatives (Lachenmann's "music with images,", Reich's "music video theatre," etc.). But I also believe that there has been a certain amount of waiting for the technology to become good enough to suit the form. Producing new opera is difficult and expensive, with the result that those who do it have to be pretty passionate about the form in the first place. This passion makes people very unwilling to dilute opera's natural strengths for the sake of including new media, even when there has been an understanding of, and enthusiasm for, the potential they offer. Very similar concerns apply in theatre, and here too, the amount of work of this type has been very small as a proportion of total output.

But really rather suddenly, the technology is ready, and not only ready, but easily available and relatively cheap. The rapid advance in computing power that we are experiencing will lead to big improvements in performance, ease of use, and stability very quickly, making the technology ever more attractive. There are, of course, a lot of new skills that need to be learnt, mainly in computing and programming, but precisely because these are computer based, there is instantly access to plenty of very active online communities where information and techniques are traded.

This is going to lead to an explosion of activity in this area, as people finally have the means to realise projects that have probably been in the back of their minds for a considerable amount of time. In a related sphere, the huge recent growth of VJing seems to bear this out. Eventually, we could see this becoming the dominant form for live dramatic performance-based art. The marriage of live and cinematic elements allowed by the incorporation of digital multimedia is irresistible, greatly expanding the narrative and dramatic possibilities. Even something as simple as the use of close-up, previously not possible on stage, can massively increase the power of a scene, if the acting is sufficiently good. With these elements meaningfully incorporated into the storytelling, we will be able to create sophisticated layered narratives that speak a language that modern, visually literate audiences have come to expect, and that have the power to engage and move those audiences. This need not be at the expense of the fundamentally musical nature of opera either. From this point of view, the form will not change at all. We can shape the use of multimedia to our musical requirements, rather than the other way round, so that one does not detract from the other, but rather strengthens what is already there.

Questions, of course, remain as to how successful the results of all this activity are, and what form the successful examples will take. The more work there is out there, in front of a critical public, and the greater the communication between practitioners, the better we will know the answers to this. Audiences will tell us what works and what does not. In the meantime, we need to develop effective working methods for both creation and performance, drawing from as many fields as possible, to create a language for this new form of an old classic.

## REFERENCES

About Pure Data. (n.d). Retrieved April 5, 2006 from http://puredata.info/

Arkaos VJ 3.6 MIDI. (2006). Retrieved April 5, 2006, from http://www.arkaos.net/software/vj_description.php

B-Control Fader BCF2000. (n.d.). Retrieved April 2, 2006, from http://www.behringer.com/BCF2000/index.cfm?lang=ENG

The Builders Association. (n.d.). Retrieved April 5, 2006, from http://www.thebuildersassociation.org/flash/flash.html?homepage

Camurri, A,. Hashimoto, S., Richetti, M., Trocca, R., Suzuki, K., & Volpe, G. (2000). EyesWeb—Toward gesture and affect recognition in interactive dance and music systems. *Computer Music Journal, 24*(1), 57-69.

Dataton Watchout. (n.d.). Retrieved April 3, 2006, from http://www.dataton.com/watchout

dbox dialog, strategy and design. (2005). Retrieved April 2, 2006, from http://www.dbox.com/

Farley, K. (2002). Digital dance theatre: The marriage of computers, choreography and techno/human reactivity *Body, Space and Technology.*

L'Amour de Loin. (n.d.). Retrieved April 3, 2006, from http://www.chesternovello.com

Manoury, P. (1993). *En Echo, the marriage of voice and electronics.* Retrieved April 5, 2006, from http://musicweb.koncon.nl/ircam/en/extending/enecho.html

McCartney, J. (n.d.). *Supercollider. A real time audio synthesis programming language.* Retrieved April 5, 2006, from http://www.audio-synth.com/

MIDI Manufacturers Association. (n.d.). Retrieved April 5, 2006, from http://www.midi.org/

Modul8. (2006). Retrieved April 3, 2006, from http://www.garagecube.com/modul8/index.php

New Ground. (2003). Retrieved April 6, 2006, from http://www.oboeclassics.com/NewGround.htm

Noa Noa. (n.d.). Retrieved April 3, 2006, from http://www.chesternovello.com

Oliva, M. (2004). Retrieved March 19, 2006, from http://www.madestrange.net/black.htm

Reich, S., & Korot, B. interviewed by David Allenby. (2001). Retrieved April 5, 2006, from http://www.boosey.com/pages/opera/OperaNews.asp?NewsID=10260&MusicID=15153

Richmond, J. (1989). *Valis points to exciting possibilities for growth of opera.* Retrieved from http://www-tech.mit.edu/V109/N28/valis.28a.html

Super Vision. (n.d.). Retrieved April 5, 2006, from http://www.superv.org/

Tools for new Media. (n.d.). Retrieved April 5, 2006 from http://www.cycling74.com/

Truax, B. (1996). Sounds and sources in *Powers of Two*: Towards a contemporary myth. *Organised Sound, 1*(1), 13-21.

Weiss, N. (1966). Film and Lulu. *Opera, 17*(9), 708.

Wind Guitar and Foot Controllers. (n.d.). Retrieved April 6, 2006, from http://www.yamaha.com/yamahavgn/CDA/ContentDetail/ModelSeriesDetail/0,,CNTID%253D1321%2526CTID%253D,00.html

Wright, M., & Freed, A. (1997). *Open sound control: A new protocol for communicating with sound synthesizers.* Paper presented at the International Computer Music Conference 1997, Thessaloniki, Greece.

Young, D. (2002). *The Hyperbow. A precision violin interface.* Paper presented at the International Computer Music conference 2002, Gothenburg, Sweden.

# Chapter IX
# Driving Sound Synthesis with a Live Audio Signal

**Cornelius Poepel**
*Academy of Media Arts, Cologne, Germany*
*& University of Birmingham, UK*

## ABSTRACT

*An overview on problems and methods to map performers' actions to a synthesized sound is presented. Approaches incorporating the audio signal are described, and a synthesis method called "audio signal driven sound synthesis" is introduced. It uses the raw audio signal of a traditional instrument to drive a synthesis algorithm. The system tries to support musicians with satisfying instrument-specific playability. In contrast to common methods that try to increase openness for the player's input, openness of the system is achieved here by leaving essential playing parameters nonformalized as far as possible. Three implementations of the method and one application are described. An empirical study and experiences with users testing the system implemented for a bowed string instrument are presented. This implementation represents a specific case of a broader range of approaches to the treatment of user input, which have applications in a wide variety of contexts involving human-computer interaction.*

## INTRODUCTION

Today's methods of sound synthesis, developed by technical progress over the last decades, arguably provide an almost inexhaustible potential for the performance of music. Thus, it would seem that what has traditionally been a task of finding acceptable solutions amongst limited possibilities has become the opposite. Today, the producer is faced with the challenge of finding the exceptional amongst a supposedly unlimited reservoir. The limitations have thus altered. For the performer they exist less in the potential of the material rather than in its availability. Regarding quantity of sonic possibilities and spectral variety, one can say that computer-based instruments outdo acoustic instruments by far. Regarding their usability for musical expression, however, due to limits in the interfaces, they are still lacking in some points (Fels, 2004).

Research on musical instruments and interfaces falls into the field of human-computer interaction, which is represented by conferences like the Conference on Human Factors in Computing Systems (CHI, 2007). A growing community working in the field of new interfaces for computer-based instruments has evolved in recent years. One important place to present outcome of research and development can be found in the international conference on New Interfaces for Musical Expression (NIME, 2001). The NIME conference evolved in 2001 out of the CHI conference. Many new interfaces have been presented there.

In contrast to the widely used MIDI keyboard, the majority of these new developments have not been commercially successful. Concerning the keyboard, one might argue that two factors were of importance for its success. Since its interface is based on the piano, there were always performers that could use existing skills to play the instrument. In addition, there was a huge body of repertoire that could be used.

Trying to replicate the success of the keyboard with other instruments like woodwinds or strings was not that effective due to the specific needs a musical interface has to meet in order to satisfy a musician. The keyboard emphasis of the MIDI protocol made it particularly difficult to adapt non-keyboard instruments as controllers.

An increasing number of researchers are addressing the questions around musical interfaces, and how the needs of musicians might be successfully met in their creation (Wanderley & Battier, 2000). Desired qualities of musical interfaces are described with terms like the "playability" of an instrument (Young & Serafin, 2003), its "feel" (O'Modhrain, 2000), its "intimacy" (Fels, 2004), or its "transparency" (Fels, Gadd, & Mulder, 2002).

Common to attempts to increase the quality of computer-based instruments is the assumption that such qualities can be realized through work on either the interface, or on the mapping method between interface and the synthesis engine. It is also common to use synthesis engines that are driven by explicit input parameters, and to control the engine with measured input that attempts to describe the actions of the performer.

According to statements of Buxton found in Buchla et al. (Buchla, Buxton, Chafe, Machover, Moog, Mathews, Risset, Sonami, & Waiswisz, 2000), a huge body of literature concerning musical interfaces has been provided in the last years without a concomitant effect on the interfaces the majority of musicians are using. This raises the question of whether it might not be helpful to study and to modify the general architectural principles of the interplay between interface and synthesis.

A main principle in building computer-based instruments has been the definition of a fixed set of formalized and measurable playing parameters derived from the actions of the performer. Therefore, studying performers' actions is crucial (Wanderley & Depalle, 2004). However, in comparison to this, an acoustic instrument, like a traditional violin, has no *explicit* formal inputs. While it is possible to define and measure those in the performer-instrument interaction from a physical point of view, it remains unclear whether this may or may not represent completely what the player does.

Taking any given formalisation of an interface based on a physical representation of the performer-instrument interaction, it arguably remains unclear whether a performer is able to make use of the full range of techniques for the creation of musical expression that she or he is used to having at her or his disposal. In order to solve the problem of such potential limitations, it is worth considering the possibility of design principles that can deal *implicitly* with playing techniques in a manner analogous to the way acoustic instruments do.

Use of an audio signal captured by means of a transducer from an acoustic instrument to drive a synthesis engine has been done by researchers like Egozy (1995), Jehan and Schoner (2001) or Janer (2005). The advantage of such an approach lies in the fact that interfaces incorporating traditional instruments, like a clarinet or a violin, can be used, including nonkeyboard instruments. In these approaches, it is assumed that an audio signal captured by means of a transducer includes all musically relevant information. It is further assumed that a synthesizer can be effectively controlled, once essential control features have been derived explicitly from the audio signal.

A method, presented by Poepel (2004), is based on an alternative interplay between interface and synthesis. It mainly uses a raw audio signal to drive synthesis algorithms and therefore does not need to formalize all essential control features. Due to the usage of implicit playing parameters, it enables a player to intuitively manipulate parameters that might not be defined and measured in the interface, such as variations in timbre or articulation. These manipulations are captured by a transducer and embedded in the resultant audio signal. One drawback of this approach is that existing synthesis methods cannot be used without modification.

It is the goal of this chapter to present actual approaches and research directions that deal with the problem of musical expression in the real-time use of computer-based systems. In addition, this chapter gives an introduction to methods that use an audio signal to drive synthesis algorithms. Included are the background, basic principles, an application using this method, and a comparison with common approaches. Comments of expert players that tested the system are provided, as well as an interview with the concertmaster of a German opera orchestra who made use of the system under discussion. Issues arising from a comparison of signal driven and parameter driven approaches are discussed with respect to the assumptions about performer-instrument

interactions that are "built into" synthesizer instruments, and with respect to problems caused by the system architecture of computer-based musical instruments.

While principles presented here will apply to many traditional musical instruments, the concrete examples discussed are based on bowed, stringed synthesizer instruments. To get a view on existing alternatives, other related developments are presented as well.

## BACKGROUND

In real-time performances of music, the performer's actions are important. These have been often described in a manner that focuses on the gestures of the performers. Research on performance using synthesized sounds has lead to the question of how sound synthesis may be controlled by gestures. Wanderley and Battier (2000) give a broad overview and present different developers, researchers, and artists with their specific points of view related to the gestural control of music. Overviews on interfaces that have been developed are found in Chadabe (1997), Paradiso (1997b), Miranda and Wanderley (2006), and of course in the proceedings of the Conference on New Interfaces for Musical Expression (NIME, 2001).

Pursuing the question of what a usable interface might look like and which quality criteria would have to be met in order to create meaningful music, many researchers (for example Hunt, 1999; Jordà, 2005; Wanderley & Depalle, 2004 ) have done extensive research. Hunt (1999) tested different mappings between the control parameters of the interface and the parameters of the synthesis. Assuming that the performance of a musical instrument is a complex task, some of the significant findings from this research include statements such as "Real-time interactive control *can* be enhanced by multiparametric interfaces," "Mappings that are *not* one-to-one are more engaging for users," and "Complex tasks may need *complex* interfaces." (p. 175). Jordà (2005) proposes interfaces that overcome the limitations of traditional acoustical instruments. He sees these limitations as having to do with the ways in which they can be played, for example, using limited gestures and in the varieties of sound they can produce. As an alternative, Jordà developed instruments like the reacTable, a multiplayer instrument that allows an instant definition of physical controls, and connections to synthesis modules in real-time on a tabletop tangible user interface.

A main question in the field of research on musical interfaces is the question of how instrumental gestures or physical movement can be mapped to sound in a way that is meaningful for the performer (Ng, 2004; Paine, 2004; Wanderley & Depalle, 2004). Wanderley and Depalle (2004) describe the research problem as breaking down into these categories: the analysis of performers' gestures, gestural capture technologies, real-time sound synthesis methods, and strategies for mapping gesture variables to sound synthesis input parameters. The basic assumption here is that a performer will make gestures, among which the musically relevant ones should be captured in order to map the resulting data to sound synthesis. Various definitions of the term "gesture" can be found among researchers (Cadoz & Wanderley, 2000). In order to avoid discussions on different understandings of "gesture," Wanderley and Depalle (2004) use the term "players' actions.".

Existing research on players' actions focuses on classifying actions of a player, determining which ones are relevant for musical output, and how they are related to the musically meaningful aspects of the sonic result. Examples of researchers working on those questions are Traube (2004), Schoonderwaldt, Rasamimanana, and Bevilacqua (2006), Askenfelt (1989), or Rasamimanana (2006). In contrast to Askenfelt (1989), who uses a purely physically based view to describe the performers actions, Traube (2004) starts from performers' verbal and phenomenological timbre descriptions such as muddy, woolly, glassy,

chocolatey, or bright. In a second step, she searches for measurements that are consistent with such descriptions.

In 1992, researchers from the MIT Media Lab developed the hypercello (Machover, 1992). The player's actions, which were captured, were derived from knowledge about instrumental performance as it pertains to expert performers of bowed stringed instruments. (Paradiso & Gershenfeld, 1997a). Schoner (2000) expanded the capturing parameters of the hypercello. Facing the fact that due to the technical limitations of measurement not all of the playing parameters one would like to measure could be captured, he provided a hierarchical order of playing parameters to capture (p. 136). He developed his hardware and software by focusing on the most relevant parameters. This approach assumes a hierarchy of playing parameters that will stay more or less constant during the performance of different playing techniques, as well as with different performers.

As mentioned in the introduction, specific terms related to the quality of instruments, like the feel, the playability, or the transparency of an interface, are discussed in the field. Regarding the requirements of interfaces, research is done to increase the potential of interactive instruments according to those quality criteria. It is one of the objectives of the Conference on New Interfaces for Musical Expression (NIME, 2001) to identify criteria for the evaluation of new musical controllers. The initial NIME workshop proposal (Poupyrev, Lyons, Fels, & Blaine, 2001) cites the history of the piano, and its technical invention, in order to compare it with the history and technical development of computer music interfaces. The topics of usability, comprehensibility, expressiveness, sensitivity, sophistication, aesthetics, and hedonics ("does it feel good?") are singled out as important for the evaluation of such new interfaces. According to the authors, such aspects are important for musicians.

However, in order to evaluate new interfaces, methods of measurement have to be developed.

Wanderley and Orio (2002) propose an evaluation based on methods derived from the field of human-computer interaction (HCI). Concerning the goal of the interactive music system, intended to be used by performers and to meet their specific musical needs, they note that "in music, it must be noted that controllers cannot be evaluated without taking into account subjective impressions of performers, ruled by personal and aesthetic considerations." Therefore, they do not recommend measuring a musical interface purely with methods based on metrics and quantitative measurement. Instead, they propose to define small musical tasks, and to let subjects perform these tasks and to rate the system on a scale.

## Performer and Synthesis Related Approaches

Summarizing the developments of the last few years in this area of research, one can find two types of approach when dealing with the playability of electronic music interfaces. These start from two different questions; one is synthesis related, one is performer related:

1.  How can I play, or increase the playability of, an algorithm that already exists? In this case, a synthesis algorithm with its inputs would be given. The inputs would have to be served, for example, by using trigger controllers like a MIDI keyboard, or continuous controllers using turning knobs, faders, sensors, and so forth.
2.  How can I "bring into the computer" what I am playing on the instrument in order to drive a synthesis algorithm using existing instrumental techniques? In this case, a traditional instrument with its attributes, and players with their existing skills, would be considered. The instrument would need an interface open to all kinds of players' actions as they relate to their instrument-specific skills.

In this chapter, we will concentrate on the second approach, because synthesis methods using the audio signal are addressed. These assume a performer creating musical expression through the application of instrumental technique to a mechanical oscillating object, and are thus performer oriented. The musically relevant features of an audio signal derived from the mechanical oscillating object have to be "brought into the computer." This approach easily enables one to build interfaces in the category of "instrument-like controllers" (Wanderley & Orio, 2002).

A focus will be the question of how electronic sounds can be played using existing instrument-specific skills. The term "instrument-specific playability" is understood here as the ability of an interface to respond to a player's input with an adequate output, as long as the player uses the skills that are essential in the instrumental education and performance of traditional Western music.

In order to "bring into the computer" what the player is doing when playing the instrument, it is an obvious and thus common approach to analyze the players' actions (Wanderley & De-palle, 2004). This approach asks what actions are done, which of them are meaningful for the music performed, and how they relate to the sound that is produced.

Facing the results, one has to find solutions to the problem of how the analyzed performance parameters can be captured, which means how they can be operationalized, measured, and formalized. The following section will outline some ideas that may be of general use in this process.

## Phenomenological and Formal Descriptors in Player-Instrument Interaction

In the process of building new instruments, one will somehow arrive at a list of requirements the instrument will have to meet. These requirements may be derived from the obvious general needs of an instrument, such as pitch or timing accuracy, as well as from practical research. Examples of the latter include appropriate haptical feedback (O'Modhrain, 2000), a high learnability, explorability feature and timing controllability (Wanderley & Orio, 2002), or an adequate intimacy (Fels, 2004). From the view of software engineering, this may be the list of specifications. Following the two development lines mentioned in the last section, we will also find here two kinds of specification types. These two kinds differ in their emphasis. These are:

- Those that emphasize the requirements of a synthesis algorithm.
- Those that emphasize the requirements of emulating a traditional instrument.

Since the formal inputs of the algorithm are the "facts" one has to deal with, the former list will already be a sort of formal specification. How, for example, could a standard MIDI keyboard be improved that was intended to control a simple frequency modulation (FM) synthesis algorithm? One could build a new interface using a theremin-like antenna to control the pitch input of the simple FM synthesis, a continuous foot pedal to control the output amplitude, and two knobs to control carrier-modulator ratio (harmonicity) and modulation index. This would increase the degree of freedom in continuous control and thus, the potential for variety in phrasing, articulation, and timbre modification. The player of this new instrument would have to adapt to it without necessarily being able to make use of the abilities, skills, musical gestures, or playing techniques she or he already has, and with the basic limitation that the player could only manipulate the fixed input parameter set of the algorithm.

It is conceivable that one might overcome these limitations by adding more parameter inputs at the side of the synthesis algorithm and by adding more parameters that can be controlled by the performer via the interface. This would result in an instrument being more complex and thus

more difficult to play. According to Wessel and Wright (2002), however, important design criteria for computer-based musical instruments lie in an initial ease of use, coupled with a long-term potential for virtuosity. The idea of increasing the musical potential by simply adding to the number of control parameters will not necessarily fulfill such requirements. It shifts the problem to the connection between control and synthesis; the mapping, where it may or may not be solved.

The latter list will be at first a list of specifications including subjective or phenomenological terms one knows from the world of instrumental performance. Those are considered here as the "facts" a performer is dealing with when playing an instrument. In a second step, the items have to be operationalized; in other words, translated into a functional specification list that can deal with a given interface and synthesis algorithm. The second step can be divided into three substeps:

1. The definition of measurable physical parameters.
2. The definition of methods of measurement.
3. The definition of a formalization of the measurement and its results.

The terms of the first list, the "facts" a musician deals with, can be studied very well in instrumental pedagogy, because it is the task of instrumental education to teach students how to interact with their instruments. While pitch, for example, correlates very well with the measurable frequency of a tone, the production of tone character or the practice of "going into the tone" is harder to operationalize. Sometimes the measurement of a parameter is a technical problem in itself (Schoner, 2000, p. 136). If measurement is possible, there might still be problems with latency and mistakes in measurement.

Many researchers see the complexity of musical performance as a difficult problem to deal with (Fels, 2004; Wanderley & Depalle, 2004).

Discussing the problem of how to capture the essential actions or gestures of a performer, already the question of what a gesture is, leads researchers to different answers (Miranda & Wanderley, 2006). Besides such diversities, a common assumption is that once the important actions have been defined, they can be adequately captured through measurement.

However, the question whether the formalization of measurement and parameters can be achieved without the loss of important factors of the specification list remains open. According to Prem (1997):

*"It was already John von Neumann who pointed out that results of measurements, choices of observables, the construction of measurement devices and the measurement process itself cannot, in principle, be formalized (von Neumann, 1955; von Neumann 1966)."* (p. 5)

Reasons *"...lie in the fact that the process of measurement is not of a purely formal nature."* because in measurement *"...two dynamical systems interact."* (p. 5)

As common in the design of empirical studies, a method of measurement that changes the object to be measured, or essential parameters of the object through the process of measurement, cannot be used, due to its influence on the object. In any case, where the process of capturing the performers' actions would lead to a disturbing effect on those actions, the formalization of the measurement can be said to be lacking.

An example of this problem coming into effect can be seen in the case of a trumpet player who plays a trumpet interface synthesizer using a pitch tracking system. Once a mistake in measured frequency is obtained and unwanted sounds have occurred, the player will change his or her behavior somehow. This could be merely an irritation to the player, or lead to a change of playing style (for example articulation) in order to "enable" the

tracking system to send pitch data correlating to played notes. According to the experience of the author, some players even decide to stop using the instrument entirely.

While one would agree that the process of measuring affects the process of playing, it might be possible to argue that the player simply would have to adapt to the new circumstances. She or he would have to focus on the measuring system.

This way of argumentation, however, would lead to an approach based on the principle of adapting the player to the facts of the system instead of adapting the system to the facts of the player and the instrument. This problem will be similar on other instruments each time measurement problems occur that disturb the instrumentalist.

Thus, the process of getting from the phenomenological level in the first list of specifications to the algorithm-necessary formalized input is a transformational process having potential problems. These may be crucial and therefore should not be ignored if one's goal is to create an instrument capable of making use of a musician's existing skills.

A question worth considering is what requirements should or should not be added to the list. Basic assumptions about instrumental performance, for instance, that a player performs tones with pitches, volumes, timbres, and articulations, will obviously be a useful starting point. Research outcomes concerning which parameters are relevant to player-instrument interaction are of course important as well. In addition, the author believes that all kinds of linguistic descriptions focusing on player-instrument interaction can be of use. The literature on computer-based instruments contains a rather small number of analyses, given the immense amount of pedagogic writing on performer-instrument interaction. Here are some examples of noted music teachers describing essential aspects of performer-instrument interaction:

The piano teacher Heinrich Neuhaus (1967, p.3) describes the essential elements of piano playing as relating to a specific quality of the resistance of an instrument against the musical idea of the performer as follows: "*Thesis—music, antithesis—musical instrument, synthesis—performance.*" (translation by the author).

This statement would require a specific resistance of the new instrument against a musical idea of the performer. Thus, it stands in contrast to the wish often stated to build a computer-based instrument that does exactly what the performer wants it to do.

The violinist Yehudi Menuhin in (Biesenbender, 1992, p. 5) "*I agree fully with Volker about the deadly effect of teaching performance from fixed visual and deliberately frozen, formulated fractional details of position when what must needs be 'learnt' is the flowing co-ordination, which incorporates a myriad of elements, themselves in a flux of speed and proportion.*"

This statement would require the possibility of the instrument to enable the player for the flowing coordination of many (performance relevant) elements, which have a changing speed, interconnection, and proportion, and are independent from fixed, formulated, and fractional gestures. This requirement is in contrast to the idea of having a fixed connection between gesture and sound.

The violin teacher Ivan Galamian (1988, p. 20): "*The tone production on the instrument does not only include the steady and clean sound, but it has to include a certain amount of knocking or accentuated noise, in order to give it character and shape.*" (translation by the author).

This statement would require the possibility of the instrument to enable the player for the creation of a steady clean sound (including timbral varieties) at any time, as well as sounds representing knocking or accentuated noise and variations of such.

Since these descriptions are done with an instrument that is already capable of fulfilling the tasks on the specification list (a traditional violin has not latency or tracking mistakes), one has to deduce the requirements arising from instrumental pedagogy by thusly: if this specific task must be accomplished by the player, the instrument must allow for this. If it is the task of the player to produce knocking and noisy sounds, then the instrument has to be capable of this.

## Interactive Bowed Stringed Instruments

Given the desire to create an instrument able to transform the player's input into a sound that indeed includes the expressivity, parameters and possibilities, we find, on the phenomenological level, what methods are commonly used? In short, this is usually done by improving the measurement, mapping, and sound synthesis itself. Figure 1 shows the basic architecture used by many computer music instruments. Explicit performance parameters are derived from measurement of physical gestures or are extracted from the audio signal. Those parameters are mapped to the sound synthesis.

The Zeta MIDI violin (Graesser, 1996), introduced in 1980, and the only commercially produced string interface currently available, uses this architecture. It tracks the pitch and amplitude of the audio signal of each string and derives corresponding MIDI signals. Taking it as an example, how could the Zeta MIDI violin be extended in order to better meet the needs of the performer? One common approach is to measure more performance parameters (figure 2, circle A).

Since the Zeta violin tracks only pitch and amplitude, we could add measuring systems. Bow speed, bow position, and bow pressure are important factors in the playing of bowed stringed instruments (Nichols, 2003). One could, for instance, add a hyperbow (Young, 1999) measuring these three parameters. Since the Zeta would be a first element to start, and other elements are added according to the users needs, this improvement can be seen as a bottom-up approach.

*Figure 1. Common architecture of computer music instruments*

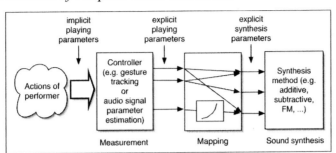

*Figure 2. Common improvements in measurement (A), mapping (B), sound synthesis (C)*

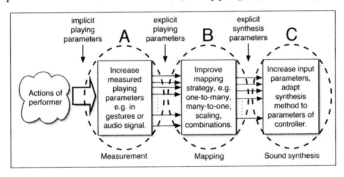

Keeping in mind the fact that changing one playing parameter often affects more than one parameter in the resultant sound (for example bow speed not only affects volume, but also the timbre of a tone), we might now consider the next aspect of the interface-synthesis connection: the mapping of input data to synthesis parameters (Figure 2, circle B).

Basic strategies for the mapping of incoming measurement parameters to outgoing synthesis control parameters include one-to-one, one-to-many, or many-to-one mappings (Hunt, 1999). The topic of mapping has been discussed in great detail, for example, by Hunt and Wanderley, (2002), Levitin, McAdams, and Adams (2002), or by Fels et al. (2002). Fels et al. talk about the need of a greater "transparency" with regard to the player's input. This desire comes close to what is described here as the goal to create "openness" to the player's input.

The synthesis algorithm can be improved by adding more input parameters affecting the sound in a meaningful way (Figure 2, circle C). Another common approach is to develop synthesis methods that have inputs that are optimized for the output of the interface. Examples can be found in cluster weighted modeling (Jehan & Schoner, 2001), or in waveguide synthesis (Jaffe & Smith, 1995), as long as those are driven with interfaces that match the synthesis inputs well. According to the conviction of the developers, this approach goes in parallel with acoustical instruments. It is assumed there that an instrument has a fixed mapping between the controls of the performer and resulting changes in sound. Under these circumstances, the developers assume that a mapping unit can be left out.

All mentioned solutions are based on the use of predefined and formalized playing parameters. They use tracking methods to create the parameters that drive the synthesis algorithms, and their success will be directly dependent on tracking latency, tracking mistakes, and the loss of untracked parameters that may be important for the player. In these solutions, the focus of the performer will have to be on the capturing system itself, which may or may not disturb the performer.

Coming back to the idea of a specification list, we want to ask what it should include. As the name of the instrument suggests, the string is the most focused part of the instrument; it is touched and modulated by a performer via fingers and the bow. According to our understanding of traditional instruments and their use, we assume that pitch accuracy, dynamics, timbre, and timing accuracy will be on the list. The instrument should be capable of transmitting articulation techniques that are common in string playing, like legato, détaché, martelé, spiccato, pizzicato, tremolo, scratching, sul ponticello, and col legno. It should react adequately to the alteration of the three basic bowing parameters: bow pressure, bow position, and bow speed. It should reproduce vibrato correctly, and give a similar account of left-hand finger pressure on the string in the sound result.

While these aspects of string playing can be seen as general and obvious, it is also necessary to include requirements resulting from player views on player-instrument interaction. These may not be so obvious.

A lot of research has been done to understand the connection between the sound derived from acoustical instruments and the actions of the performer. Examples for bowed stringed instruments can be found in Askenfelt (1989) or Rasamimanana (2006). We will start with the description of Galaminan (1988), since his idea of violin playing is often cited in literature on the construction of interactive, bowed, stringed musical instruments, for example in Nichols (2003) or in Young (1999). To summarize, one can say that the basic methods or functions a player deals with, according to Galamian (1988), are as follows:

Basic tone parameters: tone pitch, tone volume, tone consonants (similar to consonants in language, p. 20), tone character, tone color (p. 73), tone quality (p. 20, 74). Basic gestural factors of tone production: bow movement at a right-angle to the string, spring function of fingers and arm, bow speed, (p. 66), bow pressure (p. 68), bow position relative to the bridge (p. 69), various bowing techniques created by combinations of the former factors, left-hand finger pressure and left-hand finger position.

We would have to add to the list: tone consonants accuracy, tone character accuracy, tone quality accuracy, adequately responding to bow in right angle to the string and accordingly, responding to the spring function of fingers.

According to Menuhin, as cited before, the instrument would have to allow the player to get into a kind of flowing coordination of movements and other elements that are of importance during playing. To keep the instrument's features, the flowing coordination would still have to work when the elements would slightly change their proportion.

While parts of this specification list may seem to a reader somewhat esoteric and undefined, it has to be said that even in software engineering, the first specification list of a customer allows for vague terms, half developed ideas, or strange descriptions. If a string player would dislike an instrument because of a missing esoteric sounding requirement, it might be wrong to disqualify this argument just because it does not fit into the understanding of the instrument builder, or to call the player not open for new things.

One could find more, particularly individual descriptions that had to go on the specification list. Instead of collecting these, we will go on here with a look on how related work is constructed.

An early example of an interactive bowed stringed instrument is the MIT hypercello, initiated in 1990 by Tod Machover (1992). Its technical setup and its objectives are described in Paradiso and Gershenfeld (1997a). The objective of its sensing system is to measure the player's manipulation of the instrument, and to use this to control a range of sound sources (p. 72). Therefore, the hypercello senses left-hand finger position on the fingerboard. Bow wrist angle is measured, as well as bow position (longitudinal and lateral), bow speed, and right-hand finger pressure against the bow (bow pressure).

The MIT hyperbow presented in Young (1999) is an improved successor of the hypercello bow. Besides being wireless, it is lighter than its predecessor, and is capable of tracking bow position, bow speed, and bow pressure. Young and Serafin (2003) used it in order to test physical models to figure out whether the models behave similarly to the acoustic instruments with regard to changing bow position, bow speed, and bow pressure. They also use the term "playability," although this is not used in the same sense as playability in this work.

The term is used as follows:

*According to Jim Woodhouse (1993), playability of virtual instruments means that the acoustical analysis of the waveforms produced by the model fall within the region of the multidimensional space given by the parameters of the model. This is the region where good tone is obtained. In the case of the bowed string good tone refers to the Helmholtz motion, i.e. the ideal motion of a bowed string that each player is trying to achieve.* (p. 105)

Charles Nichols (2003) invented the vBow. The vBow is a virtual violin bow musical controller. It is built to allow the computer musician to use most of the gestural freedom of a bow on a violin string. *"The vBow [...] provides the performer with an amplification of their musical intent, through the translation of their physical gesture into the expressive manipulation of timbre."* (p. 12). To reach this goal, four servo motor systems track four degrees of freedom of the virtual bow: lateral, rotational, longitudinal, and vertical motion. In order not only to track the players bow movements but also to give the player a more realistic "feel" of bowing, the system is capable of simulating a haptical feedback. It is applied by using servomotors, and thus generating physical forces against the vBow.

Many more violin-related systems, like Goto (1999), Trueman and Cook (1999), and Overholt (2005), have been presented in the past. An overview can be found in Poepel and Overholt (2006). Goto (1999) has built an instrument-inspired controller (Wanderley & Depalle, 2004) that uses a wooden corpus without strings. The player's actions are caught with four slide sensors for left-hand finger position, a force sensor under the chin rest, an inclinometer, and a sensor for bow speed and position. Overholt (2005) builds a hybrid, keeping the strings and adding sensors to allow the performer new musical relevant gestures. The idea of this approach is *"to preserve the expert expressivity of the violinist [...] as well as extending/enhancing the instrument with new methods of expression that are not inherent to the conventional technique."* (p. 605).

## Using an Audio Signal to Control Sound Synthesis

In parallel to the already mentioned Zeta MIDI violin (Graesser, 1996) are guitars equipped with a guitar-to-midi controller, such as the Axon AX 100 (Axon, 2007), which work on the same principle. Features are extracted from the audio signal, providing explicit information on parameters like pitch, amplitude, or plucking position.

Egozy (1995) adapted this approach to the clarinet. He presents an overview of related topics such as which parameters to measure, understanding of timbre, and methods of analysis. Similar to Traube (2004), Egozy draws conclusions about the performer's gestural movements from the parameters extracted from the audio signal. He mentions the human voice as an interesting controller for synthesis, due to its expressivity and communicative power. Following this idea, Janer (2005) presents an approach to control sound synthesis with the voice. He uses "*spectral processing techniques, derived from the Short-Time Fourier Transform,*" and thus "*provides ways of determining a performer's vocal intentions.*" (p. 132).

Jehan and Schoner (2001) present what they call "An Audio-Driven Perceptually Meaningful Timbre Synthesizer." They assume that any sound can be fully described with the perceptual parameters pitch, loudness, brightness, and timbre of an instrument's audio signal. They further assume that "*...timbre of a musical signal is characterized by the instantaneous power spectrum of its sound output*" (p. 382). In order to drive a synthesis engine using their "Cluster Weighted Modeling" method, they analyze the audio signal in terms of frequency, amplitude, amount of noise, spectral centroid, and bark scale decomposition. Since the parameters they measure constitute what they assume to be a complete description of the analyzed sound, they in turn assume that the resulting sound will have identical perceptual qualities.

One may ask whether this assumption is valid, given the problems with measuring playing parameters in a musical performance. Interesting as well is the question of how the selection of which parameters to measure was made, and what impact on the sound result a player would have if her or his musically meaningful performance actions do not fit completely within those parameters.

In contrast to the usage of the audio signal to derive explicit parameters, one might consider the alternative of using the audio signal itself in a synthesis algorithm. Many researchers and composers have explored the use of a captured audio signal in different contexts, for instance in live-electronic music. One established approach is to derive control features from the signal, and to modify the audio signal, with an effect the parameters of which are controlled using this derived data.

The work of Furukawa and Dutilleux (2002) is one example of this approach. The audio signal is used in three ways to control algorithms. The first way is to trigger samples and to modify the playback-parameters using derived parameters (pitch and amplitude) from a clarinet audio signal. The second way is to use clarinet pitch and amplitude to control the input parameters of three sound synthesis algorithms, and the third way is to use pitch to select among three delay-loops of varying durations and to use amplitude to change the input parameters of a vocoder that transforms the clarinet audio signal.

An earlier version of the method to control input parameters of processing algorithms with analyzed parameters of its audio signal is found in the Mu-tron (Gill, 1997). The Mu-tron was introduced in the early 1970s by the company Musitronics. It was an effects box, offering the opportunity to drive a variable resonant filter via an amplitude follower.

In one of his electronic violins, Max Mathews (Pierce, 1989) used an amplitude follower to control low- and band-pass filters. The cutoff and center frequencies of these filters were modulated by the amplitude of the violin pickup signal (R. Moog, personal communication, June 5, 2004). With a sufficient number of filters, it was possible to create sounds that were similar to a human voice (Pierce, 1989, p. 159).

This principle of extending processing algorithms by controlling them with parameters derived from the input signal was described by Verfaille and Arfib (2001). They call this method "adaptive digital audio effects" (ADAFx) because of their similarity in construction to adaptive filters. Due to the fact that the basic algorithm of "audio signal driven sound synthesis" (ASDSS) is similar to the one of ADAFx, the work presented here can be seen as a subset of adaptive effects. However, it differs from the approach of Verfaille and Arfib (2001) in that it is based on the modification of algorithms from the field of sound synthesis, and in that it tries to find solutions to problems of playability arising from the interplay of interfaces and synthesis.

## METHODS OF AUDIO SIGNAL DRIVEN SOUND SYNTHESIS

The use of systems, like a Zeta MIDI violin expanded with a hyperbow (Young, 1999), will increase the ability to deal with the player's input. Due to the parameter driven approach, however, some drawbacks remain. Tracking mistakes, latency in tracking, and untracked nuances are obvious issues. Besides that, another point, mentioned in the section "Phenomenological and Formal Descriptors in the Player Instrument Interaction" (trumpet player using a pitch tracker) must be kept in mind: The reflexive relationship between a player and the measuring system. Thus, the measured object, the player's method of playing, is altered as a result of the measuring process itself.

While different mappings and parameter hierarchies are found in the playing methods of traditional musicians, it is necessary to ask how existing systems can deal with such an input. To the knowledge of the author, there are no systems available that adapt themselves to the player's input by changing their method of mapping. Instead, one mapping method has to be selected and thus, predefined. Facing these drawbacks, one can say that there are architecture immanent problems, preventing the system from doing what is on the specification list. The system is open only to the methods of playing that are predefined by the measured parameters and by the method of mapping, and thus it forces the player to adapt to the idiosyncrasies of the process of measurement.

What could be done to resolve these problems or to make the system more open or transparent to a player's input? Instead of making the system more open by formalizing, as much as possible, essentials, and structuring them in the most appropriate way, in the approach presented on the following pages, the strategy used is to create openness by leaving essentials nonformalized. The formal structure, necessary to implement any kind of software, is designed in a way to surround essentials of the players, and to generate an output that is decoded by a user as a synthesized sound. The basic principle of generating openness by leaving essentials nonformalized has been described by Trogemann and Viehoff (2005, pp. 146-147). Trogemann and Viehoff define openness of software as its capacity to be open to user scope (room for maneuver) and room for interpretation, as well as flexibility and penetrability for users' intentions. Formalizing objects requires three conditions. Those are the need to be fixed in a written form, the need to be completely schematized, and the need to be noninterpretable (translation by the author). The code of any computer program has to meet the criteria of being explicit and unambiguous. This stands in contrast with many art-related codes like musical notation, or images that allow different readings and interpretations. Formalizing the musically meaningful parameters of expression for an instrument shifts the interpretation of the instrument from the user to the developer. Leaving essentials nonformalized leaves this interpretation with the user.

The oscillating string of a traditional instrument, for example, includes all information or data the player transmits into the input, since the players' gestures, playing techniques, bowing parameters, and left-hand finger actions all serve to modify the oscillation of the string. For this reason, player-specific parameters with implicit variation in the resulting oscillation can be handled. In order to bring into the computer what the player does, one can use a formal structure surrounding the essentials of this oscillation. One can use the audio signal and formalize as it is done in an A/D converter. What is necessary now is a synthesis algorithm that can deal with this input. An approach to such algorithms and principles for their construction are presented in the following sections. In comparison to approaches that are completely "parameter driven," the approach described here is referred to as "signal driven."

## Principles of Audio Signal Driven Sound Synthesis

In "audio signal driven sound synthesis" (ASDSS), ideally one would have a synthesis algorithm that deals with the unanalyzed audio signal according to Figure 3.

However, given the sonic results of experiments with algorithms of the above architecture, the author has found that it is often necessary to use control parameters and to shape the sound result indirectly in order to make the output correspond more closely to the player's input. Therefore, the basic construction principle of ASDSS goes along with the flow chart that is seen in Figure 4. The audio signal implicitly includes all playing parameters. The synthesis is mainly driven by the audio signal. This stands in contrast to the approach described in Figures 1 and 2, where the synthesis in completely driven by explicit parameters.

While in common methods of sound synthesis, the formal parameters are the base upon which the resultant sound is built (parameter driven); in this construction principle, the unanalyzed audio signal builds the base and the control parameters shape the sound indirectly (signal driven). Nuances in sound production that are not tracked can nevertheless be present in the output signal. The latency of the whole system will be reduced to

*Figure 4. Basic construction principle of ASDSS*

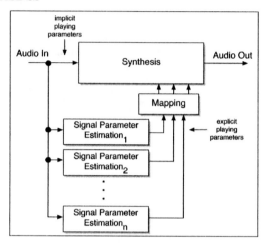

audio system latency since the throughput sound is independent of tracking latency.

In systems like the Zeta MIDI violin or those presented by Jehan and Schoner (2001), which use a parameter driven approach, a sound can be generated as soon as parameter data is available. Since measurement of frequency in an audio signal takes time, there will be a latency between the action of the player starting a tone and the synthesis unit generating the tone. This latency is crucial and disturbing to many performers (Wessel & Wright, 2002). In the signal driven approach, the sound output is effectively generated as soon as the sound input has passed the minimal delay of the system. Latency of measurement will influence the output sound as well, however, the hole of "no sound" after starting a tone is minimized. While measurement latency affects the sound indirectly, this is less disturbing than systems that do not produce sound until the results of the measurement procedure are available.

How can this kind of sound synthesis be implemented in detail? One possible solution is to modify known synthesis methods by replacing synthetic oscillators with the audio signal of the instrument. The methods presented in sections "Modified FM Synthesis" and "Modified Subtractive Synthesis" make use of this solution.

*Figure 3. Ideal ASDSS algorithm*

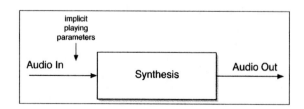

## Modified FM Synthesis

While the algorithm of a "digital cable" y(n) = x(n) does not provide the output characteristics of sound synthesis, it has the full playability the string on a bodiless stringed instrument has. It is possible to imagine synthesis as a deliberate disturbance of this digital cable with a satisfying sound result. Trying to keep this playability and experimenting with elements of sound synthesis, Poepel (2004) "disturbed" the digital cable by inserting a sine oscillator. The audio signal was amplified by scaling, and was fed into the frequency parameter input of the oscillator. While the resulting sounds were considered interesting, the amplitude of the output was not correlated to that of the input. Adding an envelope follower to drive the amplitude input of the oscillator solved this problem. However, the sound was still felt to be unnatural, due to excess brightness in the sound when playing with louder dynamics like forte or fortissimo. A transfer function (scaling table) was added, which scaled the output of the envelope follower. The result of this scaling was used to reduce the level of the audio signal before it was fed into the frequency input of the oscillator.

With this algorithm, an FM-like sound was produced. It has the ability to react to special playing techniques like sul ponticello, scratching, or hyper-soft sounds (bowing far out on the fingerboard). Similarly to traditional FM synthesis, the index can be controlled. Since it was interesting to see whether the algorithm was able to deal with FM, using constant frequency ratios, a pitch follower was inserted. Its output was multiplied by the ratio, and the result added to the amplified audio signal. A flow chart of the resulting algorithm is presented in Figure 5. Referring to the elements of Figure 4, in Figure 5, the signal parameter estimation can be found in the envelope estimator and pitch estimator. Mappings are found in the calculation of carrier to modulator ratio (using pitch estimator values)

*Figure 5. Modified FM synthesis*

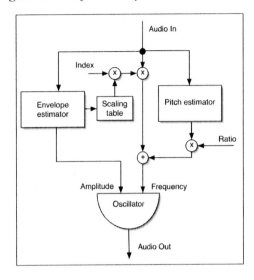

and the scaling of envelope estimator values to the index of modulation.

Testing this algorithm showed that the application of a constant frequency ratio, through the use of a pitch tracker, was indeed effective. Latency of the pitch tracker resulted in a slight change in timbre at the onset of a new tone, caused by the slight change in the frequency input of the sine oscillator.

## Modified Subtractive Synthesis

Similar to the modification of simple FM synthesis, the noise generator of a subtractive synthesis algorithm is replaced by the audio signal of the instrument. Unlike in modified FM synthesis, the algorithm is not very meaningful without the pitch tracker. The center frequencies of band-pass filters can be set to specific partials of the audio signal. The amplitude of each filtered partial can be adjusted separately. Figure 6 presents the algorithm.

Using the thusly modified subtractive synthesis enables one to create sounds with many different timbres compared to the input signal.

*Figure 6. Modified subtractive synthesis*

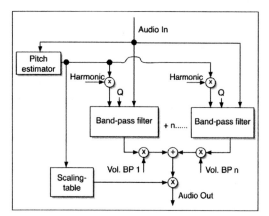

*Figure 7. Modified FM using self modulation*

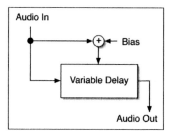

*Figure 8. Improved self modulation FM*

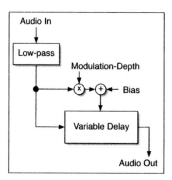

## Self Modulation

Another possibility to modify FM synthesis is called "self modulation" and is described in Poepel and Dannenberg (2005). Whereas the two methods presented before replace one oscillator, the principle here is to replace both of the oscillators of a simple FM synthesis with the audio signal of the instrument. This method was developed by the second author, Roger Dannenberg (p. 393), and is presented in Figure 7. Bias stands for a constant added to the phase in order to keep the system causal. It prevents the tap-out point of the delay from getting in front of the write-in point. The implementation was done in Aura (Dannenberg, 2004) and was tested with a trumpet as the input device.

One advantage of this approach is that neither amplitude nor pitch estimation is necessary, as the algorithm is transparent to both parameters. Similar to the case of modified FM synthesis described earlier, a disproportionate amount of brightness was achieved. To reduce this, a low-pass filter and an attenuation control, according to Figure 8, was implemented.

The sound results show a high pitch and amplitude accuracy. As reported in Poepel (2005) the filter used (12dB/Oct) ...*severely deadens the*

*tone at lower amplitudes* (p. 393). But an FM-like sound is still achieved, due to the rich spectrum that is generated as the trumpet gets louder.

## APPLICATION

The methods presented in the last section can be used for various existing instruments. Beyond that, it is conceivable that new instruments could be built using any kind of oscillating material to serve as an input device. According to the musician and sound architect Andres Bosshard (personal communication, October 7, 2004), it may even be sensible to use this algorithm with any kind of sound file in order to create new meaningful sounds.

We will, however, focus in this section on an already existing implementation, and explore various user experiences with it. This implementation was done by the author and uses a bodiless viola.

The viola was selected since the developer is an expert violist, and thus has a good base to do personal tests during development. The bodiless viola used was built by the violinmaker Arwed Harms in 2002. It is equipped with an inexpensive Shadow SH 941 pickup. In comparison with more expensive and better sounding pickups like the Schertler EV Pickup (Graesser, 1998), the Shadow pickup has a reduced transmission of higher frequencies. This setup was used in order to present a method that enables interested string players to explore electronic sounds in a way that is available, testable, affordable, and allows them to make use of their existing skills. The inexpensive pickup was used in order to check if the system works even with a low-quality audio signal, and to keep the cost of entrance to the world of electronic sounds, for interested newcomers, relatively low. The algorithms were implemented using the programming environment Max/MSP running on a Apple Macintosh G4 laptop. Pitch tracking was done using the MSP object *fiddle~* (Puckette, Abel, & Zicarelli, 1998). Figure 9 gives an impression of the setup.

## Empirical Study of an ASDSS Application

Since many advantages and disadvantages of AS-DSS had been posited in the development stage, it was considered necessary to undertake research in order to see if and how these affected real-world use. An important question is what potential for musical expression an application using ASDSS will have. Therefore, an empirical study was done by Poepel (2005) to compare three instruments. These were a Zeta MIDI viola (instrument A), the viola presented in Figure 9 performing a simple FM synthesis (instrument B), and the same viola performing the modified FM synthesis (instrument C), as described previously.

FM synthesis was selected due to the need of comparability. It is available as a signal driven, as a parameter driven, and as a MIDI driven version. All three versions use a pitch tracker, an envelope follower, and a synthesis unit. All three instruments derived from these elements were set to a fixed sound preset. Playing parameters could be altered only in the traditional way of performing them via the string.

*Figure 9. Hardware used in the application*

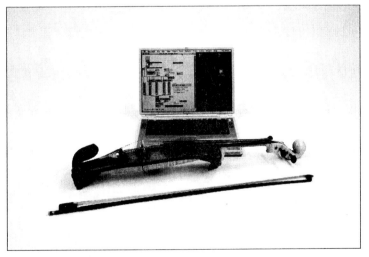

Based on findings in music psychology (Juslin, 2001), relevant cues for musical expression (tempo, sound level, timing, intonation, articulation, timbre, vibrato, tone attacks, tone decays, and pauses) were used to research how accurately the three instruments, according to the estimation of the participants, reacted when various playing techniques were applied in order to create such cues. Thirteen participants, professionals and amateurs, coming from classical backgrounds as well as from jazz and contemporary music, took part in this study. They had to perform musical tasks according to the cues, and estimate the accuracy of the sound result compared to the input they were applying.

It was hypothesized that the MIDI viola and the simple FM viola would present similar results, while the modified FM viola would be considered to be far more playable. However, the MIDI viola was estimated to have a much smaller potential for musical expression than the simple FM viola, whereas the simple FM viola and modified FM synthesis viola were closely ranked.

Details on the question of how the participants estimated the instruments, including analysis of the different playing tasks (quantitative approach), can be found in Poepel (2005). Of interest here is the qualitative approach, the question of how and *why* the instruments were estimated in terms of playability, and thus, their potential for musical expression.

Four participants rated instrument C as having the highest potential for musical expression, while two participants considered instrument B best in this regard. Seven participants estimated the potential of both instruments as equal. A notable finding was that participants with a low level of interest in electronic sounds evaluated the instruments differently from those with a high level of interest in electronic sounds. Looking at the estimated differences between instrument B and C according to the expressive cues (pitch, timing, dynamics, articulation, and timbre), interestingly, dynamic accuracy was estimated by the participants to have the widest difference.

To get a more detailed view into the reasons for these results, the participants were interviewed after they had evaluated the instruments. Two participants with a high level of interest in electronic sounds said they had expected the kind of synthesized sounds they were used to. However, instrument C was felt to have a sound in-between a string instrument and a synthesizer. Therefore, they were not quite satisfied with the sound result of instrument C. The fact that the Harms viola was heavier than a traditional viola, and thus unpleasant, was often mentioned. Four participants mentioned that instrument C reacted better to vibrato than instrument B.

It was mentioned, five times, that instrument C responded better in terms of instrument-specific playing techniques. Notable aspects of the players' experiences mentioned were: I can more effectively play the bowing technique collé; I can more effectively go "into" the tone; I feel that the tone is more effectively "in my grip"; I can more effectively "pull" the tone; I can more effectively play legato between different tones; the instrument is more transparent to my musical expression.

Four participants said that the timbre of instrument B, as well as the one of instrument C, varied too much between the lower and higher strings. In addition, four participants mentioned that the resulting "bubbling" sound, when playing sul ponticello or when playing notes with a strong noise component, was disturbing in instrument C as well as in instrument B. Two participants mentioned that they would need to have the ability to play double steps. Two participants mentioned their need for a complete system inside a mechanically stable "black box" (not a laptop) to be ready for stage performance.

This leads to the question of why the participants came to these conclusions. Interestingly, a sound driven by the audio signal was considered by some participants not to be a synthesized sound. However, the sound result in modified FM synthesis was produced by a sine oscillator. One might speculate that the character of sounds controlled by a small number of discrete parameters is probably understood as the "synthesized sound character" no matter how the sound is produced. Since vibrato is, seen in detail, not only a pitch modulation but also an amplitude and timbral modulation, it seems reasonable that vibrato was considered to be better transmitted with instrument C. Concerning dynamics that were found to be better transmitted in instrument C than in B, the reason can be seen in the fact that traditional instruments show not only a different amplitude, but also slightly different timbres when played in different dynamics. While the string and thus the audio signal already shows this timbral change, it is clear that the audio signal driven sound result can include the timbral change as well.

With this study, one of many possible implementations using ASDSS was tested. Due to the fact that only one modified and simple implementation on the base of one traditional instrument using a specific pickup has been compared, these results may not be seen to constitute a general appraisal of the potential of ASDSS. However, it shows a first empirical view into one possible implementation.

## User Tests

In addition to this study, instrument C, described in the section "Application," was given to several people in order to test its general usability under less-controlled conditions. Since this test does not compare two synthesizer instruments, it has to be expected that test candidates will refer to abilities, and thus requirements, that are related to their experiences with acoustic instruments. A set of comments, including quality criteria of the instrument mentioned in the section "Background," is presented here. The comments were translated by the author.

- *"This does not at all feel like a normal violin since I am playing here (points to the Harms viola) and the sound is coming from there*

*(points to the loudspeaker)."*

- *"The system is impressive since it is such a simple idea but with such a huge effect on playability."*

- *"It is nice but it makes no sense for me to play a bass clarinet-like sound or a pan flute on the violin."*

- *"To be playable in a string-specific manner I do not only need a string-specific reaction of the instrument, but also a string-specific sound or something close to it. You can't separate the sound from the instrumental feeling."*

- *"Such an instrument will never feel like a traditional instrument. The feedback loop between the bridge and body does not exist. Therefore the oscillation of the body will not affect the bridge and the string."*

Such statements raise questions such as: How important is the position of the speaker for the feel of the instrument? What influence does the timbre of a new instrument have on playability? Wanderley and Depalle (2004) mention sound as a "secondary feedback" (p. 633) between the instrument and the performer. The importance of timbre may play a role in questions of playability as well.

In order to focus the development of new kinds of stringed instruments and to achieve a better communication among string players, researchers, instrument builders, and composers, the author has started a special interest group called >hot_strings SIG< (Poepel & Overholt, 2006). The system was also presented and tested there. Synthesis methods used were besides modified FM, modified subtractive synthesis, as well as combinations of both and combinations with digital audio effects such as a vocoder or a single side band modulation.

The questions of which kinds of sounds the instrument should produce, whether it would be already acceptable for use, and how it could be improved, resulted in different opinions. While some players desired improvements that would make the instrument sound much closer to a traditional one, there were others that were seeking an instrument that reacted differently in sound and behavior compared to a traditional one. Asking the players about the reasons for these opinions, it became clear that aesthetic positions were important. According to these positions, the instrument was perceived and evaluated differently. The playability of an instrument is, according to this experience, not only a question of the instrument itself. It is also a question of the player.

To get a view on a personal statement of a violin player working with ASDSS, an interview with Günter Marx, principle first violin of the Dortmund Philharmonic Orchestra, Germany, is presented in the appendix.

## DISCUSSION

Obviously, the tested application differs in weight, position of sound output, and technical setup (including the required computer hard- and software know how) from the traditional instrument and thus, does not meet all of the requirements on the specification list. Criticism of those points by the test subjects is evident.

However, the question arises of why there was not a greater difference in the assessment of instruments B and C. One reason might be seen in the fact that an ASDSS algorithm is not identical with a "digital cable" in terms of transparency for all kinds of musical inputs. The algorithm will somehow cover or disturb some features of the methods applied to the string by the player. An example: playing the modified FM synthesis algorithm on a bow position far from the bridge, but at a high dynamic, will result in a typical FM sound with increased sharpness. Compared to the traditional instrument, the sound is too sharp for such a bow-bridge distance. This is an FM-specific problem, and could be reduced by adding a bow-

bridge measurement that influences the FM index based on bow position. The modified subtractive synthesis algorithm described earlier does not have this problem. However, due to the fact that rapid changes of the filters' center frequencies results in sonic artifacts, the noisy attack phase of tones may be sonically disturbing depending on the playing technique of the performer.

It is a task of the future to identify other synthesis methods that can be driven by the audio signal. According to experiences with the methods already in use, it is important to explore which kind of coverage and disturbance are found, and how one can deal with those. Besides that, it is important to ask what implication the loss of the wooden body, with all its resonances and feedback functions, has for tone production. According to discussions in the earlier mentioned >hot_strings SIG<, namely timbre, tone quality, and tone characteristics, are fields that are influenced crucially by the lack of the body.

When offering an implementation of ASDSS to download and introductions to string players, the author was often faced with rather reluctant reactions from people interested in extending their instruments. Looking at the implementations of ASDSS so far, it is true that one may not create new instruments without the player somehow needing to adapt to the new conditions. Accordingly, one may say that the new possibilities gained compared to the loss of old possibilities have not reached the point where those players could say "lets adapt to the new ways." Another reason for the need of adaptation lies in the fact that a different sound (otherwise one would stay with the traditional instrument) will always lead to a somehow different relation between gesture and sound. For instance, the use of an unfamiliar cello by a cellist already requires a certain amount of adaptation.

In comparison with sound synthesis that is purely parameter driven, ASDSS shows some notable differences. The disturbance of latency is dependent on musical material and the specific algorithm. Latency of tracking results can affect the timbre of a tone during tone start. The intensity of such a timbre change, however, depends on the distance of successive discrete parameter values. This behavior is different to latency problems in common sound synthesis, and probably offers new potential to deal with the latency problem. Latency in pitch tracking, when playing big tone intervals, leads to different timbral changes and different disturbances comparing modified FM and subtractive synthesis. This means that ASDSS offers options to deal with the problem of latency. These options lie inside and are dependant of the synthesis algorithm. Some problematic tasks usually related to the interface have thus become related to the algorithm.

One might argue that ASDSS is not synthesis but sound processing. From the author's point of view, it lies between the two. However, the author considers it to be closer to synthesis and therefore, given a "synthesis name" because the algorithms modified are derived from synthesis literature. Based on the sound results achieved so far, players perceived the system to be an instrument or a synthesizer rather than a room or a sound effect.

The basic architecture of common sound synthesis is based on a view of instruments being able to be formalized and divided into interfaces, mapping units, oscillation units, and sound radiators. As mentioned in the introduction, an acoustic instrument like a violin, however, has no formal input for pitch or amplitude, no fixed set of parameter mapping, and no parameter hierarchy. It is the player's decision when noise should become more important than pitch (e.g., ppp tremolo in slow movements can be necessarily very noisy). While one can suitably say that a string player usually wants to achieve Helmholtz motion or the "*good tone*" (Young & Serafin, 2003) as assumed in research on physical modeling, one should also keep in mind that a string player, according to Galamian (1988), necessarily needs knocking

and noisy sounds to build the "*tone consonants*" (p. 20). It is the player's task to discern what kind of sound is *good* and at what moment. The necessary process of abstraction, predefinition, and formalization in order to get to an instrument based on the common parameter driven synthesis approach results in electronic instruments that necessarily predefine the player's behavior. It may be asked whether this approach, even if the behavior is predefined as far as possible, will lead to satisfying results comparable with the expressive potential of traditional instruments.

Building a complex computer-based system trying to match an anticipated behavior of a player is a well-known problem in other areas of interaction. According to Trogemann and Viehoff (2005), the strategy to develop computer games by anticipating all possible reactions of players failed up from a specific level of complexity. Often players acted in a way the developers did not foresee. Improved development strategies do not try to anticipate any possible situation in the game. Instead, a rule-based "universe" is built proving all kinds of possible player behavior as common states of the system (p. 149). While ASDSS is not exactly the same, it is estimated here to be parallel to this approach.

An important question is how players that already have adapted to common synthesis methods, to their architecture, editing style, and sound, might deal with ASDSS. First experiences show that, for instance, laptop musicians are often not convinced of the method. Trained in working with lots of parameter driven sound synthesis, a belief and experience are found that essentials of meaningful sounds can be created in common ways. As discussions of the author have brought up, an idea or feeling for some probably missing essentials is found rather seldom.

## FUTURE WORK

In addition to all the advantages and disadvantages discussed so far, the method of driving an algorithm with an audio signal is a cheap, simple, and viable paradigm. It can be used in other instruments besides the ones presented here. Research in this approach is in its very beginning. A future task will be to analyze whether existing synthesis methods of all kinds can be modified in the presented way. While the replacement of oscillators with the audio signal is a possible modification, it will not necessarily be the only one of use.

The application presented above can be improved in many ways. The timbre differences between low and high strings should be leveled. A method to minimize plopping artifacts when bigger intervals are played would be of interest, as well a scaling of the filter bandwidth that is driven by pitch data. Many variations of modified FM synthesis, such as multiple modulator FM or feedback FM, are conceivable. Additionally, sources like oscillators could be added, ratio could be changed using nonlinear processes, or modulators could themselves be modulated by any kind of derivate of the audio signal, such as filtered partials (Poepel, 2005).

Besides stand-alone applications, plug-ins such as VST or RTAS will be of interest. The author successfully used VST plug-ins implementing the ASDSS methods of modified FM and subtractive synthesis combined with a standard live sequencer in two concerts. While features of the audio signal are used in ASDSS to modify the sound indirectly, it is possible to use gesture parameters as well. In FM synthesis bow position, bow speed and bow pressure could, for example, be used to modify amplitude, index and filters in order to obtain a highly gesture-appropriate sound.

ASDSS is not limited to the use of traditional instruments. Any kind of oscillating material may be of interest in providing an input audio signal, as long as the sound results at the output are convincing. As an important factor, the audio

pickup moves to the centre of attention. According to the authors experience, even the smallest changes in pickup position can affect the sound. It might be of interest to explore which kind of pickups work best together with which kind of algorithms.

The use of combinations with existing common synthesis methods is of interest. It might be fruitful to implement parts of some synthesis methods with an ASDSS approach. The range of possibilities is wide, and will hopefully inspire musicians and researchers in their work on interactive music.

## CONCLUSION

In summary, a new approach to sound synthesis has been described, and experiences with an application using this approach have been presented and discussed. The core idea of this method lies in the strategy to use playing parameters, playing style, and musical expression a musician applies at the input side of an instrument. In contrast to common approaches, this method does not try to define, measure, and formalize the playing parameters a musician might apply to the interface. Instead, the method presented here uses synthesis algorithms that are capable of transmitting musical input to the synthesized output with as little formalization as possible of playing parameters. In case the sound result does not go along with the player's input, parameters are defined, measured, and formalized as common. However, they do not form the core information used to create the synthesized sound, but they are used to shape the synthesized sound indirectly.

Empirical tests and user experience provide evidence that the approach presented can create meaningful results, depending on the background of the user. Furthermore, it is a meaningful addition to the collection of synthesis methods since it is already used by musicians.

This method offers a new view on the problems of player-instrument interaction. It provides, under particular circumstances, a better playability, however, with a reduced access to the variety of existing synthesis methods as long as they are not or cannot be adapted to the new method. By all means, the approach presented in this chapter may be an interesting alternative to *think* the architecture of the connection between player, interface, mapping, and synthesis.

## ACKNOWLEDGMENT

The author would like to thank J. Borchers, G. Scavone, P. Depalle, S. D. Wilson, D. Overholt, M. M. Wanderley, V. Verfaille, G. Trogemann, G. Marx, L. Scherffig, H. Hertell, E. Lee, and D. Braun for various discussions, comments, and thoughts.

## REFERENCES

Askenfelt, A. (1989). Measurement of the bowing parameters in violin playing. II: Bow-bridge distance, dynamic range, and limits of bow force. *Journal of the Acoustical Society of America, 86*(2), 503-516.

Axon. (2007). *Axon AX 100 MK II, Guitar to MIDI Controller.* Retrieved February 12, 2007, from http://audiode.terratec.net/

Biesenbender, V. (1992). *Von der unerträglichen Leichtigkeit des Instrumentalspiels.* Aarau, Switzerland: Musikedition Nepomuk.

Buchla, D., Buxton, W. A. S., Chafe, C., Machover, T., Moog, R., Mathews, M., Risset, J. C., Sonami, L., & Waiswisz, M., (2000). Round table. In M. M. Wanderley & M. Battier (Ed.), *Trends in gestural control of music* (pp. 415-437). Paris: IRCAM Centre Pompidou.

Cadoz, C., Luciani, A., & Florens, J. L. (1984). Responsive input devices and sound synthesis by simulation of instrumental mechanisms: The CORDIS system. *Computer Music Journal, 8*(2), 60-73.

Cadoz, C., & Wanderley, M. M. (2000). Gesture—Music. In M. M. Wanderley & M. Battier (Ed.), *Trends in gestural control of music* (pp. 28-65). Paris, France: IRCAM Centre Pompidou.

Chadabe, J. (1997). *Electric sound: The past and promise of electronic music.* Upper Saddle River, NJ: Prentice Hall.

CHI. (2007). *Conference on Human Factors in Computing Systems, also labeled as Conference on Human Computer Interaction (HCI).* Retrieved February 12, 2007, from http://www.chi2007.org/.

Dannenberg, R. B. (2004). Combining visual and textual representations for flexible interactive audio signal processing. In G. Tzanetakis, G. Essl, & C. Leider (Ed.), *Proceedings of the 2004 International Computer Music Conference* (pp. 240-247). Miami, FL: International Computer Music Association.

Egozy, E. B. (1995). *Deriving musical control features from a real-time timbre analysis of the clarinet.* Unpublished master's thesis. Massachusetts Institute of Technology, Cambridge, MA.

Fels, S. (2004). Designing for intimacy: Creating new interfaces for musical expression. In *Proceedings of the IEEE, 92*(4), 672-685.

Fels, S., Gadd, A., & Mulder, A. (2002). Mapping transparency through metaphor: Towards more expressive musical instrument. *Organised Sound, 7*(2), 109-126.

Furukawa, K., & Dutilleux, P. (2002). Live-electronics algorithms in the multimedia work "Swim Swan." In *Proceedings of the 5th International Conference on Digital Audio effects 2002* (pp. 263-268). Hamburg, Germany.

Galamian, I. (1988). *Grundlagen und Methoden des Violinspiels* (2nd ed.). Frankfurt/M., Berlin, Germany: Edition Sven Erik Bergh.

Gill, C. (1997). The stomping ground: Musitronics, mu-tron, and the gizmotron. *Vintage Guitar Magazine, 11*(12).

Goto, S. (1999). The aesthetics and technological aspects of virtual musical instruments: The case of the superpolm MIDI violin. *Leonardo Music Journal, 9*, 115-120.

Graesser, H. (1996). *Electric violins.* Frankfurt am Main, Germany: Verlag Erwin Bochinsky.

Hunt, A. (1999). *Radical musical interfaces for real-time musical control.* Unpublished doctoral dissertation, University of York, UK.

Hunt, A., & Wanderley, M. M. (2002). Mapping performer parameters to synthesis engines. *Organised Sound, 7*(2), 97-108.

Jaffe, D. A., & Smith, J. O., III (1995). Performance expression in commuted waveguide synthesis of bowed strings. In M. Erin (Ed.), *Proceedings of the 1995 International Computer Music Conference* (pp. 343-346). Banff, Canada: The Banff Centre for the Arts.

Janer, J. (2005). Voice-controlled plucked bass guitar through two synthesis techniques. In S. Fels & T. Blaine. (Ed.), *Proceedings of the 2005 Conference on New Interfaces for Musical Expression* (pp. 132-135). Vancouver, Canada: University of British Columbia.

Jehan, T. & Schoner, B. (2001). An audio-driven perceptually meaningful timbre synthesizer. In A. Schloss, R. Dannenberg, & P. Driessen (Ed.), *Proceedings of the 2001 International Computer Music Conference* (pp. 381-388). Havanna, Cuba: The Instituto Cubano de la Musica.

Jordà, S. (2005). *Digital lutherie. Crafting musical computers for new musics' performance and improvisation.* Unpublished doctoral dissertation.

University Pompeu Fabra, Department of Technology, Barcelona, Spain.

Juslin, P. N. (2001). Communicating emotion in music performance: A review and theoretical framework. In *Music and Emotion.* (p. 309-337). Oxford, UK: Oxford University Press.

Levitin, D. J., McAdams, S. & Adams, R. L. (2002). Control parameters for musical instruments: A foundation for new mappings of gesture to sound. *Organised Sound, 7*(2), 171-189.

Machover, T. (1992). *Hyperinstruments: A progress Report, 1987-1991.* Technical report, Massachusetts Institute of Technology, Cambridge, MA.

Mathews, M. V., & Kohut, J. (1973). Electronic simulation of violin resonances. *Journal of the Acoustical Society of America, 53*(6), 1620-1626.

Miranda, E,. & Wanderley, M. (2006). *New digital musical instruments: Control and interaction beyond the keyboard.* Middleton, WI: A-R Editions, Inc.

Mulder, A. (1998). *Design of three-dimensional instruments for sound control.* Unpublished doctoral dissertation. Simon Fraser University, Vancouver, Canada.

Neuhaus, H. (1967). *Die Kunst des Klavierspiels.* no statement of city: Bergisch Gladbach, Germany: Musikverlage Hans Gerig.

Ng, K. (2004). Music via motion: Transdomain mapping of motion and sound for interactive performances. In *Proceedings of the IEEE, 92*(4), 645-655.

Nichols, C. (2003). *The vBow an expressive musical controller haptic human-computer interface.* Unpublished doctoral dissertation, Stanford University, CA.

NIME (2001). *Conference on New Interfaces for Musical Expression.* Retrieved February 12, 2007, from http://www.nime.org

O'Modhrain, M.S. (2000). *Playing by feel: Incorporating haptic feedback into computer-cased musical instruments.* Unpublished doctoral dissertation, Stanford University, CA.

Overholt, D. (2005). The overtone violin. In A. Lewin-Richter, & X. Serra (Ed.), *Proceedings of the 2005 International Computer Music Conference* (pp. 604-607). San Francisco, CA: International Computer Music Association.

Paine, G. (2004). Gesture and musical interaction: Interactive engagement through dynamic morphology, In Y. Nagashima (Ed.), *Proceedings of the 2004 Conference on New Interfaces for Musical Expression* (pp. 80-85). Hamamatsu, Japan: Shizuoka University of Art and Culture.

Paradiso, J. A. (1997b) Electronic music interfaces: new ways to play. *IEEE Spectrum, 34*(12), 18-30.

Paradiso, J. A., & Gershenfeld, N. (1997a). Musical applications of electric field sensing. *Computer Music Journal,. 21*(2), 69-89.

Pierce, J. R. (1989). *Klang mit den Ohren der Physik* (2nd ed.). Heidelberg, Germany: Spektrum-der-Wissenschaft-Verlagsgesellschaft.

Poepel, C. (2004). Synthesized strings for string-players. In Y. Nagashima (Ed.), *Proceedings of the 2004 Conference on New Interfaces for Musical Expression* (pp. 150-153). Hamamatsu, Japan: Shizuoka University of Art and Culture.

Poepel, C. (2005). On interface expressivity: A player-based study. In S. Fels, & T. Blaine (Ed.), *Proceedings of the 2005 Conference on New Interfaces for Musical Expression* (pp. 228-231). Vancouver, Canada: University of British Columbia.

Poepel, C., & Dannenberg, R. B. (2005). Audio signal driven sound synthesis. In A. Lewin-Richter & Serra, X. (Ed.), *Proceedings of the 2005 International Computer Music Conference* (pp. 391-394). San Francisco: International Computer Music Association.

Poepel, C., & Overholt, D. (2006). Recent developments in violin-related digital musical instruments: Where are we and where are we going? In N. Schnell, N., F. Bevilacqua, M. Lyons, & A.Tanaka (Eds.), *Proceedings of the 2006 Conference on New Interfaces for Musical Expression* (pp. 228-231). Paris: IRCAM-Centre Pompidou.

Poupyrev, I., Lyons, M. J., Fels, S., & Blaine., T. (2001). Workshop proposal: New interfaces for musical expression. In *Proceedings of the 2001 Workshop on New Interfaces for Musical Expression.* Singapore: National University of Singapore.

Prem, E. (1997). Epistemic autonomy in models of living systems. In P. Husbands & I. Harvey (Eds.), *Proceedings fourth European Conference on Artificial Life* (pp. 2-9). Brighton, UK.

Puckette, M. S., Apel, T., & Zicarelli, D. D. (1998). Real-time audio analysis tools for Pd and MSP. In M. Simoni (Ed.), *Proceedings of the 1998 International Computer Music Conference* (pp. 109-112). San Francisco: International Computer Music Association.

Rasamimanana, N. (2006). Gesture analysis of violin bow strokes. In S. Gibet, N. Courty, & J.-F Kamp (Ed.), *Gesture in Human-Computer Interaction and Simulation: 6th International Gesture Workshop,* 3881, (pp. 145-155). Berlin, Heidelberg, German: Springer Verlag.

Schoner, B. (2000). *Probabilistic characterization and synthesis of complex driven systems.* Unpublished doctoral dissertation. Massachusetts Institute of Technology, Cambridge, MA.

Schoonderwaldt, E., Rasamimanana, N., & Bevilacqua, F. (2006). Combining accelerometer and video camera: Reconstruction of bow velocity profiles. In N. Schnell, F. Bevilacqua, M. Lyons, & A. Tanaka (Ed.), *Proceedings of the 2006 Conference on New Interfaces for Musical Expression* (pp. 200-203). Paris: IRCAM-Centre Pompidou.

Traube, C. (2004). *An interdisciplinary study of the timbre of the classical guitar.* Unpublished doctoral dissertation. McGill University, Montréal, Canada.

Trogemann, G., & Viehoff, J. (2005). *Code@ art, eine elementare Einführung in die Programmierung als künstlerische Praktik.* Wien, NY: Springer-Verlag.

Trueman, D., & Cook, P. (1999). BoSSA, the deconstructed violin reconstructed. In J. Fung, J. (Ed.), *Proceedings of the 1999 International Computer Music Conference* (pp. 232-239). San Francisco: International Computer Music Association.

Verfaille, V., & Arfib, D. (2001). A-dafx: Adaptive digital audio effects. In *Proceedings of the 4th International Conference on Digital Audio Effects 2001* (pp. 10-13). Limerick, Ireland.

von Neumann, J. (1955). *Mathematical foundations of quantum mechanics.* Priceton, NJ: Princeton University Press.

von Neumann, J. (1966). *The theory of self-reproducing automata.* Urbana, IL: University of Illinois Press.

Wanderley, M. M., & Battier, M. (Ed.). (2000). *Trends in gestural control of music.* CD-Rom. Paris, France: IRCAM—Centre Pompidou.

Wanderley, M. M., & Depalle, P. (2004). Gestural control of sound synthesis. In *Proceedings of the IEEE, 92*(4), 632-644.

Wanderley, M. M., & Orio, N. (2002). Evaluation of input devices for musical expression: Borrowing tools from HCI. *Computer Music Journal, 26*(3), 62-76.

Wessel, D., & Wright, M. (2002). Problems and prospects for intimate musical control of computers. *Computer Music Journal, 26*(3), 11-22.

Woodhouse, J. (1993). On the playability of violins. I: Reflection functions, on the playability of violins. II: Minimum bowforce and transients. *Acustica, 78*(3), 125-153.

Young, D. (1999). *New frontiers of expression through real-time dynamics measurement of violin bows.* Unpublished master's thesis. Massachusetts Institute of Technology, Cambridge, MA.

Young, D., & Serafin, S. (2003). Playability evaluation of a virtual bowed string instrument. In F. Thibault (Ed.), *Proceedings of the 2003 Conference on New Instruments for Musical Expression* (pp. 104-108). Montréal: McGill University.

## APPENDIX

Günter Marx is an experienced player of contemporary music and has been working for over 15 years with synthesizers and electronic violins. He tested an implementation of the methods modified FM and subtractive synthesis expanded by a modified single sideband modulation and common methods of sound processing such as filters and reverberation. Preset 3 and Preset 5 were similar to the ones used in section "Empirical Study of an ASDSS-Application." Preset 5 is instrument B (simple FM synthesis) and Preset 3 is instrument C (modified FM synthesis, according to figure 5). Günter Marx used the audio output of a Zeta MIDI violin. The interview took place in March 2006, and was translated by the author.

**Cornelius Poepel:** Günter, I am interested in your experiences and in your opinion using synthesis methods based on ASDSS. What are the reasons for you to work with this method?
**Günter Marx:** Well, I am simply interested in testing new methods to create electronic sounds as long as I can use them as a violinist. Since the first examples you presented to me were interesting, I surely wanted to figure out whether these sounds might be useful for me.

**CP:** What were your experiences in using the ASDSS software?
**GM:** After going through the presets, I tried to program my own parameter settings. Some sounds were quite exciting. Unfortunately, the software interface is not very user-friendly at present; this should be improved. Otherwise, sound editing is very circuitous.

**CP:** Readiness for marketing is indeed not yet reached; sorry for that. But focusing on the question of whether the methods of sound synthesis here do somehow improve the playing of synthesized sounds with the electric violin, what are your experiences?
**GM:** What exactly do you mean by that? Variability in terms of violin playing?

**CP:** Yes, I call it string-specific playability.
**GM:** I see, yes, I noticed immediately that this system offers a lot more in terms of violinistic playing. Much more than if I played via MIDI to drive a synthesizer.

**CP:** Could you make this more concrete?
**GM:** Well, it is more stable in terms of what I do. The reaction is more stable. And it is sensitive to the distance of the bow to the bridge.

**CP:** I would be interested in a more detailed view on the differences between the ASDSS method and common methods. Could you compare preset 3 with preset 5 and tell me about the difference?
**GM:** Sure.

**CP:** What do you think of the sound quality, or the potential of the sounds to make them interesting for a player?
**GM:** (trying for a while) I think it depends on what sound you are seeking. Let's say you want to have a relatively natural sound, close to a common violin, then preset 3 would be better. If you are more interested in an alienation to the violin, both sounds can be used. Preset 5 reminds me more of a synthesized sound.

**CP:** Could you compare the two concerning different playing techniques? I would suggest martelé, sautillé, legato usual, legato espressivo, sul ponticello.

**GM:** (trying for a while) In general I think with preset 3, the bowing techniques are better transmitted. Martelé is much better, sautillé also, legato espressivo is more expressive. With sul ponticello it is different, both do not work properly. Sounds like the pitch follower is struggling.

**CP:** Could you try to play tones with high and low tension, with different dynamics, and with different kinds of freely chosen expression?

**GM:** (trying) In terms of expression the differences are not that big. Perhaps preset 3 is a little more sensitive. But dynamical differences are much more present with preset 3 and changing tensions are similarly better represented in preset 3. From my perspective preset 3 feels more flexible and violinistic than preset 5.

**CP:** What would you suggest to improve the system?

**GM:** The biggest drawback for me is the lack of a user-friendly software interface. If this was changed I would start to use the method. At present, it is too time-consuming to edit the sounds and develop personal parameter settings. But seen from the point of violinistic variability, it is interesting.

**CP:** Günter, thanks for the interview.

# Chapter X
# How Technology Can Support Culture and Learning

**David Luigi Fuschi**
*GIUNTI Labs S.r.l., Italy*

**Bee Ong**
*University of Leeds, UK*

**David Crombie**
*DEDICON S.r.l., The Netherlands*

## ABSTRACT

*From the authors' perspective, technology is both a tool and a developing factor that can foster culture and learning development. This chapter focuses on the interrelations that interleave education, technology, content accessibility, and intercultural issues. With an introduction and related background, language learning is used as an example further to explain these issues. This chapter then discusses authoring and content development for e-learning applications (including authoring tools, virtual communities, and forums), and examines technology and accessibility issues in this context. The current state of e-learning is introduced along with a description of different tools and approaches. The chapter concludes with an overview of e-learning and the marketplace.*

## INTRODUCTION

Major developments in culture and civilisation are based on a combination of factors including personal abilities, societal, and economical environment, and so on. According to Maslow (Abraham, 1943), subsistence needs have to be met before other and "*higher*" aims are reached for (Figure 1). Nevertheless, the search for a solution to a problem (even a very practical one) may provide the core of our evolution in technology, science, culture, art, or education.

*Figure 1. Maslow's hierarchy of needs  (Adapted from Abraham Maslow, 1943)*

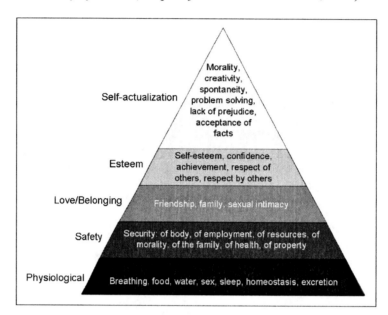

From the authors' perspective, the issue regarding the relation interleaving technology, culture, and education is twofold. On one side, technology has often been a major cause of disruptive advances in the evolution of science, culture, art, and education. On the other side, scientific and cultural progress necessarily rests upon a learning process, either formal or informal. For this very reason, the authors have focused their attention on how technology can support culture and learning.

For example, the present development of western culture has been reached thanks, in large part, to the technical innovation introduced by Gutenberg, which made possible the diffusion of culture through print, making learning affordable for everyone and therefore, also accessible. Yet were it not for Braille, all the culture and knowledge available in printed form would be totally inaccessible to visually impaired people unless they could afford to have a personal reader. This technical support is therefore a clear example of how technology can support culture and learning in the wider sense.

It is worth taking into account historical notes related to the impact of technology on the learning process and therefore, also on the evolution of society.

## SOME HISTORY NOTES

The art of teaching and learning has a long history. Initially it was a matter of subsistence and therefore, the elders in a community would act as tutors, trainers, and mentors for the younger members. This process then evolved from mere subsistence to something that became much valued by the learner and rewarding for the teacher.

Due to the very nature of this process (based on knowledge acquired through personal practical experience), teachers were numerically very limited in respect to potential learners; moreover, not everyone could benefit from mentoring, as most of the individuals would have to work hard to support the group's living needs. Therefore, only the most brilliant, or the more influential members, would be granted such a precious gift as *"formal learning"* and this had a strong social impact.

For a long period of time, education and culture has been accessible only to upper classes; religion played a relevant role in this, as knowledge was mainly held by *"priests"* or *"monks,"* who would also act as tutors and mentors for nobles, ruling classes, and their earls or illegitimate sons.

This phenomenon was so strong that during the *"Middle Ages"* the term *"clerices[1]"* was used generically to indicate the people with an education. This is also the period of the birth of the first universities like the *"Alma mater"* in Bologna (1088), the *"Sorbonne"* in Paris, *"Montpellier,"* the *"Scuola Medica Salernitana,"* *"Heidelberg,"* *"Salamanca,"* and many other ancient and prestigious universities in Europe. The *"clerices vagantes,"* in their roaming through Europe, spread culture, teaching in the various universities they visited, rivalling each other to achieve eternal fame thanks to the universal language of the time (*Latin*). A famous example is *Abelard* (the well-known character of *Abelard and Eloise*). Most people consider this as a tale while it actually was a real event in European history.

The main academic subjects at the time would have been literature, philosophy, religion, and law, while science was more limited in scope than now. In this sense, it is interesting to find out how some of the presently most reputed universities started, for example *Oxford* and *Cambridge*. Their origins date back to 1167 when Henry II ordered all English students on the Continent to return to England. Many of them decided to settle in Oxford in an attempt to create a university as they had seen in Europe. Unfortunately, disputes between the students and residents led to riots and a number of students fled to Cambridge, where they established a new university. In turn, the loss of students hurt Oxford's local economy and in 1214, traders and merchants invited them back again. The competition between Oxford and Cambridge colleges probably dates back to those times when William of Durham founded University College in

1249. Balliol was established in 1263 and Merton, the first residential college, followed a year later. Merton set the collegiate pattern, which became standard in both Oxford and Cambridge. These colleges were self-governing institutions where teachers and students lived together. Fourteen other colleges were founded by the end of the 16th century[2] (http://www.spartacus.schoolnet.co.uk/EDoxford.htm).

In another part of the world, the *"clerices"* role was covered by other scholars; it is remarkable that most of them would still be monks, hermits, or anchorites like Buddhist and Confucian scholars in Asia, or Imams and Ayatollahs in the Muslim world. Moreover, to most people, the universities previously mentioned seem to have had an extremely early start, but if we look at the records of *Nalanda,* we find out that this is actually mistaken.

*Nalanda* was a Buddhist monastic centre, often referred to as a university, in the North Indian state of Bihar. Though it is traditionally placed in the time of the Buddha (6th—5th century B.C.), archaeological excavations date its current foundations to the 5th century A.C.; it housed a population of several thousand teachers and students. The topics covered spanned logic, grammar, astronomy, and Ayurvedic Buddhist medicine; the Chinese pilgrims Xuanzang and Yijing provide vivid accounts of *Nalanda* as early as the late 7th century. *Nalanda* continued to flourish through the 12th century and became a centre of Buddhist religious sculpture, but was probably sacked during Muslim raids around 1200, and has never recovered since (http://www.ayurveda-tcm.com/Buddhist_ayurveda_monastic_college_Nalanda.htm).

In China, the First Emperor (259 B.C.) established a process to formalise a set of hierarchies and exams related to the acquisition of public roles (becoming a Mandarin or an emperor's officer). In similar fashion measures, rules, laws, and even the way of writing were standardised and formalised so that the same characters are still in use. Since then, in China, culture has always been highly valued; there is even a common saying related to this that translates as "*a word is worth a 1,000 pieces of gold.*"

The origin of this common Chinese saying can be found in the famous book Shiji (or Historical Records) by the historian Sima Qian (around 145-87 B.C.). He describes an episode from the time when Lü Buwei (the natural father of the first emperor) was prime minister. Lü Buwei was hosting and protecting over 3,000 scholars, so he compiled the best of their writings in a book, claiming that it was the encyclopaedia of his time covering science, literature, and all the knowledge that was under heaven. Actually, the prime minister did more; he had a collection of texts engraved onto rock and an edict proclaimed stating that: "*Whoever would have been able to improve all that is collected and written by simply adding or removing even a single word would have been granted a 1,000 pieces of gold.*" For fear of offending the prime minister, a very powerful man, no one dared to attempt this, but since then it was clear why even a single word

would be worth a fortune (http://www-chaos.umd.edu/history/ancient2.html, http://www-chaos.umd.edu/history/imperial.html#first, http://www-chaos.umd.edu/history/toc.html)(Mah, 2003).

Coming back to Europe, culture and education started to spread only with the rise of the middle classes and the development of the publishing industry, even though remaining the prerogative of a minority. Only in the last century, well in line with Maslow's theory (Abraham, 1943), did education become a patrimony "*for everyone.*" This is mainly due to the social and economic evolution that occurred after the industrial revolution, bringing better living conditions.

In the process of providing access to education and culture, technology had a crucial role. For example, the evolution in educational models and achievable results (in terms of educational objectives) in relation to technology innovation, along with major driving forces, is presented in Figure 2. In the diagram, the role played by economical forces as a push factor (companies demanding new learning services in order to have a more highly skilled work force) is shown. At the same time

*Figure 2. Evolution in educational models and results in relation to technology innovation*

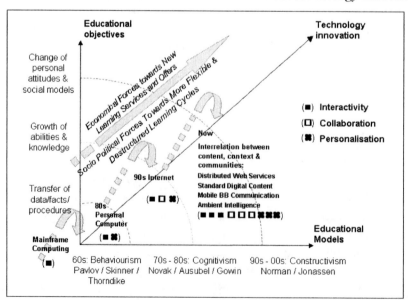

there were also socio-political forces pushing for more flexible and decentralised approaches, both in work and in education, to keep on track with society's evolution.

In all this, technology was playing a twofold role. On one side, it was a driving force providing solutions to issues and needs arising from market and production environments. On the other side, many spin-offs of this evolution were also fed back into everyday life. Education and training could also benefit from technologies by providing new tools and methods to convey content and knowledge; thanks to the introduction of factors like simulation and interactivity at first, and then collaboration and personalisation, dramatic developments were achieved. At present, the new evolutionary step will likely be lead by the effective combination of these factors and the introduction of new technologies.

To better understand this, we will look at the origin of open and distance learning (ODL). This began in areas where the educational system was facing huge challenges due to distances and the spread of population over territory, combined with a growing demand for access to education, as in the USA, Australia, and Canada. To meet the requests (coming from all levels of society) for a higher level of education/training, a form of *"distance learning"* needed to be developed. This new learning process was initially supported by regular mail, then by radio[3] and television. Then tools initially developed to support totally different scopes, like the Internet[4], started to be used for scientific and educational purposes. The initial spread of data among researchers fostered the exchange of knowledge; this brought on the rapid evolution of the so called *"wired-world"* that nowadays plays a crucial role in education, yet all previously mentioned media are still in use depending on needs and available budgets. As a matter of fact, available solutions cover almost all forms of training and teaching, from traditional class learning to e-learning.

Early examples of e-learning were the computer-based training applications often referred to as CBTs, mainly developed to foster professional (re)training. Then low-cost computers were developed, with reasonably good performance, and able to sustain multimedia applications and made available to the mass market. In more detail, it was the advent of the CD-ROM (mainly seen in this case as a mass storage device), along with easy access to the Internet that fostered the launch of the first mass-market-oriented CBT (mainly devoted to language teaching). Initially, products were conceived in a stand-alone fashion. Then hybrid versions (CD plus Internet) emerged to achieve a higher level of modularity and flexibility (including periodic product update), and now there are many online training courses.

According to IDC, e-learning means *"educational content, learning services, and delivery solutions that support and enable Internet-based learning"* (IDC, 2002). Thus, e-learning is a subset of what is defined as technology-based training (TBT) that includes CD-ROM and other technology-delivered training. In turn, TBT is a subset of what is called enhanced learning, which includes support to disability for learners, and so on. Finally, enhanced learning is a subset of the overall training and learning including instructor-led training (ILT) and text-based training, as shown in Figure 3, which elaborates on the basis

*Figure 3. Relation among the various forms of learning*

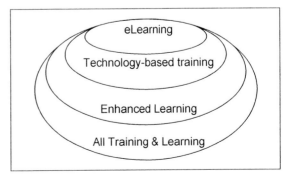

*Figure 4. The media gap (Adapted from Neuman, 1991)*

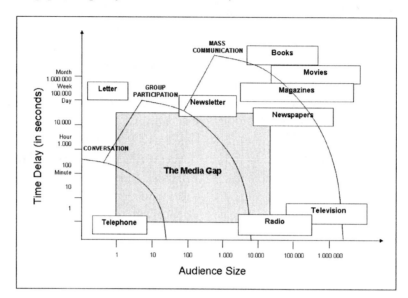

*Figure 5. Relation between learning autonomy and learner satisfaction in relation to media richness and bandwidth (Adapted from Novak, 1998)*

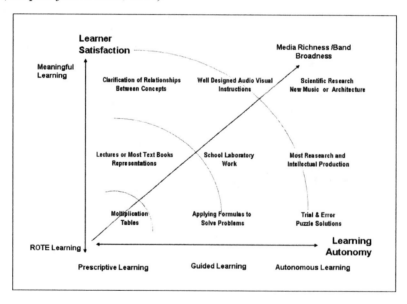

of concepts exposed from the already quoted IDC report (IDC, 2002).

According to Tomita (1980) and Neuman (1991), the scenario presented in Figure 4 shows evidence of "*a media gap.*" Blogs, Wikis, virtual communities, and many other forms of communication and social/educational experiences are quickly arising and filling this "*media gap.*"

The availability of new and more pervasive technology support, as well as the growth and spread in access to culture and education, is ultimately addressing the issue of a "*lifelong learning*" process to avoid knowledge obsolescence, especially in environments like science or technology. We must bear in mind Novak (1998), when saying that the rote-meaningful learning continuum is distinct from the reception-discovery continuum for instruction (see Figure 5). As a matter of fact, it is not enough to have availability of information and technology that can assist in accessing the related knowledge.

A common mistaken notion is that *"inquiry"* studies will assure meaningful learning. The reality is that unless learners possess at least a rudimentary conceptual understanding of the phenomenon they are investigating, the activity may lead to little or no gain in their relevant knowledge. In this respect, it is worth noting that this aspect has been taken into account in the e-learning sectors and therefore, cognitive modelling and ergonomics have been closely investigated (Sussman & Sedivy, http://www. umass.edu/psychology/div2/eyelab/).

Studies on cognitive architecture have been carried out by taking into account perception, cognition, action (motor), and memory (Hornof & Halverson) as well as studies on eye movements and visual attention (Kowler). These results are extremely interesting and promising, as the use of these technologies could be very successful if employed to foster the learning process and support full accessibility, regardless of gender, race, language, and impairment. The introduction and combination of wireless communication, agents, adaptive user profiling, virtual reality, and eye-tracking (http://www.vr.clemson.edu/ eyetracking/, http://www.nottingham.ac.uk/education/maps/eye.html) with artificial intelligence and other technologies can move the frontier for e-learning applications exactly in this direction.

The use of *"multimedia"* is probably one of the most relevant approaches to properly support education in all environments. It is an excellent way to support teaching activities, not only because it enables one to enrich the quality level of the service, but also because it allows one to attract the learner's attention, and stimulates the mind from several perspectives. However, this is not enough unless the effort involved in overcoming accessibility problems and impairments in the learning process is taken into account. To achieve this result, the accessibility issue has to be addressed in the design phase and the available and emerging technologies, regardless of their origin and major field of application, have to be fully exploited. In other words, to examine carefully how accessibility-related needs, in general, and impairment could be tackled and use whatsoever technology that could fit to solve, or work-around, the problem so as to grant full access to education and culture and therefore, also greatly contributing to societal development.

As stated, in theory (as well as in practice), it is possible to devise usage of technologies presently applied in other sectors in the learning field to empower better and more compete forms of e-learning. As an example, just think how eye tracking has been exploited in the military environment to control firing systems[5], and how it is presently used to support reading and comprehension exercises and other learning activities, but still well below its huge potential.

Another example may be the adoption of tools and methods used to teach diction, or opera singing, in the language learning environment (at least as far as pronunciation is concerned), especially when teaching languages like Chinese or Japanese to westerners or English to easterners. In this case there is a real need to learn things such as breath control, tone usage, phonation, and so on, just as it is done for opera singers or for actors.

## LANGUAGE LEARNING

Most professional sectors have adopted technologies to support the learning process. Probably the first one to do so was the professional training sector (pilots, train conductors...) and language learning. Later came the informatics sector (programmers, EDP operators…), then the finance and banking sector (initially jointly with the informatics sector, then on its own, due to the increase in complexity of the environment itself), and lastly the medical training sector (initially in imaging and diagnostic to progressively shift towards a full coverage)[6]. This section focuses on the language-learning environment as an example, given that it represents a case where technology has already been widely adopted to properly support learning processes over a long period.

It is possible to find self-learning materials based on a widespread set of technologies (from vinyl audio support, to tapes, and now CDs or DVDs) and furthermore, many different learning methods have been adopted to support different classes of learners (businesspeople, primary and secondary students, home users, and so on). This illustrates the relation between e-learning and technology as a support for culture and education.

It is widely accepted that to master a language, the four linguistic skills (speaking, listening, reading, writing) have to be acquired , but the social and cultural background also have to be understood. Therefore, the study processes can be enhanced through the guided use of contemporary media such as newspapers and magazines, film and television, video, CD-ROMs, and Internet. Certainly, literature is an important part of the study of language and culture, especially at the more advanced levels, as it constitutes the most versatile and complex of language usages. Literature essentially represents a compendium of the past and present culture(s) of the language in which it is written. Therefore, it also represents the most difficult part to master when learning a foreign language as a second language.

When using a foreign language, words will turn out to be cages for concepts the learner wants to express. Unless the learner is natively bilingual, thinking directly in another language may be achieved only partially. For some people it is easier to learn the sound of the word/sentence and to note it down in their own language. This depends on many factors, starting from the degree of knowledge and mastery of the meanings associated with a word in a specific language, to end with the personal cultural background that may bias the nuances given to a specific word or expression (just think of all forms of professional jargon and disambiguation needs encountered when translating a word or a sentence out of its context). Many problems, misunderstandings, and issues have been caused by improper usage of words among people. Therefore, there should be a basic concern when teaching/learning a foreign language:

*Concepts are expressed by words. If certain English words are missing in Chinese, it follows that the concept expressed by those words will be absent in China, and vice versa.* (Mah, 2003)

When taking all this into account, it is evident that mastering a language is much more than learning its vocabulary and grammar; it implies also learning the culture behind the language; the history, the traditions, the costumes, and the related ways of thinking. In other words, all meanings, structures, metaphors, sounds, and tastes of a language need to be learned, in the same way a child from the country in question does this. This lesson has been used by scholars working in the language-learning domain, and is progressively being widely adopted in regular language learning in primary and secondary education. For example, as far as the "*sound of a language*" is concerned, exploiting songs, and their lyrics, has become a common way to support teaching, as is evident from the following quote by LeLup and Ponterio (LeLoup & Ponterio, 2001):

*Most foreign language teachers enjoy studying song lyrics as authentic text in their classes. Songs can be used at all levels and for a wide variety of activities and purposes such as comprehension, vocabulary introduction, illustration or recogni-*

tion of grammar structures, and reinforcement of topics. Traditional or new children's songs, musical classics, or the latest pop hits are all fair game. The rhythm and melody of songs can make the words and expressions easier to remember and more enjoyable for students than other sorts of texts.

Unfortunately, teaching the culture behind a language is a long and difficult task, usually unfeasible in the timeframe of regular classroom teaching during primary and secondary education. However, this issue is being addressed more frequently than in the past, and is also often addressed by using e-learning in a lifelong learning approach. Furthermore, there exists class-based intercultural training devoted to specific audiences. Nowadays, learning words, sentences, and polite phrases in a foreign language, mainly to manage human/business relations when abroad, is becoming a common habit among far-sighted businesspeople, and therefore, it is essential to also teach proverbs, phrasal verbs, idioms, and so on. In the diplomatic environment, this has a long tradition; for example, in China, the first emperor studied Tibetan costumes and the language, to be able to properly welcome the Dalai Lama[7] (Mah, 2003). Similarly, the Jesuit missionaries in Japan or China would spend long years in training before being sent to their final destination. During their training, they would learn how to behave, talk, act as if they were locals, and this training was finalised to achieve a specific purpose: the conversion of the locals to Christianity. In this, they reached such a level of perfection that Matteo Ricci is accounted among the classical Chinese authors in maths, geography,[8] and other topics, despite the fact he was an Italian.

The power of multimedia-based e-learning lies in the possibility to convey several media and all the related content richness to the user (in a single framework). For example, on a DVD, it is possible to convey as much data as in an ordinary encyclopaedia, with high-quality audio and good quality video. The Internet allows the updating of e-learning sources and tools in a combination of self and assisted teaching, making it possible to learn at one's own pace and having tutor support only when needed. Synchronous activities can be performed along with asynchronous ones. Reinforcement tools are available, and all this is "*virtually*" usable by the learner.

There is a clear need to stress the word "*virtually*," as disability support can be provided as well, but if this is lacking, then all this power may be lost for a relevant part of the population. From a technical point of view, it is possible to take accessibility (in the wider sense) into consideration from the very beginning, thus ensuring the widest possible coverage of user needs (from impairment to aging support). Nevertheless, this implies that proper development tools and strategies have to be used.

The outcomes from a 2001 European Commission open workshop to examine the future of e-learning expected the research focus to be on virtual and remote labs, emotional characters, handwriting recognition, and eye tracking in e-learning usability. All this should be combined with situational-based training and mobile access to resources so that: "*Research on eLearning will support the development of innovative models for the provision of learning services, fully exploiting the potential of ambient intelligence technologies, enabling ubiquitous, interactive, personalized and tailored access to learning and knowledge on demand to individuals at home, at work or on the move. It will build advanced learning schemes for schools, universities, the workplace and for lifelong learning in general, reflecting the needs of the knowledge economy.*" In other words, the pillars of the knowledge society and economy are *ubiquitous access to personalized learning throughout life* for everyone.

*Figure 6. Language course levels according to several classifications*

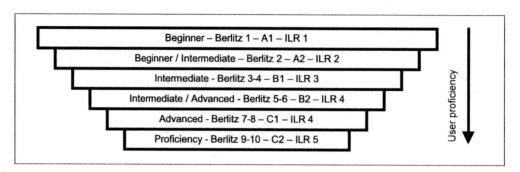

## Traditional and Innovative Language Learning

Traditional class-based language courses are structured according to a well-codified approach that regards grammar and vocabulary to be the core of the study. The main differences that are worth noting in class-based learning are mainly related to target audience and objective of the class. Basically, we can distinguish the following categories of class-based learning:

- Basic institutional curricula (primary or secondary education level).
- Advanced institutional curricula (post secondary education level).
- Specifically oriented curricula (business, summer schools).

For each of these, there are specific programmes, schedules, and methods aimed to maximise the training outcome.

Except for literature or business-oriented courses, dialogues and drill downs are considered as complementary or support activities, just like exercises. Therefore, dialogues are usually linked to curiosities and hints on culture and civilization related to the language being studied. Classes are usually organized in terms of language knowledge prerequisites that are assessed via admission texts (this applies only to noninstitutional training).

Yet even when assessment is not performed in advance, content and course structure reflect a similar approach with the presentation of the most difficult/uncommon concepts, authors, or issues at the most advanced level. A gradual approach to learning has always been adopted (see Figure 6), and is reflected in the courseware and content structure. This is certainly a harsh generalization, but still reflects a good part of the present class-based offers on the market.

The levels reported provide indications according to different classification approaches: UCLA, Berlitz (http://en.wikipedia.org/wiki/Berlitz_Language_Schools), common European framework of reference for languages (http://culture2.coe.int/portfolio/inc.asp?L=E&M=$t/208-1-0-1/documents_intro/common_framework.html), and Interagency language roundtable (http://www.utm.edu/staff/globeg/ilrhome.shtml, http://en.wikipedia.org/wiki/ILR_scale). Usually the passage from one level to the other is bound by the accomplishment of a specific (and in most cases well codified) exam. The schema also visualises the usual decline in participants from the basic to the more specialized training levels that are often not only more demanding in terms of prerequisites, but also in terms of competences and capacities of the trainees. Inside each course level, the typical learning unit could then be structured as follows (Figure 7).

*Figure 7. Typical structure of a grammar-centric learning unit*

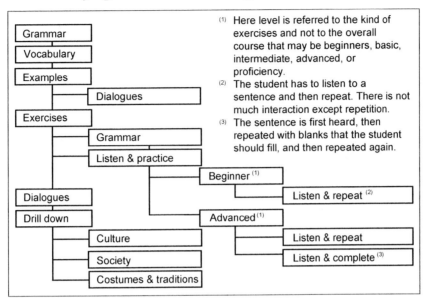

*Figure 8. Typical structure of a content-centric learning unit*

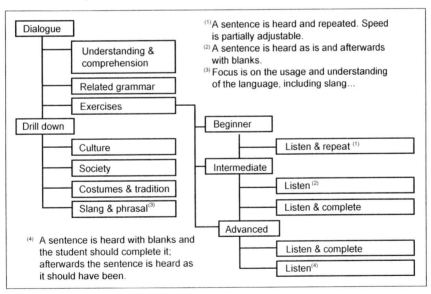

This is a harsh schematisation, as the more advanced the course is, the less such a grammar-centric schema is followed, as there is a natural shift towards a more content-centric schema that is best tailored to the form of advanced learning provided. In fact, while the grammar-centric schema perfectly suits certain pedagogical pur-poses (like teaching how to teach a language), it is not suitable for others, such as teaching literature or business/professional usage of a language. Obviously, a full range of intermediate models and combinations are also possible in order to accommodate the various needs and objectives of the training. A very similar approach has also characterised the evolution of e-learning-based language training content that was initially following the grammar-centric and is now shifting towards the content-centric unit. One of the main reasons for this shift also lays in the *"blended"* approach to teaching that combines traditional class-based to self-paced learning.

The difference in structure between the two approaches is quite apparent. Only a few products on the market are offering the user the chance to listen and modify voice samples or dialogues at playback speed. Some of the most effective online language courses, for Latin-based speakers willing to learn foreign languages, focus on reading/listening comprehension, grammar, and vocabulary. Users are provided with feedback on achieved performances, and exploit a pedagogical philosophy based on the following principles:

- The approach is student centred (user chooses own learning path).
- Each course level revolves around a central theme.
- Activities have a pedagogical rationale.

- The content is interesting and related activities are challenging.

Usually language training is divided into at least four different levels organized in about six courses. On average, each course is composed of more than 10 units plus a unit test. Units are, in turn organized, in several stimuli alternated with an average of five activities per stimulus plus tests. The course becomes progressively harder while progressing through units. For e-learning solutions foreseeing the adoption of CD/Internet-based content delivery, it is worth limiting the duration of each learning session to around 15-20 minutes for usability reasons, as schematically described in Figure 9.

On average, each stimulus is accompanied by a set of activities focused on different subskills, related to the various abilities, plus grammar and vocabulary. Listening is taught using slideshows, videos, or pictures with captions, while reading comprehension, and/or grammar are taught using texts.

*Figure 9. Typical fruition scheme of a learning unit (innovative case)*

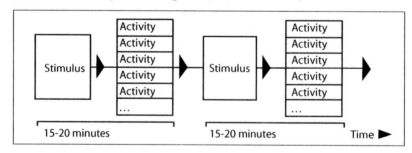

*Figure 10. Typical learner access level evaluation scheme of a language course*

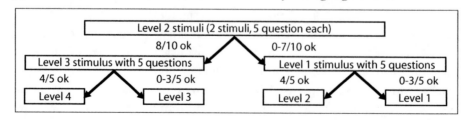

*Figure 11. Typical navigation scheme of an e-learning language course structured in levels*

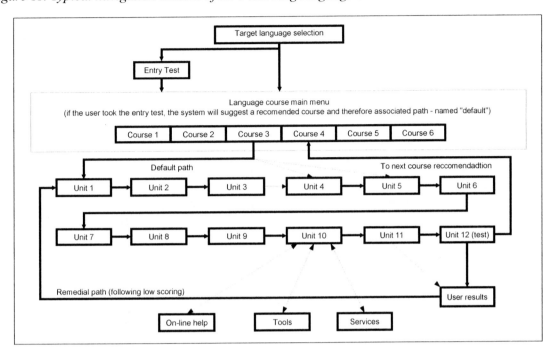

Test units are presented at the end of a set of units aiming at providing feedback on what has been learned. Units may be repeated several times and should last no more than 30 minutes each. The structure will comprise a set of stimuli, each followed by a set of questions. At the end of the session, a score is provided as feedback. The score provided is in the format X out of Y correct answers (i.e., 3/5). If the same exercise is repeated several times, only the best score is reported. There may also be entry test units focused on comprehension and containing at least three graded texts. They should last no more than 20 minutes, be timed, and drawn from a bank containing several versions of the test (at least three). These entry units assign both a level and a course to the user upon completion, based on the decision schema reported in Figure 10.

According to the SCORM standard, a tracked course expects the user to complete the full unit before being granted the chance to proceed any further. Thus, if there are exercises for knowledge

assessment, they can usually add conditions to the overall navigation procedure, for example, preventing the user from accessing any other section of the content until the present one has been completed and related tests passed positively. In general, content should be interesting and appealing. Tests should stimulate user curiosity and willingness to access the available content, providing exercises for the issues that generate most interest.

From the information presented, the structure of a typical learning course can easily be derived (see Figure 11). Please note that in most environments, the courseware structure is structured in levels according to the *"European Council Curriculum"* and to Flesch-Kincaid Grade Level Score, or to Flesch Readability Ease Score (at least as far as the English language is concerned).

Over time, several approaches to language teaching have been developed, starting from the traditional ones centred on grammar and stemming from the study of Latin and classical

Greek. This evolution has been led by the following factors:

- Recognition that "*live-languages*" (currently spoken) differ from "*dead-languages*" and are constantly evolving; therefore, Understanding & Comprehension should come first, and the implied grammar could then be studied (and in some cases even derived).
- Spoken languages often rely on a smaller set of vocabulary, and the most common phrases structure is simpler. The usage of verb tenses and cases is also typically more limited in spoken language than in literary usage.
- Recognition of different needs for different audiences (business or technical trainee undertake a learning process to be able to communicate, usually in short timeframes).
- Provision of situational training better supports the retention of acquired knowledge than the extensive study of grammar and vocabulary.

A good example is the "*Berlitz*" method, or other derived ones like "*inlingua*" (http://

www.inlingua.com/English/Services/main.asp?RefNav=rnav3). It is now clearer why there has been a progressive shift from a grammar-centric to a content-centric approach. This process greatly contributed to the need for effective and efficient self-learning[9] that is now converging towards a "*blended*" approach, where the self-led activities can be even performed on the move, with the support of specifically designed tutoring assistance. This can be summed up in terms of distinctions applied to language learning depending on learning scope, the institution providing the training, trainees' backgrounds, and domains, as illustrated in the Table 1.

## Language Labs

The setup of language labs dates back to at least the 1970s, when language teachers would use this infrastructure for practices and for assessing students' progress, especially in two of the four abilities, namely listening and speaking, while reading and writing ability would be aligned with class work. The most frequent usage of the language lab would be either in "*listening and comprehension*" or in "*listening and repeating.*" Often (but this

*Table 1. Distinctions applied to language learning*

| Environment | Provider | Learning objective | Target audience |
|---|---|---|---|
| Basic language learning | Primary and /or secondary education; Specific language schools. | Acquisition of the basic skills (read, write, listen, speak) | All categories of trainees; Businesspeople; Professionals. |
| Advanced learning education | Interpretation schools; Language universities; Specific language schools. | Linguistic refinement; Literature; Language teaching; Situational training. | All categories of trainees; University students; Businesspeople; Professionals. |
| Professional learning education | Interpretation schools; Language universities; Specific language schools. | Interpretation; Translation; Linguistic refinement; Literature; Language teaching; Situational training. | Interpreters; Translators; Dubbers; Businesspeople; Professionals (legal, science, technical or medical…). |

was much dependent on the teacher) in language labs, students would encounter audio sources that could span a wide range of topics, from read-aloud literature to radio programmes conversation, or even music (folk, traditional, pop).

In the late 1980s and early 1990s, the traditional language lab started to be sidelined by multimedia labs (initially devoted to purposes other than language learning). Only in very recent times has there been a convergence of language and multimedia labs into a single entity, a "*multimedia language lab,*" even though it is still quite popular (especially for certain forms of studies) to retain the "*classical*" configuration.

## Classical Language Lab Configuration

The classical configuration of a language lab is based on a set of audio equipment (tape recorders eventually combined with auxiliary inputs) usually divided into three categories: the teacher unit (the most richly featured and complete unit, comprising several inputs), the student unit (limited to a recording unit), and a set of supportive infrastructures (comprising the switch

and control board available to the teacher). The control console and the switch and control board are physical, even though there are implementations using a computer-based approach (Figures 12, 16 and 17).

A classroom may contain only a few workstations, depending on the target usage, availability of room, complexity of cabling, and costs. The control unit available to the teacher is usually analogical (in the most advanced perhaps computer based) and so is the student unit. In the latter case, the schema becomes the one of Figure 13.

## Multimedia Language Lab Configuration

The configuration of a multimedia language lab is based on a combination of computers and a set of equipment (including tape recorders combined with auxiliary inputs). Additionally, in this case, the whole setup is divided into three categories:

* The teacher unit
* The student unit
* A set of supportive infrastructures

*Figure 12. Typical structure of a classical language lab configuration*

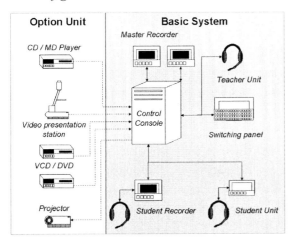

*Figure 13. Typical structure of a computer controlled language lab configuration*

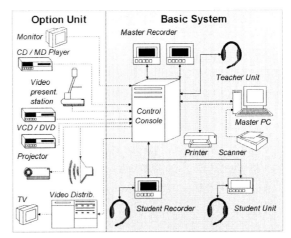

*Figure 14. Typical structure of a basic multimedia language lab configuration*

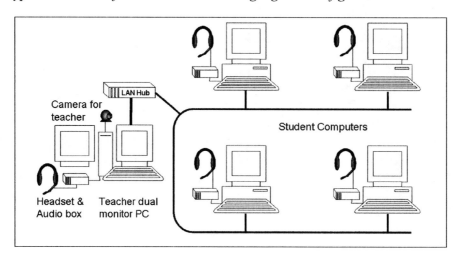

*Figure 15. Typical structure of an extended multimedia language lab configuration*

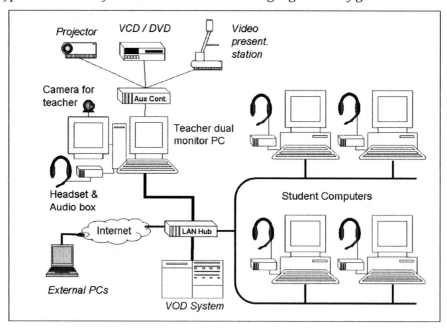

While in the traditional language lab the control unit available to the teacher is usually analogical, in multimedia labs, the control unit is implicitly computer based. Moreover, in multimedia labs, it is often possible to find equipment and applications devoted to a wider set of usages than language learning, as they were originally created to support ICT teaching and then extended to support language learning.

Presently, multimedia labs are also being provided with extensions enabling the usage of e-learning solutions. This allows for a varied set of possible configurations and setups, like the following ones (see Figures 14, 15 and 16).

*Figure 16. Typical structure of a multimedia language lab class and teacher work place*

*Figure 17. Typical structure of a multimedia language lab teacher's console*

As is apparent from the previous schemas, the usual structure is based on a network connecting the individual positions, each equipped with the specific sets of supportive tools needed, comprising specific HW (recorder) and SW (applications). The class could be either fully physically bound (all work places are in the same physical location) or dispersed (not all work places are in the same physical location, but some are remotely connected); furthermore, the class could also be connected to external resources (like a VOD server, Internet, and so forth.). Audio/video conferencing equipment can also be used to support open and distance learning.

Additionally, in this case the overall arrangement will be then complemented with a proper layout that will provide two different sets of workstations for teachers and students. Again, a classroom may contain only a few workstations, depending on the target usage, availability of rooms, complexity of cabling, and costs of the overall setup, as in the following images.

## Content Production

In the publishing environment, the content production chain follows well-codified and standardised processes that have been developing over several years. This process, and the actors involved, are schematically reported in Figure 18.

Cost control and overall IPR and copyright management are usually undertaken in a parallel

*Figure 18. Content production chain in the publishing environment*

| Activity | Task | | | Involved roles |
|---|---|---|---|---|
| Idea | | | | Management<br>Authors<br>Chief Editor<br>Press Office |
| Market survey | | | | |
| Title design | | | | |
| Go / No Go decision based on market data and production cost analysis to ensure the expected return on investment | | | | Management |
| Research of: | Sources<br>References<br>Contacts<br>Multimedia<br>...<br>Similar titles | IPR/© clearance | | Management<br>Authors<br>Editorial board<br>Editorial staff<br>Press Office<br>Legal Department |
| Draft acceptance<br>*(if positive the next step starts if not the previous is reiterated).* | | | | Management<br>Authors<br>Editorial board<br>Legal Department |
| Editing of: | Texts<br>Notes<br>Indexes<br>...<br>Multimedia<br>Captions | | | Authors<br>Chief Editor<br>Editorial board<br>Editorial staff<br>Instructional designer<br>Press Office<br>Legal Department |
| Product final acceptance<br>*(if positive the next step starts if not the previous is reiterated)* | | | | Authors<br>Chief Editor<br>Legal Department |
| Finalisation of: | Texts<br>Notes<br>Indexes<br>...<br>Multimedia<br>Captions | | | Chief Editor<br>Editorial board<br>Editorial staff<br>Instructional designer<br>Production department<br>Press Office<br>Legal Department |
| Formal authorisation to start production<br>*(if positive the next step starts if not the previous is reiterated. In this case IPR/© clearance should have been completed if not process may be suspended / stopped / cancelled)* | | | | Management<br>Chief Editor<br>Editorial board<br>Legal Department |
| Production | Books & Magazines<br>CD/ROM<br>DVD<br>Web<br>TV, iTV, PDA mobile and other new media | Cost control | IPR/© Contracts management | Production department<br>Outsourced service<br>Press Office<br>Marketing manager<br>Legal department<br>Company accountant |
| Marketing | Promoting | | | Marketing manager<br>Legal department |
| Distribution & rights selling | Revenue management | | | Marketing manager<br>Legal department<br>Company accountant |

stream, to ensure constant monitoring of high-risk factors. As far as the economic impacts are concerned, cost control has to monitor process development and ensure that it is kept in line with expectations and budgets, retaining its profitability (or even increasing it whenever possible) and therefore, is a good part of the standard management process.

On the other hand, IPR and copyright management interactions occur whenever an asset cannot be cleared and therefore, has to be replaced. This event may occur at any step, and the impact may be marginal or relevant, depending on a set of possible combinations of factors:

- The relevance for the publishing project of the object that could not be cleared.
- The reason for lack of clearance.
- The stage of the publishing process.
- The availability of a replacement/equivalent object, and so forth.

*Figure 19. Content production chain in the media environment*

| Activity | | | | | Involved roles |
|---|---|---|---|---|---|
| Idea | Storyboard drafting | | | | Author<br>Writer<br>Script editor<br>Art director<br>Director<br>Producer<br>Production accountant |
| Cost estimation | | | | | Producer<br>Production accountant |
| Go/No Go decision | | | | | Producer |
| Title design | Storyboard finalising<br>Scripting drafting<br>Casting preparation | Cost estimation refinement | | | Author<br>Script editor<br>Producer<br>Director<br>Casting director<br>Art director |
| Design & preparation | Casting<br>Scripting<br>Lighting drafting<br>Shooting plan drafting<br>Effects drafting<br>Costumes drafting<br>Sound track drafting<br>Contracts finalising | Cost estimation refinement | Distribution & sale IPR/© Contracts management | | Costume designer<br>Makeup designer<br>Composer<br>Audio Engineer<br>Graphic designer<br>Special effect designer<br>Fight arranger<br>Lighting cameramen<br>Production assistant<br>Location manager<br>Art director<br>Director<br>Casting director<br>Producer<br>Production lawyer<br>Production accountant |
| Development & shooting | Storyboard adapting<br>Lighting management<br>Shooting plan adapting<br>Effects management | Cost control | Distribution & sale IPR/© Contracts management | | |
| Post Production | Mounting<br>Sound addition<br>Effects addition<br>Packaging | | | | |
| Marketing | | | | | Marketing manager |
| Distribution & rights selling | Revenue management | | | | Marketing manager<br>Production accountant |

213

*Table 2. Documentation tools used with e-learning*

| Tool used to create e-learning courses content | Freq. of adoption |
|---|---|
| PowerPoint / Word | 66% / 63% |
| Dreamweaver (can be used by specialized and novice users) | 61% |
| Flash (can be used by specialized and novice users) | 47% |
| Code at the HTML tag level[10] | 34% |
| Traditional authoring tools[11] | 32% |
| Microsoft FrontPage | 26% |
| Learning content management system (LCMS) | 21% |
| Content authoring tools built-in to an LMS | 18% |
| Rapid e-learning development tools[12] | 13% |
| Other | 16% |

This refers to traditional, desktop and multimedia publishing as they present the highest number of contact points and overlaps.

A similar approach applies to the editorial process of any product, yet digital TV, serials, movies and in general products requiring video production are somehow different as the design and planning phase is much longer and has several by-products (storyboards, drawings, scripts, books...) that in certain cases will have their own existence and production cycle, which is reported in Figure 19 with the same approach of Figure 18.

## Authoring Tools and E-Learning Content Development Applications

Standard document creation tools rank at the top of the list of utilities used to create e-learning content. Most of them are oriented to achieve specific results and do not require specific programming skills, even if they may have extensions, they are therefore often used in combination.

According to Brandon and Hall, over 40% of companies use an e-learning solution to provide services to their own personnel, including language learning, mainly due to globalisation. Most e-learning solutions adopted are used to provide self-paced e-learning courses and live e-learning sessions using virtual classroom applications, while tracking results using a learning management system (LMS).

Unlike conventional training, a good instructor cannot rescue bad online learning; the materials' successful implementation is decided by the quality of the design. Therefore, in e-learning, content and design have remained the most critical dimensions of success. Not surprisingly, the shortage of well-designed, engaging, and relevant e-learning products is still high on the list of reasons for limited acceptance of e-learning in many organizations.

## A Contextualised Example of Content Development for E-Learning

To provide a better understanding and to highlight the benefits of the adoption of certain technologies as a support tool for the production of educational content, we examine the process followed in a successful European RTD project conducted in IST-FP5 dealing with the application of technologies developed for the support of dyslexia to adult L2 language learning, named FLIC (Foreign Language Acquisition through the Instinct of a Child)

(FLIC, 2004, 2005a, 2005b, 2006); (MediTECH, 2005a, 2005b); (Lasnier, 2005). The results of the project, in terms of pedagogical and neurological validation, have been conducted by Sheffield University, while the original idea and method at the basis of project development has been based on the experience gained by MediTECH in respect of the development of supporting tools for dyslexia treatments.

Given this content production process, it is apparent that producing content for multimedia applications, especially in the educational field for language learning, is a rather complex task per se; the introduction of new technologies that alter such a process is often opposed due to the potential cost impact. FLIC proved that the additional effort required to take into account the specific solutions that will lead to product improvement is not excessive if this is done from the product design phase (FLIC, 2004, 2005a, 2005b); (MediTECH, 2005a); (Lasnier, 2005). For the sake of reference, we will briefly report here the process followed in FLIC.

In FLIC, the audio content was using dummy stereophony (see Figure 20) for recorded sounds. The dummy head simulates the human head in an acoustic sense, as far as possible, as in place of eardrums, the dummy head has suitable microphones whose directional characteristics and other physical properties correspond to the properties of human ears (FLIC, 2005a).

The need for this special recording procedure was strictly connected with the special learning support provided by the FLIC equipment, namely the lateralisation (MediTECH, 2005a), the multichannel voice fusion (HW/SW versions) (MediTECH, 2005a, 2005b), plus the time alignment and voice modification (SW version only).

*Figure 20. Dummy head and related recording setup*

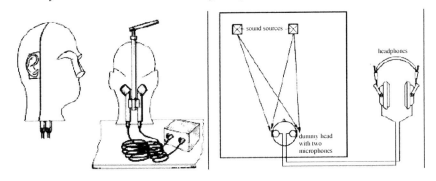

*Figure 21. Lateralisation principle: The "wandering around" voice*

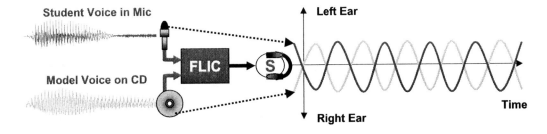

The Lateralisation process is based on a quite simple principle related to the fact that specific aural circumstances generate both a higher level of attention in the listener, and also an instinctive synchronisation effect. This is achieved in three phases, namely:

- **Phase 1:** Learner hears model voice from CD and reads along silently phoneme by phoneme hearing the model voice "*wandering from side to side.*"
- **Phase 2:** Learner silently reads along with the model voice (mouthing the words), again perceiving it as "*wandering from side to side.*"
- **Phase 3:** Learner reads aloud in synchrony with the model voice, hearing his and the model voice in opposite ears and both "*wandering from side to side*"; this automatically tends to put the two in sync.

*Figure 22. Multichannel voice fusion (MCVF) technology*

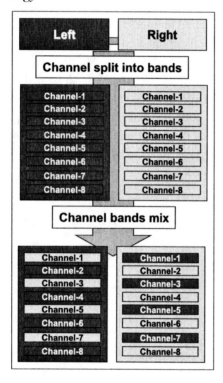

The multi channel voice fusion (MCVF) technology divides the audio information of the left and right canal into eight (8) bands each, without losing any information during the splitting. The wave bands are differentiated in the following way: Band 1 (low-pass filter till 200Hz), Band 2 (250-315 Hz), Band 3 (400-630 Hz), Band 4 (800-1000 Hz), Band 5 (1250-1600 Hz), Band 6 (2000-2500 Hz), Band 7(3150-4000 Hz), and Band 8 (high-pass filter from 5000 Hz). Consequently, two times 8 canals are generated. The mutual mixture of the canals causes an overlay of the separate audio information (left and right) to a single frequency composition of both canals. This principle is shown in Figure 22.

If MCVF and its effect are firstly used without lateralisation, while speaking through the microphone and listening to ones own voice with and without the MCVF, it is impossible to locate the direction of the voice, which is precisely the desired effect, produced by the FLIC-unit for the benefit of the learner. Furthermore, a time-alignment procedure was also implemented (SW version only) to help the learner better understand the pronunciation aspects of the reference voice. The logic diagram of the adopted solution is shown in Figure 23. Last, but not least, it was possible to modify the reference voice to enhance the possibility to understand mismatches occurring between the learner's and the reference voice. This

*Figure 23. Diagram of the time synchronization system where DTW stands for dynamic time warping and WSOLA for waveform similarity overlaps and add*

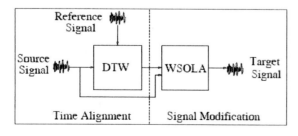

*Figure 24. Speech modification algorithm structure*

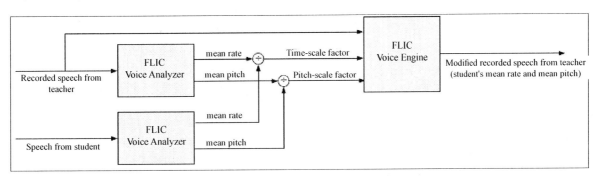

*Figure 25. Speech modification algorithm results*

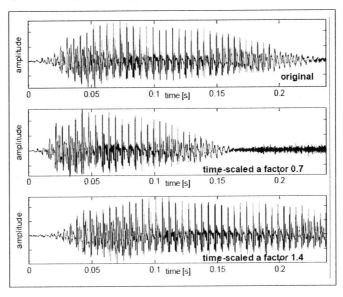

proved extremely useful (and was often needed) whenever the two voices belong to different genders. The result could be achieved with a voice modification engine (SW version only) that would operate according to the logics presented in Figure 24, transforming the original (reference voice) to achieve the result presented in Figure 25.

## TECHNOLOGY AND ACCESSIBILITY

It was mentioned that technology could support culture and learning by lowering access barriers. Technology has made access to content and sources mobile and ubiquitous, and it has also made it possible to overcome other barriers related to impairment. This is clear to a good part of the technical community, but not in totality, nor to the wider public. Such a lack of understanding of the importance of *"accessibility from scratch"* represents, at present, a real obstacle to societal evolution.

To get a clearer picture of the problem, it is sufficient to note that people with disabilities number nearly 1 billion worldwide, representing a formidable force of employees and customers.

In Europe, according to the EU Commission, people with disabilities comprise about 15% of the population, and many of them face barriers when using ICT products and services.

Despite these data, many people still consider impairment to be a marginal problem and accessibility not a relevant issue. With aging, however, everyone starts experiencing (to some extent) impairments, and accessibility is a major issue The number of elderly people is actually rising fast, according to UN figures (18% of the population was aged over 60 in 1990; while 30% will be over 60 by 2030), and very often, elderly people encounter knowledge or usage barriers when using ICT products and services. This, therefore, brings back the issues of *"lifelong learning"* and *"accessibility from scratch."*

Surprisingly, the technology required for achieving accessibility dovetails with technology required for pervasive computing, as nonimpaired customers need increasingly flexible, multimodal interfaces to accommodate IT access under varying environments, and with numerous devices. Therefore, taking impairment into account in the design phase of products and services automatically widens the market perspective and the societal benefit.

In 1998, the United States of America Congress amended the Rehabilitation Act to require Federal agencies to make their electronic and information technology accessible to people with disabilities. This decision was based on the fact that inaccessible technology interferes with an individual's ability to obtain and use information quickly and easily.

Section 508[13] was enacted to eliminate barriers in information technology, to make available new opportunities for people with disabilities, and to encourage development of technologies that will help achieve these goals. The law applies to all Federal agencies when they develop, procure, maintain, or use electronic and information technology. Under Section 508 (29 U.S.C.

'794d), agencies must give disabled employees and members of the public access to information that is comparable to the access available to others.

This process has brought about a major societal change in the USA and the upcoming spread of e-government solutions worldwide (http://www.w3.org/WAI/Policy/ http://www.w3.org/WAI/), and more specifically in Europe (Council Resolution of 25 March 2002 on the eEurope Action Plan 2002) means that the adoption, in the near future, of procedures and tools to make *"full accessibility"* a reality is now a necessity. E-learning will therefore be no more exception or something only for professionals (including or limited to training or retraining). Furthermore, the increase in the societal understanding of accessibility-related issues will favour a selection process where accessible products will be chosen over nonaccessible ones, even overriding the factors of pricing and brand name recognition.

The combination of constant availability of information and content (including in education and training sectors) and the push towards real lifelong learning is converging towards what is called *"m–learning"* (http://www.webopedia.com/, http://www.odl.org/, http://en.wikipedia.org/wiki/M-learning, http://www.pjb.co.uk/m-learning/articles.htm, http://www.e-learningcentre.co.uk/eclipse/Resources/mlearning.htm, http://www.academiccolab.org/initiatives/mlearning.html)(Metcalf, 2004a, 2004b) . In many ways, m-learning is recapitulating the evolutionary process that e-learning experienced as it emerged from traditional classroom training. In the mature e-learning markets in North America and Europe, mobile e-learning exists side by side with conventional e-learning as a general customer option. It is the product of choice over conventional e-learning for the mobile workforce.

All this leads back to the accessibility issue in the wider sense; as technology has reached a point where the objective could be reached to a great extent; what is lacking is both the application and regulation framework, along with a broad acceptance and recognition of this need for a real broad accessibility to content and education.

Previously, we have already provided a definition for e-learning and how it has come to the stage where, when talking about learning and accessibility, it is necessary to point out that e-learning is one of the terms that has emerged from the rapidly developing world of the Internet, and is broadly defined as "*Internet-enabled learning.*" This is usually referring to accessibility in terms of possibility to access, despite distance and time constraints, to sources, not in terms of impairment support. This is certainly not a minor issue.

Much expectation surrounds the Internet and its role in education, as e-learning can contribute to the improvement of standards and to the effectiveness of teaching and learning. Yet when claiming this, almost no reference is made to impairment support. Most Web-based content producers are often not even aware of W3C guidelines for accessible design of Web-based applications. The reason for this can probably be found in the fact that Internet access has generally only been available to society as a whole for the last 10-15 years, and to schools in the last 2-5 years. Such access is able to provide:

- Support for needs and individual learning requirements of both children and adults.
- A means of empowering children, helping them to learn more effectively.
- Access to vast volumes of information, mostly free.
- Communication tools and facilities that can be used on different levels.
- Access to content and learning processes that used to be confined to schools and colleges.

Summing up, the availability of Internet access provides a challenge to traditional forms of teaching and learning, and opens up opportunities previously denied to the majority. Yet all aforementioned factors are usually taken into account regardless of proper accessibility and usability related issues (in the sense that most content available on the Internet may fail either to meet accessibility issues in respect to regulations like the U.S. 508 one or similar, or usability criteria for certain user communities like elderly people or people with cognitive impairments).

This has happened largely due to the most widely adopted and common definition of e-learning. According to the IDC report "*E-learning: The Definition, the Practice, and the Promise,*" we can say that a good, working definition for e-learning (and in more general sense of e-anything) is "*electronic*" or "*Internet-enabled.*" Internet-enabled learning, or e-learning, strictly means learning activities on the Internet. Those events can be "*live*" learning that is led by an instructor or "*self-paced*" learning, where content and pace are determined by the individual learner.

The only two common elements in this process are a connection to the Internet (either physical or wireless) and learning. In 1996, a program for bringing technology into education was launched in the U.S. Its primary goals were:

- All students and teachers will have access to information technology in their classrooms, schools, communities, and homes.
- All teachers will use technology effectively to help students achieve high academic standards.
- All students will have technology and information literacy skills.
- Research and evaluation will improve the next generation of technology applications for teaching and learning.
- Digital content and networked applications will transform teaching and learning.

Presently, these objectives have almost been fully met in the U.S.[14] Furthermore, according to the report "*A Vision of eLearning for America's Workforce,*" developed by the Commission on Technology and Adult Learning, the global e-learning industry comprises approximately 5,000 suppliers offering every imaginable method of e-learning. The vast majority of these suppliers are private.

Even if it is generally accepted that the driving force behind the 21st-century economy has been knowledge, in many European countries, these objectives are still far from being realised.

What is driving the market in real time can be split among present and future trends, while drivers and inhibitors are illustrated in Tables 3 and 4.

A direct consequence of this is that technology needs to be used in order to lower costs. This can be achieved by reusing content (even if usually an increase of richness is also requested), and adding value by offering custom solutions and new approaches (performance support, customer education, and so forth.). Yet the most important issue regarding e-learning systems is related to its effectiveness in transferring knowledge to the user. Learners' comprehension depends strongly on course structure. Therefore, particular attention

*Table 3. Today and tomorrow (Source: Online Courseware Factory Ltd)*

| Today | Tomorrow |
|---|---|
| Technology training | Performance improvement |
| Classes for the masses | Personalised learning |
| Instructor centric | Learner centric |
| Training when scheduled | Learning on demand |
| Time to train | Time to perform |
| Teaching by telling | Learning by doing |
| Product-based learning | Project based learning |
| Know what | Know why |
| Skill and information (mastery basics = 3Rs) | Inquiry, discovery and knowledge basics |
| Reactive | Proactive |

*Table 4. Drivers and inhibitors (Source: Uwe Krueger, Realtech, http://www.realtech.de)*

| Drivers | Inhibitors |
|---|---|
| Lifelong learning | Technology Compatibility |
| Economic turbulence | Limitations |
| Need for continued education and staff training | Billing systems |
| Increased Internet / eCommerce usage | Security concerns |
|  | Price |

must be paid to effective navigation and look-and-feel features. In addition, content should be designed, developed, or adapted for multimodal delivery for effective content reusability. Such integrated approaches are more likely to have an impact as the meta-adaptivity system design domain emerges.

## TOOLS AND APPROACHES TO E-LEARNING

It has been pointed out that at present, there is a shift in education that is moving from an approach in which individuals undergo a specific period of training and then start their professional life to an approach in which the learning process is a lifelong one. In this second perspective, companies also have to tackle the issue of continuous education. For a rather evident set of constraints, including but not limited to time and costs, companies have been always trying to find alternative solutions to class-based learning. Thus, it is not surprising that some of the early adopters of e-learning have been major corporations like IBM, HP, AT&T, Boeing, and many others. In this respect, it is interesting to note that according to Brandon and Hall (Chapman, 2006; Chapman, 2006a Chapman & Nantel, 2006; Nantel & Vipond, 2006), "*organizations' eLearning practices are what turns tools and content into real learning.*" Furthermore, to be successful in the design of e-Learning courses, the following factors should be taken into account:

1.  **Faced problem and expected results:** Matching the e-learning solution to the problem at hand; achieving intended results.
2.  **Instructional design and integrity:** Structuring, relevance and quality of content; focus on real-world competencies; selecting the right strategies for the content and

context. This also means focussing on the intended users.
3.  **Evaluation and assessment:** Applying imagination and rigour to the design and implementation of evaluation or assessment.
4.  **Interactivity:** Using creativity and expert design practices to achieve instructionally powerful interactions of all kinds.
5.  **Usability and interface:** Creating an effective, easy-to-use interface.
6.  **Motivation and aesthetics:** Motivating learners to follow and successfully complete the training; hitting the right tone and aesthetic notes.
7.  **Media and technology:** Smart selection and application of media, development tools and delivery technologies.
8.  **Money and time:** Achieving excellence under constrained budgets and time lines. This aspect is relevant not only for companies, but also for people acquiring off-the-shelf products or online solutions to solve a specific problem like learning a language or acquiring knowledge essential for a specific purpose (re-employing, relocating, and so forth).

In this process of integrating education into the employees' daily life within a company, several aspects should be taken into account. For example, the need to keep certain components of company know-how inside the company, or how to foster practical skills acquisition, or how to handle the mapping of individual characteristics onto a professional job description to then derive, thanks to a gap analysis, the individual training needs.

Most of these items correspond in practice to one or more tool-sets that are used by the human resource department, the IT/ICT infrastructure, the employees, and the company management to address the various issues. The most relevant ones are described next, and could also be used in the "*formal*" education process to improve what is presently achievable, or to complement it in order to tackle specific issues.

## Authoring Tools, KMS and (L)CMS

Authoring tools are generally desktop, single-user applications used to construct learning content by assembling and combining text, graphics, audio, video, and animations into e-learning courses. Yet there is also a current trend to have Web-based development tools. They have been initially derived by visual HTML editors and are often used to create standard Web pages, but they can also be used for creating learning applications. In addition, there exists a growing number of authoring tools focused on rapid, template-based development of learning content, sometimes with a specific focus on a particular type of learning application, such as software simulations.

Authoring tools, even though offering a rather broad range of solutions, represent only one category of tools aimed at properly editing and formatting content/knowledge. This is undoubtedly the first step in the process. Yet once content has been prepared it has to be managed, and a set of solutions has been developed for this purpose over time. Notably the most interesting are represented by:

- **Content management systems (CMS):** Systems for organizing and facilitating collaborative creation of documents and other content, using a range of technologies and techniques, including portal systems, wiki systems, and Web-based groupware; sometimes Web based, though in many cases, requiring special client software).
- **Knowledge management systems (KMS):** Systems for organizing and facilitating collaborative creation and management of knowledge and expertise, either at company or at individual level, using a range of tech-

nologies and techniques, including portal systems, wiki systems, and Web-based groupware.

- **Learning content management system (LCMS):** A solution for the creation, management, and transfer of learning content; it is apparent that LCMS are a subcategory of CMS devoted to learning content.

## E-Learning, ODL, and Lifelong Learning

Computers are moving out of laboratories and into classrooms in learning new languages, understanding complicated math formulas, and exploring other countries. Technology is changing basic notions of schools and education and creating classrooms without walls that offer students a valuable view of the world, and enable them to experience and interact with other students and resources around the globe. With numerous forms of distance learning now available, public education is moving away from a need for students and teachers to assemble in school buildings for education to occur. This trend has far-reaching implications for the structure of state education budgets.

According to analysis performed by government and research institutions, the rapid growth in such areas as distance learning, technology-enabled assessment, and the increasingly diversified and expanded public-private learning marketplace require the development of new strategies for quality and consumers' protection. Important priorities for the public and private sectors include:

- Providing reliable and universally accessible quality information for consumers.
- Developing quality assurance mechanisms.
- Ensuring that learners have the support they need to make the right decisions about their e-learning options.

- Developing policies and practices to ensure privacy.

Traditional, institution-based approaches to assessment and certification are not well suited to an e-learning world in which the focus turns from a record of classes taken and degrees received, to measures of what an individual actually knows and is able to do. As a result, private and public sector leaders need to take steps to create new approaches such as developing and promoting outcome-based assessments of learning results, and creating an electronic system for tracking those results.

Government and commerce must play a leadership role in making quality e-learning opportunities more widely available to all, from supporting the development of common technical standards to promoting broader access in under-served communities. The challenge and the opportunity are the same: to realize e-learning potential for reducing the divide between "*haves*" and "*have nots.*" Therefore, it is necessary to:

- Create the highest-quality e-learning experiences possible.
- Implement new measures and methods for assessing/certifying what users know and are able to do.
- Ensure broad and equal access to e-learning opportunities.

The potential return on investment for both the public and private sectors is enormous. The challenge for businesses is to realize the full potential of e-learning as a driver of productivity and performance gains by making it an integral part of organizational strategy and operations. For government, the challenge is to create a nurturing policy environment for e-learning, firstly by removing barriers that restrict access to e-learning benefits and, secondly, by promoting industry self-regulation while balancing citizens' interests and needs.

By adopting e-learning standards like the one defined by IEEE, AICC, and so forth, it is possible to achieve full interoperability of e-learning platforms and to have real, full portability of produced content. A learning object respecting all features described in those standards will be available in whatsoever platform and therefore, full independence from a specific vendor is achieved. Moreover, it is possible to package objects developed with different tools and for different delivery platforms, achieving a consistent and interoperable object, where the tracking will also be kept across editing, aggregation, and reuse. Other emerging standards that focus on personalisation are likely to have an influence in the near future, such as the internationalization of the IMS AccessForAll approach in ISO, the Individualized Adaptability and Accessibility in e-learning, Education and Training Standard.

## Virtual Reality and Multisensorial Approach

The use of virtual reality is progressively becoming widespread. Usually the primary applications are either professional training or gaming. In the first case, the simulation is devoted to enable trainees to have access to equipment and situations that may be too risky and too costly to be faced otherwise. At the same time, only big organisations can presently afford costs related to simulations. On the other hand, namely in gaming, customers are demanding more and more in terms of appearance, and the huge numbers involved allow developers to achieve high levels of quality, despite the production costs.

With today's technology, it is possible to achieve results unforeseeable just a few years ago. In detail, it is now possible to achieve multisensorial stimuli by combining visual, tactile, and sound experiences into a unique new one experience. The real challenge is to be able to generate similar situations (potentially involving even smell) for edutainment purposes. What is still lacking is

*Table 5. Reasons for retention or loss within a new community*

| Reasons to stay & be active | Reasons to leave |
|---|---|
| The forum is providing interesting news | Lack of a moderator |
| The content is complete and gives a good coverage of the topic addressed | A number of participants imposing their viewpoints |
| It is possible to find replies to questions or people able to provide such replies | It is not easy to understand the content and type of mail received from the forum |
| Participants are skilled, knowledgeable and interested | Too much mail is received |
| There is enough dialogue | Shift in focus |
| There is an historical track of performed discussions | Lack of education in participants' behaviour |
| There is a service provision for FAQs | |
| Case studies, white papers, reference documents, presentations, articles and papers are available (at least for browsing, better if downloadable) | |

a paradigm to convey all those rich stimuli into a single mainstream that may be used to both entertain and educate at the same time.

## Virtual Communities and Forums

In many cases, establishing user communities is an extremely powerful and convenient way to foster a learning process. Community users will exchange ideas and cooperatively support each other in the learning process. This approach has a long history, and was initially born among scholars in the scientific domain as a way to support research results exchange, documents, and papers peer reviews, and other forms of interaction. With the wide diffusion of Internet, this approach has progressively widened its application, and presently there are thousands of communities, forums, and so forth. Given this,

it is nevertheless essential to note that starting up a new community or forum is a difficult process. Table 5 reports the most relevant factors that would cause user retention or loss.

According to Table 5, actions that help in starting up the discussion in a new-born forum/community can be summarised as follows:

- Promote forum existence by direct contact with a set of people that may be interested to take part in forum activities and provide useful cooperation.
- Provide interesting threads.
- Periodically provide contributions from experts.
- Select key themes and collect them.
- Generate FAQs starting from relevant threads.
- Simplify the process to manage messages and replies, for example introducing the concept of a follow-up message that is not a reply but a related issue.

Another success factor that has to be taken into account is "need." If the users needs to be part of a certain community, or if the users may find, in such a community, replies to their own needs, or even a sense of belonging/ownership, then community success is almost assured (the only real threat in that case may be economical sustainability). An interesting example for this is the German School Net; up to when it was strongly supported (in terms of costs and equipment) by Deutsche Telekom, it grew and developed. It turned out to be extremely important, full of users (both teachers and students) and data exchange. When Deutsche Telekom stopped supporting its activity, then community subsistence was greatly endangered. Now with the start-up of the European School Net, the German portal has also gained new vitality. Also of note is the case of eSchoolnet, the European Teachers' portal.

*Figure 26. E-learning market players and their positions*

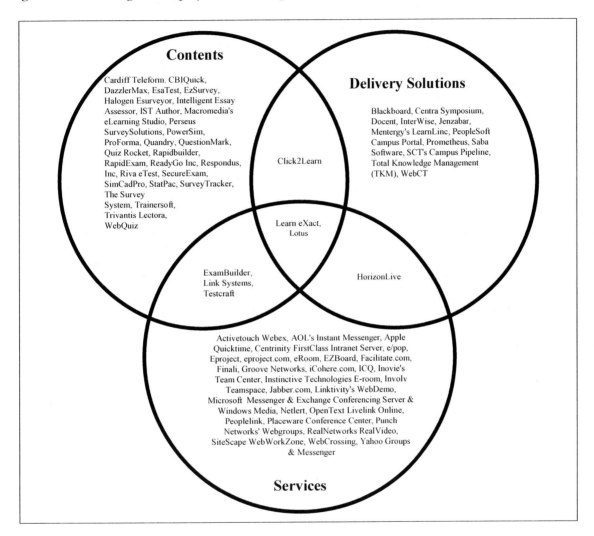

## E-LEARNING AND THE MARKET

To complete the panorama provided so far to at least the relation presently existing between e-learning and the market should be addressed. According to IDC (2002), the e-learning market is segmented in three main areas: Content, Delivery solutions, and Services.

Content providers offer courseware core material (like multimedia assets and course structure), and testing/assessments are included in their expertise. Companies that provide delivery solutions offer products oriented at course preparation and organisation, such as training authoring tools and learning management systems (LMS), including collaborative software to help course fruition. Services include all additional features that can lead to better course preparation (content design), and that are related to course maintenance (management and hosting) and CRM (online mentoring). Some products/platforms provide solutions in different areas, covering partially or totally the entire range of e-learning offers. Figure 26 describes the situation and introduces market players and their positions in the marketl as it appeared at the time of the previously mentioned IDC study.

**Asynchronous Web-based software suites** attempt to group suites of tools that quickly allow an instructor to convert existing basic electronic documents to a hierarchical system with relative ease. Although most of these suites may require limited HTML knowledge to fully exploit them, relatively little programming or other technical expertise should be needed to effectively use these software suites. Key characteristics of major players in asynchronous suites typically include capability for secure student login via standard Java browser, centralized database-centred syllabus with links to internal or external Web pages, online, time-monitored quizzes with randomised dynamically-generated testing, discussion groups, and integrated e-mail. Systems also provide instructor development tools to ease transition from other media to these products. The academic user audience is dominated by two vendors: WebCT and Blackboard, with only a few additional competitors targeting academic audiences specifically. Corporate/government learning organizations have a much larger number of competing systems.

**Synchronous (real time) Web-based training solutions** are the most appropriate to facilitate relatively formal, instructor-led, hierarchical learning events, such as a seminar or interactive classroom. A number of these products incorporate *"talking head video"*; most video-enabled products suffer from poor video quality and tend to require 128KBPS (a.k.a. ISDN class) dial-in connections for acceptable performance; although a compelling sales feature tending to appeal to instructors familiar with videoconferencing, at present current *"talking head video quality"* over dial-up Internet connections is not worth the effort; most students ignore such poor images very early into the course. Leading members of this class generally have also the following characteristics:

- Browser-based (works with Netscape and Internet Explorer, though often PC-centric).
- Online testing (designed for use over Internet dial-up connections or corporate intranets).
- Live streaming audio (generally one-way, often two-way)
- Text chat, and occasionally private text chat, among students or between participants and presenter.
- Sequencing is controlled by a presenter-leader; a secondary/copresenter is available for the higher end products.
- Ability to show PowerPoint presentations.
- Ability to record sessions and make them available for on-demand viewing at any time.
- Shared whiteboard, with ability for students and faculty to import images that can be annotated on the whiteboard.
- Web-page sharing/cobrowsing.
- Application sharing ability for presenters to share applications running on their desktop.
- Integrated polling/surveys.
- Virtual *"hand/raising,"* to indicate when participants have questions.
- Firewall friendly.

**Application service providers (ASP)** choose to make their products available as hosted solutions only; they do not sell the software for organizations to create and run their own servers under license. This license arrangement may better fit specific needs, especially where institutions do not have the in-house capability to sustain tech support teams and servers. Vendors in this category generally offer the following feature set:

- **Browser-based:** All functionality is provided within a standard browser. Updates are added automatically.

- **Presentation sharing:** allows any meeting participant to spontaneously share any presentation (generally PowerPoint).
- **Document sharing:** allows meeting attendees to view content with multilevel zooming and annotation capabilities.
- **Application sharing:** Run any software application for effective live demos and training.
- **Desktop sharing:** Presenters can share anything on their PC system, including applications.
- **Web browser sharing:** Allows easy sharing of Web-based information.
- **Polling:** Lets presenters solicit quantitative feedback from attendees online.
- **Internationalization:** ability to change the menus for selected languages.
- **Text chat:** generally available as group chat and a separate channel for interaction during a session. A controversial feature in academics, as it is perceived by faculty as the electronic equivalent of note-passing or whispering in class.
- **Record and playback:** Permits recording of all interactions in a meeting for later reference, training, or demos. Anyone can play back a recording.
- **Application share control:** The presenter can share control of any software application with others in a meeting, for unmatched interactive meetings on the Web.
- **Scalable:** Supports multiple concurrent meetings with thousands of participants.
- **File transfer:** Users can conveniently upload and download files as desired.
- **Event tech support:** ASP vendor's customer support personnel can take control of a user's PC system (with the user's approval) to instantly provide live assistance and resolve problems.

**Learning portals** are an emerging variation of Personal Collaborative Environments, and are an attempt to combine student services and community building through an integrated Web-enabled system, very much like the search engine portals Yahoo and Lycos. The use of the term "*Learning portal*" could imply either the basic software product needed to develop a portal or the actual use of such software to create a learning experience.

**Collaborative software**, an emerging category of software, allows individuals to interact one-to-one, peer-to-peer, or in small groups. The category may also be referred to as "*Instant Messaging*," or "*Buddy Systems*," although a number of products in this category also represent the older "*listserve*" e-mail-broadcast technology. This type of tool will become integral in advanced Web-based learning programs. Typically, tools in this category allow "*awareness*" of user-selected individuals and the ability to instant message (i.e., "*chat*" one-to-one) with individuals. Most programs provide for ad-hoc chatting in small groups. Some of these programs permit application sharing, voice-over-IP, or other useful over-the-Web features designed to allow individuals to interact. Currently, this category of software lacks interoperability. The Internet Engineering Task Force's Instant Message and Presence Protocol represents the current form of standards proposed in order to solve these interoperability issues.

**Team groupware** is a new subset of collaborative software aimed at creating virtual project groups. "*Team groupware*" is distinguished from personal collaborative environments by these characteristics:

- Ability to develop documents synchronously and review asynchronously.
- One-to-one, one-to-many, and many-to-many capability.
- Centralized user management.
- Real-time Internet communications by at least one of the following:
  - Enterprise-ready systems scalable to hundreds of users

Advanced software in this category includes group scheduling, ability to store and review older version of documents, and ability to route items. Systems should also require relatively little technical expertise for management after installation, as projects must be easy to create, edit, or terminate.

**Web-based education development tools** attempt to collect basic and single-purpose tools that meet specific needs but are not themselves intended to be a turnkey implementation system. They are generally visual authoring tools or programmers toolkits, or meet a very specific Web-based need. This category has undergone substantial consolidation since the high-flying days prior to the dot.com crash in 2000/2001. A late 2002 study from Market Data Retrieval revealed that one-third of K-12 schools are already offering a number of distance learning programs for their students. High schools, in particular, have been attracted to the virtual classroom environment, with 53% offering such programs to students in rural states where students do not have access to specialized teachers. Furthermore, 36% of schools reported to have distance learning programs for their teachers, allowing them to access professional development programs, which is similar to the applications corporations are finding for e-learning.

## REFERENCES

Abraham, M. (1943). A theory of human motivation. *Psychological Review,* 370-396. Reissued in 2004 as an Appendix to *The Third Force: The Psychology of Abraham Maslow* in Adobe PDF.

Brandon Hall Research. Retrieved from http://www.brandon-hall.com/

CETIS, the Centre for Educational Technology Interoperability Standards. Retrieved from http://www.cetis.ac.uk/

Chapman, B. (2006). *LMS knowledge base 2006.* Sunnyvale, CA: Brandon-Hall.

Chapman, B., & Nantel, R. (2006). *Low-cost learning management systems 2006.* Sunnyvale, CA: Brandon-Hall.

Council Resolution of 25 March 2002 on the eEurope Action Plan 2002: Accessibility of public websites and their content. (2002/C 86/02). *Official Journal of the European Communities.* Retrieved from http://eur-lex.europa.eu/LexUriServ/site/en/oj/2002/c_086/c_08620020410en00020003.pdf

EEIG. European Economic Interest Grouping (EEIG). *Activities of the European Union, Summaries of Legislation, EUROPA.EU.INT.* Retrieved from http://europa.eu.int/scadplus/leg/en/lvb/l26015.htm

FLIC Project. (2004). *D2.1 Design of a pedagogical template.*

FLIC Project. (2005a). *D2.4 Voice models recording.*

FLIC Project. (2005b). *D2.3 Development of materials for the evaluation.*

FLIC project. (2006). *Special project status report for the EC.*

Hornof, A. J., & Halverson, T. *Cognitive modeling, eye tracking and human-computer interaction.* Department of Computer and Information Science, University of Oregon. Retrieved March 23, 2007, from http://www.cs.uoregon.edu/research/cm-hci/

IDC. (2002). *Corporate eLearning: European market forecast and analysis 2001/2002.* IDC Corporate, 5 Speen Street, Framingham, MA, 01701.

Kowler, E. Eye movements and visual attention. In *MITECS: The MIT encyclopedia of the cognitive sciences.* Retrieved from http://cognet.mit.edu/MITECS/Entry/kowler

Lasnier, C. (2005). How to best exploit the VO-CODER. *AGERCEL, 2005.*

LeLoup, J. W., & Ponterio R. (2001). On the Net—Finding song lyrics online. *Language Learning & Technology, 5*(3), 4-6. Retrieved from http://llt.msu.edu/vol5num3/onthenet

Mah, A. Y. (2003). *A thousand pieces of gold—A memoir of China's past through its proverbs* (pp. 293). HarperCollins Publishers. MASIE Center's e-Learning consortium. (2002).

*Making sense of learning specifications & standards: A decision maker's guide to their adoption.* Retrieved from http://www.masie.com/standards/S3_Guide.pdf

MediTECH. (2005a). *FLIC prototype—Instruction manual.*

MediTECH. (2005b). *FLIC project public presentation.*

Metcalf, D. (2004a). *m-Learning: Technology update and best practices.* Presentation held at Training 2004, Atlanta GA. Retrieved from http://www.elearnopedia.com/mlearning/m-learning-wed.pdf

Metcalf, D., (2004b). *m-Learning evaluation.* Presentation held at Training 2004, Atlanta GA. Retrieved from http://www.elearnopedia.com/mlearning/m-learning%20evaluation.pdf

Nantel, R., & Vipond, S. (2006). *Authoring tool knowledge base 2006.* Sunnyvale, CA: Brandon-Hall.

Neuman, W. R. (1991). *The future of mass audience.* Cambridge University Press.

Novak, J. D. (1998). *Learning, creating, and using knowledge: Concept maps as facilitative tools in schools and corporations.* Mahwah, NJ: Lawrence Erlbaum Associates.

Sussman, R., & Sedivy, J. *Using Eyetracking to detect and describe Filled Gap Effects, the electronic community for scholarly research in the cognitive and brain sciences.* MIT COgNet. Retrieved from http://cognet.mit.edu/posters/poster.tcl?publication_id=45136

Tomita, T. (1980). The new electronic media and their place in the information market of the future. In A. Smith (Ed.), *Newspapers and democracy: International essays on a changing medium.* Cambridge, MA: MIT Press.

## ENDNOTES

[1] The term *"clerices"* survives in some students' organisations, named *"Goliardia,"* that can still be found in ancient European universities.

[2] St. Edmund Hall (1278), Exeter (1314), Oriel (1326), Queen's (1340), New (1379), Lincoln (1427), All Souls (1438), Magdalen (1458), Brasenose (1509), Corpus Christi (1517), Christ Church (1546), Trinity (1554), St John's (1555), and Jesus (1571).

[3] Africans (RSA and South African Radio Broadcasting Corporation), Spanish (Radio Andorra), Chinese (Radio Beijing), Jew (Israel Broadcasting Authority), French (Radio France International), Japanese (Radio Japan), Greek (Cyprus Broadcasting Corporation), English (BBC, Voice of America in Special English, Radio Australia, KGEI California, WYFR), Dutch (Radio Nederland), Polish (Radio Poland), Russian (Radio Moscow), Swedish (Radio Sweden), German (Deutsche Welle, Deutshlandfunk, Radio DDR).

[4] Originally named APPANET (from the combination of the names ARPA - Advanced Research Projects Agency and Net) was born during the late 1960s as a Defense Advanced Research Projects (DARPA) project to ensure efficient and robust communication

among military bases and the capitol, in case of a nuclear attack.

5   Some of the most well-known systems are the one used in avionics (e.g., on the Cobra attach helicopter), or in tanks and many other combat systems.

6   This is just a rough description of evolution partition and sequencing in the field

7   Actually, the first emperor ordered that a 1:1 replica of the Dalai Lama palace was built so that his guest could feel at home.

8   Matteo Ricci is the author of the first world map printed in China, which notably is China-centred, well in accordance with the Chinese definition of their land: "All that is under Heaven."

9   Initially based on a combination of books and records, then tapes, and now CD/DVD

10  NotePad or other text editor

11  Director, Authorware, ToolBook, and so forth.

12  ReadyGo, Lectora Publisher, Trainersoft, and so forth.

13  http://www.section508.gov/index.cfm

14  In 1999, 95% of schools in the U.S. have Internet access, and 63% instructional rooms with Internet access (Source: Catrina Williams .(2000). Internet Access in U.S. Public Schools and Classrooms, 1994-1999, NCES 2000-086, Washington, D.C. U.S. Department of Education, National Center for Education Statistics. For more details see http://nces.ed.gov/pubsearch/pubsinfo. asp?pubid=2000086

# Chapter XI
# Web–Based Music Intelligent Tutoring Systems

**Somnuk Phon-Amnuaisuk**
*Multimedia University, Malaysia*

**Chee Keh Siong**
*Multimedia University, Malaysia*

## ABSTRACT

*Our work bridges two interesting topics: the research in the area of Web-based applications and the area of learning technologies. We give an overall picture of the current development in Web-based music intelligent tutoring system (WMITS). The term WMITS is coined by us to describe the two main areas in our focus. In this chapter, we address the following issues: (i) the pedagogical aspect of teaching and learning music, (ii) the background of music intelligent tutoring system, and (iii) our WMITS system for teaching music theories. A Web-based environment offers strengths in terms of accessibility and self-paced learning. However, the environment has a great drawback in terms of interactivities between the users and the system. Our design addresses this issue by developing a specialised client tool. The client tool provides an interactive environment for score editing that is crucial for learning music theories. The system incorporates three major inference techniques (i.e., deductive, inductive, and Bayesian inference) in dealing with music theories and uncertain knowledge such as students' understanding.*

## INTRODUCTION

The attempt to facilitate teaching and learning music using technological knowledge has a long history. In the 1940s, Frank Cookson developed ear-training drills by recording the teaching ma-terials on a magnetic recording tape (Williams & Webster, 1999). Many computer-assisted instruction (CAI) systems had been developed as early as the 1950s. Most works around the 1950s-1970s labelled themselves as CAI systems. These systems normally presented their teaching materials with predetermined steps. The complexity of the program behaviour was obtained by implementing more branching into the program. This approach had an obvious limitation. Students were guided through the materials through a predefined navigation path. It was suitable for a learning scenario where a lot of information was pushed to students without much interactivity between the instructor and the students. The emergence of artificial intelligence offers some hope in providing a CAI with intelligence. The term intelligent tutoring system (ITS) has become a common term for researchers to use to describe their systems in the period after the 1980s. The main difference between a CAI and an ITS is in their structures. In general, an ITS is composed of three main components: *the user, the tutor,* and *the domain knowledge.* An ITS also aims to have an adaptive teaching/learning environment that can intelligently adjust its teaching to suit individual needs. To be truthful, the number of successful ITSs (especially in the music domain) is not much.

The emergence of Internet has created a lot of impact on our society and we have seen many developments in Web-based education since the 1990s. A Web-based teaching and learning environment has many appealing features. Among these are ease of accessibility, variety of resources, and self-paced learning. However, the environment still lacks support for sophisticated interactions between the system and the learners. This lack of support for sophisticated interactions can be improved on by enhancing the client's side with specialised client tools (e.g., score editing facility) suitable to the tasks faced.

In the following, we briefly discuss the background of music education and music ITS systems relevant to our study. First, we highlight the challenges. Then, we present our design and implementation concepts. We also discuss the inference mechanisms and future trend.

# BACKGROUND

Web-based learning is fast becoming a major form of learning. It is not a question of whether this can replace a real-life classroom teaching or whether we should adopt this learning environment into our education system, but it is a fact that Web-based learning is unavoidable due to knowledge delivery bottleneck. Knowledge grows at a fast speed, and it is a luxury to have real contact with an expert. Therefore, we must seek for an effective learning environment. This opens up an exciting research area that is multidisciplinary in nature; the *Web-based intelligent tutoring system* (WITS). The area of Web-based ITS encompasses a wide range of issues ranging from the design of infrastructure to the design of contents, from the design of contents to the assessment of whether the contents have been successfully delivered. Here, we focus our discussion on the *Web-based music intelligent tutoring system* (WMITS) technology.

## Nature of Music Education

Music is quite unique in terms of its theories, which are mainly concerned with music structures and the philosophy behind music education. Musicianship could never be acquired solely by reading and thinking. We may still observe the split approaches between open (e.g., learning with private teacher) and classroom education in music and other art subjects. In contrast, at present, most science education exists only in a classroom set-up.

Taking music as an academic discipline requires a good understanding of its unique structure. There exist four major schools of thought in approaching music curriculum in contemporary music education: the *Dalcroze* method, the *Orff* approach, the *Kodaly* concept, and the *Suzuki Talent Education* (Mark, 1996). These schools of thought incorporate conceptual learning materials, techniques, and practices. Here, we summarise the approaches in brief.

- The Dalcroze method places more emphasis on the expression rather than the technique; to produce music is to expressively articulate the thought and feeling through music. Therefore, the main components in the Dalcroze methods are *eurhythmics, ear training (solfege),* and *improvisation.*
- The main components of the Orff approach are *rhythm* and *improvisation.* The approach builds musical elements from rhythmic, melodic, and harmonic constructs. Improvisation cultivates creativity in the learning process.
- The Kodaly concept emphasises the following activities: singing, reading and writing music, ear training, as well as improvisation.
- The Suzuki Talent Education emphasises the so called "mother-tongue method." The concept is based on the observation that children could master their own mother tongue easily. So music should be taught as if one is going to learn a new language. The Suzuki approach facilitates learning through observation, imitation, and repetition.

There are many other variations for these mainstream approaches. The variations provide a rich source of information for knowledge engineers in designing a WMITS. For example, a WMITS should support the learning of musical elements such as rhythmic, melodic, and harmonic constructs. They should also support ear training, improvisation, and musical expression. A finalised WMITS may be an eclectic of all the approaches outlined.

## Previous Works in Intelligent Tutoring System

The common teaching activities in music education revolve around music theories, aural skills, and performing skills. Learning music is traditionally carried out in a highly interactive environment.

Students usually sing and play their instruments along with peers and teachers. Music composition is normally done in a small-group setting. Only music history and music theory can be effectively carried out in a classroom setting. It should not be a surprise from the literature reviewed that although research activities in various domains, for example, aural training (Hoffstetter, 1981), performing (Baker, 1992; Dannenberg, Sanchez, Joseph, Capell, P., Joseph, & Saul, 1990), and learning music theory (Cook, 1998; Newcomb, 1985) have been explored, the most common would be the teaching of history and music theory. One of the main reasons for this is that teaching aural and performing skills require a much more expressive and sophisticated communication mode than teaching music theories.

Holland (2000) reviewed many applications in music education. He gave a critical review of systems that offered some learning experience to users. He pointed out that music is an open-ended domain. In an open-ended domain such as music, there is no clear goal. There are many possible good solutions, and this subjectivity makes teaching music difficult. Holland suggested that an interactive environment, where problem seeking and exploratory types of activities are also emphasised (not only problem solving,) could be more suitable to the music domain. Holland summarised the activities in a music ITS into two periods; the classical period (about 1970 to about 1987) and the modern period (about 1987 onwards).

According to Holland, the classical period is characterised by its *objectivism* (i.e., there exists a well-defined body of relevant knowledge to be taught) and the emphasis of the three components: the domain model, the student model, and the teaching model. The modern period is characterised by the shift in focus from an *objectivist* approach in the classical period to other approaches such as *constructivist* and *collaborativist*. The main driving force behind this shift is mainly from the open-ended characteristic of the music domain.

Brandao et al. (Brandao, Wiggins, & Pain, 1999) provided a useful summary of instructional strategies in music applications (between the 1970s to 1990s) into four main approaches: *programmed learning/drill and practice, Socratic dialogue, coaching/monitoring, and exploratory.*

- **Programmed learning/drill and practice:** Examples of applications that base their instructional designs mainly on programmed learning and drill and practice approaches are applications in music theory and ear training for example GUIDO (Hoffstetter, 1981; Wiggins & Trewin, 2000); applications in performing skills, for example, Piano tutor (Dannenberg, 1990), pianoFORTE (Smoliar, Waterworth, & Kellock, 1995); and composition, for example, LASSO (Newcomb, 1985).
- **Coaching/monitoring:** Piano tutor and INTERPRET (Baker, 1992) are examples of systems that teach performing skills by engaging students with the task, keep monitoring students, and give appropriate feedback when suboptimum behaviour is identified.
- **Socratic dialogue:** LASSO and INTERPRET are examples of systems that employ this approach. Socratic dialogue is a discovery-learning approach. A full power of this approach requires a full power of natural language processing (NLP).
- **Exploratory:** Harmony space, LOGO, and MOTIVE (Holland, 1993) are examples of systems that support exploratory learning

Williams and Webster (1999) shared a similar opinion in categorising educational applications according to teaching and learning strategies. They reviewed many PC computer assist instructional (CAI) applications and grouped them into (1) drill-and-practice, (2) flexible practice, (3) guided instruction, (4) games, (5) exploratory, and (6) creative. Many of these applications were not constructed as knowledge intensive systems, but with appealing features such as teaching and learning through games. This breakdown highlights an important issue to us. The effectiveness of an ITS system does not result from an intelligent expert model alone, but the instructional environment also plays a major role in the effectiveness of teaching and learning of the whole system. For example, packages such as *Finale, Cakewalk, Band-in-a-Box* could be used in creativity sessions as tools to help in the teaching and learning process.

Looking from a bird's eye view into this area, we see that the systems in the early period focused on encoding expert knowledge (e.g., the focus was on the expert model). Then the focus shifted to content development, to modelling (e.g., on the learner model and the tutor model), and to interactivities between systems and users (Fober, Letz, & Orlarey, 2004). In recent years, due to the growth of the Internet, Web-based ITS has become one of the main focuses in the ITS community.

## Challenges of WMITS

The Web-based applications have many advantages in terms of accessibility and self-paced learning. Web architecture is also an appealing platform for designing an open-learning environment (Kouroupetroglou, Stamati, & Metaxaki-Kissionides, 1999; Moundridou & Virvou, 2002; Shang, Shi, & Chen, 2001). Unfortunately, there is a serious limitation when it comes to interactivity in the current Web-based environment. This is a great drawback in music learning, since exploratory and creative learning styles are important factors in music learning. To accommodate music learning in the Web-based environment, we need to overcome many challenges. Here we list some of the challenges of the present Web-based architecture.

- **Challenge from the lack of domain-specific client tools:** We need tools that support domain specific applications (e.g., teaching of singing, performing skills, and music theory, etc.). These applications require specialised interactive interface. For example, learning music theories involves learning music notations; therefore, the application must support editing tasks.

- **Challenge from the lack of observable environment:** In learning paradigm, the application must be capable of detecting any level of interaction either to or from learners, and put them into a meaningful manner. Bidirectional interactions between the instructor and the learner are necessary and must be supported (Shea, Fredericksen, Pickett, & Swan, 1999). For instance, the logging of events stream (generated by user or system) could be useful in reasoning about the student model or the system behaviour.

- **Challenge from the lack of mobility:** Although standard Web-applications are more mobile when compared to stand-alone applications, there are still difficulties in locating, accessing, and using Web-based applications. This problem will become obvious if the user is mobile styled. They always move and work around with different machines. Additionally, they have to update every piece of software they use whenever there is a change.

- **Challenge from the lack of domain specific content authoring tools:** Content development is another major issue that needs to be discussed. The system should facilitate the content-development process.

- **Challenge from the lack of intelligent behaviours:** This last point is actually common to any ITS systems, and it is probably the most challenging issue. In a way, this could be an ill-defined issue. How can we judge that a system is intelligent? Must the system pass the Turing test before we acknowledge progress in this research area?

## WEB-BASED MUSIC INTELLIGENT TUTORING SYSTEMS

Our system is a framework that utilizes the existing Web architecture. However, instead of using a standard Web browser (e.g., Internet Explorer or Firefox) as our client tool, we are going to develop our own browser so that we can address the stated deficiencies (e.g., lack of domain-specific client tool). By developing our own client tool, we need to address some design issues that will be elaborated on later. Please take note that some issues are not addressed in our current implementation (e.g., motion analysis and vocal analysis). The proposed framework should allow us to gain more control in monitoring students' learning activities within a single environment.

In this section, we describe the main components of a generic intelligent tutoring system (subsection 3.1). Only the idea of the generic components is presented. In subsection 3.2, we give a more detailed account of the design and implementation of our Web-based music ITS. Finally, in subsection 3.3, a typical interaction between the system and a learner is described.

### Main Components of ITS

In this work, our ITS consists of four main components: *user interface, expert model, tutor model,* and *student model.* The user interface (UI) acts as a communication medium that sits between the ITS system and the learners. Input/output data in any ITS systems may be categorized into three general types of user interfaces:

- **Visual interface:** Visual interface allows interactions in a visual mode, such as images, graphics, musical score, and text. In music learning, learners tend to use their eyes in acquiring information from the monitor screen. They do content browsing, content reading, or content editing. In such cases, the system will present those materials through viewable contents, such as text, score, image, and animation. Some research works have shown us that those representations have variable sensitivity towards learner's progress. This depends highly on a few factors, such as learners' behaviour, learners' preference, nature of the domain, and presentation methods. For instance, an explanation on concept "Chord," together with image will be a good presentation for a learner who prefers graphic.

- **Aural/oral interface:** Aural/oral interface allows interactions by means of audio or vocal tools, such as microphone, speakers, mouth, and ears. During learning activities, a learner listens to the sound output that is being played. If the system is equipped with "listening" capability as well, then the learner could send a vocal message to it. Normally, the content of the output could be parts of a song, conversation, instructions, and so on. But in most applications, this type of UI seems impractical, unless for those users with visual defect. Moreover, those practiced applications (games, media player, etc.) are designed to "speak out," but not "listen to." Specifically, bidirectional auditory UI is a tremendously important feature for a music-learning system.
- **Motion interface:** Motion interface allows interactions by means of movements. The movement information may be coded in any form (e.g., video, muscle signals, brainwave, etc.). Performance analysis could be done with this kind of interface.

**The Expert Model** is also known as the *Domain Model*, the domain refers to the curriculum or knowledge to be taught. Analogously, its role is similar to a human expert (e.g., musician, pianist, etc.). Therefore, this model is supposed to be *a knowledge repository*, a *solution evaluator*, and a *problem solver*. For example, it may compare the learner's solution steps with the one being generated by the system, and generate useful feedback from the discrepancies observed.

**The Tutor Model** is also known as the *Pedagogical Model*. Some of us might be confused with the role and the differences between the tutor model and the domain model. This is because in real life, these two models are situated within a single person. The tutor model provides adaptive teaching strategy to suit each individual. It makes decisions regarding the best teaching strategy based on its perception of the student from the student model.

**The Student Model** is also known as the *Learner Model*. Broadly defined, a complete student model is a representation of a learner encompassing the personal profile, action history, learning behavioural patterns, areas of understanding, misconception parts, and so on. This model aims to mirror a human learner (in computer) so that the tutor model could adjust their teaching strategy based on this information. It is not an easy job to define an accurate learner model. It is because this model contains a lot of time series or longitudinal data that are important in the study of periodicities of learning, behavioural characteristics, and for future-action prediction. To make this happen, we must record any single change of event. But these massive and high-dimensional data seem impractical from the processing point of view.

## WMITS: Infrastructure

In this section, we describe how the four main components; tutor model, student model, domain knowledge, and user interface module, are put together in our WMITS framework. In the Web-based implementation, the functionalities

*Figure 1. High-level software components inside WMITS*

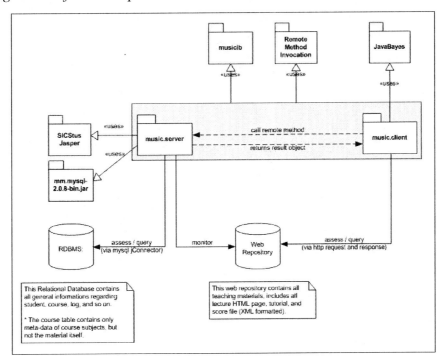

of these four main components are distributed among software components in the implemented client-server architecture.

Figure 1 shows a very brief architectural view of the system. Logically speaking, the four main software components: *music.server, music.client, RDBMS, and Web Repository* may reside in one single physical machine, or distributed among different places. However, they do communicate with each other through well-defined protocols. The so mentioned four ITS components are distributed among these software components. In our implementation, the music.server uses two other third-party packages as its extension libraries:

• **SICStusJasper:** This library allows music. server to access facilities that are provided by Prolog engine. For instance, music.server can load Prolog file and manipulate them.
• **mm.mysql-2.0.8-bin.jar:** This library is a database connector. It allows music.server

to establish connection to MySQL relational database.

In general, music.server is responsible for handling the remote method invocation (RMI) connection inside a local machine, and using it to communicate with a music.client component. Analogously, the RMI is similar to traditional remote procedural call (RPC) process, where a client can call a server's remote object and request services from it. The services provided by music. server are as listed.

• **Learner identification:** music.client can locate a remote object and ask for identity authentication and profile loading.
• **Domain problem solving:** An automated problem solver is implemented. This provides a model answer for any arbitrary question (currently connected to SICStus Prolog).

- **Event logging:** All activities are logged and used for further detailed analysis. Learners' behaviour could be analyzed using inference techniques such as a rule-based system (our own prolog music knowledge base), Bayesian inference (i.e., JavaBayes), decision tree, association rule mining, and so forth.

Currently, music.client uses JavaBayes for the Bayesian inference (open-source package for Bayesian network). This library allows music.client to access Bayesian Networks facilities. For instance, music.client can load and manipulate Bayes-compatible files. In fact, music.client is an integrated learning environment for the music domain. It provides the following main features:

- **Self-monitoring:** Periodically, learners may view their own performance profile, and adjust themselves for better results.
- **Course management:** At any time, learners may access their registered course(s). They

can register for a course if their prerequisite requirements have been fulfilled.

- **Content tree navigator:** Learners may browse through the contents of their registered courses. When they click on content node (tree node), music.client will fetch the requested material data into an attached browser.
- **Music notation editor:** This editor allows users to create, save, and manipulate music notation file (saved in XML format).
- **Observable environment:** As learners log into the system, almost all events will be logged. These events contribute towards a learner's performance assessment, inference on learning behaviour, and so forth.

## WMITS: Conceptual Framework

Figure 2 illustrates three important pieces of information: (1) Interactions between components inside the User Interface (UI) module, (2)

*Figure 2. Conceptual framework of WMITS*

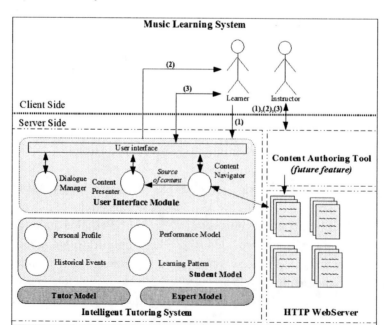

Potential components inside the Student Model, and (3) Interactions between the system components and users.

The UI model is one of the four main components to constitute a complete ITS structure. As illustrated, it contains three small, interrelated components: *Content Navigator, Content Presenter*, and *Dialogue Manager.*

- *The Content Navigator* is a component that prepares navigation plan, detects learning flow, and adjusts plans based on the learners' current and past activities. For example, when an instructor sets the content to two maximum attempts and the learner would like to go on a third attempt, the navigator may direct him/her to some prerequisite contents. So, along the learning process, the learner will be exposed to the contents that they are ready for only.
- *The Content Presenter* is a component that is responsible for presenting the content materials in the most suitable way. It detects user selection from the Navigator, obtains the source of materials from the Web server, and finally presents it. The content presenter also detects and captures the learners' interactions, such as input sequences, mouse-click patterns, or total spending time.
- *The Dialogue Manager* (Zhou, Freedman, Glass, Michael, Rovick, & Evens, 1999) is a component responsible for providing message feedback to the learner. The feedback could be a guideline, suggestion, hint, or even solution to a problem. A lot of localized factors will determine when and how to give feedback to further assist learners to learn. Basically, these components come with their own ontological commitment and agenda. They interact among themselves and with other agents, such as a student model, to form an interactive environment.

Inside the student model, there are four small, but important, modules that are able to tell us about the student in detail. These four modules carry different information, as listed.

- **Personal Profile:** This profile contains static information about the learner, such as name, registered courses, and so forth.
- **Historical Events:** This module contains a complete list of events that happen to that particular student. For example, we can know when he/she logs in and logs out.
- **Performance Model:** This module contains statistical data. These data are organized in a well-defined structure (e.g., Bayesian Network) for efficient representation and inference.
- **Learning Pattern:** This module is an inference resulting from historical events. It includes learning behaviour, navigation pattern, and and so forth. These data are tremendously important for the tutor model to set a suitable teaching plan.

During the learning process, learners interact with the UI model only. Once they log into the system, the Navigator adjusts its course structure based on the current student model and course setting. This adjustment is continuous until the learner logs out of the system. The Navigator and Presenter are the two agents that collect data from learning interactions. This data will immediately go into the student model as an input to construct. Under this conceptual framework, all users can access the deployed application through any machine that is network connectible. Here, we describe those processes in turn.

- **Process 1:** User launches application remotely.
- **Process 2:** The application will be downloaded into the client machine. However, this will be executed if and only if there is

no cached copy in the local machine, or if there is a newer version available.

- **Process 3:** Learner enrols for learning sessions. On the other end, the instructor may use it to manipulate the content materials.

Our proposed architecture provides scalability and modularity. There exists only one running server program, while there are zero or more clients connected to it. The architecture allows us to distribute resources, functions, and workloads between different machines in a very flexible way. For example, it is not necessary for a client application to contain all the information about its users, such as username, past log-in times, and so on. This information should be stored at one centre repository so that the user can access the System from anywhere, as the System "remembers" them. Our server program is state aware, that is, it remembers its interaction with every client. The interaction messages include query request, action request, and processing request. This flooding of data is later on transformed into meaningful knowledge about each individual student.

## SOLUTIONS TO CHALLENGES IN WMITS

We have listed out challenges of WMITS in section 2, and discussed our WMITS design in section 3. Indeed, challenges come from the fact that, by nature, any communication among humans is an interactive process. The attempt to transform the learning process over the Web needs to fill in many gaps. In our real world, a learner acquires knowledge from a teacher by using various communication tools. These tools include verbal conversation, body language, movement, or even changes in psychological states. But inside a virtual space, the learner is going to communicate directly with a machine. Therefore, it is compulsory to create an observable and responsive learning environ-

ment. The system must be capable of observing a learner's interaction, constructing an image that reflects the learner, and giving some feedback whenever necessary. In this section, we discuss these issues.

## WMITS Offers Domain Specific Client Tools with Observable Environment

In traditional music education, the interactions between a mentor and the learners are crucial. The learners are expected to learn important music concepts, and the mentor would probe and verify the understanding of the learners. To facilitate this activity in a Web-based environment, the system on the client's side must be very rich in terms of their interactions with the learners. This can be easily done with the standard application, but not with a Web-based application. In the proposed system, instead of using a standard Web browser, we develop our own client tools that give us the ability to offer a music-editing task and an observable environment over the Web (unlike other applications, an ITS has to be responsive at any time, even when the user is idle). In our work, we offer an observable learning browser (see Figure 3) composed from five main components, namely, Control panel, Content tree browser, Input answer interface, Content material viewer, and Status bar.

- The Control Panel contains a list of action buttons that allows students to navigate visited content materials, refresh content material, and submit answers. Simply, this panel gives students a clear view of all general actions and their availabilities.
- The Content Tree Browser is designed to populate those registered content materials in an aggregate. It is a navigable tree structure that allows students to see their courses clearly. It can be expanded or collapsed easily. The Tree Browser is a component that

*Figure 3. Distributed learning environment*

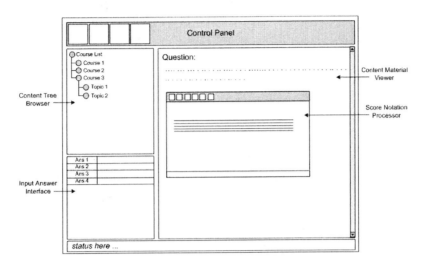

students use to browse content materials. Its high interactivity has revealed a lot of usable data, such as the navigation pattern of a student in every session. The patterns discovered in this data can tell us the past history of a student. We may use this past history to infer the next possible actions. Aggregately, these data allow us to make judgements about students' behaviours.

• The Input Answer Interface is another component that provides bidirectional interactions between a student and the system. It allows students to input their answers through flexible interfaces. The Input Answer Interface supports three input types: yes/no check box, multiple choice radio button, and subjective text fields.

• The Content Material Viewer is designed to present learning materials appropriately. These materials are authored in a hypermedia form, such as HTML files, JPEG images, and so on. One unique, observable component under this viewer is the *score notation processor*. The score processor provides music-notation editing facilities.

The answer in notation form is entered to the system via the score notation processor.

• The Status Bar provides information to students through messages and meaningful icons.

## WMITS Offers Interactive Learning Experience

Interactivity in music learning environment has been discussed in Phon-Amnuaisuk and Chee (2005). One of the main goals of an interactive environment is to enable the system to be able to quantify human learners' understanding in the music domain (e.g., music concepts such as chords, intervals, harmony, cadences, etc.), and assist them whenever possible. The following points are desired in our interactive environment:

• **The unrestricted degree of freedom in student interactions:** To promote interactive learning, it is necessary that the interface support exploratory learning. Drill and practice learning style could be implemented in a restricted and deterministic environment.

However, creative learning and exploratory learning require more freedom in interactive designs.

- **The logging of event streams and the inferences from the logged information:** Event streams are rich sources of information about the environment. Various inference tactics have been applied (e.g., logical rule-based systems, Bayesian networks, data mining, etc.) to accurately model students.

- **The feedback:** In a learning paradigm, we suggest not to delay any interaction messages between the system and the learner. The reason for this is that we believe that in solving complex question, which requires more steps to reach a solution state, beginners tend to get lost easily. For example, imagine a scenario where the learners have come to a new topic; feedback from the system would be useful. The feedback should

not be delayed, as late feedback could cause the learner to have difficulty associating the feedback and their causes.

In order to achieve this, we have designed a learning interaction architecture, as illustrated in Figure 4. Beneath the system, the messages, which flow from t1 to t7, constitute one cycle of a synchronous interaction process.

- **t1:** The system presents teaching materials to the learner through User Interface module.
- **t2:** The learner starts to interact with the system, and the activities will be logged down instantaneously.
- **t3:** The expert model is being notified. It assesses the learner's answers and puts a log on this event.
- **t4:** The learner model is being updated.
- **t5:** The tutor model is being notified as control is passed to it.
- **t6:** The tutor model fires rules to trigger feedback action.
- **t7:** The feedback actions are being executed.

*Figure 4. Learning interactions in WMITS*

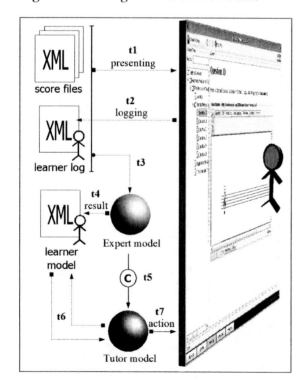

## WMITS Supports Different Inference Mechanisms

In this section, we explain three inference mechanisms employed in our WMITS system by examples. They are deductive inference, inductive inference, and probabilistic inference. Deduction is used mainly for reasoning about the domain knowledge,;where the main body of musical knowledge is coded as rules (here we use Prolog logic programming). Induction is used mainly to generalise students' behaviour, such as students' content navigation patterns. We employ Bayesian network for the reasoning of students' understanding of the topic. In the following example, we walk through different inference mechanisms involved in the example. We believe that this process is the

*Figure 5. A question for testing the knowledge of triads in different keys*

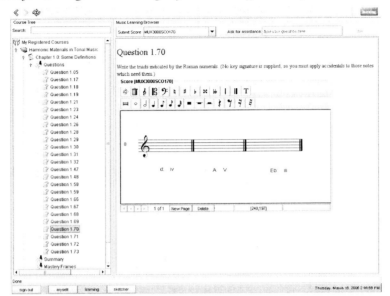

best way to highlight these inference mechanisms in our system.

Figure 5 shows a typical session after a student has registered and logged into the system. In this example, a student is asked to complete three chords in three different keys: D minor, A major, and Eb Major. The student answers this question by entering a G major chord, an E major chord, and a G major chord. The answers are all wrong in this case, due to missing the accidentals (see Figure 6a).

After submitting the answer, the student's worksheet would be converted into our proprietary score format. The expert model residing in the Sicstus prolog engine evaluates the student's answer. The inference process in this step is a conventional rule-based expert system. The correct chord for subdominant in the key of D minor is a G minor triad. The expert model has this knowledge, so it knows that the student's answers are wrong because of the missing accidentals. The expert model also gives an appropriate explanation. The level of analysis depends on the levels and the question types. An example of the system's responses is shown in Figure 6b.

Students' activities during a learning session are logged and stored in the database. This information could be mined for useful patterns. Figure 7 shows an example of logged data generated during the small session shown. The student logs in at 2:37 pm, spending around 5 minutes clicking on different content objects, and finally decides to attempt question 1.70 (see Figure 5 and Figure 7). The student answers this question by entering three triads (nine note events are recorded). Each of them is logged down with its respective coordinate. With this information, we have a precise means to infer about the students' behaviours, and we can analyse the students' answers in great detail.

Figure 8 illustrates how the Bayesian inference network is employed in our system. The purpose of this network is to infer about students' understanding of musical concepts such as pitch, interval, melody, chord, and harmony. We have decided to implement this using Bayesian network because

*Figure 6a. Wrong answers from a student*

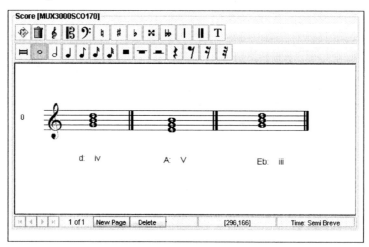

*Figure 6b. Feedback from the system*

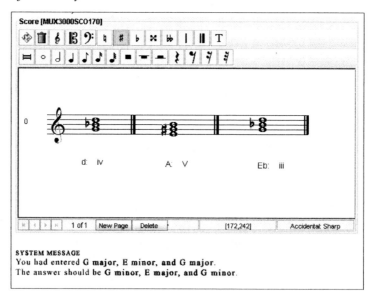

we think Bayesian network is the best method to model the understanding of these concepts, since the understanding is gradually built up after students have completed each exercise. The network in Figure 8 shows that the understanding of chords is contributed from questions 1 and 2. It may help to think of each concept (e.g., pitch, interval, etc.) as a hypothesis, and questions as a set of evidence. Answering the questions correctly increases the understanding level of concepts relevant to those questions.

## Other Challenges

We deploy our WMITS system using distributed techniques. This hides a lot of complexities and hassles from students, since their profile, history data, and other information are being stored in

*Figure 7. Student activity log data*

| Session ID | Timestamp | Action | Content | Content Object ID | Object ID | Group | Type | Page | Line | x | y |
|---|---|---|---|---|---|---|---|---|---|---|---|
| 1142491048859 | 3/16/06 2:37 PM | LOGIN | | | | -1 | -1 | -1 | -1 | -1 | -1 |
| 1142491048859 | 3/16/06 2:38 PM | CLICK | Content Object | MUX3000TOP001 | | -1 | -1 | -1 | -1 | -1 | -1 |
| 1142491048859 | 3/16/06 2:38 PM | LEAVE | Content Object | MUX3000TOP001 | | -1 | -1 | -1 | -1 | -1 | -1 |
| 1142491048859 | 3/16/06 2:44 PM | CLICK | Content Object | MUX3000QUE128 | | -1 | -1 | -1 | -1 | -1 | -1 |
| 1142491048859 | 3/16/06 2:44 PM | LEAVE | Content Object | MUX3000QUE128 | | -1 | -1 | -1 | -1 | -1 | -1 |
| 1142491048859 | 3/16/06 2:44 PM | CLICK | Content Object | MUX3000QUE170 | | -1 | -1 | -1 | -1 | -1 | -1 |
| 1142491048859 | 3/16/06 2:46 PM | CREATE | SCORE1142491583678 | MUX3000SCO170 | 1142491579362 | 5 | 1 | 1 | 0 | 136 | 102 |
| 1142491048859 | 3/16/06 2:46 PM | CREATE | SCORE1142491583678 | MUX3000SCO170 | 1142491588505 | 5 | 1 | 1 | 0 | 136 | 95 |
| 1142491048859 | 3/16/06 2:46 PM | CREATE | SCORE1142491583678 | MUX3000SCO170 | 1142491592731 | 5 | 1 | 1 | 0 | 136 | 87 |
| 1142491048859 | 3/16/06 2:46 PM | CREATE | SCORE1142491583678 | MUX3000SCO170 | 1142491602425 | 5 | 1 | 1 | 0 | 270 | 110 |
| 1142491048859 | 3/16/06 2:46 PM | CREATE | SCORE1142491583678 | MUX3000SCO170 | 1142491604218 | 5 | 1 | 1 | 0 | 270 | 102 |
| 1142491048859 | 3/16/06 2:46 PM | CREATE | SCORE1142491583678 | MUX3000SCO170 | 1142491608995 | 5 | 1 | 1 | 0 | 270 | 94 |
| 1142491048859 | 3/16/06 2:47 PM | CREATE | SCORE1142491583678 | MUX3000SCO170 | 1142491622124 | 5 | 1 | 1 | 0 | 423 | 86 |
| 1142491048859 | 3/16/06 2:47 PM | CREATE | SCORE1142491583678 | MUX3000SCO170 | 1142491625829 | 5 | 1 | 1 | 0 | 423 | 94 |
| 1142491048859 | 3/16/06 2:47 PM | CREATE | SCORE1142491583678 | MUX3000SCO170 | 1142491634922 | 5 | 1 | 1 | 0 | 423 | 102 |
| 1142491048859 | 3/16/06 2:50 PM | LEAVE | Content Object | MUX3000QUE170 | | -1 | -1 | -1 | -1 | -1 | -1 |
| 1142491048859 | 3/16/06 2:50 PM | LOGOUT | | | | -1 | -1 | -1 | -1 | -1 | -1 |

*Figure 8. Bayesian network for concept understanding*

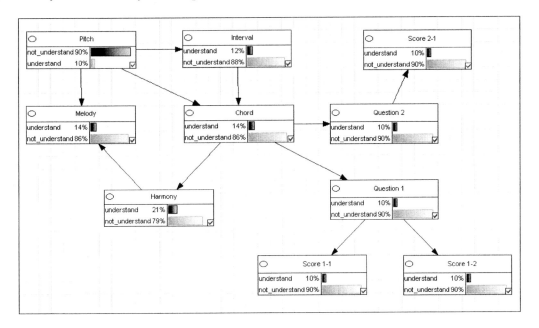

the central repository. Therefore, no matter where they are, they can connect to the system's server to continue learning. The system will always *remember* them and *understand* their needs.

The current implementation supports standard HTML tag in content-authoring process. We also devise a special tag <score> that allows the assertion of the score processor into the content-material viewer.

## FUTURE TRENDS

From a bird's-eye view, Web-based music intelligent tutoring system should receive more attention from researchers, since there are many interesting problem areas to be explored. We will now discuss some of the areas.

## Multimodal Interface

Interaction is one of the key issues in any ITS system. In a music-learning environment, visual interaction is probably the most mature and most developed area. Our application also offers score-editing facilities over the Web-based environment. Aural/oral interaction is less common, as voice recognition (for instrumental or vocal) over the Web is still at the initial stage. Motion interaction is also at its infant stage. To our knowledge, we have not seen any music applications that employ any kind of motion interaction over the Web. The research in this area should gain more interest from the community.

## Standardisation of Teaching Materials

The standardisation of teaching materials is the area that deserves real attention. The development of a shareable content object reference model (SCORM) (ADL, 2004; Sabbir, 2004) is one example of the attempts to standardise the content-representation schemes. Standardisation of music content is an important research issue. Music has many unique features; hence, the teaching and learning of music is multimodal by nature. It involves seeing, hearing, singing, and performing. Standardisation of framework in this area is very important in order to have a seamless Web-based music education environment.

## Problem Solving, Analysis, Data Mining, and Knowledge Discovery

The main ingredients that make intelligent tutoring systems appear to be intelligent are the abilities to analyse problems and explain its analysis in an effective manner. These kinds of problem solving and problem analysis are knowledge intensive tasks. In this area, we have achieved a certain level of success in coding domain knowledge and using the knowledge for problem solving and

analysis. The symbolic computation approach is effective in dealing with domain knowledge. In recent years, we have also seen a lot of activities in data mining and knowledge discovery in the music domain. Data-mining techniques could be very useful for modelling a student. These techniques are very suitable when dealing with a lot of noisy information. Our work explores data mining and Bayesian network in the modelling of a student.

## CONCLUSION

In this chapter, we discuss the Web-based music intelligent tutoring system. We list out five main challenges: (1) the lack of domain specific client tools, (2) the lack of observable environment, (3) the lack of mobility, (4) the lack of domain specific content authoring tools, and (5) the lack of intelligent behaviours. We have presented our design and implementation with those issues in mind.

We developed our own client tool for music-score editing. This is very much like the editing tools in the application such as *Finale*. However, our client tool is Web-based, and it also provides an observable environment. This means we can detect and log students' activities. This information can be used in further processing steps (e.g., data mining) to gain more understanding about each individual student.

We have described three main inference mechanisms in our system: deductive, inductive, and Bayesian inference. Each of them is suitable for different objectives. Inference in deductive rule-based style is used mainly with the domain knowledge (e.g., reasoning about music structures: pitch, chord, interval, harmony, etc.). Inference in inductive style (e.g., induction decision tree, association rules mining) is suitable for mining students' behaviours (e.g., patterns observed from student activity logs). Finally, the students' understanding of learned concepts is suitable to be modelled using Bayesian network.

## ACKNOWLEDGMENT

We acknowledge the financial support extended by the Ministry of Science, Technology and Innovation through the IRPA grant. We would like to thank our anonymous reviewers, who have provided constructive and useful comments to us during the preparation of this chapter.

## REFERENCES

ADL Technical Team. (2004). *SCORM Specifications v1.3*. Retrieved from http://www.adlnet.org/

Baker M. J. (1992). Design of an intelligent tutoring system for musical structure and interpretation. In M. Balaban, K. Ebcioglu, & O. Laske (Eds.), *Understanding music with AI: Perspectives on music cognition* (pp. 467-489). The AAAI Press/ The MIT Press.

Brandão, M., Wiggins, G., & Pain, H. (1999). Computers in music education. In G. Wiggins (Ed.), *Proceedings of The AISB'99 Symposium on Musical Creativity* (pp. 82-88). AISB.

Chee, K. S., & Phon-Amnuaisuk, S. (2005, July). Intelligent learning environment: Building hybrid system from standard application and Web application. In *The 5th IEEE International Conference on Advanced Learning Technologies* (pp. 506-510). Kaohsiung, Taiwan.

Cook., J. (1998). Mentoring, metacognition and music: Interaction analyses and implications for intelligent learning environments. *Journal of Artificial Intelligence in Education, 9*.

Dannenberg, R., Sanchez, M., Joseph, A., Capell, P., Joseph, R., & Saul, R. (1990). A computer-based multi-media tutor for beginning piano students. *Interface-Journal of New Music Research, 19*(2-3), 155-173.

Fober, D., Letz, S., & Orlarey, Y. (2004, October 20-24). Imutus: An interactive music tuition system. In C. Agon & G. Assayag (Eds.), *Sound and music computing, International Conference, smc'04, Paris, Proceedings* (pp. 91-95). IRCAM.

Hoffstetter, F. (1981). Computer-based aural training: The GUIDO system. *Journal of Computer-based Instruction, 7*(3), 84-92.

Holland, S. (2000). Artificial intelligence in music education: A critical review. *Readings in Music and Artificial Intelligence, Contemporary Music Studies, 20*, 239-274. London: Harwood Academic Publishers.

Holland, S. (1993). Learning about harmony with harmony space: An overview. In M. Smith, A. Smaill, & G. Wiggins (Eds.), *Music education: An artificial intelligence approach. Workshops in Computing* (pp. 25-40). Montreal, Canada: Springer-Verlag.

Kouroupetroglou, G., Stamati, M., & Metaxaki-Kissionides, C. (1999). World-Wide-Web supporting for the learning of non-orthographic languages. *International Conference on Computers in Education*. Amsterdam: IOS Press.

Mark, M. L. (1996). *Contemporary music education* (3rd ed). New York: Schirmer Books.

Moundridou, M., & Virvou, M. (2002). Authoring intelligent tutoring systems over the World Wide Web. *1st International IEEE Symposium Intelligent System* (pp. 160-165).

Newcomb, S. R. (1985). Lasso: An intelligent computer based tutorial in sixteenth century counterpoint. *Computer Music Journal, 9*(4), 49-61.

Phon-Amnuaisuk, S., & Chee K. S. (2005). *Reviewing interactivity issues in music tutoring system*. Presented at The Fifth Music Network Open Workshop: Integration of Music in Multimedia Applications, Universität für Musik und darstellende Kunst Wien, Vienna, Austria, July 4-5, 2005.

Sabbir, A. K. (2004, Aug 30 -Sep 1). A conceptual framework for Web-based intelligent learning environments using SCORM-2004. In *Proceedings of the IEEE International Conference on Advanced Learning Technologies* (ICALT'04) (pp. 10-15). Finland.

Shang, Y., Shi, H., & Chen, S. (2001). An intelligent distributed environment for active learning. In *Proceedings of the Tenth International Conference on World Wide Web* (pp. 308-315). Hong Kong.

Shea, P., Fredericksen, E., Pickett, A., & Swan, K. (1999). Student satisfaction and perceived learning in Internet-based higher education. *Advanced Research in Internet-Based Higher Education. Advanced Research in Computers and Communications in Education.* Amsterdam: IOS Press.

Smoliar, S. W., Waterworth, J. A., & Kellock, P. R. (1995). Pianoforte: A system for piano education beyond notation literacy. In *Proceedings of ACM Multimedia 95* (pp. 457-465). San Francisco.

Wiggins, G. A., & Trewin, S. (2000). A system for concerned teaching of musical aural skills. In *Proceedings of the 5th International Conference on Intelligent Tutoring System* (pp. 494-503) Montreal, Canada: Springer-Verlag.

Williams, D. A., & Webster, P. R. (1999). *Experiencing music technology: Software, data, and hardware* (2nd ed.). Belmont, CA: Wadsworth Group/Thomson Learning.

Zhou, Y. Freedman, R., Glass, M., Michael, J., Rovick, A., & Evens, M. (1999). Delivering hints in a dialogue-based intelligent tutoring system. In *Proceedings of the Sixteenth National Conference on AI (AAAI-99)* (pp. 128-134). Orlando, FL.

# Chapter XII
# Digital Rights Management Technologies and Standards

**Jaime Delgado**
*Universitat Politècnica de Catalunya, Spain*

**Eva Rodríguez**
*Universitat Politècnica de Catalunya, Spain*

## ABSTRACT

*This chapter discusses technologies and standards related to digital rights management (DRM). Firstly, it presents DRM systems that are multimedia information management systems that take into account digital rights and protection. These systems enable the controlled distribution and use of multimedia content through the digital value chain. Then, this chapter presents current initiatives, standard and proprietary, that specify a DRM system. It focuses in the MPEG-21 standard initiative, mainly in the parts of this standard that normatively specify the different pieces and formats needed by a complete DRM system. Finally, this chapter presents one of the key components of DRM systems, rights expression languages (RELs) that have been defined to express content usage rules.*

## INTRODUCTION

Distribution and use of digital content is continuously growing. In the context of this Digital Revolution, it is important to prevent unauthorised distribution and use of copyrighted content.

Digital rights management (DRM) systems provide a means for content creators and distributors to address the unauthorised copying issue. These systems enable the creation, distribution, and consumption of digital content according to the permissions and constraints stated by the content creator. A DRM system provides intellectual property protection by encrypting, or protecting in other ways, the digital content, so that it can only be accessed and used by authorized users according to the digital rights governing this content. The different elements that form a DRM system are the digital objects declaration languages, rights expression languages, intellectual property management and protection, rights enforcement, adaptation, distribution and consumption of content, and notification of events within these systems.

Digital rights management and content protection are necessary in different business models that include the management and distribution of digital content as music, movies, or e-books. DRM is also useful for managing the user privileges and content access, for example, in a virtual collaboration environment. It is also useful in B2B environments, when adapting or aggregating digital content, for example, in the edition process of an encyclopaedia. Moreover, it could be necessary in financial services or in health care, for example, to manage the access to patient medical records.

In order to illustrate how a DRM system works, a simple music distribution scenario is presented. A music producer has produced a new album and granted, to a distributor, permission to distribute this album. Then, the distributor makes available the music album, which has been protected and packaged in a digital object, publishing it in the distributor's Web site. When a user downloads the digital object with the protected album, he cannot render it until he obtains the appropriate license containing the usage rules and the key for unprotecting the content. The license also has been protected and bounded to the user devices.

Nowadays, different companies have developed their proprietary systems for distributing digital content in a controlled way. For instance, Apple, Microsoft, and Sony have their own proprietary systems. Then, the major problem for DRM systems is the lack of interoperability among them. This is a big problem for consumers because if they have purchased content protected by a concrete DRM system, they only can reproduce this content in players that support this concrete

DRM. In order to provide interoperability among existing DRM systems, there are different initiatives, such as Coral Consortium (http://www.coral-interop.org/) or DReaM (Fernando, 2005), working on interoperability issues.

## DRM SYSTEMS

Conventionally, digital assets were managed by digital management systems that do not control the distribution or consumption of these assets according to the terms imposed by their creators. Occasionally, metadata related to the use of the digital content was generated, associated to the asset, and stored for later search and retrieval.

Nowadays, digital objects are managed in a controlled way by digital rights management (DRM) systems. These systems enable the creation, distribution, and consumption of multimedia content according to the permissions and constraints stated by content creators and rights issuers. DRM permits the governance of multimedia content throughout the complete digital value chain. For example, when a distributor buys content, he agrees to certain permissions and constraints, as to distribute freely a low-quality version of a track, and to distribute the complete music album to the members of a music club with a special fee.

There are different initiatives, standard and proprietary, that specify a DRM system or the elements that form it. These initiatives consider different concepts as those detailed next.

### Creation of Digital Objects

The creation of digital objects process involves combining the protected digital assets with associated metadata to create digital objects that include the usage rules, information regarding the protection tools, and other data as the creator of the asset.

On the other hand, licenses could be issued to users separately from the content; then governance information is not associated to digital objects at this stage.

## Definition of Rights Expressions

Rights expressions are defined to be the terms that govern the usage of digital assets through the complete value chain. These permissions and constraints are usually presented to the actors of the value chain as an XML file, usually called license, that is expressed according to a rights expression language (REL). RELs specify the syntax and semantics of a language for expressing the rights and conditions of use of digital content. Licenses are generated according to a specific REL, with the digital content usage rules, permissions, and constraints associated to an entity. Then, licenses are associated to a digital asset, and could be interpreted and enforced by a DRM system. In some cases, licenses also contain information related to the protection of digital objects, for example, the key needed to decipher the digital object or asset. Usually, licenses are signed to provide integrity and authenticity to the rights expressions that govern the digital object.

## Intellectual Property Protection Tools

Nowadays, different technical protection measures are used, for example, encryption, watermarking, or fingerprinting. Among them, the most used to protect digital objects or part of these digital objects is encryption. The other technologies, watermarking, fingerprinting, or hashing technologies, are used for embedding information in content to facilitate tracking or to verify the integrity of the content itself.

## Distribution of Content

Protected and governed digital objects are distributed to the different actors of the value chain. This process requires the digital rights management system to provide to the associated distribution service the digital object, and to the license creator service the associated encryption keys. Governed digital objects can be distributed with the management rules, or these rules can be distributed separately of the content. Different processes can carry out the distribution, as broadcast, download streaming, and so forth.

## Content Consumption

DRM players consume digital objects according to the terms and conditions specified in the associated licenses. Then, they make use of authorisation tools that resolve if users are authorized to consume digital objects according to the permissions and constraints specified within users' licenses. If the user is authorised, then the content is deciphered and consumed. Typically, DRM players have secure storage, execution, and consumption environments where unauthorised parties cannot access keys and status information.

## Notification of Events

Some participants of the distribution chain, as content creators or distributors, could want to monitor usage of their copyrighted material. Therefore, some mechanisms will be necessary to allow systems to share information about events referred to multimedia content and peers that interact with the content.

## DRM INITIATIVES

Currently, there are standard and commercial initiatives that specify DRM systems. The most relevant ones are as follows.

## MPEG-21 Standard

MPEG-21 (MPEG-21 standard, 2007) aims to identify and define the different mechanisms and elements needed to support the multimedia delivery chain, the relationships, and the operations supported by them. In the different parts of the standard, these elements are standardised by defining the syntax and semantics of their characteristics, such as interfaces to these elements.

## Open Mobile Alliance (OMA) DRM

The scope of OMA DRM (OMA DRM, 2006) is to enable the controlled management and use of protected digital content. OMA DRM specification enables to content providers the ability to manage previews of DRM content, and it also enables superdistribution of DRM content and the transfer of this content between DRM agents.

## TV-Anytime DRM

TV-Anytime Forum (http://www.tv-anytime.org/) is developing open specifications for interoperable systems that will allow service providers, manufacturers, content creators, and telecommunications companies to use high-volume digital storage most effectively in consumer devices. The TV-Anytime Working Group on Rights Management and Protection is developing standards to enable the expression and enforcement of digital rights for content distributed to personal digital recorders.

## DReaM

DReaM (Fernando, Jacobs, & Swaminathan, 2005) is a Sun Labs (http://research.sun.com/) initiative that aims to develop a digital rights management solution based on open standards to provide interoperability for user requirements, and that will also integrate with proprietary DRM solutions. This initiative enables the protection of content and management of the digital rights during its entire lifetime, from content creation to consumption. Sun Labs tries to move the industry toward an open, scalable, and adaptable solution. Then, Sun launched the Open Media Commons (OMC) initiative that hosts a community forum where the technical and legal issues can be discussed. Sun has agreed that DReaM will be open source without royalty.

## CORAL

The Coral Consortium is a cross-industry group that has, as promoter members, Hewlett-Packard Corporation, IFPI, Intertrust Technologies Corporation, Koninklijke Philips Electronics N.V., LG Electronics, Matsushita Electric Industrial Co., Ltd., NBC Universal, Inc., Samsung Electronics Co., Ltd, Sony Corporation, and Twentieth Century Fox Film Corp. The main objective of this consortium is to promote the interoperability between DRM technologies. The goal of this initiative is to create a common framework for content, device, and service providers independently of the DRM solution that they use. This interoperability framework will ensure that users can access to protected content regardless of the DRM technology for the device, and the content format. Coral specification addresses trusted interoperability among applications, services, and devices compliant with these specifications.

Coral specifications also define a framework architecture that has, as objective, to provide a common trust framework that can bridge the differences in trust management between different trusted DRM systems. In this context, trust management has two main characteristics, certified identities and trusted roles. Every device in the Coral Framework architecture receives a unique certified identity that is used as a basis for trust with other DRM Coral compliant systems. On the other hand, the Coral Framework architecture defines 30 roles that represent the various functions typical in interoperability transactions.

Some of these roles simply provide information, while others make sophisticated policy decisions. In the Coral Framework, every device or system must be certified for one or more roles. Systems that control the expression of rights adopt a role, and license servers that translate these rights expressions according to different rights expression languages adopt another role.

## Internet Streaming Media Alliance (ISMA) DRM

ISMA (http://www.isma.tv/) is composed of companies from the information technology, consumer electronics, and media industries. They are jointly specifying protocols for media streaming over IP networks. ISMA/DRM must preserve the ISMA interoperability goals using standard encryption, authentication, and integrity validation for ISMA conforming media and protocols.

## Organization for the Advancement of Structured Information Standards (OASIS)

OASIS (http://www.oasis-open.org/home/index.php) is a not-for-profit, global consortium contributing to the development and adoption of e-business standards. OASIS produces worldwide standards for security, Web services, XML conformance, business transactions, electronic publishing, topic maps, and interoperability within and between marketplaces. OASIS has more than 600 corporate and individual members in 100 countries around the world. OASIS and the United Nations jointly sponsor ebXML (http://www.ebxml.org/), a global framework for e-business data exchange.

One of the current OASIS technical committees is the OASIS Rights Language Technical Committee (RLTC). The purpose of the RLTC is to define the industry standard for a rights expression language that supports a wide variety of business models. Moreover, it has an architecture that provides the flexibility to address the needs of the diverse communities that have the need of a rights language. OASIS RLTC uses XrML as the basis in defining the industry standard rights language.

## Open eBook Forum (OeBF)

OeBF (http://www.openebook.org/) is the standards group for e-book industry. It is formed by more than 70 members worldwide; this independent organization is guided by board of directors and membership. The Rights and Rules Working Group (Rights and Rules, 2003) aims to create an open standard for interoperability of DRM systems, providing trusted exchange of electronic publications among rights holders, intermediaries, and users. The Rights and Rules group has specified a Rights Grammar, that has taken as basis the MPEG-21 Rights Expression Language (ISO/IEC, 2004b). The rights and rules specification will provide to the publishing community a standard way of expressing business rules by granting access permissions and constraints.

## Publishing Requirements for Industrial Standard Metadata (PRISM)

PRISM Working Group (PRISM, 2007) was established by a group of companies, including publishers, content aggregators, systems integrators, and software developers. This group is involved in the production of serial and Web-based editorial content that recognizes the value of content standards. PRISM specification (PRISM specification, 2005) defines an XML metadata vocabulary for managing, postprocessing, and aggregating digital content such as magazines, news, catalogues, books, and so forth. PRISM specification provides mechanisms to describe the most common rights associated with content and conditions for the use of digital content, In addition, PRISM provides a framework for the interchange of content, a collection of elements to describe that content, and a set of vocabularies that define the values for these elements.

## Windows Media DRM

Windows Media DRM (Windows Media, 2007) is a platform that enables the protection and secure delivery of content for playback on different devices, such as computers, portable devices, or network devices. Windows Media DRM platform has been designed to support a wide range of business models, for example, single downloads and physical format delivery.

## Real Networks DRM

RealNetworks, Inc. (http://www.realnetworks. com/) provides a universal platform for the distribution of any media across any network to any actor of the value chain on any Internet-enabled device. For this purpose, RealNetworks, Inc. has introduced the Helix Initiative, and the Helix Servers and RealProducer product families. Helix DRM (Helix DRM, 2007) replaces the Real Networks Media Commerce Suite (MCS) (Real Networks, 2007) that provided DRM only for RealAudio and RealVideo formats. Helix DRM is the first multiformat digital rights management platform for secure distribution of digital content to any Internet-enabled device. It is a standards-based platform for the secure content delivery, including RealAudio, RealVideo, MP3, MPEG-4, AAC, H.263, and AMR. Helix DRM makes possible to deliver these formats to any Internet-enabled device, not only to PCs.

## STARDARDISATION ACTIVITIES

## MPEG-21 Standard

Moving Picture Experts Group aims to define a Multimedia Framework that enables systems

delivering multimedia content to interoperate, and to simplify and automate the transactions between these systems. This approach should apply to the infrastructure requirements for content delivery, content processing and adaptation, content security, and digital rights management. The result is an open framework for multimedia delivery and consumption for use by all the actors in the digital value chain. This open framework will provide to the actors of the digital value chain, as content creators, aggregators, adapters, distributors, end users…, with equal opportunities in the MPEG-21 open market. End users will benefit, as they will be able to access a large variety of content in an interoperable manner.

MPEG-21 aims to identify and define the different mechanisms and elements needed to support the multimedia delivery chain, the relationships, and the operations supported by them. In the different parts of the MPEG-21 standard, these elements are elaborated by defining the syntax and semantics of their characteristics, such as interfaces to these elements.

In the MPEG-21 context, the information is structured in Digital Items, which are the fundamental units of distribution and transaction. Digital Items are digital documents written in XML according to an XML Schema. A Digital Item is constituted by the digital content, which can be embedded or referenced from the Digital Item, plus related metadata that describes additional information regarding the content, such as intellectual property management and protection information, rights expressions information, and others.

MPEG-21 standard is divided into 18 parts that deal with different aspects of multimedia information management. The parts of MPEG-21 standard normatively specify different pieces and formats needed by a complete DRM system. This parts are MPEG-21 Digital Item Declaration (DID, Part 2) (ISO/IEC, 2006a), which specifies the model for a DI that is constituted by the digital content, referenced or embedded, plus related metadata that describes additional information regarding the content, for example, protection, governance and processing information. MPEG-21 Rights Expression Language (REL, Part 5) (ISO/IEC, 2004b) defines as a machine-readable language to declare rights and permissions using the terms as defined in the Rights Data Dictionary. MPEG-21 Rights Data Dictionary (RDD, Part 6) (ISO/IEC, 2004c) comprises a set of clear, consistent, structured, integrated, and uniquely identified terms. The structure of the RDD is designed to provide a set of well-defined terms for use in rights expressions. MPEG-21 Intellectual Property Management and Protection Components (IPMP, Part 4) (ISO/IEC, 2006b) deals with the standardisation of a general solution for the management and protection of intellectual property. digital items, which can be protected in order to ensure that the access to the contents is done according to the license terms. The solution lies in the use of digital signatures and encryption techniques over the digital content, which makes it possible to deploy a business model that ensures the accomplishment of the license terms in a controlled way. MPEG-21 Event Reporting (ER, Part 15) (ISO/IEC, 2006) provides a standardised means for sharing information about events amongst peers und Users. Such events are related to digital items and/or peers that interact with them.

Most of the parts of the MPEG-21 standard have achieved the International Standard status, except the Digital Item Streaming part. Currently, profiles for some parts of the MPEG-21 standard are under development. For example, three profiles have been defined for the MPEG-21 REL, for the mobile, optical media and broadcasting environments, and for open release, and two for the MPEG-21 IPMP Components.

The parts of the MPEG-21 standard are detailed as follows:

**Part 1:** Vision, Technologies and Strategy (ISO/IEC, 2004a). The purpose of this part of the standard is to define a vision and strategy for the MPEG-21 multimedia framework to enable transparent and augmented use of digital content across a wide range of networks and devices to meet the needs of all users. The objective of this part is to achieve the integration of technologies for the creation, management, distribution, and consumption of digital items. Moreover, it shall define a strategy for achieving a multimedia framework based on well-defined functional requirements.

**Part 2:** Digital Item Declaration (DID) (ISO/IEC, 2006a). The second part of the MPEG-21 standard specifies a model for defining Digital Items, describing a set of abstract terms and concepts. Digital Items are the representation of digital content, and as such, they are managed, described, and exchanged within the model.

**Part 3:** Digital Item Identification (DII) (ISO/IEC, 2003). This part of the standard provides a schema that can be used to include identifiers into a Digital Item Declaration. Then, Digital Items and parts thereof (such as items, components, or resources) can be uniquely identified.

**Part 4:** Intellectual Property Management and Protection (IPMP) (ISO/IEC, 2006b). This part of MPEG-21 will define an interoperable framework for Intellectual Property Management and Protection. It includes standardized ways of describing IPMP tools and for retrieving these tools from remote locations. It also addresses authentication of IPMP tools, and the association of protection information and rights expressions according to the Rights Data Dictionary and the Rights Expression Language to governed Digital Items.

**Part 5:** Rights Expression Language (REL) (ISO/IEC, 2004b). Part 5 of the MPEG-21 standard defines a Rights Expression Language that can be seen as a machine-readable language for declaring permissions and constraints for digital content. The semantics for the terms of this REL are defined in the Rights Data Dictionary. The REL is intended to provide flexible and interoperable mechanisms to support the usage of digital resources in such a way that the rights, conditions, and fees specified for digital contents will be respected. Moreover, it is intended to support specification of access and use of digital content.

**Part 6:** Rights Data Dictionary (RDD) (ISO/IEC, 2004c). The Rights Data Dictionary comprises a set of clear, consistent, structured, integrated, and uniquely identified Terms to support the MPEG-21 Rights Expression Language. This part of the standard also specifies the hierarchy for the terms of the RDD Dictionary, and specifies how further terms may be defined under the governance of a registration Authority. The RDD System is made up of the RDD Dictionary and RDD Database.

**Part 7:** Digital Item Adaptation (DIA) (ISO/IEC, 2004d). One of the goals of MPEG-21 is to achieve interoperable transparent access to multimedia content. This will enable the distribution and use of multimedia content to a wide range of devices, always with the agreed or contracted quality, reliability, and flexibility. Towards this goal, the adaptation of Digital Items is required. Digital Items are subject to resource and descriptor adaptation engines that produce the adapted Digital Items.

The goal for this part of the standard is to specify tools that provide the inputs and outputs to the adaptation engine, so that constraints on the distribution and consumption of resources can be satisfied.

**Part 8:** Reference Software (ISO/IEC, 2006c). In the eighth part of the standard is presented the normative and informative reference software developed in other parts of the MPEG-21 standard, such as REL, RDD, DID, DIA, DIP.... In part 8, software modules that integrate the functionalities of the other parts of the standard are also specified. Then, this part of the standard will define specifications for MPEG-21 related systems. The development of the Reference Software will be based on the requirements that have been defined in the different parts of MPEG-21.

**Part 9:** File Format (ISO/IEC, 2005a). In this part of the MPEG-21 standard, a file format is defined. An MPEG-21 Digital Item can be a complex collection of information, such as Digital Item information, metadata, and layout information. It can include both textual data and binary data.

**Part 10:** Digital Item Processing (DIP) (ISO/IEC, 2006d). The objective of this part of the standard is to provide a normative set of tools for specifying processing of Digital Items in a predefined manner. In this way, processing information can be described in Digital Item Declarations. Therefore, the standardisation of Digital Item Processing will allow interoperability at the processing level. The main idea behind the Digital Item Processing Architecture is that a list of DI Methods can be presented to Users and applied to Digital Items. After that, the User chooses one Method that is then executed by the DIP Engine.

**Part 11:** Evaluation Methods for Persistent Association Technologies (ISO/IEC, 2004e). This part consists of the comparison of technical report documents that evaluate persistent association technologies, for example, technologies that link information to identify and describe content using the content itself.

This part of the MPEG-21 standard does not contain any normative behaviour. Its purpose is to allow evaluations of such technologies to be conducted using a common methodology rather than to standardise the technologies themselves.

**Part 12:** Test Bed for MPEG-21 Resource Delivery (ISO/IEC, 2005b). This part of the MPEG-21 standard provides a software-based test bed for the delivery of scalable media delivery, and testing or evaluating this scalable media delivery in streaming environments, for example, by taking into account varying network environments.

**Part 13:** It was moved out.

**Part 14:** Conformance Testing (ISO/IEC, 2007a). The purpose of this part is to define conformance testing for other parts of the MPEG-21 standard.

**Part 15:** Event Reporting (ER) (ISO/IEC, 2006e). The purpose of this part of the MPEG-21 standard is to provide a standardised way for sharing information about events, referred to Digital Items, and peers that interact with them, within the MPEG-21 multimedia framework. Use cases that help to understand the necessity of event reporting are the monitoring of usage of copyrighted material, and the necessity for network nodes to know the connectivity condition between peers within a network when trying to deliver multimedia content.

**Part 16:** Binary Format (ISO/IEC, 2005c). This part of the standard describes the methods to binarise MPEG-21 documents.

**Part 17:** Fragment Identification of MPEG Resources (ISO/IEC, 2006f), specifies a normative syntax for URI Fragment Identifiers.

**Part 18:** Digital Item Streaming (ISO/IEC, 2007b) specifies tools for Digital Item Streaming. The first tool is the Bitstream Binding Language, which describes how Digital Items (comprising the Digital Item Declaration, metadata, and resources) can be mapped to delivery channels such as MPEG-2 Transport Streams or the Real Time Protocol.

## Digital Item Declaration (DID)

The two major goals of the Digital Item Declaration part (ISO/IEC, 2006a) within MPEG-21 are first to establish a flexible and interoperable schema for declaring Digital Items, and second to be as general and flexible as possible, providing hooks to enable higher-level functionality and interoperability.

A Digital Item is defined as a structured digital object including a standard representation, identification, and metadata. It is the fundamental unit of distribution and transaction inside MPEG-21.

The Digital Item Declaration technology is defined in three normative parts: DID Model, Representation, and Schema. Digital Item Declaration Model is defined in (ISO/IEC, 2006a).

It consists of the description of a set of abstract terms and concepts to form a useful model for defining Digital Items. Within this model, a Digital Item is the digital representation of a work, and as such, it is the thing that is acted upon within the model. The model provides a common set of abstract concepts and terms that can be used to represent a Digital Item.

The terms that form the model are described as follows:

- **Container:** This element allows items and containers to be grouped.
- **Item:** A grouping of subitems and components bounded to relevant descriptors. Descriptors can contain information about the item.
- **Component:** The binding of a resource to a set of descriptors that contain information about all or part of the digital resource. These descriptors contain control or structural information about the resource, as the bit rate, usage rules, protection information, and so forth.
- **Anchor:** This element allows the binding of descriptors to a fragment. A fragment corresponds to a specific location or a part of a resource.
- **Descriptor:** This element associates information with the enclosing element. This information may be a component or textual information.
- **Condition:** This element describes the enclosing element as being optional. Multiple conditions associated with an element are combined as a disjunction when determining if include or not the element.
- **Choice:** This element describes a set of related selections that can be used when determining the configuration of an item.
- **Selection:** describes a specific decision that will affect the conditions of an item.
- **Annotation:** This element can be used to describe another element of the model.

- **Assertion:** This element defines a configured state of a choice by asserting true, false, or undecided values for the predicates associated with the selections for that choice.
- **Resource:** This element contains a digital asset such as an image, audio, video clip, or a textual asset. It may also potentially be a physical object. Resources shall be locatable via an unambiguous address.
- **Fragment:** designates a specific point or range within a resource.
- **Statement:** This element contains a textual value with descriptive, control, or identifying information.
- **Predicate:** This element represents an unambiguous declaration that can be true, false, or undecided.

Figure 1 shows an example of a Digital Item Declaration, and illustrates the relationship among some of the terms of the model defined. The digital item represented has a container, which inside groups some items together with their descriptors and components.

*Figure 1. Example Digital Item Declaration*

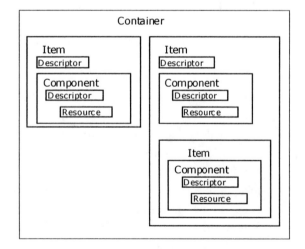

## Intellectual Property Management and Protection (IPMP)

Intellectual Property Management and Protection Components (ISO/IEC, 2006b), part 4 of the MPEG-21 standard, shall specify an interoperable framework for Intellectual Property Management and Protection. This part of the standard includes the expression and enforcement of rights that are associated with digital item distribution, management, and usage by all members of the value chain.

IPMP defined their requirements on March 2004. Then, a Call for Proposals was opened until end of June 2004, where submissions fulfilling some or all of the IPMP requirements were presented. After evaluating the proposals received against the requirements, it was agreed that the technologies that form part of the IPMP Components standard specification were the IPMP DIDL extension and the IPMP Information Description specification.

The IPMP Digital Item Description language (IPMP DIDL) was defined to enable the protection and governance of any part of a Digital Item, from a complete Digital Item to a specific asset. Digital Items are represented using the Digital Item Declaration Language (DIDL) (ISO/IEC, 2006a), which is defined by an XML schema. Then, the IPMP DIDL has been designed to allow the protection of a part of the hierarchy of a Digital Item, and to enable the association of the appropriate identification and protection information with it. For each element of the DID model, an IPMP DIDL element is provided as a protected representation of the element. The IPMP DIDL elements have the same semantics as its DIDL counterpart. Each one of these elements consists of the Identifier, Info, ContentInfo, and Contents elements. The Identifier element contains the unique identification for the protected element. The Info element contains information about the protection tools and the rights expressions that govern the element. The ContentInfo element

*Figure 2. Structure of IPMP DIDL elements*

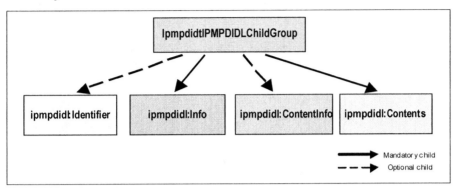

*Figure 3. IPMPGeneralInfoDescriptor element*

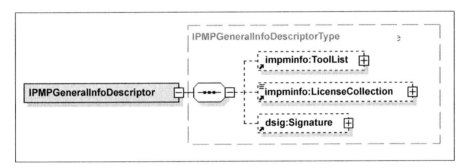

acts as a placeholder for the protected contents. Figure 2 presents the structure of IPMP DIDL elements.

This part of the MPEG-21 standard also defines how protection information can be described in a standardised way. The description of protection and governance information for a specific asset is required to satisfy intellectual property management, and protection and enforcement of governance rules for multimedia content. The protection information falls into two categories: the first one includes general protection and governance information, and the second one information about protection and governance of specific parts of a Digital Item. The syntax of IPMP information has been defined using an XML schema as specified in W3C XMLSCHEMA (XML Shema, 2007). In this schema, the two categories of protection and governance information are expressed with two

top-level elements, the IPMPGeneralInfoDescriptor and IPMPInfoDescriptor, respectively.

The IPMPGeneralInfoDescriptor element contains general information about protection and governance related to a complete Digital Item. Under this element can be included the list of IPMP tools and licenses packaged in a Digital Item. On the other hand, the IMP Info Descriptor has been designed to contain information about the protection and governance of a specific part of a Digital Item. Figure 3 shows the structure of the IPMPGeneralInfoDescriptor element. In order to associate general protection and governance information to digital objects, the IPMPGeneralInfoDescriptor should be carried at the outmost place of the protected DIDL. Therefore, it should be placed in the Statement element of the Descriptor under the Declarations element of the DIDL.

*Figure 4. IPMPInfoDescriptor element*

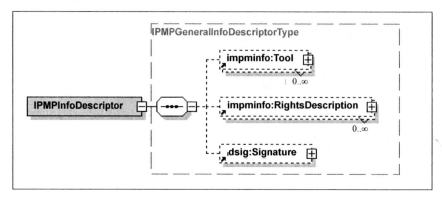

The IPMPInfoDescriptor element, see Figure 4, has been defined for declaring specific IPMP information. This element includes three different types of information related to protection, governance, integrity, and authenticity: IPMP Tool information includes specific information about protection tools and mechanisms. This information could be directly described within the descriptor or through reference. Governance information specifies the usage for the IPMP Tools and/or multimedia content. Finally, a digital signature for the specific IPMP information in order to provide integrity and authenticity to the information specified.

## Rights Expression Language (REL)

Part 5 of the MPEG-21 standard specifies the syntax and semantics of a Rights Expression Language. The most important concept of the MPEG-21 REL are licenses that can be conceptualized as container of grant elements, each one of which conveys to a particular principal the sanction to exercise some identified right against some identified resource, possibly subject to the need for some condition to be first fulfilled. A Grant is an XML structure that is at the heart of the rights management and authorization policy semantics that REL is designed to express. Another important element of a license is the issuer element, which may contain the identification of the issuer and a set of issuer-specific details about the circumstances under which the license is issued. The optional issuer-specific details may include any of the following information: the specific date and time at which this issuer has issued the license, and the description of the mechanisms by which the issuer of the license will notice the revocation of the license, if later revoked. When checking for revocation, REL systems may choose to use any one of these identified mechanisms.

More details on MPEG-21 REL are given in section 6.1.

## Rights Data Dictionary (RDD)

Part 6 of the MPEG-21 standard defines a Rights Data Dictionary (ISO/IEC, 2004c) that comprises a set of clear, consistent, structured, and uniquely identified terms to support the MPEG-21 Rights Expression language (REL). The RDD Dictionary has the characteristics of a structured ontology, in which meaning, once it has been defined, can be passed on from one term to another by logical rules of association such as inheritance and opposition. In this context, an ontology can be conceptualized as a structured catalogue of entities. The structure of this ontology is designed to provide a set of terms that can be used in rights expressions governing the use of Digital Items.

In recognition of the great diversity of actions associated with digital content, the ontology has been designed to allow the representation of as many specializations of meaning for the rights as required by users, and to show their relationships in a structured way.

The methodology described has been used to create the standardized terms for the RDD Dictionary, and may be used, in future, for introducing new terms as specializations of the existing ones under the governance of a Registration Authority. Then, the standardized terms in the RDD Dictionary are not a closed list; they are the foundations of a widely extensible Rights Data Dictionary.

On the other hand, the RDD System is comprised of the following three elements, the specifications contained in the RDD standard, a Dictionary with the terms, and a Database that contains the dictionary and supports its maintenance.

The use of the RDD System will facilitate the exchange and processing of information between interested parties involved in the digital rights management and in the use of digital content. The RDD Dictionary is a prescriptive Dictionary since it defines a single meaning for each term in the dictionary, but it is also inclusive, as it can recognize terms of other authorities, and it can incorporate them through mappings. Moreover, the RDD supports different definitions for a name under different authorities.

The RDD Dictionary defines the meaning for the terms defined in the REL. Table 1 summarizes the terms of the dictionary that have been defined in response to the requirements identified in the process of developing the MPEG-21 REL. These rights are focussed on common processes in the use and adaptation of digital resources.

*Table 1. RDD ActType and its parent and definition*

| ActType | Parent | Definition |
|---------|--------|------------|
| Adapt | Derive, ChangeTransiently | To ChangeTransiently an existing Resource to Derive a new Resource. |
| Delete | Destroy | To Destroy a DigitalResource. |
| Diminish | Adapt | To Derive a new Resource which is smaller than its Source. |
| Embed | Relate | To put a Resource into another Resource. |
| Enhance | Adapt | To Derive a new Resource which is larger than its Source. |
| Enlarge | Modify | To Modify a Resource by adding to it. |
| Execute | Activate | To execute a DigitalResource. |
| Install | UseTool | To follow the instructions provided by an InstallingResource. |
| Modify | Change | To Change a Resource, preserving the alterations made. |
| Move | Modify | To relocate a Resource from one Place to another. |
| Play | Render, Perform | To Derive a Transient and directly Perceivable representation of a Resource. |
| Print | Render, Fix | To Derive a Fixed and directly Perceivable representation of a Resource. |
| Reduce | Modify | To Modify a Resource by taking away from it. |
| Move | Modify | To relocate a Resource from one Place to another. |
| Play | Render, Perform | To Derive a Transient and directly Perceivable representation of a Resource. |
| Uninstall | UseTool | To follow the instructions provided by an UninstallingResource. |

## Event Reporting

Event Reporting (ISO/IEC, 2006e) is required within the MPEG-21 Multimedia Framework to provide a standardised means for sharing information about events amongst peers and users. Peers are defined in MPEG-21 as devices or applications that compliantly process a Digital Item, and Users as the entities that make use of Digital Items or interact in the MPEG-21 environment. Such events are related to Digital Items and peers that interact with them. In the MPEG-21 context, the reporting messages that include information about different aspects of media usage are called Event Reports.

Event Reporting could be useful, for example, when monitoring the usage of copyrighted material. A distributor offering Digital Items would specify in an Event Report Request (ER-R) that whenever a Resource is rendered, he/she would receive an Event Report (ER) containing information about the resource, the user, and the conditions under which the resource has been rendered. Peers, upon rendering the resource, will generate an Event Report that will be delivered to the distributor specified, in the Event Report Request. Then, the distributor could manage his/her royalties Event Reporting aims to facilitate interoperability between consumers and creators, enabling multimedia usage information to be requested and represented in a normalized way. Other examples where Event Reports can be requested include usage reports, copyright reports, financial reports, and technical reports.

On the other hand, an event occurs when a set of specified conditions are met. Then, the Event Reporting standard specifies the elements that may be used to define conditions under which an event is deemed to have occurred. These conditions could be:

- Time based operations that define the period at which the event will occur.

- DI-related operations that have been exercised over the specified resource, this operation has been defined by the MPEG-21 Rights Data Dictionary.
- Peer related operations that describe the events related to the peer.
- Combinations thereof.

MPEG-21 Event Reporting standard specification defines a basic model of Event Reporting. This model indicates that events that shall be reported may be specified by interested parties in an ER-R, which is used to define the conditions under which an event is deemed to have occurred. The events defined by ER-Rs determine the creation of ERs, which contain information that describes the event. An ER contains the following information: the Peer having created it, information that describes the event, a reference to the originating ER-R, and status information regarding its completion and creation, along with a free-form description.

The elements that form this model are the ERR that serves as the root element for describing an entire Event Report Request. It consists of three elements: the ERRDescriptor, the ERSpecification, and the EventConditionDescriptor. Figure 5 depicts the structure of the ERR element. The ERRDescriptor provides a descriptor of the Event Report Request including aspects of the lifetime of the ER-R, the history of the ER-R, and the priority of the ER-R. The ERSpecification element provides information about the Event Reports that have been created. The ERConditionDescriptor element specifies the event conditions, and then the occurrence of the event will trigger the creation and delivery of the ER. The ERConditionDescriptor could contain operators, and at least one condition represented by the TimeCondition, DIOperationCondition, or PeerCondition elements. The Operator element is used when the event will occur by the combinations of conditions.

On the other hand, in order to represent Event Reports, the ER element has been defined as con-

*Figure 5. ER-R element*

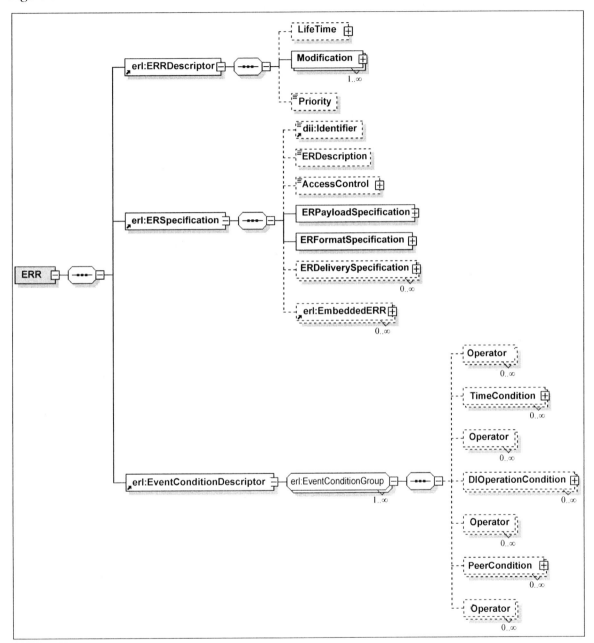

sisting of three main elements: the ER Descriptor, the ER Data, and the Embedded ERR, as shown in Figure 6.

The ER Descriptor element describes the Event Report. It contains the Description element that can be used to provide comments on the Event

Report. The Recipient element contains the identity of the user or peer that will receive the ER. The Status element provides information describing if the peer can compliantly generate the ER. The Modification element contains the history of modifications of the ER. Finally, the

*Figure 6. ER-element*

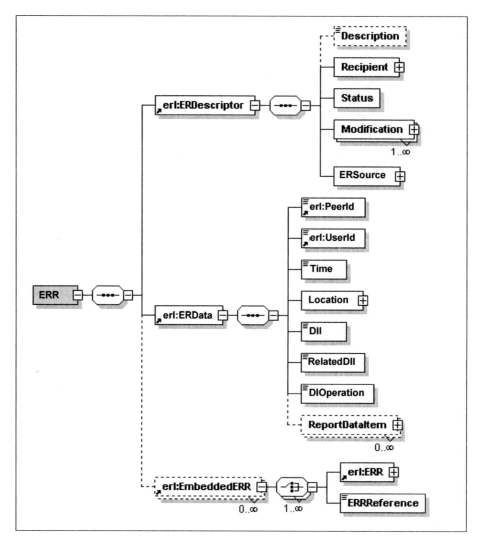

ERSource element indicates the original source that requests the generation of an ER, for example, an ER-R or a source application.

## OMA DRM

OMA digital rights management (OMA DRM, 2006) aims to enable the controlled use of digital content by allowing content providers the abil-

ity to manage previews of content, and to enable superdistribution and transfer of content between DRM agents. The OMA DRM specifications provide mechanisms for secure authentication of trusted DRM agents, and for the definition and issuance of usage rights of content. Then, OMA DRM defines the format for DRM Content, a rights expression language for expressing conditions of use of content, protection mechanisms for content and for rights objects, and a security model for management of encryption keys. The OMA DRM specifications also define how DRM Content and Rights Objects can be transported to devices using a wide range of transport mechanisms.

## OMA DRM System

OMA DRM system enables the distribution of protected content in a controlled way. The DRM system defined by OMA is independent of the object formats, operating systems, and runtime environments. Figure 7 depicts OMA DRM system architecture (OMA DRM Architecture, 2006).

The OMA DRM system enables content issuers to distribute protected content, and rights issuers to define the permissions and constraints for the protected content. Then, users acquire rights objects, with the appropriate rights for the protected content, by contacting rights issuers. The content is cryptographically protected when distributed, and it can be delivered to the device by any means, but the Rights Objects are distributed by the rights issuer in a controlled manner. The

Rights Objects can be delivered to the device together with the protected content or separately. Rights Objects have to be enforced when consuming the content. For this purpose, OMA has specified the DRM Agent that is the responsible for enforcing permissions and constraints for DRM Content on the device. A Rights Object is cryptographically bound to a specific DRM Agent; then, only that DRM Agent can access it, and DRM Content can be freely distributed, enabling superdistribution.

OMA DRM specification also defines the basic steps for distributing DRM Content. First, the content is encrypted with a symmetric content encryption key and packaged in a secure content container. DRM agents have a unique private/public key pair and a certificate that allow content and rights issuers to securely authenticate a DRM Agent. Rights Objects contain the permissions and constraints associated with the content and the content encryption key; this ensures that DRM Content cannot be used without an associated Rights Object. Before delivering the Rights Object, sensitive parts are encrypted; this ensures that

*Figure 7. OMA architecture*

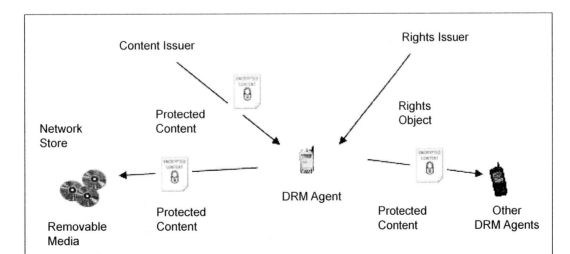

only the target DRM agent can access the Rights Object. Then, the Rights Object and the content can be delivered using any transport mechanism to the target DRM Agent.

## OMA Rights Expression Language

OMA has developed the OMA DRM Rights Expression Language (OMA DRM REL, 2006) based on the Open Digital Rights Language (ODRL, 2007). OMA specification defines six different models to group rights elements according to their functionality. The foundation model constitutes the basis for rights. The agreement model expresses the rights granted over content. The context model provides metainformation about the rights. This model is used for expressing additional information. The permission model enables the definition of permissions over digital assets specifying the access granted to a device. The constraint model enhances the permission model by providing fine-grained consumption control of content. The inheritance model describes how a parent Rights Object can specify permissions and constraints for different pieces of content, each governed by a child Rights Object. This model uses a limited subset of the ODRL inheritance model. Finally, the security model provides confidentiality for the content encryption key of Rights Objects, integrity to the association of the Rights Objects to content, and Rights Object integrity and authenticity. This model is based on the ODRL security model that is based on XM-LENC (XML Encryption, 2002) and XMLSIG (XML Signature, 2002). More details on OMA DRM REL are given in section 6.3.

## TV-Anytime

TV-Anytime Forum is an association of organizations that aims to develop specifications to enable services based on mass-market high-volume digital storage in consumer platforms. The TV-Anytime Forum was formed in California on September 1999. It has started work to develop open specifications designed to allow consumer electronics manufacturers, content creators, broadcasters, and service providers to exploit local storage.

TV-Anytime Forum has established four objectives for the organization. It will define specifications that will enable applications to exploit local persistent storage in consumer electronics platforms. It will be network independent with regard to the means for content delivery to consumer electronics equipment. It will develop specifications for interoperable systems, from content creators to consumers, and will specify the necessary security structures to protect the interests of all parties involved.

TV-Anytime specification enables the search, selection, acquisition, and rightful use of content on local and remote personal storage systems from broadcast and online services. For enabling these features, TV-Anytime has defined the specification for metadata, content referencing, rights management, and bidirectional metadata delivery protection.

## Rights Management and Protection

TV-Anytime has specified, in TV-Anytime Rights (2005), a minimum set of usage rules to enable controlled use of broadcast digital television content within a Rights Management and Protection (RMP) compliant domain. When RMP Information (RMPI) is associated with a broadcast signal, it is called RMPI-Micro Broadcast (RMPI-MB); when this information is associated with content present in a TVA RMP compliant domain, it is called RMPI-Micro (RMPI-M).

RMP information consists of three main elements: principals, rights, and conditions. TV-Anytime DRM specification also defines the syntax for the RMPI and RMPI payload. The payload describes the minimum set of rights and conditions that can be associated with a digital television broadcast. It consists of at most four grants, one for the receiving domain and other for any domain that signals the rights and conditions that apply to content once it has entered a receiving domain; and a grant for any domain and other for the receiving domain that signals the extended rights and associated conditions. The encoding of the payload allows for signalling the conditions for each of the rights in a grant. In TV-Anytime, RMPI-MB rights are granted to the RMP System, and they are positively asserted, never implied.

TV-Anytime also specifies how Rights Management and Protection Information can be bounded to content. This specification defines binding as the process of associating a set of RMPI to the content to which it applies. It defines two different types of binding, which are secure and nonsecure binding. Secure binding is defined as a binding adequate to ensure that bound RMPI cannot be reassigned to unintended content without detection. There are two kinds of secure binding: the first one by content scrambling, and the second one by watermark and RPMI authentication. Nonsecure binding is a binding that is not secure, and does not include sufficient mechanisms to protect against tampering and/or modifications to RMPI.

## INDUSTRY SOLUTIONS

### Windows Media DRM 10

Windows Media digital rights management (DRM) (Windows Media, 2007) is a platform that enables the protection and secure distribution of content to be rendered on a computer, portable device, or network device. It is designed to support a wide range of business models from single downloads or physical format delivery, for example, it enables direct and indirect license acquisition, subscription services, purchase and download single tracks, rental services, video-on-demand, and pay-per-view.

Windows Media Rights Manager allows content providers to deliver digital media content over the Internet in a protected way by packaging digital media files. The packaged media file can only be rendered by users that have obtained a license, as it contains the encrypted version of a media file, and it is bundled with additional information from the content provider.

Microsoft is introducing two new technologies that allow devices to use media files that are protected with Microsoft Windows Media Digital Rights Management (DRM) technology: (1) Microsoft Windows Media DRM 10 for portable devices is a lightweight DRM technology that enables portable devices to use protected content according to the rights defined in licenses, and (2) Microsoft Windows Media DRM 10 for Network Devices is used by network devices to render protected content from a computer running Microsoft Windows XP or Windows XP Media Center Edition over a home network. These devices only request protected content and render it immediately. They cannot store or perform any other actions on content.

### Architecture

The basic Windows Media Rights Manager process results as follows. First, the digital media files are encrypted and packaged by the Windows Media Rights Manager. The key used for locking the media file is stored in an encrypted license, which is distributed separately form the content. The packaged digital media file is saved in Windows media audio or video format. Then, the packaged media file is distributed; it can be placed on a Web site or on a media server, or delivered in any other way to end-users who, in turn, can send copies of the protected digital media files to their friends. Then, a License Server is established, and the license clearinghouse stores the specific usage rules for the content, and implements the Windows Media Rights Manager license services. The clearinghouse will authenticate consumer requests for licenses. When the license clearinghouse needs to issue a license, a key must be recreated by retrieving the key ID from the packaged file. The Windows Media License Service uses the license key seed and the key ID from the packaged file to create a key.

Finally, if a consumer wants to play a packaged digital media file, first he/she must acquire a license with the key to unlock the file. The consumer can then play the digital media file according to the rights and conditions specified in the license. Licenses can have different rights and conditions, such as play, or copy, or start times and dates, duration, and counted operations. The range of different business rules that licenses in Windows Media Rights Manager can support are:

- How many times a file can be played.
- Which devices a file can be played or transferred on.
- If the file can be transferred to a CD recorder.
- If the user can back up and restore the license.
- What security level is required on the client to play the Windows Media file.

Licenses are not transferable; if a consumer sends a copy of a digital media file to a friend, his/her friend must acquire his/her own license to play the file. In this way, only the computer that has acquired the license can play the packaged digital media files.

## Helix DRM

RealNetworks develops end-to-end solutions for the distribution of digital content across any network to any Internet-enabled device. RealNetworks Helix initiative (RealNetworks, 2007), and the product families Helix Servers and RealProducer, enable the secure distribution of any digital content to media player users across any network. The formats supported by Helix DRM

are RealAudio, RealVideo, AAC, MP3, MPEG-4, H.263, AMP, WAV, AV1, H.261, GIP, JPEG, PNG, and MPEG-1.

Helix DRM is comprised of three key components:

- **Helix DRM Packager:** It protects digital content using strong encryption algorithms, packages the protected content, and associates to it the appropriate business rules. The content and the business rules for unlocking and using the protected content are stored separately; then, protected content can be governed by different business rules. When used in conjunction with RealProducer, it can deliver secure, live content.
- **Helix DRM License Server:** The functionalities of the license server regarding governance of digital content are the following: it verifies content licensing requests; it issues licenses containing the usage rules of protected content to authenticated users; it facilitates the revocation of licenses by content owners, and it enforces digital rights governing multimedia content. On the other hand, the license server also provides auditing information that will facilitate royalty payments.
- **Helix DRM Client:** It enables download and streaming playback according to the terms stated in the licenses governing protected digital content in tamper-resistant environments. On the top of the Helix DRM client, different client applications can be built. One example of a customised client application is the Real Player.

Helix DRM provides scalability in the overall platform architecture and specifications. It can be adapted to changing business rules, as content and licenses are distributed separately. Therefore, content owners can change the usage rules in licenses without repackaging the protected content. Helix DRM supports multiple content delivery modes, as content can be distributed via streaming, downloads, peer-to-peer file sharing, or physical media. Nevertheless, Helix DRM only supports a very limited set of usage rights. The different types of licenses supported include the following combination of permissions and constraints:

- Playback of a specific duration.
- Playback during a specific window of time.
- Playback a limited number of times.

Helix DRM supports consumer electronic devices in two different models of integration: are native device support and secure receiver support.

## RIGHTS EXPRESSION LANGUAGES

The different parties involved in the online distribution and consumption of multimedia resources need to exchange information about the rights, terms, and conditions associated with each resource at each step in the multimedia resource lifecycle. For example, in distribution and super distribution business models, the information related to the rights and the terms and conditions under which the rights may be exercised needs to be communicated to each participant in the distribution chain.

In an end-to-end system, other considerations, such as authenticity and integrity of Rights Expressions, become important. For example, any content provider or distributor who issues rights to use or distribute resources must be identified and authorized. In addition, a Rights Expression may be accessed by different participants, which requires mechanisms and semantics for validating the authenticity and integrity of the Rights Expression. A common Rights Expression Language that can be shared among all participants in this digital workflow is required.

Right expression languages (RELs) are languages devised to express conditions of use of digital content. They have been proposed to describe licenses governing the terms and conditions of content access. Right expression languages can be used, for example, to describe an agreement between a content provider and a distributor; or between a distributor and an end user; or can be used to express the copyright associated to a given digital content, such as video, an e-book, or a piece of music, by specifying under which conditions the user is allowed to exercise a right, such as play, print, or copy.

The most relevant right expression languages are MPEG-21 REL based on the eXtensible rights Markup Language (XrML) (XrML Specifications, 2007) proposed by ContentGuard, Inc. (http://www.contentguard.com/), and the Open Digital Rights Language (ODRL) (ODRL, 2007) proposed by Renato Ianella form IPR Systems (http://www.iprsystems.com/). XrML and ODRL syntactically are based on XML, while structurally they both conform to the axiomatic principles of rights modelling first laid down by, among others, Dr. Mark Stefik of Xerox PARC, the designer of the Digital Property Rights Language (DPRL) (DPRL, 2007). Main differences between both languages are that ODRL has some media-specific constructs that XrML does not specify, as the inheritance model and the ability of specifying attributes of digital objects, as file formats or encoding rates, among others. On the other hand, ODRL has the advantage that it is more concise, then resultant licenses are more compact than their equivalents in XrML. This is important for example in mobile environments; then, this is one of the reasons why OMA chose ODRL instead of XrML.

License Script (Chong, Corin, Etalle, Hartel, Jonker, & Law, 2003) is a logic-based rights expression language that tries to avoid some intrinsic disadvantages of XML-based RELs, such as the complicated syntax of them when the conditions of use become complex, and the lack of formal semantics. License Script has a declarative as well a procedural reading, and this makes it possible to capture a multitude of sophisticated usage patterns precisely and unambiguously.

## MPEG-21 REL

Part 5 of the MPEG-21 standard specifies the syntax and semantics of a Rights Expression Language. MPEG chose XrML as the basis for the development of the MPEG-21 Rights expression language. MPEG-21 Rights Expression Language (REL) (ISO/IEC, 2004b) specifies the syntax and semantics of a language for issuing rights for users to act on Digital Items and elements within them.

The most important concept in REL is the license that, conceptually, is a container of grants, each one of which conveys to a principal the sanction to exercise a right against a resource. A license is formed by the elements title, inventory, grant or grantGroup, and otherInfo. Title element provides a descriptive phrase about the License, which is intended for human consumption in user

*Figure 8. REL License Structure*

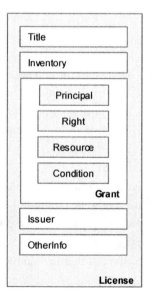

interfaces. Inventory element is used for defining variables within a License. The Grants and GrantGroups contained in a license are the means by which authorization policies are conveyed in the REL architecture. In the other information element, additional information relevant to the license can be placed. It uses the wildcard construct from XML Schema. It is important to take into account that not all processors of REL licenses will understand the semantics of the fields within the elements. Figure 8 shows the structure of a REL License.

The most important concept within a license is the grant that conveys to a particular principal the sanction to exercise some identified right against some identified resource, possibly subject to the need for some condition to be first fulfilled. A Grant is an XML structure that is at the heart of the rights management and authorization policy semantics that REL is designed to express.

A grant is formed by four elements: A Principal that represents the unique identification of an entity involved in the granting of rights; A Right that specifies an action or activity that a Principal may perform on, or using some associated target Resource; A Resource that represents the digital object against which the Principal of a Grant can exercise a Right; The Condition element that represents grammatical terms, conditions, and obligations that a Principal must satisfy before it may take advantage of an authorization conveyed to it in a Grant. The issuer element may contain two pieces of information: an identification of the issuer, possibly coupled with a digital signature for the license, and a set of issuer-specific details about the circumstances under which the license has been issued. The optional issuer-specific element may include any of the following information: the specific date and time at which this issuer has issued the license; and the mechanisms by which the issuer of the license will, if he/she later revokes it, post notice of such revocation.

The structure of an REL license is the described if it is in clear text, but it can contain

*Table 2. Namespace prefixes*

| Part | Namespace prefix | Namespace |
|------|------------------|-----------|
| Core | r | urn:mpeg:mpeg21:2003:01-REL-R-NS |
| Standard | sx | urn:mpeg:mpeg21:2003:01-REL-SX-NS |
| Multimedia | mx | urn:mpeg:mpeg21:2003:01-REL-MX-NS |

an encryptedLicense element if the license is encrypted. The encryptedLicense element provides a mechanism by which the contents of a License can be protected and then not accessed by unauthorised parties. This mechanism is based on the XML Encryption Syntax and Processing (XML Encryption).

The principals, rights, resources, and conditions of the REL are organized in three main groups. The first one, the Core, specifies structural elements and types and how are they related. The standard extension and the multimedia extension specify standard or multimedia principals, rights, resources, and conditions. Each one of the parts is related to a namespace. Table 2 gives the prefix and the corresponding namespace.

At the heart of REL is the REL Core Schema, whose elements and types define the core structural and validation semantics that comprises the essence of the specification. The REL Core Schema includes different elements and types organised in four main groups:

## Principals

Within REL, principals represent the unique identification of an entity involved in the granting or exercising of rights. They identify the entity that is permitted to exercise granted rights. The principal element and its type are both, conceptually, abstracts. Then, principal elements do not indicate how a particular principal identified and authenticated. For this purpose, types that are derivations of the principal element have been defined. These types have been defined in extensions to REL. However, there are derivations that

are important and central enough to be defined within the REL core itself:

- **allPrincipals:** This element is a simple container of Principals. Semantically, it represents the conjunction of all the principals represented by all of its children.
- **keyHolder:** Instances of the KeyHolder element represent entities that are identified by their possession of a certain cryptographic key.

## Rights

Within REL, right represents a verb that a principal may be authorized to carry out. Typically, a right specifies an action or activity that a principal may exercise over a digital resource. The element right and its type are conceptually abstract. Therefore, the type right itself does not indicate any action or activity to be exercised. These actions or activities are defined in types that are derivations of the right element. Such derived types also have been defined in extensions to REL. However, the following rights pertain to the REL core itself:

- **issue:** When the right of a license is to issue, then the resource against which the right is applied shall be a grant or grantGroup that conveys the authorization for the principal to issue the resource.
- **obtain:** This right can be conceptualized as an offer or advertisement for the sale of the contained grant. When the right of a license is to obtain, then the resource shall be a grant or a grantGroup.

- **possessProperty:** It represents the right for the associated principal to claim ownership of a particular characteristic, for example, that this principal is member of a video club, which is listed as the resource associated to this right.
- **revoke:** This right represents the authorized act of exercising the revoke right by a principal.

## Resources

An instance of type resource represents the object against which a principal of a grant can evoke some right. The element resource and its type are conceptually abstract. Therefore, the type resource does not indicate any digital object. The digital objects have been defined in types that are derivations of the resource element in extensions to REL. The relevant resources defined within the REL core are:

- **digitalResource:** This element provides the means by which an arbitrary sequence of digital bits can be identified as being the target object of a grant within a license
- **propertyAbstract:** An instance of type propertyAbstract represents some kind of property that can be possessed by principals via possessProperty right.

## Conditions

Within REL, instances of the type condition represent restrictions and constraints that a Principal must satisfy before it can exercise the granted rights. The semantic specification of each condition indicates the details of the obligations and constraints that use of the condition imposes. Then, when these requirements are fulfilled, the condition is satisfied. The condition element and its type are conceptually abstracts. Therefore, the type Condition does not indicate any restriction or constraint. The conditions have been defined in types that are derivations of the condition element in extensions to REL. The conditions defined within the REL core that we consider relevant to detail:

- **AllConditions:** This element is a simple container of conditions
- **validityInterval:** A validityInterval condition indicates a contiguous, unbroken interval of time in which rights can be exercised. The start and end of this interval are specified by the child elements of the validityInterval element:
  - ○ notBefore element indicates the instant in time at which the interval begins
  - ○ notAfter element indicates the instant in time at which the interval ends

The Standard Extension schema defines terms to extend the usability of the Core Schema, some of them are:

- **Right Extensions:** Right Uri.
- **Resource Extensions:** Property Extensions and Revocable.
- **Condition Extensions:** Stateful Condition, State Reference Value Pattern, Exercise Limit Condition, Transfer Control Condition, Seek Approval Condition, Track Report Condition, Track Query Condition, Validity Interval Floating Condition, Validity Time Metered Condition, Validity Time Periodic Condition, Fee Condition and Territory Condition.
- **Payment Abstract and its Extensions:** Payment Abstract, Rate, Payment Flat, Payment Metered, Payment per Interval, Payment per Use, Best Price Under, Call for Price, and Markup.
- **Service Description:** WSDL and UDDI
- **Country, Region and Currency Qualified Names:** Namespace URI Structure, Country Qualified Names, Region Qualified Names, and Currency Qualified Names.

- **Matches XPath Function:** Regular Expression Syntax and Flags.

The REL Multimedia Extension expands the Core Schema by specifying terms that relate to digital works. It specifically describes rights, conditions, and metadata for digital works that include:

- **Rights:** Modify, Enlarge, Reduce, Move, Adapt, Extract, Embed, Play, Print, Execute, Install, Uninstall, and Delete.
- **Resources:** Digital Item Resources.
- **Conditions:** Resource Attribute Conditions, Digital Item Conditions, Marking Conditions, Security Conditions, and Transactional Conditions.

- **Resource Attribute Set Definitions:** Complement, Intersection, Set, and Union.

A typical example of an REL license issued to an end-user. In this case a distributor, MusicDist, issues to a user, Alice, a license that permits her the right to play a song, TheEnd.mp3, during this year. The license is sketched in Figure 9.

The main elements of the license are the grant and the issuer. The grant element is formed by four elements. The keyHolder that represents the user, Alice, who is identified by her possession of a certain cryptographic key. Then, she is identified as the Principal that possess the private key that corresponds to this-here public key. The play element that represents the granted right. The definition of Play in the Rights Data Dictionary is to derive a

*Figure 9. REL license example*

```
<r:license xmlns:r="urn:mpeg:mpeg21:2003:01-REL-R-NS" xmlns:sx="urn:mpeg:mpeg21:2003:01-REL-SX-NS"
           xmlns:mx="urn:mpeg:mpeg21:2003:01-REL-MX-NS" xmlns:dsig="http://www.w3.org/2000/09/xmldsig#"
           xmlns:xsi="http://www.w3.org/2001/XMLSchema-instance">
  <r:grant>
    <r:keyHolder licensePartId="Alice">
      <r:info>
        <dsig:KeyValue>
          <dsig:RSAKeyValue>
            <dsig:Modulus>KtdToQQyzA==</dsig:Modulus>
            <dsig:Exponent>AQABAA==</dsig:Exponent>
          </dsig:RSAKeyValue>
        </dsig:KeyValue>
      </r:info>
    </r:keyHolder>
    <mx:play/>
    <r:digitalResource>
      <r:nonSecureIndirect URI="http://www.onlinemusic.com/mySong.mp3"/>
    </r:digitalResource>
    <r:validityInterval>
      <r:notBefore>2006-01-01 T00:00:00</r:notBefore>
      <r:notAfter>2006-12-31 T12:59:59</r:notAfter>
    </r:validityInterval>
  </r:grant>
  <r:issuer>
    <r:keyHolder licensePartId="MusicDist">
      <r:info>
        <dsig:KeyValue>
          <dsig:RSAKeyValue>
            <dsig:Modulus>X0j9q99yzA==</dsig:Modulus>
            <dsig:Exponent>AQABAA==</dsig:Exponent>
          </dsig:RSAKeyValue>
        </dsig:KeyValue>
      </r:info>
    </r:keyHolder>
  </r:issuer>
</r:license>
```

transient and directly perceivable representation of a resource. The DigitalResource element that provides a means by which an arbitrary sequence of digital bits can be identified as being the target object within the grant. Conceptually, an instance of DigitalResource defines an algorithm by which a sequence of bits is to be located. If the bits are to be physically located at some external location, as for this example, they are located on a Web site, we use that nonSecureIndirect element child, where we indicate the algorithm used to allocate the bits. In this example, we indicate that the song is in the URI http://www.webmusic.com/TheEnd.mp3. And the fourth one, the ValidityInterval element that represents the condition. It indicates a contiguous, unbroken, interval of time. The semantics of this Condition is that the interval of the exercise of a Right to which a ValidityInterval is applied must lie wholly within this interval. The delineation of the interval is expressed by the presence, as children of the Condition, of up to two specific fixed time instants. notBefore of type xsd:dateTime, indicates the inclusive instant in time at which the interval begins, 1 January 2006. notAfter element of type xsd:dateTime, indicates the inclusive instant in time at which the interval ends, 31 December 2006. Therefore, with this license, the user can play the song during this year. The issuer element indicates the entity that issues the license. In this example, it represents the music distributor that has the right to issue this kind of license to end-users.

Another important concept of the REL is the authorization model, which may be used by any implementation of software that makes an authorization decision using REL licenses. The central question that lies in this decision making process *"Is a principal authorized to exercise a right against a resource?"*. The REL Authorization Model makes use of an authorization request (see Figure 10), an authorization context, an authorization story, and an authorizer.

An authorization request can be conceptualized as representing the question if it is permitted for a given Principal to perform a given Right upon a given Resource during a given time interval based on a given authorization context, a given set of Licenses, and a given trust root. The authorization request contains the following members:

- The principal element, which is the identity of the entity for which permission is requested.
- the right element, which embodies the semantics of the action which is requested to be permitted.
- The resource element identifying the Resource upon which permission is requested.
- The interval of time during which the requested performance of the right by the principal upon the resource is considered to take place. This may be either an instantaneous point in time or an unbroken interval of time.
- The authorization context containing properties representing statements that are to be considered true for the purposes of establishing the requested permission.

*Figure 10. REL authorization request*

| Authorization Request |
|---|
| Principal |
| Right |
| Resource |
| Interval of time |
| Authorization context |
| License elements |
| Grant elements that do not require an authorizer |

- The set of license elements that may be consulted to establish the requested permission. The algorithm will attempt to find authorized grants or grantGroups within this license that it can use to establish a basis for an affirmative authorization decision.
- The set of grant elements that do not require an authorizer for the purposes of establishing the requested permission.

The authorization story (see Figure 11) contains the following elements:

- A primitive grant, it is used to demonstrate to which authorization requests the authorization story applies.
- Either a grant or a grantGroup, it represents the actual grant or grant group that is authorized by the authorizer of the authorization story.
- An authorizer, it contains the following members:
  - The license in which the principal is authorized.

  - The principal that authorized the license above.
  - The time instant in which the license was issued.
  - The authorization context that contains the properties representing statements that were considered true for the purposes of establishing the permission.
  - An authorization story.

## ODRL

The Open Digital Rights Language (ODRL) (ODRL, 2007) is a proposed language for the DRM community for the standardisation of expressing rights information over content. The ODRL is intended to provide flexible and interoperable mechanisms to support transparent and innovative use of digital resources in publishing, distributing, and consuming of electronic publications, digital images, audio and movies, learning objects, computer software, and other creations in digital form. This is an XML-based usage grammar. ODRL is focused on the semantics of expressing rights languages and definitions of elements in the data dictionary. ODRL can be used within trusted or untrusted systems for both digital and physical assets (resources).

ODRL is based on an extensible model for rights expressions that involves three core entities

*Figure 11. REL authorization story*

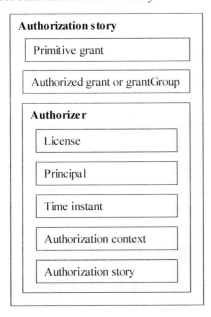

*Figure 12. ODRL license*

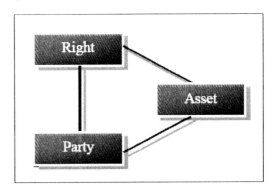

and their relationships. They are sketched in Figure 12 and detailed as follows: Party includes end users and Rights Holders. Parties can be humans, organisations, and defined roles. In the previous example, Alice is the party. Right includes permissions, which can then contain constraints, requirements, and conditions. Permissions are the actual usages or activities allowed over the assets (e.g., play, print, etc.) Constraints are limits to these permissions (e.g., print an e-book for a maximum of three times) Requirements are the obligations needed to exercise the permission. Conditions specify exceptions that, if they become true, expire the permissions and renegotiation may be required. In the previous example, print is the right that includes the constrain of "3 times." Asset includes any physical or digital content. They must be uniquely identified and may consist of many subparts and be in many different formats. Assets can also be nontangible expressions of works and/or manifested in particular renditions. In the previous example, the book is the asset.

## OMA DRM v2 REL

The Open Mobile Alliance (OMA) defines a DRM system to enable the consumption of digital content in a controlled manner, taking into account the special requirements and characteristics of the mobile domain. OMA has developed the OMA DRM Rights Expression Language (OMA DRM REL, 2006) based on ODRL (ODRL, 2007), as previously presented in section 2.7.1. In this section, we present the OMA DRM REL specification, and we will provide more details about the models and schemas defined by OMA for the OMA DRM REL v2 and Data Dictionary. OMA DRM REL is defined as a mobile profile of ODRL, and specifies the rights expression language used to describe mechanisms for expressing rights over DRM Content in an OMA DRM system. There are two different versions of OMA DRM REL specification: OMA DRM REL specification v1.0 and OMA DRM REL specification v.2.0. Security

constitutes an important part of a DRM System, and OMA DRM REL v1.0 and, in a deeper way OMA DRM REL v2.0, provide the specification of the elements that are needed to get confidentiality and other security features. Version 2.0 of OMA DRM specification includes new rights and conditions and new concept of inheritance that allow a license to inherit rights and conditions from other external licenses.

OMA specification uses models to group rights elements according to their functionality. The following models have been defined.

## Foundation Model

This model constitutes the basis for rights. It contains the rights element that contains metainformation and agreement information. The foundation model is the starting point for incorporating other models specified as the agreement and the context models.

## Agreement Model

This model has been defined to express the rights granted over a digital content. It consists of the agreement element that associates a set of rights with the corresponding DRM content specified within the asset element. The agreement model incorporates the permission and security models.

## Context Model

This model provides metainformation about the rights. It augments other models by expressing additional information.

## Permission Model

This model facilitates the expression of permissions over digital assets by specifying the access granted to a device. This incorporates the constraint model, enabling the controlled consumption of DRM Content. The set of permissions defined comprises play, display, execute, print, and export. The usage of the DRM Content must only be granted according to the permissions specified by Rights Objects. Then, this model enables the control of content access, as content can only be accessed if the corresponding Rights Object is available. Similarly, encrypted content can be superdistributed, since DRM Content without the decryption key cannot be accessed if the user does not have the appropriate Rights Object with the decryption key.

## Constraint Model

This model enhances the permission model by providing fine-grained consumption control of content. Constraints are associated with one permission element.

## Inheritance Model

Describes how a parent Rights Object can specify permissions and constraints for different DRM Content, each governed by a child Rights Object. This model uses a limited subset of the ODRL inheritance model.

## Security Model

OMA DRM 2.0 provides confidentiality for the content encryption key of Rights Objects, integrity to the association between Rights Objects and DRM Content, and Rights Object integrity and authenticity. This model takes as basis the ODRL security model based on XMLENC (XML Encryption, 2002) and XMLSIG (XML Signature, 2002).

## TV-Anytime Rights Expressions

TV-Anytime (TV-Anytime Rights, 2005) has defined four elements to represent the conditions and constraints to access multimedia content. The elements defined are grants principals, rights, and conditions.

The principals defined are the receiving domain, which is the first domain that receives the content, and any domain, which is any compliant domain that can respond to the usage conditions. The rights specified are play, analogue export, digital export standard and high definition, and extend rights. Finally, the conditions specified are geographical control, which limits the use of a right within one or more specified territories. Single point of control allows the implementation of device-bounded rights. Physical proximity condition limits the use of a right to devices within close physical proximity of the receiver that first received the content. Buffer duration condition limits the use of a right in such a way that each frame of content is used only within a specified duration after that frame was broadcast. Standard and high-definition digital export control conditions forward content management rules to external content protection systems. Analogue export signalling condition forwards content management rules to external content protection systems for immediate viewing. Analogue standard definition control condition constrains the resolution of the exported analogue signal. Security level condition constrains the execution of rights based on the level of robustness of the invoked components. Simultaneous rendering count condition limits the number of simultaneous plays, analogue exports, and digital exports of content within a domain. Source of additional rights condition identifies the authority that may assign new rights to the content.

## Creative Commons

Creative Commons (http://www.creativecommons.org/) does not specify a Rights Expression Language, but it defines different types of licenses that can be used to express the terms of use of digital content.

CC was founded in 2001 with the support of the Center for the Public Domain. It is led by a Board of Directors that includes cyber law and intellectual property experts, and public domain Web publishers. It is a nonprofit organization founded on the notion that some people would prefer to share their creative works instead of exercising all of the restrictions of copyright law.

Creative Commons first project, in December 2002, was the release of a set of copyright licenses free for public use. They consider the philosophy of the GNU General Public License (GNU GPL) from the Free Software Foundation's. Creative Commons has developed a Web application that helps content creators to decide if they dedicate their digital works to the public domain or retain their copyright.

Creative Commons' licenses are designed for digital works such as music, videos, photography, e-books, and so forth. The aim of CC is to make access to online digital content, which is growing continuously, in a cheap and easy way. To this end, they have specified metadata to associate digital works with their public domain or license status in a machine-readable way. This will enable people to use CC search application and other online applications to find digital content that can be used with no restrictions.

## Creative Commons Licenses

Creative Commons has defined six different types of licenses that can be chosen by content creators when publishing their work. These licenses are listed starting with the most restrictive license type that content creators can chose.

### Attribution Noncommercial No Derivatives (by-nc-nd)

This is the most restrictive CC license. It allows other people to download, use, and share with others original Works, as long as they mention the creator and link back to the creator. This license does not permit one to change original works in any way or to use them commercially.

### Attribution Noncommercial Share Alike (by-nc-sa)

With this license, work creators lets others remix, tweak, and build upon the original work noncommercially, but they have to credit the creator and license their creations under identical terms as stated by the original work creator. Therefore, other people can download and redistribute the work if they use a same kind of license, but they can also translate, make remixes, and produce new derivative works based on the original. These derivations will carry the same license, then any derivatives will also be of noncommercial type.

### Attribution Noncommercial (by-nc)

With this license, work creators let others remix, tweak, and build upon the original work noncommercially. The new derived works must credit the creator and be noncommercial, but they must not be licensed under identical terms as stated by the original work creator.

### Attribution No Derivatives (by-nd)

This license allows for redistribution, commercially and noncommerciallt, as long as it is passed along unchanged and in whole, with credit to you.

### Attribution Share Alike (by-sa)

These kinds of licenses let others remix, tweak, and build upon the original work for commercial and noncommercial purposes, as long as they credit the creator and license their new creations under the identical terms. As new derived works will carry the same license, they will also allow commercial use.

### Attribution (by)

These kinds of licenses lets others distribute, remix, tweak, and build upon the original work, even commercially, as long as they credit the creator of the original work.

## CC Rights and Permissions

Creative Commons licenses have some common features. They will help creators retain their copyright, to announce that other people have fair use or first sale.

The use of CC licenses requires that rights issuers issue licenses governing derivative works according to the terms and conditions stated by the original creator of the work.

Every license requires that creators of derivative works respect the terms stated by the original creator of the work, to keep any copyright notice intact on all the copies of the creator's work; to link to original license from copies or derivations of the work; to not alter the terms of the license, and not use technology to restrict other uses of the work by other licensees.

It is important to accentuate that every license applies worldwide, lasts for the duration of the copyright of the work, and is not revocable.

## CC Metadata Files

Creative Commons metadata files have two major parts: a work description and a license description. The work description uses Dublin Core properties to provide information about the work. The properties used are the title or name for the resource (dc:title), a text description of the resource (dc:description, the key words and phrases describing the topic of the resource (dc:subject), an agent responsible for making the resource available (dc:publisher), the agent who created the resource (dc:creator), the agent who contributed to the creation of the resource (dc:contributor), the cc:Agent who holds the copyright on the resource (dc:rights),

the copyright date for the resource (dc:date), the media type of the resource (dc:format), the DCMI type or schema of the resource (dc:type), the work that the resource was derived from (dc:source), the Work that was derived from the resource (cc:derivativeWork), and the copyright license for the resource (cc:license). Figure 13 shows how a full file will look like.

## Interoperability between Rights Expression Languages

One of the key issues for the real deployment of DRM systems is interoperability. Interoperability may apply to different aspects of DRM, for example, to Rights Expression Languages (RELs). In this context, MPEG-21 REL is defining profiles in order to facilitate the interoperability with other RELs.

MPEG-21 REL can be extended to support new business models defining extensions. On the other hand, it can be profiled to trade off complexity and interoperability. The extensions mechanism that MPEG-21 REL specifies allows the addition of new elements to address the requirements of a new application domain.

The first of the three MPEG-21 REL profiles is the Mobile and Optical Media (MAM) profile (Wang, Delgado, & Barlas, 2006) that addresses the needs of the mobile and optical media domains. Moreover, it facilitates the interoperability with OMA DRM REL v2. The Dissemination and Capture (DAC) profile (Kim, Chiariglione, & Wang, 2007) has been designed to be able to represent the concept of the OMA DRM v2.0 Extensions for Broadcast Support. The aim of this profile is to facilitate the interoperability with TV Anytime REL. Finally, the third profile still under development is Open Release Content (ORC) profile (Kim, Delgado, Schreiner, & Barlas, 2006) that is defined to support some of the concepts expressed in the different types of Creative Commons licenses.

*Figure 13. Creative Commons file*

```
<rdf:RDF xmlns="http://web.resource.org/cc"
    xmlns :dc="http://purl.org/dc/elements/1.1"
    xmlns :rdf="http://www.w3.org/1999/02/22-rdf-syntax-ns#">
    <Work rdf:about="http://webMusic.org/MySong.mp3">
        <dc:title>Summer Nights</dc:title>
        <dc:description>My first song</dc:description>
        <dc:creator><Agent>
            <dc:title>Sue Sue</dc:title>
        </Agent></dc:creator>
            <dc:rights><Agent>
            <dc:title>Manhattan</dc:title>
            <dc:date>10/10/2006</dc:date>
            <dc:format>audio/mpeg</dc:format>
        <dc:type rdf:resource="http://purl.org/dc/dcmittype/Sound" />
        <dc:source rdf:resource="http://webMusic.org/sd_first.mp3" />
        <license rdf:resource="http://creativecommons.org/licenses/by-nc-nd/2.0" />
        <license rdf:resource="http://ww.eff.org/IP/Open_licenses/eff_oal.html" />
    </Work>
    <License rdf:about="http://creativecommons.org/licenses/by-nc-nd/2.0">
        <permits rdf:resource="http://web.resource.org/cc/Reproduction" />
        <permits rdf:resource="http://web.resource.org/cc/Distribution" />
        <requires rdf:resource="http://web.resource.org/cc/Notice" />'
        <requires rdf:resource="http://web.resource.org/cc/Attribution" />
        <prohibits rdf:resource="http://webresource.org/cc/CommercialUse" />
    </License>
</rdf:RDF>
```

## CONCLUSION

This chapter presented the background, requirements, and developments related to Digital Rights Management (DRM). Firstly, it discussed a number of selected initiatives, standard and proprietary, that specify a DRM system, including the MPEG-21 standard, Open Mobile Alliance (OMA) DRM, TV-Anytime DRM, and DReaM. This chapter then focussed on the MPEG-21 standard initiative, particularly on the parts of this standard that normatively specify the different pieces and formats needed by a complete DRM system. This chapter also discussed industry solutions, such as Windows Media DRM 10 and Helix DRM, and identified common elements for existing DRM systems, such as the creation of digital objects.

Finally, this chapter presented Rights Expression Languages (RELs), which is one of the key components of DRM systems. Current initiatives that specify an REL, such as MPEG-21 REL and OMA DRM REL, are discussed. Additionally, this chapter presented different types of Creative Commons licenses that can be used to express the terms of use of the digital content. Interoperability issues among existing RELs have also been discussed, together with MPEG-21 REL profiles to facilitate interoperability of MPEG-21 REL with other RELs.

## REFERENCES

Chong, C., Corin, R., Etalle, S., Hartel, P., Jonker, W., & Law, Y. (2003). LicenseScript: A novel digital rights language and its semantics. In IEEE

Computer Socitety *Proceedings of the Third International Conference WEB Delivering of Music (WEDELMUSIC'03)* (pp. 122-129).

DPRL. (2007). Retrieved April 3, 2007, from http://www.oasis-open.org/cover/DPRLmanual-XML2.htm

Fernando, G., Jacobs, T., & Swaminathan, V. (2005). *Project DReaM: An architectural overview.* Retrieved April 3, 2007, from http://www.openmediacommons.org/collateral/DReaM-Overview.pdf

Helix DRM. (2007). Retrieved April 3, 2007, from http://www.realnetworks.com/products/drm/index.html

ISO/IEC. (2003). *ISO/IEC IS 21000-3—Digital Item Identification.* Geneva, Switzerland: ISO.

ISO/IEC. (2004a). *ISO/IEC 2nd Edition TR 21000-1—Vision, Technologies and Strategy.* Geneva, Switzerland: ISO.

ISO/IEC. (2004b). *ISO/IEC IS 21000-5—Rights Expression Language.* Geneva, Switzerland: ISO.

ISO/IEC. (2004c). *ISO/IEC IS 21000-6—Rights Data Dictionary.* Geneva, Switzerland: ISO.

ISO/IEC. (2004d). *ISO/IEC IS 21000-7—Digital Item Adaptation.* Geneva, Switzerland: ISO.

ISO/IEC. (2004e). *ISO/IEC 21000-11—TR Evaluation Methods for Persistent Association Technologies.* Geneva, Switzerland: ISO.

ISO/IEC. (2005a). *ISO/IEC 21000-9—IS File Format.* Geneva, Switzerland: ISO.

ISO/IEC. (2006a). *ISO/IEC 2ⁿᵈ Edition IS 21000-2—Digital Item Declaration.* Geneva, Switzerland: ISO.

ISO/IEC. (2005b). *ISO/IEC 21000-12—TR Test Bed for MPEG-21 Resource Delivery.* Geneva, Switzerland: ISO.

ISO/IEC. (2005c). *ISO/IEC IS 21000-16—Binary Format.* Geneva, Switzerland: ISO.

ISO/IEC. (2006b). *ISO/IEC CD 21000-4—Intellectual Property Management and Protection.* Geneva, Switzerland: ISO.

ISO/IEC. (2006c). *ISO/IEC IS 21000-8—Referente Software.* Geneva, Switzerland: ISO.

ISO/IEC. (2006d). *ISO/IEC 21000-10—IS Digital Item Processing.* Geneva, Switzerland: ISO.

ISO/IEC. (2006e). *ISO/IEC IS 21000-15—Event Reporting.* Geneva, Switzerland: ISO.

ISO/IEC. (2006f). *ISO/IEC IS 21000-17—Fragment Identification of MPEG Resources.* Geneva, Switzerland: ISO.

ISO/IEC. (2007a). *ISO/IEC 21000-14—FCD MPEG-21 Conformance Testing.* Geneva, Switzerland: ISO.

ISO/IEC. (2007b). *ISO/IEC FDIS 21000-18–MPEG-21 DI Streaming.* Geneva, Switzerland: ISO.

Kim, T., Chiariglione, F. & Wang, X. (2007). ISO/IEC 21000-5/FPDAM 2 Rights Expression Language: the DAC profile. In *ISO/IEC JTC 1/SC 29/WG 11/N8344* (pp. 1-39).

Kim, T., Delgado, J., Schreiner, F. & Barlas C. (2006). ISO/IEC 21000-5:2004/PDAM 3: ORC (Open Release Content) Profile. In *ISO/IEC JTC 1/SC 29/WG 11/N8566* (pp. 1-34).

MPEG-21 standard. (2007). Retrieved April 3, 2007, from http://www.chiariglione.org/mpeg/standards/mpeg-21/mpeg-21.htm

OMA DRM Architecture. (2006). Retrieved April 3, 2007, from http://www.openmobilealliance.org/release_program/docs/DRM/V2_0-20060303-A/OMA-AD-DRM-V2_0-20060303-A.pdf

OMA DRM Rights Expression Language. (2006). Retrieved April 3, 2007, from http://www.openmobilealliance.org/release_program/docs/DRM/ V2_0-20060303-A/OMA-TS-DRM-REL-V2_0- 20060303-A.pdf

OMA DRM Specification. (2006). Retrieved April 3, 2007, from http://www.openmobilealliance. org/release_program/drm_archive.html#V2_0- 20050915-C

Open Digital Rights Language. (2007). Retrieved April 3, 2007, from http://odrl.net

PRISM specification. (2005). Retrieved April 3, 2007, from http://www.prismstandard.org/speci- fications/

PRISM to Focus on Web Content. (2007). Re- trieved April 3, 2007, from http://www.prismstan- dard.org/

Real Networks Media Commerce Suite. (2007). Retrieved April 3, 2007, from http://www.real- networks.com/products/commerce/description. html

Rights and Rules Working Group. (2003). Re- trieved April 3, 2007, from http://www.openebook. org/oebf_groups/rrwg.htm

TV-Anytime Rights Management and Protection Information for Broadcast Applications. (2005). Retrieved April 3, 2007, from http://www.tv- anytime.org/

Wang, X., Delgado, J., & Barlas C. (2006). ISO/ IEC 21000-5/FDAM 1 Rights Expression Lan- guage: the MAM profile. In *ISO/IEC JTC 1/SC 29/WG 11/N8342* (pp. 1- 49).

Windows Media Digital Rights Management. (2007). Retrieved April 3, 2007, from http://www. microsoft.com/windows/windowsmedia/es/drm/ default.aspx

XML Encryption Syntax and Processing, W3C Candidate Recommendation. (2002). Retrieved April 3, 2007, from http://www.w3.org/TR/2002/ REC-xmlenc-core-20021210/

XML Shema. (2007). Retrieved April 3, 2007, from http://www.w3.org/XML/Schema

XML Signature Syntax and Processing, W3C Recommendation 12. (2002). Retrieved April 3, 2007, from http://www.w3.org/TR/2002/REC- xmldsig-core-20020212/

XrML Specifications. (2007). Retrieved April 3, 2007, from http://www.xrml.org/get_XrML.asp

# Chapter XIII
# Possibilities, Limitations, and the Future of Audiovisual Content Protection

**Martin Schmucker**
*Fraunhofer Institute for Computer Graphics Research IGD, Darmstadt, Germany*

## ABSTRACT

*This chapter explains the fundamental principles of audiovisual content protection. It explains the basic knowledge that is needed to understand the fundamentals of digital rights management (DRM) systems and their problems. Starting with a general introduction about copyright and content protection, available protection technologies are described and analyzed. The basic concepts of DRM solutions are explained and problems discussed. Potentials and practical limitations are analysed based on the digital music industry value chain. An outlook is given on solutions that are under development and that stronger consider the needs of the customers. In the conclusion, future solutions are discussed.*

## INTRODUCTION

*I am about to put forward some major ideas; they will be heard and pondered. If not all of them please, surely a few will; in some sort, then, I shall have contributed to the progress of our age, and shall be content.*
Marquis de Sade

Social and technical progress is one of the key issues of mankind. It is driven by the desire to disburden and to beautify life. Technical progress can be perceived in tangible goods like new devices, tools, and machines, while social progress cannot be perceived as easily. Both are based on a creative process resulting in new inventions and new ideas.

In law, the importance of this creative process is reflected by intellectual property (IP). "The term intellectual property reflects the idea that this subject matter is the product of the mind or the intellect" as explained in "Intellectual property" (Wikipedia). Furthermore, it is explained, that IP rights (IPR) are more complex in the digital domain.

As the aim of IPR protection is to encourage new inventions, inventors, as well as authors, are granted (time-limited) exclusive rights for the exploitation of their works. Wikipedia identifies different intangible subject matters that are protected by IP laws:

- Copyright
- Patent
- Trademark
- Industrial design right
- Trade secret

As this chapter deals with digital (audiovisual) content, its focus is on copyright. The reader, however, should be aware that the described technologies are protected by patents and the mentioned products are protected by trademarks. This chapter is an updated summary of the technical report by Schmucker (2005c).

Copyright's main purpose is to prevent people from copying a person's original work. Copyright lasts for a specific duration.[1] After this well-defined period of time, the work enters public domain. The term copyright is generally equivalent to author's rights. Although certain organizations, like World Intellectual Property Organisation (WIPO), prefer the term author's rights, copyright is used within the area of DRM. The United States Copyright Office provides some general information on copyright and related issues (http://www.copyright.gov/).

Cohen (2002) describes how copyright changed due to the appearance of online work: Initially, copyright did not control access to, or private use of, an already purchased copy. Neither did copyright interfere with fair use derivatives. Nowadays, content owners claim the rights to control the access to, and the use of, content.

## Music Copyright

Music copyright is a negative right, which means it gives the composer the right to restrict others from certain activities including copying music. Third parties who do not acknowledge these restrictions are liable for copyright infringements. Copyright automatically arises upon the creation of content without any formal registration process. Thus, copyright is distinct from other subsequent copyrights.

Music copyright includes different exclusive rights. As described in detail by Bell (2007), according to the U.S. copyright, a copyright owner has the right to:

- Reproduce copyrighted work
- Prepare derivative works
- Distribute copies
- Perform the work publicly
- Perform sound recordings of the work publicly

Further information on (music) copyright can be found, at:

- World Intellectual Property Organization (http://www.wipo.int/)
- Euro-Copyrights.org (http://www.euro-copyrights.org/)
- United States Copyright Office (http://www.copyright.gov/)
- Copyright for music librarians (http://www.lib.jmu.edu/org/mla/)
- "Copyright Issues for Music" at University of Buffalo Libraries
- 10 Big Myths about copyright explained by Templeton (2007)

## Publishing Rights and Licensing

Copyright owners have the exclusive right to reproduce or make copies of their work. The copyright owner also has the exclusive right to perform publicly a copyrighted work, directly or indirectly through means of communication or transmissions.

While these two rights (recording and public performance rights) were clearly separated before the digital distribution of content via the Internet, today this is not so clear anymore. Hence, service providers are forced to obtain multiple licenses from different parties. This process can be very difficult, as typically each right is connected with certain limitations, for example, geographical restrictions that can hardly be verified in the Internet. Rights can be negotiated either with the rights owner or with collection societies.

## Legislation

International agreements that protect artistic and literary works aim to harmonize legal definitions and terms of protection. In the Berne convention, which was signed by more than 1,979 member states in 1979, such an international framework was determined. Yet, this framework has a degree of freedom to deviate from: As described by Cohen (2002), the copyright industries had secured an international commitment to additional legal protection for technological protection regimes in the 1996 WIPO Copyright Treaty, which leaves member states substantial flexibility in implementation.

The Digital Millennium Copyright Act of 1998 (DMCA, U.S.) forbids circumvention of access control technologies, and also the manufacture and distribution of circumvention devices. Hence, usage controls are protected indirectly. One side effect of the DMCA is shown by Craver et al. (Craver, Wu, Liu, Stubblefield, Swartzlander, Wallach, Dean & Felten, 2001) in the SDMI hack where the content industry tried to stop Felten distributing his research knowledge, cf. Felten (2001).

In Europe, the digital copyright directive was approved. This results in the classification of a range of devices that are to be prohibited. Yet, it leaves member states free to define what constitutes adequate legal protection against the act of circumvention. Member states may require preservation of exceptions (e.g., private noncommercial copying)

Furthermore, there are other legal frameworks, for example, the Uniform Computer Information Transactions Act (UCITA), which would validate consume "assent" to these restrictions, and legitimise the accompanying technological controls as part and parcel of the agreement.

Other potential areas of conflict are fair use and privacy. The possibilities of DRM are usage control. A qualification of the usage, however, is difficult. For example, devices and computers cannot distinguish between legal and illegal copying. Thus, a restrictive policy is enforced by DRM: No copying is allowed.

This led to interesting court decisions like in France, where the French court ruled that copy protection schemes have to be removed from DVDs, as described by Orlowski (2005). Similarly, the Deutsche Bibliothek (now German National Library) signed an agreement with the content industry that allows one to crack and to duplicate DRM-protected digital media. Here, DRM opposes the legal mandate of the German National Library.

The storage and exchange of personal information is sometimes considered critical as well. For example, a customer exchanges information with a third trusted party, which stores this information. This potentially infringes privacy of the customers, which is analysed, for example, by Grimm (2005).

## Illegal File Sharing

Obviously, for very good reasons, content sharing is restricted. In the digital world, IP theft is not as obvious as theft in the physical world. In contrast to physical goods, digital content can be easily reproduced without quality loss. The copy is the original. Thus no other person experiences a lack of the digital content that was stolen.

Nevertheless, file sharing is against the copyright unless:

- The content is in public domain.
- The owner/creator gave permission to share it.
- The content is available under prosharing license (e.g., Creative Commons, http://creativecommons.org/).

As a result, the content industry successfully identified, and still identifies, users who illegally distribute digital content on the Internet via Web sites or via Peer-to-Peer (P2P) networks. Each user can be identified through the corresponding unique IP-address. This is required to receive information from the Internet. For permanent IP addresses, this is very easy (e.g., in the case of companies). In the case of dynamic IP-addresses (dial-in access), the Internet Service Providers (ISPs) temporarily store this information. The content industry was successful in identifying users by requesting user-related data from the ISPs.[2]

Nevertheless, this procedure is under strong discussion, and different verdicts exist in the different countries. Also the resulting lawsuits and their success are heavily discussed. Rudish (2005) states that "Eight of nine lawsuits filed last summer against Emory students accusing them of illegally sharing copyrighted music files have been dismissed, according to Senior Vice President and General Counsel Kent Alexander. The Recording Industry Association of America (RIAA) spokesperson Jenni Engebretsen said that one of the Emory cases has been settled, but she could not confirm the dismissal of the others."

## Digital Rights Management

The term digital rights management (DRM) comprises technologies that allow the usage control of digital content. This goes beyond the possibilities copyright holders had before, thus DRM threatens user privileges. For example, fair use[3] or archiving of content is also restricted, as DRM systems restrict access to content. Unfortunately, there is no unique definition for DRM. Thus, when somebody faces the term DRM, the connotation associated with it must not be neglected.

In "Digital Rights Management and Libraries," a selection of different connotations is given:

- "Digital rights management technologies are aimed at increasing the kinds and/or scope of control that rights-holders can assert over their intellectual property assets." (as taken from *Electronic Frontier Foundation*, http://www.eff.org/)
- "DRM must be about the 'digital management of rights' not the "management of digital rights." (as described by the *W3C Workshop Report on DRM for the Web*, http://www.w3.org/2000/12/drm-ws/)
- "The purpose of DRM technology is to control access to, track and limit uses of digital works." (as seen by *The American Library Association*, http://www.ala.org/, itself)
- "DRM are the technologies, tools and processes that protect intellectual property during digital content commerce..." (as defined by the *Publishers' Requirements for DRM, W3C Workshop Report on DRM for the Web*, http://www.w3.org/2000/12/drm-ws/minutes/publishers.html)
- "DRM systems restrict the use of digital files in order to protect the interests of copyright holders." (as taken from *Electronic Privacy Information Center*, http://www.epic.org/)

Camp (2003) outlined the copyright system's legal, technological, and economic foundations with the aim to support the design of DRM systems. She identified several key functions[4], which should be considered in the requirements of a DRM system. Among these key functions identified by Camp are:

- Protection of the author's reputation
- Protection of the work's monetary value
- Archiving of content
- Ensuring of content integrity
- Providing surety through persistence[5]
- Facilitating personalization through filtering and annotation[6]

Although copyright defines under which circumstances copying is legal and when copying is illegal, copyright infringements are ubiquitous. Therefore several campaigns were launched addressing this topic. As discussed by Walter (2003), the MPAA launched an advertising campaign, copying is stealing, to sensitive public that IPR infringement by private people can be compared to stealing a CD from a record shop.

Similar threats to music can be identified even before the predigital age (before the 1980s), for example, shortly after the completion of the first pianolas in 1895 (http://www.pianola.org/), a Pianola copyright ruling was cited in 1899, according to Rhodes: "Boosey vs Whight (1899) involved copyright charges arising over the production of pianola rolls, in which the court found that the reproduction of the perforated pianola rolls did not infringe the English copyright act protecting sheets of music."

When analogue audio tapes and also video tapes emerged, potential threats caused by illegal copies were realized. As by Walter (2003), in the predigital age, several legal disputes are known where copyright owners claimed copyright infringement offences:

- Ames Records allowed subscribers to hire records from it for a small rental charge.
- Amstrad supplied tape-to-tape recording equipment.
- Sony's video recorders were used for illegal copying.

Interestingly, neither Ames nor Amstrad nor Sony was liable for copyright infringement. Before the introduction of the compact disk (CD) in 1982, music was typically sold on long playing (LP) vinyl records. The sales of LPs slowly declined with the introduction of the music cassette (MC), which allowed copying of music, cf. Lewis (2003). Content was, however, stored in an analogue representation. Copying this analogue content was not possible without loss of quality. Therefore a natural barrier existed limiting the amount of recopies. In addition to these natural barriers, copy prevention systems were developed. This natural barrier no longer exists in the digital world.

Nowadays, copying digital data is much easier, and commercially oriented pirates, as well as some consumers certainly do misuse this: Digital data can be copied without any loss of information, and distributed fast world wide via the Internet. Especially P2P file-sharing networks—the most popular one was probably Napster (http://www.napster.com/)—enable users to share content. After the US courts shut down the first version of Napster[7], rights holders still claim that Napster's descendants cost billions of dollars in revenues.

While the rights holders were quite successful against Napster, actions against other P2P-software suppliers like Grokster (http://www.grokster.com) and StreamCast (http://www.streamcastnetworks.com/) failed. These service suppliers cannot control the use of the technology by the end user, and the users' communication is entirely outside the control of the service suppliers. Today's descendants have a decentralized architecture and cannot be shutdown easily. As a consequence, rights holders now target consumers, ISPs, operators, and even founders of file sharing systems.

The content industry, especially the music and movie industry, nowadays sues P2P users who exchange content illegally. At the beginning of these activities, the P2P users reduced their illegal file exchange as outlined by Greek (2004). This resulted from the news that P2P users are sued for their IPR infringements. Additionally, the content industry started PR campaigns to raise the users' awareness for the illegality of the file sharing of copyright protected content. Despite these activities, illegal P2P-usage seems to have increased again, and users have identified other ways of exchanging content, as discussed in Madden and Rainie (2005): "Beyond MP3 players, email and instant messaging, these alternative sources include music and movie Web sites, blogs and online review sites." Also, with portable storage devices, sharing content is very easy and convenient. Recent news related to P2P systems is available, for example, on People to People net (http://p2pnet.net/).

Although Verizon RIAA won a court order forcing an Internet Service Provider to disclose the identity of individual consumers who traded music files, technologies like Freenet[8] (http://freenet.sourceforge.net/) allow users to share any kind of content strongly reduced risk of being identified by rights holders. Obviously, P2P developments reacted on the content industries activities: While the first generation of P2P-file sharing networks has a centralised file list, the second generation is a purely distributed architecture. And the third generation addresses the anonymity of its users as outlined in "Peer-to-Peer" (Wikipedia).

Business aspects cannot be neglected when discussing and analysing protection technologies and illegal distribution. Unfortunately, there is no unique view on the influence of P2P exchange to the development of the traditional and the online market. On the one hand, each copied file is considered as a loss. On the other hand, some people consider downloaded content as an appetizer. Different reports and studies exist where common people have been interrogated about the influence of P2P networks. The results of the studies are contradicting, comparable to the results of studies trying to identify the reasons for the decrease in CD sales.

Besides these previously discussed methods and procedure, the technical endeavours of controlling the usage of content are summarized in the term digital rights management (DRM), and were first focused on security and encryption addressing the problem of unauthorized copying. But DRM evolved, and now it covers various issues including:

- The description of content
- The identification of content
- Trading and exchanging content
- Protection of content
- Monitoring/tracking of content distribution and its usage

As emphasised by Iannella (2001), DRM is the "digital management of rights" and not the "management of digital rights." Thus, it has become a very complex area addressing issues far beyond security and encryption.

The first section gives an overview of the current situation of copyright and content distribution. Section two introduces the available technologies for active and passive content protection. The following section, three, describes the application of individual techniques in DRM solutions. Their possibilities and limitations are discussed in the next section. New developments that try to embrace user requirements are described in the fifth section. An outlook discusses the future development of content protection of digital audiovisual content.

## AVAILABLE TECHNOLOGY FOR AUDIOVISUAL CONTENT PROTECTION

*Engineers like to solve problems. If there are no problems handily available, they will create their own problems.*
Scott Adams

In this section, the basic technologies are described that are available for content protection. Some of these technologies are also relevant for other areas, like the content identification and the linkage of content and metadata.

## Content Identification, Content Description, and Content Management

As already outlined before, content identification is an important aspect when content-related information has to be identified. For example, this is a central aspect of libraries and archives, where content-related metadata is managed.

Whenever data has to be accessed or retrieved, two issues are important:

- Content identification
- Content description

These issues are independent of DRM. But also DRM has to somehow identify content, as usage and rights information relate to specific pieces of content. In the following, a very brief overview on different standards for content identification and descriptions are given.

### Content Identification

Content identification should be accomplished with an open standardized mechanism. Several open standards have been created for this purpose in the digital world. They allow identifying content or resources uniquely. Among the most commonly used are:

- International Standard Book Number (ISBN, cf. http://isbn-international.org/ or http://www.isbn.org/)
- International Standard Serial Number (ISSN, cf. http://www.issn.org)
- International Standard Music Number (ISMN, cf. "International Standard Music Number")
- Uniform Resource Identifier (URI, cf. "RFC1736", "RFC1737" and "RFC2396")
- Digital Object Identifier (DOI, cf. http://www.doi.org/)
- International Standard Text Code (ISTC, cf. "International Standard Text Code")

### Content Description

Within a DRM system itself, the most significant content description is the licensing information. For completeness, general content description is summarized briefly.

According to Iannella (2001), content description should be based on the most appropriate metadata standard for each genre. Any overlap with other metadata systems might result in difficulties in the implementation due to redundant information.

Among the existing standards for content description are:

- Online Information Exchange (ONIX) as developed by EDItEUR (http://www.editeur.org/).
- IMS Learning Resource Metadata Information Model by IMS ( http://www.imsproject.org/)
- Dublin Core Metadata Initiative (DCMI, http://dublincore.org/)
- Interoperability of data in eCommerce systems <indecs> (http://www.indecs.org/)

- "EBU metadata specifications" from the European Broadcasting Union
- Standard Media Exchange Format (SMEF), cf. "SMEF Data Model"
- MPEG-4 defines a stream management framework. This framework includes a rudimentary representation of metadata for the "description, identification and logical dependencies of the elementary streams" (http://www.chiariglione.org/mpeg/).
- MPEG-7 addresses the describing of and searching for content. "MPEG-7, formally named *Multimedia Content Description Interface*," is a standard for describing the multimedia content data that supports some degree of interpretation of the information's meaning, which can be passed onto, or accessed by, a device or a computer code." (http://www.chiariglione.org/mpeg/).

## Rights Management and Rights Description Languages

As DRM is the digital management of rights, they have to be represented in a digital format to be digitally manageable. These digital representations must consider several aspects, as also described by Rosenblatt et al. (Rosenblatt, Trippe, & Mooney, 2002):

- **Content rights transactions:** Traditional business models.
- **Components of rights models:** Types of rights and their attributes.
- **Fundamental rights:** Render rights (print, view, play), transport rights (copy, move, loan), derivative work rights (extract, edit, embed).
- **Rights attributes:** (considerations, extends, types of users)

A general problem of DRM systems is the fact that they are not able to qualitatively distinguish between the different kinds of usage. For example, copying for personal purpose and copying for friends or even unknown persons is represented as the same action within a DRM system. This is what Rosenblatt et al. (2002) expressed as "they [digital rights models] don't do a great job of modeling the actual uses of content."

This is a potential starting point for further developments. The complexity of such an approach, however, might be beyond the relatively simple license (models), not only due to the potential dynamics of sociocultural aspects.

Today's licenses can have a strongly varying range of usage rights and conditions reflecting everything from simple to complex rights situations. Therefore, the language used for the description of rights should be able to model even very complex situations, which can appear easily when dealing with digital content (e.g., audiovisual material).

## Rights Description Languages

The purpose of a digital license is to express who can do what with a specific content under certain conditions. For the digital management of rights, obviously, this license has to be expressed in a machine-readable way.

The extensible markup language (XML) is a de facto standard for the exchange and storage of data. Due to its flexibility, several rights description languages are based on XML. An overview of different XML-based rights description languages can be found in "XML and Digital Rights Management (DRM)." The currently most relevant ones are:

- Digital Property Rights Language (DPRL) and its successor eXtensible Rights Management Language (XRML, http://www.xrml.org/) are implemented by ContentGuard (http://www.contentguard.com/) and became an official standard within MPEG-21 (ISO/IEC 21000).

- Open Digital Rights Language (ODRL, http://www.odrl.net) was adopted by the Open Mobile Alliance (OMA).

## Rights Processing

Expressing the rights in a machine-readable way is only the first step. Ideally the rights are processed automatically whenever content is created, derived, or exchange. This cannot be achieved yet as different terminology, especially when dealing with multinational content, and even different legal foundations complicate an automation process. Thus a rights ontology or thesaurus is inevitable.

## Current Status of REL Standardisation

MPEG so far chose XrML as a basis for the MPEG Rights Expression Language (REL). Nevertheless, OMA was in favor of ODRL. This competition between XrML and OMA is very interesting, as XrML is patented and ODRL is royalty free. Nevertheless, "ContentGuard asserts that because its patents cover DRM implementations based on any rights language, even ODRL implementations should be subject to patent licensing from ContentGuard. The OMA tacitly disagreed with ContentGuard's assessment when it chose ODRL; the issue has yet to be tested, in the courts or otherwise" as pointed out by Rosenblatt (2004).

MPEG REL seems to be too complex and is hardly accepted by the market. Microsoft still prefers XrML. In March 2007, the first publicly known DRM patent licensing deal was done by ContentGuard. LG Electronics will apply XrML in it mobile handsets. A more recent overview of DRM related activities can be found at DRMWatch (http://www.drmwatch.com).

## Encryption

Whenever data is transmitted over an insecure channel, which indeed is the Internet, the only possible protection mechanism to guarantee confidentiality is encryption.[9] The methods used for encryption can be attacked. These attacks are not limited to the encryption algorithm itself. Attacks are also possible against keys or protocols. In this section, we will address some general aspects of encryption to allow a basic understanding of distribution systems and related requirements. Detailed information on encryption and cryptography was given, for example, by Menezes et al. (Memezes, Oorschot, & van, Vanstone, 1996) or Schneier (1996).

## Cryptography

Cryptography is the art of encryption and is several thousand years old. Encryption transforms the content by using an encryption algorithm or a cipher. Retransformation of the original message (or plain text) from the encrypted form (or cipher text) is known as decryption. To prevent others from reading the cipher text, the method could kept secret or the algorithm uses a secret to determine the transformation. Kerkhoff (1883) already formulated in 1883 that security by obscurity is not possible: Keeping the encryption method secret does not increase the security of the method. The security of an algorithm therefore must not be based on its secrecy but on the usage of a key.

Different methods exist:

- Symmetric encryption methods
- Asymmetric encryption methods

## Symmetric Encryption Methods

Whenever data is exchanged, communication partners agree on a common key for the encryption of the data, as shown in Figure 1. As the same key is used for encryption and decryption by symmetric encryption methods, everybody who has access to the key can decrypt encrypted data.

*Figure 1. Symmetric encryption methods use the same key for encryption and decryption. The key determines the transformation for the plain text to the cipher text. Thus, everybody who has knowledge about the secret key can decrypt the cipher texts, which have been encrypted with this key.*

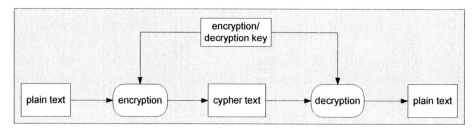

*Figure 2. In contrast to the symmetric encryption algorithm, the asymmetric encryption methods use different keys for encryption and decryption. The public key can be accessed by everybody interested in encrypting a message for a certain receiver. The private key is kept secret.*

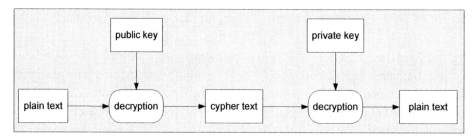

Symmetric encryption algorithms include:

- **Substitution algorithm:** By using a table every character is replaced by another one.
- **Vignere method:** A password determines the mapping.

One severe attack is the knowledge of an instance of encrypted and the decrypted data, that allows the calculation of the mapping and therefore, the decryption of other encrypted messages. But also statistical attacks can be applied. Of course the system security depends on the length of the password or key. If the key has the same length as the message maximum, security is achieved. In this case the key is also called a one-time pad.

There are two main types of symmetric encryption algorithms that differ in the size of the data the cipher works on:[10]

- Block ciphers process a number of bits simultaneously, for example DES, 3DES, IDEA, AES, Blowfish, Twofish, and RC6.
- Stream ciphers process a single bit at a time, for example, RC4.

## Asymmetric Encryption Methods

The general problem of the symmetric schemes is the exchange of secret keys. As the secret key has to remain secret, the transmission of keys in plain text is not possible. This problem is addressed by public-key or asymmetric encryption methods.

Asymmetric encryption methods use two keys:

1. The public key is for the encryption of data. This key can be distributed freely.
2. The private key is used for the decryption of the data.

Thus, no keys have to be exchanged. One can even think of a "telephone book" that publishes the e-mail addresses and the corresponding public keys. Yet, public key encryption is computationally expensive.

The existing solutions for the asymmetric methods are based on the computation of mathematical calculations that are extremely difficult for very large numbers, like done, for example, in:

- ElGamal
- RSA
- Elliptic Curve Ciphers (ECC) probably will replace RSA in the future

## Key Length

The comparison of different ciphers based on their key lengths is meaning less: The security is influenced by the design of the ciphers. One example is public key algorithms' key length: They require much longer key lengths than symmetric algorithms.

Recommendations on the key lengths are given by different national organizations. A collection can be found at http://www.keylength.com/. These recommendations consider that advance of cryptoanalysis.

## Cryptoanalysis

Cryptoanalysis deals with the analysis of cryptographic methods. For example, the "brute force" attack is a straight forward attack that calculates and verifies all possible keys. Of course this can be very time-consuming, but for certain encryption algorithms, hardware was developed to speed up this task, and even distributed calculations that use a huge amount of computers connected via the Internet are performed. A method can be considered as secure when the most effective attack is the "brute force" attack. However, cryptoanalysis is not limited to the decryption of the secret message: collecting any kind of information, which provides more information about the secret message, represents an attack.

## Dangers and Attacks

The security of all asymmetric encryption methods depends on the computational complexity of the corresponding mathematical problems. A tricky calculation or quantum computers might endanger the security of all asymmetric encryption methods in the future.

Besides this potential risk, attackers can exploit other leaks like the previously mentioned randomness of a PRN generator. Further possible leaks are cryptographic protocols, chosen keys, short pass phrases, and so forth. Even more sophisticated attacks are applicable, like the ones based on the power consumption or the time delay of cryptographic coprocessors.

## One-Way Encryption

Encryption with one-way algorithms[11] cannot be reversed. Typical applications are scenarios, where the plain text must not be recovered, and include the storage of passwords. One of those one-way hash algorithms is the secure hashing algorithm (SHA) that creates a 160-bit hash value. As these one-way encryption functions typically base their calculations on a password, they can be used to sign data with a digital signature.

Depending on the application, for example, like for authentication/verification of digital content, the security of one-way encryption is very significant. Recent attacks on MD5, as shown by

Wang et al. (Wang, Feng, Lai, & Yu, 2004) or on SHA-1 MD5, as outlined by Wang et al. (Wang, Yin, & Yu, 2005), show that collisions are possible, and that MD5 and SHA-1 can no longer be considered secure.

## Applications in DRM Systems

Encryption technologies are primarily used to secure the communication between different parties, and the storage at the parties' storage media. While this is reasonable in business environments, concerns have to be raised with respect to the encrypted storage of content at the consumers' side. As consumers access the encrypted data, an unencrypted version must be temporarily available in the memory of the computer. As a matter of fact, consumers that are capable of handling debugging software are also able to access this decrypted content as long as trusted hardware solutions are not available. This is discussed next.

Besides the secure communication and storage of content encryption, technology is used for further applications:

- Verifying content based on digests.
- Verifying identities based on certificates.
- Verifying identities and content based on signatures.

## Watermarking

Besides the active protection technologies, like the previously described encryption and cryptography, passive protection technologies provide further possibilities in protecting content. For example, passive protection technologies address the identification of content or the identification of content owners. Thus, they do not prevent copying, per-se. These mechanisms, nevertheless, can be used for the detection of IPR infringements, as shown in the different movie piracy cases where several Oscar screeners—among them

were *The Last Samurai*, *Shattered Glass*, and *In America*—were illegally distributed on the Internet in illegal file-sharing networks (cf. "Arrest In 'Screener' Upload Case," "FBI Arrests Internet Movie Pirate," and "Man nabbed for uploading Oscar 'screener'").

This section describes digital watermarking techniques, which allow embedding arbitrary information directly into the any multimedia content imperceptibly. The embedded information depends on the application. For the protection of intellectual property, typically, information about the rights holder is embedded. Information about the content itself, or a link to corresponding metadata, can be embedded, which supports the identification of content. Other scenarios embed information relevant for authentication[12] or even information related to marketing and PR.[13] In some applications, for example, for transaction tracing, as it was in the case of the Oscar screeners, the embedded information might consist of a customer identifier.

On the one hand, perceptible watermarking techniques influence the quality of the multimedia content. On the other hand, a successful removal can be easily verified by an attacker. Therefore we will limit this discussion on imperceptible watermarking techniques.[14]

In contrast to steganography, where the most important requirement is that the communication remains undiscovered, in digital watermarking, the information, if a message was embedded or not, can be publicly available. This knowledge leads to increased requirements on the robustness and the security of the communication respective of the embedded message. Thus, a good watermarking system maximizes robustness for a constraint-perceived quality degradation.

## Characteristics and Requirements

The general principle of watermarking methods can be compared with the symmetrical encryption.[15] Both methods require the same key for

*Figure 3. During the watermarking embedding process the watermarking message is interwoven with the original content*

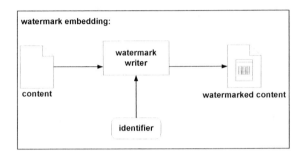

*Figure 4. During the retrieval process the embedded watermark message is restored*

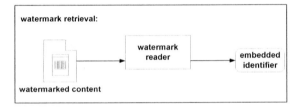

encoding and decoding the information. A watermarking system consists of two subsystems: the watermark writer (encoder) and the watermark reader (decoder).

The embedding process is shown in Figure. Watermarking technologies' most important characteristic is the active embedding of a watermark message (e.g., an identifier) in the content. Thus, the content is modified (imperceptibly). This message is read during the retrieval process, as shown in Figure 4. This has severe implications to the protection scenario as in some cases, unmarked content that is already distributed has to be considered carefully.

The retrieval processes (as shown in Figure 4) of existing methods differ in the detection itself as well as in the number of input parameters. Blind[16] detection schemes require only the marked content and the detection key for the detection. In contrast to the blind detection schemes, the

nonblind[17] methods require, in addition to the previous parameters, the original and sometimes the embedded watermark message. Semiblind methods require, in addition to the blind detection schemes, the watermark message as a retrieval parameter.

Nonblind methods are practically relevant only for a very limited number of application scenarios due to the necessary input of the original. In the typical application scenarios, like broadcast monitoring or the automatic identification of the copyright owner, the original is either not known or not immediately accessible.

General requirements on watermarking techniques are:

- The quality can be considered as the most important criteria. In general, the embedding of a message into the content should not affect the perceived quality of the content (the information carrier). As perceived quality always depends on the media type, watermarking techniques have to be developed or adapted to individual media types (e.g., choosing a suitable perceptual model to minimize distortions).[18]
- The robustness is defined by the types and numbers of operations (and their parameters) applied to the watermarked content, which can be survived by the watermark message. From a watermark developer's and user's view, these processing operations are called attacks. Depending on the intention of the operations, they can be distinguished between intentional and unintentional attacks. Although an attacker has numerous attack operations available, their combination and their parameters cannot be chosen arbitrarily, as the result also has to fulfill a certain quality requirement as well. The operations a watermarking scheme should be robust against are defined by the individual application scenario. For the identification of content and protection of IPR robustness can

be considered as the second most important criteria.

- The capacity is the amount of information, which can be embedded in the content. It is the third most important criteria. Due to the mutual dependencies between quality, robustness, and capacity, a certain quality level is defined (according to the application scenario), and the robustness is chosen dependent on the deserved quality. Capacity is finally defined by quality and robustness.
- The complexity of an algorithm is important for certain application scenarios where real-time embedding or detection is important.
- The security of a watermarking scheme does not only depend on the robustness, but also on other issues like the used key and the message embedding method. Also, its implementation and integration into the overall system cannot be neglected.

General information on watermarking techniques was collected by Katzenbeisser and Petitcolas (2000). Cox et al. (Cox, Miller, & Bloom, 2002) provide a detailed technical inside on watermarking schemes for images. An application-oriented introduction and detailed information about requirements and application scenarios is given by Arnold et al. (Arnold, Schmucker, & Wolthusen, 2003).

## Limitations

Watermarking schemes are advantageous as they allow the embedding of arbitrary information directly into content. This embedded information can survive processing and media conversion. In the sense that compression techniques remove imperceptible information, they can be regarded as competitors. Thus, the effect of future emerging compression techniques on the embedded information is unclear.

In IPR protection scenarios, watermarking techniques certainly have some limitations. For example, the robustness of watermarking schemes might not be sufficient, and an attacker might be able to remove, or maybe copy, a watermark message. Nevertheless, an attacker cannot be 100% secure about the success of his attack.

Available objective tests and performance analysis of existing watermarking techniques address a limited scope. These benchmarking suites like Stirmark by Peticolas (2006) or Certimark (http://www.certimark.org) do not fully consider practical requirements. Here, standardized application scenarios defining requirements would be advantageous. Another limitation is the missing standardization of the embedded information.

## Applications in DRM systems

Although watermarking techniques must be developed for individual media types, a broad range of watermarking algorithms are available for various media types including audio, images, video, geometry data, text, music scores, and so forth. Several requirements can be addressed by integrating watermarking techniques into DRM solutions, as also described by Rosenblatt (2002):

- Source identification can be achieved by imperceptible watermarking techniques, which do not affect the perceived quality. The information embedded links to the content owner or to a rights owner.
- Tracking and tracing by embedding so-called transaction watermarks, which is information about people involved in transactions, might allow the detection of leaks within the distribution chain.
- Metadata labelling stores a link to a database containing metadata information.

From a security point of view, applications involving encrypted watermarks and encrypted files with watermarks should be considered critically if they are used for access control in end-user devices. Yet, Rosenblatt et al. (2002) concludes "a scheme that incorporated both encryption and watermarking is not foolproof, but (all else being equal) it's the best DRM scheme available."

## Fingerprinting or Perceptual Hashing

In contrast to watermarking techniques, which modify content, fingerprinting, or perceptual hashing techniques can identify content and fragments thereof without prior modifications. Thus, they have an inherent advantage if used in application scenarios where content cannot be modified, for example, as already distributed or due to workflow limitations. In this section, we explain shortly the idea and application of fingerprinting technologies.

### General Principle

Fingerprinting techniques calculate a content-dependent identifier, as shown in Figure 5. This content-dependent fingerprint can be compared with a human fingerprint: It is a unique identifier for renderings, and the original content cannot be created out of this identifier. Thus these techniques are also related to the cryptographic one-way functions. The significant difference to cryptographic hash functions is that cryptographic hash functions map similar input values not to similar

*Figure 5. The fingerprinting method calculates the content dependent identifier directly from the original content. Thus the content has not to be modified.*

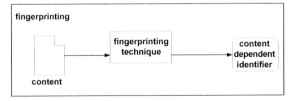

hash values. For fingerprinting techniques, the opposite requirement must hold. Therefore, they are also called perceptual or soft hashing functions.[19] Perceptual hash reflects the fact that perceptual similar content should result in a similar hash value. Fingerprinting techniques are methods for content based identification (CBID).

Due to this property, fingerprinting solutions are very suitable for identification applications, like automatic play list generation or broadcast monitoring, as described by Allamanche et al. (Allamanche, Herre, Hellmuth, Froba, & Cremer, 2001). Further potential applications include the tracking of content flow or even restricting the content flow (e.g., in corporate networks). Due to these characteristics, fingerprinting techniques have attracted increased attention recently. A very good overview on the basis of audio fingerprinting is given by Cano et al. (Cano, Baltle, Kalker, & Haitsma, 2002).

### Characteristics and Requirements

Fingerprinting techniques are related to content-based retrieval (CBR). CBR methods create a content-dependent signature directly from the content. This signature is also compared to pre-calculated and stored content signatures.

Figure 6 shows the principle steps necessary for the calculation of a unique identifier. First, features are extracted from the content. These extracted features typically have very high dimensions and are processed further, resulting in unique identifiers.

The feature extraction process itself might extract features that are directly perceived by humans, like the frequency characteristics (melody) in the case of audio signals. On the contrary, features that do not directly depend on the human perceptions can also be used, as long as they allow the automatic discrimination of content. A typical example is the sign of the difference between neighboring (frequency) energy bands,

*Figure 6. For calculating a unique identifier, (perceptually) relevant features are extracted. These features are processed to reduce their dimensionality.*

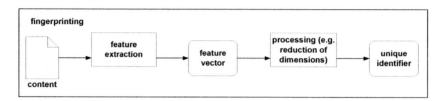

as proposed by Haitsma et al. (Haitsma, van der Veen, Kalker, & Brueker, 2000).

Without a following processing step, the dimensionality of the feature vector would be very high. Therefore, the dimensionality is reduced by removing redundant information. During this processing step, further improvements, for example, error resilience, can be achieved. Although the aim is to receive a compact digest, the discriminability of this digest still has to be sufficient.

In addition to the feature vector, a suitable distance measure is required. This is also related to CBR methods, where it defines similarity. Typical distance measures are the Euclidean or related distance measures or distance measures based on correlation.

The retrieval architecture strongly influences the complexity and the scalability of the fingerprinting technique. Efficient spatial access structures have been developed like indices, or application-oriented approach like the ones used for DNA information processing. In the retrieval architecture, a final hypothesis test calculates the probability of the correct identification of the content.

In the case of content identification, a good performance in discriminating a huge amount of data and corresponding fingerprints is crucial. Similarly to watermarking techniques, requirements can be identified:

- The robustness can be defined by the types and numbers of operations and their parameters applied the content, which does not

effect the retrieval of the content. Typical operations depend on the application scenario where the fingerprinting method will be integrated in. For example, when a system should be able to recover the song from a radio transmission that is recorded via a mobile phone, the fingerprinting system should be capable of the reduced frequency band available due to the mobile phone. Also small audio extracts somewhere within the song must not result in misidentification, as humans will rather realize in the middle or at the end of the song that is worth being remembered or purchased. Finally, a noisy background will probably be the general recording place, for example, in a car, bar, club, or café.

- The discriminability determines the capability of how many content items can be identified.

- The scalability is an important practical criterion. Today, millions of different types of audio content exist. Some of them are even available in different editions, for example, studio or live performance recordings. In this case, a system should be capable of handling all available works in a reasonable amount of time, where "reasonable" is again defined by the application scenario.

- The complexity of an algorithm is important for certain application scenarios where real-time identification is important.

In contrast to watermarking applications, so far security is hardly considered. This might be caused due to the fact that perceptual hashing techniques, so far, are mainly applied in CBID scenarios, where security can be neglected. In authentication scenarios, however, security is crucial and requirements are different.

## Limitations and Comparison to Watermarking

Different limitations have to be considered when a fingerprinting technology is deployed. As already mentioned, fingerprinting techniques do not modify the content, but calculate an identifier directly from the content itself. This is an obvious advantage when content is already available in a nonmarked version. Yet, this is also a drawback in comparison to watermarking schemes: personalization is not possible. Therefore, applications like leakage tracking are not possible. Although content can be tracked, tracking users is not possible, as content is generally not unique for individual users.

Instead of being marked, content must be registered. That means that only content can be identified if its fingerprint was previously calcu-

lated and stored in a database. And if the identifier is stored in a database, this database has to be accessible during the identification process.

Another limitation of fingerprinting techniques have to consider when using fingerprinting for controlling the data transfer networking infrastructure: encrypted content or scrambled content cannot be identified. Identification is only possible with content that is accessible as it is intended for rendering.

A comparison between the different properties of watermarking and fingerprinting is shown in Table 1.

## Applications in DRM systems

Besides the previously listed applications of fingerprinting systems in automatic play list generation, broadcast monitoring, content tracking, and content flow limitations, another application is very interesting for fingerprinting techniques: royalty distribution. Content can be monitored in peer-to-peer networks with the help of fingerprinting techniques. This information can be combined with other information available, for example, metadata within the peer-to-peer networks used by humans for content identification. Keeping in

*Table 1. Principle characteristics of watermarking and fingerprinting schemes are summarised.*

|  | **Watermarking** | **Fingerprinting** |
|---|---|---|
| **Development** | Has to be developed for individual media types | |
| **Availability** | Audio, video, images, 3D, music scores | Various media types with a focus on audio, video, images |
| **Alteration** | Content is altered by embedding | Not necessary but registration in database necessary instead |
| **Registration** | Not necessary (cf. alteration) | Prior to identification |
| **Attacks** | Vulnerable | Limited vulnerability (perceptual features) |
| **Capacity** | Varying on content (minimum requirement should be 64bit for creating a link) | Indirectly in the content and the method's ability to discriminate content |
| **Infrastructure** | Depending on application (can be implemented as an independent solution) | Needed (connection to a database) |

mind the future revenue stream, new possibilities can be created when new technologies are considered, as discussed in the following section.

## Summary

For each of the different basic technologies different realizations exist. This allows some flexibility for system developers in combining different solutions. For example, a DRM system can be implemented as an open source system. Nevertheless, this flexibility provides difficulties, especially for the compatibility of the different DRM systems.

From a security point of view, it has to be considered that the whole system is as secure as its weakest part. This does not only address the individual components but also their interactions. Thus, components, as well as their integration, have to be chosen carefully.

## DRM TECHNOLOGIES

*If everything seems under control, you're just not going fast enough.*

Mario Andretti

In this section, the principle components of DRM systems are described. This general principle is more or less underlying each implementation of a DRM system. From an operational point of view, the typical parties involved are the content owner who distributes content, the customer or the consumer who purchases content, and a clearinghouse that manages licenses. For simplicity, we assume that the content owner is also the content distributor, which is not generally the case. If this is not the case, the relationship between the content distributor and the content owner might influence the DRM architecture, as content can be exchanged between these two parties at different security levels.

## General Aspects

Sellers of traditional goods benefit from online shops as they are accessible without any time constraint. Product information as well as purchase related information can be made available. But not only traditional goods can be sold on the Internet. Especially content providers of digital content have a general interest in, and strongly benefit from, online distribution. Several advantages can be identified including:

- **Availability:** 24 hours a day and 7 days a week
- **Reduced costs:** Not only complete collections are sold
- **Try before buy:** Customers can have a prelistening/preview
- **Customer relationship:** Direct contact to customers like personalized offers, increased feedback possibilities, and so forth.
- **Reduction of shipping costs:** No physical goods have to be distributed
- **Reduction of storage costs:** Only a digital storage solution is need

Content providers deserve the protection of their content. Therefore content is encrypted before its distribution. As a result, this encrypted content can be distributed in various ways, including download or e-mail transmission. For content usage and rendering, a license is needed, which can be stored locally or on a remote server. This license is used by the client device or client player for decrypting content.

Today's protection solutions, however, are device dependent. Therefore content usage and rendering is device dependent. This is a general problem today. Customers do not want to be restricted by protection solutions. As most available distribution platforms strongly restrict customers (e.g., content can be rendered only on one certain device) in the numerous customers' view DRM is the acronym for digital restriction management.

When analyzing a system's security, different assumptions have to be made as described by Arnold et al. (2003). These assumptions include the knowledge of the attacker. It is quite difficult to estimate this, as software patches ("hackz" or "crackz") can be often downloaded from the Internet ("break once, run everywhere"—BORE). These patches allow even users with almost no knowledge to circumvent certain protection mechanisms. Furthermore, the applied security solutions can be secure while the runtime system is not secure at all. This allows potential hackers to successfully attack the runtime system while not interfering with the applied security solutions. Thus, a secure system is vital for the security of content. Therefore the hardware industry is targeting at secure devices[20].

## DRM Architecture

The general architecture of a DRM system is shown in Figure 7. Primary technology components can be identified (according to):

- Packagers[21] collect license information, metadata, and the requested content in encrypted files. These secure files are called packages, containers, and so forth.
- Controllers[22] realize local rights management systems at the client side and are responsible for authentication of the device or the user, decryption of the content, provision of access to the content, and sometimes for financial transactions.

*Figure 7. This figure illustrated the principle architecture of a DRM system. The important aspect is that content is always encrypted outside of the DRM environment. Whenever an application wants to access information, the local rights management system is called to decrypt the content, and it also influences the functionality of the application. Thus a user cannot access any data outside the DRM system.*

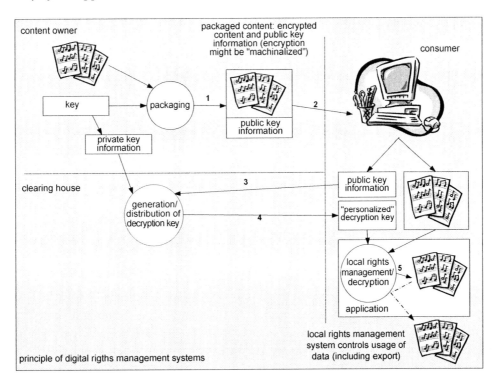

- License servers or clearinghouses are run by third trusted parties, and create and distribute licenses that grant access to the requested content via the local rights management system and can also contain access conditions.

As described by Rosenblatt et al. (2002), a broader definition of DRM encompasses everything that can be done to define, manage, and track rights to digital content. Thus further elements are included in this definition:

- Business rights (or contract rights) are typically associated with some content in certain scenarios. For example, the right to use a certain audio sequence in a commercial spot might be granted while processing of the audio sequence is prohibited.
- Access tracking, or tracking of operations on content, provides valuable information for content providers, even if they do not charge for access to the content. This information also helps to improve business models or relationships to customers.
- Rights licensing is an important issue, especially when content can be modified and is redistributed. Yet, technical solutions are strongly limited, for example, when the modification is translation.

## Content Owner

Whenever content is distributed, this content is encrypted. The encrypted content is transmitted to the customer with public information about the encryption key. This process is called "packaging" and is step "1" in the figure 7. One has to keep in mind that this is just a simplified view on the package and the packaging itself. Typically, rights information is also included in the package to permit or to restrict certain types of operations, certain operations intervals, or the amount of operations, as well as additional product information (metadata). This rights information is stored in the license.

Content is stored in a repository. Either the repository is built within the DRM solution or it is part of a content management system (CMS). If a CMS stores the content and the packaging system is not able in managing arbitrary file types, the storage format of the content must be chosen according to the capabilities of the packaging respective the DRM system.

Again, it is also necessary to protect the content distribution system. Typical attacks might come from the Internet. These attacks can be faced by a well-configured firewall. Yet, attacks from users with physical access to the content distribution system are also possible. Thus, a certain level of trust in the people working at the content distributor's side is also necessary.

After packaging, content is distributed to the consumers. This can be done using different transmission channels. The Internet via download is probably the most common channel, but also, a transmission via e-mail, floppy disk, or CD is possible. The transmission processes is indicated in step "2."

## Consumer

Whenever the consumer receives the content, it is initially useless as it is encrypted. Thus, the corresponding decryption key is needed. Of course it is possible to distribute the keys directly to the customer. Yet, this would reduce the security of the system drastically. Therefore, a local rights management component is responsible for this task. This component requests the keys from the clearinghouse (step "3"), which is a third trusted party. To increase the security, this local rights management component is unique and can be identified. Thus, personalized keys are sent to the local rights management component (step "4"), which makes them only useable for one certain local rights management component.

After receiving the decryption key the content is decrypted. For security reasons, neither the decryption key nor the decrypted content[23] must be stored locally.[24] Therefore, a strong connection between the local rights management component and the application rendering the content is necessary, as content exchange is not only possible via files but also through other channels, like the clipboard or via screenshots.

We would like to stress that the previously described functionality is not restricted to a personal computer. It can also be deployed in other devices. But certain ,for example, mobile consumer devices will result in certain requirements on the complexity of the involved algorithms as their computational power is weaker, and the usability of devices is directly correlated to the execution speed of certain operations.

One important aspect, not only when dealing with mobile devices, is the problem if the DRM solution should also be functional in an offline environment. This requirement increases security threats considerably.

## Clearinghouse

The clearinghouse enables the consumer to render the content. The minimalist version transmits "personified" decryption keys to consumers. A more sophisticated version considers licensing issues: The valid content usage period or the amount of rendering. The clearinghouse is also able to initiate financial transaction, for example, when pay-per-use is demanded in the license.

## Rendering Applications

As described, a strong connection between the local rights management is necessary. Rosenblatt et al. (2002) distinguish different rendering applications: stand-alone, plug-in, and java rendering applications:

- Stand-alone rendering applications allow a maximum control of the content. Yet, this advantage has to be paid with several drawbacks: First, the software has to be distributed to the consumers. Second, the consumer has to install the proprietary software on his hardware. Generally, users prefer ready-to-use solutions. They do not want to be bothered with technical details.

- Plug-in rendering applications are common solutions that integrate themselves into existing software. As a direct consequence, the functionality of the "hosting" software is augmented. In the case of DRM plug-ins, it is able to render an increased number of files types. Of course, the plug-in has to modify the "hosting" software's behavior to control data exchange and to avoid any content leakage.

Unfortunately these solutions have to be developed for each hardware platform. From a content distributor's point of view, *Java* combines the advantages of stand-alone and plug-in applications, and additionally throws away the hardware dependency, as Java programs are not run directly on the microprocessor but are executed on a simulated processor, which is called the Java Virtual Machine (JVM). DRM solutions implemented in Java can be run on every processor for which a JVM exists.[25] Today this is the case for most Web browsers. Although Rosenblatt et al. (2002) raise the problem of incompatibilities, an efficient platform-independent DRM solution is currently addressed, for example, by Sun Microsystems.

## Security Issues

The main purpose of a DRM solution is the protection of content respective of its license conform usage: content security. Security is always related to certain assumptions. For example, the described assumption of the technical skills of an attacker.

But other security issues are directly related to the user and the involved hardware and software platforms.

Digital rights management systems for general content distribution scenarios require the identification of the user. For example, this is very important for secret information exchanged within a company. Similarly, an identification of a customer is important in the music distribution scenario as consumers can be seen as a business partner. For the business transaction, a credit card number might be sufficient. Practically, content usage cannot be limited to the person who purchased it. Thus, information about the person rendering the content is necessary. This information may be a simple e-mail address, a user ID, a password, or other personal information. In other application scenarios, biometric identification systems are used. For example, one can think of personalized mobile devices with biometric sensors: a "lost" mobile device is useless for its "finder." Yet, simple biometric solutions—and these are all current solutions which can be integrated into mass products for monetary reasons—can be easily fooled. Other solutions exist, like the "typewriting style," and are considered by music distribution solution providers. For identification, other possibilities include digital certificates (created by a third trusted party) or smart cards.

Besides user identification, device identification plays an important role. This can be done, for example, by a unique identification number or by the media access control (MAC) address.[26] The advantage of using the MAC address instead of the IP address is the fact that IP addresses can be dynamic addresses, and also IP addresses can correspond to multiple users.

Device identification is not sufficient at all. One aspect that is generally neglected is the device integrity. The device integrity includes hardware as well as software integrity, which is very difficult. First, hardware and software are under total control of a user.[27] But even if the customer is trustworthy, "external influences" like Trojan horses might violate the device's integrity.

The problem of the device integrity is addressed by the "trusted computing" activities like the Trusted Computing Group (TCG, https://www.trustedcomputinggroup.org/), Trusted Computing Platform Alliance (TCPA, http://www.trustedcomputing.org/), or "Next Generation Secure Computing Base" (NGSCB, http://www.microsoft.com/resources/ngscb).

A trusted environment is typically assumed as a precondition. Yet, this is difficult to achieve, especially whenever the hardware and software cannot be fully controlled, which is usually the case whenever a consumer owns a device.

The trusted computing idea, which is supported by the most hardware and software players, aims to a standard for a PC with increased security level. Although this goal is very important in commercial scenarios (e.g., document security, information assurance...), such a standard is ambivalent for consumers. The danger is that control of individual hardware is transferred from the hardware owner to other parties, like the software vendor implementing the operating system or the content industry in general.

While this is interesting for content distributors, consumers might neglect this standard as from their point of view, the system is less trustworthy, and what is even more important, somebody has to pay for the additional components. The resulting trusted devices will not allow access to decrypted data, for example, through debugging software, will not start modified software, and they will also control the input and output devices.

## Integrating DRM Systems with Existing Systems

Although DRM systems can be used as standalone solutions, it is more fruitful to combine DRM systems with other systems to maximize their common benefit. As DRM systems manage content access they can be used whenever content is involved. Thus DRM systems address the complete content "life cycle" and related tools or systems, including:

- Content Creation Tools
- Content Management Systems (CMS)
- Customer Relationship Management (CRM)
- Web publishing systems
- Access Control
- And so forth

In companies, a certain workflow process is established. As modifications of an existing workflow process is very expensive or maybe not possible, deploying DRM systems must not result in any change. This is even more important when techniques or solutions are applied for the protection of content. The protection level of some protection technology is time dependent; it might depend on the time and effort attackers spent in breaking it. If some content requires the highest protection level, the involved protection technology must be updated regularly. Therefore, changes of the workflow process are not manageable. But DRM systems must not only fit in the workflow process, but should also support it.

The general interest in DRM system is reflected in Microsoft's ambitious goal to include a complete DRM system within their operating system. However, there are strong concerns about the integration of DRM functionality in operating systems as discussed, for example, by Anderson (2003, 2004) and the Electronic Frontier Foundation (EFF, http://www.eff.org/).

## Content Creation and Management

In business application scenarios dealing with content creation and management, DRM technology can be integrated in the content creation tools and the content management system. The main motivation for this is that content is always stored together with metadata. This metadata may include contract rights or licensing rights.

As an alternative, rights metadata can be created by a manual input. Yet, manual input is expensive as well as error-prone. Thus, a DRM system allows the automation of metadata creation and guarantees its consistency, even if compound works are created. For example, an audiovisual presentation might contain several individual images, video sequences, songs, and speech, which have their individual rights. Content creation and authoring software involving a DRM system can automatically deal with these rights issues, and also solve problems when extracts of such a kind of audiovisual sequence are created.

Besides the storage of rights in a DRM system, fingerprinting and watermarking technologies can link media to the corresponding set of rights. Thus, even a link between the rights and the rights is possible when a media break happened. These content management systems (CMS) integration issues are addressed by Rosenblatt and Dykstra (2003a, 2003b).

## Web Publishing and Customer Relationship Management

Deployment of DRM solutions in consumer-related areas typically involve the sales of digital content. This has to be done via an online catalogue or portal. DRM solutions provide the necessary technologies to achieve different business models that better suit the wishes of customers. These business models may include subscription-based services, free time-limited trials, or pay-per-rendering, and can be chosen independently for different customers.

Further improvements are possible when DRM technologies are integrated with customer relationship management systems. Therefore, the offers can be chosen, exactly matching the customers' behavior. For example, whenever a customer purchases a rendering right for a certain content, free time-limited trial rights can be created for related content. Also, the prices for products can be adapted to the usage, allowing a subtle change between pay-per-rendering and subscription based services, for example, as addressed by Rosenblatt and Dykstra (2003a, 2003b).

## Access Control

Access control is a desired criterion for content providers and contet owners. Yet, this is not a desired criterion for customers, as they generally do not accept any restrictions on content they purchased. Additionally, access control might interfere with privacy, as discussed by Cohen (2002) and considered by the EU in "Digital Rights—Background, Systems, Assessment."

This is different from companies that want to keep confidential material within their domain. Thus, enterprise content management (ECM) can be regarded as an application that very strongly demands efficient rights management systems. NGSCB and TCG lay the necessary foundation for a secure environment within business applications.[28] As the computers involved in this area are under the control of one administrator, the security assumptions within this scenario are different from the previous scenario. Also DRM systems do not interfere with privacy in this scenario. But DRM systems might interfere with other laws, as access to information can be limited to a certain time interval. And not to forget that also companies, like users, want to define when content is accessible. Both will not accept restriction imposed by third parties, which includes hardware and operating system developers.

## Examples for Conflicts between Security and Consumer Issues

Here, two examples are given how the security intention of DRM systems can interfere with consumer issues and sometimes even with law. These incompatibilities can be created artificially

for the protection of content, for example, in the case of Macrovision. Also, a proprietary format can result in incompatibilities, for example, in the case of Sony.

- Macrovision's video copy protection system (http://www.macrovision.com/) is a popular product for protecting video content. It was originally developed for video home systems (VHS). An additional copy protection signal is inserted in the part of the video signal used to control the TV (vertical blanking interval and extra synchronization pulses). The idea is that this kind of noise does not interfere with the screen representation of the visual content. But if a video cassette recorder (VCR) tries to make an exact copy of the video signal containing the copy protection signal, it will fail drastically (for the visual content). Interestingly, this idea worked fine with TVs produced before Macrovision's protection system was developed. However, with the growing numbers of DVD devices, people found out that for some TV sets, the only possibility is to connect the DVD to the screen via the VCR. Although the signal is passed only through the VCR in this case, some activate their video-scrambling chip, leading to the same distortion as descried earlier. Additionally some TVs are not capable of resolving the Macrovision signal due to the bas synchronisation pulses. And the Macrovision's video copy protection system delayed the development of DVD players with a progressive[29] output signal.
- Not only Apple with iTunes insists on proprietary format and unrevealed applicaton programming interfaces (APIs); also does (or did) Sony. BETAMAX is an example where Sony failed with a proprietary format. Sony founder Akio Morita saw the reason in the missing license possibilities, resulting in the fact that the inferior VHS system reached a critical mass. Besides BETAMAX, Mi-

croMV was another proprietary format that was abandoned, although it was introduced recently in 2002. Another proprieraty format is ATRAC3, Sony Minidisc format. Even the memory sticks used in Sony's digital cameras and PDAs are proprietary.

Incompatibility, as it regularly has happened with Macrovision's video copy protection system, is also an issue for the protection of music CDs. Incompatibilities interfering with a trouble-free enjoyment led to the creation of "negative lists" like UnCD (cf. http://www.heise.de/ct/cd-register/). Proprietary formats are always critical. For example, Microsoft Office documents can hardly be exported to software products produced by other vendors. But for protected content, this is even more critical. On the one hand content encryption parameters have to be known. On the other hand the representation is unknown.

Potential problems can be foreseen not only in the case of a proprietary format: Customers will not be happy if a proprietary format is abandoned. But furthermore, there is one aspect that is never considered by industry. Archives must provide access to content, even after years of its creation and distribution. They will fail poorly. Today it is already a problem to access content in old formats stored on outdated devices, as hardware and software for access is missing. This problem will become much more severe with encrypted content whose decryption keys are not accessible anymore.

## Further Criteria

In addition to the previously mentioned characteristics that should be considered, further criteria that should be evaluated include:

- **Degree of protection:** As described before, one has to be clear who the potential attackers are and what kind of attacks can be performed. On the one hand, typical customers should not be able to break the system. On the other hand, commercially oriented product pirates should not be able to attack a DRM-system successfully. Both groups can be distinguished by their knowledge and the available tools. Especially for commercially oriented pirates there is almost always a possibility to break the security of a DRM-system, as they expect a monetary benefit. Firstly, they can hire professional security experts[30] who have the necessary knowledge. Secondly, they can buy the necessary equipment. Therefore, a huge variety of attacks can be performed, including attacks penetrating hardware.[31]

- **Known attacks:** Considering the security of DRM-systems, one important question is: Are there any known attacks against the complete DRM-system or against individual components? As any DRM system is as strong as its weakest component, one has to consider this aspect carefully. In some cases the weakest points might even be humans. For example, if people are interested in hacking a server, sometimes the easiest way might be to bribe its administrator for creating security holes, which can be exploited easily. Besides the knowledge of successful attacks, details about the attack itself are important, including the effort and the consequences. On the one hand a successful attack might take a lot of time, involve expert knowledge, and has to be performed on each digital item. On the other hand an exploit of the system might have been discovered, resulting in a software patch available on the Internet. Balancing the negative effects, it is obvious that the second kind of attack is much more severe and might almost destroy the security of the whole DRM-system. This is not a theoretic or potential threat. The software industry experienced that hackers[32] react fast and sometimes publish new exploits within a few days in the Internet.

- **Usability:** Any hindrance to content access caused by DRM systems directly reduces user acceptance. Thus, an ideal DRM-system should not be experienced by any user unless a user has the intention to violate the licensing conditions. Unfortunately, this is practically not realizable, as operations cannot be qualified in (current) DRM-systems. For example, a DRM-system cannot distinguish between a legal[33] format conversion and an illegal one. As a consequence, a DRM system prevents all operations that potentially lead to a violation of licensing conditions.[34] One of these effects is the denial of copying in DRM-systems, leading to strong impacts on accustomed ease of handling content.

- **Compatibility:** An important aspect of usability is compatibility. The rendering of content should not be limited to a specific class of devices. This is a major obstacle of today's DRM systems. Although there are ongoing standardization issues, no compatible DRM exists yet.

- **Current popularity:** Obviously, content owners and distributors are in favor of DRM as it supports them in protecting content. Due to restrictions imposed by DRM systems and due to privacy issues most users are against DRM systems. However, the success of iTunes shows that DRM solutions, which are not as restrictive or obvious, are acceptable for customers.

- **Future trends:** DRM is a relatively young issue and one which addresses not only rationality, but also feelings. Also little experience was gained so far with its application. The development of new DRM systems with different kinds of restrictions will show what will be acceptable for customers, practically.

## Summary

Obviously, DRM covers a wide range of technologies and also touches legal issues, which makes this topic quite complex. DRM's main purpose is the protection of content. Content security is a very important issue, although not easy to achieve. As a consequence, operating systems implement more and more functionality needed for the protection of content. Their initial implementations, TCG and TCPA, experienced strong resistance, for example, as privacy and traditional content usage are not guaranteed. Nevertheless, there are a lot of hardware systems, especially laptops and mobile phones, that already include the basic functionality. This is almost unknown to most users as this functionality is not used yet.

As explained before, user acceptance is very crucial for the success of business models as well as for the success of DRM systems. Among the important aspects is compatibility and traditional content usage. This does not mean that customers will not accept DRM. Apple shows with its iTunes Music Store—it has a less restrictive content protection policy—that customers indeed are actually willing to pay for DRM-protected content. Nevertheless, iTunes is under strong discussions due to its restrictive DRM solution, from a legal point of view, for example, as in Norway or in France.

## TECHNOLOGICAL POSSIBILITIES AND PRACTICAL LIMITATIONS

*In dreams and in love there are no impossibilities.*

Janos Arany

Content distribution depends on the underlying business model. Therefore, the objective of this section is to describe how DRM can support different business models. For further information, the reader is suggested to consult Rosenblatt

*Figure 8. The traditional music value chain involves different players for composition, selection, production, and recording, copyright and licensing, marketing and promotion, manufacturing, distribution, sales, consumption, and innovation.*

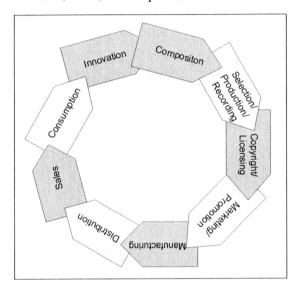

(2002), Dubosson-Torbay et al. (Dubosson-Torbay, Pigneur, & Usunier, 2004) or Bockstedt et al. (Bockstedt, Kauffman, & Riggins, 2005).

## Traditional Music Industry Value Chain

A simplified traditional music industry value chain is shown in Figure 8. Its purpose is to exemplify the influence of digital representation and DRM on content distribution. For specific content like audio or sheet music, the content value chain varies. Different chain links can be identified in the general content value chain:

1. Composition
2. Selection, production, and recording
3. Copyright and licensing
4. Marketing and promotion
5. Manufacturing
6. Distribution

7. Sales
8. Consumption
9. Innovation

This value chain can be considered as a value circle: Existing content is typically the starting point for innovation, which is already the case for the traditional value chain.[35]

## Digital Music Industry Value Chain

The digital content representation strongly influences the production and distribution of music. Music has become or is becoming a digital good. As a consequence of the digital representation of music, the processing and distribution possibilities are extended. These new possibilities not only blur the boundaries in the traditional content value chain. The result is a downsized content value chain, as shown in Figure 9:

1. Composition, production, and recording
2. Copyright and licensing
3. Marketing and promotion, distribution, sales
4. Consumption
5. Innovation

## Influence of DRM on the Digital Music Industry Value Chain

In Figure 9 we showed the influence of digitalization. DRM provides further potentials for content creators and content owners: DRM enables control on content usage. Thus content consumption and innovation can be influenced or controlled with DRM. As the basis for DRM are digital (representation of) license, copyright and licensing can be simplified, also as shown in Figure 10. This is so far ongoing development. For example in the AXMEDIS (http://www.axmedis.org) project, the simplification of licensing issues is a central aspect.

*Figure 9. The digital music industry value chain is downsized through the possibilities of digital content representation and its distribution. From content and rights owners' point of view, this allows more efficient content distribution to customers. Furthermore, due to the loss of hardware costs and the capabilities of the computers, more tasks can be performed with less equipment. Obviously, the cycles are rigorously shorter than in the traditional content value chain.*

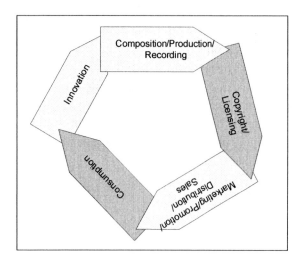

Traditionally, a content creator benefits from the composition of the new content and its sale or derived contents thereof. Due to the digitalization, the content creator benefits as selection, production, and recording, marketing and promotion, manufacturing, and distribution is easier and more strongly connected. DRM furthermore has potentials in copyright and licensing, consumption, and innovation. This is shown in Figure 10.

## Business and License Models

Different business and corresponding license models can be implemented considering the potentials of digital distribution and DRM. The common ones are listed. Further business and license models are described by Dubosson-Torbay et al.

*Figure 10. Influence of digitalization and DRM on the content value chain: Traditionally, a content creator benefits from the composition of the new content and its sale or derived contents thereof (labeled with "1"). Due to the digitalization the content creator benefits as selection, production, and recording, marketing and promotion, manufacturing, and distribution is easier and more strongly connected (labeled with "2"). Due to DRM, potentials can be exploited in the areas copyright and licensing, consumption, and innovation (labeled with "3").*

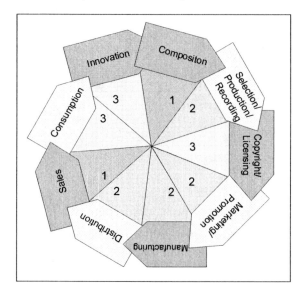

(2004). They focus on the influence of emerged P2P legal distribution of free content and illegal distribution of copyright protected content:

• License per content and license per collection of content (paid downloads).
• License per rendering (pay-per-view, pay-per-listen, …).
• License for a specific number of renderings or for a specific time frame.
• Distributed retail by distributing content to retailers (super distribution).
• Super distribution in P2P environments.

- Subscription based services.
- License according to usage.

## Licensing Rights

Instead of distributing the content, the rights can be "sold." Of course digital rights management also should address these business models, as selling rights involves rights transactions among commercial organizations.

## Summary

DRM provides the possibility to implement a different business model, for example, based on the content consumption. The success of DRM-enabled business models is decided by the customers' acceptance. Furthermore, a successful DRM solution supports business models and does not require the business models to be adapted to the DRM system.

Practically, it does not matter if the business models are adopted models from the physical world, new business models, or a combination of both. Naturally, the business models must be derived from the needs of the customers, which is a well-known fact from the physical world. Yet, new technologies provide possibilities for further products and services.

It should be also stressed here that only few content creators' primary income in the music domain is based on the commercial distribution of their music or songs. A huge part lives on secondary sources, like live performances or ring tones. Thus, limiting access to content is not in the interest for these artists. As a consequence, each artist has to decide carefully the personal pros and cons before applying existing DRM technologies to her/his content.

## TOWARDS THE CUSTOMERS

*All government—indeed, every human benefit and enjoyment, every virtue and every prudent act—is founded on compromise and barter.*

Edmund Burke

Although music labels were strongly in favor of CD copy protection technologies, more and more music labels do not apply CD copy protection technologies anymore. Users did not appreciate this technology that they practically realized as an obstacle.

This is something content owners and distributors have to understand. Maybe the following statement explains the users' restrictions best: "I will accept your DRM protected content if you accept my DRM-protected money!" Thus, new solutions are needed considering the customers' requirements and objections. Similarly, the decision of a French court against DVD copy protection shows that new approaches have to be developed. In this section, we summarize recently developed and on-going developments that better consider customers' requirements.

Obviously, DRM and content protection is still a hot topic. But as shown by Apple's iTunes MusicStore, and some others that want to get a share from Apple's success, users potentially accept content protection technologies. Nevertheless, there are ongoing developments that focus on the user requirements that have not been sufficiently considered yet.

### Interoperable DRM

One of the major reasons customers are very reluctant against it is compatibility, respectively, the lack of compatibility. "Buy once, listen anywhere and anytime" is not possible with current DRM systems. Actually, this was one of the reasons why customers reject copy protected CDs: They cannot be played on all consumer devices (including computers).

In the digital world the situation is even more complex: Having different storage carriers, different media encodings and recently, different DRM containers dramatically increases the difficulties in exchanging content.[36] And for ordinary users this is a big issue: they are interested in enjoying content; they neither want to be bothered with any technical detail nor with any problem.

As described before, there are ongoing efforts that address compatible DRM, which we include:

- **CORAL:** The Coral Consortium is "a cross-industry group to promote interoperability between digital rights management (DRM) technologies used in the consumer media market. The Consortium's goal is to create a common technology framework for content, device, and service providers, regardless of the DRM technologies they use. This open technology framework will enable a simple and consistent digital entertainment experience for consumers." (http://www.coral-interop.org/)
- **DMP:** The Digital Media Project is a not-for-profit organization with the mission to "promote continuing successful development, deployment and use of Digital Media that respect the rights of creators and rights holders to exploit their works, the wish of end users to fully enjoy the benefits of Digital Media and the interests of various value-chain players to provide products and services." (http://www.dmpf.org/)
- **ISMA:** The Internet Streaming Media Alliance's goal is "to accelerate the adoption and deployment of open standards for streaming rich media content such as video, audio, and associated data, over Internet protocols." (http://www.isma.tv/)
- **OMA:** Open Mobile Alliance is similar to ISMA, which is not limited to a specific technology, but is in favor of a certain range of applications, OMA wants to promote the

usage of mobile devices. Its mission is "to facilitate global user adoption of mobile data services by specifying market driven mobile service enablers that ensure service interoperability across devices, geographies, service providers, operators, and networks, while allowing businesses to compete through innovation and differentiation." (http://www.openmobilealliance.org/)

Unfortunately, there is a competition between the different standardization activities. It is very interesting to see how the different standardization activities developed during the last years a good summary is given by Rosenblatt (2004, 2005, 2006, 2006b).

In the mobile area, OMA so far succeeded in the sense that new mobile phones already integrate OMA-DRM. The new extension of OMA addressing entertainment devices at home thus seems promising, although OMA seems to have slowed down. DMP seems to lack a user group and electronics companies, and still is in the specification phase in contrast to CORAL, which already showed how to build interoperable DRM, for example, with Microsoft Windows Media DRM. CORAL would benefit from Apple that should publish their interfaces. In addition to these activities, Sun initiated a project called Open Media Commons (http://www.openmediacommons.org/). For this open source "DRM/everywhere available" (DReaM), no license cost should limit its usage. If a reliable security level can be guaranteed in open source, DRM has to be proven in the future. The first implementation, however, is already limited to IPTV. The first implementations are expected in 2007.

## Less Interfering DRM

Developing interoperable DRM systems is only one direction for improving the usability of DRM-protected content. Another direction is not to develop new formats and devices, but to use existing formats and embedding customer information. This has been described before as transaction watermarks.

One example for this is the Light Weight Digital Rights Management (http://www.lwdrm.com/), which cooperates with consumers. It distinguishes between locally bound and signed content in which user certificates are enclosed. As these user certificates link the content to users, users are expected to be very reluctant in distributing this personalized content.

The philosophy behind this is quite simple, like the car's license plate: In principle, the users can do anything with their content. There is no restriction unless the content is not distributed to others. If such personified content occurs on illegal file sharing networks, the responsible user can be identified and blamed for this. This is similar if a driver violates a speed limit and can be punished for this.

Besides the usage aspect—traditional content usage is not prevented—user awareness is increased: Users become responsible for the content they purchase.

## New Developments in P2P-Networks

There are also ongoing developments that try to commercialize the distribution in P2P networks. One approach is to distribute DRM-protected content via P2P networks. Examples are Napster (http://www.napster.com/) for audio content or in-2movies (http://www.in2movies.de/in2movies/) for video content. Besides these traditional approaches, new developments that avoid classical DRM protection methods have been developed.

## Music2Share

Kalker et al. (Kalker, Epema, Hartel, Lagendijk, & van Steen, 2004) presented a solution where each client integrates fingerprinting and watermarking techniques. By this the system allows the identification of the content exchanged. Simplified,

before a client is allowed to receive content, his/her request is evaluated from a trusted third party to identify, if he/she already licensed the content. If so, the content is transferred to the customer. This allows putting different business models on top of existing P2P networks. After receiving the content, the content is encrypted or put in a DRM container, together with the licensing information retrieved from the TTP. Again, users experience restrictions when content is DRM protected.

## The "Social Distribution Network" (SDN)

User awareness and user responsibility are the key concepts of the so-called social distribution networks (SDNs), as presented by Schmucker (2004) and Schmucker and Ebinger (2005a).[37]

The authors motivate them by the following train of thoughts:

- Perfect content protection is not possible. There are always security leaks like the analog hole. This has to be considered when efforts are spent for the development, integration, or usage of DRM. This means that at least specialists "unprotect" DRM protected content.
- Content exchange via the Internet cannot be controlled.
- Unknown artists do not care about DRM and illegal distribution, as their primary income is not from record sales but from performances, ring tones, and so forth. Nevertheless, they deserve a platform for the exchange, and especially the promotion of their content. This platform requires the possibility to stop the delivering of content upon request.
- Users are not bad. Costumers will not redistribute illegal copies to harm artists. Instead they are willing to pay a reasonable amount of money for music that is unrestricted in its usage.

- Costumers will support artists by promoting content. Additionally, they will create additional metadata. This additional metadata further promotes artists' content.

Commercial DRM-protected content is less attractive and competes with illegally distributed content that does not have any usage limitations.

A distribution system that integrates consumers is most attractive if it is based on P2P networks: "Let them make work (pay) for you" is the direct benefit for artists. P2P users pay for storage and bandwidth. A P2P-based architecture was presented by Schmucker and Ebinger (2005b) that considered those issues mentioned earlier, and provides a framework for the secure exchange of unprotected content.

Everybody who is registered can distribute content in the P2P network. User awareness is a central issue. It is achieved by the feedback to the customers: If the content that should be distributed is already registered as nonsharable, the user gets a message and cannot distribute this content. In contrast, if this content is not registered, the user has to register it to him/her. After this registration, content can be distributed freely within the P2P network.

Due to the fact that content itself is not DRM protected, this distribution network is very interesting for the promotional distribution of content, especially for relatively unknown artists.

## New Licensing and Business Models

In addition to the technological developments, new licensing and business models are being developed. In general, they are not limited to a certain distribution channel. Some of them are presented here.

## Super Distribution

The Potato-System (http://www.potatosystem.com/) and WeedShare (http://www.weedshare.com/) are typical super distribution business models. The users who distribute content of artists get money for the distribution if the recipient buys the music.

## Creative Commons

Creative Commons provides a set of copyright licenses free for public use. (http://creativecommons.org/). One can select a suitable license easily, based upon some preferences/selections. This license model is related to GNU Public License (GPL) and EFF Open Audio License. Some projects evolved from creative commons like science commons (http://sciencecommons.org/) or iCommons, which aims at a "united global commons front" (http://icommons.org/).

## Fisher's License Model

Fisher's license model is based on a low-rate subscription. Fisher (2004) showed in detail how such a model could work, and Orlowski (2004) analyzed it.

## German Academic Publisher

German Academic Publishers (http://www.gap-portal.de/) is developing a new model for the design and administration of electronic publications. It is especially interested in the scientist's need for "Open Access."

## Summary

Customers' acceptance is the most critical issue of content protection technology. Thus, current developments try to solve today's systems' flaws. An interesting aspects is to raise consumers awareness and their responsibility, while incorporating them in the distribution of content either buy online reputation systems or by using their resources. There is a huge potential in the user communities, as examples in other areas show. Interestingly, the successful content distribution platforms, like YouTube (http://www.youtube.com) or BeSonic (http://www.besonic.com), incorporate users in producing, rating, and ranking content, but not in its distribution.

Return on investment (ROI) or return on capital employed (ROCE) plays an important role for nonprofit as well as for commercial organizations. Both judge solutions' and technologies' benefit according to their ROI. ROI is even more important if venture capital is involved, or a company is listed in the stock market.

One problem of general security solutions is to measure this return on investment. Costs for new technology can be measured accurately, but what about the saved amount of money? The problem return on security invest (ROSI) is currently highly debated.

As DRM belongs to the category of security mechanisms, the same problems arise here. Yet, additional return on investment factors can be identified:

- Cost saving resulting from electronic stock.
- Cost saving resulting from traditional content delivery (including packaging or redelivery).
- Flexibility and scalability of the online solution (business model can be changed or adopted easily).
- Improved services to customers (e.g., availability, transmission speed, …).
- Improved customer relationship management.
- Improved monitoring capabilities.
- Improved brand loyalty.

Again, these returns are difficult to measure. But it should be clear that the benefit of a modern combined distribution and DRM solution is far beyond the return on investment by protection of content after the point of purchase.

Bomsel and Geffroy (2004) characterized the economic characteristics of DRM. Two main economic functions of DRM are defined: content protection and versioning. Then, the mechanisms of DRM adaptations are analyzed. Network effects are considered in this analysis. Interestingly, this analysis distinguishes between open and dedicated networks for content delivery. For example, mobiles are considered a one-way dedicated channel for content delivery. Although the analysis identified the DRM's significance for content delivery, three obstacles are identified for DRM's roll-out in open architectures (in contrast to dedicated networks).

1. "The current economic model of Internet access … does not favour non free open services."
2. "In broadband networks, pay content distribution conflicts with the network effects pulling the roll-out."
3. "Content owners may push alternative networks."

According to Bomsel and Geffroy (2004), one consequence is that "broadband open networks may give priority to two way communication services … rather than to pay models for digital media content distribution."

## THE FUTURE SOLUTION

Again we would like to emphasize that DRM systems integration within other solutions, like content management systems, will increase their benefit most. Aspects that cannot be neglected in the design and decision process include the business models and the workflow process. Depending on the customers, a less-restrictive DRM, for example, lightweight DRM, might even be the better solution.

The change in the hardware and software solutions for content distribution is still ongoing. Their tendency is going into the direction of "trusted computers" or "trusted devices." Independently how long it takes to achieve these ambitious goals, which have some advantages and also some drawbacks, customers have to accept these solutions and also to pay for them. This development towards "trusted devices" is highly debated, as it seems to endanger the right for "free speech" and free information exchange. Future solutions of trusted computers might allow the customers a more flexible key management away from hardware keys stored in machines, but with keys stored in smart cards. This will also be influenced by other standardization activities like DMP, OMA, CRF, or CORAL.

So what the future might bring is hard to say, as history already told us that not the best solution must succeed in the long run.[38] Nevertheless, GartnerG2 and the Berkman Center for Internet & Society presented "five possible scenarios for copyright law applicable to digital media in the United States" in the report "Five Scenarios for Digital Media in a Post-Napster World." These scenarios predicted losses and gains for consumer values, and costs and revenues for content owners, artists, technology CE vendors, and Internet service providers:

1.  The no-change scenario is based on the assumption that DMCA is still enforced: "This scenario is the least likely to play out, as the entertainment industries are not likely to sit still and see their business models slowly destroyed. Media companies have already attempted to address piracy via legal, regulatory and technology solutions. They will continue to pursue solutions to what they perceive as an attack on their traditional business models. However, it is likely that the no-change scenario will prevail in the immediate future as efforts so far have yielded minimal results and piracy is still widespread."

2.  The taking property rights seriously scenario is based on the assumption that content owners and providers strongly succeed in protection of their IPRs. As a result, the gains for content owners and artists will increase together with increased cost on the overhead with violation prosecution. Technology and Internet service providers will gain marginally and the consumers will be the losers. "This scenario certainly plays to the interests of those in the media industry and copyright holders who would seek to maintain existing business models based on complete control of the content. However, it is probably the one scenario that best illustrates the chasm separating content owners/media companies from large segments of the consumer population. It is also the scenario that, if realized, would most emphatically underscore the regional differences in intellectual property laws and enforcement. "

3.  The effective technology defense scenario assumptions are that content will be distributed physically and digitally. Content is copy protected while still meeting consumers' needs. It also includes the assumption that copy protection is an ongoing cycle, which is indeed the case. "This scenario can be described as 'technology rescues the content industries from wanton copyright piracy.' However, the technological challenges are compounded by the numbers of increasingly tech-savvy consumers around the world. There is very little margin for error and the transition to universal copy protection must be relatively quick. Otherwise, media companies and artists may find that large

numbers of consumers are seeking digital content from sources other than traditional music labels, movie studios and publishers." The difference between this scenario and the second scenario is that the second scenario assumes legal reforms while the third scenario assumes technological changes.[39]

4. The compulsory license scenario assumes that the current copyright system is replaced by a system in which the creators and producers of content are compensated by the government in proportion to the "consumption" frequency. "While this scenario has its own risks—giving a government entity significant discretionary power and assuring the virtual annihilation of the physical retail market—the potential for reducing litigation, lowering the costs of enforcement and eliminating the incentive for an ongoing encryption 'arms race' make it very attractive."

5. The utility model scenario considers digital content as a public utility. Regulations are enforced by a federal regulatory body. Concerning the estimated effects, this scenario is most interesting. "Of all five scenarios presented here, this one countenances major legal, business and consumer behaviors changes. From a technology perspective, it is less complicated than might be considered. At least one technology provider currently has an offering that could track content distribution to the end user in much the same way power companies use meter-reading systems. However, music and movie producers and their businesses—not to mention conventional retail distribution entities—will be violently opposed. Music and movie producers would see their revenue models altered greatly, with the costs associated with distributing content and usage eliminated."

Thus the "utility model scenario," as described in the report "Five Scenarios for Digital Media in a Post-Napster World" by GartnerG2 and the Berkman Center for Internet & Society, might be the best solution to the current problem of the content owner. But before such a final solution is publicly accepted and established, content providers have to find their individual solutions.

## The Evolution of P2P Networks

P2P technology is constantly evolving. Thus, it is interesting to see what will be the next step in this evolution. Biddle et al. (Biddle, *England, Peinado, & Willman*, 2002) from Microsoft expect that "interconnected small world darknets" will come into existence. In this network type, small groups of people exchange content within. The different groups are connected through people being a member of several groups. Due to the structure, it is very difficult to control and therefore to stop exchange within it.

This development has gone far beyond from shared file systems. Friendster (http://www.friendster.com/) indicated this development and was also one of Napster's success factors according to Roettgers (2004): Communities were part of Napster. And solutions like AllPeers (http://www.allpeers.com/) enable content sharing with friends and family directly via a Web browser plug-in.

Current P2P rather satisfies the users' need for anonymity due to the legal pressure. "The Free Network Project" (http://freenet.sourceforge.net/) is probably the P2P network addressing this requirement for anonymity best. It "is entirely decentralized and publishers and consumers of information are anonymous. Without anonymity there can never be true freedom of speech, and without decentralization the network will be vulnerable to attack." Although its intended aim is to stop censorship, it can also be misused for illegal content exchange. And other developments are ongoing as well.

This is in contradiction to the trust-based communities like Friendster. Incorporating trusted communities in P2P networks will result in "social P2P networks." They will exist in parallel to the anonymous P2P networks.

Besides legal measures and court trials, the evolution of P2P technology also resulted in the evolution of technology, which can be used as countermeasures against illegal distribution. One popular approach is the introduction of wrong or manipulated files in the P2P networks. Fingerprinting solutions are used in commercial and educational environments as well as in the P2P-networks, for example, in Napster. Also, the Internet traffic is statistically analyzed to identify potential P2P applications. Early 2007, YouTube announced that it will also deploy fingerprinting technologies for IPR protection.

Instead of fighting P2P networks, advantages are more and more realized. For example, P2P networks can be used for promotion of new material. Additionally, P2P networks are a distribution channel, as recently used by George Michael. Furthermore, content is exchanged between people. Statistical analysis can be performed on this exchange with the aim to identify new trends in music, as done by Big Champagne (http://www.bigchampagne.com/).

## The Analogue Hole

DRM developments aim at trusted systems: Systems that cannot be "manipulated" by users. But there is a general flaw in trying to protect content: the analogue hole. There must be a version of the content that can be accessed by humans: Images and videos are visualized and audio is played. The resulting signal, which is intended for human spectators or listeners, can also be recorded in a digital format again. In this case, watermarking, if it is sufficiently robust, presents the only possibility to trace back the origin of the leakage. This might not be possible somewhere in the future, when electrodes directly stimulate the brain. But in the meantime, an analog signal has to be presented to the ears or the eyes.

There are already companies trying to address exactly this problem. For example, DarkNoiseTechnologies[40] tries to insert a "dark noise" in the signal, with the aim that recorded versions of the signal suffer severe distortions.

## Examples for Music Distribution

Within this chapter, an overview about the technological aspects of audiovisual protection was provided. As already discussed, protection solutions have to form a unity with other technologies, for example, CMS or CRMS, in distribution systems. Different online music distribution services are described in several reports at the Interactive Musicnetwork (http://www.interactivemusicnetwork.org).

All of them apply DRM technology. Although in the case of Apple iTunes MusicStore, the DRM is less restrictive and allows burning CDs. Maybe this is one of the reasons why Apple's approach is the most successful so far.

## Summary

In spite of all efforts, the current situation is controversial: From a consumer's perspective, any usage restriction reduces content value. From a content owner's perspective, digital content cannot be distributed without any protection. Hence, a compromise must be found between the consumers and the content owners. So far DRM is not generally accepted.

Nevertheless, DRM has the potential to be part of this compromise. For example, the versioning, as identified by Bomsel and Geffroy (2004), provides interesting opportunities. However, the content owners have to be aware that the new possibilities in usage control that are offered by DRM, are neither wanted nor enjoyed by customers today. It seems that in early 2007, the music industry realizes the problems caused by current DRM systems. But alternatives that are attractive for content owners and customers so far are still missing.

Thus, each content owner has to perform an objective analysis on the individual DRM usage. This analysis has to consider his/her needs and the needs and the requirements of the customers as well. Only by this, realistic opportunities can be identified in contrast to the hopes and expectations that were initially created by technology developers. Only then, DRM has realistic chances to be a valuable technology.

Not to be forgotten, that technology is often used in different ways, as initially intended by its developers. The potentials and the future usage of DRM might also be different from its initial intensions. Thus, continuously analyzing new application scenarios and technologies that were initially not covered by DRM technology is mndatory.

# REFERENCES

Allamanche. E., Herre. J., Hellmuth. O., Froba. B., & Cremer, M. (2001). AudioID: Toward content-based identification of audio material, In *Proceedings 110th AES*, Amsterdam, The Netherlands.

American Library Association. (2005). *Digital rights management and libraries*. Retrieved March 20, 2007, from http://www.ala.org/ala/washoff/WOissues/copyrightb/digitalrights/digitalrightsmanagement.htm

Anderson, R. (2003). *Trusted computing—Frequently asked questions*, August, 2003. Retrieved March 21, 2007, from http://www.cl.cam.ac.uk/~rja14/tcpa-faq.html

Anderson, R. (2004). *Economics and security resource page, 2004*. Retrieved March 21, 2007, from http://www.cl.cam.ac.uk/~rja14/econsec.html

Arnold, M., Schmucker, M., & Wolthusen, S. (2003). *Techniques and applications of digital wtermarking and content protection*. Boston: Artech House.

Arrest in 'Screener' Upload Case. *CBS News*, Los Angeles, January 23, 2004. Retrieved March 21, 2007, from http://www.cbsnews.com/stories/2004/02/18/entertainment/main600881.shtml

Bell, T. W. (2007). *Music copyrights table*. Retrieved March 20, 2007, from http://www.tomwbell.com/teaching/Music(C)s.html

Biddle, P., England, P., Peinado, M., & Willman, B. (2002). The darknet and the future of content distribution. *Microsoft Corporation, 2002 ACM Workshop on Digital Rights Management*. Retrieved from http://crypto.stanford.edu/DRM2002/darknet5.doc

Bockstedt, J. C., Kauffman, R. J., & Riggins, F. J. (2005). The move to artist-led online music distribution: Explaining structural changes in the digital music market. In *Proceedings of the 38th Hawaii International Conference on System Sciences, 2005*. Retrieved from http://misrc.umn.edu/workingpapers/fullpapers/2004/0422_091204.pdf

Bomsel, O., & Geffroy, A. G. (2004). *Economic analysis of digital rights management systems (DRMs)*. MediaNet Project Paper, December, 2004. Retrieved from http://www.cerna.ensmp.fr/Documents/OB-AGG-EtudeDRM.pdf

Camp, L. J. (2003). First principles of copyright for DRM Design. *IEEE Internet Computing, 7*(3).

Cano, P., Baltle, E., Kalker, T., & Haitsma, J. (2002). A review of algorithms for audio fingerprinting. *IEEE Workshop on Multimedia Signal Processing*.

Cohnen, J. E. (2002). *DRM and privacy*. Research Paper Series, Research Paper No. 372741, Georgetown University Law Center.

Commission Staff Working Paper, SEC. (2002). *Digital rights—Background, systems, assessment, 197*, February, Brussels.

*Copyright Issues for Music.* Music Library, University at Buffalo. Retrieved March 20, 2007, from http://ublib.buffalo.edu/libraries/units/music/copyright.html

Cox, I. J., Miller, M. L., & Bloom, J. A. (2002). Digital watermarking. In *The Morgan Kaufmann Series in Multimedia Information and Systems.* San Francisco: Morgan Kaufmann Publishers.

Craver, S. A., Wu, M., Liu B., Stubblefield, A., Swartzlander, B., Wallach, D. S., Dean, D., & Felten, E. W. (2001). Reading between the lines: Lessons from the SDMI challenge. In *Proceedings of the 10ᵗʰ USENIX Security Symposium*, Washington, DC.

Dubosson-Torbay, M., Pigneur, Y., & Usunier, J. C. (2004). Business models for music distribution after the P2P revolution. In *WEDELMUSIC '04: Proceedings of the Web Delivering of Music, Fourth International Conference on Web Delivery Of Music.* Washington, DC: IEEE Computer Society.

EBU metadata specifications. *European Broadcasting Union (EBU).* Retrieved March 21, 2007, from http://www.ebu.ch/en/technical/metadata/specifications/index.php

FBI Arrests Internet Movie Pirate. *FOX News*, January 23, 2004. Retrieved March 21, 2007, from http://www.foxnews.com/story/0,2933,109272,00.html

Felten, E. (2001). *Statement at the fourth international information hiding workshop in Pittsburgh.* Retrieved from http://www.cs.princeton.edu/sip/sdmi/sdmimessage.txt

Fisher, W. (2004). Promises to keep—*Technology, law, and the future of rntertainment.* Retrieved March 23, 2007, from http://www.tfisher.org/PTK.htm

GartnerG2 and the Berkman Center for Internet & Society. (2003). *Five scenarios for digital media in a post-Napster world.* Retrieved March 21, 2007, from http://cyber.law.harvard.edu/home/research_publication_series

Greek, D. (2004). *RIAA crackdown shows signs of success.* Retrieved March 20, 2007, from http://www.vnunet.com/vnunet/news/2124044/riaa-crackdown-shows-signs-success

Grimm, R. (2005). *Privacy for digital rights management products and their business cases.* Virtual Goods Workshop at IEEE Axmedis 2005, Firence, Italy, December.

Haitsma, J., van der Veen, M., Kalker, K., & Brueker, F. (2000). *Audio watermarking for monitoring and copy protection.* ACM Multimedia Workshops.

Iannella, R. (2001). Digital rights management architectures. *D-Lib Magazine, 7*(6). Retrieved March 20, 2007, from http://webdoc.sub.gwdg.de/edoc/aw/d-lib/dlib/june01/iannella/06iannella.html

Intellectual property. *Wikipedia.* Retrieved March 20, 2007, from http://en.wikipedia.org/wiki/Intellectual_property

International Standard Text Code. *ISO/TC 46/SC 9 WG3 Project 21047.* Retrieved March 20, 2007, from http://www.nlc-bnc.ca/iso/tc46sc9/wg3.htm

Kalker, T., Epema, D. H. J., Hartel, P. H., Lagendijk, R. L., & van Steen, M. (2004). Music2Share—Copyright-compliant music sharing in P2P systems. *Proceedings of the IEEE, 92*(6), 961-970.

Katzenbeisser, S., & Petitcolas, F. A. P. (Eds.). (2000). *Information hiding: Techniques for steganography and digital watermarking.* Boston: Artech House.

Kerkhoffs, A. (1883). La Cryptographie Militaire. *Journal des Sciences Militaires*, 9ᵗʰ series, 5-38,161-191.

Lewis, G. J. (2003). *The German e-music industry.* Leonardo de Vinci, Faculty of Business Administration, University of Applied Sciences, Dresden, Germany. Retrieved from http://imec. hud.ac.uk/imec/iMEC%20GermanFINALrepo rt110902.pdf

Library and Archives Canada. *International Standard Music Number.* Retrieved March 20, 2007, from http://www.collectionscanada.ca/ismn/

Madden, M., & Rainie, L. (2005). *Music and video downloading moves beyond P2P.* Pew Internet & American Life Project, Retrieved from http://www.pewinternet.org/pdfs/PIP_Filesharing_March05.pdf

Man nabbed for uploading Oscar "screener." *CNet News.com*, February 22, 2007. Retrieved March 21, 2007, from http://news.com.com/2061-10802_3-6161586.html

Marion, A., & Hacking, E. H. (1998). Educational publishing and the World Wide Web. *Journal of Interactive Media in Education, 98*(2). Retrieved from http://www-jime.open.ac.uk/98/2

Menezes, A., Oorschot, P. & van Vanstone, S. (1996). *Handbook of applied cryptography.* CRC Press.

Network Working Group, The Internet Society. *RFC 1737: Functional Requirements for Uniform Resource Names.* Retrieved March 20, 2007, from http://www.ietf.org/rfc/rfc1737.txt

Network Working Group, The Internet Society. (1995). *RFC 1736: Functional Recommendations for Internet Resource Locators.* Retrieved March 20, 2007, from http://www.ietf.org/rfc/rfc1736. txt

Network Working Group, The Internet Society. (1998). *RFC 2396: Uniform Resource Identifiers (URI): Generic Syntax,* Retrieved March 20, 2007, from http://www.ietf.org/rfc/rfc2396.txt

Orlowski, A. (2004). Free legal downloads for 6$ a month. DRM free. The artists get paid. We explain how... *The Register*, February, 2004. Retrieved March 23, 2007, from http://www.theregister. co.uk/content/6/35260.html

Orlowski, A. (2005). French court bans DVD DRM. *The Register*, 26/04/2005. Retrieved March 20, 2007, from http://www.theregister. co.uk/2005/04/26/french_drm_non/

Peer-To-Peer. *Wikipedia.* Retrieved March 20, 2007, from http://en.wikipedia.org/wiki/Peer-to-peer

Peticolas, F. (2006). *Stirmark benchmark 4.0,* 06 February 2006. Retrieved March 22, 2007, from http://www.petitcolas.net/fabien/watermarking/stirmark/

Rhodes, R. (1899). *Pianola copyright ruling cited.* Retrieved March 20, 2007, from http://mmd.foxtail. com/Archives/Digests/200406/2004.06.05.03. html

Roettgers, J. (2004). *Social networks: The Future of P2P file sharing.* Retrieved from http://freebit-flows.t0.or.at/f/about/roettgers

Rosenblatt, B., Trippe, B., & Mooney, S. (2002). *Digital rights management—Business and technology.* New York: M&T Books,

Rosenblatt, B., & Dykstra, G. (2003a). *Technology integration opportunities*, November, 14, 2003. Retrieved March 21, 2007 from http://www. drmwatch.com/resources/whitepapers/article. php/11655_3112011_3

Rosenblatt, B., & Dykstra, G. (2003b). *Integrating content management with digital rights management—Imperatives and opportunities for digital content.* Lifecycles. GiantSteps, Media Technology Strategies, Technical Report. Retrieved from http://www.xrml.org/reference/CM-DRMwhite-paper.pdf

Rosenblatt, B. (2004). *Review: DRM Standards*, January 5, 2004. Retrieved March 21, 2007 from http://www.drmwatch.com/standards/article.php/3295291

Rosenblatt, B. (2005). *Review: DRM Standards*, January 6, 2005. Retrieved March 21, 2007 from http://www.drmwatch.com/standards/article.php/3455231

Rosenblatt, B. (2006). *Review: DRM Standards*, January 2, 2006. Retrieved March 21, 2007 from http://www.drmwatch.com/standards/article.php/3574511

Rosenblatt, B. (2006b). *Review: DRM Standards*, December 27, 2006. Retrieved March 21, 2007 from http://www.drmwatch.com/standards/article.php/3651126

Rudish, J. (2005). Illegal file sharing lawsuits dismissed; Emory withholds defendants' names. *The Emory Wheel Online*, April 15, 2005. Retrieved March 20, 2007, from http://media.www.emorywheel.com/media/storage/paper919/news/2005/04/15/News/Illegal.Filesharing.Lawsuits.Dismissed.Emory.Witholds.Defendants.Names-1647598.shtml

Schmucker, M. (2004). *Enlightening the Dark-Net.* IST-Workshop, November, 15th, 2004, Den Hague, Netherlands.

Schmucker, M., & Rantasa, P. (2005a). *Ein soziales Verteilungsnetzwerk—Beispiel eines alternativen Distributionsmodells.* CAST-Workshop, February 2nd, 2005, Darmstadt, Germany.

Schmucker, M., & Ebinger, P. (2005b). *Promotional and commercial content distribution based on a legal and trusted P2P framework.* CEC 2005. Seventh IEEE International Conference on E-Commerce Technology.

Scmucker, M. (2005c). *Protection of coded music.* The Interactive Musicnework. Retrieved from http://www.interactivemusicnetwork.org/documenti/view_document.php?file_id=1195

Schneier, B. (1996). *Applied cryptography* (2nd ed.). Hoboken, NJ: John Wiley & Sons.

SMEF Data Model. *British Broadcasting Corporation.* Retrieved March 21, 2007, from http://www.bbc.co.uk/guidelines/smef/

Templeton, B, (2007). *10 big myths about copyright explained.* Retrieved March 20, 2007, from http://www.templetons.com/brad/copymyths.html

Walton, T. (2003). *Golden age of free music vs. Copying is stealing.* Retrieved March 20, 2007, from http://www.theregister.co.uk/2003/08/06/golden_age_of_free_music/

Wang, X., Feng, D., Lai, x., & Yu, H. (2004). Collisions for hash functions MD4, MD5, HAVAL-128 and RIPEMD. *Cryptology ePrint Archive, Report 2004/199.* Retrieved from http://eprint.iacr.org/2004/199

Wang, X., Yin, X. L., & Yu, H. (2005). *Collision search attacks on SHA1*, February 13, 2005. Retrieved from http://theory.csail.mit.edu/~yiqun/shanote.pdf

XML and Digital Rights Management (DRM). *Cover Pages* (hosted by OASIS). Retrieved March 21, 2007, from http://xml.coverpages.org/drm.html

## ENDNOTES

[1]   For example, in the U.S., the copyright for a new composition lasts for the lifetime of the composer and additional 70 years after his death.

[2]   Generally, user anonymity is not given. All users can be traced back by their IP and with the support of the ISP. It is very important for wireless-LAN (WLAN) operator to secure access to their WLAN against misuse, as these operators are responsible for any kind of misuse.

[3]   Fair use is a statutory exemption to the copyright law.

[4]   Interestingly, the existing solutions analysed by Camp, which included copy protection as well as circumvention technologies, only partially fulfilled these requirements.

[5]   The analogue mass production ensured that a document survives unaltered and can be located.

[6]   The publishers' and broadcasting investment results in a careful selection of content.

[7]   An information collection is available at RIAA (http://www.riaa.com/).

[8]   Freenet can be summarized as a decentralized network of file-sharing nodes tied together with strong encryption and further technology, which allows anonymous users.

[9]   Besides confidentiality, other relevant aspects might be authentication, integrity, or copyright protection, which has to be addressed using different techniques.

[10]   Yet this distinction is somewhat hazy as block ciphers can be used as stream ciphers, and vice versa.

[11]   These algorithms are also known as one-way hash algorithms.

[12]   Typically a soft-hash or perceptual hash value is embedded, which is another term for fingerprinting.

[13]   A watermark in an image or audio can be used to start a plug-in in a Web browser for automatic linking the content to a certain Web site.

[14]   More or less a perceptible watermark in music scores already exists: the copyright information.

[15]   Asymmetric watermarking schemes have been developed as well, but they have some drawbacks.

[16]   Blind watermarking schemes are also called public watermarking schemes.

[17]   These are also called private watermarking schemes.

[18]   For some media types (e.g., text or music scores), embedding a watermark directly in the content is very difficult. Here, the representation is modified, which effects robustness against conversion and potentially the perceived quality.

[19]   Sometimes even the term "passive watermarking" is used, which we consider as misleading as no mark is embedded.

[20]   These secure devices are also called trusted devices, reflecting the assumption that trusts in the security of the systems can be provided.

[21]   Typically, content servers provide this functionality.

[22]   Controllers are sometimes also called "DRM controllers."

[23]   Local storage of the decrypted content depends on the business model. Some business models might allow this. Some might only allow local storage with poor quality (e.g., strongly compressed audio files).

[24]   Current solutions implement a key cache to increase the systems flexibility. But this also increases the systems vulnerability.

[25]   Of course the processing power must be sufficient.

[26]   The MAC address is a unique value associated with a network adapter, and are also

known as hardware addresses or physical addresses.

27    At least this is the case nowadays. This might change in the future if the "trusted computing" initiatives succeed. Yet consumers have to pay for this technology and they do not only benefit from it.

28    Other possible consequences, for example, software monopoles, have to be considered carefully, and a thorough observation is necessary to avoid negative effects to economy.

29    Typically, a TV set uses interlacing, which combines two "half"-images into one. DVD players are capable of producing a progressive output signal; one complete frame at once.

30    Due to their motivation "semiprofessional" hackers can be considered as a big threat.

31    Thus, people interested in the protection of their content have to be aware that the higher the monetary benefit is, the bigger is the potential danger that an attacker has commercial interests.

32    Sometimes this kind of hacker is also called crackers.

33    For example, archiving or providing access to visually impaired people are most often allowed by law.

34    Interestingly in the physical world, such a practise is not manageable or allowed. For example, knives are still sold although people can potentially be hurt.

35    There are different opinions on this on other areas, for example, as expressed by Marion and Hacking (1998). For the digital value chain this might be more evident, as content available in digital format can be processed more easily. Thus the cycles are rigorously shorter.

36    This is a general problem especially for digital archives, even without DRM: Will any device to read the content stored on a specific carrier be available in 20 or 30 years?

37    This, and the resulting architecture, was a direct result of the discussion within the MUSICNETWORK when looking for a possible decentralised solution for unknown musicians.

38    One example is the success of VHS against Betamax or Video 2000, although VHS was inferior against its competitors.

39    Although the second and the third scenarios are linked due to the results, the difference is in how rights are established and enforced.

40    Dark Noise Technologies was bought by SunnComm (http://www.sunncomm.com).

# Chapter XIV
# Online Music Distribution

**Francesco Spadoni**
*Rigel Engineering S.r.l., Italy*

## ABSTRACT

*This chapter analyses multiple aspects of online music distribution, investigating the major problems, the different approaches, and business models, considering the different points of view and perspectives, presenting the emerging technologies and digital rights management standards, analysing issues for rights clearing, intellectual property protection, content retrieval, and metadata management. The chapter presents the structure of the developing market of digital music and multimedia content distribution, considering all the stakeholders and their mutual relationships, as well as the legal framework. It highlights the importance of the needs of end users and consumers of music when considering the major problems, as well as the new behaviours and possibilities originated by the availability of music in digital form. This chapter is aimed at many different audiences, from policy makers to music end users and consumers to content creators, publishers, and distributors, as well as technology providers, and in general, to all the players in the digital music content value chain.*

## INTRODUCTION

This chapter investigates the development of *multimedia content distribution*, analysing the major problems, the different approaches, and business models, considering different aspects and views of the phenomenon. The main focus is on distribution of multimedia content using the Internet to perform transactions and/or content delivery. Key issues are business models, new technologies, and distribution media (mobile environments, Web

services, XML, Web-TV and streaming), rights clearing and content protection aspects (digital rights management), content information retrieval (metadata management). It will also consider the legal framework and the developing market of digital music, as well as the quality and accessibility of music distribution services.

The chapter analyses in depth the *structure of the market* of digital music and multimedia content distribution, considering all the stakeholders and their mutual relationships. The next sections present data and evaluate the bleeding-edge of technologies and products, systems, tools, and research, considering, at the same time, business and user needs. A section of the chapter presents and analyses the most important issues, problems, or barriers affecting the development of the multimedia content distribution sector.

The analysis revealed *the increasing importance of the needs of end users and consumers* of music when considering the major problems, as well as the new behaviours and possibilities originated by the availability of music in digital format. To this aim, copyright can represent the tool to get a trade-off between the sometimes conflicting interests of users and publishers-majors-authors, balancing the needs of the rights holder against those of society, users, and consumers.

More and more authors, copyright collecting societies, and independent labels are embracing the conviction that economic and business models generated or based on new communication and transaction schemas, like P2P, are totally *positive* in terms of distribution, selling, and knowledge of music. Such authors and their representatives are inviting the major labels to start a new innovative and creative approach, involving also the Internet Service Providers in the process, and allowing the user, paying a fee, to access music and possibly redistribute rights via the peer-to-peer and a new licensing scheme.

Adoption and proposition of *emerging standards* are considered for critical aspects of multimedia content delivery systems, as for instance, for the protected communication protocol used for communications and transactions management between the delivery systems and the related clients or third-party applications. Standardisation activities can play a primary role for the full exploitation of the Internet in terms of content exchange. In particular, the still evolving MPEG-21 ISO standard appears to fit well the music distribution scenario, providing an interoperable multimedia framework and

supporting users in accessing, exchanging, and manipulating digital music.

This chapter is aimed at *many different audiences,* from policy makers to music end users and consumers to content creators, publishers, and distributors as well as technology providers, and in general, to all the players in the digital music content value chain. Each one of the players is characterised by having a deep and very specific knowledge concerning his/her core business, but sometimes a limited understanding of the needs and processes of other players, partners, and (sometimes) even customers. Considering such a widespread target audience, every attempt has been made to make this chapter as readable and usable as possible to such differentiated audiences, while still retaining the accuracy and clarity needed in a technical report. The author tried to present an objective overview of the digital content distribution phenomenon, abstracting as much as possible from ethical and philosophical considerations concerning the boundaries of individuals' freedom of action against the enforcement of intellectual property rights.

Part of the content of this chapter is the outcome of different *activities* and initiatives performed under the framework of the Working Group on Distribution of Coded Music of the MUSICNET-WORK Project, a centre of excellence financed by the IST Program of the European Commission.

The following sections present an overview of the market for online distribution of digital music, a description of the main players in the content value chain, an overview of the major products and services, a discussion on the major problems affecting the market and the major stakeholders; a list of the basic enabling technologies; a description of emerging and promising technologies that can be used to solve some of the existing problems and/or to moderately improve the current situation; existing and emerging business models for the online distribution of digital music; new business models and approaches to the market better

*Table 1. Roles in the content distribution value-chain*

| Role | Description |
| --- | --- |
| Content Creators | Artists, multimedia creators, performers |
| Content Distributors | Broadcasters, TV, retailers (shops), Webcasters, labels, score publishers, recording industries |
| Technology Providers | Develop the technology enabling the distribution market |
| Collecting Societies | Organizations devoted to the collection of IPR payments |
| End Users | Multimedia content users (musicians, amateurs, audiophiles, …) |
| Independent Organizations | Standardisation bodies, industry organizations, independent market researchers, other special purpose organizations |
| Governmental Organizations | Policy and decision makers |
| Law Experts | Experts in legal aspects of IPR protection |
| Projects & Research Centres | Large projects, Universities, Research Centres |

accommodating the transformational change in the usage environment and users needs.

## BACKGROUND

### Main Actors in the Market

The market of digital music and multimedia content distribution can be structured according to the following categories of players and their role in the market (see Table 1).

In general these categories can present overlapping, since, for instance, a technology provider can also play the role of music distributor. Examples in such sense are Liquid Music Network and Real Networks, which provides both multimedia content distribution technologies (servers, systems, and models) and music download services (Content Village, 2004).

Content creators generally are music authors, musicians, multimedia artists, and they represent the first step in the content value chain. They are often also the very holder of the intellectual pro-

priety rights for a piece of music or multimedia content in general.

Content distributors are companies and organizations that make business at providing music to end users or resellers, buying the rights form the respective rights holders. They exploit technologies and the Internet to provide their services. Music pieces and licences are the core business for content distributors, but other revenues and value added also come from providing background information and additional services, like selling events tickets or providing direct contact between performers/authors and their fans. In some cases, publishers and labels of any dimension directly sell their music on their Internet, playing both the roles of publishers and content distributors.

Music authors and content creators are usually represented by their labels, major or Indies, or their publishers. In some (rare) cases, they might directly distribute their own music. There is also an unexplored space of the market, at this moment, however, new authors of multimedia content in various formats.

The main online content distributors currently in (or approaching) the market can be divided into the following categories (1) Music labels; (2) Publishers and distributors of music scores, which are converting their musical archives from papers to digital images and need to distribute music and multimedia content at a lower cost and to a wider audience with a strong control on the rights; (3) Company addressing the market of music and multimedia authors interested in new, direct methods of distributing their works, and promote their art and skills without companies financing costs for the distribution. As an example, *ARTISTdirect Network* (http://www.artistdirect.com) is a company that enables artists to control their own Websites, online stores, and downloadable music.

Concerning music scores, big publishers (such as Casa Ricordi) prefer to delegate the online distribution of music scores to third companies that are more focused on delivery and service for distribution of music and multimedia content. This is mainly due to the fact that the current core business for major publishers is mainly on CD audio distribution rather than on music scores or multimedia objects, their name, the label, is mainly connected to those of the authors and not the product.

## Technology Providers

Technology providers are innovators, know-how, and software developers providing technology transfers and/or tools for the management of multimedia content and related distribution and commercialisation in the net/digital world. The following list presents an overview of the main technology providers active in the market. Technology providers and software developers' typically provide their technologies to (1) content owners, (2) music publishers and music labels; (3) content providers and distributors; (4) end users.

For example, *Liquid Music Network* (Liquid Digital Media) is composed of hundreds of music and lifestyle Web sites that offer Liquid Audio downloads including Amazon.com, Barnes & Noble, Best Buy, CDNow.com, Hard Rock, HMV, J&R Music World, Sam Goody/Musicland, and Sony Music Club.

Liquid Audio is partnering with content owners and Web sites interested in promoting and selling music on the Internet. Liquid Audio also partners with consumer electronic manufactures, chipset manufacturers, and embedded operating system developers who are interested in using this technology to create secure digital music players. Liquid Audio's Consumer Electronics Partner Program provides device manufacturers, chipset providers, and embedded operating systems developers with a comprehensive digital music solution to get to market quickly with digital audio devices. Liquid Music Network also distributes its Liquid Audio Player enabling end users.

Currently there is a battle between some major technology providers. They are aggressively pushing their proprietary technologies to become market leaders. This might imply that their licensing schemes are dictating the content distribution, which is an undesired side effect. Thus, open formats and standards might be important to avoid content distribution affected by technology providers. Again, formats are not only a matter of compatibility but also a business model influencing issue.

## Copyright Collecting Societies

Copyright collecting societies are nongovernmental organizations that represent rights holders (authors, creators, and publishers), and look after the enforcement of their rights, ensuring that authors are rewarded for their creativity. The societies negotiate licences with users and receive payments that they pass on to their members. Each collecting society represents a different aspect of copyright.

Typically, Copyright Collecting Societies services their affiliates (content creators, author's, rights holders) by (CISAC 2004): (1) licensing copyrights with record companies; (2) collecting and distributing the income (royalties) earned from the exploitation of copyrights; (3) advancing the economic and creative interests of the rights holders that they represent; (4) registering copyrights throughout the world and collect mechanical and performance royalties; (5) entering into reciprocal arrangements with foreign collecting societies to collect and distribute local royalties to foreign and to receive and distribute royalties earned overseas to local rights holders; (6) providing regular royalty statements, personal service, and ongoing, aggressive pursuit of unpaid royalties; (7) issuing synchronization licenses to film, television, radio, advertising agencies, and new technologies and media (e.g., gaming, mobile phones ring-tones, flash productions); (8) additional services including subpublishing and exploitation of copyrights; (9) legal support, such as drawing up of model contracts, issuing licences, and authorising uses; negotiate rates and terms of use with users; (10) political action in favour of the effective protection of author's rights; such action can be undertaken before national or international bodies representing the author's rights community.

Copyright collecting societies fulfil their functions by means of collective administration. The status of collective administration bodies is recognised in European Union community law and national law. They are typically and historically organized on a country basis, each society dealing with and providing expertise for the specific national regulation, market, and legal framework. There is no single collective rights management body covering all countries or the entire Web. As the market has become internationalised, especially in the last decade, due to the Internet and digital revolution, and the legal framework evolved towards unified models, collecting societies started to group together at the international level.

A Brussels-based European-level umbrella body, *GESAC* (http://www.gesac.org), was created in December 1990 in the form of an EEIG (European Economic Interest Grouping) and encompasses 25 of the largest authors' societies in the EU, Norway, and Switzerland. GESAC represents around 480,000 authors or their successors in title in the area of music, visual arts, literary, dramatic works, audiovisual, and music publishers.

The International Confederation of Societies of Authors and Composers, CISAC, works towards increased recognition and protection of creator's rights. As of January 2004, CISAC represents *210 authors' societies in 109 countries*. Thus, CISAC indirectly represents more than 2 million creators, covering all the artistic repertoires: music, drama, literature, audiovisual works, graphic, and visual arts.

Another international association for music copyright is the *European Music Office* (http://www.musicineurope.org), an international not-for-profit association (under Belgium law is termed "Asbl," Association sans but lucratif) gathering professional organizations, associations, and federations from the music sector in the European Union. It represents more than 600 000 people from all music genres and sectors (authors, composers, performers, publishers, producers, managers; those involved in live music, education, and training…). EMO's mission is to promote the interests of the music sector at the European Union level. Its main objective is thus the conception and implementation by the European Union of a music policy, a specific and necessary support to the European music industry.

## End Users

Users of digital music distribution systems can be roughly divided into business users and end users.

*Business users* are music distribution organizations and companies, music labels, which are described above as current players in the market. Besides, there are a lot of smaller entities willing to enter the market of digital music, multimedia, and online distribution/interaction. They are potentially interested in acquiring a system for music and multimedia content distribution, even for small-scale distribution (for instance, distribution within their organizations). Such entities are mainly orchestras, theatres, conservatories and music schools, libraries, and mediatheques.

*End users* are mainly interested in using and interacting with music and multimedia content, accessing the catalogue from the Web, selecting and purchasing the content they need, downloading it in a protected way, and finally using it by the proper music/multimedia players. They are typically the business users' customers. By now, it is convenient to highlight the importance of the needs of users and consumers when considering the major problems, as well as the new behaviours and possibilities originated by the availability of music in digital format. As in widely adopted design models (Moore, 1991; Norman, 1998), from ICT to building houses to developing appliances, the final user should stand at the centrel of the development process and should be involved in the design process from the early stages.

Briefly, the main objective of users of digital music is to have access to the desired music, at a "good enough" quality, "reasonable" cost, and in "short" time. On the other hand, authors, creators, publishers, and other rights holders aims at widely distributing and (in the most cases) selling their music at a competitive price while maximising revenues and profit. Copyright can represent the tool to get a trade-off between these sometime conflicting interests. Copyright should be based on a *balancing principle*: the needs of the rights holder should be balanced against those of society, users, and consumers. Copyright law lists the exclusive rights (generally Publication, Reproduction, Adaptation, Public performance or display, Broadcasting) of the rights holder, which

will normally be balanced by making the work available to the public (Chiariglione, 2005).

While copyright law has existed for hundreds of years, founding a balance in the market, the advent of new technologies such as electronic storage and Internet distribution have broken such balance. The balancing principle behind copyright should be redefined in terms of the *new digital environment* to ensure that users have sufficient and easy access to music, while still protecting the interests of rights holders. This will involve publishers, recording labels, authors and users working together to understand each others needs and experimenting new solutions.

## Independent Organizations

Within the present document, and coherently to the WG activities, the term "Independent Organizations" refers to a heterogeneous group of entities composed of standardisation bodies, independent market researchers, industrial organizations, special purpose organizations.

Table 2 lists the most relevant organizations, and these organizations are briefly described in the following paragraphs.

The *Audio Engineering Society* (AES) is a professional society devoted exclusively to audio technology. Members are of leading engineers, scientists, and other authorities throughout the world. The AES serves its members, the industry, and the public by stimulating and facilitating advances in the constantly changing field of audio. It encourages and disseminates new developments through annual technical meetings and exhibitions of professional equipment, and through the Journal of the Audio Engineering Society, the professional archival publication in the audio industry.

The *AXMEDIS* (Automating Production of Cross Media Content for Multi-channel Distribution), is a resourceful large integrated project cofinanced by the European Commission. The AXMEDIS consortium consists of leading

Table 2. Independent organizations involved in music distribution

| Organization | URL |
|---|---|
| AES (Audio Engineering Society) | http://www.aes.org |
| AXMEDIS (Automating Production of Cross Media Content for Multi-channel Distribution) | http://www.axmedis.org |
| CC (Creative Commons) | http://creativecommons.org/ |
| CRF (Content Reference Forum) | http://www.crforum.org |
| DMP (Digital Media Project) | http://www.chiariglione.org/project/ |
| ISMA (Internet Streaming Media Alliance) | http://www.isma.tv |
| MPEG (Motion Picture Expert Group) | http://www.mpeg.org |
| OASIS (Organization for advancement in Structured Information Standards) | http://www.oasis-open.org |
| OeB (Open eBook Forum) | http://www.openebook.org |
| OMA (Open Mobile Alliance) | http://www.openmobilealliance.org |
| RIAA (Recording Industry Association of America) | http://www.riaa.com |
| SDMI (Secure Digital Music Initiative) | http://www.sdmi.org |
| SMPTE (Society of Motion Picture and Television Engineers) | http://www.smpte.org |
| TV-Anytime Forum | http://www.tv-anytime.org |
| WIPO (World Intellectual Property Organization) | http://www.wipo.int |
| WS-I (Web Services Interoperability Organization) | http://www.ws-i.org |
| MUSICNETWORK (Interactive MusicNetwork Project) | http://www.interactivemusicnetwork.org/ |

European digital content producers, integrators, aggregators, and distributors, as well as information technology companies and research groups. It mainly aims to build the "AXMEDIS framework" to provide innovative methods and tools to speed up and optimise content production and distribution, up to the production-on-demand capability, for leisure, entertainment, and digital content valorisation, and exploitation in general., providing new methods and tools for innovative, flexible, and interoperable digital rights management, including the exploitation of MPEG-21, and overcoming its limitations, and supporting different business and transactions models.

*Creative Commons* (CC) was founded in 2001 with the generous support of the Centre for the Public Domain. It is led by a Board of Directors that includes cyberlaw and intellectual property experts James Boyle, Michael Carroll, Molly Shaffer Van Houweling, and Lawrence Lessig, MIT computer science professor Hal Abelson, noted Japanese entrepreneur Joi Ito, and public domain Web publisher Eric Eldred. The aim of Creative Commons is to offer creators a best-of-both-worlds way to protect their works while encouraging certain uses of them, to declare "some rights reserved." Thus, a single goal unites Creative Commons' current and future projects: to build a layer of reasonable, flexible copyright in the face of increasingly restrictive default rules.

The *Content Reference Forum* (CRF) is a newly formed standards group of leading technology and content-related companies chartered to develop a universal way to distribute digital content across various mediums and geographies. Its goal is to create a dynamic marketplace where consumers can get and share the right content for their platform and preferences, and where underlying commercial agreements and rights are respected.

The *Digital Media Project* (DMP), incorporated on December 2003, is led by Dr. Leonardo Chiariglione of MPEG. DMP is still in its starting phase, having recently named a board of directors and established a membership policy. It also issued a call for submissions of information about traditional content rights and how they might map to sets of precisely described rights in the digital media world. Three major vendors of consumer media technology have expressed interest in joining the DMP and may do so after their respective internal reviews. This is good news for this very well-intentioned though wildly ambitious metastandards initiative. The bad news is that there appears to be no interest so far from any of the major media companies. Such interest will be necessary if the DMP is to have any credibility with the standards processes it intends to influence.

The *Internet Streaming Media Alliance* (ISMA) is a nonprofit corporation formed to provide a forum for the creation of specifications that define an interoperable implementation for streaming rich media (video, audio, and associated data) over Internet Protocol (IP) networks. This alliance of streaming media innovators is actively involved in the development of rights language requirements and to contribute specific domain knowledge about DRM interoperability.

The *Moving Picture Experts Group* (MPEG) is a Working Group of ISO/IEC, JTC 1 / SC 29 / WG 11 in charge of the development of international standards for compression, decompression, processing, and coded representation of moving pictures, audio, and their combination. It is expected to be advanced to International Standard by this ballot.

The *Organization for the Advancement of Structured Information Standards* (OASIS) develops standards largely based on XML, providing an open forum with broad industry participation, for the future development of the Rights Languages. OASIS founding members include Hewlett Packard, Microsoft, Reuters, VeriSign, IBM, and ContentGuard.

The *Open eBook Forum* (OeBF) is the leading international trade and standards organization for the eBook industry, running a Rights and Rules and an IP Policy Working Groups. The Rights and Rules Working Group (RRWG) has selected XrML as a foundation rights expression language for developing detailed material in its Rights Grammar specification. The Working Group has also established a formal liaison with MPEG-21.

Formed in June 2002, the *Open Mobile Alliance* (OMA) delivers open specifications for the mobile industry, helping to create interoperable services that work across countries, operators, and mobile terminals, and are driven by users' needs. To expand the mobile market, companies that support OMA work to stimulate the fast-and-wide adoption of a variety of new and enhanced mobile information, communication, and entertainment services.

The *Recording Industry Association of America* is the trade group that represents the U.S. recording industry. Its mission is to foster a business and legal climate that supports and promotes our members' creative and financial vitality. Its members are the record companies that comprise the most vibrant national music industry in the world. RIAA members create, manufacture, and/or distribute approximately

90% of all legitimate sound recordings produced and sold in the United States.

The *Secure Digital Music Initiative* (SDMI) is a forum that has brought together more than 200 companies and organizations representing information technology, consumer electronics, security technology, the worldwide recording industry, and Internet service providers. SDMI's objective is to develop open technology specifications that protect the playing, storing, and distributing of digital music such that a new market for digital music may emerge. DMAT (Digital Music Access Technology) is the trademark for products that are compliant with SDMI specifications.

The *Society of Motion Picture and Television Engineers* (SMTPE) is the leading technical society for the motion imaging industry. ContentGuard is actively engaging the Digital Cinema Technology Committee of this organization.

The *TV-Anytime* Forum is an association of organizations that seeks to develop specifications to enable audiovisual and other services based on mass-market high-volume digital storage in consumer platforms. XrML is under consideration as a standard rights expression language by their Rights Management and Protection Working Group. The Rights Management and Protection Information subgroup has developed tvax, an XrML extension for TV-Anytime.

The *World Intellectual Property Organization* is an international organization dedicated to promoting the use and protection of works of the human spirit. With headquarters in Geneva, Switzerland, WIPO is one of the 16 specialized agencies of the United Nations system of organizations. It administers 23 international treaties dealing with different aspects of intellectual property protection. The Organization counts 180 nations as member states.

The *Web Services Interoperability Organization* (WS-I) is an open, industry organization chartered to promote Web services interoperability across platforms, operating systems, and programming languages. ContentGuard is a member and will support initiatives to address Web Services security.

The *MUSICNETWORK* is "a distributed Centre of Excellence to bring the music industry, content providers and research institutions together" offering a comprehensive package of valuable services to professionals and to "everyone who is interested in the future of music and multimedia technologies" (Nesi, Zoia, Bellini, & Barthelemy 2003).

## Copyright, Author's Rights, Intellectual Property, and Fair Use

### What is Copyright

When a person creates a musical, scientific, literary, or artistic work, she/he is the owner of that work and is free to decide on its use. That person (i.e., the "creator" or the "author" or "owner of rights") can control the usage of the work. Since, by law, the work is protected by copyright from the moment it comes into being, there is no formality to be complied with, such as registration or deposit, as a condition for such protection. Ideas in themselves are not protected, only the way in which they are expressed.

*Copyright* is the legal protection extended to the owner of the rights in an original work that he/she has created. It comprises two main sets of rights: the economic rights and the moral rights (WIPO, 2004).

The *economic rights* are the rights of reproduction, broadcasting, public performance, adaptation, translation, public recitation, public display, distribution, and so on. The moral rights include the author's right to object to any distortion, mutilation, or other modification of his/her work that might be prejudicial to his/her honour or reputation (CISAC, 2004). This entitlement, which belongs initially to the author, may be transferred in order to allow a work to be exploited. In return for the transfer of rights, the author will receive remuneration, which must be proportional to the revenues generated by the exploitation of the work.

Both sets of rights belong to the creator who can exercise them. The exercise of rights means that he/she can use the work himself/herself, can give permission to someone else to use the work, or can prohibit someone else from using the work. The general principle is that copyright protected works cannot be used without the authorization of the owner of rights. Limited exceptions to this rule, however, are contained in national copyright laws. In principle, the term of protection is the creator's lifetime and a minimum of 50 years after his/her death.

At the international level, the economic and moral rights are conferred by *the Berne Convention for the Protection of Literary and Artistic Works*, commonly known as the "Berne Convention." This Convention, which was adopted in 1886, has been revised several times to take into account the impact of new technology on the level of protection that it provides. It is administered by the World Intellectual Property Organization (WIPO), one of the special-purpose international agencies of the United Nations.

The terminology concerning rights and obligations related to the use of the intellectual work of others can be quite confusing. From one country to another, people speak of author's right and copyright as if it were the same thing. Underlying this verbal blur are two differing conceptions of author's right, on which the legal systems in the world are based. *Author's right*, ("droit d'auteur" in French) is founded on the idea, born in continental Europe, that a work of creation is intimately linked with its creator. The copyright concept stems from the Anglo-Saxon tradition, according to which authors hold a property right to their creations that can be traded on the basis of economic principles (CISAC, 2004). Usually, copyright laws in most countries support a wide definition of author's right, combining the idea of "droit d'auteur" and that of copyright.

Closely linked to the discussion about copyright and author's right are the two theories, which are at the heart of current international copyright law. The first theory establishes economic rights. It provides that authors need to be rewarded for their unique creative abilities. The second theory supports the intimate connection between *author* and *work* and states that authors should be given a moral right to limit the alteration and display of their works, even after they have transferred their economic rights to a third party such as a publisher.

Authors enjoy an exclusive right to certain forms of exploitation of their works. Every time that such a work–a book, a play, a song, a painting, a film–is created, its author becomes the owner of the copyright of that work; he or she acquires the author's right. Basically, this means that the creator decides if and how his/her work will be used. To become holder of this right generally requires no formalities whatsoever. All that is needed is that a creative work becomes fixed in a tangible form. From that moment on, an author is granted legal protection, the nature of which is provided by copyright law.

The international standard for protection, established by the Berne Convention, is the life of the author and fifty years after his/her death. However, in many countries, such as the United States and in those of the European Community, the protection is extended for the life of a work's author plus an additional *70* years. Once the term expires, the work enters the public domain, where it can be freely used by anyone and in particular, it can be (1) copied by anyone without fees and form-filling; (2) published and edited in different versions and editions; (3) commercialised at fair prices with value-added features like critics and special editions.

Before the term, works are still subject to copyright, meaning in brief that only the rights holder, usually a publisher who acquired the rights after the death of the author, can decide (1) how much the work costs; (2) if the works can be published or not; (3) who distributes the work and how.

The copyright extension after the author's life was introduced at the beginning of the 18th century in the UK for an ethic consideration: to ensure an economic support to the author's family for a reasonable period. In 1790 in the U.S., a similar law established that the reasonable period was intended as *14 years*. From the original 14 years, the "reasonable" period is now 70 years (and will probably become 95 years in the future in the US).

## Different Categories of Rights

Rights management is complex and concerns widely differing rights such as:

- Reproduction rights (e.g., copying by publishers, schools, businesses, government agencies).
- Public performance rights.
- Resale rights.
- Lending and rental rights.
- Broadcasting and cable retransmission rights.

We should consider at least four different scenarios corresponding to the four main rights categories:

- Purchase of sheet music or audio recordings.
- Public Performance rights, paid by for the public performance (live or broadcasted) of a sound recording and music works.
- Mechanical Rights, paid for audio recording of songs and music works.
- Special rights (Synchronisation, Arrangements, Productions, Sampling).

Names used for such kind of rights can vary from country to country: the words "Licenses" and "Royalties" are all used in some cases to refer to "Rights."

The *purchase* of sheet music or audio recordings gives the right to use each single copy purchased. It does not give the right to produce additional copies (photocopying or digital copying), nor to perform the work in a live public performance, nor to record the work, nor to broadcast a recording or live performance.

*Mechanical Rights* cover the mechanical reproduction of a recording in multiple copies. All recordings must be licensed, even noncommercial recordings. They may be licensed by Rights Collecting Societies or directly from the copyright owner by payment of fees. Mechanical Rights are issued only for the recording of a copyrighted musical composition or the duplication of a sound recording, or its synchronization to an audiovisual presentation, not for the public performance of the sound recording. A Mechanical Right can be sometimes issued for the streaming of the sound recording. The Mechanical Rights for the duplication is only issued after a sound recording has been distributed (released to the public). The license is then granted on a compulsory basis thereafter.

*Public Performance Rights* concern the public execution of a musical work, covering live performance situations and broadcasts of recordings, (however, Public performance rights do not provide the right to make a recording). Public performance rights may be licensed directly from the copyright owner or from one of the Performing Rights organizations. Performing Rights Organizations represent the musicians that performed on a specific sound recording that is publicly performed in bars, dance halls, amusement parks, entertainment functions, retail shopping facilities, hotels, waiting areas, elevators.

The *Special Rights* category groups different kind of rights, like Synchronisation Rights, Arrangements Rights, and Grand Rights. The latter covers production of music with associated dramatic action, dancing, or staging. It must be licensed directly from the copyright owner. Audio utilized from production music libraries also requires licensing for replication. The licensing may be in various forms depending upon the music library vendor. Traditionally, a Master Use Agreement will be issued by the music library vendor when the specific usage fees for the chosen music are paid. Synchronization Rights allow using music as part of video or film, film, television works, advertising, and new technologies. Often Synchronisation Rights are considered as a special case of Mechanical Rights. Arrangements Rights concerns the creation of arrangements on music pieces, while Sampling is when portions of a previously recorded audio track are utilized in creating a new audio track. For tracks to be sampled, appropriate audio licensing for the sampled track are required from the recorded track IPR owner and music publisher.

Consequently recorded audio tracks require, for instance, two different types of licensing: (1) a license for the recorded track from the artist; (2) a license for the published song used in the recording from the music publisher (mechanical rights). The recorded track license must demonstrate a chain-of-title from the actual recording artist or organization representing the artist to the individual or organization recording the music. Use of a published song on an audio recording requires a per copy fee to be paid to the music publisher (mechanical rights) that can be paid directly to the publisher, or the publisher can establish a relationship with an agency to handle the negotiation of royalty payments, collections, and disbursement to publishers.

A term commonly used in the music industry is *Compulsory License*, considering a published song that has been previously recorded by an artist. When another artist wishes to rerecord it, federal copyright law allows for a compulsory license, which gives an artist the ability to rerecord a song and pay a predefined mechanical royalty rate. Compulsory licenses only apply when the song has already been recorded by another artist.

## Collective Administration

It is increasingly difficult, if not impossible, for individual authors to monitor the uses of their work. Numbers of performance are overwhelming and authors are not supposed to spend their time going after their rights. On the other hand, users of creative works would find it as impossible to address the proper right holder every time they use one, especially if this work, a film for instance, consists of the work of different authors of different creative disciplines. The solution that individual creators have found to bridge the gap between themselves and the users of their works, has been to unite and to administer their rights collectively. Creating and organising *collective administration* societies. Collective administration is the exercise of author's right by copyright collecting organizations (WIPO, 2004).

For individual owners, it is often difficult to maximise the economic value of their rights and to protect those rights. Similarly, third parties who wish to use those rights must incur the trouble and expense of finding the appropriate rights owners, negotiating individual deals, and administering and accounting to a vast number of such rights owners. The collective administration of copyright is often the most effective method of managing the rights, both for the owners of the rights and those who need access to them.

In much of the world, collective administration is performed by a network of not-for-profit copyright collecting societies, sometimes known as authors' societies or reproduction rights organizations (RROs). They often have a statutory basis and may enjoy monopoly powers. In the US and some other jurisdictions administration is by for-profit entities on an almost competitive basis.

Collective administration, particularly of secondary uses such as broadcasting, has developed with the proliferation of rights and uses. Collective administration *spreads the cost of administration* (e.g., establishment and maintenance of databases, exemplary litigation, and employment of advocates) over all members of the society. "Blanket licensing" reduces the cost to consumers, with users paying a single fee for access to the whole of a society's repertoire, thereby eliminating high transaction costs that would be incurred through clearing rights with every individual author, publisher, composer, lyricist, artist, performer, and record company. Rights management costs are deducted from the sums collected. Collective licensing applies to a single territory, but reciprocal agreements between societies mean that it allows rights holders to gain remuneration for uses across the globe.

The process of collective administration is activated as soon as a creator has finished a work, and aims to ensure the enforcement of his or her rights, and it ends when the creator receives the benefits of his/her creation. The process is made up of a number of steps. The first step is the *registration and documentation:* a creative work is protected by copyright law from the moment of its creation. It only needs to be tangible. Nevertheless, authors' societies encourage authors to register all the works they create. This will allow effective exercise of their rights. Some conditions for the registration of works vary from society to society. The basic information required to protect intellectual property rights effectively are details on the creator and on his or her works. This documentation allows collective administration to carry out its task. The next step is the license issue, for which collective administration societies deal with the authorisation of the use of the author's work. If a user meets the conditions set by the society, he/she will be licensed to use a specific work. The major condition for use will be the payment of royalty. Tariffs are generally set as a result of negotiation between author's societies and users. Sometimes, the law prescribes the tariff, like in the case of "droit de suite" (resale right) or of private copying.

According to the kind of work involved (music, literature, audiovisual works, "multimedia"

productions, etc.), authors' societies will manage different kinds of rights, depending on the forms of exploitation of the repertoire it represents.

For *Multimedia* works, on account of growing popularity of "multimedia" productions, there is a growing tendency to set up "one-stop-shops.". These are a sort of coalition of separate collective management organizations, which offer a centralised source where authorisations can be easily and quickly obtained. This to suit users in the multimedia field, where the majority of productions are composed of, or created from, several types of work that require a wide variety of authorisations.

The rights management of *audiovisual* works (feature films, short films, TV films, serials, cartoons, and works involving multimedia and still images) can be compared to that of music. On behalf of audiovisual creators, the collective management society negotiates general representation contracts with broadcasters like television stations, cable networks, and satellite packages. Societies may also assist individual authors negotiate production contracts for cinema, TV, radio, and multimedia, providing them with standard contracts, for instance.

Concerning *musical works*, the author's society generally deals with the collective management of the rights of public performance and broadcasting. It negotiates with users, such as television stations, discotheques, cinemas, bars, and determines the payment for the use of copyrighted works from its repertoire and the conditions under which users are authorised.

## Online Music Distribution Services

This section presents some thoughts on emerging online music distribution services and their business models. As often, the pioneers in this market are US-based companies servicing only the US market. Besides the readiness of the US market, the reasons for this limit are basically related to the agreement with music labels and publishers that are easier to set up on a national basis. Only recently, starting from May 2004, some of the big players like Sony, Apple, Napster, and OD2 entered the European market.

Napster constituted a potential threat to the dominance of OD2 as the dominant online music distributor in the UK and the rest of Europe. Napster owns music distribution infrastructure, which its parent, Roxio, acquired from Sony Music and Universal Music, as well as a single retail site in each country. OD2, in contrast, is solely a distributor, but it has about two dozen different retail partners, some of which (such as MTV and Tiscali) cover multiple countries themselves.

The markets for distribution of physical media have evolved to near-monopoly distributorships over time. For each major type of physical media (CDs, books, videotapes, etc.), there are only one or two major distributors behind the many online retail sites, usually Amazon.com and maybe one other. There is little reason for the situation to be any different with digitally downloaded content. Too much competition for essentially the same services will drive prices down and turn already-thin profit margins into loss-leading fights for market share. The result will be what is already the reality in Europe. Of course, consumers will benefit of the extremely fierce competition in the market, as each company is cutting its prices for downloads and gathering momentum with an increasing number of retail partnerships.

There are many different online music services and many others are appearing, while some of them close down or are being acquired by other companies in a somewhat necessary consolidation of the market. Instead of presenting few words describing each online service, this section focuses on giving some details about the very successful Apple iTunes Music Store, selected as one of the most significant ventures in the sector and an interesting business case.

## Apple iTunes Music Store

Several research markets showed that, at the moment, a healthy number of file traders are willing to pay for fee-based online music. As already discussed, among the reasons for the failure of current fee-based online music distribution sites are subscription-based services (instead of pay-per-download) and the mediocrity of their offerings:

- Prices are too high.
- Music selection is too limited.
- Usage of licensed music is too restrictive for customers.
- The quality is not better than in free (illegal) offers.

A great potential to make significant revenue is there if the pay music service would only compete directly with free P2P services, leveraging their limitations. Additionally, P2P networks are not considered as competitors to CDs, but are seen as a promotional method like radio. Piracy is not the number one reason why the record industry wants to eliminate the free P2P services. New CD sales have dropped, that's true, but marginally. Used CD sales meanwhile have skyrocketed (Rosenblatt, 2005).

Thus, Apple iTunes Music Store's success is not as astonishing: In less than 24 hours it nearly sold 300,000 tracks at $0.99. However, according to many customers feedbacks, pricing is still too expensive especially considering the free, but illegal, P2P alternative. One of the key factors for iTunes booming success resides in its usability, user friendliness, and attractive user interface, as in the typical, traditional Apple-style.

So far, the success of Apple iTunes Music Store shows that a successful business model for online music distribution can be established. The model's major advantages are increased service and decreased restrictions. This also states the fact that a major interest of participants in illegal

P2P-exchange networks is the fact of the broad variety available in these illegal networks, which is beyond the daily mainstream, the advantage of prelistening or evaluation and easily download. If the market is the place where offer and demand meet, then Apple seems to have moved a step in the right direction, and customers showed their appreciation.

Thus it is interesting to see what might happen with the future of other online music distribution services: Apple's success put some pressure on the existing services that are partially owned by the record industry. Therefore the existing services will try to copy the model adopted in Apples iTunes Music Store. This will lead to a decrease of prices, as the copyright fees have to be lowered. When the business of commercialising electronic music distribution will succeed, the winners will be the record industry, as more music is distributed, the online music services as more music is distributed online and customers who benefit from the increased service and who might benefit from the reduced prices.

## MAJOR PROBLEMS AND REQUIREMENTS

The market of music and multimedia content distribution over the Internet currently presents different problems, related to the different market actors and sectors. Up to now, the major problems have been identified in the market structure, basically caused by the evolving technologies and digitization of contents. Other issues are related to systems, solutions, and technologies currently available on the ICT market for securely distributing multimedia content. Technology providers need to guarantee the music content protection to copyright owners, together with acceptable performances in content retrieval and delivery. Moreover, end users must consider these new distribution systems convenient compared to the traditional ones.

## Impact of Digital Technologies on Copyrights

The wide availability of music in *digital format* and of broadband connections, as well as the proliferation of effective hardware and software tools for digital processing of music, dramatically changed the way music is consumed, exchanged, and created. Such digital revolution is having a side effect too, making what was previously a series of relatively onerous unproductive tasks something of relative ease, leaving large gaps in the traditional business models, which started soon to fall apart.

The digital revolution has facilitated many once heavy content production, enrichment, and distribution activities like *copying* from disk to disk (carrier to carrier); recording music, which can be now digital, allowing identical copies; music distribution, which can leverage the ubiquity and speed of the Internet or massive copying of disks; creative tasks such as music production and adaptation, which has gone digital (and computer aided); music compression (mp3, divX, ogg, ...), which reduces the size of music pieces, makes it easier to exchange and transport music over the Internet as well as other media (CDs, DVDs, media cards).

Anyone can now become a publisher, a distributor, and a music store (of other people's music) as well as reducing the cost of being a producer, adapter, and author of one's (or partially) own music. The separation of the content from the carrier has severely complicated the business model and the control of IPR implications to the extent that legal music sales have actually fallen, reversing a long growth trail

At first sight, one might be tempted to look at the Internet and the digital revolution as a threat to authors and their rights. The music industry was shocked when Mp3 technology and peer-to-peer services enabled worldwide use of copyrighted musical works for free. Furthermore, not only music is involved, since creative works of all kinds can be distributed over the Internet. According to figures from the majors, the global music pirate business is believed to be worth about €4 billion in 2001, whereas it is estimated that the audiovisual sector looses €2.8 billion per year due to illegal downloading.

More and more, however, creators and their representatives remember what was clear from the beginning: the World Wide Web also offers unprecedented opportunities to the world of creation. Never before had authors the possibility to make their works known to so many people, wherever they are.

Such considerations leads to a two-fold approach to the distribution of digital music, aiming both to protect the work of creators and to stimulate the distribution of music as a chance of strong social, cultural, and economic growth.

The digital revolution has facilitated:

- Copy from disk to disk (carrier to carrier)
- Music can be recorded digitally.
- Distribution can be made on the Internet or by massive copying of disks.
- Music can be digitally produced or adapted (usually, a creative task?).

Anyone can now become publisher, distributor, and music store (of other people's music), as well as reducing the cost of being a producer, adapter, and author of one's (or partially) own music. The separation of the content from the carrier has severely complicated the business model and the control of IPR implications, to the extent that legal music sales have actually fallen, reversing a long growth trail

From a technological and infrastructure point of view, the major problems are identified in:

- Need for efficient, secure, nonintrusive content protection mechanisms.
- Lack for interoperability and compatibility among the different solutions and systems

for multimedia content distribution, needs for standards.
- Infrastructure aspects like insufficient availability and limited geographic distribution of broadband connections, network of trusted content (re)distributors.
- Protection and security issues related to the extension of online distribution to mobile technology (UMTS, Wi-Fi).
- Limited availability of secure micro-payments systems needed to enable mass purchasing of inexpensive items (e.g., like single music pieces, single "hits," special offer album).

From a technical point of view, a fundamental feature of a system for the distribution of coded music according to the rights of the owners of the musical contents is the *security*, which is the capability to protect and avoid unauthorised uses of these contents. To accomplish it, this system should fulfil at least the following guidelines:

- Avoid intrusions into the server system through bugs and exploits of the server software.
- Avoid intrusions into the server system through bugs and exploits of the operating system and the Web server.
- Avoid intrusions into the network where the server system is located.
- Provide a secure and protected way to perform transactions via the Internet.
- Avoid illegal copies of the digital content.
- Allow only authorized/selected operations on the music/multimedia object.

Keep control of the operations performed on the various packaged objects constituting the content.

Another important aspect to be considered when providing a suitable environment for hosting music delivering applications and multimedia content servers is related to the *performance* of the whole system. The cost in terms of performance of each step and operation involved in the content distribution, from the digitalisation to uploading in the server to downloading to remote clients, should be investigated. Documents and data sheets containing information about performances should be extremely useful to help content providers, publishers, and content distributors to choose the proper system according to their needs and expectations. This should avoid problems arising from the installation of a good tool in unfitting computers. In fact, in many cases, organizations willing to adopt a music distribution system may have not skilled people available to properly configure and dimension an installation, or even to properly carry on the decision process.

## Market Issues

The major problems affecting the structure and efficiency of the market can be summarized in:

- Lack of efficient Business Models, which are sustainable and satisfactory for all the stakeholders.
- Uncertainty due to new untested business models.
- The Complexity of business models often generates confusion in customers.
- Lack of confidence in content providers and distributors, due to the reduced barriers to entry (it is also an opportunity, indeed), piracy threats, fears of adopting of the "wrong" technology.
- Lack of content offer, in general, due to publishers' lack of confidence into currently available systems for protection of IPR (DRM, watermarking).
- Lack of content specifically in highly specialized niche markets, posing the need for valorisation of cultural heritages (traditional music and representations, ancient music).

- Also the high cost and resources required to digitize existing content and prepare the multimedia objects with the proper quality level is preventing the content offer to spread and grow.
- Political aspects, such as the high competition in the market, the presence of contradictions at any level of the digital value chain, the major changes to come in the traditional structure, and the shifting in the role of traditional content distributors/retailers.
- Social aspects, such as the needs to provide wider accessibility for everyone to digital resources.
- Excess of investments in the past without support of sound business plan (euphoric financial markets of the late 1990s).
- Lag in e-publishing at European Level, with respect to US market.

## General Requirements

Concerning music authors, one of the most important requirements is to improve their control on the music distribution chain and payments of rights, as they are now usually represented at national and international level by a few, very large institutions for the collection of property rights. At the same time, artists are interested in increasing the knowledge and distribution of their works to end users, so to raise their profits.

Content providers and distributors, such as major labels or companies providing only distribution systems, are mainly focused on the security aspects and on protection of copyrights in particular. The main issue here is to enhance their confidence and thrust in the new technology for online content distribution.

Protection of copyrights should preferably cover the spell of content providers' ownership of these rights. On the other hand, the cost of applying this protection must be acceptable, in terms of needed resources. In general, the application of protection systems to coded music is a time-consuming and space-consuming process. The more robust the protection algorithm is, the more time and space it requires to be applied.

Another important aspect in the distribution of coded music via Internet is related to the time needed to send the purchased bits to end users. This problem is related mainly to the size of the files to be delivered and to the type of connection purchasers are using. In turn, the size of the digitalized music depends on its quality. Usually the distribution system creates compressed files so as to make the delivering of music files via Internet as a matter of minutes. But the algorithms that perform this compression cause a loss of quality, which can be more or less patent. In general, a compression algorithm can reduce this loss so to let it be detectable only to a professional musician. The cost is in part an increasing of the time to create the compressed file, the growing of the size of these files.

From the point of view of end users, besides quality of downloaded files and time needed for the downloading process, there is a great interest in the functionality provided by the system, and especially in the tools for downloading and using the multimedia content. Additionally, they want simple systems, user friendly and easy to customize for their own needs (Norman, 2002). The main issue related to end users is to give the most possible visibility to music distribution systems.

Another important aspect is the restrictions in the use of downloaded files. In fact, in the traditional music market, a purchased item, such as a CD, is regarded by the vendee as something that can be used without limitations. In the online music market, content owners want to keep control of the delivered files, even if they have been legally bought, by applying restrictions in the use of these files.

These restrictions could keep away users from joining the online music market, all the more so as many people have been accustomed to free

downloading and usage of music files, because of the success of peer-to-peer distribution systems without control of copyrights, such as Napster, KaZaA, and WinMX. On the other hand, avoiding of illegal use of coded music appears to be a feature not to be set aside from the point of view of the content owners. Consequently, whatever online distribution system aims at conquering the major discography labels, confidence has to cope with the preventing of illegal use of downloaded files. Since it is accomplished by applying restrictions to the use of the downloaded files, it is important not to over restrict this use, not to run the risk of having a secure but boycotted system.

Finally, *music notation* and related applications require a special consideration since their wide and dynamically evolving usage scenarios. Music notation applications have been extensively identified in Nesi (2003). Some examples for the broad range of varying usage are:

- Distribution of music and associated (background) information (e.g., text), publishing music notation pieces.
- Rendering (including printing, rendering to audio, Braille music, Spoken Music...).
- Music editing (audio, sheet music...), music formatting (conductor, piano, guitar tablature...), music manipulation, music synchronization, comparison of music pieces, recognition of notes, pitch recognition, cooperative work.
- Annotating, semantic annotations, integration of multimedia aspects (including AR and VR), associated information: education (on various devices including i-TV) and training (feedback, pull-push scenario), games scenarios, direct connection, play along, separated (independent) media annotations.
- Adding, navigating, and playing multimedia music, bi-(multi-) directional.
- Providing simple and complex queries, multimedia music navigation in all domains,

music searching in all domains, structuring and searching, query (humming, MIDI, instrument, sequence of notes, rhythm, segment), cataloguing, logical combinations of queries.

## Political Problems: The SDMI Case and the P2P Case

On 15 December 1998, leaders of the recording industry announced the SDMI, Secure Digital Music Initiative, with executive director Leonardo Chiariglione, leading figure of the MPEG standard. SDMI published its first specification on 13 July 1999. It aimed to ensure that there is an interoperable standard for downloading and that copyright is protected. Manufacturers should use this standard to develop new portable devices expected for the end of 1999; this activity failed the commercialisation. This had the intention of preventing consumers to play illegal content including existing CDs or MP3 files when phase II technology will filter out pirated copies of music. Moving to Phase II will require consumers with existing phase I devices to voluntarily upgrade their systems. SDMI then decided that watermarking will be the screening technology. This initiative required collaboration by all parties, and set an example of music and IT industries working together, involving 130 representatives of the music (including collecting societies), consumer electronics, and IT industries (http://www.sdmi. org). On 9 August 1999, SDMI announced that it had selected an audio watermarking technology to indicate consumers that they can upgrade their portable devices so as to only record lawful copies.

In parallel to the SDMI initiative, software firms are working on coming up with a definitive format that will rival MP3 and offer both copyright protection and a way of charging fees. IBM and Real Networks have paired to develop a secure delivery system. Universal joined AT&T, Matsushita, and BMG to develop a secure technol-

ogy to digitally deliver music. In relation to DVD Audio and Super CD launch, hardware manufacturers have already announced the development of watermarking and encryption technologies to provide some copy protection for music made available on the new formats. In short, it provides consumers with the ability to make one digital copy, per recorder of the original, for personal use, at a sound quality equal to CD-Audio or less. More copying might be possible if authorised by the content owner. Technical solutions will also have to be implemented by digital broadcasters, Webcasters and Internet radio, if rights are to be enforced for all forms of commercial exploitation. Failure to carry the technical mechanism or identifier along the audio signal will mean the inability to control copying or collect royalties.

In effect, SDMI failed with its initial intention and time schedule. SDMI is capable to cope with a limited protection and digital right management (DRM) model. This is probably the limitation that has partially stopped its evolution. SDMI has been mainly produced for audio content while today, several other types of content are distributed on the network and via traditional supports.

Peer-to-peer applications (P2P) such as Napster, Gnutella, Morpheus, KaZaA, AudioGalaxy, iMesh, LimeWire, and so forth, are the perfect examples of optimal distribution systems. Their cost is practically null for the publishers; they are capable of reaching a very huge number of consumers, destroying barriers of nations with a very efficient distribution in terms of delivered number of copies. The "only" problem is that the lack of control about the distribution of copyright protected content without authorisation or recognition of the fees due to the copyright owner.

## Legal Issues

### Two Views on Rights

The Internet offers several new opportunities to the music distribution market. But every new business model has to cope with the pre-Internet laws about music trade, such as copyright. In fact, many of these laws apply in cyberspace. Moreover, several new measures were enacted in the last few years to address issues that could not previously have been identified.

From the point of view of music contents owners, such as the *Recording Industry Association of America (RIAA)*, the central issue is copyright that can be defined as the "protection of the original expression of an idea, whatever form is used to express it." It is considered a sort of "financial incentive for individuals to share ideas and inventions by granting that everyone is able to protect his or her artistic work." Hence, copyright owners believe that downloading music online does not breach copyright laws.

Current laws protect content owners by granting their right to control the reproduction, distribution, and adaptation of their work, including public performance and display of it. There is not an international copyright law, but many treaties establishing mutual respect for countries' copyright laws have been signed. The basic reference for these treaties is the *Berne Convention for the Protection of Literary and Artistic Works*, administered by the World Intellectual Property Organization.

Moreover, specific legislation has been passed to best cope with digital matters. For example, the *No Electronic Theft (NET) Act* "criminalizes sound recording copyright infringements occurring on the Internet regardless of whether there is financial gain from such infringements." To infringe copyright, it is sufficient making a music piece available to the public without authorization from the copyright owner, by whatever mechanism (uploading it to an Internet site to be downloaded by other people, sending it via e-mail or chat service…).

Copyright is breached with or without money exchange for the music (civil cases), and whenever there is a possibility of financial loss to the copyright owner or financial gain to the infringer

(criminal cases). "The NET Act defines 'financial gain' as the receipt or expectation of receipt of anything of value, including receipt of other copyrighted works (as in MP3 trading)" (RIAA, 2005).

On the other side, the *Electronic Frontier Foundation (EFF)* promotes "rights to think, speak, and share ideas, thoughts, and needs using new technologies, such as the Internet and the World Wide Web."

In EFF opinion about copyright law, "the movie and recording studios are trying to dumb down technology to serve their 'bottom lines' and manipulate copyright laws to tip the delicate balance toward intellectual property ownership and away from the right to think and speak freely"(EFF, 2005).

## Consumer Rights and Fair Use

*Fair use* is a copyright principle based on the belief that the public is entitled to freely use portions of copyrighted materials for purposes of commentary and criticism. Without this freedom, copyright owners could stifle any negative comments about their work (WIPO, 2004).

Unfortunately, if the copyright owner disagrees with the fair use interpretation, the dispute will have to be resolved by courts or arbitration, and in case of not a fair use, then the user is infringing upon the rights of the copyright owner and may be liable for damages.

The only guidance is provided by a set of *fair use factors* outlined in the US copyright law. These factors are weighed in each case to determine whether a use qualifies as a fair use. For example, one important factor is whether your use will deprive the copyright owner of income. Unfortunately, weighing the fair use factors is often quite subjective. For this reason, the fair use road map is often tricky to navigate.

In its most general sense, a fair use is any copying of copyrighted material done for a limited and "*transformative*" purpose. such as to comment upon, criticize, or parody a copyrighted work. Such uses can be done without permission from the copyright owner.

There are no hard-and-fast rules, only general rules and varying court decisions. That's because the judges and lawmakers who created the fair use exception did not want to limit the definition of fair use. They wanted it, like free speech, to have an expansive meaning that could be open to interpretation

Most fair use analysis falls into two categories: *commentary/criticism* and parody. Unfortunately, the only way to get a definitive answer on whether a particular use is a fair use is to have it resolved in federal court. Judges use four factors in resolving fair use disputes, which are discussed in detail below. It is important to understand that these factors are only guidelines, and the courts are free to adapt them to particular situations on a case-by-case basis. In other words, a judge has a great deal of freedom when making a fair use determination, and the outcome in any given case can be hard to predict.

The four key criteria to discern fair use can be summarised in (1) the purpose and character of use, (2) the nature of the copyrighted work, (3) the amount and substantiality of the portion taken, and (4) the effect of the use upon the potential market.

After the enactment of the *Digital Millennium Copyright Act (DMCA)* in the United States, and the adoption, 2 years later, of anticircumvention regulations in the European Copyright Directive, the legal framework surrounding digital rights management systems has been severely criticized for hampering fair use and burdening free speech in the digital environment. While one approach to solve this tension between fair use and DRM is to change the legal framework by legislative amendments and influential court decisions, another approach is to address it directly at the technological design level of DRM systems.

Current copyright law in both the US and *Europe* does not recognize affirmative "user rights"

to fair use, but merely acknowledges certain exceptions to the exclusive rights of the copyright owner as a defence to an infringement action. To preserve a balance between the interests of content producers and content users, it would be easier and more efficient to address such aspects not at the level of the legal DRM framework, but at the technological design level of DRM systems. The law might assist this development by influencing the technological design (Bechtold, 2001).

A better solution to the tension between fair use and DRM systems may therefore be to design DRM systems in a way that such problems do not occur in the first place. This may include the use of *rights management languages* as a way to preserve fair use in DRM systems and the avoidance of the "security through obscurity" approach, as well as the use of privacy-enhancing technologies. This approach provides also an international reach, since DRM applications are usually developed for a global market.

## SOLUTIONS AND RECOMMENDATIONS

## Technologies and Products for Online Music Distribution

The basic technologies supporting current and emerging products and services can be classified according to the following points[2] (Chiariglione, 2004, 2005):

- Web technologies.
- Electronic payment.
- Information technologies (Databases, Middleware, Application Servers).
- User devices (hardware and software music players, mobile devices).
- Encryption and watermarking (audio watermarking, perceptual hashing).

Baseline features of such technologies are:

- A protection mechanism to avoid unauthorized communications (for instance based on encryption).
- Information to register and identify the actors of the communication.
- Messages to perform transactions.
- Messages to request downloads.
- Messages to resume failed downloads.

Some of the most relevant technologies are briefly described in the following paragraphs. We can anticipate that there exists a common feeling in the music industry that outside of Apple's iTunes service, Windows Media DRM is becoming a *de facto standard* for digital music distribution (Lenzi & Spadoni, 2003).

In the following sections, some of the most relevant technologies for content distribution are considered and described.

## Online Music Services, Technologies, and Standards

### Adobe Digital Editions and Adobe Policy Server

Adobe Digital Editions (http://labs.adobe.com/technologies/digitaleditions) is a Rich Internet Application (RIA) built from the ground up for digital publishing, with native support for Adobe Portable Document Format (PDF), Flash as well as a XHTML support. Initially available as a free public beta for Windows, Digital Editions will support Macintosh systems as a universal binary application, Linux® platforms, as well as mobile phones and other embedded devices in future versions. The DRM for Digital Editions, Adobe Digital Editions Protection Service, is derived from LiveCycle Policy Server, Adobe's Enterprise DRM solution. Digital Editions Protection Service is backward compatible with the DRM in the now-discontinued Adobe Content

Server, previous Adobe's DRM solution for PDF, an e-book publishing, largely used by the libraries community.

The new format uses Flash for animation and video, which became a natural step after Adobe's acquisition of Macromedia in April of last year. Adobe also provided some basic support to help publishers to manage layout-oriented PDF documents as XML-based digital contents, exploiting XHTML.

Digital Editions Protection Service uses user ID-based authentication rather than the combination of user and device authentication used in Adobe Content Server, thus eliminating the device-based limitations, loosening in the process the protection against sharing of documents.

Adobe DRM enterprise solution is Adobe Live-Cycle Policy Server Enterprise. The key feature of the latest versions is its client-side integration with Microsoft Word and Excel, and the high-end CAD/CAM package CATIA from Dassault Systemes. Previous versions of LiveCycle Policy Server only worked with Adobe Acrobat and PDF format documents. LiveCycle Policy Server features a full set of dynamic rights capabilities, and integrates smoothly with Microsoft Outlook e-mail via Adobe's existing Acrobat plug-in for Outlook (which enables documents to be e-mailed as PDF). If a user sends an encrypted document to a recipient who is not in the sender's company, then the recipient must create an Adobe ID in order to get credentials to access the document. Within the corporate firewall, Policy Server integrates with several popular identity management schemes.

### Apple iTunes, the iPod, and iPhone

The technology behind Apple iTunes Music Store distribution service (http://www.apple.com/music/store/) is *iTunes*. iTunes is the Mac/Windows application ("jukebox software") that enables users to enter the iTunes Music Store. Its music player supports the new AAC audio format, and lets users share their music with other Mac computers on local Ethernet or AirPort wireless networks. Using a Mac with a SuperDrive, it is possible to archive music to DVDs. iTunes has a Music Sharing feature that uses Rendezvous technology to give user remote streaming access to his/her personal music library. It automatically synchronises with the iPod device (a digital audio player, cf. below) at high speeds over FireWire, by connecting iPod to a Mac computer with FireWire.

iTunes DRM technologies is *FairPlay*, a good compromise in protection and ease-of-use, although lacking significantly in flexibility and interoperability.

*iPod* is the well known digital audio player that can download music files and hold up to thousands of songs. It is a very slim device and includes 2 to 80 GB flash cards or hard drives. Some models have a docking station to make them able to charge and sync via FireWire or USB 2.0. They can be connected to a home stereo system, too. iPod supports several audio formats, including MP3 (up to 320 kbps), MP3 Variable Bit Rate (VBR), WAV, and the native AAC.

Apple recently announced the release of a new product, the *iPhone*, merging the functionality of an iPod, a Personal Digital Assistant, and a mobile phone, which can bring to Apple iTunes an even higher share in the music distribution market.

## ContentGuard XrML

Launched in April 2000, ContentGuard (http://www.contentguard.com, http://www.xrml.org) conducts its operations in Bethesda, MD, and El Segundo, CA. The company is owned by Xerox Corporation, with Microsoft Corporation holding a minority position. The company focuses on the distribution and management of digital works (content or services), including the use of a rights language, and its right language, XrML, were originally developed at the Xerox Palo Alto Research Centre (PARC).

These core technologies enable the efficient creation of DRM applications, simplify the digital distribution process, and increase revenue opportunities for content or service providers deploying varied business models, while protecting their intellectual property.

The company is focused on creating a single worldwide standard Digital Rights Language. It believes that such a standard will enable interoperability across DRM systems for digital content or services, including Web services. Towards this end, ContentGuard has proposed XrML to numerous standards bodies, and provides technical expertise in support of their work. MPEG, officially known as ISO/IEC JTC1/SC29/WG11, selected XrML as the basis for the development of the MPEG-21 REL.

Foundation technologies, such as the XrML, will accelerate high-value digital content distribution and Web Services initiatives by enabling standards-based interoperability, and alleviating the concerns of being restricted to a technology platform, a business model, a media type, a format, a proprietary solution, or a particular vendor. XrML is extensible and fully compliant with XML namespaces using XML schema technology.

## Coral DRM Interoperability Standard

Coral is a DRM interoperability standard based on the same underlying messaging technology as Marlin, a technology developed by Intertrust and known as NEMO. Coral is a practical approach to DRM interoperability; it is meant to be used by service providers that have an incentive to offer it, such as customer lock-in or cross-sell. The first public Coral spec was published in June, and shortly thereafter, the Coral working group published a white paper showing how Microsoft Windows Media DRM can interoperate with Coral "out of the box," that is, with no changes to the technology. This is an important result; the Coral group has already shown interoperability with both Marlin and OMA DRM (Rosenblatt, 2007).

Major disadvantages of Coral interoperability are in the current lack of support from Apple, and in the lack of involvement of major service providers.

## Digital Media Project IDP-2 Interoperability Standard

Leonardo Chiariglione's Digital Media Project (DMP) released its second major spec, IDP-2, in May 2006. IDP-2 shows DMP's approach to interoperability, which was missing from the previous spec (IDP-1). IDP-2 is a spec for a new, device-centric DRM that includes a small amount of required core functionality, and enables particular devices to include extended DRM features. The idea is that everyone should adopt IDP-2 and choose the set of DRM features that makes the most sense for any particular device (Rosenblatt, 2007).

A major disadvantage of Digital Media Project's interoperability standard is the lack of support from big consumer electronics players and content providers.

## Digital World Services ADo²RA System

ADo²RA from Digital World Services (http://www.dwsco.com) is a content independent digital distribution solution. It is a system that makes the creation, protection, and distribution of digital content—text, music, software, games, and video—possible to access and enjoy from all mobile devices and methods.

## DMDfusion

DMDfusion (http://www.dmdfusion.com/) is a product consisting of flexible software components and applications, including Digital Rights Management and Conditional Access technologies, that manages the access, usage, protection, and licensing of digital content. Central to DMD-fusion is the concept of a separation of layers that each performs its own tasks. DMDfusion is a server-side product and does not involve client side software or a plug-in. In fact, DMDfusion leverages on existing trusted software player and devices, and allows for the delivery of content to desktops and (mobile) devices without the use of proprietary plug-ins, thus maximising the end user experience. DMDfusion is designed for, and typically operates within, the content delivery supply chain involving content creation, management, and distribution. It incorporates both Digital Rights Enforcement (DRE) and Digital Rights Management (DRM) in one solution.

DMDfusion provides server side license delivery conditions (e.g., geolocation) as DRM technology agnostic mechanisms to allow for more diverse business models than would be enabled by the various proprietary DRM technologies alone. The separation of protected content from licenses is a fundamental principle of DMDfusion. This allows for content to be delivered using a wide variety of distribution channels such as content delivery networks, peer-to-peer distribution systems, physical carriers, and so forth.

## Element 5 E-Sales

E-sales is element 5's (http://www.element5.com) solution to perform online sales of software through unique marketing campaigns to lower distribution costs, develop new international markets, increase customer loyalty, and implement new licensing models. The element 5 Control Panel enables a complete overview of online activities and sales data, to adjust sales activities at any time to meet individual needs. element 5 e-sales offers order processing and all associated communications in 10 major languages. It supports local payment options for various countries, and all forms of payment commonly accepted across the globe, including credit cards, checks, purchase orders, cash, and bank transfers.

## RealNetworks Rhapsody, and Helix

Rhapsody (http://www.rhapsody.com/) is RealNetworks' membership-based music service that gives users unlimited access to a catalogue of millions of full length, CD-quality tracks. They also provide a free 25-songs-month limited membership.

Helix from RealNetworks is both a platform and community that enable creation of digital media products and applications for any format, operating system, or device. The Helix platform combines extensive, proven digital software technology with a rich set of application interfaces. It empowers developers, information technology and consumer electronics companies to easily integrate digital media. The Helix community enables companies, institutions, and individual developers to license Helix DNA platform source code in order to build Helix-powered server and client products.

RealNetworks has recently taken Helix DRM off the market; it is no longer selling the server software, though it will continue to support existing customers, as well as its own services such as Rhapsody. The company is investigating plans to incorporate the technology into its Real Broadcast Networks infrastructure, to offer on a service-provider basis to customers (Rosenblatt, 2007).

RealNetworks did not succeed in getting the technology established in the PC market, lead by Apple and Microsoft, or the mobile market. As part of its transition, RealNetworks has been offering some of its server software for free or under open-source licensing.

RealNetworks Rhapsody content services support both Windows DRM and Apple's FairPlay as part of the company's Harmony interoperability platform.

## Liquid Music Network (Liquid Digital Media)

The Liquid Music Network system from Liquid Audio (http://www.liquidaudio.com) is based on two products for final users, the Player and the Secure Portable Player Platform (SP3), and a Server. The Liquid Music Network system from Liquid Audio is based on two products for final users, the Player and the Secure Portable Player Platform (SP3), and a Server. Liquid Player for Windows enables streaming, downloading, purchasing, playback, ripping, and CD burning of digital audio. Liquid Plug-Ins enable third-party music players to access secure music in the Liquid Audio format.

Liquid Audio's SP3 provides consumer electronics companies, chipset manufacturers, and embedded operating systems developers with a digital music solution to get to market with digital audio devices. Combined with a custom-branded version of Liquid Player Plus software, SP3 enables the rapid development of secure digital audio devices that are compliant with the guidelines established using the Secure Digital Music Initiative (SDMI).

## Microsoft Windows Media DRM

(http://www.microsoft.com/windows/windows-media/forpros/drm/default.mspx)

Microsoft Windows Media DRM is a suite of programs that form a complete platform for digital media distribution. The components of the Microsoft Windows Media 10 Series are the Player, for audio and video, both online and offline; the Encoder, a tool for producing audio and video contents; the Server, for media streaming; Codecs for audio and video compression; and a DRM, an end-to-end system that offers content providers and retailers a platform for the secure distribution of digital media files. The Windows Media Rights Manager includes both server and client software development kits (SDKs) that enable applications to protect and play back digital media files.

Using the server SDK, developers can create applications that encrypt (package) digital media files and issue licenses for those digital media files. A packaged Windows Media file contains a version of the file that has been encrypted with a key so that only the person who has obtained a license for that file can play it. The license is separate from the packaged Windows Media file, which means that the content and license for that content can be acquired at different times. Encrypted files can be either streamed or downloaded to the consumer's computer. To enable digital media playback applications to play packaged Windows Media files, acquire licenses for them, back up and restore licenses, and issue security upgrades for its DRM component, developers should use the client SDK.

In an attempt to emulate the successful iTunes/iPod model by Apple, Microsoft proposed the Zune Marketplace/Zune player combo, incompatible with Microsoft Windows Media DRM. The initiative at the moment gained scarce support from clients.

## Napster

Napster was a pioneer of "free" music distribution, and after fighting with majors' lawyers, eventually turned into a legal and paid distribution service. It now offers a roster of services including free, Web-based music listening and sharing, subscription and portable subscription services, and an advanced mobile music platform. Recently, under the consolidation forces driving the present more mature online music market, two online music services based on Windows Media decided to transfer their subscriber bases to Napster.

In fact, Napster acquired the MusicNow subscription service from AOL (about 350,000 subscribers) for $15.6 Million. AOL had originally acquired in 2004 from the electronics retail chain Circuit City. MusicNow started life

as FullAudio, one of the first paid music sites, predating Apple's iTunes. As a result, Napster becomes the featured online music subscription service on AOL. Virgin Digital also recently shut down its US subscription music service and sent its subscribers an e-mail offer to transition their accounts to Napster. Virgin's service launched in 2004; it was one of several online music services that was owned by traditional music retailers and used MusicNet's infrastructure. After the two deals, Napster's paid subscribers are circa one million. There are dozens of online music services based on Windows Media, none of which have made much impact on iTunes's dominance of Internet music delivery. Further consolidation is inevitable. At the same time, Microsoft itself has threatened to marginalize all of these services with its integrated Zune player/service stack, while RealNetworks is attempting to do the same with Rhapsody and its partnership with SanDisk. Consolidation may simplify consumer choice, giving Windows Media-based services a collective boost in the market, but any benefit to consumers is undone by fragmentation without interoperability (Rosenblatt, 2007).

## OMA DRM Enabler Release (Version 2.0)

In an ongoing effort to accelerate the wireless industry's adoption of rich and accessible mobile services, the Open Mobile Alliance (OMA) (http://www.openmobilealliance.org), an industry organization delivering specifications for interoperable mobile service enablers across the world, recently (Feb. 2, 2004) announced the release of the OMA DRM 2.0 Enabler Release, designed to protect high-value content produced and distributed by a wide range of content and service providers. The OMA expects to release the specification during the first half of this year.

OMA DRM 2.0 is backward compatible with OMA DRM 1.0, but goes considerably beyond it in the functionality it supports. OMA DRM 1.0

was designed for a world of simple, low-cost devices with not much memory, no trusted system clocks, and no sophisticated content rendering capabilities, that is, it was designed to support ring tones and wallpaper graphics. OMA DRM 2.0, in contrast, is designed for more powerful devices that have the ability to play higher-resolution audio (such as actual music tracks) and video, send content to other devices and storage, and so on.

## STARBAK Torrent Origin Streaming Appliance

The Torrent Origin Streaming Appliance (http://www.starbak.com/products/origin_streaming_servers.html) from STARBAK (http://www.starbak.com) is a network appliance. A network appliance is a specialized device that is dedicated to performing one function very well. The Torrent OSA was specifically designed to stream media. Since it is not a normal multipurpose server, it is very easy to use.

The Torrent OSA utilizes Web-based administration. This means that it can be controlled from any computer that has a Web browser. No special software needs to be installed. It can also be administered from any location on the network.

The Torrent OSA streams all major streaming formats including Microsoft Windows Media, Apple QuickTime, MPEG-1, and MPEG-2. All formats can be streamed simultaneously from a single Torrent OSA.

## Sun Open DReaM

Sun Microsystems introduced Project DReaM (DRM/everywhere available), a project to create an open-source standard for interoperable DRM. Sun's COO Jonathan Schwartz announced the initiative at the Progress and Freedom Foundation Summit in Aspen, Colorado, in September 2005. The standard calls for DRM that relies on user authentication alone and does not bind content

to hardware devices. The project results will be made available on a royalty-free basis under Sun's Common Development and Distribution License (CDDL), a licensing scheme similar to an open-source license like the GNU General Public License, but which affords Sun some control. Project DReaM includes a DRM architecture called DRM-OPERA as well as some technology components for digital video management and distribution.

DRM-OPERA is the result of the Project OPERA, a Eurescom R&D initiative sponsored by the European Union and the European telecommunications industry. Sun's R&D lab contributed heavily to Project OPERA, which produced architecture for interoperable DRM in 2003. OPERA achieves interoperability among DRM systems, essentially by reducing DRM licenses down to a lowest common denominator of authenticating users only and providing "play once" as an atomic licensing term that all DRM systems can understand and support. Each of the DRM systems involved in a specific instance of interoperability can manage more complex licensing terms internally, and communicate them through the OPERA architecture via "play once" licenses.

## WebWare ActiveMedia

ActiveMedia software from WebWare (http://www.webwarecorp.com) provides a secure repository to manage, share, distribute, and publish rich media content, such as graphics, images, layouts, animation, video, and documents. ActiveMedia is designed for wide-scale deployment, and allows content sharing throughout global organizations among employees, partners, agencies, and distributors. WebWare ActiveMedia can be used as a stand-alone content management system, or incorporated into an existing enterprise content management system (ECM) as the backend digital media repository. It can be implemented as installed software in-house or as an outsourced service.

## WEDELMUSIC

WEDELMUSIC (http://www.wedelmusic.org) is a complete system for distribution and sharing of interactive music via Internet, totally respecting the publisher rights and protecting them from copyright violation.

WEDELMUSIC allows publishers, archives, and consumers (theatres, orchestras, music schools, libraries, music shops, musicians) to manage interactive music; that is, music that can be manipulated: arranged, transposed, modified, reformatted, printed, and so forth, respecting copyright. It is an innovative support for preparing performances, studying music, analysing music, learning instruments, distributing music at low cost, and so forth. The same music objects will be available for traditional media and Braille. These innovative features are possible thanks to the definition and implementation of a unified XML-based format for modelling music including audio, symbolic, image, document, and so forth; reliable mechanisms for protecting music in symbolic, image, and audio formats; a full set of tools for building, converting, storing, distributing music on the Internet. The WEDELMUSIC system is composed by the following applications: (1) the Music Editors and Visualisers, to edit, view, and manipulate music scores, and create multimedia musical objects, including images, video, audio, lyrics, documents, and so on; (2) the Server for preparing and delivering WEDELMUSIC objects considering protection and accounting, fast retrieval of any component: images of music sheets, scores, audio files, documents, video, and so forth; (3) the Local Distributor for locally storing and distributing music in the local area, suitable for music shops, theatre archives, music schools, conservatories, libraries, and so forth.

## Balancing Author's Rights and User Rights

Copyright can represent the tool to get a trade-off between the sometimes conflicting interests of users and publishers-majors-authors. Copyright should be based on a *balancing principle*: the needs of the rights holder should be balanced against those of society, users, and consumers. Such balancing principle behind copyright should be translated in terms of the new technologies, and the digital scenario to ensure that users have sufficient and easy access to music, while still protecting the interests of rights holders.

As an example iTunes, provide users with the possibility to burn CDs in unprotected formats. Even id this can appear as a gaping security hole, having to buy blank CDs and spend the time burning them is a serious deterrent to large-scale piracy. Being able to burn CDs is a convenient feature that helps meet reasonable usage expectations; Apple, and the record companies who have licensed their material to iTunes, are betting that the value of that convenience is larger than the size of the piracy loophole

## Business Models

Transaction and business models are really at the heart of the problem. An industry that had very clear business models is finding that all previous assumptions on conducting its normal line of business are gradually becoming extinct, whilst, at the same time, many new opportunities are developing. However, many of the players in the industry are purely creative, lacking in many of the basic marketing, administrative, or even technical skills required to take advantage of the new opportunities offered and, at the same time, unable to defend themselves from the challenges of a shrinking market in other segments.

New technologies are opening up new market opportunities for the music business, as the digital world is converting the mass market into a mass of niche markets. Also, opportunities for content from economically marginal groups or regions could be promoted.

The large variety of software and hardware devices, players, DRM systems, and other software involved in the whole music content chain, particularly in the end user side, makes it very difficult to find a business model that will satisfy the needs of consumers, authors, publishers, and soft or hardware device manufacturers. The market scarce responsiveness to technological advancement and changes in the way end users consume music has kept traditional business model in place, without giving birth to an accepted alternative, further complicated by the traditionally slow legal response of the lawmakers.

A further issue is the difference between Anglo-Saxon and other European legal systems and tax laws. All these conflicting interests make it difficult for a new model to emerge.

*Business to Business (B2B)* is the most important part of the total electronic commerce (70%-80% of the total). Despite the different trends that are present in different countries, the total trend foreseen for Europe is similar to that of US.

B2B e-commerce provide benefits for managing inventory more efficiently, adjusting more quickly to customer demand, getting products to market faster, cutting the cost of paperwork, reigning in rogue purchases, obtaining lower prices on some supplies.

Potential applications of B2B approach to the online music distribution are:

- Online licensing of music for "traditional" multimedia content productions like advertisement, movies, cover songs, derivative works.
- Online licensing of music and multimedia for new rich media content productions like flash and Web productions, entertainment and infotainment, especially directed to SMEs.

- Online licensing of music and multimedia content for education and e-learning services.
- Online licensing of music for developers and publishers of interactive entertainment software for personal computers and advanced entertainment systems such as the PlayStation®2 Computer Entertainment System, the PlayStation®, Xbox™ video game console from Microsoft, the Nintendo GameCube™, and the Game Boy® Advance.
- Levy-based licensing of music and audio/video content (for instance, a certain small amount of royalties is paid from consumer electronics producers to music labels for each player/storage device sold).
- Value added services such as online music collaborations and services for DJs.
- Artist management and relationships services.

*Business to Consumer (B2C)* applies to any business or organization that sells its products or services to consumers over the Internet for their own use like, for example, Apple iTunes or Amazon. Examples of innovative models of online music distribution services based on the B2C approach are:

- Webcasting.
- Niche-market subscription services.
- Subscription services for mobile content and wireless devices.
- "Direct from the artist" services.

From a business model perspective, *Peer to Peer (P2P)* leverages the P2P communication paradigm to build a business case and provide revenue from the distribution of content according to a file-sharing schema. P2P communication (also called peer to peer and file sharing) is the hottest and fastest growing media breakthrough in the world. The "Napster phenomenon," which was responsible for single-handily developing

*Figure 1. Current status of the online music distribution market (February 2007)*

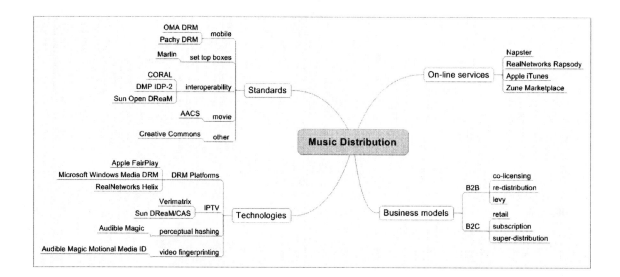

the unique and simple idea of P2P File Sharing, allowed users to keep files on their computer, add a naming scheme, and create and use different identities, regardless of their IP number. Peer-to-peer networks are generally simpler and less expensive, but they usually do not offer the same performance under heavy loads.

But now, with legal issues and lawsuit risks surrounding the use of a P2P file sharing program, many people are turning to "legitimately licensed" music download Web sites instead of the controversial "Napster alternative" file sharing sites that are popping up all over the Web. However, there are legal ways to implement a P2P music distribution system, even if at the cost of minor restrictions to the operations users can perform on their digital music.

Fraunhofer IDMT's Potato System, as an example, comes up with an innovative solution to this problem, particularly developed for unknown authors and independent music labels and operators of music download portals. It is based

on a commission model: the consumer receives a commission for redistributing a music file. That means, within the Potato System, the user does not just pay for the right to hold a music file, but also for the right of redistribution.

An even more significant argument in favour of P2P business models is contained in a study titled "Peer-to-Peer: un autre modèle économique" (P2P: another business model), by French collecting society ADAMI. The study, developed by a pool of experts coordinated by P2P-supporter Tariq Krim, presents the different possible P2P business models, their advantages and disadvantages, and proposes P2P-based solutions preserving authors- and rights owners' interests, but also of the interests of users and consumers.

The following map summarizes the current status of the online music distribution market, showing the most adopted and visible technologies, standards, online services and business models at the moment (February 2007).

# FUTURE TRENDS

## An Innovative Approach, a New Strategic Vision

Innovation at level of multimedia and music content management and online distribution can be introduced both at levels of technologies and at level of market structure and business models. From the technological side, different solutions and system exist, still with some significant drawbacks, to partially solve some of the problems, and more attention is needed towards standardization of protocols, procedures, mechanisms, as well as on interoperability and compatibility of systems. In such direction, the emerging of Web Services and the work on MPEG standardization is surely promising. In particular, the activities performed under the *MPEG21* and MPEG7 frameworks are relevant to content protection and classification issues respectively.

From the marketing side, new and efficient business models and licensing schemes still need to emerge to cope with the new, different nature of the multimedia products and the new needs and demands from customers.

To have a better idea of the structure and the complexity of the music distribution market, it can be convenient to consider the different categories of actors involved, as described in chapter 2.1 (Main actors in the market).

Each one of these categories has different objectives, interests, points of view, competencies, organizations, and size, bringing into the "distribution." From a strictly technical point of view, the several different aspects involved in multimedia content management and online distribution are mainly related to Intellectual Property Rights (IPR) clearing, content protection and Digital Right Management (DRM) systems, and can be summarized as:

- Encryption of data.
- Managing of online transactions.
- Compression and storing of digital content files.
- Managing of delivering of digital content files.
- Prevention of illegal use of digital content.

But as mentioned before, the large gap to cover is on the market side, where new business models and licensing scheme are most than needed, and where political aspects and competition are the major driving forces.

More and more authors, copyright collecting societies, and independent labels are embracing the conviction that economic and business models generated or based on peer-to-peer communication schemas are totally positive in terms of distribution, selling, and knowledge of music.

Moreover, such models are considered as the basis to recover from the decreasing sells of CDs, a model which is outdated for certain specific targets. Some of the authors and their representatives, in some countries (e.g., ADAMI in France), are inviting the major labels to stop a war sometimes directed against their direct customers and against their own revenue streams, and to start instead a new innovative and creative approach, involving also the Internet Service Providers in the process and allowing the user, paying a fee, to access music and possibly redistribute rights via the peer-to-peer and a new licensing scheme.

The approach aims to remunerate rights holder without limiting too much the freedom of end users, providing value to all the players in the content value chain.

## Towards Less DRM

The analysis of future trends for the online music distribution market suggests that in the near future we will see less DRM, especially encryption-based DRM. A set of market driving forces encompassing the whole online distribution value-chain can make this happen.

Firstly, music labels aim to increase digital music sales by making digital products more attractive by improving DRM and making them lighter and more user friendly (and more flexible, and more interoperable). Moreover, major music companies are unhappy with Apple's restrictive scheme for music licensing, including lack of variable pricing and DRM flexibility.

For content distributors and technology providers, creating digital music services with DRM that is looser than Apple's FairPlay is certainly a sound and appealing competitive strategy aimed at dragging users away from iTunes. This makes especially good sense to consumer electronics firms and service providers, because less DRM means less cost to them.

Different technical solutions are emerging to reduce the impact of DRM on end users: acoustic fingerprinting (i.e., examining the bits of a file to determine the identity of its content, then acting accordingly) is gaining traction, as are certain advanced variations on digital watermarking, such as so-called transactional watermarking (i.e., embedding the identity of the user into a downloaded file). Both techniques are used in content services that are licensed by major music and video content owners. Both can be used either as a substitution of or in addition to encryption. (Rosenblatt, 2007).

In addition, the usage and diffusion of encryption-based DRM for digital music can be significantly affected and reduced by the development of levies-based business models. Such models are based on evidence that the majority of music transferred to portable devices, like Apple iPods, is not purchased online with DRM, but instead is ripped from CDs (whether those of the device owner or not) or obtained through file-sharing networks or other sources.

Levies-based business models can be both market-inspired (e.g., the deal between Universal Music and Microsoft for Microsoft's audio player Zune) or government-imposed (like in many European countries).

## New Business Models from Emerging Online Music Services and Web2.0

The business model for *iTunes* is really something of a throwback compared to other online media models. It is not much more than a purely digital version of a traditional record store; the only real difference is that users can buy their choice of individual tracks instead of having to buy either an entire album or those tracks the record company selects as singles. Rhapsody, as well as others, like MusicMatch and MusicNow, charges a monthly subscription fee. While that arrangement may not be appropriate for everyone, it does offer value in the form of unlimited streaming, artist information, recommendations, radio-like listening experiences, and so on.

The advantage of "owning" vs. "renting" music, provided by online stores like iTunes over others like Rhapsody, is quite limited in benefits for "advanced" users: ownership of music in performance form is a concept of convenience that did not exist a century ago, and it need not exist in the not-so-distant future when most music will be *ubiquitously available on demand*, in one form or another.

The real problem is that Rhapsody and other services, to say nothing of record companies, have done a terrible job of educating the public on music-listening modes other than purchasing individual items of music; the only modes that people understand are record stores and radio stations (and, at a stretch, jukeboxes and libraries). The new technologies and the Internet enable many interesting new business models, but some serious marketing is mandatory to gain confidence from end users.

Lately, innovative business models emerged to address the wide issue of making a content–based business profitable, or at least sustainable, as in the case of public organizations needing to cover high costs and efforts for content digitization, maintenance, and creation. The objective is to develop and activate new revenue streams and new distribution channels, by targeting *small, niche markets*, both repurposing and reusing the available content, and adopting major search engines' contextual advertisement business models, like Google AdSense or Yahoo! Search Marketing (formerly Overture).

Such approach project aims to provide low-cost tools and methodologies to exploit the opportunity of the many emerging niche markets for digital music and other cultural content, ensuring economic sustainability of no-profit content services (public organizations, governments, public-private partnerships) and the success of digital content related business services and enterprises.

The competitive threat from niche markets is related to the cost of establishing and maintaining them, and the bother required for readers to track multiple small Web sites. Such costs can be dramatically reduced by leveraging customer self service and algorithmic data management to reach out to the entire Web, to the edges and not just the centre, to the *long tail* and not just the head. Contextual advertisement business models are a way for Web site and content publishers to display relevant ads on their Web site's content pages, and obtain an economic compensation in return. The ads are related to what the visitors are looking for on a Web site. It is also a way for Web site publishers to provide advanced Web and site search (Google, Yahoo, MSN engine, et al.) to their visitors, displaying ads on the search results pages. Contextual advertisement models allow content publishers and distributors to sell advertising space for other people's ads on their Web site, and not just any ads that the ads provider (e.g., Google AdSense) chooses, but ads that are relevant to the specific content pages. The service is free, and the publisher receives a fee every time someone clicks on an ad. The amount of the fee varies, and the company does not disclose its payments.

Google AdSense, for instance, places relevant CPC (cost-per-click) and CPM (cost per thousand impressions) ads into the same auction and lets them compete against one another. The auction takes place instantaneously and when it is over, AdSense will automatically display the text or image ads that will generate the maximum revenue for a page. Google AdSense technology aims to understand page content and deliver ads that are relevant to specific pages. And since ads are also targeted by country, global businesses can display local advertising with no additional effort. Other AdSense features allow to block competitive ads and to filter out ads that may be inappropriate for some pages. AdSense has become a popular method of placing advertising on a Web site because the ads are less intrusive than most banners, and the content of the ads is often relevant to the Web site.

Google AdSense assesses the content of the Web page and supplies ads that might interest the end user (visitor). For example, in our case of an educational-oriented Web service providing regional music content, when a user is accessing a page concerning a Paganini performance, Google is likely to serve ads for used violins, rare recordings of "Cantabile in re maggiore" and tickets for some "Quartetto" concert. That kind of relevance is important, because Google does not recognize a fee when somebody sees an ad, but rather when somebody clicks an ad, so it is in the interest of the Web publisher/content distributor to provide the best context (content metadata, ancillary information, words, page structure, and formatting) so that Google will provide ads most likely to interest the specific user. Google's AdSense engine, as with everything Google, is rather sophisticated. Rather than simply serving up random ads from its advertiser base, Google periodically analyses the page content to make sure the ads users see are likely to pique their interest.

These emerging business models fit well in Web2.0 and participation context, where strategies are in place to mash up and remix existing content, content provided by end users and content provided by external sources and leverage the use of search engines' contextual advertisement to differentiate content providers' revenue streams.

## Common Aspects of Advanced Business Models

Whatever approach is selected, more efficient and satisfactory business models need at least to have the following features:

- They address new ways of delivering and consuming music (digital revolution).
- They address the diversity of targeted market sectors and final customers.
- There are efficient, safe, performing, and possibly standard protection mechanisms, enabling the operation of the business models.
- They are flexible, and their flexibility is supported by the underlying technologies.
- They are developed and diffused by more dynamic and flexible companies with respect to the existing, often static, giants.
- They leverage the interactive and multimedia aspects of the digital content and music in particular.
- The revenue streams are mainly from added value services and features, focusing on what the customers really want and need.
- They leverage the reduction in distribution costs to make niche markets (vanity publishing, national and regional markets, cultural heritages) as new revenue streams.
- They are based on multiple revenue streams and on reuse of content for different markets and markets sectors (entertainment, advertising, multimedia content production, infotainment, education).

Solving the above addressed issues, or at least finding a path to improve the situation, would bring the online digital music market into a new era of expansion and development. In fact, a widely trusted environment, from the point of view of

protection and security, would increase supply and demand of digital music via the Internet. Consequently, more people would be stimulated to provide themselves with high-speed Internet connections. This would increase the average availability of bandwidth, inducing other markets (such as movies or software ones) to increase investments on online market.

In particular, a list of possible benefits can be summarized in the following points:

- Reduction in distribution costs.
- Chances to reach a wider audience.
- Higher flexibility in the offer.
- Access to "niche" markets previously not economical to enter.
- Exploitation of new services (infotainment, edutainment, e-learning, …) and new media (3G mobile, Wi-fi, broadband Internet).
- Valorisation of existing archives, valorisation of cultural heritage.
- Creation of a standard in content protection: new distribution systems could refer to a proved and trusted way of protecting digital content. This could be the starting point to develop new online markets that distribute other kind of content, such as e-books, digital movies, or software.
- Improvement in quality of digitalized content: the digitalized content quality could almost match the quality of the nondigitalized one. Customers could find more and more convenient buying digital content.
- Increasing in quantity of online distributed content: this could reduce the prices of digital content. Moreover, the traditional distribution system (shops) should improve their supply to try to regain positions in the market.
- Increasing of average availability of bandwidth: if Internet users had a better quality Internet connection, digital markets would increase the amount of sold digital content.

- Impulse in developing of online distribution to mobile technology (UMTS, Wi-fi): a robust online distribution market would naturally expand to alternative way of selling digital content.
- Creation of a standard in distribution systems: it would be easier to develop new distribution systems.
- Creation of a standard in exchange formats: the distribution systems could refer to a unique way of exchanging format, so to improve the interoperability among them.

## Evolution and Adoption of MPEG-21

MPEG-21 aims at defining a normative open framework for multimedia delivery and consumption for use by all the players in the delivery and consumption chain. This open framework will provide content creators, producers, distributors, and service providers with equal opportunities in the MPEG-21-enabled open market. This will also be to the benefit of the content consumer providing them access to a large variety of content in an interoperable manner (Bormans, 2002).

MPEG-21 is based on two essential concepts: the definition of a fundamental unit of distribution and transaction (the Digital Item), and the concept of Users interacting with Digital Items. The Digital Items can be considered the "what" of the Multimedia Framework (e.g., a video collection, a music album), and the Users can be considered the "who" of the Multimedia Framework.

The goal of MPEG-21 can thus be rephrased to defining the technology needed to support Users to exchange, access, consume, trade, and otherwise manipulate Digital Items in an efficient, transparent, and interoperable way.

During the MPEG-21 standardization process, Calls for Proposals, based upon requirements, have been and continue to be issued by MPEG. Eventually the responses to the calls result in different parts of the MPEG-21 standard (i.e., ISO/IEC 21000-N) after intensive discussion,

*Table 3. MPEG standards covering different parts of the digital content value chain*

| MPEG Standard | Targeted Usage |
|---|---|
| MPEG-1<br>MPEG-2<br>MPEG-4 | Coding of audio/visual content |
| MPEG-7 | Providing metadata that describes multimedia content |
| MPEG-21 | Providing a framework for the all-electronic creation, production, delivery, and trade of content. Within the framework we can use the other MPEG standards where appropriate. |

consultation, and harmonisation efforts between MPEG experts, representatives of industry, and other standardization bodies.

MPEG-21 identifies and defines the mechanisms and elements needed to support the multimedia delivery chain as described, as well as the relationships between and the operations supported by them. Within the parts of MPEG-21, these elements are elaborated by defining the syntax and semantics of their characteristics, such as interfaces to the elements.

MPEG-21 will create an open framework for multimedia delivery and consumption, with both the content creator and content consumer as focal points. It will define a multimedia framework to enable transparent and augmented use of multimedia resources across a wide range of networks and devices used by different communities (called simply "*Users*").

MPEG21 aims to enable electronic creation, delivery, trade of digital multimedia content, to provide access to information and services from almost anywhere at anytime with ubiquitous terminals and networks, and to identify, describe, manage, and protect the content in order to the *entire multimedia content delivery chain* encompassing content creation, production, delivery, and consumption. Many standards exist for delivery and consumption of multimedia contents, but there is no "big picture" to describe how these elements relate to each other.

Table 3 table shows how MPEG21 relates to other MPEG standards that cover different areas.

Different advantages can be identified for the major content chain actors when applying MPEG-21 compliant solutions (Girer, Günther, Schmucker, & Spadoni, 2004), namely:

- Standardised exchange formats and technologies allows the device-independent protection of intellectual property. Protection is not limited to certain hardware devices or operating systems. Stakeholders can easily exchange content without the need to take care about media formats or hardware-related issues.
- An increased level of trust will be established between Composers, Publishers, Distributor,s and End users. The intellectual protection management and protection allows the control of the usage of content.
- Contractual aspects can be directly incorporated in license files, which are automatically evaluated and enforced.
- A standardised IPMP solution is accepted by customers as they can use content independent of their hardware or software solutions.
- The distribution of the content is independent of the information carrier. Information can be transmitted, for example, by CD-ROM, e-mail, or via download.
- Content identifiers allow the creation of references that are useful for IPMP, as well as for metadata related issues.
- Cooperation between content owners, publishers, distributors, and collecting societies is improved, as all the necessary information including usage rights exists, and can be easily transferred to the collecting societies.

- As the content identifiers can also be connected with different media representations (e.g., audio files of performances) automatic monitoring of the usage rights is improved, and collecting societies are supported in collecting royalties.
- Promotion activities are improved as a license clearly identifies allowed operations and a valid period of time of these operations.

## CONCLUSION

The "Online Distribution of content" is a complex phenomenon. The *scope* of the problem is very wide, and the analysis work quite laborious due to the complexity and heterogeneity of the market, the quick and dynamic evolution of the enabling technologies, the contrasting interests and opposite driving forces.

The analysis work put good effort in highlighting *the importance of the needs of end users and consumers* of music when considering the major problems, as well as the new behaviours and possibilities originated by the availability of music in digital format. Copyright can represent the tool to get a trade-off between the sometimes conflicting interests of users and publishers-majors-authors. Copyright should be based on a balancing principle: the needs of the rights holder should be balanced against those of society, users, and consumers. Such balancing principle behind copyright should be translated in terms of the new technologies and the digital scenario to ensure that users have sufficient and easy access to music, while still protecting the interests of rights holders.

More and more authors, copyright collecting societies, and independent labels are embracing the conviction that economic and business models, generated or based on *peer-to-peer* communication schemas, are totally positive in terms of distribution, selling, and knowledge of music.

Such authors and their representatives are inviting the major labels to start a new *innovative* and creative approach, involving also the Internet Service Providers in the process, and allowing the user, paying a fee, to access music and possibly redistribute rights via the peer-to-peer and a new licensing scheme. The approach aims to remunerate rights holder without limiting too much the freedom of end users, providing value to all the players in the content value chain.

However, the lack of standards for interoperability between proprietary technologies is a serious impediment to the broad deployment of consumer-friendly legitimate media distribution. *Standards* can play a primary role for the full exploitation of the Internet in terms of content exchange. Within these activities, protocols and interfaces are standardized to enable exchange of content. MPEG initially addressed the issues of coding of moving pictures and audios. Areas addressed by MPEG include (de-) compression, processing, and coded representation of moving pictures, audio, and multimedia content. Within the "MPEG family," each member is addressing specific issues: the still evolving MPEG-21 ISO standard aims to provide an interoperable multimedia framework and to support users in accessing, exchanging, and manipulating digital items. MPEG-21 appears to fit well the music distribution scenario, providing an interoperable multimedia framework and supporting users in accessing, exchanging, and manipulating digital music

As always, user requirements have to be considered carefully. And if so, they are only one part of standardisation activities, as potential users have to be aware of the benefits of standards. To shorten the time between creation of a standard and its real world establishment, potential users have to be integrated as soon as possible in the standardisation process.

Besides the traditional use cases, the digital distribution of content provides new possibilities and roles. For example, some users might be interested in the Event Reporting to gain information about distribution numbers. This might provide new opportunities for software vendors who are paid according to the actual number of performed transactions done with their software solution. This results in a constant revision of the user requirements, determined by real-world users and real-world applications.

Concerning DRM technology providers, Sun's Open DReaM initiative and open standard DRM efforts should be highlighted and followed for future development, in particular concerning (1) potential new partnerships with big players in consumer electronics and (2) the Participation Age, that is digital media activity outside the mainstream, Web2.0-style microcontent, or consumer created content.

In short, transaction and *business models* are key to stimulate the growth of the online content distribution market However, many of the players in the industry are purely creative, lacking in many of the basic marketing, administrative, or even technical skills required to take advantage of the new opportunities offered and, at the same time, unable to defend themselves from the challenges of a shrinking market in other segments. New technologies are opening up new market opportunities for the music business, as the digital world is converting the mass market into a mass of niche markets. Also, opportunities for content from economically marginal groups or regions could be promoted.

Lately, innovative business models emerged to address the wide issue of making a content–based business profitable, or at least sustainable, as in the case of public organizations needing to cover high costs, and efforts for content digitization, maintenance, and creation. The objective is to develop and activate new revenue streams and new distribution channels, by targeting *small, niche markets*, both repurposing and reusing the available content and adopting major search engines' contextual advertisement business models, like Google AdSense or Yahoo! Search Marketing (formerly Overture).

## ACKNOWLEDGMENT

Part of the work needed in writing this chapter was performed in the framework of the Music-Network Centre of Excellence, cosupported by the European Communities IST (Information Society Technology) 5th Framework Programme, and coordinated by Prof. Paolo Nesi of the University of Florence, Dipartimento di Sistemi and Informatica.

The author would like to thank all participants of the MUSICNETWORK *Open Workshops* held in Darmstadt (December 2002), Leeds (September 2003), Munich (March 2004), Barcelona (September 2004), and Wien (July 2005), who provided valuable contribution to the thoughts presented in this chapter.

## REFERENCES

Barthelemy, J., Gunther, B., Nesi, P., N,g K. C., Schmucker, M., & Spadoni, F. (2003). *Interactive MUSICNETWORK portal*. Retrieved September 2004, from http://www.interactivemusicnetowork.org

Bechtold, S. (2001). *Fair use by design or by law*. Universitat Tuebingen and Stanford Law School. Retrieved from http://www.jura.uni-tuebingen.de/~s-bes1/pub/2001/Fair_Use_By_Design.pdf

Bormans, J., & Hill K. (2002). *MPEG-21 Overview v.5*. ISO/IEC JTC1/SC29/WG11, Shanghai, October 2002.

Chiariglione, L. (1999). *Technologies for e-content*, Paper presented at WIPO International Conference on Electronic Commerce and Intellectual Property, Geneva, August 1999. Retrieved September 2004, from http://www.chiariglione.org/leonardo/publications/wipo99/index.htm

Chiariglione, L. (2004). *The MPEG home page*. Retrieved September 2004, from http://www.chiariglione.org/mpeg

Chiariglione, L. (2005). *Media and rights management. The future digital economy: Digital content – creation, distribution*. January 2006. Retrieved February 2006, from http://www.chiariglione.org/leonardo/publications/oecd2006/index.htm

CISAC. (2004). *International Confederation of Societies of Authors and Composers Web site*. Retrieved September 2004, from http://www.cisac.org

Content Village. (2004). *An accompanying measure of the eContent programme*. Retrieved January 2004, from http://www.content-village.org

Creative Commons. (2004). *Creative Commons licenses*. Retrieved September 2004, from http://creativecommons.org/

DigiCULT. (2004). *Digital heritage and cultural content*. Access to cultural heritage is in the IST priority area within the 6th Framework Programme of the European Commission (2002-2006). Retrieved January 2005, from http://www.cordis.lu/digicult

DMP. (2005). *Digital Media Project Web site*. Retrieved May 2005, from http://www.dmpf.org/

EFF. (2005). *Electronic Frontier Foundation Web site*. Retrieved May 2005, from http://www.eff.org

Fontanelli, S. (2003). *MPEG21 easy. A tutorial on MPEG21 framework activities.* Interactive MUSICNETWORK Project, Working Group on Distribution of Coded Music. Retrieved September 2004, from http://www.interactiveMUSICNETWORK.org/documenti/view_document.php?file_id=727

Girer, M., Günther, B., Schmucker, M, & Spadoni, F. (2004). MPEG-21 and music notation applications. In J. Delgado, P. Nesi, & K. Ng (Eds.), *4th IEEE Conference on Web Delivering of Music Scores*, Barcelona (E), September 13-14, 2004. Retrieved from http://csdl.computer.

org/comp/proceedings/wedelmusic/2004/2157/
00/21570028abs.htm

Günther, B., Schmucker, M., & Spadoni, F. (2004). *Music notation requirements for the protection of coded music.* Interactive MUSICNETWORK Project. Retrieved September 2004, from http://www.interactiveMUSICNETWORK.org/documenti/view_document.php?file_id=790

ISO/IEC. (2004). Syntax and semantics of a Rights Expression Language. ISO/IEC 21000 Technical Report.

Kosch, H. (2003). *Distributed multimedia database technologies supported by MPEG-7 and MPEG-21.* CRC Press. Retrieved from http://www-itec.uni-klu.ac.at/~harald/mmbook/

Lenzi, R., & Spadoni F. (2003). *DRM technology survey, technical report.* Interactive MUSICNETWORK Project, Working Group on Distribution of Coded Music. Retrieved September 2004, from http://www.interactiveMUSICNETWORK.org/documenti/view_document.php?file_id=361

Moore, G. A. (1991). Crossing the chasm: Marketing and selling mainstream customers. NY: HarperCollins.

Nesi, P., Zoia, G., Bellini, P., & Barthelemy, J (2003). Music notation application requirements and MPEG technology.

Norman, D. A. (1998). *The invisible computer: Why good products can fail, the personal computer is so complex, and information appliances are the solution.* Cambridge, MA: MIT Press.

Norman, D. A. (2002). *The design of everyday things.* New York: Basic Books.

OMA. (2004). *Open Mobile Alliance Web site.* Retrieved September 2004, from http://www.openmobilealliance.org/

RIAA. (2005). *Recording Industry Association of America Web site.* Retrieved May 2005, from http://www.riaa.com

Rosenblath, B. (2005). *DRMwatch Web site.* Retrieved May 2005, from http://www.drmwatch.com

Rosenblath, B. (2007). *DRMwatch Web site.* Retrieved February 2007, from http://www.drmwatch.com

Spadoni, F., Lenzi, R., & Schmucker, M. (2005). Distribution of coded music. In M. Mitolo, P. Nesi, & K. Ng (Eds.), *Proceedings of the 5th MUSICNETWORK Open Workshop*, Vienna (A), July 2005.

WIPO, World Intellectual Property Organization. (2004). *Copyright definitions.* Retrieved September 2004, from http://www.wipo.int

## ENDNOTES

[1]   Human-centred or user-centred approach. See bibliography for more details.

[2]   This is an extension of classification of technologies for distribution of digital content from [DMP].

364

# Compilation of References

About Pure Data. (n.d). Retrieved April 5, 2006 from http://puredata.info/

Abraham, M. (1943). A theory of human motivation. *Psychological Review,* 370-396. Reissued in 2004 as an Appendix to *The Third Force: The Psychology of Abraham Maslow* in Adobe PDF.

ADL Technical Team. (2004). *SCORM Specifications v1.3.* Retrieved from http://www.adlnet.org/

Adler, S., Berglund, A., *et al.* (2001). *Extensible stylesheet language (XSL) Version 1.0.* Retrieved March 16, 2006, from http://www.w3.org/TR/xsl/

Allamanche. E., Herre. J., Hellmuth. O., Froba. B., & Cremer, M. (2001). AudioID: Toward content-based identification of audio material, In *Proceedings 110ᵗʰ AES,* Amsterdam, The Netherlands, 2001.

Altheim, M., & McCarron, S. (2001). *XHTML 1.1—Module-based XHTML.* Retrieved March 16, 2006, from http://www.w3.org/TR/xhtml11

American Library Association. (2005). *Digital rights management and libraries.* Retrieved March 20, 2007, from http://www.ala.org/ala/washoff/WOissues/copyrightb/digitalrights/digitalrightsmanagement.htm

Anderson, R. (2003). *Trusted computing—Frequently asked questions,* August, 2003. Retrieved March 21, 2007, from http://www.cl.cam.ac.uk/~rja14/tcpa-faq.html

Anderson, R. (2004). *Economics and security resource page, 2004.* Retrieved March 21, 2007, from http://www.cl.cam.ac.uk/~rja14/econsec.html

Apparao, V., Byrne, S., Champion, M., Isaacs, S., Le Hors, A., Nicol, G. et al. (1998). *DOM1: Document object model level 1.* Retrieved March 16, 2006, from http://www.w3.org/TR/REC-DOM-Level-1

Arkaos VJ 3.6 MIDI. (2006). Retrieved April 5, 2006, from http://www.arkaos.net/software/vj_description.php

Arnold, M., Schmucker, M., & Wolthusen, S. (2003). *Techniques and applications of digital wtermarking and content protection.* Boston: Artech House.

Arrest in 'Screener' Upload Case. *CBS News,* Los Angeles, January 23, 2004. Retrieved March 21, 2007, from http://www.cbsnews.com/stories/2004/02/18/entertainment/main600881.shtml

Askenfelt, A. (1989). Measurement of the bowing parameters in violin playing. II: Bow-bridge distance, dynamic range, and limits of bow force. *Journal of the Acoustical Society of America, 86*(2), 503-516.

Axon. (2007). *Axon AX 100 MK II, Guitar to MIDI Controller.* Retrieved February 12, 2007, from http://audiode.terratec.net/

Bainbridge, D., & Bell, T. (2001). The challenge of optical music recognition. *Computers and the Humanities, 35,* 95-121.

Bainbridge, D., & Bell, T. (2003). A music notation construction engine for optical music recognition. *Software—Practice & Experience, 33*(2), 173-200.

Bainbridge, D., & Bell, T.. (1996). An extensible optical music recognition system. *Australian Computer Science Communications, 18*(1), 308-317.

Bainbridge, D., & Carter, N. (1997). Automatic recognition of music notation. In H. Bunke & P. Wang (Eds.), *Handbook of optical character recognition and document image analysis* (pp. 557–603). Hackensack, NJ: World Scientific.

Bainbridge, D., & Wijaya, K. (1999). Bulk processing of optically scanned music. In *Proceedings of the 7th International Conference on Image Processing and Its Applications* (pp. 474–478).

Baker, M. J. (1992). Design of an intelligent tutoring system for musical structure and interpretation. In M. Balaban, K. Ebcioglu, & O. Laske (Eds.), *Understanding music with AI: Perspectives on music cognition* (pp. 467-489). The AAAI Press/The MIT Press.

Barthelemy, J., Gunther, B., Nesi, P., N,g K. C., Schmukker, M., & Spadoni, F. (2003). *Interactive MUSIC-NETWORK portal.* Retrieved September 2004, from http://www.interactivemusicnetowork.org

B-Control Fader BCF2000. (n.d.). Retrieved April 2, 2006, from http://www.behringer.com/BCF2000/index.cfm?lang=ENG

Bechtold, S. (2001). *Fair use by design or by law.* Universitat Tuebingen and Stanford Law School. Retrieved from http://www.jura.uni-tuebingen.de/~s-bes1/pub/2001/Fair_Use_By_Design.pdf

Bell, T. W. (2007). *Music copyrights table.* Retrieved March 20, 2007, from http://www.tomwbell.com/teaching/Music(C)s.html

Bellini, P., & Nesi, P. (2001, November 23-24). WEDEL-MUSIC FORMAT: An XML music notation format for emerging applications. In *Proceedings of the 1st International Conference of Web Delivering of Music*, Florence, Italy, (pp. 79-86). IEEE press.

Bellini, P., & Nesi, P. (2004). Modeling music notation in the Internet multimedia age. In S. E. George (Ed.),

*Visual perception of music notation: On-line and off-line recognition.* Hershey, PA: IRM Press.

Bellini, P., Barthelemy, J., Bruno, I., Nesi, P., & Spinu, M. B. (2003). Multimedia music sharing among mediateques: Archives and distribution to their attendees. *Journal on Applied Artificial Intelligence, 17*(8-9), 773-795.

Bellini, P., Bruno, I., & Nesi, P. (2001). Optical music sheet segmentation. In *Proceedings of the First International Conference on WEB Delivering of MUSIC* (pp. 183–190).

Bellini, P., Bruno, I., & Nesi, P. (2004). An off-line optical music sheet recognition. In S. E. George (Ed.), *Visual perception of music notation: On-line and off-line recognition.* Hershey, PA: Idea Group Inc.

Bellini, P., Bruno, I., & Nesi, P. (2004). Multilingual lyric modeling and management. In S. E. George (Ed.), *Visual perception of music notation: On-line and off-line recognition.* Hershey, PA: IRM Press.

Bellini, P., Bruno, I., & Nesi, P. (2005). Automatic formatting of music sheets through MILLA rule-based language and engine. *Journal of New Music Research, 34*(3), 237-257.

Bellini, P., Bruno, I., & Nesi, P. Assessing optical music recognition tools. *Computer Music Journal, 31*(1), 68-93.

Bellini, P., Crombie, D., & Nesi, P. (2003). MUSICNET-WORK: To bring music industry into the interactive multimedia age. In *Proceedings of the EVA Florence, Italy.*

Bellini, P., Della Santa, R., & Nesi, P. (2001, November 23-24). Automatic formatting of music sheet. In *Proceedings of the 1st International Conference on WEB Delivering of Music* (pp. 170-177). Florence, Italy: IEEE press.

Bellini, P., Fioravanti, F., & Nesi, P. (1999). Managing music in orchestras. *IEEE Computer, September,* 26-34. Retrieved from http://www.dsi.unifi.it/~moods/

Bellini, P., Nesi, P., & Spinu, M. B. (2002). Cooperative visual manipulation of music notation. *ACM Transactions on Computer-Human Interaction, 9*(3), 194-237.

Bellini, P., Nesi, P., & Zoia, G. (2005). Symbolic music representation in MPEG for new multimedia applications. *IEEE Multimedia, 12*(4), 42-49.

Berners-Lee, T. (2000). *Weaving the Web: The past present and future of the World Wide Web by its inventor.* London: Texere.

Biddle, P., England, P., Peinado, M., & Willman, B. (2002). The darknet and the future of content distribution. *Microsoft Corporation,* 2002 ACM Workshop on Digital Rights Management. Retrieved from http://crypto.stanford.edu/DRM2002/darknet5.doc

Biesenbender, V. (1992). *Von der unerträglichen Leichtigkeit des Instrumentalspiels.* Aarau, Switzerland: Musikedition Nepomuk.

Biron, P. V., Permanente, K., & Malhotra, A. (Eds.). (2004). *XML schema part 2: Datatypes*(2nd ed.). Retrieved March 16, 2006, from http://www.w3.org/TR/xmlschema-2/

Blostein, D. & Haken, L. (1991). Justification of printed music. *Communications of the ACM, 34*(3), 88-99.

Blostein, D., & Baird, H. S. (1992). A critical survey of music image analysis. In H. S. Baird, H. Bunke, & K. Yamamoto (Eds.), *Structured document image analysis* (pp. 405–434). Berlin: Springer-Verlag.

Blostein, D., & Haken, L. (1991). Justification of printed music. *Communications of the ACM, 34*(3), 88-99.

Bockstedt, J. C., Kauffman, R. J., & Riggins, F. J. (2005). The move to artist-led online music distribution: Explaining structural changes in the digital music market. In *Proceedings of the 38th Hawaii International Conference on System Sciences, 2005.* Retrieved from http://misrc.umn.edu/workingpapers/fullpapers/2004/0422_091204.pdf

Boehm, C. (undated) *MuTaTeD (Music Tagging Type definition).* Retrieved March 16, 2006, from http://www.music.gla.ac.uk/CMT/projects/MuTaTeD1/mutated.html

Boll, S., Klas, U., & Westermann, W. (1999). *A comparison of multimedia document models concerning advanced requirements.* Technical Report—Ulmer Informatik-Berichte No 99-01. Department of Computer Science, University of Ulm, Germany.

Bomsel, O., & Geffroy, A. G. (2004). *Economic analysis of digital rights management systems (DRMs).* MediaNet Project Paper, December, 2004. Retrieved from http://www.cerna.ensmp.fr/Documents/OB-AGG-EtudeDRM.pdf

Bormans, J., & Hill K. (2002). *MPEG-21 Overview v.5.* ISO/IEC JTC1/SC29/WG11, Shanghai, October 2002.

Bos, B. (1997). *Some thoughts and software on XML.* Retrieved March 16, 2006, from http://www.w3.org/XML/notes.html

Bos, B., Lie, H. W., Lilley, C., & Jacobs, I. (Eds). (1998). *Cascading style sheets, level 2.* Retrieved March 16, 2006, from http://www.w3.org/TR/REC-CSS2

Bosak, J. (1997). *XML, Java, and the future of the Web.* Retrieved from http://www.ibiblio.org/pub/sun-info/standards/xml/why/xmlapps.htm

Bosak, J. (1998). Media-independent publishing: Four myths about XML. *IEEE Computer, 31*(10), 120-122.

Brandão, M., Wiggins, G., & Pain, H. (1999). Computers in music education. In G. Wiggins (Ed.), *Proceedings of The AISB'99 Symposium on Musical Creativity* (pp. 82-88). AISB.

Brandon Hall Research. Retrieved from http://www.brandon-hall.com/

Bray, T. (1998). *Annotated XML specification.* Retrieved March 16, 2006, from http://www.xml.com/axml/testaxml.htm

Bray, T., Paoli, J., Sperberg-McQueen, C. M., & Maler, E. (1998). *Extensible markup language (XML) 1.0* (2nd ed.). Retrieved from http://www.w3.org/TR/REC-xml

Brueggemann-Klein, A., & Wood, D. (2004). A conceptual model for XML. In P. King & E. V. Munson (Eds.). *Digital documents: Systems and principles* (pp. 176-189). Berlin: Springer.

Bruno, I. (2003). *Music score image analysis: Methods and tools for automatic recognition and indexing.* PhD Thesis, Department of Systems and Informatics, University of Florence, Italy.

Bruno, I., & Nesi, P. (2002). *Multimedia music imaging: Digitisation, restoration, recognition and preservation of music scores and music manuscripts.* 1st MUSICNET-WORK Open Workshop, Darmstadt, Germany, 2002.

Buchla, D., Buxton, W. A. S., Chafe, C., Machover, T., Moog, R., Mathews, M., Risset, J. C., Sonami, L., & Waiswisz, M., (2000). Round table. In M. M. Wanderley & M. Battier (Ed.), *Trends in gestural control of music* (pp. 415-437). Paris, France: IRCAM Centre Pompidou.

Bulterman, D., Grassel, G., Jansen, J., Koivisto, A., Laya-ïda, N.,Michel, T., Mullender, S., & Zucker, D. (Eds.). (2005). *Synchronized multimedia integration language (SMIL 2.1).* Retrieved from http://www.w3.org/TR/2005/CR-SMIL2-20050513/

Byrd, D. (2001). Music-notation searching and digital libraries. In *Proceedings of 2001 Joint Conference on Digital Libraries* (JCDL 2001) (pp.239-246).

Byrd, D. (2006). *OMR (Optical Music Recognition) Systems.* School of Informatics and School of Music, Indiana University. Retrieved from http://mypage.iu.edu/~donbyrd/OMRSystemsTable.html

Byrd, D. A. (1984). Music notation by computer. (Doctoral Dissertation, Indiana University). *UMI, Dissertation Service.* Retrieved from http://umi.com

Cadoz, C., & Wanderley, M. M. (2000). Gesture—Music. In M. M. Wanderley & M. Battier (Ed.), *Trends in gestural control of music* (pp. 28-65), Paris, France: IRCAM Centre Pompidou.

Cadoz, C., Luciani, A., & Florens, J. L. (1984). Responsive input devices and sound synthesis by simulation of instrumental mechanisms: The CORDIS system. *Computer Music Journal, 8*(2), 60-73.

Camp, L. J. (2003). First principles of copyright for DRM Design. *IEEE Internet Computing, 7*(3).

Camurri, A,. Hashimoto, S., Richetti, M., Trocca, R., Suzuki, K., & Volpe, G. (2000). EyesWeb—Toward gesture and affect recognition in interactive dance and music systems. *Computer Music Journal, 24*(1), 57-69.

Cano, P., Baltle, E., Kalker, T., & Haitsma, J. (2002). A review of algorithms for audio fingerprinting. *IEEE Workshop on Multimedia Signal Processing.*

CANTATE project. (1994). *Deliverable 3.3: Report on SMDL evaluation, WP3.* CANTATE. Retrieved from http://projects.fnb.nl

Capella. (2005). *CAPXML.* Retrieved from http://www.whc.de/capella.cfm

capella-scan (n.d.). *capella Software,* Retrieved February 9, 2003, from http://www.whc.de/

Carlisle, D., Ion, P., Miner, R., & Poppelier, N. (Eds.). (2003). *Mathematical markup language (MathML) version 2.0* (2nd ed.). Retrieved March 16, 2006, from http://www.w3.org/TR/2003/REC-MathML2-20031021/

Carter, N. P. (1989). *Automatic recognition of printed music in the context of electronic publishing.* Doctoral dissertation, University of Surrey, UK.

Carter, N. P. (1992). Segmentation and preliminary recognition of madrigals notated in white mensural notation. *Machine Vision and Applications, 5*(3), 223-30.

Carter, N. P. (1994). Conversion of the Haydn symphonies into electronic form using automatic score recognition: A pilot study. In L. M. Vincent & T. Pavlidis (Eds.), *Proceedings of the SPIE—Document Recognition, 2181,* (pp. 279–290).

Carter, N. P. (1994). Music score recognition: Problems and prospects. *Computing in Musicology, 9,* 152-158.

Carter, N. P., & Bacon, R. A. (1990). Automatic recognition of music notation. In *Proceedings of the International Association for Pattern Recognition Workshop on Syntactic and Structural Pattern Recognition,* 482.

Castan, G. (2000). *MusiXML.* Retrieved March 16, 2006, from http://www.music-notation.info/en/musixml/MusiXML.html

CETIS, the Centre for Educational Technology Interoperability Standards. Retrieved from http://www.cetis.ac.uk/

Chadabe, J. (1997). *Electric sound: The past and promise of electronic music.* Upper Saddle River, NJ: Prentice Hall.

Chapman, B. (2006). *LMS knowledge base 2006.* Sunnyvale, CA: Brandon-Hall.

Chapman, B., & Nantel, R. (2006). *Low-cost learning management systems 2006.* Sunnyvale, CA: Brandon-Hall.

Chastanet, F. (undated) *MusiqueXML* Retrieved March 16, 2006, from http://francois.chastanet.free.fr/musiquexml/MusiqueXML.htm

Chee, K. S., & Phon-Amnuaisuk, S. (2005). Intelligent learning environment: Building hybrid system from standard application and Web application. In *The 5ᵗʰ IEEE International Conference on Advanced Learning Technologie*s (pp. 506-510). Kaohsiung, Taiwan, July 2005.

CHI. (2007). *Conference on Human Factors in Computing Systems, also labeled as Conference on Human Computer Interaction (HCI).* Retrieved February 12, 2007, from http://www.chi2007.org/.

Chiariglione, L. (1999). *Technologies for e-content,* Paper presented at WIPO International Conference on Electronic Commerce and Intellectual Property, Geneva, August 1999. Retrieved September 2004, from http://www.chiariglione.org/leonardo/publications/wipo99/index.htm

Chiariglione, L. (2004). *The MPEG home page.* Retrieved September 2004, from http://www.chiariglione.org/mpeg

Chiariglione, L. (2005). *Media and rights management. The future digital economy: Digital content – creation, distribution.* January 2006. Retrieved February 2006, from http://www.chiariglione.org/leonardo/publications/oecd2006/index.htm

Chong, C., Corin, R., Etalle, S., Hartel, P., Jonker, W., & Law, Y. (2003). LicenseScript: A novel digital rights language and its semantics. In IEEE Computer Socitety *Proceedings of the Third International Conference WEB Delivering of Music (WEDELMUSIC'03)* (pp. 122-129).

Choudhury, G. S., DiLauro, T., Droettboom, M., Fujinaga, I., Harrington, B., & MacMillan, K. (2000). *Optical music recognition system within a large-scale digitization project.* International Conference on Music Information Retrieval.

CISAC. (2004). *International Confederation of Societies of Authors and Composers Web site.* Retrieved September 2004, from http://www.cisac.org

Clark, J. (1999). *XSL transformations (XSLT) Version 1.0.* Retrieved from http://www.w3.org/TR/1999/REC-xslt-19991116

Clark, J., & DeRose, S. (1999). *XML path language (Xpath) version 1.0.* Retrieved from http://www.w3.org/TR/1999/REC-xpath-19991116

Code, D. L. (2002). Grove.Max: An adaptive tuning system for MIDI Pianos. *Computer Music Journal, 26*(2), 50-61.

Cohnen, J. E. (2002). *DRM and privacy.* Research Paper Series, Research Paper No. 372741, Georgetown University Law Center.

Commission Staff Working Paper, SEC. (2002). *Digital rights—Background, systems, assessment, 197,* February, 2002, Brussels

Content Village. (2004). *An accompanying measure of the eContent programme.* Retrieved January 2004, from http://www.content-village.org

Cook., J. (1998). Mentoring, metacognition and music: Interaction analyses and implications for intelligent learning environments. *Journal of Artificial Intelligence in Education, 9.*

Cooper, D., Ng, K. C., & Boyle, R. D. (1997). An extension of the MIDI file format: expressive MIDI—exp-MIDI. In E. Selfridge-Field (Ed.), *Beyond MIDI: The handbook of musical codes* (pp. 80–98) Cambridge, MA: MIT Press.

Cooper, D., Ng, K. C., & Boyle, R. D. (1997). MIDI extensions for musical notation: Expressive MIDI. In E. Selfridge-Field (Ed.), *Beyond MIDIL: The handbook of musical codes* (pp. 402-447). London, UK: The MIT Press.

*Copyright Issues for Music.* Music Library, University at Buffalo. Retrieved March 20, 2007, from http://ublib. buffalo.edu/libraries/units/music/copyright.html

Coüasnon, B. (2002). *Improving optical music recognition.* Position paper, First MUSICNETWORK Open Workshop, Darmstadt, Germany, 2002.

Coüasnon, B., & Camillerapp, J.. (1995). A way to separate knowledge from program in structured document analysis: Application to optical music recognition. In *International Conference on Document Analysis and Recognition* (pp. 1092-1097).

Coüasnon, B., & Rétif, B. (1995). Using a grammar for a reliable full score recognition system. In *Proceedings of the International Computer Music Conference (ICMC)* (pp. 187-194).

Council Resolution of 25 March 2002 on the eEurope Action Plan 2002: Accessibility of public websites and their content. (2002/C 86/02). *Official Journal of the European Communities.* Retrieved from http:// eur-lex.europa.eu/LexUriServ/site/en/oj/2002/c_086/ c_08620020410en00020003.pdf

Cover, R. (2006). *Cover pages: XML and music.* Retrieved March 16, 2006, from http://xml.coverpages. org/xmlMusic.html

Cox, I. J., Miller, M. L., & Bloom, J. A. (2002). Digital watermarking. In *The Morgan Kaufmann Series in Multimedia Information and Systems.* San Francisco, CA: Morgan Kaufmann Publishers.

Craver, S. A., Wu, M., Liu B., Stubblefield, A., Swartzlander, B., Wallach, D. S., Dean, D., & Felten, E. W. (2001). Reading between the lines: Lessons from the SDMI challenge. In *Proceedings of the 10th USENIX Security Symposium*, Washington DC.

Creative Commons. (2004). *Creative Commons licenses.* Retrieved September 2004, from http://creativecommons.org/

Crombie, D., Fuschi, D., Mitolo, N., Nesi, P., Ng, K., & Ong, B. (2005). **Bringing music industry into the interactive multimedia age.** *AXMEDIS International Conference*, Florence, Italy. IEEE Computer Society Press.

CUIDADO project. *Processing of music and Mpeg7.* Retrieved from http://www.ircam.fr/cuidad/

Dancing dots (n.d.). *Goodfeel Braille Music Translator.* Retrieved August 8, 2002, from http://www.dancingdots.com

Dannenberg, R. B. (2004). Combining visual and textual representations for flexible interactive audio signal processing. In G. Tzanetakis, G. Essl, & C. Leider (Ed.), *Proceedings of the 2004 International Computer Music Conference* (pp. 240-247). Miami, FL: International Computer Music Association.

Dannenberg, R., Sanchez, M., Joseph, A., Capell, P., Joseph, R., & Saul, R. (1990). A computer-based multimedia tutor for beginning piano students. *Interface-Journal of New Music Research, 19*(2-3),155-173.

Dataton Watchout. (n.d.). Retrieved April 3, 2006, from http://www.dataton.com/watchout

dbox dialog, strategy and design. (2005). Retrieved April 2, 2006, from http://www.dbox.com/

Delgado, J., Nesi, P., & Ng, K. C. (Eds.). (2004). In *Proceedings of the Fourth International Conference on WEB Delivering of Music (WEDELMUSIC-2004).* IEEE Computer Society Press, Barcelona, Spain.

DeRose, S. J., & Durand, D. G. (1994). *Making hypermedia work: A user's guide to HyTime.* Boston: Kluwer Academic.

DeRose, S. J., Maler, E., Orchard, D., & Trafford, B. (2001). *XML linking language (Xlink)*. Retrieved from http://www.w3.org/TR/xlink/

DigiCULT. (2004). *Digital heritage and cultural content*. Access to cultural heritage is in the IST priority area within the 6th Framework Programme of the European Commission (2002-2006). Retrieved January 2005, from http://www.cordis.lu/digicult

DMP. (2005). *Digital Media Project Web site*. Retrieved May 2005, from http://www.dmpf.org/

DPRL. (2007). Retrieved April 3, 2007, from http://www.oasis-open.org/cover/DPRLmanual-XML2.htm

DSSSL 1996 (ISO/IEC 10179). Retrieved March, 2006, from http://www.ibiblio.org/pub/sun-info/standards/dsssl/draft/

Dubosson-Torbay, M., Pigneur, Y., & Usunier, J. C. (2004). Business models for music distribution after the P2P revolution. In *WEDELMUSIC '04: Proceedings of the Web Delivering of Music, Fourth International Conference on Web Delivery Of Music*. Washington, DC: IEEE Computer Society.

EBU metadata specifications. *European Broadcasting Union (EBU)*. Retrieved March 21, 2007, from http://www.ebu.ch/en/technical/metadata/specifications/index.php

EEIG. European Economic Interest Grouping (EEIG). *Activities of the European Union, Summaries of Legislation, EUROPA.EU.INT*. Retrieved from http://europa.eu.int/scadplus/leg/en/lvb/l26015.htm

EFF. (2005). *Electronic Frontier Foundation Web site*. Retrieved May 2005, from http://www.eff.org

Egozy, E. B. (1995). *Deriving musical control features from a real-time timbre analysis of the clarinet*. Unpublished master's thesis. Massachusetts Institute of Technology, Cambridge, MA.

Fahmy, H., & Blostein, D. (1994). A graph-rewriting approach to discrete relaxation: Application to music recognition. In *Proceedings of the SPIE*, 2181, (pp. 291-302).

Fahmy, H., & Blostein, D. (1998). A graph-rewriting paradigm for discrete relaxation: Application to sheet-music recognition. *International Journal of Pattern Recognition and Artificial Intelligence, 12*(6), 763-99.

Farley, K. (2002). Digital dance theatre: The marriage of computers, choreography and techno/human reactivity *Body, Space and Technology*.

FBI Arrests Internet Movie Pirate. *FOX News*, January 23, 2004. Retrieved March 21, 2007, from http://www.foxnews.com/story/0,2933,109272,00.html

Fels, S. (2004). Designing for intimacy: Creating new interfaces for musical expression. In *Proceedings of the IEEE, 92*(4), 672-685.

Fels, S., Gadd, A., & Mulder, A. (2002). Mapping transparency through metaphor: Towards more expressive musical instrument. *Organised Sound, 7*(2), 109-126.

Felten, E. (2001). *Statement at the fourth international information hiding workshop in Pittsburgh*. Retrieved from http://www.cs.princeton.edu/sip/sdmi/sdmimessage.txt

Fernando, G., Jacobs, T., & Swaminathan, V. (2005). *Project DReaM: An architectural overview*. Retrieved April 3, 2007, from http://www.openmediacommons.org/collateral/DReaM-Overview.pdf

Ferraiolo, J. (2001). *Scalable vector graphics specification*. Retrieved March 16, 2006, from http://www.w3.org/TR/SVG

Ferris, R. (1995). *A HyTime application development guide*. Retrieved from ftp://ftp.techno.com/HyTime/Application_Development_Guide

Finale of Coda. Retrieved from http://www.finalemusic.com/

Fisher, W. (2004). Promises to keep—*Technology, law, and the future of rntertainment*. Retrieved March 23, 2007, from http://www.tfisher.org/PTK.htm

FLIC Project. (2004). *D2.1 Design of a pedagogical template*.

FLIC Project. (2005). *D2.4 Voice models recording.*

FLIC Project. (2005). *D2.3 Development of materials for the evaluation.*

FLIC project. (2006). *Special project status report for the EC.*

Flynn, P. (Ed.). (1999). *Frequently asked questions about the extensible markup language.* XML Special Interest Group FAQ.

Fober, D., Letz, S., & Orlarey, Y. (2004). Imutus: An interactive music tuition system. In C. Agon & G. Assayag (Eds.), *Sound and music computing, International Conference, smc'04, Paris, France, October 20-24, 2004, Proceedings* (pp. 91-95). IRCAM, 2004.

Fontanelli, S. (2003). *MPEG21 easy. A tutorial on MPEG21 framework activities.* Interactive MUSICNETWORK Project, Working Group on Distribution of Coded Music. Retrieved September 2004, from http://www.interactiveMUSICNETWORK.org/documenti/view_document.php?file_id=727

Frederico, G. (1999). ChordML. Retrieved March 16, 2006, from http://www.cifranet.org/xml/ChordML.html

Freehand. Retrieved from http://www.freehandsystems.com/

Fujinaga, I. (1988). *Optical music recognition using projections.* Master Thesis, McGill University, Montreal, Canada.

Fujinaga, I. (1988). *Optical music recognition using projections.* M.A: Thesis.

Fujinaga, I. (1996). *Adaptive optical music recognition.* Ph.D. Dissertation, Music, McGill University.

Fujinaga, I. (1996). Exemplar-based learning in adaptive optical music recognition system. In *Proceedings of the International Computer Music Conference* (pp. 55-56).

Fujinaga, I. (2001). An adaptive optical music recognition system. In D. Greer (Ed.). Musicology and sister disci-

plines. In *Past, Present, Future: Proceedings of the 16th International Congress of the International Musicological Society.* Oxford: Oxford University Press.

Fujinaga, I., & Riley, J. (2002). Digital image capture of musical scores. In *Proceedings of the 3rd International Conference on Music Information Retrieval (ISMIR 2002), IRCAM*—Centre Pompidou, Paris, France.

Fujinaga, I., Alphonce, B., & Pennycook, B. (1992). Interactive optical music recognition. In *Proceedings of the International Computer Music Conference* (pp. 117-120).

Furukawa, K., & Dutilleux, P. (2002). Live-electronics algorithms in the multimedia work "Swim Swan." In *Proceedings of the 5th International Conference on Digital Audio effects 2002* (pp. 263-268). Hamburg, Germany.

Fuss, C., Gatzemeier, F., Kirchhof, M., & Meyer, O. (2004). Inferring structure information form typography. In P. King & E. V. Munson (Eds.), *Digital documents: Systems and Principles* (pp. 44-55). Berlin: Springer.

Galamian, I. (1988). *Grundlagen und Methoden des Violinspiels* (2nd ed.). Frankfurt/M., Berlin, Germany: Edition Sven Erik Bergh.

GartnerG2 and the Berkman Center for Internet & Society. (2003). *Five scenarios for digital media in a post-Napster world.* Retrieved March 21, 2007, from http://cyber.law.harvard.edu/home/research_publication_series

Gezerlis, V. G., & Theodoridis, S. (2000). *An optical music recognition system for the notation of the Orthodox Hellenic Byzantine Music.* International Conference of Pattern Recognition (ICPR-2000), Barcelona, Spain.

Gill, C. (1997). The stomping ground: Musitronics, mu-tron, and the gizmotron. *Vintage Guitar Magazine, 11*(12).

Girer, M., Günther, B., Schmucker, M, & Spadoni, F. (2004). MPEG-21 and music notation applications. In J. Delgado, P. Nesi, & K. Ng (Eds.), *4th IEEE Conference on Web Delivering of Music Scores,* Barcelona

(E), September 13-14, 2004. Retrieved from http://csdl. computer.org/comp/proceedings/wedelmusic/2004/2157/ 00/21570028abs.htm

Goldfarb C. F., & Prescod, P. (1998). *The XML handbook.* NJ: Prentice Hall.

Goldfarb, C., Newcomb, P. J., & Kimberm, W. E. (1997). A reader's guide to the HyTime standard. Retrieved March 16, 2006, from http://www.hytime.org/papers/ htguide.html

Good, M. (2000). *MusicXML.* Retrieved March 16, 2006, from http://www.recordare.com

Good, M. (2001). MusicXML for notation and analysis. In W. B. Hewlett & E. Selfridge-Field (Eds.), *The virtual score: Representation, retrieval, restoration* (pp. 113-124). Cambridge, MA: The MIT Press. Retrieved from http://www.recordare.com

Good, M. (2002). MusicXML in practice: Issues in translation and analysis. In G. Haus & M. Longari (Eds.), *MAX 2002: Musical applications using XML. Proceedings First International Conference* (pp. 47-54). Laboratoria di Informatica Musicale, Computer Science Dept, State University of Milan.

Goto, S. (1999). The aesthetics and technological aspects of virtual musical instruments: The case of the superpolm MIDI violin. *Leonardo Music Journal, 9,* 115-120.

Graesser, H. (1996). *Electric violins.* Frankfurt am Main, Germany: Verlag Erwin Bochinsky.

Greek, D. (2004). *RIAA crackdown shows signs of success.* Retrieved March 20, 2007, from http://www. vnunet.com/vnunet/news/2124044/riaa-crackdown-shows-signs-success

Grigaitis, R. J. (1998). *XScore (eXtensible Score language).* Retrieved March 16, 2006, from http://grigaitis. net/xscore/

Grimm, R. (2005). *Privacy for digital rights management products and their business cases.* Virtual Goods Workshop at IEEE Axmedis 2005, Firence, Italy, December 2005.

Günther, B., Schmucker, M., & Spadoni, F. (2004). *Music notation requirements for the protection of coded music.* Interactive MUSICNETWORK Project. Retrieved September 2004, from http://www.interactiveMUSICNETWORK.org/documenti/view_document. php?file_id=790

Haitsma, J., van der Veen, M., Kalker, K., & Brueker, F. (2000). *Audio watermarking for monitoring and copy protection.* ACM Multimedia Workshops

HARMONICA. Retrieved from http://projects.fnb. nl/harmonica

Harris, R. (1987). *Reading Saussure.* London: Duckworth.

Haus, G., & Longari, M. (Eds.). (2002). *MAX 2002: Musical applications using XML.* In Proceedings First International Conference. Laboratoria di Informatica Musicale, Computer Science Dept, State University of Milan.

Haus, G., & Longari. M. (2002a). Towards a symbolic/ time-based music language based on XML. In G. Haus & M. Longari (Eds.). *MAX 2002: Musical applications using XML.* In *Proceedings First International Conference* (pp. 38-46). Laboratoria di Informatica Musicale, Computer Science Dept, State University of Milan.

Haus, G., & Longari. M. (2002b). Music information description by mark-up languages within DB-Web applications. In G. Haus & M. Longari (Eds.), *MAX 2002: Musical Applications using XML.* In *Proceedings First International Conference* (pp. 83-90). Laboratoria di Informatica Musicale, Computer Science Dept, State University of Milan.

Haus, G., & Longari. M. (2005). A multi-layered, time-based music description approach based on XML. *Computer Music Journal, 29*(1), 70-85.

Helix DRM. (2007). Retrieved April 3, 2007, from http:// www.realnetworks.com/products/drm/index.html

Herwijnen, E., van (1994). *Practical SGML* (2nd ed.). Boston: Kluwer Academic.

Heussenstamm, G. (1987). *The Norton manual of music notation*. W.W. Norton & Company, Inc.

Hoffstetter, F. (1981). Computer-based aural training: The GUIDO system. *Journal of Computer-based Instruction, 7*(3), 84-92.

Holland, S. (1993). Learning about harmony with harmony space: An overview. In M. Smith, A. Smaill, & G. Wiggins (Eds.), *Music education: An artificial intelligence approach. Workshops in Computing* (pp. 25-40). Montreal, Canada: Springer-Verlag.

Holland, S. (2000). Artificial intelligence in music education: A critical review. *Readings in Music and Artificial Intelligence, Contemporary Music Studies, 20*, 239-274. London: Harwood Academic Publishers.

Honing, H. (2001). From time to time: The representation of timing and tempo. *Computer Music Journal, 25*(3), 50-61.

Hoos, H. H., Hamel, K. A., Renz, K., & Kilian, J. (1998). The GUIDO music notation format—A novel approach for adequately representing score-level music. In *Proceedings of the International Computer Music Conference* (pp. 451–454).

Hornof, A. J., & Halverson, T. *Cognitive modeling, eye tracking and human-computer interaction*. Department of Computer and Information Science, University of Oregon. Retrieved March 23, 2007, from http://www.cs.uoregon.edu/research/cm-hci/

Hoschka, P. (1998). *Synchronized multimedia integration language (SMIL) 1.0 specification*. Retrieved from http://www.w3.org/TR/REC-smil

Hunt, A. (1999). *Radical musical interfaces for real-time musical control*. Unpublished doctoral dissertation, University of York, UK.

Hunt, A., & Wanderley, M. M. (2002). Mapping performer parameters to synthesis engines. *Organised Sound, 7*(2), 97-108.

Iannella, R. (2001). Digital rights management architectures. *D-Lib Magazine, 7*(6). Retrieved March 20, 2007, from http://webdoc.sub.gwdg.de/edoc/aw/d-lib/dlib/june01/iannella/06iannella.html

IDC. (2002). *Corporate eLearning: European market forecast and analysis 2001/2002*. IDC Corporate, 5 Speen Street, Framingham, MA , 01701.

I-MAETRO project. *EC IST FP6*. Retrieved from http://www.i-maestro.org

IMUTUS project. Retrieved from http://www.exodus.gr/imutus/

IMUTUS. (2004). *Interactive Music Tuition System*. Retrieved from http://www.exodus.gr/imutus

Ingram, J. (1985, 1999). *The notation of time*. Personal copy.

Ingram, J. (2002). *Developing traditions of music notation and performance on the Web*. Personal copy.

Ingram, J. (2002). *Music notation*. Personal copy.

Intellectual property. *Wikipedia*. Retrieved March 20, 2007, from http://en.wikipedia.org/wiki/Intellectual_property

International Standard Text Code. *ISO/TC 46/SC 9 WG3 Project 21047*. Retrieved March 20, 2007, from http://www.nlc-bnc.ca/iso/tc46sc9/wg3.htm

Ion, P., & Miner, R. (Eds.). (1999). *Mathematical markup language (MathML) 1.01 specification*. Retrieved March 16, 2006, from http://www.w3.org/1999/07/REC-MathML-19990707

IPA International Phonetic Association. Retrieved March 16, 2006, from http://www2.arts.gla.ac.uk/IPA/ipa.html

*ISO/IEC JTC1/SC29/WG11 W6689*. Call for proposals on symbolic music representation, Audio Subgroup, July 2004, Redmond, USA.

ISO/IEC. (2003). *ISO/IEC IS 21000-3—Digital Item Identification*. Geneva, Switzerland: ISO.

ISO/IEC. (2004). Syntax and semantics of a Rights Expression Language. ISO/IEC 21000 Technical Report.

ISO/IEC. (2004). *ISO/IEC 2nd Edition TR 21000-1—Vision, Technologies and Strategy.* Geneva, Switzerland: ISO.

ISO/IEC. (2004). *ISO/IEC IS 21000-5—Rights Expression Language.* Geneva, Switzerland: ISO.

ISO/IEC. (2004). *ISO/IEC IS 21000-6—Rights Data Dictionary.* Geneva, Switzerland: ISO.

ISO/IEC. (2004). *ISO/IEC IS 21000-7—Digital Item Adaptation.* Geneva, Switzerland: ISO.

ISO/IEC. (2004). *ISO/IEC 21000-11—TR Evaluation Methods for Persistent Association Technologies.* Geneva, Switzerland: ISO.

ISO/IEC. (2005). *ISO/IEC 21000-9—IS File Format.* Geneva, Switzerland: ISO.

ISO/IEC. (2005). *ISO/IEC 21000-12—TR Test Bed for MPEG-21 Resource Delivery.* Geneva, Switzerland: ISO.

ISO/IEC. (2005). *ISO/IEC IS 21000-16—Binary Format.* Geneva, Switzerland: ISO.

ISO/IEC. (2006). *ISO/IEC 2nd Edition IS 21000-2—Digital Item Declaration.* Geneva, Switzerland: ISO.

ISO/IEC. (2006). *ISO/IEC CD 21000-4—Intellectual Property Management and Protection.* Geneva, Switzerland: ISO.

ISO/IEC. (2006). *ISO/IEC IS 21000-8—Referente Software.* Geneva, Switzerland: ISO.

ISO/IEC. (2006). *ISO/IEC 21000-10—IS Digital Item Processing.* Geneva, Switzerland: ISO.

ISO/IEC. (2006). *ISO/IEC IS 21000-15—Event Reporting.* Geneva, Switzerland: ISO.

ISO/IEC. (2006). *ISO/IEC IS 21000-17—Fragment Identification of MPEG Resources.* Geneva, Switzerland: ISO.

ISO/IEC. (2007). *ISO/IEC 21000-14—FCD MPEG-21 Conformance Testing.* Geneva, Switzerland: ISO.

ISO/IEC. (2007). *ISO/IEC FDIS 21000-18– MPEG-21 DI Streaming.* Geneva, Switzerland: ISO.

Jaffe, D. A., & Smith, J. O., III (1995). Performance expression in commuted waveguide synthesis of bowed strings. In M. Erin (Ed.), *Proceedings of the 1995 International Computer Music Conference* (pp. 343-346). Banff, Canada: The Banff Centre for the Arts.

Janer, J. (2005). Voice-controlled plucked bass guitar through two synthesis techniques. In S. Fels & T. Blaine. (Ed.), *Proceedings of the 2005 Conference on New Interfaces for Musical Expression* (pp. 132-135). Vancouver, Canada: University of British Columbia.

Jehan, T. & Schoner, B. (2001). An audio-driven perceptually meaningful timbre synthesizer. In A. Schloss, R. Dannenberg, & P. Driessen (Ed.), *Proceedings of the 2001 International Computer Music Conference* (pp. 381-388). Havanna, Cuba: The Instituto Cubano de la Musica.

Jones, G. (in press). *Using a shape classifier as part of a larger system.*

Jordà, S. (2005). *Digital lutherie. Crafting musical computers for new musics' performance and improvisation.* Unpublished doctoral dissertation. University Pompeu Fabra, Department of Technology, Barcelona, Spain.

Joung, Y., & Kim, K. (2002). An XMT API for generation of the MPEG-4 scene description. In *Proceedings of the Tenth ACM International Conference on Multimedia,* December.

Juslin, P. N. (2001). Communicating emotion in music performance: A review and theoretical framework. In *Music and Emotion.* (p. 309-337). Oxford, UK: Oxford University Press.

Kalke,r T., Epema, D. H. J., Hartel, P. H., Lagendijk, R. L., & van Steen, M. (2004). Music2Share—Copyright-compliant music sharing in P2P systems. *Proceedings of the IEEE, 92*(6), 961 - 970.

Kanai, J., Rice, S. V., Nartker, T. A., & Nagy, G. (1995). Automated evaluation of OCR zoning. *IEEE Transac-*

*tions on Pattern Analysis and Machine Intelligence, 17*(1), 86–90.

Kato, H., & S. Inokuchi. (1990). The recognition system for printed piano music using musical knowledge and constraints. In *Proceedings of the International Association for Pattern Recognition Workshop on Syntactic and Structural Pattern Recognition* (pp. 231-48).

Katzenbeisser, S., & Petitcolas, F. A. P. (Eds.). (2000). *Information hiding: Techniques for steganography and digital watermarking*. Boston: Artech House.

Kerkhoffs, A. (1883). La Cryptographie Militaire. *Journal des Sciences Militaires*, 9th series, 5-38,161-191.

Kim, K., Lee, I., & Ki, M. (2002). Interactive contents authoring system based on XMT and BIFS. In *Proceedings of the Tenth ACM International Conference on Multimedia*, December.

Kim, M., & Wood, S. *XMT: MPEG-4 textual format for cross-standard interoperability*. Retrieved from http://www.research.ibm.com/mpeg4/Projects/XMTInterop.htm

Kim, M., Wood, S., & Cheok, L. T.. (2000). Extensible MPEG-4 textual format (XMT). International Multimedia Conference. In *Proceedings of the 2000 ACM workshops on Multimedia*. November.

Kim, T., Chiariglione, F. & Wang, X. (2007). ISO/IEC 21000-5/FPDAM 2 Rights Expression Language: the DAC profile. In *ISO/IEC JTC 1/SC 29/WG 11/N8344* (pp. 1-39).

Kim, T., Delgado, J., Schreiner, F. & Barlas C. (2006). ISO/IEC 21000-5:2004/PDAM 3: ORC (Open Release Content) Profile. In *ISO/IEC JTC 1/SC 29/WG 11/N8566* (pp. 1-34).

Kobayakawa, T. (1993). Auto music score recognition system. In *Proceedings SPIE: Character Recognition Technologies 1906* (pp. 112-23).

Kosch, H. (2003). *Distributed multimedia database technologies supported by MPEG-7 and MPEG-21*. CRC Press. Retrieved from http://www-itec.uni-klu.ac.at/~harald/mmbook/

Kouroupetroglou, G., Stamati, M., & Metaxaki-Kissionides, C. (1999). World-Wide-Web supporting for the learning of non-orthographic languages. *International Conference on Computers in Education*. Amsterdam: IOS Press.

Kowler, E. Eye movements and visual attention. In *MITECS: The MIT encyclopedia of the cognitive sciences*. Retrieved from http://cognet.mit.edu/MITECS/Entry/kowler

Krolick B. (2000). *New international manual of braille music notation, braille music*. Subcommittee of the World Blind Union. Retrieved from **http://www.opustec.com/products/newintl/newprint.html**

L'Amour de Loin. (n.d.). Retrieved April 3, 2006, from http://www.chesternovello.com

Lasnier, C. (2005). How to best exploit the VOCODER. *AGERCEL, 2005*.

Lazzaro, J., & Wawrzynek, K. (2000). *MPEG-4 structured audio*. Retrieved from http://www.cs.berkeley.edu/~lazzaro/sa/book/index.html=

Le Hors, A., Le Hégaret, P., Wood, L., Nicol, G., Robie, J., Champion, M., & Byrne, S. (2000). *Document object model (DOM) level 2 core specification*. Retrieved from http://www.w3.org/TR/DOM-Level-2-Core/

LeLoup, J. W., & Ponterio R. (2001). On the Net—Finding song lyrics online. *Language Learning & Technology, 5*(3), 4-6. Retrieved from http://llt.msu.edu/vol5num3/onthenet

Lenzi, R., & Spadoni F. (2003). *DRM technology survey, technical report*. Interactive MUSICNETWORK Project, Working Group on Distribution of Coded Music. Retrieved September 2004, from http://www.interactiveMUSICNETWORK.org/documenti/view_document.php?file_id=361

Levitin, D. J., McAdams, S. & Adams, R. L. (2002). Control parameters for musical instruments: A foundation for new mappings of gesture to sound. *Organised Sound, 7*(2), 171-189.

Lewis, G. J. (2003). *The German e-music industry.* Leonardo de Vinci, Faculty of Business Administration, University of Applied Sciences, Dresden, Germany. Retrieved from http://imec.hud.ac.uk/imec/iMEC%20 GermanFINALreport110902.pdf

Library and Archives Canada. *International Standard Music Number.* Retrieved March 20, 2007, from http://www.collectionscanada.ca/ismn/

Lie, H. W., & Bos, B. (1996). *Cascading style sheets, level 1.* Retrieved March 16, 2006, from http://www.w3.org/TR/REC-CSS1

Machover, T. (1992). *Hyperinstruments: A progress Report, 1987-1991.* Technical report, Massachusetts Institute of Technology, Cambridge, MA.

Madden, M., & Rainie, L. (2005). *Music and video downloading moves beyond P2P.* Pew Internet & American Life Project, Retrieved from http://www.pewinternet.org/pdfs/PIP_Filesharing_March05.pdf

Mah, A. Y. (2003). *A thousand pieces of gold—A memoir of China's past through its proverbs* (pp. 293). Harper Collins Publishers. MASIE Center's e-Learning consortium. (2002).

*Making sense of learning specifications & standards: A decision maker's guide to their adoption.* Retrieved from http://www.masie.com/standards/S3_Guide.pdf

Malyankar, R. (2002). *Vocabulary development for markup languages—a case study with maritime information.* ACM 1-58113-449-5/02/0005 674-685.

Man nabbed for uploading Oscar "screener." *CNet News.com*, February 22, 2007. Retrieved March 21, 2007, from http://news.com.com/2061-10802_3-6161586.html

Manoury, P. (1993). *En Echo, the marriage of voice and electronics.* Retrieved April 5, 2006, from http://music-web.koncon.nl/ircam/en/extending/enecho.html

Marion, A., & Hacking, E. H. (1998). Educational publishing and the World Wide Web. *Journal of Interactive Media in Education, 98*(2). Retrieved from http://www-jime.open.ac.uk/98/2

Mark, M. L. (1996). *Contemporary music education* (3rd ed). New York: Schirmer Books.

Mason (1997). SGML and related standards: New directions as the second decade begins. *Journal of American Society of Information Science, 48*(7) 593-596.

Mason, J. D. (1997). SGML and related standards: New directions as the second decade begins. *Journal of American Society of Information Science, 1*(7), 593-596.

Mathews, M. V., & Kohut, J. (1973). Electronic simulation of violin resonances. *Journal of the Acoustical Society of America, 53*(6), 1620-1626.

Matsushima, T., Harada, T., Sonomoto, I., Kanamori, K., Uesugi, A., Nimura, Y., Hashimoto, S., & Ohteru, S. (1985). Automated recognition system for musical score: The vision system of WABOT-2. *Bulletin of Science and Engineering Research Laboratory,* Waseda University.

McCartney, J. (n.d.). *Supercollider. A real time audio synthesis programming language.* Retrieved April 5, 2006, from http://www.audiosynth.com/

McPherson, J. R. (2002). *Introducing feedback into an optical music recognition system.* Third International Conference on Music Information Retrieval, Paris, France.

MediTECH. (2005). *FLIC prototype—Instruction manual.*

MediTECH. (2005). *FLIC project public presentation.*

Menezes, A., Oorschot, P. & van Vanstone, S. (1996). *Handbook of applied cryptography.* CRC Press.

Metcalf, D. (2004). *m-Learning: Technology update and best practices.* Presentation held at Training 2004, Atlanta GA. Retrieved from http://www.elearnopedia.com/mlearning/m-learning-wed.pdf

Metcalf, D., (2004). *m-Learning evaluation.* Presentation held at Training 2004, Atlanta GA. Retrieved from http://www.elearnopedia.com/mlearning/m-learning%20evaluation.pdf

MIDI Manufacturers Association. (n.d.). Retrieved April 5, 2006, from http://www.midi.org/

Miranda, E,. & Wanderley, M. (2006). *New digital musical instruments: Control and interaction beyond the keyboard.* Middleton, WI: A-R Editions, Inc.

Mitolo, N., Nesi, P., & Ng, K. C. (Eds.). (2005). In *Proceedings of the 5th MUSICNETWORK Open Workshop,* Universität für Musik und darstellende Kunst Wien, Vienna, Austria, 2-4 July 2005.

Miyao, H., & Haralick, R. M. (2000). Format of ground truth data used in the evaluation of the results of an optical music recognition system. In *IAPR Workshop on Document Analysis Systems* (pp. 497-506).

mLAN (undated). Retrieved March 16, 2006, from http://www.mlancentral.com/mlan_info/mlan_ppf.php

Modayur, B. R. (1996). *Music score recognition - a selective attention approach using mathematical morphology.* Seattle, University of Washington, Electrical Engineering Department.

Modul8. (2006). Retrieved April 3, 2006, from http://www.garagecube.com/modul8/index.php

Montgomery, L. (2001). *4ML (Music and lyrics markup language).* Retrieved March 16, 2006, from http://xml.coverpages.org/ni2001-03-03-b.html

MOODS project. Retrieved from http://www.dsi.unifi.it/~moods

Moore, G. A. (1991). Crossing the chasm: Marketing and selling mainstream customers. NY: HarperCollins.

Mosterd, E. (2001). *EMNML (Enhanced musical notation markup language).* Retrieved March 16, 2006, from http://www.usd.edu/csci/research/theses/graduate/sp2001/emosterd.pdf

Moundridou, M., & Virvou, M. (2002). Authoring intelligent tutoring systems over the World Wide Web. *1st International IEEE Symposium Intelligent System* (pp. 160-165).

MPEG ISO SMR group web page. Retrieved from http://www.interactivemusicnetwork.org/mpeg-ahg

*MPEG SMR AHG Web page.* Retrieved from http://www.interactivemusicnetwork.org/mpeg-ahg

MPEG-21 standard. (2007). Retrieved April 3, 2007, from http://www.chiariglione.org/mpeg/standards/mpeg-21/mpeg-21.htm

Mulder, A. (1998). *Design of three-dimensional instruments for sound control.* Unpublished doctoral dissertation. Simon Fraser University, Vancouver, Canada.

MUSICALIS project. Retrieved from http://www.musicalis.fr/

Musitek (2002). SmartScore. Retrieved from http://www.musitek.com/

Nantel, R., & Vipond, S. (2006). *Authoring tool knowledge base 2006.* Sunnyvale, CA: Brandon-Hall.

Nesi, P., Ng, K., & Delgado, J. (Eds). (2005). In *Proceedings of the 1st International Conference on Automating Production of Cross Media Content for Multi-channel Distribution Conference* (AXMEDIS 2005): Workshops and Industrial, 30 Nov - 2 Dec 2005, Convitto della Calza, Florence, Italy, Firenze University Press.

Nesi, P., Zoia, G., Bellini, P., & Barthelemy, J (2003). Music notation application requirements and MPEG technology.

Network Working Group, The Internet Society. (1995). *RFC 1736: Functional Recommendations for Internet Resource Locators.* Retrieved March 20, 2007, from http://www.ietf.org/rfc/rfc1736.txt

Network Working Group, The Internet Society. (1998). *RFC 2396: Uniform Resource Identifiers (URI): Generic Syntax,* Retrieved March 20, 2007, from http://www.ietf.org/rfc/rfc2396.txt

Network Working Group, The Internet Society. *RFC 1737: Functional Requirements for Uniform Resource Names.* Retrieved March 20, 2007, from http://www.ietf.org/rfc/rfc1737.txt

Neuhaus, H. (1967). *Die Kunst des Klavierspiels.* Bergisch Gladbach, Germany: Musikverlage Hans Gerig.

Neuman, W. R. (1991). *The future of mass audience*. Cambridge University Press.

New Ground. (2003). Retrieved April 6, 2006, from http://www.oboeclassics.com/NewGround.htm

Newcomb, S. R. (1985). Lasso: An intelligent computer based tutorial in sixteenth century counterpoint. *Computer Music Journal, 9*(4), 49-61.

Newcomb, S., *et al.* (1995). *Standard music description language*. ISO/IEC DIS 10743. Retrieved from ftp://ftp.techno.com

Ng, K. (2004). Music via motion: Transdomain mapping of motion and sound for interactive performances. In *Proceedings of the IEEE, 92*(4), 645-655.

Ng, K. C. (1995). *Automated computer recognition of music scores*. PhD Thesis, School of Computing, University of Leeds, UK.

Ng, K. C. (2001). Music manuscript tracing. *Proceedings of the Fourth IAPR International Workshop on Graphics Recognition (GREC 2001),* Canada (pp. 470–481).

Ng, K. C. (2002). Document imaging for music manuscript. In *Proceedings of the Sixth World Multiconference on Systemics, Cybernetics and Informatics* (SCI 2002), Orlando, USA, XVIII (pp. 546–549).

Ng, K. C. (Ed.). (2005). *Journal of New Music Research* (JNMR), *34*(2).

Ng, K. C. (guest editor). (2005). *Journal of New Music Research (JNMR) special issue on Multimedia Music and the World Wide Web, 34*(2).

Ng, K. C., & Boyle, R. D. (1994). *Reconstruction of music scores from primitive Sub-segmentation*. School of Computer Studies, University of Leeds.

Ng, K. C., & Boyle, R. D. (1996). Recognition and reconstruction of primitives in music scores. *Image and Vision Computing, 14*(1), pp.39-46.

Ng, K. C., & Cooper D. (2000). *Enhancement of optical music recognition using metric analysis*. Proceedings of the XIII CIM 2000—Colloquium on Musical Informatics, Italy.

Ng, K. C., Badii, A., & Bellini, P. (Eds). (2006). In *Proceedings of the 2nd International Conference on Automated Production of Cross Media Content for Multichannel Distribution*, 13-15 December 2006, University of Leeds, UK: Firenze University Press.

Ng, K. C., Boyle, R. D., & Cooper, D. (1996). Automatic detection of tonality using note distribution. *Journal of New Music Research, 25*(4): 369–381.

Ng, K. C., Busch, C., & Nesi, P. (Eds.). (2003). In *Proceedings of the third International Conference on WEB Delivering of Music* (WEDELMUSIC-2003), Leeds, UK.

Ng, K. C., Cooper, D., Stefani, E., Boyle, R. D., & Bailey, N. (1999). Embracing the composer: Optical recognition of hand-written manuscripts. In *Proceedings of the International Computer Music Conference (ICMC'99)—Embracing Mankind*, Tsinghua University, Beijing, China (pp. 500–503).

Ng, K. C., Crombie, D., Bellini, P., & Nesi, P. (2003). Musicnetwork: Music industry with interactive multimedia technology. In *Proceedings of Electronic Imaging and the Visual Arts* (EVA London 2003), UCL, London, UK.

Ng, K. C., Ong, S. B., Nesi, P., Mitolo, N., Fuschi, D., & Crombie, D. (2005). *Interactive Multimedia Technologies for Music*, EVA 2005 London International Conference, UK, 25-29 July 2005.

Ng, K.C. (Ed.). (2006). In *Proceedings of the COST287-ConGAS 2nd International Symposium on Gesture Interface for Multimedia Systems* (GIMS2006), 9-10 May 2006, Leeds, UK.

Nichols, C. (2003). *The vBow an expressive musical controller haptic human-computer interface*. Unpublished doctoral dissertation, Stanford University, CA.

NIFF Consortium. (1995). *NIFF 6a: Notation interchange file format*.

NIFF. (1995). *NIFF 6a: Notation Interchange File Format*.

NIME (2001). *Conference on New Interfaces for Musical Expression*. Retrieved February 12, 2007, from http://www.nime.org.

Noa Noa. (n.d.). Retrieved April 3, 2006, from http://www.chesternovello.com

Norman, D. A. (1998). *The invisible computer: Why good products can fail, the personal computer is so complex, and information appliances are the solution*. Cambridge, MA: MIT Press.

Norman, D. A. (2002). *The design of everyday things*. New York: Basic Books.

Novak, J. D. (1998). *Learning, creating, and using knowledge: Concept maps as facilitative tools in schools and corporations*. Mahwah, NJ: Lawrence Erlbaum Associates.

O'Modhrain, M.S. (2000). *Playing by feel: Incorporating haptic feedback into computer-cased musical instruments*. Unpublished doctoral dissertation, Stanford University, CA.

Oliva, M. (2004). Retrieved March 19, 2006, from http://www.madestrange.net/black.htm

OMA DRM Architecture. (2006). Retrieved April 3, 2007, from http://www.openmobilealliance.org/release_program/docs/DRM/V2_0-20060303-A/OMA-AD-DRM-V2_0-20060303-A.pdf

OMA DRM Rights Expression Language. (2006). Retrieved April 3, 2007, from http://www.openmobilealliance.org/release_program/docs/DRM/V2_0-20060303-A/OMA-TS-DRM-REL-V2_0-20060303-A.pdf

OMA DRM Specification. (2006). Retrieved April 3, 2007, from http://www.openmobilealliance.org/release_program/drm_archive.html#V2_0-20050915-C

OMA. (2004). *Open Mobile Alliance Web site*. Retrieved September 2004, from http://www.openmobilealliance.org/

OMeR (n.d.). *Optical Music easy Reader, Myriad Software*, Retrieved February 8, 2003, from http://www.myriad-online.com/omer.htm

Ong, B., Ng, K., Mitolo, N., & Nesi, P. (2006). i-Maestro: Interactive multimedia environments for music education. In Kia Ng, Atta Badii, & Pierfrancesco Bellini (Eds.), In *Proceedings of the AXMEDIS2006 International Conference on Automated Production of Cross Media Content for Multi-channel Distribution, 2<sup>nd</sup> i-Maestro Workshop* (pp. 87-91). Firenze, Italy: Firenze University Press.

Open Digital Rights Language. (2007). Retrieved April 3, 2007, from http://odrl.net

OPENDRAMA project. Retrieved from http://www.iua.upf.es/mtg/opendrama/

Orlowski, A. (2004). Free legal downloads for 6$ a month. DRM free. The artists get paid. We explain how... *The Register*, February, 2004. Retrieved March 23, 2007, from http://www.theregister.co.uk/content/6/35260.html

Orlowski, A. (2005). French court bans DVD DRM. *The Register*, 26/04/2005. Retrieved March 20, 2007, from http://www.theregister.co.uk/2005/04/26/french_drm_non/

Overholt, D. (2005). The overtone violin. In A. Lewin-Richter, & X. Serra (Ed.), *Proceedings of the 2005 International Computer Music Conference* (pp. 604-607). San Francisco, CA: International Computer Music Association.

Paine, G. (2004). Gesture and musical interaction: Interactive engagement through dynamic morphology, In Y. Nagashima (Ed.), *Proceedings of the 2004 Conference on New Interfaces for Musical Expression* (pp. 80-85). Hamamatsu, Japan: Shizuoka University of Art and Culture.

Paradiso, J. A. (1997b) Electronic music interfaces: new ways to play. *IEEE Spectrum, 34*(12), 18-30.

Paradiso, J. A., & Gershenfeld, N. (1997a). Musical applications of electric field sensing. *Computer Music Journal,. 21*(2), 69–89.

Peer-To-Peer. *Wikipedia.* Retrieved March 20, 2007, from http://en.wikipedia.org/wiki/Peer-to-peer

Pemberton, S, Austin, D. *et al.* (2000). *XHTML™ 1.0 The extensible hypertext markup language* (2nd ed.). Retrieved from http://www.w3.org/TR/xhtml1

Pennycook, B., *et al.* (1995). The music library of the future: A pilot project. In *Proceedings of the 1995 International Computer Music Conference.* San Fransisco: ICMA.

Pennycook, B., *et al.* (1995). Music and audio markup tools for the World Wide Web. In *Proceedings of the 99th Audio Engineering Society.* New York.

Pereira, F., & Ebrahimi, T. (Eds.) (2002). *The MPEG-4 book.* Los Angeles, CA: IMSC Press.

Peticolas, F. (2006). *Stirmark benchmark 4.0,* 06 February 2006. Retrieved March 22, 2007, from http://www.petitcolas.net/fabien/watermarking/stirmark/

Phon-Amnuaisuk, S., & Chee K. S. (2005). *Reviewing interactivity issues in music tutoring system.* Presented at The Fifth Music Network Open Workshop: Integration of Music in Multimedia Applications, Universität für Musik und darstellende Kunst Wien, Vienna, Austria, July 4-5, 2005.

PhotoScore (n.d.). *Neuratron.* Retrieved February 8, 2003, from http://www.neuratron.com/photoscore.htm

Pierce, J. R. (1989). *Klang mit den Ohren der Physik* (2nd ed.). Heidelberg, Germany: Spektrum-der-Wissenschaft-Verlagsgesellschaft.

Pinto, J., Vieira, P., Ramalho, M., Mengucci, M., Pina, P., & Muge, F. (2000). *Ancient music recovery for digital libraries.* Fourth European Conference on Research and Advanced Technology for Digital Libraries (ECDL 2000), Lisbon.

Poepel, C. (2004). Synthesized strings for string-players. In Y. Nagashima (Ed.), *Proceedings of the 2004 Conference on New Interfaces for Musical Expression* (pp. 150-153). Hamamatsu, Japan: Shizuoka University of Art and Culture.

Poepel, C. (2005). On interface expressivity: A player-based study. In S. Fels, & T. Blaine (Ed.), *Proceedings of the 2005 Conference on New Interfaces for Musical Expression* (pp. 228-231). Vancouver, Canada: University of British Columbia.

Poepel, C., & Dannenberg, R. B. (2005). Audio signal driven sound synthesis. In A. Lewin-Richter & Serra, X. (Ed.), *Proceedings of the 2005 International Computer Music Conference* (pp. 391-394). San Francisco, CA: International Computer Music Association.

Poepel, C., & Overholt, D. (2006). Recent developments in violin-related digital musical instruments: Where are we and where are we going? In N. Schnell, N., F. Bevilacqua, M. Lyons, & A. Tanaka (Eds.), *Proceedings of the 2006 Conference on New Interfaces for Musical Expression* (pp. 228-231). Paris, France: IRCAM-Centre Pompidou.

Porck, H. J., & Teygeler, R. (2000). *Preservation science survey: An overview of recent developments in research on the conservation of selected analogue library and archival materials.* Washington, D.C.: Council on Library and Information Resources.

Poupyrev, I., Lyons, M. J., Fels, S., & Blaine., T. (2001). Workshop proposal: New interfaces for musical expression. In *Proceedings of the 2001 Workshop on New Interfaces for Musical Expression.* Singapore: National University of Singapore.

Prem, E. (1997). Epistemic autonomy in models of living systems. In P. Husbands & I. Harvey (Eds.), *Proceedings fourth European Conference on Artificial Life* (p. 2-9). Brighton, UK.

Prerau, D. S. (1970). *Computer pattern recognition of standard engraved music notation.* Ph.D. Dissertation, Massachusetts Institute of Technology.

PRISM specification. (2005). Retrieved April 3, 2007, from http://www.prismstandard.org/specifications/

PRISM to Focus on Web Content. (2007). Retrieved April 3, 2007, from http://www.prismstandard.org/

Pruslin, D. H. (1966). *Automated recognition of sheet music*. Doctor of Science dissertation, Massachusetts Institute of Technology.

Puckette, M. S., Apel, T., & Zicarelli, D. D. (1998). Real-time audio analysis tools for Pd and MSP. In M. Simoni (Ed.), *Proceedings of the 1998 International Computer Music Conference* (pp. 109-112). San Francisco, CA: International Computer Music Association.

Rader, G. M. (1996). Creating printed music automatically. *IEEE Computer,* June, 61-68.

Raggett, D., Le Hors, A., & Jacobs, I. (1999). *HTML 4.01 specification*. Retrieved from http://www.w3.org/TR/html401/

Rasamimanana, N. (2006). Gesture analysis of violin bow strokes. In S. Gibet, N. Courty, & J.-F Kamp (Ed.), *Gesture in Human-Computer Interaction and Simulation: 6th International Gesture Workshop*, 3881, (pp. 145-155). Berlin, Heidelberg, German: Springer Verlag.

Rastall, R. (1983). *The notation of western music*. London: J.M.Dent & Sons Ltd.

Real Networks Media Commerce Suite. (2007). Retrieved April 3, 2007, from http://www.realnetworks.com/products/commerce/description.html

Reich, S., & Korot, B. interviewed by David Allenby. (2001). Retrieved April 5, 2006, from http://www.boosey.com/pages/opera/OperaNews.asp?NewsID=10260&MusicID=15153

Renfrew, C., & Bahn, P. (2004). *Archaeology: Theories, methods and practice*. London: Thames & Hudson.

Rhodes, R. (1899). *Pianola copyright ruling cited*. Retrieved March 20, 2007, from http://mmd.foxtail.com/Archives/Digests/200406/2004.06.05.03.html

RIAA. (2005). *Recording Industry Association of America Web site*. Retrieved May 2005, from http://www.riaa.com

Richmond, J. (1989). *Valis points to exciting possibilities for growth of opera*. Retrieved from http://www-tech.mit.edu/V109/N28/valis.28a.html

Rights and Rules Working Group. (2003). Retrieved April 3, 2007, from http://www.openebook.org/oebf_groups/rrwg.htm

Roads, C. (1986). The Tsukuba musical robot. *Computer Music Journal, 10*(2), 39-43.

Roettgers, J. (2004). *Social networks: The Future of P2P file sharing*. Retrieved from http://freebitflows.t0.or.at/f/about/roettgers

Roland, P. (2001). *MEI (Music encoding initiative)*. Retrieved March 16, 2006, from http://www.lib.virginia.edu/digital/resndev/mei/

Roland, P. (2002). The music encoding initiative (MEI). In G. Haus & M. Longari (Eds.), *MAX 2002: Musical applications using XML. Proceedings First International Conference* (pp. 55-59). Laboratoria di Informatica Musicale, Computer Science Dept, State University of Milan.

Rosenblath, B. (2005). *DRMwatch Web site*. Retrieved May 2005, from http://www.drmwatch.com

Rosenblath, B. (2007). *DRMwatch Web site*. Retrieved February 2007, from http://www.drmwatch.com

Rosenblatt, B. (2004). *Review: DRM Standards*, January 5, 2004. Retrieved March 21, 2007 from http://www.drmwatch.com/standards/article.php/3295291

Rosenblatt, B. (2005). *Review: DRM Standards*, January 6, 2005. Retrieved March 21, 2007 from http://www.drmwatch.com/standards/article.php/3455231

Rosenblatt, B. (2006). *Review: DRM Standards*, January 2, 2006. Retrieved March 21, 2007 from http://www.drmwatch.com/standards/article.php/3574511

Rosenblatt, B. (2006). *Review: DRM Standards*, December 27, 2006. Retrieved March 21, 2007 from http://www.drmwatch.com/standards/article.php/3651126

Rosenblatt, B., & Dykstra, G. (2003). *Technology integration opportunities*, November, 14, 2003. Retrieved March 21, 2007 from http://www.drmwatch.com/resources/whitepapers/article.php/11655_3112011_3

Rosenblatt, B., & Dykstra, G. (2003). *Integrating content management with digital rights management—Imperatives and opportunities for digital content.* Lifecycles. GiantSteps, Media Technology Strategies , Technical Report. Retrieved from http://www.xrml.org/reference/CM-DRMwhitepaper.pdf

Rosenblatt, B., Trippe, B., & Mooney, S. (2002). *Digital rights management—Business and technology.* New York, NY: M&T Books,

Ross, T. (1970). *The art of music engraving and processing.* Miami: Hansen Books.

Roth, M. (1994). *An approach to recognition of printed music.* Diploma thesis, Department of Computer Science, Swiss Federal Institute of Technology, Zurich, Switzerland.

Rudish, J. (2005). Illegal file sharing lawsuits dismissed; Emory withholds defendants' names. *The Emory Wheel Online*, April 15, 2005. Retrieved March 20, 2007, from http://media.www.emorywheel.com/media/storage/paper919/news/2005/04/15/News/Illegal.Filesharing.Lawsuits.Dismissed.Emory.Witholds.Defendants.Names-1647598.shtml

Rumelhart, D. E., Hinton, G. E., & McClelland, J. L. (1986). A general framework for parallel distributed processing. In D. E. Rumelhart, J. L. McClelland, and the PDP Research Group (Eds.), *Parallel distributed processing: Explorations in the microstructure of cognition, vol. 1: Foundations.* Cambridge, MA: MIT Press.

Sabbir, A. K. (2004). A conceptual framework for Web-based intelligent learning environments using SCORM-2004. In *Proceedings of the IEEE International Conference on Advanced Learning Technologies* (ICALT'04) (pp. 10-15). Finland, Aug 30-Sep 1, 2004.

Saussure, F. de. (1916, 1986). *Course in general linguistics.* Translated by R. Harris. London: Duckworth.

Schiettecatte, B. (2000). *FlowML.* Retrieved March 16, 2006, from http://xml.coverpages.org/FlowML.html

Schmucker, M. (2004). *Enlightening the DarkNet.* IST-Workshop, November, 15th, 2004, Den Hague, Netherlands.

Schmucker, M., & Ebinger, P. (2005). *Promotional and commercial content distribution based on a legal and trusted P2P framework.* CEC 2005. Seventh IEEE International Conference on E-Commerce Technology.

Schmucker, M., & Rantasa, P. (2005). *Ein soziales Verteilungsnetzwerk—Beispiel eines alternativen Distributionsmodells.* CAST-Workshop, February 2nd, 2005, Darmstadt, Germany.

Schneier, B. (1996). *Applied cryptography* (2nd ed.). Hoboken, NJ: John Wiley & Sons.

Schoner, B. (2000). *Probabilistic characterization and synthesis of complex driven systems.* Unpublished doctoral dissertation. Massachusetts Institute of Technology, Cambridge, MA.

Schoonderwaldt, E., Rasamimanana, N., & Bevilacqua, F. (2006). Combining accelerometer and video camera: Reconstruction of bow velocity profiles. In N. Schnell, F. Bevilacqua, M. Lyons, & A. Tanaka (Ed.), *Proceedings of the 2006 Conference on New Interfaces for Musical Expression* (pp. 200-203). Paris, France: IRCAM-Centre Pompidou.

Scmucker, M. (2005). *Protection of coded music.* The Interactive Musicnework. Retrieved from http://www.interactivemusicnetwork.org/documenti/view_document.php?file_id=1195

Scorscan (n.d.). *npc Imaging.* Retrieved August 8, 2002, from http://www.npcimaging.com

Selfridge-Field E. (Ed.) (1997). *Beyond MIDI—The handbook of musical codes.* London: The MIT Press.

Selfridge-Field E., (1997). *Beyond MIDI - The handbook of musical codes.* London: The MIT Press.

Selfridge-Field, E. (1993). Optical recognition of musical notation: A survey of current work. *Computing in Musicology, 9,* 109-145.

Selfridge-Field, E. (1994). Optical recognition of music notation: A survey of current work. In W. B. Hewlett & E. Selfridge-Field (Eds.), *Computing in Musicology: An International Directory of Applications, 9,* 109–145.

Selfridge-Field, E. (Ed.) (1997). *Beyond MIDI—The handbook of musical codes.* London, UK: The MIT Press.

SGML SIGhyper. (1994). *A brief history of the development of SMDL and HyTime.* Retrieved from http://www.sgmlsorce.com/history/hthist.htm

SGML Users' Group (1990). *A brief history of the development of SGML.* Retrieved from http://www.sgmlsource.com/history/sgmlhist.htm

Shang, Y., Shi, H., & Chen, S. (2001). An intelligent distributed environment for active learning. In *Proceedings of the Tenth International Conference on World Wide Web* (pp. 308-315). Hong Kong.

SharpEye (n.d.). *visiv.* Retrieved August 8, 2002, from http://www.visiv.co.uk

Shea, P., Fredericksen, E., Pickett, A., & Swan, K. (1999). Student satisfaction and perceived learning in Internet-based higher education. *Advanced Research in Internet-Based Higher Education. Advanced Research in Computers and Communications in Education.* Amsterdam: IOS Press.

SIBELIUS. Retrieved from http://www.sibelius.com

Sloan, D. (1993). Aspects of music representation in HyTime/SMDL. *Computer Music Journal, 17*(4).

Sloan, D. (2002). Learning our lessons from SMDL. In G. Haus & M. Longari (Eds). *MAX 2002: Musical applications using XML. Proceedings First International Conference* (pp. 69-73). Laboratoria di Informatica Musicale, Computer Science Dept, State University of Milan

Sloan, D. (2002). Learning our lessons from SMDL. In G. Haus & M. Longari (Eds.), *MAX 2002: Musical applications using XML. Proceedings First International Conference* (pp. 69-73). Laboratoria di Informatica Musicale, Computer Science Dept, State University of Milan.

SmartScore (n.d.). *Musitek.* Retrieved February 8, 2002, from http://www.musitek.com/

SMDL ISO/IEC. (1995). *Standard Music Description Language.* ISO/IEC DIS 10743.

SMDL. (1995). *ISO/IEC, standard music description language.* ISO/IEC DIS 10743.

SMEF Data Model. *British Broadcasting Corporation.* Retrieved March 21, 2007, from http://www.bbc.co.uk/guidelines/smef/

Smith, L. (1997). SCORE. Beyond MIDI - The handbook of musical codes, (E. Selfridge-Field, Ed.). London : The MIT Press.

Smoliar, S. W., Waterworth, J. A., & Kellock, P. R. (1995). Pianoforte: A system for piano education beyond notation literacy. In *Proceedings of ACM Multimedia 95* (pp. 457-465). San Francisco, CA.

Spadoni, F., Lenzi, R., & Schmucker, M. (2005). Distribution of coded music. In M. Mitolo, P. Nesi, & K. Ng (Eds.), *Proceedings of the 5th MUSICNETWORK Open Workshop,* Vienna (A), July 2005.

Sperberg-McQueen, C. M., & Huitfield, C. (2004). GODDAG: A data structure for overlapping hierarchies. In P. King & E. V. Munson (Eds), *Digital documents: Systems and principles* (pp. 139-160). Berlin: Springer.

Steyn, J. (1999). *Music markup language.* Retrieved March 16, 2006, from http://www.musicmarkup.info/

Steyn, J. (2002). Framework for a music markup language. In G. Haus & M. Longari (Eds.), *MAX 2002: Musical applications using XML.* In *Proceedings First International Conference* (pp. 22-29). Laboratoria di Informatica Musicale, Computer Science Dept, State University of Milan

Steyn, J. (2004). *Introducing Music Space.* Retrieved March 16, 2006, from http://www.musicmarkup.info/papers/musicspace/musicspace.html

Stückelberg, M. V., & Doermann, D. (1999). On musical score recognition using probabilistic reasoning. In *Pro-*

*ceedings of the Fifth International Conference on Document Analysis and Recognition*. Bangolore, India.

Stückelberg, M. V., Pellegrini, C., & Hilario, M. (1997). An architecture for musical score recognition using high-level domain knowledge. In *Proceedings of the Fourth International Conference on Document Analysis and Recognition, 2*, (pp. 813-818).

Suen, C. Y., & Wang, P. S. P. (1994). Thinning methodologies for pattern recognition. *Series in Machine Perception and Artificial Intelligence, 8*.

Sundberg, J. (1991) *The science of musical sounds*. New York: Academic Press, INC.

Super Vision. (n.d.). Retrieved April 5, 2006, from http://www.superv.org/

Sussman, R., & Sedivy, J. *Using Eyetracking to detect and describe Filled Gap Effects, the electronic community for scholarly research in the cognitive and brain sciences*. MIT COgNet. Retrieved from http://cognet.mit. edu/posters/poster.tcl?publication_id=45136

Tardieu, D. (undated). *VMML (Virtual musician markup language)*. Retrieved March 16, 2006, from http://vrlab. epfl.ch/research/S_VMML.pdf

Templeton, B, (2007). *10 big myths about copyright explained*. Retrieved March 20, 2007, from http://www. templetons.com/brad/copymyths.html

The Builders Association. (n.d.). Retrieved April 5, 2006, from http://www.thebuildersassociation.org/flash/flash. html?homepage

Thompson, H. S., Beech, D., Maloney, M., & Mendelsohn, N. (Eds). (2004). *XML schema part 1: Structures* (2nd ed.).. Retrieved from http://www.w3.org/TR/xmlschema-1/

Tojo, A., & Aoyama, H. (1982). Automatic recognition of music score. In *Proceedings of 6th International Conference on Pattern Recognition, 1223*.

Tomita, T. (1980). The new electronic media and their place in the information market of the future. In A. Smith (Ed.), *Newspapers and democracy: International essays on a changing medium*. Cambridge, MA: MIT Press.

Tools for new Media. (n.d.). Retrieved April 5, 2006 from http://www.cycling74.com/

Traube, C. (2004). *An interdisciplinary study of the timbre of the classical guitar*. Unpublished doctoral dissertation. McGill University, Montréal, Canada.

Trogemann, G., & Viehoff, J. (2005). *Code@art, eine elementare Einführung in die Programmierung als künstlerische Praktik*. Wien, NY: Springer-Verlag.

Truax, B. (1996). Sounds and sources in *Powers of Two*: Towards a contemporary myth. *Organised Sound, 1*(1), 13-21.

Trueman, D., & Cook, P. (1999). BoSSA, the deconstructed violin reconstructed. In J. Fung, J. (Ed.), *Proceedings of the 1999 International Computer Music Conference* (pp. 232-239). San Francisco, CA: International Computer Music Association.

TV-Anytime Rights Management and Protection Information for Broadcast Applications. (2005). Retrieved April 3, 2007, from http://www.tv-anytime.org/

Van Rotterdam, J. (1998). *MusicML*. Retrieved March 16, 2006, from http://lists.xml.org/archives/xml-dev/199803/ msg00091.html

Verfaille, V., & Arfib, D. (2001). A-dafx: Adaptive digital audio effects. In *Proceedings of the 4th International Conference on Digital Audio Effects 2001* (pp. 10-13). Limerick, Ireland.

Visiv. (2005). *Sharpeye*. Retrieved from http://www. visiv.co.uk/

Vivaldi Scan (n.d.). *VivaldiStudio*. Retrieved February 8, 2003, from http://www.vivaldistudio.com/Eng/VivaldiS-can.asp

von Neumann, J. (1955). *Mathematical foundations of quantum mechanics*. Priceton, NJ: Princeton University Press.

von Neumann, J. (1966). *The theory of self-reproducing automata*. Urbana, IL: University of Illinois Press.

Wächter, W., Liers, J., & Becker, E. (1996). Paper splitting at the German Library in Leipzig. *Development from Craftsmanship to Full Mechanisation. Restaurator, 17*, 32–42.

Walsh, N., & Muellner, L. (1999). *DocBook: The definitive guide*. Cambridge: O'Reilly.

Walton, T. (2003). *Golden age of free music vs. Copying is stealing*. Retrieved March 20, 2007, from http://www.theregister.co.uk/2003/08/06/golden_age_of_free_music/

Wanderley, M. M., & Battier, M. (Ed.). (2000). *Trends in gestural control of music*. CD-Rom. Paris, France: IRCAM—Centre Pompidou.

Wanderley, M. M., & Depalle, P. (2004). Gestural control of sound synthesis. In *Proceedings of the IEEE, 92*(4), 632-644.

Wanderley, M. M., & Orio, N. (2002). Evaluation of input devices for musical expression: Borrowing tools from HCI. *Computer Music Journal, 26*(3), 62-76.

Wang, X., Delgado, J., & Barlas C. (2006). ISO/IEC 21000-5/FDAM 1 Rights Expression Language: the MAM profile. In *ISO/IEC JTC 1/SC 29/WG 11/N8342* (pp. 1- 49).

Wang, X., Feng, D., Lai, x., & Yu, H. (2004). Collisions for hash functions MD4, MD5, HAVAL-128 and RIPEMD. *Cryptology ePrint Archive, Report 2004/199*. Retrieved from http://eprint.iacr.org/2004/199

Wang, X., Yin, X. L., & Yu, H. (2005). *Collision search attacks on SHA1*, February 13, 2005. Retrieved from http://theory.csail.mit.edu/~yiqun/shanote.pdf

WEDELMUSIC. Retrieved from http://www.wedelmusic.org

Weinkauf, D. (undated). *JscoreML*. Retrieved March 16, 2006, from http://nide.snow.utoronto.ca/music/

Weiss, N. (1966). Film and Lulu. *Opera, 17*(9), 708.

Wessel, D., & Wright, M. (2002). Problems and prospects for intimate musical control of computers. *Computer Music Journal, 26*(3), 11-22.

Wiggins, G. A., & Trewin, S. (2000). A system for concerned teaching of musical aural skills. In *Proceedings of the 5th International Conference on Intelligent Tutoring System* (pp. 494-503) Montreal, Canada: Springer-Verlag.

Williams, C. F. (1903, 1969). *The story of notation*. New York: Haskell House

Williams, D. A., & Webster, P. R. (1999). *Experiencing music technology: Software, data, and hardware* (2nd ed.). Belmont, CA: Wadsworth Group/Thomson Learning.

Wind Guitar and Foot Controllers. (n.d.). Retrieved April 6, 2006, from http://www.yamaha.com/yamahavgn/CDA/ContentDetail/ModelSeriesDetail/0,,CNTID%253D1321%2526CTID%253D,00.html

Windows Media Digital Rights Management. (2007). Retrieved April 3, 2007, from http://www.microsoft.com/windows/windowsmedia/es/drm/default.aspx

WIPO, World Intellectual Property Organisation. (2004). *Copyright definitions*. Retrieved September 2004, from http://www.wipo.int

Woodhouse, J. (1993). On the playability of violins. I: Reflection functions, on the playability of violins. II: Minimum bowforce and transients. *Acustica, 78*(3), 125-153.

Wright, M., & Freed, A. (1997). *Open sound control: A new protocol for communicating with sound synthesizers*. Paper presented at the International Computer Music Conference 1997, Thessaloniki, Greece.

XML and Digital Rights Management (DRM). *Cover Pages* (hosted by OASIS). Retrieved March 21, 2007, from http://xml.coverpages.org/drm.html

XML Encryption Syntax and Processing, W3C Candidate Recommendation. (2002). Retrieved April 3, 2007, from http://www.w3.org/TR/2002/REC-xmlenc-core-20021210/

XML Shema. (2007). Retrieved April 3, 2007, from http://www.w3.org/XML/Schema

XML Signature Syntax and Processing, W3C Recommendation 12. (2002). Retrieved April 3, 2007, from http://www.w3.org/TR/2002/REC-xmldsig-core-20020212/

XrML Specifications. (2007). Retrieved April 3, 2007, from http://www.xrml.org/get_XrML.asp

Young, D. (1999). *New frontiers of expression through real-time dynamics measurement of violin bows.* Unpublished master's thesis. Massachusetts Institute of Technology, Cambridge, MA.

Young, D. (2002). *The Hyperbow. A precision violin interface.* Paper presented at the International Computer Music conference 2002, Gothenburg, Sweden.

Young, D., & Serafin, S. (2003). Playability evaluation of a virtual bowed string instrument. In F. Thibault (Ed.), *Proceedings of the 2003 Conference on New Instruments for Musical Expression* (pp. 104-108). Montréal: McGill University.

Zhou, Y. Freedman, R., Glass, M., Michael, J., Rovick, A., & Evens, M. (1999). Delivering hints in a dialogue-based intelligent tutoring system. In *Proceedings of the Sixteenth National Conference on AI (AAAI-99)* (pp. 128-134), Orlando, FL.

# About the Contributors

**Kia Ng** obtained his PhD in computer science from the University of Leeds, where he is director and cofounder of the Interdisciplinary Centre for Scientific Research in Music (ICSRiM), and senior lecturer in computing and music. Ng's research links together work in the School of Computing and the School of Music on computer vision, computer music, and AI. Currently, he is the president of the International Association of Interactive Multimedia MUSICNETWORK. Ng is involved in several domains and initiatives relating to 2-D and 3-D imaging including document imaging (printed and handwritten music manuscripts, paper watermark, etc.), gestural interfaces, and interactive multimedia systems, in collaboration with many European and international organisations and individuals in the field. His Music via Motion (MvM) system, which provides interactive gestural control of musical sound, has been widely featured in the media, including the BBC and Sky TV. Ng has served as general chair and programme committees for many national and international conferences including WEDELMUSIC, AXMEDIS, AISB, and so forth. He is a fellow of the Royal Society of Arts, a chartered engineer, and a chartered scientist. For more information, visit http://www.kcng.org.

**Paolo Nesi** (nesi@dsi.unifi.it) is a full professor at the University of Florence, Department of Systems and Informatics, and head of the Distributed Systems and Internet Technology research group. Nesi received a PhD in electronic and informatics engineering from the University of Padoa. His research interests include object-oriented technology, real-time systems, quality, system assessment, testing, formal languages, physical models, computer music, and parallel and distributed architectures. He has been the general chair of IEEE ICSM, IEEE ICECCS, WEDELMUSIC international conferences, and program chair of several others. He has been the coordinator of several R&D multipartner international R&D projects of the European Commission such as MOODS, WEDELMUSIC, AXMEDIS, VARIAZIONI, and MUSICNETWORK (The Interactive Music Network, http://www.interactivemusicnetwork.org) and involved in many other projects. Currently, he is co-editor of the MPEG SMR ISO standard, with P. Bellini and G. Zoia.

\* \* \*

**Pierfrancesco Bellini** is a contract professor at the University of Florence, Department of Systems and Informatics. His research interests include object-oriented technology, real-time systems, formal languages, computer music. Bellini received a PhD in electronic and informatics engineering from the University of Florence, and has worked on MOODS, WEDELMUSIC, IMUTUS, MUSICNETWORK,

AXMEDIS, VARIAZIONI, and many other projects funded by the European Commission. He is presently co-editor of the MPEG SMR ISO standard, with P. Nesi and G. Zoia.

**Ivan Bruno** is a contract professor at the University of Florence, Department of Systems and Informatics. His research interests include optical music recognition, audio processing, computer music, object-oriented technologies, grid computing, and software engineering. Bruno obtained his PhD in software and telecommunication engineering from the University of Florence. He has worked on many projects, including WEDELMUSIC, VISICON, IMUTUS, MUSICNETWORK, VARIAZIONI, and AXMEDIS, that have been cosupported by the European Commission.

**David Crombie** is coordinating research strategies at the Utrecht Research & Design Institute for Digital Cultures (part of Utrecht School of the Arts); is head of International Projects at DEDICON in Amsterdam, and a cofounder and director of Openfocus Consultancy. He has worked on many European e-Inclusion and Cultural Heritage projects, and has collaborated with many of the major European organisations and individuals in these fields. He has coordinated or participated in EC-funded projects such as HARMONICA, TESTLAB, MIRACLE, WEDELMUSIC, TEDUB, MULTIREADER, MUSIC NETWORK, eBRASS, CONTRAPUNCTUS, I-MAESTRO, and PRO-ACCESS, and runs the European Accessible Information Network (EUAIN). He has been active in standardisation activities such as DAISY, MPEG SMR, and he established the CEN WS/DPA. He is currently involved in several research domains and related commercial initiatives relating to accessible software architectures, information modelling, and intelligent knowledge management strategies.

**Jaime Delgado** obtained his PhD in telecommunication engineering in 1987. Since 1999, he has been a professor of computer networks and computer architecture at the Universitat Pompeu Fabra (UPF), and is currently a professor at the Computer Architecture Department of the Universitat Politècnica de Catalunya (UPC), Barcelona. He is head and founder of the Distributed Multimedia Applications Group (DMAG) of the UPF and UPC. Delgado has been a project manager for several European and national research projects in the areas of electronic commerce, digital rights management, metadata, multimedia content, security, and distributed applications. Since 1989, Delgado has actively participated in international standardisation activities, as editor of standards and chairman of groups in ISO/IEC, EWOS, ETSI, ITU-T, and CEN/ISSS. He serves as a reviewer for the European Commission in different research programs, and as an advisor to the Spanish Ministry of Science. He has over 100 publications, and he has served as chair or programme committee member of many international conferences.

**David Luigi Fuschi** obtained his MSc in electronic engineering (Politecnico di Milano) with additional qualifications in ICT system management (SDA-Bocconi) and software engineering (IBM-IFDA). Currently, Fuschi is a senior project manager for GIUNTI. His works involve many national and international SMEs, institutions, and corporations in the IT/ICT domains, with particular focus on software development, security, and quality assurance. He has many publications, including a market analysis that has been adopted by the CEE Special Task Force for Multimedia and Education. Fuschi is a member of: IEEE (Computer Society, Communication Society, Technical Committee on Engineering of Computer Based Systems, Technical Council for Software Engineering, Standards Association), ACM, U.S. Digital Society, PMI, and IST Experts Group of the Socio-Economic Trends Assessment for the Digital Revolution (STAR) programme. He also serves as a project expert evaluator/reviewer for EU-IST, Regione Emilia Romagna and Piemonte, lecturer for Fondazione Clerici and Politecnico di Milano, scientific committee of several international conferences, judge for Brandon Hall Excellence Award and IEEE Computer Society CSIDC.

**Graham Jones** studied mathematics at Cambridge and Warwick universtities, obtaining a PhD in group theory in 1983. He then made his living as a landscape artist and later as a programmer, and has specialised in the field of pattern recognition since 1992. His first major application was a commercial text OCR program called Sleuth, marketed by Beebug. He started work on the music OCR program, SharpEye, in 1996. He released the first version of SharpEye in 1999, with improved versions following in later years. SharpEye was taken over by another company in 2006.

**Günter Marx** is the principal violinist at the Opera in Dortmund, Germany. He also performs as a soloist, and is a member of several chamber ensembles including the Brahms Quartet Hamburg, the Leonardo Quartet, Cologne, and Trionys, Bad Urach, a trio performing experimental electronic music. As a computer violinist, he performed at events like the International Computer Music Conference (ICMC), or the Conference of the Society for Electro-Acoustic Music in the United States (SEAMUS). He has collaborated on performance projects with composers Thomas Kessler, Mesias Maiguashca, Wilfried Jentzsch and Rainer Bürck among others.

**Michael Oliva** trained as a biochemist and is now area leader for Electroacoustic Music at the Royal College of Music as well as a composer with a fondness for writing operas and music for electronics and woodwind. In addition to live laptop improvisations, regular performances with the ensemble *rarescale,* both in Europe and in the U.S., and well over 40 theatre scores, Oliva's compositions include *Xas-Orion* for oboe/cor and electronics, *Into the Light* for oboe/cor and piano (both recorded by Paul Goodey on his CD "New Ground"), *Torso* for wind orchestra, *Cyclone* for wind quintet with piano, and *Apparition and Release* for quartertone alto flute and electronics. Michael also runs *madestrange opera,* which premiered his multimedia operas *Black & Blue* and *Midsummer* at BAC in 2004 and 2005, and *The Girl Who Liked to be Thrown Around* at An Tuireann in autumn 2006.

**Bee Ong** is a research officer at the Interdisciplinary Centre for Scientific Research in Music (IC-SRiM), University of Leeds. She has been involved in a number of interactive multimedia projects, including the Optical Music Recognition project funded by the Arts and Humanities Research Board of the British Academy, and Music via Motion (MvM) project funded by the Arts Council, UK, and several European projects including MUSICNETWORK, I-MAESTRO, and AXMEDIS that are co-supported by the European Community under the IST Framework Programme. She has obtained her degrees in mathematics and statistics (BSc), information systems and office automation (MSc) from the University of Leeds, UK.

**Somnuk Phon-Amnuaisuk** obtained his PhD from the Department of Artificial Intelligence, Edinburgh University, Scotland. He currently lectures at Multimedia University, Malaysia. He is the chairman of the Centre for Artificial Intelligence and Intelligent Computing (CAIIC), and also leads the Music Informatics Research group at the same centre. His current research works span over multimedia information retrieval, polyphonic music transcription, algorithmic composition, ITS, data mining, and machine learning.

**C. Poepel** (Diplom Orchestra Musician (viola), Diplom Audio Designer) performs as an orchestra musician in Europe and the U.S., and has appeared in radio and TV-recordings, for example, at the Salzburg Festival or the Festival Vienna modern. Poepel has also created sound design and productions for Swiss and German TV and radio. Other activities include performances of live electronic music, software development for live-electronics, interactive multimedia installations, sound synthesis, and data sonification. Currently, Poepel is a lecturer at the Music University Hannover, and research associate at ZKM Karlsruhe (Centre for Art and Media). He has had directive positions in applied computer sciences for example, for the interactive multimedia opera "Heptameron" of Gerhard Winkler, Biennale Munich 2002. Since October 2002, he has been working on his dissertation at the University of Birmingham in music research. Poepel has been an artistic and academic staff member at the Academy of Media Arts Cologne since April 2003, with research focus on human-computer interaction, interface-design, and sound synthesis.

**Eva Rodríguez** obtained her PhD in computer science in 2007 and her BSc in telecommunication engineering in 2001. She is an associate professor at the Department of Computer Architecture in the Universitat Politècnica de Catalunya (UPC). Her PhD thesis focuses in the standardisation of the protection and governance of multimedia content. She has been a member of the Distributed Multimedia Applications Group (DMAG) since 2002 and a participant in several IST projects in the areas of multimedia publishing, electronic commerce, and distributed applications. Her research interests include digital rights management, content protection, MPEG-21 intellectual property management and protection, and multimedia framework. Other work includes active participation, since 2003, in MPEG-21 standard, several contributions to MPEG-21 REL, RDD, DIP and Reference Software, and coeditor of ISO/IEC 21000-4 "Intellectual Property Management and Protection Components" standard and of ISO/IEC 23000-7 "Open release MAF." Rodgríguez is the author of several published papers in international journals and conferences.

**Martin Schmucker** has been working with Fraunhofer IGD since 2000 in the security technology department. He received his diploma in computer science from the University of Ulm. Before that, he worked in industry in the field of telematics and traffic control systems. He has been working at Fraunhofer IGD on several European and national projects like AXMEDIS (content identification and authentication), eCrypt (in the watermarking virtual laboratory WAVILAB), MusicNetwork (protection workgroup), Certimark (benchmarking of watermarking techniques), and WEDELMUSIC (music score watermarking). In addition to the above projects, he is responsible for projects dealing with secure content distribution via P2P networks and the protection of symbolic media, particularly on the identification of music scores by watermarking and perceptual hashing (fingerprinting) techniques. Besides identification technology for sheet music, he works on fingerprinting techniques for images and videos.

**Chee Keh Siong** obtained his Bachelor in Information Technology from Multimedia University, Malaysia. He is a researcher under the Music Informatics Research group, and he is currently doing research on music intelligent tutoring system. This project is funded by the MOSTI (Ministry of Science, Technology and Innovation).

**Francesco Spadoni** is head of research and development at Rigel Engineering S.r.l., an Italian ICT company focused on developing turn-key solutions for digital content and rights management, knowledge management, and human-machine interfaces. He participated in several R&D projects funded by different EU Programmes: WEDELMUSIC (design and development of a complete and secure solution for digital music rights management), MusicNetwork (a centre of excellence for multimedia and interactive digital content, where he coordinates the Working Group on Distribution of Coded Music). He is currently involved in the eContentPlus VARIAZIONI project, a content enrichment effort aimed to add relevant metadata and tags to music scholarly content according to both an ontology-based and a participative-Web2.0-style approach.

**Jacques Steyn** has been Associate Professor of Multimedia at the University of Pretoria, and now Head of the School of IT at Monash University's South African campus. In the 1990s, he was a multimedia and Web technologies, and information design consultant. In 1999, he developed the concept of an XML-based general markup language for music. He participated in the ISO/MPEG work group's Symbolic Music Representation initiative. His present research focus is on development informatics.

**Giorgio Zoia** is a scientific advisor at the Signal Processing Institute of the Ecole Polytechnique Fédérale de Lausanne (EPFL). In April 2001 he received his PhD "es Sciences Techniques" from EPFL with a thesis on fast prototyping of architectures for audio and multimedia. His research interests evolved from digital video, digital design, and CAD synthesis optimization in submicron technology to compilers, virtual architectures, and fast execution engines for digital audio. Fields of interest in audio include 3-D spatialization, audio synthesis and coding, representations and description of sound, interaction, and intelligent user interfaces for media control. He has been actively collaborating with MPEG since 1997, with several contributions concerning structured audio, audio composition (systems), and analysis of computational complexity. Currently, he is a coeditor of the SMR standard with P. Bellini and P. Nesi.

# Index